HISTORY OF SYRIA

A restoration by John Dibs, Beirut

MODEL OF THE TEMPLE OF BAʻLABAKK, HELIOPOLIS

This temple of Jupiter was enlarged and completed by members of the Syrian dynasty of Roman emperors in the second and third Christian centuries

Frontispiece

HISTORY OF SYRIA

INCLUDING
LEBANON AND PALESTINE

BY

PHILIP K. HITTI

PROFESSOR OF SEMITIC LITERATURE ON THE
WILLIAM AND ANNIE S. PATON FOUNDATION
PRINCETON UNIVERSITY

NEW YORK
THE MACMILLAN COMPANY
1951

PRINTED IN GREAT BRITAIN

TO

MY WIFE

WHOSE UNFAILING ENCOURAGEMENT
SUSTAINED ME THROUGH THE MANY YEARS
OF HARD LABOUR ON THIS VOLUME

PREFACE

THE history of Syria, using the name in its geographic meaning, is in a sense the history of the civilized world in miniature. It is a cross-section of the history of the cradle of our civilization and of a significant part of our spiritual and intellectual heritage. To do justice to it one must not only control the ancient Semitic languages and medieval Arabic literature but should also have competence in the Greco-Roman histories and the Turkish and Persian fields — to say nothing of modern Western European languages and historical material.

No such claim can be made by the author. His studies have been limited to the Semitic field and his researches to the Arabic and Islamic one. Impressed, however, by the fact that, while numberless monographs have been written dealing with some region in Syria or covering a certain epoch in its long and chequered history, there is hardly a single work that gives a balanced comprehensive picture of the life of the whole area as a unit from the earliest times to the present, he felt bold to make the attempt. The Phoenicians of Lebanon — it should be remembered —, the Hebrews of Palestine, the Arabs of Damascus, all of whom have been the subject of comparatively intensive historical research, cannot be fully understood unless treated as integral parts of the people of greater Syria and projected against a common background of contemporary Near Eastern culture.

The task was far from an easy one. How to keep in hand, through the maze, the golden thread upon which to hang the chronicle of significant events in the life of a country which had been normally an adjunct of other states presented in itself a major problem. The attempt to sift the store of available data, utilize its essential elements, interpret their relevance and integrate the whole into a consecutive story that would be serviceable to the student as well as to the cultured layman had its own difficulties If the result, which lays no claim to originality and holds no aspiration to definiteness, meets the present-day need for a readable, non-technical, yet reliable account of the story of the people of Syria, Lebanon, Palestine and Transjordan and meantime serves as a general background for the understanding of the many complicated problems that beset the rising nationalities in those localities, the effort would not have been in vain. Two extensive trips undertaken by the author in the summers of 1946 and 1947 to these and neighbouring lands served to refresh his memory on ancient sites and historic scenes and give him first-hand contact with current thoughts and modern trends. If it is true that no present can be understood without a study of the past, it is equally true that no past can be fully comprehended without adequate acquaintance with the present.

Experts in their fields cast critical eyes over portions of the manuscript submitted to them. Professor Glenn L. Jepsen of Princeton read the introductory anthropological material. Professor William T. Thom and Dr. John C. Maxwell, also of Princeton, scrutinized the geological section. Professor Cyrus H. Gordon of the Dropsie College examined the chapters dealing with the Canaanites and Aramaeans and my colleague Henry S. Gehman criticized the data on the Hebrews. Another colleague, T. Cuyler Young, reviewed the material on the Persian period. The chapters dealing with Alexander and the Seleucids were submitted to Professor Alfred R. Bellinger, those on the Roman period and Christianity to Professor Carl H. Kraeling, both of Yale. Dr. Glanville Downey of Dumbarton Oaks Research Library, Harvard University, went over the chapters on the Byzantine era. Professor Harald Inghold of Yale reviewed the sections dealing with the Nabataeans, Palmyrenes and Ghassānids. The last two chapters, which treat of the Ottoman age, were read by my colleague Dr. Lewis V. Thomas. To all these scholars, as well as to the host of others here and abroad whose aid I sought and received, my heartfelt thanks are due. Needless to add for any errors or shortcomings that remain the responsibility is entirely mine.

I also owe a debt of gratitude to Dr. George C. Miles of the American Numismatic Society, who provided me with most of the coin illustrations, and to several students in my seminar — chief among whom were Harry W. Hazard, Wilfred C. Smith, R. Bayly Winder and C. Ernest Dawn — who read almost the entire manuscript and gave me the benefit of their criticism. Most of the maps were sketched by Dr. Winder. The secretarial assistance in preparing the manuscript for publication and compiling the index was generously contributed through the Risq G. Haddad Foundation of New York.

As I read and re-read the manuscript and corrected the proofs, the words of a twelfth century Syrian judge repeatedly came to my mind:

> Never have I met an author who is not ready to proclaim on the morrow of finishing his book, " O, had I expressed this differently, how much better would it have been! Had such a statement been added, how much more correct it would have been! Had this been moved forward, it would have read better and had that been omitted it would have certainly been preferable." In such experience there is indeed a great lesson; it provides full evidence that defect characterizes all works of man.

P. K. H.

March 15, 1950

CONTENTS

PART I

THE PRE-LITERARY AGE

CHAPTER I

CHAPTER II

CHAPTER III

CHAPTER IV

CHAPTER V

PART II

ANCIENT SEMITIC TIMES

CHAPTER VI

CHAPTER VII

CHAPTER VIII

CHAPTER IX

CHAPTER X

CHAPTER XI

CHAPTER XXVI

CHAPTER XXVII

CHAPTER XXVIII

CHAPTER XXIX

PART IV
THE ARAB ERA

CHAPTER XXX

CHAPTER XXXVIII

CHAPTER XXXIX

CHAPTER XL

CHAPTER XLI

CHAPTER XLII

CHAPTER XLIII

CHAPTER XLIV

CHAPTER XLV

CHAPTER XLVI

CHAPTER XLVII

PART V

UNDER THE OTTOMAN TURKS

CHAPTER XLVIII

CHAPTER XLIX

CHAPTER L

LIST OF ILLUSTRATIONS

LIST OF MAPS

LIST OF COINS

PART I

THE PRE-LITERARY AGE

CHAPTER I

PLACE IN HISTORY

SYRIA occupies a unique place in the annals of the world. Especially because of the inclusion of Palestine and Lebanon in its ancient boundaries, it has made a more significant contribution to the progress of mankind intellectually and spiritually than any other land. It is perhaps the largest small country on the map, microscopic in size but cosmic in influence.

As the cradle of Judaism and the birthplace of Christianity it provided the civilized world with two monotheistic religions and held close relationship with the rise and development of the third — the only other there is — Islam. The eye of the Christian, the Moslem and the Jew — no matter where the Christian, the Moslem or the Jew may be — may always be turned to some sacred spot in Syria for religious inspiration, and the foot turned there for guidance. Almost any civilized man can claim two countries: his own and Syria.

Closely associated with its religious contribution was the ethical message southern Syria conveyed. Its people were the first to promulgate the doctrine that man is created in the image of God and that each is the brother of every other man under God's fatherhood, thereby they laid the basis of the democratic way of life. They were the first to emphasize the supremacy of spiritual values and to believe in the ultimate triumph of the forces of righteousness, and thereby they became the moral teachers of mankind.

Not only did those early Syrians provide the world with its finest and highest thought but they implemented it with the provision of those simple-looking magic-working signs, called alphabet, through which most of the major literatures of the world are enshrined. No invention compares in importance with that of the alphabet, developed and disseminated by the ancient Lebanese. It was from the Phoenicians, or Canaanites as they called themselves, that the Greeks, to the west, derived their characters and passed them on to the Romans and hence to the modern peoples of Europe, and the Aramaeans, to the east, borrowed theirs and passed them on to the Arabs, the Persians and Indians and other peoples of Asia and Africa. Had those people of Syria rendered no other service, this would have been enough to mark them out among the greatest benefactors of humanity.

But their contribution did not cease therewith. Into their narrow land more historical and cultural events, colourful and dynamic, were squeezed than perhaps into any land of equal size — events that made the history of Syria-Palestine the history of the civilized world in a miniature form. In the Hellenistic and Roman periods the sons of this land furnished the classical world with some of its leading thinkers, teachers and historians. Some of the founders of the Stoic and Neo-Platonic philosophies were Syrians. One of the greatest schools of Roman law flourished in Beirut, Lebanon, and certain of its professors had their legal opinions embedded in the Justinian Code, rightly considered the greatest gift of the Roman genius to later generations.

Shortly after the spread of Islam, the Syrian capital Damascus became the seat of the illustrious Umayyad empire, whose caliphs pushed their conquests into Spain and France at one end and into India and the confines of China at the other end — an empire greater than that of Rome at its zenith. Throughout that vast domain the word of the Damascene caliph was law. With the ʿAbbāsid caliphate in Baghdād, which ensued, the Arab world entered upon a period of intellectual activity, involving translation from Greek, that had hardly a parallel in its history. Greek philosophy and thought was then the most important legacy that the classical world had bequeathed to the medieval. In this process of transmitting Greek science and philosophy, the Christian Syrians took a leading part; their language Syriac served as a stepping-stone over which Greek learning found its way into the Arabic tongue.

In the Middle Ages Syria was the scene of one of the most sensational dramas in the annals of contact between the Moslem East and the Christian West. From France, England, Italy and Germany crusading hordes poured into the maritime plain of

Syria and the highlands of Palestine, seeking the dead Christ whom they did not possess as a living reality. Thus was started a movement of far-reaching consequences in both Europe and Asia. The Crusades, however, were but an episode in the long and chequered military history of this land which, because of its position at the gateway of Asia on the crossroads of the nations, has acted as an international battlefield in time of war and a thoroughfare of trade in time of peace. What land other than Syria could claim to have witnessed such a galaxy of warriors and world conquerors, beginning with Thutmose, Nebuchadnezzar, Alexander and Julius Caesar and continuing through Khālid ibn-al-Walīd, Saladin and Baybars down to Napoleon?

In recent years the people of this country, after an eclipse of centuries under Turks and Mamlūks, have provided the Arab East with its intellectual leadership. Syrians, more particularly Lebanese, were the first to establish in the last century vital contacts with the West through education, emigration and travel and thus to act as the medium through which European and American influences seeped into the Near East. Their modern colonies in Cairo, Paris, New York, São Paulo and Sydney are living monuments to their industry and adventure.

The historical importance of Syria does not arise solely from its original contributions to the higher life of man. It results partly from its strategic position between the three historic continents, Europe, Asia and Africa, and its functioning as a bridge for transmitting cultural influences from its neighbouring foci of civilization as well as commercial wares. This function is well illustrated in the career of the Phoenicians, who became the earliest international traders. Lying at the core of the Near East, which in itself lay at the centre of the ancient world, Syria early became the culture carrier of antiquity. On one side stretched the valley of the two rivers, on the other the valley of the one river. No other region can vie in antiquity, activity and continuity with these three. It was here that the dawn of continuous history broke. In it we can observe more or less the same peoples for fifty or sixty centuries of uninterrupted history. Their civilization has been a going concern since the fourth millennium before Christ. The early culture of Europe, we now know, was for long but a pale reflection of this civilization of the Eastern Mediterranean.[1] Certain fundamental elements of the ancient Chinese civilization, we are beginning to learn, seem to have penetrated from the eastern horn of the Fertile Crescent.

Even in pre-history Syria has, in recent years and as a result of archaeological investigation, loomed high in significance as the probable scene of the first domestication of wheat, the discovery of copper, the invention of local pottery, which resulted in changing the pattern of life from a hunting, nomadic way to an agricultural sedentary one. This region, therefore, may have experienced settled life in villages and towns before any other place we know. Earlier still, as we shall learn in the next chapter, it may have served as the nursery of one of our direct ancestors, the emerging Homo sapiens.

[1] V. Gordon Childe, *New Light on the Most Ancient East* (London, 1934), ch. 1.

CHAPTER II

CULTURAL BACKGROUND: STONE IMPLEMENTS

JUST as in an iceberg the visible part above the surface of the water is but a small fraction of the huge mass, so in the history of Syria and the Syrians the literary period is but a small portion of the whole. The literary history in this country dawned toward the beginning of the third millennium B.C., subsequent to the invention of writing in the two neighbouring nurseries of civilization, lower Mesopotamia and Egypt, and its spread therefrom. The pre-literary period, for the knowledge of which we have to depend upon archaeological remains rather than written records, goes back through the New Stone Age (Neolithic) to the Old Stone Age (Palaeolithic) tens of thousands of long years. Excavations conducted in the last three decades in the unexplored wastes of northern and eastern Syria, the caves of Lebanon, the tells of Palestine and the sand-buried cities of Transjordan have been yielding the secrets of long-forgotten civilizations. They leave no doubt that this archaeologically long-neglected and little-known region was much more advanced in the earliest ages than has hitherto been suspected.

The earliest relics: stone implements

As we endeavour to catch our first glimpse of man in this region he eludes us as a person, but his traces we can detect in the form of stone implements in cave deposits or surface finds strewn like *cartes de visite* over a wide area. These tools and weapons consist of roughly chipped or irregularly flaked flints which he used as fist hatchets, scrapers or choppers and belong to the end of the early Palaeolithic Age, some 150,000 years ago.[1] The fist hatchet in this area was the earliest certain implement manufactured by primitive man and consisted of a core of flint from which fragments had been flaked off to make it easy to grasp and use for cutting or pounding. No unmistakable earlier implements of the ruder type termed eoliths

[1] Corresponding to the Acheulean culture in Europe, so called from a type station in France.

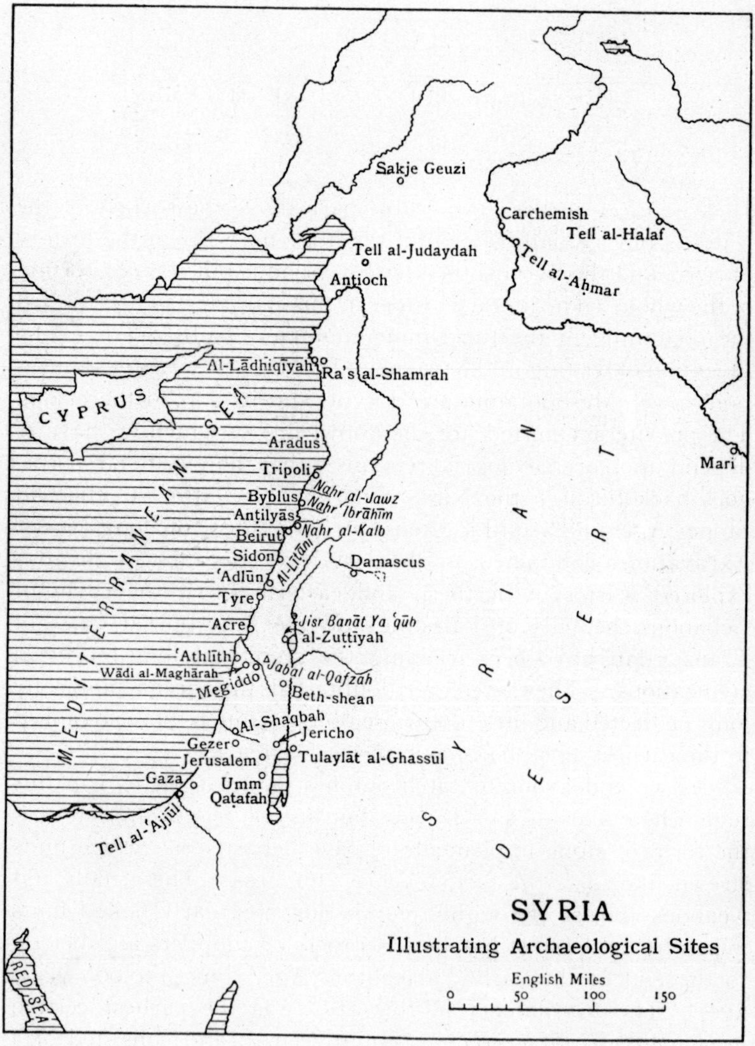

SYRIA

Illustrating Archaeological Sites

(" dawn stones ") have been discovered. The difficulty lies in the ability to distinguish such man-made implements from naturally fractured stones. Any branches of trees or other pieces of wood which primitive man may have used concurrently or before could not by their nature have left traces that are readily discovered.

Among the caves in Lebanon and Palestine in which Palaeolithic artifacts have been found and studied are those of ʻAdlūn,[1] Mount Carmel,[2] Umm Qaṭafah [3] and al-Zuṭṭīyah.[4] Hand axes belonging to the same general period have been found among other places in the Jordan River bed (below Jisr Banāt Yaʻqūb) [5] and in Ra's al-Shamrah, ancient Ugarit [6] The axe is triangular or ovoid and more extensively processed than the hatchet

The humans who left us those stone traces of their existence were presumably a primitive and unspecialized type of the white man whose culture is still undifferentiated. They lived at least at times in caves as a measure of protection against rain, wild animals and enemies, and because, in a still earlier age, the severity of climate had forced such mode of life on them. Though the ice-sheet never reached as far south as Syria, the climate of this country must have been affected by it. The climatic phase at the end of the early Palaeolithic was pluvial — rainy, damp and tropical — with a fauna, the species of which are today almost completely extinct, which flourished amidst luxuriant growths. The animal remains found include bones of the rhinoceros, the hippopotamus and an elephant-like creature.

1 Half-way between Sidon and Tyre. This and the other caves of Nahr Ibrāhīm, Nahr al-Kalb and Anṭilyās were explored by G. Zumoffen; see his *La Phénicie avant les Phéniciens* (Beirut, 1900), pp. 4-16; " L'Age de la pierre en Phénicie ", *Anthropos*, vol. iii (1908), pp. 431-55.

2 Excavated in 1929–34 by Dorothy A. E. Garrod and D. M. A. Bate; see their *The Stone Age of Mount Carmel*, vol. i (Oxford, 1937), ch. 8.

3 North-west of the Dead Sea. Explored by René Neuville; see his " L'Acheuléen supérieur de la grotte d'Oumm Qatafa ", *L'Anthropologie*, vol. xli (1931), pp. 13-51, 249-63; " Le Préhistorique de Palestine ", *Revue biblique*, vol. xliii (1934), pp. 237-59.

4 North-west of the Sea of Galilee. Excavated by F. Turville-Petre; see his *Researches in Prehistoric Galilee* (London, 1927), §§ 5, 6; cf. Garrod and Bate, pp. 113-15.

5 " Jisr Banāt Yaʻqūb ", *The Quarterly of the Department of Antiquities in Palestine*, vol. vi (1936), pp. 214-15.

6 Claude F. A. Schaeffer, *The Cuneiform Texts of Ras Shamra-Ugarit* (London, 1939), p. 1.

At this time Europe was suffering from the rigours of the Ice Age, allowing the Near East an earlier start for the career of man.

Earliest human skeletons

The earliest human skeletal remains in the Near East come from the middle Palaeolithic They were mostly found in two

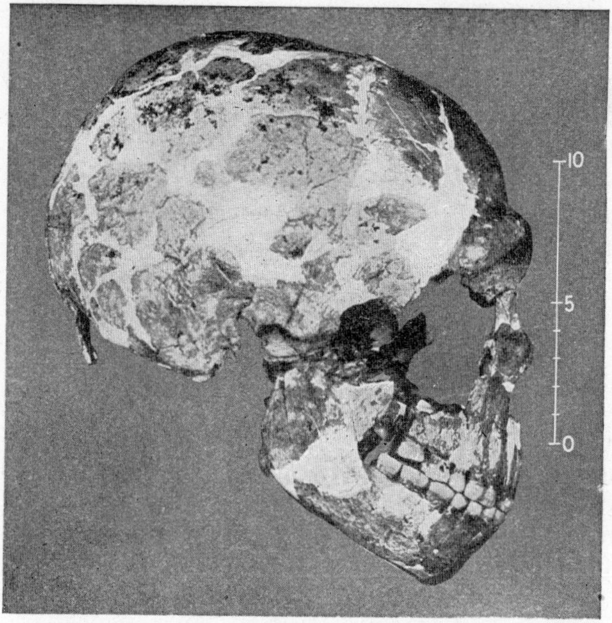

From T. D. McCown and A. Keith, " The Stone Age of Mount Carmel ", vol. ii (Clarendon Press)

RIGHT LATERAL ASPECT OF SKULL, FOUND AT MAGHĀRAT AL-ṬĀBŪN

caves of Mount Carmel by Miss Garrod,[1] one south of Nazareth [2] and one to the north-west of the Sea of Galilee.[3] Their discovery constitutes an epoch-marking event for the pre-history of the Near East. All belong to the Mousterian type of culture (so called from a cave in France) and must be dated at least 100,000

[1] Maghārat al-Ṭābūn (cave of the oven) and Maghārat al-Sukhūl (cave of the kids); Garrod and Bate, chs. 4-7.

[2] Jabal al-Qafzah. Explored by René Neuville in 1934, still unpublished; see " Jabal Qafze ", *The Quarterly of the Department of Antiquities in Palestine*, vol. iv (1934), p. 202.

[3] Al-Zuṭṭīyah; Turville-Petre, § 9, " Report on the Galilee Skull " by Edward Keith.

years ago. They present an entire series of skeletal material ranging from the Neanderthal type (from a valley in the Rhine Province) through progressive forms to some that are nearly human. Short in stature and stocky in build the Neanderthal man stood almost but not quite erect. What is especially striking about some Carmel skeletons is that they show certain anatomical

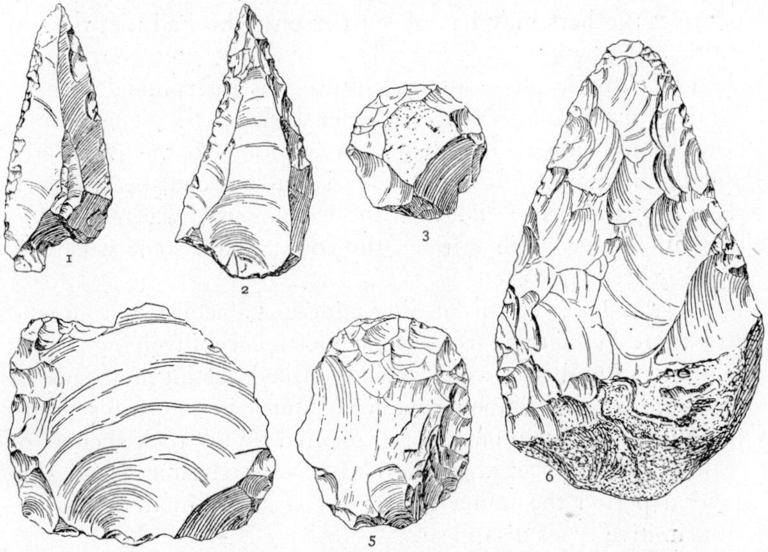

From D. A. E. Garrod and D. M. A. Bate, "Mount Carmel", vol. i (Clarendon Press)

IMPLEMENTS FROM MAGHĀRAT AL-SUKHŪL, LOWER MOUSTERIAN

Nos. 1, 2 are triangular flakes; Nos. 3, 4, 5 are cores; No. 6 is flint

features of Homo sapiens.[1] The skull capacity was larger than that of their European counterpart; the chin was larger but yet lacked the structure associated with coherent speech. They thus seem to constitute a significant link in the evolution of man and render this region in the Near East the scene of the genesis of an intermediate between the primitive and the modern man.

Our man in the middle Palaeolithic still lived in caves. His industry, as before, consisted of preparing irregular flakes and

[1] Theodore D. McCown and Arthur Keith, *The Stone Age of Mount Carmel*, vol. ii (Oxford, 1939), ch. 2; cf. Earnest A. Hooton, *Up from the Ape* (New York, 1946), pp. 336-9; Alfred S. Romer, *Man and the Vertebrates* (Chicago, 1941), pp. 219-22.

rough chunks of flint which he employed as hand-axes, scrapers, choppers and hammers.[1] The social organization was no doubt crude and primitive, centring on units of groups or herds subsisting on the produce of nature in terms of plants and animals in their natural condition. Expertly cracked human bones from which the coveted marrow was extracted point to cannibalistic practices. The victims were captured enemies or inconvenient relatives; others may have been persons who had met natural death.

The climatic phase of this culture was interpluvial with an evident gradual alteration to drier conditions. The animal remains indicate the existence, in addition to the rhinoceros and hippopotamus, of the gazelle, spotted hyena, bear, camel, river hog and deer.[2] Though the weather was warm and dry, permanent rivers still watered the country and some woody or scrubby areas persisted.

In the later epoch of the middle Palaeolithic a drastic alteration in climatic conditions took place involving heavy rainfall. Another pluvial period ensued lasting for tens of thousands of years, about which not much is known for Syria-Palestine. In Lebanon it is represented by the rock shelters of Nahr al-Jawz (near al-Batrūn) and Nahr Ibrāhīm.[3] In this general period the fauna begins to assume a modern aspect; all primitive types disappear.

Late Palaeolithic

Throughout the long epoch of the late or upper Palaeolithic there is evidence of increased desiccation with the exception of one damper interlude. Archaeological remains point to an alternation of warm and cool Mediterranean climates extending down to the late Palaeolithic.[4] The culture of late Palaeolithic corresponds to the Aurignacian in Europe (so called from a type station in France) and is represented by finds in the caves of Anṭilyās and Nahr al-Kalb [5] and one near the Sea of Galilee.[6]

[1] Garrod and Bate, pp. 88-90, 109-12; Turville-Petre, §§ 3, 6; Neuville in *Revue biblique* (1934), pp. 237 *seq.*

[2] Garrod and Bate, p. 226; Turville-Petre, §§ 4, 8.

[3] Zumoffen, *La Phénicie*, pp. 29-48; *Anthropos*, pp. 443 *seq.*

[4] Leo Picard, *Structure and Evolution of Palestine* (Jerusalem, 1943), pp. 119-120.

[5] Alfred E. Day, "Āthār al-Insān al-Awwal al-Muktashafah ḥadīthan fi Anṭilyāṣ", *al-Kullīyah*, vol. xii (Beirut, 1926), pp. 496-9; Zumoffen, *La Phénicie*, pp. 20-28, 49-87; *Anthropos*, pp. 443 *seq.*

[6] Maghārat al-Amīrah; Turville-Petre, § 2.

Recent excavations (1938) at Kasār ʿAqīl, near Anṭilyās, yielded skeletal remains of deer, hyenas, rhinoceros, foxes and goats as well as of human beings.[1] The Museum of the American University of Beirut is especially rich in Stone Age implements

Among animal remains those of the gazelle assume a dominant place. While the industry in this epoch does not radically vary from the preceding, the stone implements manifest a tendency to diminish in size, becoming pygmy or microlithic. This indicates that man had begun to mount his tools and weapons in wooden or bone hafts as members of a composite body. The wood being perishable left no traces, but bones suspected of such use have been discovered.

Fire: charcoal

The earliest fragments of charcoal thus far discovered in our area come from one of the lowest levels in a Carmel cave [2] and belong to the end of early Palaeolithic, some 150,000 years ago. Others, belonging to the late Palaeolithic (Aurignacian), were unearthed in a neighbouring cave [3] and suggest oak, tamarisk, olive and the grape-vine types of structure.[4] In his slow and arduous ascent from lower mental levels primitive man presumably stumbled by accident, rather than design, upon discoveries that gave him superior advantages, reacted upon his dormant inventive faculty and developed it. Among the earliest of these discoveries was fire.

The early Palaeolithic man must have witnessed, even utilized, fires engendered by lightning, falling meteors and other natural occurrences. Bits of fresh meat, green fruit, edible roots must have fallen accidentally into fires. The resulting tenderness and improved flavour no doubt invited experimentation on the part of the intellectually alert or curious. He, moreover, must have experienced repeatedly sparks and blazes generated by the accident of friction or percussion as he chipped or flaked flints and other hard stones; but he had to wait for generations before the appearance of some unnamed Edison, or rather Edisons, who pondered over that phenomenon and

[1] J. Franklin Ewing, "Aurignacian Man in Syria", *American Journal of Physical Anthropology*, n.s., vol. iv (1946), pp. 252-3; do., *al-Mashriq*, vol. xli, No. 2 (1947), pp. 74-104. Archaeological finds of 1948 indicate continuous human habitation in the Anṭilyās valley as far back as 75,000 B.C.

[2] Al-Ṭābūn; Garrod and Bate, p. 129.

[3] Maghārat al-Wādi, near the western edge of Carmel.

[4] Garrod and Bate, p. 129.

tried to generate and control it for their purposes. Thereby was ushered in one of the greatest revolutions in the history of the progressive march of mankind. The value of a blaze was gradually realized not only for preparing new dishes but also as a measure of protection against cold and as a means of warding off wild beasts and driving game out of woods.

Language

Another dynamic achievement of early Palaeolithic times was the development of that distinctive means of communication between one human being and another called language. The origins of language should be sought in the workings of a mind that was only beginning to be human and therefore beyond the reach of our scrutiny. As a purposive activity designed to establish mental contact between man and man, language helped to weld isolated individuals into groups. Its whole process of evolution and acquisition was one of progressive socialization. But since it could have left no tangible traces until the invention of writing millenniums later, we have no archaeological data for its investigation.

The middle Stone Age

The Old Stone Age shades off imperceptibly into the New Stone Age, in which man used polished stone implements. The transitional period has been termed Mesolithic, or middle Stone Age, and lasted some four thousand years beginning about 10,000 B.C. Not only did the Mesolithic man polish flint, basalt and other stone weapons and tools and thus render them more effective for his purposes but he also for the first time exploited to an appreciable extent his environmental resources. In Palestine this culture is well represented by the Naṭūfian, so called from Wādi al-Naṭūf, north-west of Jerusalem, whose cave (al-Shaqbah) was excavated in 1928 by Miss Garrod.[1] Elements of Naṭūfian culture were later discovered in Maghārat al-Wādi and other sites.

The Naṭūfian culture

The Naṭūfian culture had its start early in the Mesolithic and lasted to the sixth millennium. Its human constituents belonged to a race smaller in stature than the earlier one, slender and round-headed, resembling the Chalcolithic man of Byblus (Jubayl) and the pre-dynastic Egyptians. Evidently they were members of the same race to which the Hamites and Semites of

[1] Dorothy A. E. Garrod, "Excavation of a Palaeolithic Cave in Western Judaea", *Palestine Exploration Fund Quarterly Statement* (1928), pp. 182-5; Garrod and Bate, p. 114.

later times belonged.[1] In the Naṭūfian the fauna, though of the general modern type, reveals important differences from that of the present day. Gazelle remains are still plentiful but are those of the fallow deer, now rare, suggesting a condition of aridity; the hyena was then spotted, of the species now found only south of the Sahara; the hedgehog was quite distinct from the short-eared species now extant.[2] Climatic conditions may have been responsible for the later disappearance of such animals as the horse and the red deer. The industry is rich in

From John and J. B. E. Garstang, " Story of Jericho " (Marshall, Morgan & Scott)

VOTIVE CLAY FIGURINES OF COWS, GOATS, SHEEP, PIGS AND DOGS FOUND IN THE REMAINS OF A JERICHO SHRINE OF NOT LATER THAN 5000 B.C.

worked and carved bones and notched arrowheads. Its implements are of the small or microlithic type, a characteristic of Mesolithic culture.

Domestication of animals

The discovery of an almost complete skull of a large dog in the strata of a Carmel cave[3] provides the first evidence of the domestication of animals — another epoch-making event in man's upward march towards a civilized life. The dog was domesticated when man was still a hunter. Besides his usefulness in hunting and guarding, the dog was the first garbage

[1] W. F. Albright, " The Present State of Syro-Palestinian Archaeology ", *The Haverford Symposium on Archaeology and the Bible* (New Haven, 1938), p. 7.

[2] Garrod and Bate, p. 153.

[3] Al-Wādi; Garrod and Bate, pp. 175-7.

collector. Other evidence shows that the domestication of cattle, which led to a life of herding with a more reliable supply of food than hunting, came later. Man had to domesticate himself before he could domesticate other animals. Votive figurines of clay representing such domestic animals as cows, goats, sheep and pigs were found in a Jericho shrine of the late sixth millennium before Christ.[1] The domestication of animals usually takes place while man is still in a nomadic stage and, therefore, precedes the practice of agriculture. Some Mesolithic man in the Near East must have hit upon the idea of animal domestication by chance. Moved by pity or love, he on some occasion spared the young of some beast, after the mother had been killed, and the puppy or ewe was reared with that man's own children. It worked. The experiment was repeated and expanded. Man offered protection and in return received from the beast milk and service in terms of hunting and burden bearing. The primitive society of Palaeolithic culture was giving way to a higher state.

Agri-culture

While man was a hunter, his movements were dictated by those of the wild animals he sought for food. With the domestication of animals, in the pastoral stage, he remained a wanderer but with this difference: his movements were dictated by his quest of green pastures for his herds. The Naṭūfian culture, however, witnessed in the late Mesolithic or perhaps early Neolithic Age the initiation of another movement which tended toward a sedentary mode of life and exercised an even more abiding influence upon man, the practice of agriculture.

Syria was fortunate in being the home of noble animals adaptable for taming as it was in being the home of useful grasses capable of domestication. Wild wheat and barley grow native in North Syria and in Palestine [2] and their nutritive value must have been discovered very early. Flint sickles and other implements left by Naṭūfians [3] in considerable numbers evince the fact that they and their contemporaries, the North Syrians, were the first in the Near East to practise some form of agri-

[1] John Garstang and J. B. E. Garstang, *The Story of Jericho* (London, 1940), pp. 49-51.

[2] Childe, p. 45; René Neuville, "Les Débuts de l'agriculture et la faucille préhistorique en Palestine", *Journal of the Jewish Palestine Exploration Society* (1934–5), pp. xvii *seq.*

[3] D. A. E. Garrod, "A New Mesolithic Industry: The Natufian of Palestine", *Journal Royal Anthropological Institute of Great Britain*, vol. lxii (1932), pp. 261, 263, 265.

culture. The people were still mostly cave-dwellers (troglodytes) related to those of Egypt,[1] living on hunting and fishing. Some were pastoral. The practice of agriculture no doubt began as rude hoe culture, necessitating movement from place to place as the surface soil became exhausted. The initial steps were taken presumably prior to the sixth millennium, centuries before the appearance of pottery or metals. The food gatherer now became a food producer. Gourds and skin bags were still used for storing and transporting food and liquids. There is no evidence of agricultural practice by any other people so early in history. It is evidently from Syria that early Semitic emigrants into Egypt introduced wheat as well as viticulture.[2] In ancient Egyptian the word for wheat (*qmḥw*) and the word for vineyard (*ka*(*r*)*mu*) are of undoubted Semitic, more specifically Canaanite, etymology.[3] Pictures of ploughs from Babylonia, Egypt and modern Syria look strikingly alike (see below, p. 145, fig.).

How the Mesolithic man discovered the possibility of the domestication of plants no one can exactly tell. Hitherto man had been wont to include wild grain kernels in his food. Some of this wild grain must have accidentally spilled on the ground at a certain time and some man, or rather superman, noticed the dense growth of grain about the preceding year's camping-ground. Then the great idea dawned upon his consciousness. No less of a superman must have been he who by force or by persuasion prevailed upon his tribe to refrain from consuming all the seeds gathered at a given season and spare some — yea, even select the best — to insure a future crop and even to improve it. The cultivation of wheat and barley opened the way for other cereals, such as millet (*dhurah*), and later for fruits, such as olives, grapes and figs, and to vegetables of varied kinds — all of which were cultivated and improved before recorded history.

Settled life

Plant husbandry was more revolutionary for the progress of man than animal husbandry. As it advanced, man began living in clay huts or mud-brick houses. Remnants of primitive habitats have been found in the earliest levels of the human

[1] Strabo, *Geography*, Bk. XVII, ch. 1, § 2.
[2] H. R. Hall, *The Ancient History of the Near East*, 8th ed. (New York, 1935), pp. 89-90.
[3] W. F. Albright, "Palestine in the Earliest Historical Period", *Journal of the Palestine Oriental Society*, vol. xv (1935), pp. 212-13.

occupation of Jericho dating back to about 5000 B.C.,[1] followed by those of Tell al-Judaydah,[2] Ra's al-Shamrah[3] and, among others, Byblus.[4] No earlier settlements of man have been found anywhere else. Jericho has perhaps the longest continuous existence of any city in the world. With the full adoption of stock and crop raising, Mesolithic man, hitherto a nomad, now became a creative settler, a master of the sources of his food supply. Caves and rock shelters in highlands were gradually abandoned in favour of settlements in plains. Land ownership arose. While man was still a wanderer, not fixed to one place to be sufficiently impressed by his environment, his environment could not radically alter him or give him its local colour. His experience tended to become scattered, dissimilar. Now, however, fixity of abode made for accumulation and transmission of similar experience in the form of cultural tradition. Thus did the sedentary man develop store-houses not only of food but also of ideas which enabled him better to transmit his experience to future generations.

Higher life

One important result of community life was the strong impetus it gave to the evolution of language. What astounds us today is the degree of elaborateness to which language was developed by the Palaeolithic mind. A comparison of modern colloquial Arabic, for example, with the reconstructed mother Semitic tongue reveals a continuing process of simplification from the high and remote prehistoric level.

Another relic of the higher life of Mesolithic man is religious belief in some deity or deities and a crude idea of some life for the departed person after death. This is indicated by the presence of food vessels and offerings in burial places. Traces of such hazy belief in an after-life go back to the Mousterian culture. But now the practice of agriculture and animal husbandry made religion more complex. In the pastoral stage people were presumably devotees of the Moon-God, who in a warm country like Syria-Palestine was more beneficent and kindly disposed

[1] Garstang and Garstang, pp. 47-8.

[2] In North Syria; its ancient name still unknown. See below, p. 20, n. 4.

[3] Claude F. Schaeffer, *Ugaritica* (Paris, 1939), pp. 3-4.

[4] Maurice Dunand, *Fouilles de Byblos*, vol. i (Paris, 1939), text, pp. 295-6, considers the Byblus buildings of about 3200 B.C. the earliest monumental stone construction in the Orient and perhaps in the world. The builders were probably pre-Semitic. The necropolis goes back to the first half of the fourth millennium.

than the sun. He dispelled the terrors of darkness and brought about coolness in which the flocks could comfortably graze. He, rather than the sun, was the shepherd's friend. The Jericho shrine of the late sixth millennium B.C. may have been dedicated to this god.[1]

In the agricultural stage man established in his mind association between growth and sun, which then began to take precedence over the moon. Besides the worship of the Sun-Goddess, the worship of earth mother in the person of a goddess of fertility who had charge of plantation then had its start. For still another reason religion assumed a distinctly feminine cast: agriculture could be practised by woman with more ease than hunting. Cultic symbolism and mythology associated with the goddess of fertility, which reached their full bloom later in the Adonis-Ishtar and the Osiris-Isis cycles of Phoenicia and Egypt, have their origins in this period. A triad of plastic statues from early Jericho, consisting of father, mother and son,[2] must have a cultic significance and suggest that in the fifth millennium family organization had taken the form it later permanently assumed.

Along with the religious growth of Mesolithic man went his artistic evolution. Like language art is a distinctive mark of humanity. It was born when the possibility of deliberate imitation awoke in the consciousness of some Stone Age man. Thereupon man's soul entered a new world, that of imagination and beauty. Art

In its earliest manifestation art was closely associated with magic; the image of the animal supposedly gave the painter power over the object represented. The head of a bull carved in bone by a Mesolithic man has been found in a Carmel cave. Aware of the forces surrounding him and conscious of his helplessness, man evolved a system of magic, implemented with amulets of bone and stone, whereby he sought protection from objects he feared. Fear was a basic element in his early religion. Later he sought through magic advantages including increase in the produce of his herd or crop. Animism and magic presumably lay at the base of primitive religion. Animism made him endow all objects around him with an indwelling spirit which should be placated if maleficent or catered to if beneficent.

[1] See above, p. 16.

[2] Garstang and Garstang, p. 57.

Naṭūfian carvings in bone and stone are numerous, the best being the statuette of a fawn made from the end of a bone. Apparently " the earliest known examples of plastic art, at any rate in Palestine ",[1] are those votive offerings in the form of images of domestic animals found in Jericho.[2]

Neolithic culture

In the Neolithic, or late Stone Age, which lasted about two millenniums beginning about 6000 B.C., marked advance was made in agriculture, animal breeding, the use of polished stone implements and settled life. It also saw the invention of pottery and the discovery of metal. The Mesolithic culture of Syria-Palestine differs from other Mesolithic cultures in that its two characteristic features of cattle breeding and agriculture antedate pottery and metals.

When man learned to mould pots out of clay and bake them, he hit upon another momentous discovery in his cultural progress. Earthenware vessels soon replaced gourds, skins and hollowed-out pieces of stone or wood which had hitherto served, albeit imperfectly, his economic needs. The new invention meant that man could now safely live some distance from the source of his water supply, could truly cook his food and not only eat it raw or roasted, and — what is even more important — could conveniently store, for future use, what he could not consume at a given time. To his control over food supply man now added control over its preservation. The food gatherer of the nomadic stage who turned food producer in the agricultural stage now became, in addition, food conserver. This gave him leisure from the all-time consuming search for means of sustenance, and leisure was an essential in the furtherance of the higher things of life

Pottery

Pottery makes its appearance in Palestine in one of the lowest strata of Jericho. Garstang believes it was invented there.[3] It first took the form of basins scooped in the earth and lined with a limy coat, then simple jars with plain rims, flat bases and loop (or knob) handles. In Syria the earliest pottery comes from the Mesopotamian part of the country; monochrome North Syrian pottery may date from about 5000 B.C This was followed by painted pottery from Tell al-Judaydah,[4]

[1] Garstang and Garstang, p. 54. [2] See above, p. 15.

[3] Garstang and Garstang, pp. 53-4.

[4] Excavated by Robert J. Braidwood; see his *Mounds in the Plain of Antioch* (Chicago, 1937), p. 7

north-east of Antioch, dating from about the middle of the fifth millennium and decorated with designs of a most primitive type. To the same cultural level belongs the painted pottery found in Sakje Geuzi, in the far north of Syria, the earliest of which is black incised ware, followed by new fabrics of coloured decoration.[1] Sherds of North Syrian pottery have been found as far east as Sāmarra on the Tigris. The potter's wheel must have been invented before 4000 B.C., but was not used masterfully in southern Palestine until about 2000 B.C. Prior to its invention, pottery was all hand-fashioned.

The late fifth and early fourth millenniums witnessed the highest stage in the early history of decorative art. North Syria and Mesopotamia was its centre. The culture may be termed Ḥalafian, from Tell al-Ḥalaf[2] (ancient Gozan) on the Khābūr River. In the west it is represented by Marsīn in Cilicia. Its exponents were vase painters who evidently worked in emulation of skill already attained by basket makers and rug weavers. Technically and artistically their wares, including dishes, bowls, platters, jars and cups, rank among the finest hand-made fabrics of antiquity. They used intricate polychrome geometrical and floral designs that "have not been surpassed in beauty, at least from our modern viewpoint, at any subsequent time in history".[3] Nor do we have reason to believe that man's mental capacity has greatly increased since that time. From this painted pottery era the greatest number of settlements, the thickest deposits and the highest cultural remains come from North Syria-Mesopotamia, leaving no doubt that the main stream of civilization in Western Asia flowed then through that region, leaving all surrounding zones relatively unaffected.

The addition of pottery to man's household goods serves incidentally a most useful scientific purpose. Pottery is imperishable, though it may be smashed into innumerable sherds; its make and decoration reflect the tastes and fashions of the age as women's clothing does in our day; its distribution affords

[1] John Garstang, "Excavations at Sakje-Geuzi, in North Syria", *Annals of Archaeology and Anthropology*, University of Liverpool, vol. i (1908), pp. 114-17.

[2] Excavated by Max F. von Oppenheim; see his *Der Tell Halaf* (Leipzig, 1931). "Tell" is an artificial mound made up of the ruins of many cities one on top of the other. It is a phenomenon peculiar to Western Asia, where it was represented as early as 2000 B.C. The word is Arabic of Sumerian origin.

[3] William F. Albright, *From the Stone Age to Christianity* (Baltimore, 1940), p. 98.

the best index of early trade relations. Therefore its study opens up before the modern scholar one of the widest windows through which he can peep into the obscure realm of the past. Metallurgy provides a later window. With ceramics and metallurgy we pass from prehistory to protohistory.

CHAPTER III

METAL IMPLEMENTS

THE discovery of metal initiated a new and significant stage in the ascent of man, the metal stage, in which metal displaced stone as the dominant material for the manufacture of implements.

Chalcolithic

The discovery may have been made in Western Asia not long after the invention of pottery, but the wide use of its first important representative, copper, must have been delayed a thousand years or so. In Syria-Palestine copper began to be more or less widely used around 4000 B.C., but it did not displace stone as the dominant material of tools and weapons till after 3000 B.C. This millennium, the fourth, may be designated the Chalcolithic Age; in it copper was utilized by the most progressive communities, but flint undoubtedly remained the principal material. Traces of Chalcolithic culture abound in Ugarit and other sites in northern Syria and in Tulaylāt al-Ghassūl [1] (whence some of the earliest metal implements so far found in Palestine come) and other Palestinian sites. About 3000 B.C. the Copper Age begins, often wrongly designated the Bronze Age. The discovery about 2000 B.C. of ore deposits in Edom, south and east of the Dead Sea, completed the triumph of copper.

In the Chalcolithic as in the Neolithic period, North Syria remains the main cultural focus of the entire Near East. Someone here must have hit upon copper as he happened to bank his camp fire with pieces of ore and noticed the next morning, as he stirred the embers, the shining beads of metal. Little did that Neolithic North Syrian realize that he had taken thereby a step in a revolutionary movement destined to raise the whole level of culture from the stone to the metal plane. With the

[1] Excavated in 1929–32 by the Pontifical Biblical Institute; see Alexis Mallon *et al.*, *Teleilāt Ghassūl* I (Rome, 1934); Robert Koeppel *et al.*, *Teleilāt Ghassūl* II (Rome, 1940).

discovery of metal and the realization of its properties man stood at the threshold of a new era that lasted until our modern times. Bronze followed copper and iron followed bronze. The beginning of the bronze era coincided with the invention of the alphabet. The illiterate cultures of Syria then come to an end; the literate culture begins.

From Syria the knowledge of copper was disseminated in all directions. Pre-dynastic Egypt very likely received it from this source through the Semitic invasion.[1] The region of Nineveh may likewise have acquired this knowledge from its western neighbour.[2] Thus did the Syrian Saddle,[3] straddling the area from the Gulf of Alexandretta to the bend of the Euphrates, loom in significance as the scene of the domestication of wheat, the local invention of pottery and the discovery of metal.

The relics of man in this region indicate that he used first copper, later its harder alloy bronze, for the manufacture of weapons of war before he used it for tools of peaceful pursuit Tribes or communities employing weapons of such malleable, ductile and tenacious metal enjoyed a preponderant advantage over those employing stone. But the arts of peace benefited equally. The art of building markedly improved. Sizable structures make their appearance. Remains of houses reveal that they were rectangular in plan, but the shrines were circular.

The Ghassūlian culture

In the Chalcolithic city of Tulaylāt al-Ghassūl, north of the Dead Sea, one of the largest sides of the rectangular houses often faced a courtyard. The walls were of mud brick, the foundations of uncut stone. The roofs were made of reeds covered with mud. Under the floors were buried infants within jars; some of the dead were cremated — a distinctly un-Semitic practice. A cave was set aside by the Gezirite cave-dwellers for burning the bodies of their deceased companions. Burning provided the simplest way of disposing of the dead body; through it the ghost was safely laid away and no harm could reach the survivors. Similar jars containing the dead, not burned but set upright in the embryonic (contracted)

[1] Hall, p. 90; see above, p. 17.

[2] The Sumerians in the south probably discovered this metal earlier and independently received their supply from 'Umān; see Hitti, *History of the Arabs*, 4th ed. (London, 1949), p. 36; "Sumerian Copper", *Report British Association for the Advancement of Science*, 1928 (London, 1929), pp. 437-41.

[3] See below, p. 70.

position and buried under the earth floors of Neolithic homes, have been found as far north as Ugarit,[1] and also at Carchemish (Jarābulus) of later date.[2] Pot burials were discovered elsewhere as in Gezer [3] (Tell al-Jazar), south-east of modern al-Ramlah, which belonged to the same early culture. In Gezer the cave-dweller can be noticed on his way to becoming a house-dweller. The later village was encircled by a rude wall, as many other villages of the Bronze Age were, to afford protection against enemies. City fortifications begin with that age. With a burned corpse found in a Gezer cave was placed pottery filled with food and drink,[4] showing increased interest in the dead.

Beneath Gezer's shrine a heap of bones indicates that the pig, long domesticated by Palestinians, was the preferred animal for sacrifice — a fact that made it an object of abhorrence to their enemies and successors, the Semites.[5] In Gezer grapes and olives were grown and trodden in pits with a lower cup for the dregs.[6] Such simple forms of rock-cut fruit presses have been found elsewhere, too. The grape-vine and olive tree were evidently indigenous to the Mediterranean basin and were first intensively cultivated and fully domesticated in its eastern end, whence they spread later to the west through the distributing agencies of trade and colonization. The same is true of the fig tree. Olives and olive oil, grapes, figs, wheat and barley are until the present day the staple articles in Syrian diet. In the generally poor soil of such a country as Palestine the yield of barley is far in excess of that of wheat. China's wheat is precisely the same as that of the Near East, and the wild ancestors of her domestic ox and sheep appear to be derived from the Near Eastern wild forms.[7]

Other Chalcolithic towns of the Ghassūlian type have been

[1] Claude F. A. Schaeffer, "Les Fouilles de Ras-Shamra", *Syria*, vol. xv (1934), pp. 111-12, pl. xi, No. 2, facing p. 110.

[2] C. Leonard Woolley, "Hittite Burial Customs", *Annals of Archaeology and Anthropology*, University of Liverpool, vol. vi (1914), p. 88; *Carchemish*, vol. ii (London, 1921), pp. 38-9.

[3] Excavated 1902–8 by R. A. Macalister; see his *The Excavation of Gezer*, 3 vols. (London, 1912).

[4] Macalister, vol. i, pp. 74 *seq.*, 285 *seq.*

[5] Macalister, vol. ii, pp. 379-80.

[6] Macalister, vol. ii, p. 49.

[7] Carl W. Bishop, "The Beginnings of Civilization in Eastern Asia", *Journal of the American Oriental Society*, vol. lix, suppl. (Dec. 1939).

[8] Robert M. Engberg and Geoffrey M. Shipton, *Notes on the Chalcolithic and Early Bronze Age Pottery of Megiddo* (Chicago, 1934).

excavated at Jericho, Megiddo[8] (Tell al-Mutasallim), ʿAffūlah, Beth-shean (Baysān), Lachish (Tell al-Duwayr), Ugarit and Byblus. The Ghassūlian culture of Palestine corresponds to that of the Ḥalafian of North Syria and Mesopotamia, though coming a little later.

Irrigation agriculture

In the meantime impetus was given to agriculture and animal husbandry. The ox, sheep and goat, whose domestication began in the Neolithic, were now widely used, as evidenced by their frequent appearance on figurines. Other common domestic animal figures represent pigs and doves. From later evidence we learn that the dove was associated with the mother goddess, the deity representing the principle of life and fertility. Almost all of the Chalcolithic settlements had their location in river valleys or alluvial plains and depended upon irrigation. In the realm of agriculture the outstanding Chalcolithic achievement thus came to be irrigation culture, involving the cultivation of several varieties of garden vegetables: lettuce, onions, garlic, chick-peas, horse-beans and condiments. This increase in the variety and quantity of available food is reflected in the noticeable rise of the median human stature in the late Chalcolithic.

Ethnic relationship

The ethnic composition of the population of the varied settlements at this time is not clear. The prevailing element was surely not Semitic; the Semites, as we shall see later, are still to come and occupy both North and South Syria. Their advent must have taken place toward the close of the Chalcolithic period. It may be assumed that some of the population of this period belonged to the same original stock from which Semites and Hamites were later differentiated. Others were evidently members of the so-called Armenoid family, as a study of the skeletal finds of Gezer in the south suggests.[1] Other archaeological remains unearthed in Carchemish and Sakje Geuzi in the north suggest affiliation and evince the wide prevalence of this type throughout Chalcolithic Syria. This is corroborated by the fact that many early place names in Central and North Syria, including Dimashq (Damascus) and Tadmur[2] (Palmyra), admit of no certain Semitic etymology; they may be survivals of pre-Semitic nomenclature. The Armenoid, which is the eastern branch of the Alpine, is characterized by the prominent nose and broad, short skull. The Hurrians and pre-Indo-

[1] Macalister, vol. i, pp. 58-9.

[2] See below, pp. 163, 388-9.

Europeans among the ancients and the Armenians and Jews among the moderns are its representatives. Reinforced by later movements, such as the Hittite, the type has its characteristic features still conspicuous throughout the land.

That varied ethnic strains entered into the composition of the population cannot be doubted, but that there was a strange race

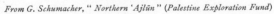

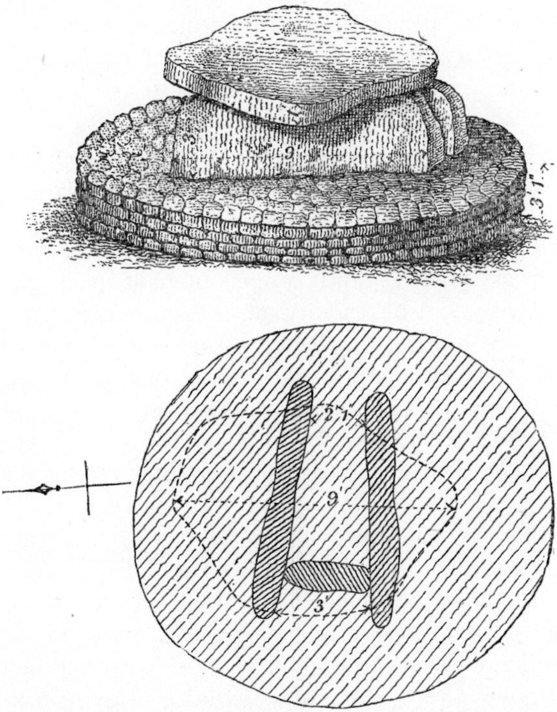

From G. Schumacher, "Northern 'Ajlūn" (Palestine Exploration Fund)

DOLMEN NEAR KAFR YŪBA, SOUTH-WEST OF IRBID IN NORTHERN TRANSJORDAN

of "giants in the earth in those days" [1] cannot be proved. The widely scattered huge cave tombs, some of which are hundreds of feet in length, together with the monumental tomb structures called dolmens, built by unworked boulders (megaliths) on solid circular foundations, must have so greatly impressed the newcomers as to give rise to such legends. Those relating to the

[1] Gen. 6:4.

" sons of Anak "[1] and to the Amalekites have perpetuated themselves in the Arabic and Islamic literature. The name of a Palestinian town in the district from which Goliath came, Bayt Jibrīn (Heb. Beth Gubrin), means " home of the giants "

Dolmens abound until today in Transjordan, the hill country of Palestine and the uplands of Syria as well as in Asia Minor. The marks of metal implements on the walls of certain huge caves and the copper rings unearthed in one of the Transjordan dolmens[2] prove their Chalcolithic date. The most primitive among them are found in the land of Canaan and go back to the Neolithic, 5000 B.C. The megalithic structures of Western Europe came a thousand or more years later and gave rise to similarly fantastic stories about prehistoric giants.

Aesthetic development

Art in general and its plastic variety in particular took a long stride forward subsequent to the introduction of metal. Seals, jewelry articles and copper utensils from this period abound. The artistic quality of these and similar products improved. Sculpture, which had its inception at the Mesolithic Age as we learned before, began now to be seriously cultivated. Figures of men and animals were discovered on paving-stones of late Chalcolithic levels of Megiddo. Contemporaneous mural paintings from Tulaylāt al-Ghassūl, depicted on the plastered inner surfaces of mud-brick walls, represent human or divine figures in several colours.[3] This was the earliest known attempt at decorating a house's interior. But it was ceramic decoration which continued to provide the artist with the best opportunity for the exercise of his talent. By the end of the fourth millennium the technique of glaze painting had reached early Minoan Crete and early dynastic Egypt from North Syria. Vases decorated with glaze paint in the North Syrian tradition occur as imports in the graves of the first Pharaohs at Abydos. From Tell al-Judaydah in North Syria there has come a hoard of cast copper statuettes, including a god and a goddess of fertility,[4] believed to be the earliest known representation of the human form in metal.

[1] Num. 13:33.

[2] Gottlieb Schumacher, *Northern ʿAjlūn* (London, 1890), p. 176.

[3] Millar Burrows, *What Mean These Stones* (New Haven, 1941), p. 188; Chester C. McCown, *The Ladder of Progress in Palestine* (New York, 1943), pp. 61-3.

[4] Now in the Oriental Institute of the University of Chicago; consult its *Handbook and Museum Guide* (Chicago, 1941), pp. 6-7.

The development of metallurgy and ceramics which featured the late Chalcolithic and the early Copper Ages gave rise to different trades, increased business relations between villages and towns and resulted in a higher degree of specialization in labour. Populous towns flourished in plains and valleys and in hitherto uninhabitable places. Trade began to assume international proportions. Expansion of commercial and cultural contacts between Syria-Palestine-Lebanon, on one hand, and Egypt and Babylonia, on the other, was a factor of primary significance for the future life of all these lands. The whole tempo of life in the Near East was speeded up, just as it was in modern times by the discovery of steam and electric power.

Only one great invention is lacking before we can make our entry into the full light of history: writing. The first inscribed documents thus far discovered came from Sumer about 3500 B.C. From lower Mesopotamia the art spread into North Syria. It became well advanced in the early third millennium. With it history begins. But before we enter the historic period in the life of Syria let us catch a glimpse of the history of the land itself which set the stage for the historic events.

CHAPTER IV

THE SETTING OF THE STAGE

THE ruling feature of Syrian topography is an alternation of lowland and highland that runs generally parallel with a north-to-south orientation. Between sea and desert a series of five such longitudinal strips may be delineated.

Maritime plain

On the west the first of these strips is the maritime plain stretching along the shore of the eastern Mediterranean from the peninsula of Sinai to the Gulf of Alexandretta (ancient Issus, Ar. Iskandarūnah).[1] Hemmed in between sea and mountain the plain widens in the north and in the south and dwindles to a mere ribbon at the feet of Lebanon. Nowhere is it, adjoining Lebanon, more than four miles wide, whereas in ʿAsqalān (Ascalon) it extends twenty miles. The rise from the coast plain is at times strikingly abrupt. At Jūniyah, north of Beirut, the one-mile-wide plain is succeeded by foothills that rise 2500 feet within four miles from the sea. About three miles south, at the mouth of Nahr al-Kalb (the Dog River, classical Lycus),[2] the mountain cliffs plunge into the very sea providing the natives with a strategic position for intercepting the passage of enemy hordes. Again at Carmel the promontory effaces the plain leaving a passage barely 200 yards wide along the coast and deflects inland the great international highway of ancient times, which had its start in Egypt and followed the coast northward.[3]

Most of the maritime plain owes its origin to a lift of the old sea floor in that remote geological age termed Tertiary. Its chalk deposits were later overlaid in places by alluvium dragged and spread by the running water from the mountain-sides. Around Beirut its overlying sand deposit has been left by the waves of the Mediterranean, which in turn receives it from the Nile. Thus formed of beaches and sea-beds and enriched as well as watered by the adjoining highlands, the coast is every-

[1] See below, pp. 231-2. [2] See below, p. 134, n. 1. [3] See below, pp. 59-60, 63.

where remarkably fertile. In the south it comprises the anciently renowned plains of Sharon and Philistia, whence the name Palestine,[1] in the north the Nuṣayrīyah littoral and in the middle the Sāḥil of Lebanon.

The coastal line throughout is one of the straightest in the world with no deep estuary or gulf except at the very north, Alexandretta. From there to the Egyptian border, a distance of some 440 miles, there is hardly a harbour worthy of the name.

The western range

Overlooking the Syrian littoral is a line of mountains and plateaus that begins with the Amanus in the north and extends to the towering massif of Sinai in the south and whose backbone is western Lebanon, the Lebanon *par excellence*. Lebanon is the skeleton upon which the flesh — the adjoining plains and lowlands — are hung. This is the second of the longitudinal strips. It forms the first barrier to communication between the sea and its eastern hinterland, a barrier that is seriously breached only at each extremity, at the Gulf of Alexandretta, through which access is established via the Syrian Saddle [2] to the Mesopotamian plains, and at the Isthmus of Suez, through which access was maintained to the Red Sea or the Arabian Desert. Between these two extremities the highland barrier is pierced at only the valley of al-Nahr al-Kabīr (the great river, Eleutherus), north of Tripoli, and at the faulted plain of Esdraelon (Marj ibn-ʻĀmir), east of ʻAkka (Acre) and Ḥayfa (Haifa).

The Amanus [3] is a short offshoot or fold sent southward by the Tauric system — which separates Syria from Asia Minor — as if to join hands with the Syrian system to the south. It rounds the Gulf of Alexandretta, forming a barrier between Syria and Cilicia, and rises to a height of some 5000 feet above sea level. Its southern fringe is cleft by the ʻĀṣi (the rebel, Orontes) gorge as this river seeks passage into the sea. The mountain is crossed by roads to Antioch and Aleppo, the chief pass being Baylān (Belian, Pylae Syriae), the celebrated Syrian Gates. The rock formation is partly limestone, as in Lebanon,

[1] See below, pp. 180-81.

[2] See below, p. 70. The modern *sanjāq* (district) of Alexandretta, which includes Antioch, was ceded to Turkey by the French mandatory power over Syria, with the consent of Britain, in the summer of 1939, the eve of the second world war.

[3] Ar. al-Lukkām (from Syr. *ukkāma*, black), Tur. Gavur Daghi (Giaour Dagh, mountain of the unbelievers, i.e. Christians), for it formed during a long period the rampart of the Byzantine Empire against Islam.

partly igneous; near Alexandretta are serpentine rocks with ores of chrome, in which the Turkish mountains are especially rich.[1]

The range is continued south of the mouth of the Orontes by the naked Mount al-Aqraʿ (the bald, classical Casius), which rises to a height of 4500 feet and stretches down to the vicinity of al-Lādhiqīyah (Laodicea), where it bears the name of Jibāl al-Nuṣayrīyah (Bargylus),[2] down to its break at al-Nahr al-Kabīr.[3] This river, which has its source in the Nuṣayrīyah Mountains, marks the division between them and the Lebanon. It also marks the present political division between Lebanon and Syria. The Nuṣayrīyah chain is of Jurassic limestone with basaltic intrusions.[4] Its general outline is comparatively simple but encloses several deep valleys, rugged ravines and steep cliffs which provided the Syrian branch of the Assassins in the Middle Ages with their stronghold and the schismatic Moslems called Nuṣayrīyah with their retreat. Some of its hills are still crowned with the imposing ruins of ancient Crusading castles.

Lebanon

The western range rises to alpine heights in the Lebanon massif which extends from the Nahr al-Kabīr to al-Qāsimīyah,[5] north of Tyre, a distance of 105 miles. The name Lebanon comes from a Semitic root *lāban*, to be white. The mountain is so called from the snow which now caps its peaks about six months of the year. In the crevices at the summits ice lingers all the year round. The highest peak in Lebanon, al-Qurnat al-Sawdā' (the black corner), is 11,024 feet above the sea; its neighbour Ḍahr al-Qaḍīb, in whose lap the large surviving grove of ancient cedars nestles, is about a hundred feet lower, and majestic Ṣannīn, overlooking Beirut and its St. George Bay, is another hundred feet lower.

This cedar grove rests in an amphitheatre pronounced by

[1] Max Blanckenhorn, *Handbuch der regionalen Geologie*, vol. v, pt. 4, *Syrien und Mesopotamien* (Heidelberg, 1914), pp. 5, 14, 29; Alfred E. Day, *Geology of Lebanon* (Beirut, 1930), p. 30.

[2] Pliny, *Natural History*, Bk. V, ch. 17, § 20. On the Nuṣayrīyah see below, pp. 586 *seq*.

[3] The tenth century Arab geographer al-Iṣṭakhri, *Masālik al-Mamālik*, ed. M. J. de Goeje (Leyden, 1870), p. 55, makes al-Lukkām extend as far south as al-Lādhiqīyah and calls the Nuṣayrīyah Mountains Bahrā'; see René Dussaud, *Topographie historique de la Syrie antique et médiévale* (Paris, 1927), p. 146.

[4] Louis Dubertret *et al.*, *Contributions à l'étude géologique de la Syrie septentrionale* (Paris, 1933), vol. i, pp. 23-4.

[5] See below, p 39.

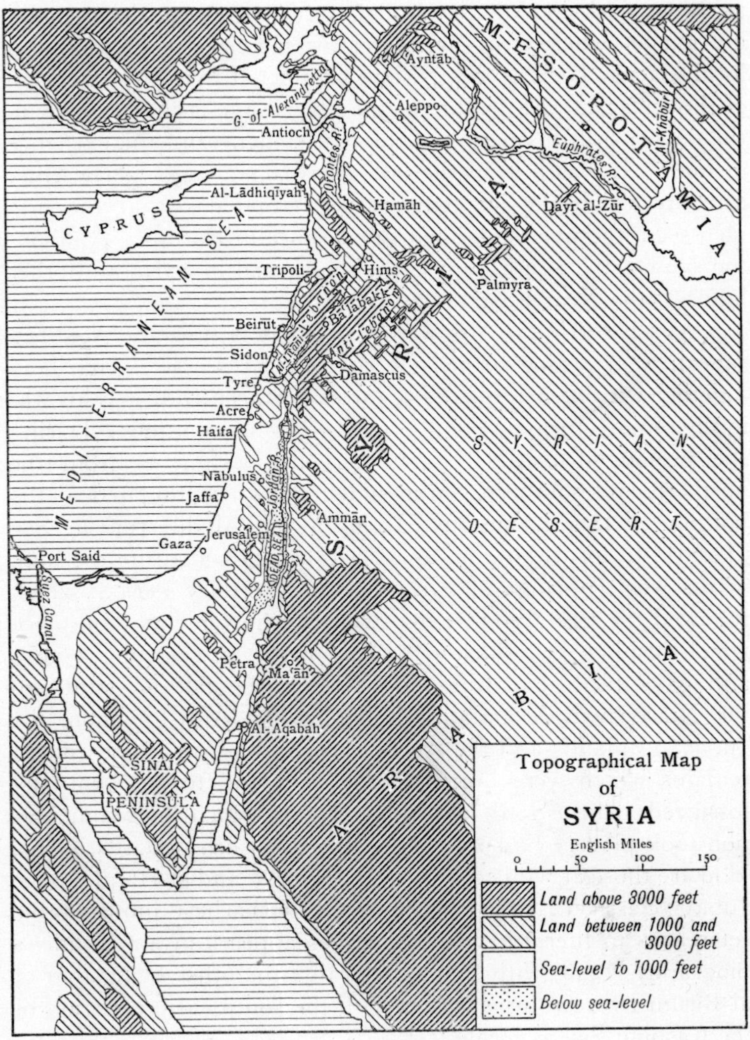

Topographical Map
of
SYRIA
English Miles
0 50 100 150
Land above 3000 feet
Land between 1000 and 3000 feet
Sea-level to 1000 feet
Below sea-level
MESOPOTAMIA
SYRIAN DESERT
ARABIA
SYRIA
MEDITERRANEAN SEA
CYPRUS
SINAI PENINSULA
G. of Alexandretta
Ayntāb
Aleppo
Antioch
Orontes R.
Euphrates R.
Al-Khābūr
Al-Lādhiqīyah
Hamāh
Dayr al-Zūr
Tripoli
Hims
Palmyra
Lebanon
Ba'labakk
Anti-Lebanon
Beirut
Sidon
Tyre
Damascus
Acre
Haifa
Nābulus
Jordan R.
Jaffa
Ammān
Jerusalem
Gaza
DEAD SEA
Port Said
Suez Canal
Petra
Ma'ān
Al-'Aqabah

geologists to have been the terminus of a prehistoric glacier.[1] While the ice of the glacial epoch, which reached south as far as New York in America and covered northern Europe, did not get anywhere near Syria, yet the increased cold produced local glaciers such as this. More significant than the extension of the ice sheet as a feature of the glacial age is the presence in the deposits of this period of the first evidences of the existence of man. It was during the last interglacial stage — a warmer time in which the ice temporarily retreated — that the first men seem to have made their appearance in Europe. At about the same time, if not earlier, they appeared in Syria and other lands of the Near East.

Ages before that, the waters of what is now the Mediterranean Sea, geologists tell us, covered the whole Syrian land together with its neighbours as far as northern India. This was in the remote Jurassic [2] and Cretaceous (chalky) times. During the prolonged periods of submergence sediments from the northern and southern continental masses accumulated at the bottom of this former extension of the Mediterranean Sea (Tethys) to form the limestone rocks which constitute the bulk of the western range of Syria. In the Tertiary Period, which followed the Cretaceous, extensive earth movements took place which resulted in reducing the size of the far-reaching Tethys and gave birth, by lifting and folding the bottom strata, to the Nuṣayrīyah Mountains, Lebanon and Anti-Lebanon, the Judaean uplands and the Arabian desert plateau. The animal remains which were buried in the sediment, to be eventually fossilized, help us to determine the age in which the sedimentation took place. Famous among the fossil fish deposits of this kind are those at Sāḥil ʿAlma (near Jūniyah) and at Ḥāqil (above Jubayl, classical Byblus).[3] One of the two earliest unmistakable references in literature to fossil fishes appears in a Crusader's biography (1248) with Sidon as locale,[4] the other being that of al-Bīrūni two centuries earlier with the south-eastern region of the Caspian Sea as locale.[5]

[1] G. Zumoffen, *Géologie du Liban* (Paris, 1926), pp. 152-3; Day, p. 21.

[2] So called from the Jura Mountains between Switzerland and France, which belong to the same age.

[3] Zumoffen, pp. 137-41.

[4] Joinville, *Histoire de Saint Louis*, ed. Naralis de Wailly (Paris, 1874), § 602.

[5] *Ṣifat al-Maʿmūr*, ed. A. Zaki Valīdī Togan (New Delhi, 1941), p. 56.

The rocks of Lebanon comprise an upper and lower limestone series with an intermediate sandstone. The upper series of limestone strata in Lebanon forms the summits and varies in thickness from a few hundred feet to five thousand feet; the base of the lower series is nowhere exposed to determine its thickness. While forming the bottom of the deepest valleys, the lower series has by foldings been elevated to the height of some 4000 feet in Kisrawān to 7000 near Tawmāt Nīḥa (the twin peaks near Jazzīn east of Sidon) and to about 9000 feet at Mount Hermon. Strewn in abundance on the surface of the lower limestone in both Lebanon and Anti-Lebanon, where that formation happens to crop out, are lumps of iron ore, the smelting of which has been carried on in rude furnaces up to recent times and has contributed to making Lebanon as bare of trees as it is.[1]

It is the limestone of the upper strata that has through the ages dominated the Lebanese scene. Its greyish colour has given the landscape its tone. Its erosion yielded the soil for agriculture and rendered its roads dusty in summer. Its stones provided building material. Through the upper limestone strata rain water has always seeped through as far as the complex of sands and clays, which overlies the lower limestone series and retains the water to create those sparkling gushing springs that bestow their life-giving contents upon the slopes and valleys.

The sandstone series of strata, sandwiched in between the upper limestone, which is late Cretaceous, and the lower limestone, which is late Jurassic, is itself in part early Cretaceous. It constitutes a northward extension of the Nubian sandstone of Egypt, Sinai, Arabia and Transjordan. The thickness of the sandstone layers in Lebanon ranges from a few hundred to a thousand feet. They are devoid of fossils but have thin strata of lignite which has been mined in modern times to supply fuel for silk factories and for the railway during the first world war. In certain districts, such as Kisrawān and al-Matn, east of Beirūt, where erosion has removed the entire upper limestone, the sandstone and the lower limestone are exposed. The latter, usually a reddish brown, has in places a rich diversity of coloration that manifests itself at its best not in Lebanon but in Petra. It produces a soil particularly favourable for the growth of stone pines. Mixed with clay and irrigated by water, it provides the

[1] Day, pp. 29-30.

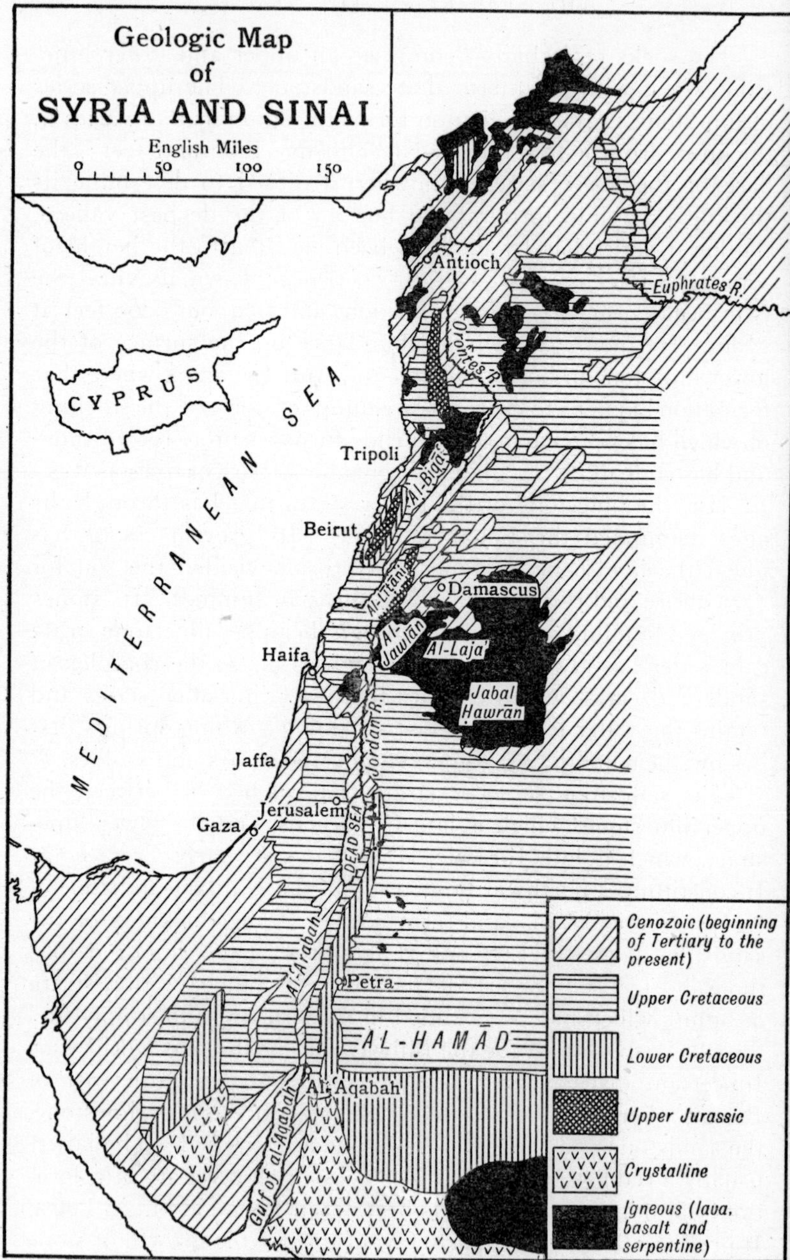

Based on "Carte géologique de la Syrie et du Liban" by L. Dubertret, Beirut, 1933

fertile soil for the fruit and mulberry orchards in which much of the prosperity of the maritime plain around Beirut lies.

The Lebanese landscape sets off the austere outlines of boldly sculptured multicoloured highlands against a sunlit sea whose surface, usually a rich indigo blue, displays every shade of colour. The scenery draws its distinction from its clear sky, distant horizon and that lucid atmosphere in which the outline and colour of its physical features are sharply perceived and in which the pervasive contrast between land and sea, mountain and valley, is distinctly discerned. Such beauty has never ceased to exercise its charm upon poets and bards from Hebrew to Arab times.

Home of the lost cause

The strata of Lebanon, being generally inclined, bent and twisted — often vertical and seldom horizontal — result in a jumble of hills, cliffs and ravines that make communication difficult between one part of the country and the other. This is further complicated by the fact that the whole region is broken by faults along which the different tracts of the country have pressed against and crumbled one another as the tormented crust was in ancient times being subjected to compression and folding. Such terrain has through the ages provided places of refuge for communities and individuals with unpopular loyalties and peculiar beliefs, and at the same time afforded an unusually large proportion of high valleys and fertile tracts which attracted the more enterprising and freedom-loving of the neighbouring population. Maronites, Druzes and Shīʿites (called in Syria Matāwilah) have nestled and maintained their identity in the fastnesses of Lebanon. Armenians and Assyrians, fleeing from Ottoman misrule, were among the last to find haven there. Christian hermits and anchorites preferred its caves to the pleasures of this world, and ancient robber tribes resorted to them for other reasons.[1] Numberless grottoes are today dedicated to the Virgin and other saints, and a whole valley, that of the Qādīsha River[2] extending from the neighbourhood of the large cedar grove to Tripoli, has retained its Syriac name meaning " holy ".

A true mountain, the Lebanon has been through the ages the home of lost causes and the last of the lines to fall to foreign invaders.

[1] Strabo, *Geography*, Bk. XVI, ch. 2, §§ 18, 20. [2] Called abu-ʿAli near the sea.

Galilee

Palestine is geologically a southern continuation of Lebanon.[1] The Lebanese maritime plain is continued through the undulating plain of Sharon,[2] which extends from Carmel to a little south of Jaffa, and connects with the littoral of Philistia.[3] The western Syrian range is continued, south of al-Qāsimīyah cleft, through the plateau and highlands of Upper Galilee, virtually an outlier of the Lebanon, and the chain of low hills termed Lower Galilee. The Upper Galilee highlands attain at al-Jarmaq, north of Ṣafad, an elevation of 3935 feet, the highest in Palestine; Lower Galilee rises to a height of 1843 feet at Mount Tabor near Nazareth. The range then suffers its greatest separation in Esdraelon, which intersects the whole of Palestine, dividing the hill country of Galilee in the north from the hill country of Samaria and Judaea to the south. The hills of Samaria, interspersed with valleys, are represented by Ebal (al-Jabal al-Shamāli, northern mount, 3077 feet) and Gerizim (2849 feet), the holy mountain of the Samaritans. They pass imperceptibly to the rugged and compact limestone tableland of Judaea, which culminates south of Hebron, where Juttah [4] rises 3747 feet above the sea. Jerusalem lies 2550 feet high. The Judaean plateau then rolls down in broad undulations to Beer-sheba (Bi'r al-Sabʻ, the lion's well). This barren southern region was appropriately called Negeb (parched land) by the Hebrews.

Caves

The widespread limestone formations which in Lebanon run out seaward in bold white promontories, hollowed in places by the surf into caves, are symbolized here by Mount Carmel, which rises 1742 feet above the sea and in whose caves the skeletons of the earliest Near Eastern man have been found.[5] Some caves may now be far inland where the sea or its underground river tributaries once penetrated. The troglodytes may have enlarged or altered the grottoes and caves which they used for habitats. As in Lebanon, such caves provided refuge for the persecuted whether on religious or political grounds. Elijah, fleeing from the wrath of Ahab's wife, and David, escaping from Saul's vengeance, sought shelter in caves.[6] Other caves served as burial

[1] Day, p. 24; cf. Dubertret, pp. 70-73.

[2] Heb. *shārōn* means plain; there is no modern Arabic name for it.

[3] See below, pp. 180 *seq.*

[4] In Ar. Bible (Josh. 15: 15) Yūṭah; modern Yaṭṭa; see F.-M. Abel, *Géographie de la Palestine*, vol. ii (Paris, 1938), p. 91.

[5] See above, p. 10.

[6] 1 K. 19:9; 1 Sam. 22:1.

places.[1] It was presumably such a grotto that received Christ's body and thereby became the holiest shrine in Christendom.

The median depression

The third longitudinal strip in the structure of Syria is a long, narrow trough occupying a median position in the scheme of the land. Starting at the north at the western bend of al-ʿĀṣi in a broadish plain called al-ʿAmq,[2] the trough ascends at Ḥamāh to about 1015 feet above the sea, becomes al-Biqāʿ between the two Lebanons and continues south through the Jordan to the Dead Sea and thence through al-ʿArabah to al-ʿAqabah, the eastern arm of the Red Sea. The rift was brought about by the down-dropping of a zone between two great linear faults or fractures in the earth's crust in fairly recent geologic times.[3] This Biqāʿ-Jordan-ʿArabah valley, especially in its southern part, is one of the most singular features of the earth's surface. At al-Ḥūlah its floor is 7 feet above the sea, at Lake Tiberias it is 685 feet below the sea, at the Dead Sea it is 1292 feet below — so rapid is the descent.[4] Here is the real " cellar of the world ", nowhere else is there such a visible depression.

Al-Biqāʿ

Al-Biqāʿ,[5] or the Lebanon trough, varies in breadth from six to ten miles and rises near Baʿlabakk to 3770 feet above the sea. Near by is the swampy watershed whence al-ʿĀṣi starts on its leisurely course northward and al-Līṭāni (Leontes) moves southward. The ʿĀṣi is the largest Syrian river, the Euphrates being Syrian neither in birth nor in demise. The ʿĀṣi and the Jordan are the only two large rivers in Syria. The Līṭāni duplicates the career of al-ʿĀṣi when, in its lower course, it makes an abrupt turn westward at the feet of the Crusading castle Belfort,[6] breaks a passage through the Upper Cretaceous limestone of Lebanon and becomes known as al-Qāsimīyah debouching between Tyre and Sidon.

[1] Gen. 23:9; 49:29-31.

[2] " Unqi " of Assyrian records; see Daniel D. Luckenbill, *Ancient Records of Assyria and Babylonia*, vol. i (Chicago, 1926), §§ 769, 772, 821.

[3] Picard, pp. 4 *seq*.

[4] " Jordan " comes from Heb. *yardēn*, descender. Lake Tiberias is called Gennesaret in New Testament (Luke 5:1; John 6:1), Chinnereth (harp-like) in Old Testament (Num. 34:11; cf. 1 K. 15:20). Al-Ḥūlah is classical Lake Semechonitis.

[5] Literally " places where water stagnates "; classical Coele-Syria, Hollow Syria, which in the Greco-Roman period had a more extensive application as to include Ḥawrān and part of Transjordan; Strabo, Bk. XVI, ch. 2, § 21; Josephus, *Antiquities of the Jews*, Bk. I, ch. 11, § 5; Bk. XIII, ch. 13, §§ 2, 3.

[6] Qalʿat al-Shaqīf; see below, p. 602.

Drained by these twin streams the Biqāʿ affords the largest and best pastoral areas of all Syria. Blanketed with deposits of recent alluvium and loam it provides the most favourable soil for agriculture. But like many other Syrian rivers, the bed of al-ʿĀṣi is so low that its water cannot be readily utilized. Hence those water-wheels,[1] for raising water to the level of the land, whose perpetual monotonous wailing has lulled to sleep successive generations of Ḥamātites since Roman days.

The Jordan valley[2] is some sixty-five miles in length and three to fourteen in width. This singular crevasse receives considerable streams from the west watershed, which makes Palestine the overdrained land that it is, and ultimately spreads its water into the bitterest lake in the world. The unusual salinity of the water of the Dead Sea may be accounted for not only by the lack of an outlet but also by a prehistoric connection with the ocean. It has a high percentage of bromine, potash and magnesium chloride. Bituminous limestone and asphalt of excellent quality are found in and around the Dead Sea as well as in Ḥāṣbayya at the south-western foot of Hermon.

Earthquakes, volcanoes

The faulted scarps of the Lebanon blocks and the long-drawn rift valley continued in the Jordan-Dead Sea depression mark the zone of intense earthquake activity. But the zone of seismic unrest is not limited to the great fracture area. Part of the plateau east of Hermon and south of Damascus is crossed by lines of extinct volcanoes and overlaid here and there by old lava fields. Certain areas are sprinkled with thermal springs as in Tiberias, the region of the Dead Sea and Palmyra.

The history of Syria is more punctuated with earthquakes than its geography with volcanoes. At the northern extremity Antioch was scourged by earthquakes through the ages. In the first six centuries before Christ it was thereby damaged no less than ten times.[3] The walls of the world-renowned temple of the Sun in Baʿlabakk bear scars of seismic disturbances, as do the extant Crusading castles. The sudden collapse of Jericho's walls on the occasion of the Israelite invasion as well

[1] Ar. sing. *nāʿūrah*, whence noria; see below, pp. 292-3.

[2] Ar. Ghawr al-Urdunn, or al-Ghawr. The Jordan is also called Nahr al-Sharīʿah (the watering-place); abu-al-Fidā', *Taqwīm al-Buldān*, ed. M. Reinaud and M. de Slane (Paris, 1840), p. 48.

[3] Ellen C. Semple, *The Geography of the Mediterranean Region* (London, 1932), p. 42.

as the spectacular destruction of Sodom and Gomorrah, at the south-west extremity of the Dead Sea, point to earthquakes, assisted in the case of the last two cities by fire due to earthquake-induced oil exudations and asphalt springs. Hebrew prophets, poets and historians drew upon their personal experience of seismic disturbances accompanied by tidal waves or the often-used imagery connected therewith when they made their early essays to describe the power and might of Jehovah.[1] An earthquake is reported in the New Testament to have occurred at the Crucifixion as well as at the Resurrection.

Such tidal waves were especially destructive along the Phoenician coast. Tyre and Sidon frequently suffered from them as well as from shocks.[2] What made Tyre particularly vulnerable was its "skyscraper" style of buildings, some of which were seventy feet or more high.[3] The last severe earthquake in northern Syria occurred in 1822 and converted Aleppo, among other cities, into a heap of ruins, destroying tens of thousands of human lives; the last in Palestine took place in 1837 and utterly demolished Ṣafad.[4]

The eastern range

The eastern range constitutes the fourth strip in the Syrian relief. Rising from a place south of Ḥimṣ, it opposes Lebanon by Anti-Lebanon[5] in almost equal length and height, falls swiftly from Hermon[6] upon the plateau of Ḥawrān with its hilly neighbour to the west, al-Jawlān,[7] whence it continues in Transjordan through the hills of Gilead into the high tableland of Moab, ending in Mount Seir,[8] south of the Dead Sea.

Anti-Lebanon

Anti-Lebanon is divided by the plateau and gorge of Barada (ancient Abana) into a northern part,[9] on the western

[1] Amos 5:8; 9:6; Is. 29:6; Job 9:5-6; 28:9; Ps. 60:2, 114:3-4; 1 K. 19:11; Num. 16:31-2.

[2] Seneca, *Questiones naturales*, Bk. VI, ch. 1, §§ 11, 13; ch. 24, § 5; Strabo, Bk. I, ch. 3, § 16.

[3] Strabo, Bk. V, ch. 3, § 7.

[4] Francis R. Chesney, *The Expedition for the Survey of the Euphrates and Tigris* (London, 1850), vol. i, pp. 436, 441; H. B. Tristram, *The Land of Israel*, 3rd ed. (London, 1876), p. 567.

[5] Lubnān al-Sharqi, the eastern Lebanon.

[6] Sirion in Ps. 29:6; Deut. 3:9; modern al-Jabal al-Shaykh, the grey-haired mountain; Jabal al-Thalj, the mountain of snow, in al-Maqdisi, *Aḥsan al-Taqāsīm fi Maʿrifat al-Aqālīm*, ed. M. J. de Goeje (Leyden, 1877), p. 160; abu-al-Fidā', pp. 48, 68.

[7] From Heb. Golān (circuit), classical Gaulanitis. Al-Jawlān is mentioned by Yāqūt, *Muʿjam al-Buldān*, ed. F. Wüstenfeld, vol. ii (Leipzig, 1867), p. 159.

[8] Heb. Seʿir, practically synonymous with Edom.

[9] Called Sanīr by Arab geographers; Yāqūt, vol. iii, p. 170.

flank of which there is hardly a village, and a southern part featuring Hermon, which is one of the highest (9383 feet) and most majestic peaks of Syria, and on the western slopes of which many villages flourish. Largely on account of its lower rainfall and sparseness of vegetation, Anti-Lebanon has a more scattered and less progressive population than Lebanon. Its population has always gravitated to it from eastern Syria.[1] The eastern boundary of present-day Republic of Lebanon passes over Hermon, makes a detour around al-Zabadāni and follows the crest of northern Anti-Lebanon. The Beirut-Damascus railway follows the Zabadāni-Barada gorge.

Arising in the rich upland valley of al-Zabadāni village, Barada flows east, reclaims for Syria a large portion of what otherwise would have been a desert and creates Damascus, civilization's outpost in the desert. After irrigating Damascus' celebrated orchards called al-Ghūṭah, whose fragrance bestowed upon the city its Arabic honorific title al-Fayḥā', the river sends off five arms or channels for the benefit of the streets and homes of the ancient metropolis. The present Damascus water system owes its origin to the early Umayyad caliphs.[2]

Hawrān

The surface of the Ḥawrān [3] plateau has the distinction of being predominantly volcanic with basalt rocks and rich soil. The lava field begins in the Tulūl, south of Damascus, and covers an area of nearly sixty miles long by as many wide, the largest in Syria.[4] On the north-east the field is bounded by the black stony fastness of al-Laja',[5] a refuge — as its Arabic name indicates — at all times to turbulent tribes, and on the south-east by the mountainous region called Jabal Ḥawrān, or Jabal al-Durūz. The Druze occupation, however, is a comparatively recent event. It dates from the early eighteenth century subse-

[1] *Ahl al-Jabal* or *Jabalīyūn* (people of the mountain, mountaineers) ordinarily refers to the inhabitants of the western range.

[2] See below, p. 482

[3] Classical Auranitis, biblical Bashan, Assyrian Ḥauranu (cf. Luckenbill, vol. i, §§ 672, 821), " hollow land ". In the narrow sense Ḥawrān is limited to the great plain east of al-Jawlān west of al-Laja' and Jabal al-Durūz; in the broad sense and as a *mutaṣarrifīyah* (political division) under the Turks it comprised all these three districts as well as 'Ajlūn.

[4] D. G. Hogarth, *The Nearer East* (New York, 1915), p. 66.

[5] The Arabs refer to it and its eastern neighbour al-Ṣafa as *al-wa'r*, which corresponds to Trachon, its classical name. George A. Smith, *The Historical Geography of the Holy Land*, 11th ed. (New York, 1904), pp. 615 *seq.*; do., *Syria and the Holy Land* (London, 1918), p. 29.

quent to party disturbances in the Lebanon.[1] This eastern bulwark of Ḥawrān has an average height of 4000 to 5000 feet and intervenes between it and the desert. The volcanic region extends west to include al-Jawlān. Treeless and with very few springs, Ḥawrān bears abundant wheat and good pasture. The soil consists of disintegrated black lava and red loam, rich in plant food and retentive of moisture, overlying the limestone which elsewhere forms the surface rock. The archaeological remains range from dolmens — handiwork of primitive man — to ruins of Roman and Byzantine roads, aqueducts, reservoirs, buildings and fortifications which testify to its once thriving condition and to the fact that it was at one time a granary of the empire. Today it still provides Palestine and Lebanon with wheat as it did in the days of the Hebrews and the Phoenicians.

The volcanic tracts of the Ḥawrān region extend south-east through the Ḥamād desert into those stony fields of al-Ḥijāz called *ḥarrahs*.[2] Transjordan proper continues the Upper Cretaceous layers of the eastern range and culminates in the north in Mount ʿAjlūn (4137 feet) and its neighbour Mount Gilead[3] (3397 feet). In the south near al-Karak[4] it rises to a height of 3775 feet above the sea, while the sandstone strata near Petra attain the height of 4430 feet.

Syrian Desert

The plateaus of north-eastern Ḥawrān and Transjordan pass gradually into steppes, ḥarrahs and sands merging at last into the great wasteland called the Syrian Desert.[5] This is the fifth and last distinct zone in Syrian structure. The desert plains are often rocky and calcareous but seldom stony. This desert is a continuation of the great Arabian Desert, the Syrian part of the Arabian oblong, and separates Syria from al-ʿIrāq. It is the desert bay that intervenes between the eastern and the western horns of the Fertile Crescent. The desert bordering on the eastern horn, or al-ʿIrāq, is called in its northern part Bādiyat al-Jazīrah (Mesopotamian Desert) and in its southern part Bādiyat al-ʿIrāq or al-Samāwah. The surface of the south-western half of the Syrian Desert, al-Ḥamād, is partly stony and partly sandy and is covered with grass in spring. The Syro-

[1] Sulaymān abu-ʿIzz-al-Dīn, "Tawaṭṭun al-Durūz fi Ḥawrān", *al-Kullīyah*, vol. xii (1926), pp. 313-23; see below, pp. 686-7.

[2] Ar. for volcanic tracts.

[3] Heb. for hard, stony region; Ar. Jilʿād.

[4] Le Crac of the Crusades, see below, pp. 596, 601.

[5] Bādiyat al-Sha'm.

ʿIrāqi desert is a huge triangle whose base rests on the Gulf of al-ʿAqabah on the west and the Gulf of al-Kuwayt on the east and whose apex reaches toward Aleppo in the north. At its widest this desert is some 800 miles. Its nomadic denizens trade with the settled population on both sides, act as middlemen, guides and caravaneers and in remote times built such cities as Palmyra, which lay on the trans-desert route between the east and the west. Their blood throughout the ages served as a perennial reservoir of biological vitality to the urban population, supplying it with fresh infusion either through conquest or by peaceful penetration. But normally Bedouins resist the temptation to settle down, and in quest of pasture for their flocks they roam the desert plains which are blanketed with grass after the rain. Bedouin hospitality to guests is not reflected in hospitality to innovations. If the mainspring of progress in a settled community lies in the attempt to change and adapt the conditions of life and environment, the secret of survival in a nomadic community consists in accepting those conditions and adapting one's self to them.

Several of the streams which trickle down the eastern slopes of the Syrian eastern range are vanquished in the struggle with the desert and lie buried in its barren soil. The struggle between the sown and the desert, old as time, is a central fact in the physical geography of that part of the country. The desert, which in many of its aspects resembles the sea, has in its movement through history behaved like a mighty one, endlessly repeating the pattern of ebb and flow. The struggle has its counterpart in the equally ancient conflict between the Bedouins, the " have-not " nomads of the desert, and the settled agriculturists, the " haves " of the fertile plains. Centuries before and centuries after the Israelites, covetous eyes from the desert turned toward the neighbouring lands " flowing with milk and honey ".

CHAPTER V

PHYSICAL ENVIRONMENT

THE stage on which the drama of Syrian history was played has been described in its geologic and geographic setting in the last chapter. In this chapter it will be further described in its physical features including climate, flora and fauna.

The ruling feature of Syrian climate is an alternation of a Climate rainy season from mid-November to the end of March and a dry season covering the rest of the year. This is in general true of the whole Mediterranean region and is due to its location on the margin between two zones of sharply contrasted precipitations: the dry trade wind or desert tract of Africa on the south and the westerly winds on the north. It is these moisture-bearing westerlies which all the year round bring rain from the Atlantic to middle and northern Europe. They are in winter the prevailing winds in Syria; in summer the heat belt moves northward from the equator, and the country for months approaches the arid conditions of the Sahara. The variability of climate which characterizes the northern United States and is said to promote energy does not obtain anywhere there.

As the prevalent westerlies, at times associated with cyclonic storms, sweep over the Mediterranean they become more filled with moisture. They then encounter the Lebanon and the central hilly ridge of Palestine and rise. In rising the air expands and is forced to part with some of its contents in the form of rain. Proximity to the sea, the relief of the land, altitude, distance from the desert and the interplay of Mediterranean and Saharan influences are therefore the determining climatic factors. The result is that the coastal strip of the western flank of the Syrian highlands receives the largest amount of yearly precipitation, which decreases as one goes from west to east and from north to south.

Records bear witness to this result. The average annual rainfall in Beirut for the forty-one years ending July 1926 was

35·9 inches. On the Palestinian coast the mean annual rainfall has been 23 inches. Four thousand feet above Beirut in al-Shuwayr, the average for the twenty-five years ending July 1926 was 59·7 inches; in Jerusalem, 2550 feet above the Palestinian coast, 25·6 inches. At Kasārah, in the central trench flanked by the parallel highlands, the general average is 24·8 inches; in the Jordan valley 5·5 inches. After the central Palestinian highlands little precipitation occurs until farther east where the hills of Transjordan cause the air to ascend and part with what remains of its moisture, thus almost skipping the southern Jordan valley. Behind the double rain-screen of Lebanon, Damascus receives only 10 inches. On the summit of the Transjordan escarpment the mean annual rainfall is 27·55 inches; but east Transjordan receives only 3·9.[1] On the whole the Palestine-Lebanon coast receives more than twice as much precipitation as the corresponding coast of southern California and lower California.

The mean annual temperature in Beirut is 68° F. The maximum degree of temperature recorded in the observatory of the American University of Beirut was 107·06° F. on May 18, 1916; the lowest was 29·82° on December 30, 1897, and January 25, 1907.[2] In the Lebanon coastlands humidity reaches its maximum, strangely enough, in July with an average of 75 per cent, its minimum in December with an average of 60 per cent.[3] In winter the dense, cold, dry anti-cyclonic influences of Central Asia spread over the eastern plateau region of Syria giving it frost and snow, a phenomenon hardly ever experienced along the coast.

Along the littoral, the temperature is moderated by the influence of the sea, which is warmer in winter and colder in summer than the earth. The double-wall barrier and the in-between moat serve to shut off the cooling sea winds from the interior. The dust-laden winds blow from the desert and the summer heat in such cities as Damascus and Aleppo becomes intense. The thermometer occasionally registers in Palestine as

[1] Manṣūr Jurdāq, "Hawā' Jabal Lubnān", *al-Kullīyah*, vol. xii (1926), pp. 413-14; cf. D. Ashbel, "Rainfall Map of Palestine, Transjordan, Southern Syria, Southern Lebanon", 3rd ed. (Jerusalem, 1942).

[2] Jurdāq in *al-Kullīyah*, vol. xii (1926), p. 412.

[3] W. B. Fish, "The Lebanon", *The Geographical Review*, vol. xxxiv (1944), p. 243.

high as 100° F. in the shade; in the Jordan valley it may reach 130°. Most dreaded of the east and south-east hot winds is the simoom, or sirocco,[1] which is particularly oppressive and dry, with a humidity at times under 10 per cent, making it difficult to breathe. It is frequent through spring and autumn, when it often reaches the coast and announces the coming of rain. On the fringe of the desert it is often laden with fine penetrating sand. It was probably a day in which such a wind blew that was chosen by Arabian Moslem generalship for confronting the Byzantine army defending Syria at the decisive battle of Yarmūk in 636.[2]

Erosion

Much of the rain water percolates through large expanses of limestone rock and is thus lost. Some of it gathers in subterranean channels and gushes out in the form of springs. The prevalence of limestone in the Lebanons and Palestine thus introduces another unfavourable factor in addition to the minor one of a shimmering dusty landscape, noticed above. It restricts the water-supply and results in reducing human settlement especially in Anti-Lebanon.

Whatever water does not soak through the calcareous layers flows into streams and rivers which swell into torrents after every heavy rain-pour and shrink in the drought of summer into mere dribbles if not disappear altogether. The onrush of water down the highlands, with its concomitant processes of erosion and denudation, has resulted through the ages in rendering barren tracts of land which were once flourishing. This phenomenon has misled certain scholars to the belief that there have been substantial climatic changes within historic times in Syria and neighbouring lands in the direction of desiccation.[3] As we shall see later,[4] this hypothesis is based on entirely fallacious evidence. No climatic changes or rainfall fluctuations suffice to explain the seemingly strange phenomenon, commonly encountered in eastern Syria, involving vast tracts once thriving

[1] "Simoom" comes from Ar. *samūm*, poisonous, pestilential; "sirocco" from Ar. *sharq*, east, through Italian. The sirocco, popularly supposed to last three days, corresponds to the *khamsīn* (Ar. for fifty) in Egypt.

[2] See below, pp. 413-16. For up-to-date charts of temperature, rain and wind consult Charles Combier, *Aperçu sur les climats de la Syrie et du Liban* (Beirut, 1945).

[3] Ellsworth Huntington, *Palestine and its Transformation* (Boston, 1911), chs. 12-14.

[4] Below, p. 293.

and populous but now impoverished and depopulated. The practical identity of crops since ancient times (exclusive of plants introduced by Arabs from the east in medieval times and by natives from the New World in modern times), the persistence of tillage methods and the preservation through the ages of virtually the same seasonal dates for ploughing and harvesting militate against any theory of desiccation through climatic changes. The real causes of decline in land productivity have been the denudation of the hillside by the running rain water and winds, the failure of certain springs, deforestation and grazing which have deprived the loose soil of roots to hold it together, neglect or destruction of irrigation works by barbarian invasion or nomadic attacks and the possible exhaustion of the soil in certain spots.[1]

Vegetation

Three contrasted zones of vegetation lie side by side in the Syrian area. The coastal plain and the lower levels of the western highlands have the ordinary vegetation of the Mediterranean littoral. Evergreen shrubs and quickly flowering, strongly scented spring plants characterize this zone. The plants that have provided the main food crops of man, e.g. wheat, barley, millet (*dhurah*), which were first domesticated there,[2] still flourish. Maize was introduced later. To onions, garlic, cucumbers and other vegetables known from earliest times [3] were added in modern times tomatoes, potatoes and tobacco from the New World. Almost all American cereals (except maize and some forms of oats), vegetable crops, and common temperate zone fruit trees (except pecan and persimmon) came from Asia, more particularly the Near East, through Europe [4] The Lādhiqīyah (Latakia) tobacco is famous all over the world. The crop of ancient fruits, including figs, olives, dates and grapes, was later enriched by the introduction of new varieties such as bananas and citrus products. Sugar-cane came from the east with the Arab conquerors. The absence of summer rains necessitates irrigation for some of these crops, and the baking Mediterranean sun, whose relentless rays reach the parched land almost daily throughout the dry season, ripens the fruit to perfection. The predominant trees in this zone

[1] Semple, p. 100. [2] See above, p. 16. [3] See above, p. 26.

[4] Walter T. Swingle, "Trees and Plants We Owe to Asia", *Asia*, vol. xliii (1943), p. 634.

are scrub oaks, Mediterranean pines, mulberry and beeches (*zān*). Deciduous trees were formerly, no doubt, more plentiful. The shrinkage of the wooded zone was detrimental to the extent that forests retarded the erosion of the soil in the uplands.

Along the crests of Lebanon and Anti-Lebanon the lowered winter temperature kills off the subtropical palms and shrubs of the coastal region and only such hardy trees as firs, cedars and other coniferous plants survive. This constitutes the second floral zone. Arid in their northern portion the Anti-Lebanon heights present a striking contrast to western Lebanon.

In the third floral zone, represented by the canyon-like trough and the plateaus of eastern Syria, the intense heat in association with a diminished rainfall produces a steppe régime in which trees all but disappear, grasses tend to have a seasonal existence and only coarse shrubs or bushes survive. Poverty of trees and prevalence of dry, thorny bushes likewise characterize the plateau at the fringe of the Syrian Desert. The Orontes and the Jordan flow in deep beds and are of little use for irrigation.

The Transjordan and Ḥawrān plateaus are fortunately so situated as to face the broad wind-gap formed by the comparatively low Samaritan and Galilean hills and to be high enough to condense enough of the moisture left to permit pasturage. In ancient as in modern times Ḥawrān was the granary of Syria and the probable source of wheat export from Palestine to Tyre,[1] and even to Greece.

These three zones of vegetation result from the fact that two distinct floral regions meet in Syria: that of the Mediterranean with that of the West Asiatic steppeland. The interposition of the Lebanon Mountains introduces a new element and imposes a change due directly to the effects of altitude. It makes the transition from Mediterranean to continental influences unusually abrupt.[2] Banana plantations, winter-sport resorts and desert oases are therefore encountered within a range of sixty miles from the sea. But everywhere the contrast between the landscape in spring, when the foliage is at its best, and in summer, when the increased heat has burned up vegetation, is very striking.

[1] 1 K. 5:11; see below, p. 293.

[2] Cf. H. B. Tristram, *The Survey of Western Palestine: The Fauna and Flora of Palestine* (London, 1888), pp. xix-xxii.

The olive tree

In ancient times the only fruit plants cultivated on a large scale were the three drought-resisting species: the fig, the vine and the olive. The vine was introduced by the Phoenicians into the Greek lands and thence into Italy. The olive accompanied or followed the vine on its travel from east to west.[1] The olive tree demands little and yields much. Its fruit formed and still forms one of the main dishes in the diet of the lower classes. To the south of Beirut one of the largest olive orchards in the world stretches for miles. Olive oil was consumed as food,[2] taking the place of butter which is more difficult to preserve, and used for burning in lamps,[3] for ointment and making perfume [4] and for medicinal purposes.[5] It filled the horn of Samuel when he anointed the first king over Israel [6] and acquired such sacredness that to this day it is used in smearing the brow of the dying. The pulp of the fruit after it was crushed was fed to animals and the crushed stones served as fuel. Ever since Noah's dove returned with an olive branch, its leaf has been an emblem of peace, a sign of happiness. In the arboreal convention reported in the Book of Judges (9 : 8), the Palestinian plants acknowledged the superiority of the olive tree by naming it first to be king over them.

The cedar

The most magnificent and renowned among the trees of Lebanon is the cedar (*Cedrus libani*), whose virtues of strength (Ps. 29 : 5), durability (Jer. 22 : 14), majesty (2 K. 14 : 9; Zech. 11 : 1-2) and suitability for carving (Is. 44 : 14-15) were sung by ancient poets, prophets and historians. The cedar provided the early Lebanese with the finest timber for constructing their seafaring ships and attracted kings from the Tigro-Euphrates and the Nile valleys, where no large trees could flourish. Unfortunately today it does not constitute as much of the glory of Lebanon as it anciently did (Is. 35 : 2; 60 : 13). It survives only in small batches — bouquets on the bare breast of Lebanon — the best known of which is that above Bisharri, where upward of four hundred trees, some perhaps a thousand years old, still grow.[7]

[1] For other Syrian trees introduced into Italy see below, pp. 293-4.

[2] 1 Ch. 12:40; Ezek. 16:13.

[3] Ex. 25:6; Matt. 25:3.

[4] Ex. 30:25; 2 Sam. 14:2; Ps. 23:5.

[5] Is. 1:6; Mk. 6:13; Luke 10:34.

[6] 1 Sam. 10:1.

[7] Consult George E. Post, *The Botanical Geography of Syria and Palestine* (London, 1885?), pp. 36-7. Albert E. Rüthy, *Die Pflanze und ihre Teile im biblisch-hebräischen Sprachgebrauch* (Bern, 1942), pp. 41-2.

The highest is about eighty feet. They are popularly referred to as *arz al-Rabb*, the cedars of the Lord. One of them was adopted as the emblem of the modern Republic of Lebanon. A smaller and younger grove survives above al-Bārūk, to the

CEDAR OF LEBANON

This is the cedar tree in the grove above Bisharri chosen as emblem of the Republic of Lebanon and of the American University of Beirut

south, where it is called *ubhul*.[1] Centuries of exploitation of the groves, culminating in their use by the Ottoman Turks for railroad fuel in 1914–18, have not only stripped the mountains of their best trees but have also accelerated the process of

[1] Strictly a species of juniper (*Juniperus sabina*); Heb. *erez*, Ar. *arz* is cedar. But the two words are often confused. The *erez* wood used in the ritual of cleaning after defilement by contact with a leper (Lev. 14:4) or a dead body (Num. 19:6) is evidently juniper, which grew in the wilderness and by the water (Num. 24:6).

erosion, which is always a hindrance to reforestation.

Fauna

Goats and sheep, particularly goats, contributed to facilitating the process of erosion by eating up grass and young sprouts on the hillsides, leaving the soil loose and more exposed to the action of running water. Because of the relief of the Lebanon Mountains and the overdrainage of the Palestinian highlands Syria has always had scant natural grazing for cattle and horses, but the sheep and goats can find enough forage.

The horse

Originally an American wild animal, the horse found its way in remote prehistoric times, when America and Asia formed one single continent, into Eastern Asia. In its wild form it appears as early as Naṭūfian times in Palestine.[1] It was domesticated in early antiquity somewhere east of the Caspian Sea by Indo-European nomads. It was later imported into Mesopotamia on a large scale by the Kassites and through them made its way into Western Asia some two millenniums before Christ. The Hittites passed it on to the Lydians, and the Lydians to the Greeks. The Hyksos introduced the horse into Syria and thence into Egypt some eighteen centuries before the Christian era. From Syria it was also introduced before the beginning of our era into Arabia where, as the Arabian horse, it has succeeded more than anywhere else in keeping its blood free from admixture.[2]

The camel

Like the horse the camel is of American origin and migrated to North-eastern Asia millions of years ago. Thence it made its way through Kashmir and India, where its fossil bones have been found, into north-western Arabia and thence southern Syria. The first known reference to the camel in literature is in Judges 6 : 5, describing the Midianite invasion of Palestine in the eleventh pre-Christian century. The earliest known drawings of this animal belong to Stone Age days and were recently found in Kilwah,[3] Transjordan, where it is rendered in two carvings in one of which it is poised in space behind a Mesolithic ibex.[4] The representation is that of a small one-humped camel, still the typical Arabian camel of today. A fine picture of a

[1] Dorothea M. A. Bate, " A Note on the Fauna of the Athlit Caves ", *Journal of the Royal Anthropological Institute*, vol. xlii (1932), pp. 277-8.

[2] Hitti, *History of the Arabs*, pp. 20-21.

[3] In Jabal al-Ṭubayq, at the south-eastern boundary of Transjordan.

[4] Hans Rhotert, *Transjordanien: vorgeschichtliche Forschungen* (Stuttgart, 1938), p. 176, pl. 15, No. 2; p. 224, pl. 26, No. 1; Agnes Horsefield, " Journey to Kilwah ", *The Geographical Journal*, vol. cii (1943), pp. 71-7.

dromedary, with rider, was found at Tell al-Ḥalaf and dated 3000 to 2900 B.C.[1] The presence of a rider leaves no doubt that the animal was domesticated. At Jubayl a figurine of Egyptian origin, dating from the first half of the second millennium before Christ, represents a camel lying in the characteristic recumbent position.[2] Other Egyptian statuettes belonging to the Old Kingdom (*ca.* 2500 B.C.) and found in Jubayl leave no doubt of the existence of the camel at that time as a beast of burden.

Another animal introduced from arid Asia through Arabia is the ancient breed of broad fat-tailed, long-fleeced sheep, which is still the common type. It is mentioned in biblical and classical literature.[3] The strange practice of fattening sheep that has survived in Lebanon by forcing food through the mouth and manipulating the jaw by the hand was known in ancient Egypt as evidenced by relief sculptures of animals that look like gazelles or goats on tombs going back to the Sixth Dynasty.

Besides the camel and horse Syria has the donkey, mule and other draught animals, and in addition to goats and sheep its domestic animals comprise cows, dogs and cats domesticated from the earliest of times.[4] Cattle, sheep, goats, hogs and chickens are all Asiatic animals which were domesticated and introduced into Europe and thence America.[5] The characteristic wild animals are the hyena, wolf (now rare), fox and jackal, roe and fallow deer. The gazelles, which can go without water for a long period, are rapidly disappearing. The amazing oryx, that can live in the fastnesses of the desert and survive without water, is now probably extinct. The last ostriches were evidently killed in the late twenties of this century in Jabal al-Ṭubayq. Lions and leopards, common in Crusading times,[6] have now disappeared. Snakes, lizards and scorpions are common, especially in the southern part of the country. The characteristic birds are the eagle, vulture, owl, partridge and others familiar to students of biblical literature

[1] Von Oppenheim, *Tell Halaf*, p. 140, and pl. xxi a, facing p. 136.

[2] Pierre Montet, *Byblos et l'Égypte* (Paris, 1928), p. 91, No. 179; "Atlas" vol. (1929), pl. lii. No. 179.

[3] Ex 29:22; Lev. 3:9; Herodotus, *History*, Bk. III, ch. 113.

[4] See above, pp. 15-16.

[5] Swingle in *Asia*, vol. xliii (1943), p. 634; Childe, p. 46.

[6] Usāmah ibn-Munqidh, *Kitāb al-I'tibār*, ed. Philip K. Hitti (Princeton, 1930), pp. 104 *seq.*, 144; tr. *An Arab-Syrian Gentleman and Warrior in the Period of the Crusades* (New York, 1929), pp. 134 *seq.*, 173.

PART II

ANCIENT SEMITIC TIMES

CHAPTER VI

THE ADVENT OF THE SEMITES

IN its broad outline the history of the peoples of Syria may be divided into five main divisions:

(1) The pre-literary age, treated in the preceding chapters;
(2) The Semitic period, beginning with the Amorites (*ca.* 2500 B.C.) and ending with the fall of the Neo-Babylonian (Chaldaean) Empire in 538 B.C., followed by the Persian hegemony;
(3) The Greco-Roman period, ushered in by the conquest of Alexander the Great in 333 B.C. and ended with the Arab invasion of A.D. 633–40;
(4) The Arab Moslem period, which lasted until the Ottoman Turkish conquest in 1516;
(5) The Ottoman period, which came to an end with the first world war.

Throughout this long and chequered history there was hardly a time in which Syria in its entirety stood as an independent sovereign state by itself under native rulers. Its forced unity was always accomplished by the will of an external power. Ordinarily it was either submerged in a larger whole or partitioned among native or foreign states. Only during the second phase of the Seleucid kingdom (301–141 B.C.),[1] with its capital at Antioch, and during the Umayyad caliphate (A.D. 661–750), with its capital at Damascus, did the political centre of gravity lie in Syria itself. Under the Moslem Mamlūks (1250–1516), it formed an adjunct of Egypt. The Nile in Egypt and the Euphrates in Mesopotamia were unifying forces. Syria had no corresponding physical agency. In fact its physical structure tended to produce diversity rather than unity.

Nomenclature

The name Syria is Greek in form. It appears as SHRYN in

[1] See below, pp. 237, 245.

Ugaritic literature [1] and as Siryōn in Hebrew,[2] where it is used for Anti-Lebanon. The name of a part was later extended to include the whole. The word Lebanon is also Semitic,[3] but appears in earlier Cuneiform records. A north Euphratean district was known to the Babylonians as SU-RI.[4] Between "Syria" and "Assyria" there is probably no etymological relation.[5] In Greek and post-Greek times the term was expanded and applied to the entire country, and was thus used until the end of the first world war. Generally it covered the area between the Taurus and Sinai, the Mediterranean and the 'Irāq desert. To Herodotus [6] Palestine was a part of Syria — as it was to the Turks — and its inhabitants were the Syrians of Palestine. William of Tyre [7] and other historians of the Crusades also considered Palestine a part of Syria. "Palestine" also comes from Greek, but was originally "Philistia", which perpetuates the name of the Indo-European Philistines, who occupied the coastal region in the latter part of the thirteenth pre-Christian century, about the same time that the Israelites from Egypt were endeavouring to occupy the interior.[8] Thence the name spread to include the whole area as far as the desert.

The terms Syria and Syrian do not occur in the original Hebrew of the Scriptures but are used in the Septuagint for Aram and Aramaeans. Some classical writers mistakenly speak of the Syrians as identical with the Assyrians. The Arabs gave the country a new name, al-Sha'm, the one to the left (i.e. north), in opposition to al-Yaman, the one to the right (south), all from the standpoint of al-Ḥijāz.[9] In English "Syrian" has been applied until recently as an ethnic term to the population of all Syria, but now it is used only to designate a citizen of the Syrian

[1] Early fourteenth century B.C.; Cyrus H. Gordon, *Ugaritic Handbook* (Rome, 1948), p. 142.

[2] Deut. 3:9; Ps. 29:6. [3] See above, p. 32. [4] See below, p. 74.

[5] Cf. Ernst Herzfeld in *Majallat al-Majma' al-'Ilmi al-'Arabi*, vol. xxii (1947), pp. 178-81, where this etymology is accepted.

[6] Bk. I, ch. 105; Bk. II, chs. 104, 106; Bk. III, chs. 5, 91. Cf. Josephus, *Antiquities*, Bk. I, ch. 6, § 2.

[7] *A History of Deeds Done Beyond the Sea*, tr. Emily A. Babcock and A. C. Krey (New York, 1943), vol. ii, p. 5.

[8] See below, pp. 180-81.

[9] Maqdisi, p. 152; abu-al-Fidā', p. 225; see below, p. 547. For the limits of al-Sha'm consult ibn-Ḥawqal, *al-Masālik w-al-Mamālik*, ed. M. J. de Goeje (Leyden, 1872), p. 108; Yāqūt, vol. iii, p. 240; Gaudefroy-Demombynes, *La Syrie à l'époque des Mamelouks* (Paris, 1923), pp. 6 *seq*.

Republic. As a linguistic term it refers to all Syriac (Aramaic)-speaking peoples, including those of al-ʿIrāq and Persia, and as a religious term to the followers of the old Christian church of Syria, some of whom settled as far away as southern India.[1]

To the Romans *Syrus* meant any Syriac-speaking person, but the Roman province of Syria extended from the Euphrates to Egypt. It was so bounded by Arab geographers [2] and was so recognized until the end of the Ottoman period.[3] The physical unity of this area, in the past popularly called Syria, has its correspondence in cultural unity, though not in ethnic or in political unity. It constitutes a roughly homogeneous area of civilization sharply distinguished from the adjacent areas. Only between it and the other horn of the Fertile Crescent, the eastern one, has the cultural boundary been always fluid.

Determining historical factors

The determining factors in the history of Syria and its people are three: first its geographic configuration as a conglomeration of different regions reflected in a hodge-podge of population — a crazy quilt of ethnic groups and religious denominations. So cut up is the surface of the land that nowhere did the geography provide wide enough locale for the development of a strong comprehensive state. The second factor is its strategic position as a connecting link between the three historic continents, which exposed it to hazards and invasions from all sides. Babylonians and Assyrians, Egyptians, Hittites, Persians, Macedonians and Romans, Arabians, Mongols and Turks, Crusaders and sundry others attacked at different times and occupied the land in part or in full. The third factor is its proximity to the two earliest seats of dynamic culture, the Sumero-Babylonian on the east and the Egyptian on the south. In subsequent times the country was open by sea to Indo-European influences from Crete, Greece and Rome, and by land to Indo-Iranian influences from Persia and India.

The great international highway

Perpetually and easily brought into touch with the outside world through the great international highway, Syria was ex-

[1] Arabic makes a distinction, using *Sūri* in the first sense and Suryāni in the last two. See below, p. 171.

[2] E.g. Iṣṭakhri, p. 55; abu-al-Fidā', p. 225.

[3] See Smith, *Historical Geography*, pp. 3-4; Arnold J. Toynbee, *Survey of International Affairs*, vol. i, *The Islamic World* (London, 1927), pp. 347-8; Cornelius Van Dyck, *al-Mir'āt al-Waḍīyah fi al-Kurah al-Arḍīyah* (Beirut, 1886), pp. 119-20; cf. Dussaud, p. 1.

posed to cosmopolitan influences and to the onrush of remnants of broken communities. In its southern part modern Bahā'ism has been shielded from destruction and exists side by side with such a fossil of ancient faith as Samaritanism. In its central section Druze and Maronite communities of medieval origin still flourish. In the north Nuṣayri and Assassin sects still subsist.

This great international highway may be traced from its rudiments in the Delta of the Nile, along the coast of Sinai — whence it sends a branch south to the copper and turquoise mines of the peninsula and another branch, farther east, to the frankincense lands of South Arabia. It then turns northward along the Palestinian coast, not very close to the sea, to Carmel. Here it bifurcates, with one part skirting the coast through Tyre, Sidon, Byblus and other Syrian ports, and the other part turning inland through the plain of Megiddo, over the Jordan at its northern course and then straight north-east to Damascus. Here a branch goes through the Syrian Desert via Palmyra to link the centre of Syria with the centre of Mesopotamia, successively represented by Babylon, Ctesiphon and Baghdād. From Damascus the main highway turns west, crosses the Anti-Lebanon at the Zabadāni corridor and shoots north through Hollow Syria, following the Orontes through Qadesh into northern Syria. On its way at Qadesh it sends a branch that connects with the Mediterranean through the Nahr al-Kabīr gorge ; the same course is followed by the present-day railway After sending a branch in northern Syria through the Syrian Gates of the Amanus to the sea and another north-west through the Cilician Gates of the Taurus into Asia Minor, the highway swerves east through the Syrian Saddle [1] to the Euphrates and thence on to the Tigris and southward to the Persian Gulf.

Sargon, Sennacherib, Nebuchadnezzar, Alexander, Pompey, 'Amr ibn-al-'Āṣ, Napoleon, Allenby, Abraham, Moses, the Holy Family, all these and many others trod some part of this great caravan trade route. On it flowed in ancient and medieval times cargoes of ivory and gold from Africa, myrrh, frankincense and condiments from India and South Arabia, amber and silk from Central Asia and China, wheat and lumber from the plains and mountains of Syria. But the caravans carried more

[1] See below, p. 70.

than that; they bore an invisible cargo of ideas. The wheat was consumed. The amber was used to satisfy the passing fancy of some damsel. But the ideas were not all lost. Some germinated in Syrian minds and contributed to the production of that composite culture, called Syrian, which was a fusion of native elements plus others from the surrounding cultures. The native element itself represented deposits which numberless migrations and invasions had left.

Tent-dwellers versus house-dwellers

The fourth of the determining historic factors is the fact that throughout its history the land, especially in its eastern and southern margins, has been the scene of unceasing struggle between the nomads and the settled. One great pulse through the whole of Near Eastern history has been recurring raids and invasions by Bedouins who coveted the fuller life enjoyed by the urban population of adjacent lands. A large part of the history of Syria is the story of that surge and resurge on the part of restless, half-starved desert neighbours who by peaceful or forceful penetration set their hearts upon the occupation of the tilled land. With little property, greater mobility and more endurance the tent-dweller had the advantage over the house-dweller. The story of the early Israelites, as recorded on the pages of the Old Testament, provides the most elaborate illustration of this perennial transition from nomadism to urbanism. But the Israelites were not the first Semites to experience this transition. Many Semites before them and many after them passed through the same stages in their relation to Syria.[1]

Who were the Semites?

The term Semite comes from Shem in the Old Testament through the Latin of the Vulgate, the assumption being that the Semites were the descendants of Noah's eldest son. According to scientific usage, however, the term is a linguistic one; it applies to him who speaks or spoke a Semitic tongue. The Semitic languages are now recognized as a distinct family comprising Assyro-Babylonian (Akkadian),[2] Canaanite (Phoenician), Aramaic, Hebrew, Arabic and Ethiopic. Within this family the members manifest striking points of similarity, and as a group differ from other linguistic groups, the Hamitic being

[1] Cf. above, p. 44.

[2] *Akkad(u)*, Semitic equivalent of Sumerian *Agadē*, was originally the name of the capital of Sargon, founder of the first Semitic empire, but later applied to the country. The city lay where the Tigris and Euphrates came close together and is mentioned in Gen. 10:10.

the nearest of kin. Chief among the points of similarity within this linguistic family are: a basic verbal triconsonantal stem, a tense system with only two forms (really aspects) — perfect and imperfect —, and a verbal conjugation that follows the same pattern. In all the members of the Semitic family the basic words — such as personal pronouns, nouns denoting blood kinship, numbers and chief members of the body — are almost alike.

This linguistic kinship among the Semitic-speaking peoples is the most important bond that justifies their inclusion under one name, but is not the only bond. A comparison of their social institutions, religious beliefs, psychological traits and physical features reveal impressive points of resemblance. The inference is inescapable: at least certain ancestors of those who spoke Babylonian, Assyrian, Amoritic, Canaanite, Hebrew, Aramaic, Arabic and Abyssinian — before they became thus differentiated — must have formed one community speaking the same tongue and occupying one locale.

Arabia, the cradle of the Semites

Where was the home of that community? The most plausible theory makes it the Arabian peninsula. The geographical argument presented in favour of Arabia brings out the desert nature of the land with the sea encircling it on three sides. Whenever the population increases beyond the capacity of the narrow habitable margin of land to support it, it tends to seek elbow-room available only in the northern and more fertile neighbouring land. This involves the economic argument according to which the Arabian [1] nomads have always lived on the verge of starvation, and the Fertile Crescent provided the nearest place for the supply of their needs

Around 3500 B.C. a Semitic migration from the peninsula moved north-eastward and spread its component nomadic parts over the settled and highly civilized Sumerian population of Mesopotamia, producing the Akkadians (later called Babylonians) of history. As the Semites intermarried and intermixed with their non-Semitic predecessors in the Tigro-Euphrates region they acquired from them the knowledge of building and living in homes, planting and irrigating lands and, what is

[1] The distinction between the use of "Arabians" for the inhabitants of the peninsula and of "Arabs" for all Arabic-speaking peoples — who may have been by nationality Persian, Mesopotamian, Syrian, Egyptian, etc., and as a result of the Moslem conquest adopted the Arabic tongue and were mostly Islamized — was first recommended in Hitti, *History of the Arabs*, p. 43, n. 3.

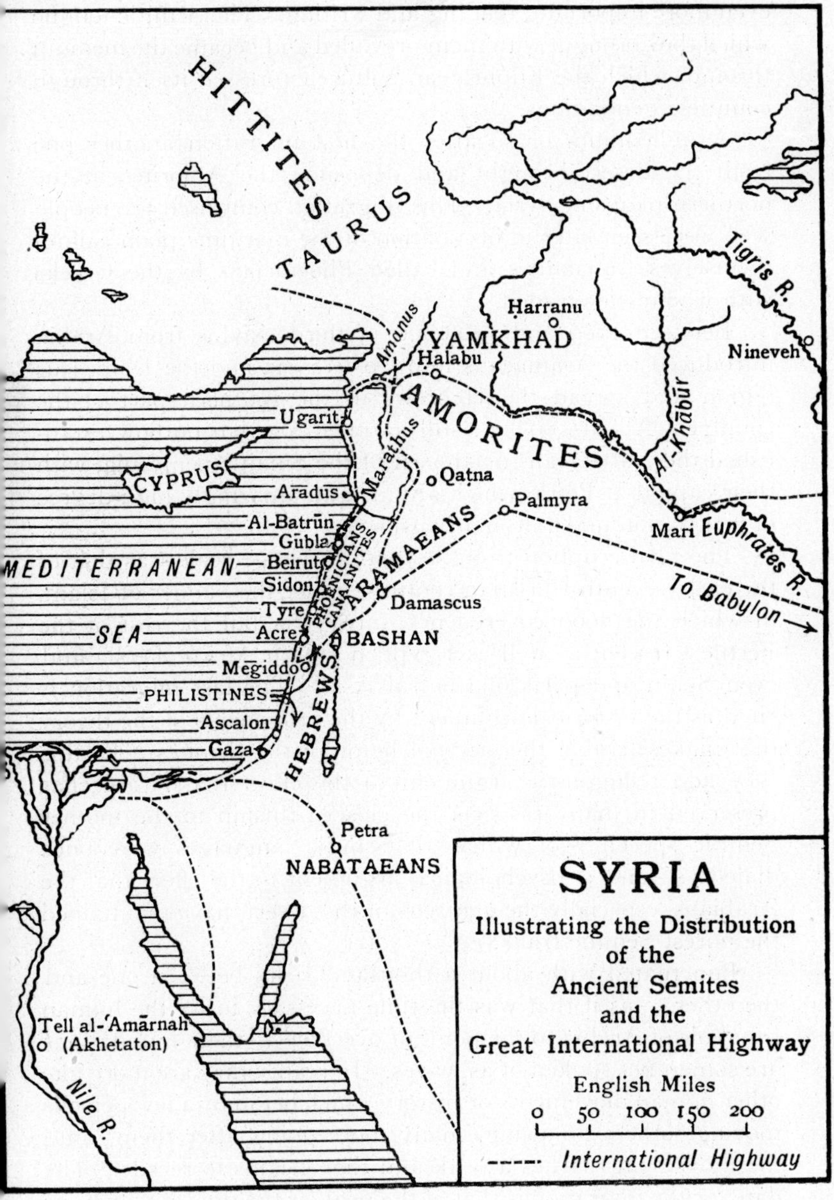
HITTITES
TAURUS
Amanus
YAMKHAD
Halabu
Harranu
Nineveh
Tigris R.
AMORITES
Ugarit
CYPRUS
Aradus
Marathus
Qatna
Palmyra
Al-Khābūr
Al-Batrūn
Gubla
Mari
Euphrates R.
MEDITERRANEAN
Beirut
Sidon
PHOENICIANS
CANAANITES
ARAMAEANS
To Babylon
Damascus
Tyre
SEA
Acre
BASHAN
Megiddo
PHILISTINES
HEBREWS
Ascalon
Gaza
Petra
NABATAEANS
Tell al-ʿAmārnah
(Akhetaton)
Nile R.
SYRIA
Illustrating the Distribution
of the
Ancient Semites
and the
Great International Highway
English Miles
0 50 100 150 200
International Highway

even more important, reading and writing. The Semitic tongue which they brought with them prevailed and became the medium through which the Euphratean culture expressed itself through countless generations.

A millennium or so after the first migration another one from the desert brought and deposited the Amorites in the northern plains of Syria. This migration comprised the people who were seen later in occupation of the maritime plain calling themselves Canaanites and called Phoenicians by the Greeks with whom they traded.

Between 1500 and 1200 B.C. a third exodus from Arabia introduced the Aramaeans into Coele-Syria and the Damascus region and spread the Hebrews in the southern part of the country. About 500 B.C. still another Arabian outflow established the Nabataeans north-east of the Sinaitic peninsula, with their capital at Petra, which attained an amazingly high degree of civilization under Roman auspices.

The final eruption from Arabia on a huge scale was that of the early seventh Christian century, under the banner of Islam, in which the flood covered not only Syria but the rest of the Fertile Crescent as well as Egypt, northern Africa, Persia and even Spain and parts of Central Asia. The last migration is cited as the historical argument by the proponents of the theory that makes Arabia the original home of the Semites. To this they add a linguistic argument to the effect that Arabic has preserved in many respects the closest kinship to the mother Semitic speech — of which all Semitic languages were once dialects — and a psychological argument to the effect that the Arabians, especially the denizens of the desert, have maintained the purest Semitic traits.

Punctuated with about a thousand years between one and the other — as if that was the time necessary to fill the human reservoir of Arabia to the point of overflow — these inundations are sometimes spoken of as waves. In reality they are more like other human movements of history which begin by a few persons moving, others following, many more going after them, until the movement reaches a peak and then begins to recede. The date for the migration is that of the peak or the time in which the movement became widely noticeable, though it may in actuality have covered scores of years before and after.

CHAPTER VII

THE AMORITES: FIRST MAJOR SEMITIC COMMUNITY IN SYRIA

Enter the Amorites

FIRST among the major Semitic peoples to seek and find abode in the Syrian area were a group whose name for themselves is unknown, but who were called Amorites by their eastern neighbours, the Sumerians. The word is therefore non-Semitic. It means westerners. The Amorite capital city Mari, just below the mouth of the Khābūr (also a Sumerian word), is etymologically identical with the name of the country A-MUR-RU, MAR-TU, westland, which was likewise the name of their early deity, a god of war and hunting. Later the Babylonians extended the name to cover the whole of Syria, and called the Mediterranean " the great sea of Amurru ".

The first reference to the land of the Amorites appears as early as the time of Sargon (*ca.* 2450 B.C.), the first great name in Semitic history.[1] Gradually Amorites begin to make their appearance in Central Syria, Lebanon and as far south as Palestine. " Lebanon ", " Sidon " and " Ascalon " are said to have Amoritic endings. Modern ʽAmrīt[2] on the north Phoenician coast perpetuates the name. It was then that Syria, exclusive of some pockets inhabited by Hurrians and other non-Semites, was first Semitized — an aspect which it has maintained through the ages until the present day. Before Sargon overran Amurru, its capital Mari was the seat of one of the early Sumerian dynasties. Sargon deposed the Sumerian conqueror, Lugal-zaggisi of Erech, who claims in one of his inscriptions that " he had conquered the lands from the rising of the sun unto the setting of the sun " and that " he made straight his path from the Lower Sea, from the Euphrates and Tigris, unto the Upper Sea ".[3] In the course of the twentieth

[1] Arno Poebel, *Historical Texts* (Philadelphia, 1914), p. 177.

[2] Egyptian ʽMRṮ, classical Marathus.

[3] F. Thureau-Dangin, *Die sumerischen und akkadischen Königsinschriften* (Leipzig, 1907), p. 155.

century the city and the country around it became Amorite in population, culture and control. The Semitic invaders must have established themselves on top of an earlier and more civilized Mesopotamian society, and it may be assumed that prior to that they roamed over the northern territory and al-Biqāʿ as Bedouins following their flocks and herds.

This transition from the pastoral to the agricultural stage has been dramatized by a Sumerian poet who lived shortly before 2000 B.C., when Amorites were occupying Babylonia:

> For the Amorite the weapon [is his] companion,
> . . . he knows no submission.
> He eats uncooked meat,
> Through his whole life he does not possess a house,
> His dead companion he does not bury.
> [Now] Martu possesses a house [?] . . .
> [Now] Martu possesses grain.[1]

His nomadism was perhaps based on the ass; the camel was not yet in wide use as a domesticated animal.[2] In the eighteenth century he was still using the ass for sacrifice.

Not only did the Amorites establish a state in the middle Euphrates and overrun all Syria, but they also overran and ruled Mesopotamia proper. Between 2100 and 1800 B.C. they founded several dynasties from Assur in the north to Larsa in the south. Most important among these was that of Babylon, the first to arise in that city, to which the earliest great lawgiver of antiquity Hammurabi (d. *ca.* 1700), belonged.[3] It was this Hammurabi who conquered Amurru and incorporated it in his Babylonian empire.

The archives of Mari

This conquest consigned Mari into oblivion until only a few years ago when a site called Tell al-Ḥarīri (mound of the silk man) was excavated [4] and turned out to be ancient Mari (Māri).

[1] Edward Chiera, *Sumerian Religious Texts* (Upland, 1924), pp. 20-21.

[2] Albright, *The Stone Age*, pp. 120-21.

[3] Albert T. Clay's thesis in his *Amurru: The Land of the Northern Semites* (Philadelphia, 1909), and *The Empire of the Amorites* (New Haven, 1919), that the culture of the Semitic Babylonians had, if not its origin, at least a long development in the land of the Amorites, that the Amorites had a vast empire as early as the fourth and fifth millenniums and that the generally accepted theory of the Arabian origin of the Semites is utterly baseless, has not been sustained.

[4] By André Parrot; see his reports, "Les Peintures du palais de Mari", *Syria*, vol. xviii (1937), pp. 324-54; "Les Fouilles de Mari", *Syria*, vol. xix (1938), pp. 1-29; vol. xx (1939), pp. 1-22. Now over a mile west of the Euphrates the city in antiquity stood on the bank of the river.

The finds proved to be among the most notable discoveries of modern times. They comprised over 20,000 cuneiform tablets, a number unsurpassed by any outside of Nineveh. The

From "Syria", vol. xix (Librairie Orientaliste Paul Geuthner, Paris)

CUNEIFORM TABLET OF YAḪDUN-LIM, FATHER OF ZIMRI-LIM, FOUND IN THE ROYAL PALACE OF MARI

language is mostly Akkadian, but the vocabulary and grammatical peculiarities leave no doubt that those who wrote them spoke Amoritic or West Semitic as distinct from Akkadian or

East Semitic. The tablets represent the archives of Zimri-Lim (*ca.* 1730–1700),[1] the last king of Mari, whose kingdom was destroyed by the greatest monarch of the age, Hammurabi. Among the tablets are letters by kings and officials, business, administrative and economic documents and valuable reports.[2] One letter reveals that horse-drawn chariots were already known, another that fire signals were used as a measure of national defence or flashing news. The civilization of the Amorites, as reflected in the language they wrote, was a blend of Amoritic, Hurrian and Babylonian elements.

In these tablets Ḥalabu (Ar. Ḥalab, Aleppo) appears as the capital of Yamkhad,[3] Gubla (Jubayl, Byblus) as a centre for the manufacture of cloth and garments, Qaṭana (later Qaṭna, modern al-Mushrifah, north-east of Ḥimṣ) as an important centre, and Ḥarranu (Ar. Ḥarrān, biblical Haran) — one of the stopping stations of Abraham as a nomadic shaykh on his way to found the Hebrew nation in Palestine — as an Amorite princedom. In fact the documents reveal that all these cities were centres of Amorite dynasties or under Amorite princes, and not only that, but that around 1800 B.C. practically the whole region from the Mediterranean to the highlands of Elam was dominated by Amorite princes. The name of a Byblus prince Yantin-ʿAmmu suggests Amorite origin; *ʿammu* means clan.

The palace of Zimri-Lim, which yielded the tablets, comprised some 300 rooms with elaborate mural frescoes with panels, borders and well-executed figures of men and deities — one of the show places of the world, as one of the tablets puts it. It covered more than six acres and was provided with bathroom and toilet facilities.[4] Two rooms with benches and desks look like school-rooms. One brilliantly coloured painting represents the king receiving the emblems of power from Ishtar.

[1] W. F. Albright, "An Indirect Synchronism between Egypt and Mesopotamia, *cir.* 1730 B.C.", *Bulletin, American Schools of Oriental Research*, No. 99 (1945), pp. 9-10.

[2] Georges Dossin, "Les Archives épistolaires du palais de Mari", *Syria*, vol. xix (1938), pp. 105-26; "Les Archives économiques du palais de Mari", vol. xx (1939), pp. 97-113.

[3] Its king Yarīm-Lim had an Amoritic name; W. F. Albright, "Western Asia in the Twentieth Century B.C.: The Archives of Mari", *Bulletin, American Schools of Oriental Research*, No. 67 (1937), p. 27.

[4] A picture in *Syria*, vol. xvii (1936), pl. iii, fig. 2 (opposite p. 16), shows two terracotta bath-tubs (one for hot water and one for cold?) at the right and a toilet at the left.

From "Syria," vol. xviii (Librairie Orientaliste Paul Geuthner, Paris)

ROYAL INVESTITURE: THE KING OF MARI RECEIVES FROM ISHTAR THE INSIGNIA OF POWER

The bearded royal personage, assisted by a goddess behind him, receives from Ishtar with his left hand the stick and circle while his right is raised in adoration. His turban and garment are characteristic of those of the first Babylonian dynasty. Ishtar appears in her military aspect, armed and with her right foot on a couchant lion. She is assisted by a god and a goddess standing

From " Syria ", vol. xviii (Librairie Orientaliste Paul Geuthner, Paris)

ROYAL INVESTITURE: THE KING OF MARI RECEIVES FROM ISHTAR THE INSIGNIA OF POWER

The bearded royal personage, assisted by a goddess behind him, receives from Ishtar with his left hand the stick and circle while his right is raised in adoration. His turban and garment are characteristic of those of the first Babylonian dynasty. Ishtar appears in her military aspect, armed and with her right foot on a couchant lion. She is assisted by a god and a goddess standing behind her. Below them two goddesses hold vases from which water spouts and in which fish move up and down, the theme being fertility. On the right hand of the panel are stylized trees and animals and a date palm

The palace architecture and the documents reveal a state of culture undreamt of before, and rivalling those of Egypt and Mesopotamia.

The Syrian Saddle

The prosperity of the Amorite land was partly based on its irrigation agriculture and partly on its commercial relations with its neighbours. From the Gulf of Alexandretta, where the sea takes its largest bite from the land, to the western bend of the Euphrates — a distance of some 100 miles — the land forms a natural corridor between the littoral and the Mesopotamian region. Corridors are important in both commercial geography and the history of ideas; they give direction to the process of cultural fusion. Here the multiple barrier of mountains from the north and the west and of desert from the south is reduced to a single low passage which gives access to a valley on one hand and to a sea on the other, and has therefore been properly called the Syrian Saddle.[1] The Saddle lies at the foot of the Taurus Mountains and is therefore referred to at times as the "piedmont". It is the terminus of the line of communication which, starting from the Persian Gulf, goes up the Tigris to the environs of Nineveh and there turns west to the Syrian seaports, linking Tell al-Ḥalaf, Ḥarrān, Mari, Aleppo and other ancient towns. It is on this plain that continuous Syrian history commences, with the Amorites as its first Semitic representatives. Since then, as transit land, Babylonians, Egyptians, Assyrians, Chaldaeans, Persians and Macedonians have endeavoured in turn to control it. Its grassy plain receives 10 to 20 inches of annual rain, enough to maintain ample herbage for animals and passing caravans. After the rains parts of it look like golf links. Streamlets from the Taurus and waters from the Euphrates irrigated its cities.

Amorite centre shifts south

At the turn of the second pre-Christian millennium the focus in Syrian affairs was on the north with Amorites playing the leading rôle. A century after the middle of that millennium the focus shifts to Central Syria, with the Amorites still occupying the centre of the stage. Meanwhile Egypt, setting out upon its first career as an imperialist power, had brought under its sway, thanks to the mighty sword of Thutmose (d. 1447), the Napoleon of the Eighteenth Dynasty, a large part of Syria.[2] Another gigantic power and a rival of Egypt was looming high in

[1] Semple, p. 184. [2] See below, p. 129.

the northern horizon, the Hittites.[1] In between was caught the Amorite state or states of Central Syria which, judging from the Tell al-ʿAmārnah tablets — our most important source — covered at their height a large part of northern Lebanon with its seaboard, Coele-Syria, eastern Lebanon and the Damascus region. One of their dynasts, Abd-Ashirta,[2] an Egyptian vassal, bursts onto the pages of history with a letter in poor Akkadian — the lingua franca of the age — to Pharaoh Amenhotep III (d. 1375) introduced by clichés which sound servile and abject to us now but which were a part of the protocol of the day:

> To the king, the sun, my lord, thus saith Abd Ashirta, thy slave, the dust of thy feet. At the feet of the king, my lord, seven times and seven I fall down. Behold, I am the servant of the king and the dog of his house and all Amurru for the king, my lord, I guard.[3]

International double dealing

At the time of writing, Abd-Ashirta was in the Phoenician town Irqat,[4] which he had conquered, but the centre of his kingdom evidently lay on the upper Orontes. He had helped the Hittites to conquer Amki [5] and was now playing the two ends against the middle — professing loyalty to Egypt, seemingly co-operating with the advancing Hittites, but in reality attempting the conquest of new territories on his own account. One city after the other, both inland and on the coast, fell into the hands of Abd-Ashirta and his son Aziru, or were plundered by them and by those who made common cause with them. Certain vassals of Egypt were bought off; others were disposed of. Qaṭna was occupied, so was Ḥamāh. Ubi (the region of Damascus) [6] was threatened and Damascus itself was later seized. Arwād, Shigata, Ambi, al-Batrūn [7] and others on the coast were all captured. The Arwadites, perhaps due to trade

[1] See below, pp. 130-31.

[2] " The slave of Ashirta " or Ashirat; see below, p. 118.

[3] J. A. Knudtzon, *Die el-Amarna-Tafeln* (Leipzig, 1908), No. 60; cf. A. H. Sayce, *Records of the Past*, new series, vol. v (London, 1891), pp. 97-8; Samuel A. B. Mercer, *The Tell el-Amarna Tablets* (Toronto, 1939), No. 60.

[4] ʿRQT of the Egyptian annals, classical Arka, modern ʿArqah, about 12 miles north-east of Tripoli; referred to in Gen. 10:17; 1 Ch. 1:15.

[5] Plain between Antioch and the Amanus; see above, p. 39, n. 2.

[6] DI-MASH-QA of the tablets. See below, p. 163.

[7] AR-WA-DA, SHI-GA-TA, AM-BI, BAT-RU-NA. Shigata is not modern Zagharta (Sagarātim of the Mari letters) but Shaqqa north of al-Batrūn. Ambi, Ampa of the Assyrians, Anafa of the Arabs, Nephin of the Crusaders, is modern Anfah between Shaqqa and Tripoli. Batruna, Gr. Botrys, is modern al-Batrūn. Abel, *Géographie*, vol. ii, p. 4; Dussaud, p. 117.

rivalry with the Gublites, seem to have been since the days of Thutmose anti-Egyptian. Only Simyra,[1] the residence of the Egyptian deputy, and Gubla,[2] seat of the pro-Egyptian Canaanite Rib Addi, who also held a portion of the interior and claimed authority over the coast as far as Simyra, held out. At last Simyra succumbed and Gubla, cut off from her hinterland and unable to carry on her lumber trade with Egypt, could not survive. One wailing letter after another — some fifty in all [3] — did the loyal Rib Addi dispatch to his sovereign in Egypt reporting the treachery of Abd-Ashirta " the dog " [4] and Aziru, and fervently praying for aid, but all to no avail.

At one time Amenhotep bestirred himself and sent a detachment — instead of an army with himself at its head as his predecessor Thutmose would have done — which succeeded in recovering Simyra and temporarily quelling the revolt but which could not cope with the threatening danger from the north represented by the Hittite advance.

The death by violence of Abd-Ashirta removed the actor from the scene but not the act. His son and successor Aziru carried on with the same Machiavellian technique. Nor did the accession of Amenhotep IV (Ikhnaton, 1375–1358) [5] change the Egyptian side of the picture ; if anything it made it worse. The new Pharaoh was apparently more interested in his religious reforms than in the defence of the realm.

As Aziru and his brothers and allies start capturing more cities, Rib Addi starts a new series of tales of woe expressed on clay tablets in cuneiform and dispatched to the Pharaoh and his agents. " Formerly at the sight of an Egyptian, the kings of Canaan fled from before him, but now, the sons of Abd-Ashirta

[1] ṢU-MUR, ḌMR of Egyptian annals, classical Simyros, perhaps modern Sumra, just north of the mouth of al-Nahr al-Kabīr ; referred to in Gen. 10 : 18.

[2] Biblical Gebal (mountain, surviving in modern Jubayl), Eg. KBN, KPN, KPNI Gr. Byblos, L. Byblus.

[3] Some preserved in London, others in Berlin ; C. Bezold, *The Tell el-Amarna Tablets in the British Museum* (London, 1892), Nos. 12-25 ; C. R. Conder, *The Tell Amarna Tablets*, 2nd ed. (London, 1894), pp. 48 *seq.* ; Knudtzon, Nos. 68 *seq.* ; Mercer, Nos. 68 *seq.*

[4] Nos. 75, 85.

[5] An innovator in religion, he substituted the worship of Aten (Aton, sun's disk) for that of Amon, changed his name accordingly (splendour of the sun's disk) and transferred his capital from Thebes to Akhetaton, whose site is now called Tell al-ʻAmārnah (hill of the ʻAmārnah, more correctly ʻAmārinah, plural of [banu-] ʻAmrān, name of an Arab tribe which settled there at the beginning of the eighteenth century).

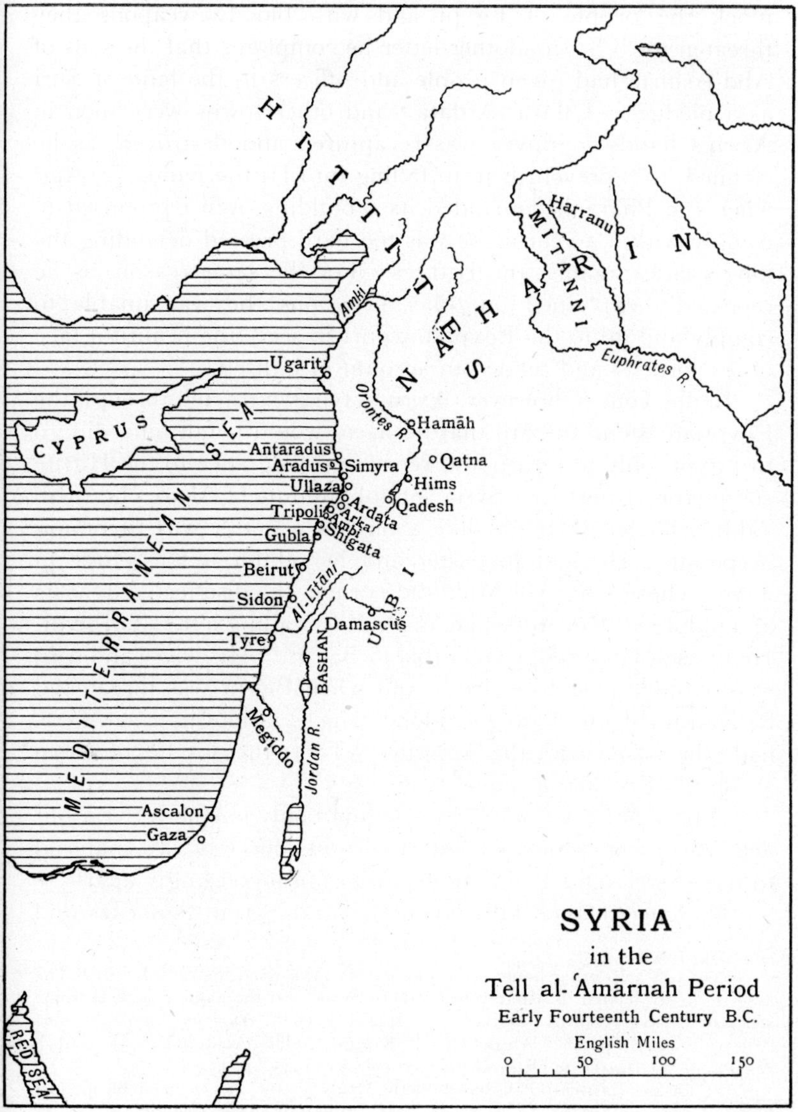

HITTITES
NAHARIN
MITANNI
Harranu
Amki
Euphrates R.
Ugarit
Orontes R.
Hamāh
CYPRUS
MEDITERRANEAN SEA
Antaradus
Aradus
Simyra
Qatna
Ullaza
Hims
Ardata
Qadesh
Tripoli
Arka
Ambi
Gubla
Shigata
Beirut
Al-Lītāni
Sidon
UBI
Damascus
Tyre
BASHAN
Megiddo
Jordan R.
Ascalon
Gaza
RED SEA
SYRIA
in the
Tell al-ʿAmārnah Period
Early Fourteenth Century B.C.
English Miles
0
50
100
150

mock the people of Egypt and with bloody weapons they threaten me." [1] In another letter he complains that the sons of Abd-Ashirta had given people and officers to the land of Suri as a pledge.[2] Ullaza, Ardata [3] and other towns were soon in Aziru's hands. Simyra was recaptured and destroyed, as he claimed, to " prevent it from falling into Hittite hands ". And when the Pharaoh demanded its rebuilding Aziru promised to comply within a year as he was too hard pressed defending the king's cities against the Hittites. For the same reason, as he repeatedly explained on other occasions, he was unable to comply and go to the Egyptian court to see " the beautiful face of my lord " [4] and render an account of himself.

In due course, however, Aziru, having extracted through the Egyptian agent an oath that no harm would befall him, did go to Egypt, only to return and renew his allegiance to the Hittite conqueror of northern Syria, Shubbiluliuma.[5] Meanwhile Rib Addi, who felt " caught like a bird in a net ", was becoming desperate. He sent his sister and her children for refuge in Tyre,[6] whose king Abi-Milki did not join the disaffected dynasts and indulged, Rib Addi-like, in sending wailing letters to Egypt. He himself later fled from Gubla to Beirut.[7] His wives and sons were handed over to Aziru. And when Beirut was threatened he continued his flight to Sidon [8] which, unlike its rival Tyre, had allied itself with the Amorites. There the clutches of Aziru at long last overtook him.

Thus was Egypt obliged to yield not only northern Syria but also Phoenicia, which was an important source of raw material to her. Syria and Palestine began to fall increasingly apart.

The Amorites in Palestine

The curtain then falls on the Central Syrian Amorites and

[1] No. 109.

[2] No. 108. In other letters SU-BA-RI, ZU-BA-RI, is used instead of Suri. The land is closely related to Mitanni in northern Syria, and the name is said by some scholars to have given us " Syria "; cf. Ignace J. Gelb, *Hurrians and Subarians* (Chicago, 1944), p. 48; Alexander H. Krappe, " The Anatolian Lion God ", *Journal of the American Oriental Society*, vol. lxv (1945), p. 153.

[3] UL-LA-ZA, classical Orthosia, modern Artūsi, at the mouth of al-Bārid, just north of Tripoli; AR-DA-TA is Ardat, near Zagharta; Abel, *Géographie*, vol. ii, p. 4; Dussaud, p. 85.

[4] Nos. 164-7.

[5] See below, pp. 130-31.

[6] ṢUR-RI, preserved in the modern name Ṣūr.

[7] BE-RU-TA, Egyptian BI-'RU-TA, today the most flourishing city from among all those cited; *b'ēroth* means wells; Zellig S. Harris, *A Grammar of the Phoenician Language* (New Haven, 1936), p. 85. Cf. Josh. 9:17; 18:25.

[8] ṢI-DU-NA, so named after a god of fishing and hunting.

the centre of interest shifts farther south. The Hittites were entrenched in North and Central Syria, and the immediate successors of Ikhnaton carried on no serious campaigns. The Tell al-ʿAmārnah letters show that while the Hittites were occupying the northern territory the southern territory was being invaded by new hordes, the Khabiru,[1] drifting evidently with the Aramaeans, the new Semitic wanderers, from the desert. Certain scholars identify the Khabiru with the Sa-Gaz, mercenaries in the Hittite army co-operating with Abd-Ashirta. In one of his last letters to Ikhnaton, Rib Addi refers to them: "Since thy father returned from Sidon, since that time, the lands have fallen into the hands of the Gaz".[2]

As the Khabiru penetrated into Palestine they found it, at least in part, occupied by earlier Semites, the Amorites. The historical links between the many Amorite kingdoms and communities in Syria widely scattered, in time and place, are missing. Nor can we be certain that the Amorite movement into the south was a mass movement. The term Amorite, like the term Hittite, evidently shifted its meaning in course of time and was loosely applied. The Amorites may have been in the south as the ruling class.[3] One of the principal sources used by Old Testament historians and prophets gives them a dominant position in pre-Israelitish Palestine and makes all the inhabitants of the mountain land and of Transjordan, prior to the influx of the Israelites,[4] Amorite.[5] The other principal source makes the inhabitants, especially of the wasteland, Canaanite. It is evident that in the thirteenth century Amorites were in control of strategic sites and hill-tops in southern Syria, and that they founded some of the settlements that later developed into those mighty Canaanite cities before whose walls and towers the Israelitish newcomers stood aghast.

In due course the Israelites succeeded in wresting the control from Amorite and Canaanite hands. By overrunning Sihon and its more northerly Amorite neighbour, Bashan, Transjordanic Syria was gained.[6] The chief of Bashan, Og, "the

[1] See below, pp. 160-61. [2] No. 85.

[3] Albrecht Alt, "Völker und Staaten Syriens im frühen Altertum", *Der alte Orient*, vol. xxxiv, No. 4 (1936), p. 2.

[4] Descendants of Israel, i.e. Jacob (Ex. 9:7), grandson of Abraham.

[5] Num. 13:29; Josh. 24:8, 18; Amos 2:10; Ezek. 16:3, 45.

[6] Deut. 2:30 *seq.*; 3:1 *seq.*

remnant of the giants", had a gigantic stature; his "iron bedstead" (basalt sarcophagus ?) measured nine by four cubits.[1] To Amos (2 : 9) the Amorites were cedar-high and oak-like in strength. On the monuments Amorite statures appear tall and martial. Their size and culture must have so impressed the primitive and short troglodytic inhabitants of southern Syria that legends grew that a giant race came and intermarried with the daughters of men — legends which were passed on to the Israelites.[2] Such legends, common to many other peoples, seem to have some connection with the appearance of metal-using newcomers.[3] In this case it must have been bronze. The early Amorites hardened their copper spearheads, daggers and knives by hammering, then by alloying with tin. The earliest Palestinian bronze daggers bear affinity to those of North Syria. Thence the smelting of bronze was introduced into Palestine prior to 2500 B.C.

Amorite physiognomy belongs to the so-called Armenoid type, characterized by brachycephalic (round) heads and prominent noses. The same type is found among South Arabians.[4] The earliest representations of Asiatic captives, those of Pharaoh Sahure (*ca.* 2553–2541), belong to this type. The same is true of those represented in the mural paintings of Bani Ḥasan bringing kohl (Ar. *kuḥl*) to the "administrator of the eastern desert" (*ca.* 1900 B.C.). Here the Amorite shaykh Absha, probably from South Palestine, appears with his clansmen and clanswomen in elaborately woven multicoloured tunics, with leather sandals on the feet of men and shoes or socks on those of women. The men are black-bearded with bird-like faces, hooked noses, grey irises and black pupils. Absha leads the procession. Following the women are a man and his donkey with a water-skin slung upon his back and a plectrum in his hand to play his eight-stringed lyre. The patient-looking donkey bears a saddle-cloth to which are tied a throw-stick and a spear. Other arms borne by the men include javelins and composite bows. A carved ivory from the latter part of the First Dynasty (*ca.* 2800 B.C.) reproduces a Semite in a costume

[1] Deut. 3 : 11.
[2] For still earlier legends see above, pp. 27-8.
[3] M. E. Kirk, "An Outline of the Cultural History of Palestine", *Palestine Exploration Quarterly*, vol. lxxv (1943), p. 22.
[4] Hitti, *History of the Arabs*, p. 30.

THE AAMU GROUP

From Percy Newberry, "Beni Hasan" (Egypt Exploration Society)

THE AAMU SHAYKH, ABSHA

GROUP OF SEMITIC WOMEN

From Nina M. Davies, "Ancient Egyptian Paintings" (University of Chicago Press)

SEMITE WITH HIS DONKEY

he presumably wore in battle — a fringed loin-cloth reaching almost to the knees

The Amorite language left us no inscriptions of importance; only names of places and princes remain. Nevertheless, we can be sure that it differed only dialectally from Canaanite. In fact it may be considered East Canaanite as opposed to West Canaanite or Phoenician.

Amorite religion

In its primitive form Amorite religion could not have differed from the Semitic nature worship prevailing among the early nomads of the Syrian Desert and Arabia. Behind the tribal martial deity Amurru stood a host of ill-defined gods, many of whom later figured in the Canaanite pantheon. Chief among these was Hadad (in Akkadian Adad or Addu),[1] also known as Rammanu (thunderer), a god of rain and storms exemplifying a prevalent type throughout Western Asia and represented in association with the bull and thunderbolt. Later he became the great Baʻal. As chief god of the West he was known as Martu. Another prominent deity, Rashap,[2] may have had some connection with fire. The Egyptians of the New Empire adopted him from the Canaanites. Dagon, worshipped by the Amorite conquerors of Babylon, was basically a food god. A temple dedicated to him has been excavated at Ugarit. The Philistines adopted him as a fish god and he was especially revered at Gaza (Ghazzah). All these gods are cited in the Mari tablets.

Amurru had a consort in the person of Ashirat, mistress of lusty energy and joy — of the common Ishtar type. She was the chief female deity. Pre-Israelitish serpent worship appears to be associated with a female deity and may have been introduced by Amorites. In the South Arabian pantheon this goddess is associated with the Moon-God. The name corresponds to Hebrew *ashērāh*, the sacred pole or tree trunk, a well-known cult object.[3]

Conspicuous among the cults introduced into southern Syria by the Amorites was that of the sacred pillar (monolith), which evidently represented the tribal deity and was set up in some

[1] In a Tell al-ʻAmārnah letter (No. 52) from the king of Qaṭna begging Amenhotep III for aid, probably against the Hittites, the king calls the Pharaoh "my Addu". The Qaṭna letters (Nos. 52-5) have a number of Hurrian glosses. See below, p. 172.

[2] See below, p. 174.

[3] See below, p. 121.

ritually clean spot, usually a cave with a limestone altar near by polluted by no tool.[1] The Semites who in Gezer displaced the earlier population and practised sacrifice of the first-born as well as foundation sacrifice and built the megalithic high places were Amorites.[2] One of the earliest references to foundation sacrifice occurs in a Sumerian poem cited in part above,[3] where we are told the Amorite raised his temple court " upon a dead man ". The Amorite religious institutions and practices were carried on by their kinsmen and successors, the Canaanites.

[1] Cf. Ex. 20:25. [2] See above, pp. 24-5; cf. below, p. 123. [3] P. 66.

CHAPTER VIII

THE CANAANITES: SECOND MAJOR SEMITIC PEOPLE IN SYRIA

THE Canaanites, later called Phoenicians by the Greeks, were the second Semitic community, after the Amorites, to figure prominently in Syrian affairs. Both Canaanites and Amorites belonged to the same migration. The ethnic difference between them is therefore basically nil, though the Amorites must have gradually assimilated Sumerian and Hurrian elements while the Phoenicians assimilated other native elements. The cultural difference stems from the fact that the Amorites had their original centre in northern Syria and therefore came under Sumero-Babylonian influence; the Canaanites had their geographic centre in the littoral and were oriented Egypt-ward. The religious difference was mainly one of development and adaptation to local environments. The linguistic difference was merely dialectal, both being members of the Western Semitic branch to which Hebrew belongs.[1] This same branch could be designated north-western in distinction from the south-western, which is Arabic.

Canaan

The name of the land, Canaan, hitherto considered Semitic meaning lowland,[2] as opposed to the highlands of Lebanon, has recently been suspected of being non-Semitic in origin. The new etymology makes it Hurrian *knaggi*, purple dye, which gave Nuzi Akkadian *kinakhni* (*Kinakhkhi* of the Tell al-ʿAmārnah cuneiform), Phoenician *Kenaʿ*, Hebrew *Kenaʿan*, land of purple.[3] At the time in which the Hurrians came into close contact with the Mediterranean coast, in the eighteenth or seventeenth century, the purple industry must have been the

[1] See above, pp. 67-8.

[2] From the stem *kanaʿ*, be low or humble. See Smith, *Historical Geography*, pp. 4-5; Claude R. Conder, *Syrian Stone-Lore* (London, 1896), pp. 2-3; C. Autran, *Phéniciens* (Paris, 1920), p. 4; cf. Lewis B. Paton, *The Early History of Syria and Palestine* (New York, 1901), pp. 68-9.

[3] W. F. Albright, "The Role of the Canaanites in the History of Civilization", *Studies in the History of Culture* (Menasha, 1942), p. 25; cf. Alt in *Der alte Orient* vol. xxxiv, No. 4 (1936), p. 25.

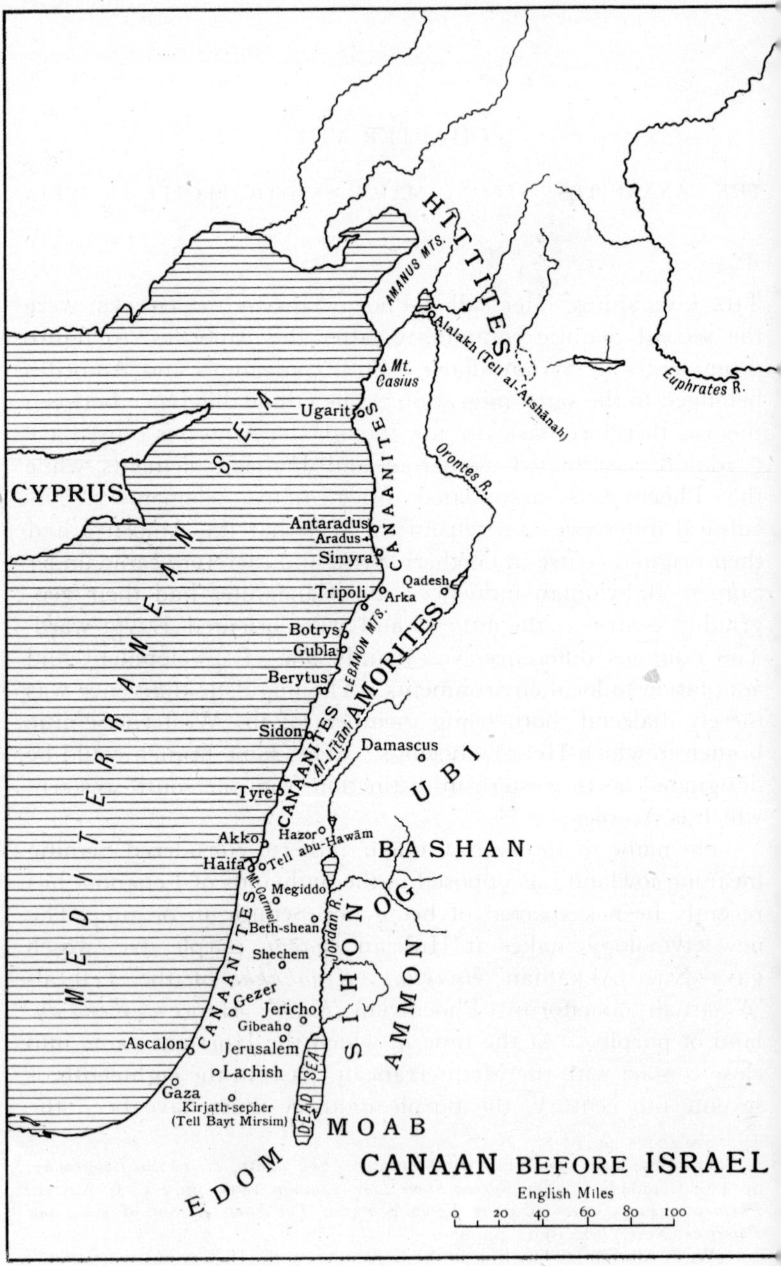

CANAAN BEFORE ISRAEL

dominant one in the land. Likewise the term Phoenicia, from Greek *phoinix*,[1] means purple red and refers to the same industry. First applied by the Greeks to those of the Canaanites with whom they traded, the term Phoenician became after about 1200 B.C. synonymous with Canaanite. These Semites of Syria, not unlike many other ancient peoples, must have been made up of communities more conscious of tribal and local differences than of national unity and had to await a foreigner to give them a general name.

First applied to the sea-coast and western Palestine, the name Canaan became the standard geographical designation of Palestine and a large part of Syria. This was the first designation of Palestine; all others are secondary. In the early documents of the Old Testament the term Canaanite was applied in a broad sense to all inhabitants of the land without any racial connotation, and "the language of Canaan"[2] was used as the general designation of the Semitic tongue of Palestine.

Canaanite religion and language begin to emerge from the mists of Semitic antiquity toward the beginning of the second millennium before Christ, but the ancestors of those called Canaanites must have been in occupation of the land for a millennium or more before. This may be inferred from place names as revealed by modern archaeology. Such cities as Jericho,[3] Beth-shean,[4] and Megiddo,[5] with clear Canaanite names were founded prior to 3000 B.C. Others like Akko,[6] Tyre,[7] Sidon,[8] Gubla, Arka and Simyra,[9] with good Semitic names which may be considered Canaanite, make their appearance in inscriptions in the first half of the second millennium.

City-states

In consequence of the configuration of Canaan and its strategic position between the seats of mighty powers that arose in the valley of the Nile, the valley of the Tigris and Asia Minor, the Canaanites never succeeded in establishing a strong unified state. They were rather grouped into small communities, each

[1] Cf. G. Bonfante, "The Name of the Phoenicians", *Classical Philology*, vol. xxxvi (1941), pp. 1 *seq.*

[2] Is. 19:18.

[3] *Yerēḥō*, moon city, modern Arīḥa.

[4] Or Beth-shan (*bēth-shan*, house of the god Sha'an), modern Baysān. See below, p. 120.

[5] Or Megiddon, derived from *gadad*, to cut or hew, modern Tell al-Mutasallim.

[6] Acco (*'akkō*, sultriners, hot sand), Gr. Ptolemais, modern 'Akka.

[7] *Sōr*, rock, modern Ṣūr.

[8] *Sīdon*, fishery, modern Ṣaydā'.

[9] See above, p. 72.

headed by a king who had presumably risen to power from a landed nobility. Each community would be nucleated round a city fortified by crenelated walls and defensive towers,[1] to which the rustic population would rush in time of danger for refuge and would repair in time of peace as a market and social centre. Such fortified cities constituted the chief defence against invasions from strong neighbours or raids from nomads. But the partition of the land into petty city-states, often at war among themselves and internally unstable through discord among nobles aspiring for local sovereignty, left the whole country at the mercy of aggressive neighbouring powers.

The earliest Canaanite settlements spread themselves all along the coast from Casius to south of the Carmel,[2] but the few indentations of the coast-line limited the number of natural harbours. The Amanus and Casius in the north, however, and the Palestinian highlands in the south afforded no adequate bulwark against rear attacks as did the lofty Lebanon. It was at the feet of Lebanon, therefore, that the great and enduring settlements clustered and flourished: Tripoli,[3] Botrys,[4] Byblus, Berytus, Sidon, Tyre. These, with Arka, Simyra, Aradus[5] to the north, and others formed a mosaic of diminutive, self-sufficient, autonomous city-states. In southern Syria, Gaza[6] and Ascalon[7] lie on the coast, but a number of other Canaanite cities — Gezer, Lachish, Megiddo, Hazor, Shechem, Jerusalem[8] — lie inland. All these and several others are mentioned in the campaign reports of Thutmose III (early fifteenth century before Christ) and the Tell al-ʿAmārnah letters and are described in the Books of Joshua and Judges.

The cities were small in area. Gezer and Hazor,[9] two of the largest, covered fifteen to sixteen acres; Jericho covered only six. An easily defended mound or a water spring may have been the determining factor in the choice of the site. But Gezer's

[1] Sing. *migdol*; the Semitic form has survived in Arabic *majdal* appearing in place names.

[2] Ar. Kirmil, from Sem. *karmel*, garden land.

[3] Gr. (three cities), modern Ṭarābulus. The name of the ancient Phoenician town, which stood on the shore and did not figure prominently until the Persian period, is still unknown. See below, p. 224.

[4] See above, p. 71.

[5] A non-Semitic name.

[6] From *ʿazzāh*, strength, firmness, modern Ghazzah.

[7] Heb. *Ashqelōn*, modern ʿAsqalān.

[8] See below, p. 161.

[9] See below, p. 147.

wall, as revealed by modern excavation, was as thick as sixteen feet; Jericho's ramparts rose to a height of twenty-one feet.[1] Such were the mighty Canaanite strongholds that scared Moses' spies.[2] The military chariot which the Canaanites introduced into the land was their chief weapon of defence. The horse was introduced about the time of the Hyksos[3] (*ca.* 1750 B.C.). Other offensive weapons included a bow and a bronze- or flint-tipped arrow, a short dagger, a curved knife — remains of all of which have been found — and a heavy club of hard wood.

The rural population must have been sparse, and the entire number of inhabitants of pre-Israelite Palestine could not have exceeded a quarter of a million.[4] Cities simply grew and followed no pre-arranged scheme. Canaanite houses of the fifteenth century, as unearthed by the archaeologist's spade, were, on the whole, poor in construction and irregular in plan. The houses of the poor were small in size and crowded together as in old-style villages of today. Those of the well-to-do had for a centre a courtyard around which the rooms were grouped. Some were evidently provided with a granary and a special cistern.[5]

Island cities

Certain cities — Aradus, Sidon, Tyre — had a double line of defence. Their citizens occupied in each case twin settlements, one on the mainland, where they traded or cultivated their orchards, and the other on adjacent islets, to which they scampered whenever the Assyrian wolf pack, for instance, burst through the mountain passes. The Aradians, whose coast settlement was called in Hellenistic days Antaradus,[6] huddled themselves on their rocky islet, Manhattan-wise, in diminutive skyscrapers. Their ingenuity was manifested in achieving water-supply for their isle. Rain water from roofs was stored in cisterns and supplemented by tapping a submarine spring by sinking over it a huge inverted funnel to which a leathern hose was attached.[7] This is perhaps the earliest record of a fresh-water submarine spring.

[1] Garstang, *Heritage of Solomon*, pp. 109-10; A.-G. Barrois. *Manuel d'archéologie biblique*, vol. i (Paris, 1939), pp. 145 *seq.*

[2] Num. 13:28.

[3] On this people see below, p. 146.

[4] Garstang, *Heritage of Solomon*, p. 107.

[5] Macalister, *Excavation of Gezer*, vol. i, p. 169; for description of other houses consult Barrois, pp. 251 *seq.*

[6] Tortosa of the Crusades, modern Ṭarṭūs, north of ʻAmrīt, where some of the most remarkable of Phoenician ruins — a shrine and tombs — are still observable.

[7] Strabo, Bk. XVI, ch. 2, § 13.

Tyre on the islet was "built in the same manner as Aradus".[1] The islet was joined to the mainland by a half-mile mole which Alexander built when besieging it.[2] Recent excavations under the sea and photographs from the air reveal that the main harbour was on the south side of the isle, that the breakwater protecting it, now fifty feet below the surface, was 750 metres long, about 8 metres thick, and that the whole was commanded by the city walls with detached towers at each end.[3] These massive works were supposedly built by King Hiram, contemporary of Solomon, under whom the city reached its height. This made Tyre one of the strongest ports on the eastern Mediterranean. Hers, however, was then as always an empire of trade and wealth, rather than of land and conquest.

Tyre's northern sister Sidon stood on a promontory, chosen doubtless because of the excellent harbour formed by a series of tiny islets later joined together by artificial embankments. This harbour lay to the north; on the south was another harbour, styled the Egyptian, larger but less secure. A wall protected the land side of the town. Its present castle, Qalʿat al-Baḥr (castle of the sea), owes its origin to the Crusades and stands on the largest of the islets. In the early seventeenth century the Lebanese prince Fakhr-al-Dīn al-Maʿni caused the entrance of the ancient harbour to be filled up in order to prevent the approach of the Ottoman fleet.[4]

Leagues

The political isolation of these city-states, reflecting the physical dismemberment of the land, could best be overcome only temporarily and locally when a political hegemony under the leadership of some one city was effected. Common interests at times impelled voluntary federation. Ugarit in the late sixteenth century, Gubla in the fourteenth, Sidon before the eleventh, Tyre after it and Tripoli in the fifth acted as such leaders. Especially under the stress of pending danger did these cities join hands to form leagues and alliances. One of the few great alliances recorded was that crushed by Thutmose III at Megiddo in 1479 B.C., but the leading spirit in the coalition then was distant Qadesh on the Orontes. The Tell al-ʿAmārnah

[1] Strabo, Bk. XVI, ch. 2, § 23. [2] See below, p. 232.
[3] A. Poidebard, *Un Grand Port disparu: Tyr* (Paris, 1939), pp. 25-6.
[4] See below, p. 683.

correspondence of a century later betrays not only lack of concerted action but an attempt on the part of the Phoenician kings to seek favours from the Egyptian suzerain at the expense of one another. Most of these kings addressed their letters to the Pharaoh personally and individually. Throughout their long history the Canaanites proved themselves to be peace loving and not military minded. The centre of their interest lay in the field of trade, art and religion rather than that of war. As a rule their cities bowed their heads before the storms of conquest from Egypt, Babylonia, Hittiteland, Persia or Macedonia. They purchased immunity from undue interference by payment of tribute and hoped to be at least partly compensated by an enlarged hinterland market.

Economy: agriculture

The people of Canaan developed the types of economy conditioned by their land and its natural resources. Agriculture, fishing and trade were the earliest major pursuits. Farming was a chief interest; it profoundly influenced their religion. Sowing, first done by hand, received an impetus when the plough was introduced from Babylonia; the southern part of the country may have received it through Egypt.[1] Vestiges of Canaanite farming between 1500 and 1300 B.C. have been found at Tell Bayt Mirsim (Kirjath-sepher). A bronze hoe has been unearthed at Ra's al-Shamrah. Harvest was reaped with a sickle made of flint teeth fastened with plaster into a bone or wooden handle. This type of implement was used until about 1000 B.C., when displaced by the iron sickle. From about the same time comes the earliest datable iron implement excavated in central Palestine, a plough point found in Gibeah, home of Saul, modern Tell al-Fūl.[2] Tell Bayt Mirsim has yielded iron ploughshares and sickles alongside Philistine pottery, helping to date these finds. Threshing was done by a sledge whose bottom was studded with small stones. Grain was winnowed with a large wooden fork. Flour was ground in stone hand-mills and bread was baked in cylindrical mud-brick ovens. The whole picture did not differ radically from the rural practice of present-day Syria as can be judged by a cursory examination of sickles, grinding mills, pounding stones, mortars and other utensils unearthed in recent years.

Nor did crops differ much from today's. Wheat, oats, barley,

[1] See above, p. 17. [2] See below, p. 186.

beans, vetch, grapes, olives, figs, pomegranates and nuts were representative products.[1] Grains, vines and olives have been rightly called the Mediterranean trio of farm produce. In order to adjust his tillage to the constant threat of inadequate rainfall, the farmer resorted to dry-farming procedure, which involved an alternate year of crop and fallow. The Canaanite society included a class of serfs or free-born tenants termed *khapshi*, which corresponded to the *mushkēnu* in the Babylonian society.[2] In rural Lebanon, as the population outstripped local means of subsistence, the mountain-sides were terraced, by means of walls one a few yards from the other, with a view to extending the arable land and protecting its soil against erosion. Such terraced slopes were better adapted to gardens, vineyards and orchards than to field agriculture. The earliest references to these terraces, still a feature in Lebanese landscape, occur in an inscription of Thutmose III.[3]

The domesticated animals were led by cows, sheep, asses, goats, pigs and dogs. The last three were the only scavengers. Meat, eaten only on special and festive occasions, was boiled in wide-mouthed pots. Food was eaten with the hand or with bone-handled spoons. Drinking-water was lifted from cisterns or received from springs and carried on the head in water-skins or large jars. Lamps were simple clay saucers with a slightly pinched place in the rim to hold the wick. The earliest go back to the first half of the second millennium. Numberless kitchen utensils, including jars, vases and stone bowls, have been dug out from ancient sites, revealing that the main features of domestic life have been perpetuated until the present day.

Industry

Craftsmen and traders occupied a medial position in Canaanite society between the feudal aristocracy — composed of landed nobility and chariot warriors — and the lowest class composed of serfs and slaves.

The sons as a rule took up the same profession as their fathers, a practice that continued till later times.[4] There is reason to believe that the craftsmen organized themselves into

[1] Cf. above, p. 48; Barrois, pp. 309 *seq.*

[2] Code of Hammurabi, §§ 198, 201, 204, 205, 208, etc. *mushkēnu* has survived in Ar. *miskīn*, poor, Anglicized " mesquin " through Sp. and Fr. *khapshi* comes from a stem surviving in Ar. *khabutha*, to be base.

[3] See below, p. 130. Ar. word for terrace is *jall*.

[4] See below, pp. 549-50, 649-50; cf. p. 640, ll. 12-15.

guilds. The guilds consisted of closely related groups bound together by profession and blood and living in separate quarters. Such organizations existed in Palestine as early as the eighteenth pre-Christian century.

Pottery, one of the earliest and most successful of Syrian industries, attained its zenith prior to 1500 B.C. Babylonian influence was manifest as early as 2000 B.C. The use of the potter's wheel, beginning early in the second millennium,[1] gave Canaanite ceramics new quality and more symmetrical form. The clay then used became more refined. Early Amorite characteristics began to vanish and imitation of foreign patterns, mainly Egyptian, Cretan and Mycenaean, became common. Egyptian glazed earthenware and alabaster vessels were imported in considerable numbers. Cypriote pieces also served as models, as indicated by finds in Ugarit[2] and other sites. Ugarit lay on the Syrian coast just across from Cyprus. After 1500 B.C. Cypriote and Mycenaean influences became particularly strong. Special designs for cult objects and votive offerings were worked out. Tin was used in glazing and for giving pottery special lustre. Remains in tombs display considerable taste and technical skill. Sculpture reached its height in the sixteenth century.

Metallurgy

As metallurgists the Canaanites of the middle and late Bronze Ages (*ca.* 2100–1200 B.C.) were probably unexcelled. Copper and its alloy bronze were freely worked. Chemical analysis of the blade of an early fourteenth-century axe found at Ra's al-Shamrah revealed not only knowledge of smelting iron but of mixing it with other metals to form steel[3] — a hitherto unknown fact. In quest of tin for hardening copper into bronze and iron into steel, and in search of gold and silver, they undertook long journeys outside of their own homeland. Silver dishes were included in the Syrian booty of the Pharaohs. The art of the goldsmith attained its height in the sixteenth century. A jeweller's scales and weights have been found at Ra's al-Shamrah. Silver, not coined but weighed, served as currency throughout Western Asia, though trade took largely the form of barter. Sennacherib (705–681), one of the Assyrian conquerors of Syria, refers to such weights made by him: "I built a form of clay and poured bronze into it as in making

[1] Cf. above, p. 21. [2] See below, p. 116.
[3] Schaeffer, *Ugaritica*, p. 110, No. 2.

half-shekel pieces ".[1] Knives, lance-heads, battle-axes, awls and tweezers have been found in pre-Israelite Jericho. After 1500 B.C. Hittite, Cypriote and Mycenaean forms of weapons make their appearance in Palestine. Bronze, gold and silver bracelets, anklets, ear-rings, nose-rings and brooches have been found in various sites. Small brass cymbals of the fourteenth century were unearthed at Tell abu-Hawām, near Haifa. Monuments show harps, flutes, oboes, lutes and tambourines which, being perishable, have left no remains. As Canaanite merchants began to import from Egypt amulets, scarabs, seals, beads, vessels, vases, arms and other objects, Canaanite metal-workers began to imitate them. Homer's poems extol Phoenician metal work

From Dussaud, Deschamps & Seyrig, " La Syrie "
(Librairie Orientaliste Paul Geuthner, Paris)

A ROYAL COLLAR IN GOLD REPOUSSÉ FOUND IN TOMB III BYBLUS

The central motif is formed by a falcon with spread wings. Each extremity of the collar holds a falcon's head. It is an imitation of the Egyptian pectoral

and arts. A bowl of silver which " Sidonians, well skilled in deft handiwork, had wrought cunningly " was " in beauty far the goodliest in all the earth ".[2]

Ivory

The adornment of the common people included necklaces and rings of limestone, quartzite and carnelian, of which specimens have been found. Only a few cases of ivory beads and amulets have been unearthed. Bone took the place of ivory though the elephant must have existed in Central Syria, as

[1] Daniel D. Luckenbill, *The Annals of Sennacherib* (Chicago, 1924), p. 123.

[2] *Iliad* xxiii. 740-45. " Sidonians " and " Phoenicians " were used synonymously.

By courtesy of Prof. F. A. Schaeffer

THE MOTHER GODDESS ON A MYCENAEAN IVORY FOUND AT AL-MĪNA AL-BAYḌĀ' (THE PORT OF RA'S AL-SHAMRAH)

The goddess, dressed in Mycenaean fashion, and seated on an altar with a lion on each side, holds an ear of corn. The motif was of Oriental origin, particularly Sumerian, but became popular throughout the Aegean Sea

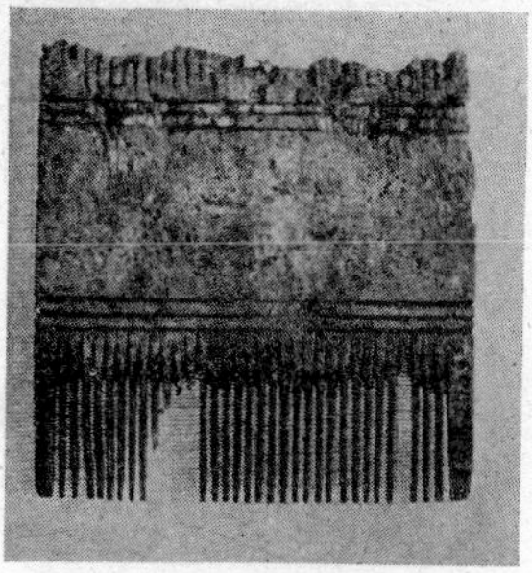

(*a*)

(*b*)

From Gordon Loud, " The Megiddo Ivories " (University of Chicago Press)

DOUBLE IVORY COMB

Front (*a*) with surface rising from teeth to central ridge and with sides bevelled; black inlay in decoration. Back (*b*) flat with black inlay in decoration

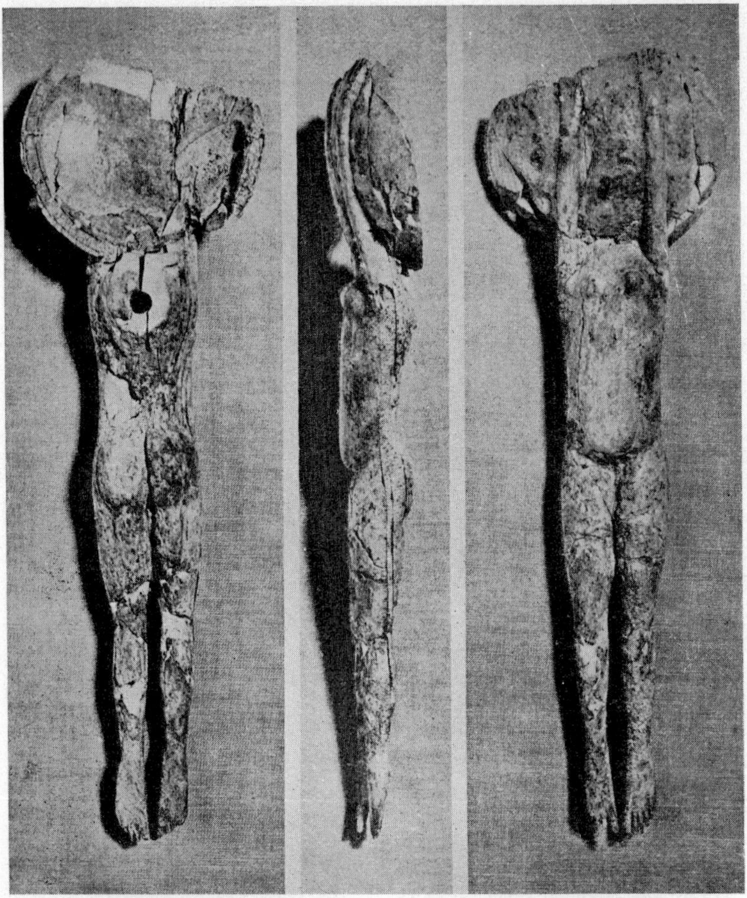

FRAGMENTARY IVORY SPOON WITH FEMALE FIGURINE HANDLE

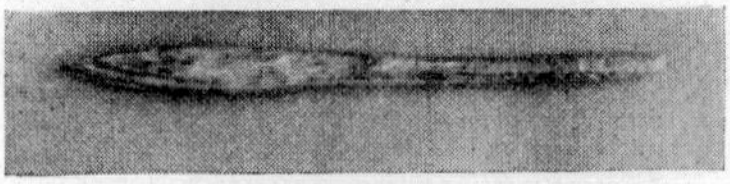

(a)

(b)

(c)

(d)

From Gordon Loud, " The Megiddo Ivories " (University of Chicago Press)

IVORY PINS

Large end of (*c*) broken where once pierced as if for use as a toggle

Pharaonic reports of hunting trips into that region indicate. The earliest Phoenician ivories go back to the fourteenth century; those of Megiddo were found in an early twelfth century palace, but may be of earlier origin. Combs found in tombs in Spain carry on the Megiddo tradition but belong to the eighth century. The earliest known Greek imitation of Phoenician works belongs to this century. A Megiddo ivory of the twelfth or thirteenth century shows a minstrel playing a lyre. Certain Phoenician ivories are of such exquisite workmanship and beauty as to render them among the most prized relics of ancient Eastern art.

Glass

The manufacture of glass was another industry in which the Canaanites excelled. Classical tradition credits them with the discovery of glass but we now know that the Egyptians manufactured glass long before the Canaanites. The Canaanite tradition is represented in Pliny's [1] report that merchants while preparing their repast on the shore near ʿAkka employed lumps of nitre, with which their ship was laden, for supporting their cauldrons and discovered transparent streams when the nitre was subjected to the action of fire and combined with the sand. The fact, however, remains that it was the Phoenicians who trafficked in Egyptian glass and who perfected the ancient art of producing glass.

Cloth industry

Spinning and weaving were a regular industry carried on at home. Vestiges of whorls of stone and bone as well as loom weights of stone and clay, dating from the early third millennium, have been found. Wool was no doubt the earliest fabric; Nuzi documents of about 1500 B.C. mention Canaanite wool.[2] Cotton, originally an Indian plant, was introduced by Sennacherib into Assyria, as he refers in an inscription to "the trees that bore wool" which his men "clipped and carded for garment".[3] It was never common in those days. The Phoenicians introduced this material into the Greek world in the early Hellenistic period, and with it its Semitic name.[4] Linen was evidently produced in southern Syria in the tenth century as the Gezer calendar of that date mentions a "month of pulling

[1] Bk. XXVI, ch. 65.
[2] *Annual, American Schools of Oriental Research*, vol. xvi (1936), No. 77.
[3] James H. Breasted, *Ancient Times*, 2nd ed. (New York, 1935), p. 203.
[4] *Kitōn, chitōn*, tunic. Eng. "cotton" comes from Ar. *quṭn*, a cognate of the ancient Semitic word, which survived in Ar. *kittān*, linen.

flax ".[1] Silk was presumably known in Tyre in the sixth century if the translation of a word in Ezekiel 16: 10, 13 is correct.[2] Needles and pins have been found in pre-Israelite Palestine in bronze cases and loose. The needles are eyed and the pins are

From Nina M. Davies, " Egyptian Paintings " (University of Chicago Press)

SYRIAN TRIBUTE BEARERS, FROM A THEBES TOMB, REIGN OF THUTMOSE IV (1420–1411 B.C.)

The tribute bearers present their choicest vessels of gold and silver. The foremost prostrate themselves or raise their arms in adoration before the Pharaoh. The faces are bearded though two of the heads are bald. In the upper register the first of the two standing men leads a nude girl whose head is shaven except for long hanging bunches. The other standing man holds an ointment horn. In the lower register the first standing man has a bow case slung over his arm. He and the man behind him carry blue jars which might be of lapis lazuli. The hindmost bears on a dish a drinking vase in the shape of a conventionalized bird's head

long with ribbed heads or are toggle.[3] Round buttons with two holes have been discovered. The buttons of the poor were made of broken pottery; those of the rich, of bone or ivory.

Illustrations in mural paintings of the rock tombs of Egypt,

[1] Gustaf Dalman, *Arbeit und Sitte in Palästina* (Gütersloh, 1928), vol. i, p. 7.
[2] See below, p. 275.
[3] See above, p. 90, figs. (*a*)-(*d*).

dating from the early Hyksos period (*ca.* 1750 B.C.), show Canaanites wearing long garments reaching from shoulder to knee, made of dyed cloth and trimmed with braid, often elaborately embroidered. Originally worn by the king and the priest, the style was gradually extended to the commonality. Syrian tribute bearers appear on the Theban tombs of the Eighteenth Dynasty with a white shawl edged with red or blue and wound round the body from the waist downwards. Canaanite captives on Egyptian monuments appear wearing shirts or short tunics, kilts and overgarments consisting of a long narrow strip wound spirally round the body. The whole outfit, including the head-gear, resembles the Bedouin's. Not only Canaanites but Aramaeans and other Semites are represented by Egyptian artists as heavier in physique than the Egyptian and often with long hair and dark heavy beards ending in a point. The hair from behind falls in thick masses as low as the neck and above the forehead is confined by a sort of fillet. The priests shaved their heads as in Egypt. In later times women hid their hair under veils, and after marriage wore close-fitting bonnets with "round tires like the moon" attached to them.[1]

From Gordon Loud, "The Megiddo Ivories"
(University of Chicago Press)

A CANAANITE MAIDEN OF THE TWELFTH OR THIRTEENTH CENTURY, AS RESTORED FROM A MEGIDDO IVORY

The flowing robe and long hair were characteristic of the fashion of the day

Another industry which throve along the coast was fishing. Sidon owes its very name to this industry.[2] The pasture of the Purple

[1] Is. 3:18. [2] See above, p. 81, n. 8.

land was at times disappointing or uncertain owing to the poor soil or variable rainfall, but the pasture of the deep furnished abundant fish, especially of the tunny variety, salt and purple dye.

The earliest occurrence of the word for purple is in a Ra's al-Shamrah text stating that a certain quantity of wool was delivered for distribution among weavers charged with the fabrication of *argmn*.[1] Not only the eastern but the entire Mediterranean littoral had in varying measure the murex from which the purple fluid was extracted, and peoples other than the Phoenicians, for example the Minoans and Greeks, utilized this mollusk. Greek legend asserts that Helen of Troy, while strolling along the beach to while away her captivity, noticed how a shellfish which her dog chewed turned its mouth into a deep purple colour, which she so admired that she expected any suitor before receiving any favour to produce a dress dyed with *porphyra*. But the Tyrian purple was the most famous and precious of the dyes of antiquity. In the neighbourhood of Tyre and Sidon a superior variety of the mollusc flourished, and the Phoenicians, anxious to conserve their native supply, discovered and imported the dye

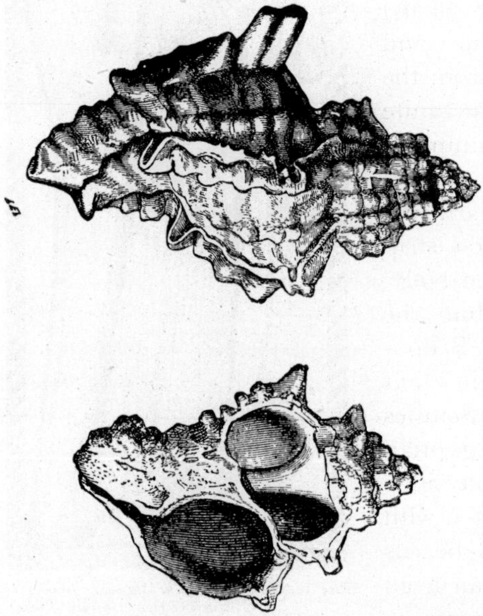

From Rawlinson, "Phoenicia" (Longmans Green)

SHELL OF THE *MUREX TRUNCULUS*, WHICH YIELDED THE PURPLE DYE

Large heaps of these shells can be seen near Tyre and outside the south gate of Sidon

[1] Virolleaud in *Journal asiatique*, vol. ccxxx (1938), p. 146. In Assyrian the word takes the form *argamānu*, in Heb. *argāmān* (2 Ch. 2 : 7), Ar. *urjuwān*, of non-Semitic origin.

from as far as the port of Sparta and the neighbourhood of Carthage and Utica. The trade was not in the dye but in the dyed cloths, which could be wool, hair, flax or hemp. What purpose the fluid serves in the economy of the animal is not known; but certainly it is not naturally exuded so as to colour the water as a protective measure against its enemies, as claimed by some.

Considerable and painstaking labour was required to extract the few drops from the tiny mollusc and distil it. Hence its high cost, in so far as it was not a monopoly product. Since only the wealthy could afford it, robes in purple colour became a mark of distinction,[1] ultimately giving rise to the phrase "born to the purple". In Homeric[2] as well as Hellenistic days[3] purple raiment was associated with royalty. Like Helen of Troy, Cleopatra of Egypt was especially fond of it. As an indication of pontifical dignity the Jewish high priest wore purple dress as did the chief priest of Hierapolis in North Syria[4] and the priest of Jupiter at Magnesia in Asia Minor.[5]

The exact process of preparing the dye is not known from Phoenician sources. Pliny[6] describes it as starting with the taking of the fish alive — for when it dies it spits out this juice — extracting the fluid from a vein, adding salt and leaving it to steep for three days, after which it is boiled by moderate heat. While boiling, the liquid is skimmed from time to time. About the tenth day, when the contents of the cauldron are in a liquefied state, the fleece is plunged into it and left to soak for five hours. Then it is carded and thrown in again until it has fully imbibed the colour. It is considered of the best quality when it has exactly the colour of clotted blood.

The influx of wealth into Rome in the first pre-Christian century made possible great extension in purple use and later occasioned the imitation of the dye in Italy and other lands. In the East its manufacture continued after the Moslem conquest; "Tyrian purple" is mentioned among the articles of luxury imported by Venetian merchants in the late eighth century. After the fall of the Byzantine Empire, where the

[1] Esth. 8:15; Prov. 31:22; Luke 16:19.
[2] *Iliad*, iv, 141-5.
[3] 1 Macc. 8:14.
[4] Lucian, *De Dea Syria*, § 42. See below, p. 172.
[5] Strabo, Bk. XIV, ch. 1, § 41.
[6] Bk. IX, ch. 62.

privilege of making the dye was confined to a small group, the knowledge of it was completely lost in the East. In England, where it was carried from the East, it survived in isolated regions as late as the seventeenth century.

Besides the purple dye the early Lebanese introduced kermes [1] into ancient commerce. This is the scarlet of the Old Testament [2] and was made from insects found on a species of oak [3] growing around the eastern shores of the Mediterranean. When dried and dissolved in some acid the insects yielded the scarlet or crimson colour. At first wild, the insects were cultivated by Persians and later by Armenians.

[1] Eng. " crimson " comes from Ar. *qirmiz*, originally Persian or Armenian.
[2] Lev. 14:4; Num. 19:6.
[3] Theophrastus, *De historia plantarum*, Bk. III, ch. 16, § 1.

CHAPTER IX

MARITIME ACTIVITY AND COLONIAL EXPANSION

THE Phoenicians were the first maritime nation of history. As the Lebanon hindered intercourse with the hinterland but provided excellent timber for shipbuilding, the Mediterranean beckoned these Semites on its eastern shore to its surface and they responded by turning their nomadism of the desert into that of the sea. The deep held no horrors for them, and the unknown fascinated rather than scared them. Starting with coastwise sailings to peddle their tunny fish, glass, earthenware and other local products, they later struck across the open sea and established east and west trunk routes which long remained their monopoly. The pedlars developed into merchant princes. Typical colonizers, they disseminated elements of their own culture and their neighbours', which they made acceptable to foreigners. Especially after the thirteenth and twelfth centuries, when squeezed out of Central Syria by the Aramaeans and out of southern Syria by the Israelites and Philistines, did the Canaanites bend their energies seaward to become, relatively speaking, the greatest mariners and traders of all history.

Sea routes

The Phoenicians were not the sea rovers pictured by tradition. They rather followed well-charted routes which they first explored and then utilized, almost monopolized. Their earliest international routes connected Byblus and other ports with Egypt. The main later trunks ran from Sidon and Tyre by Egypt or directly north to Cyprus, turned west in the lee of the Taurus, past Lycia, then on the south side of Rhodes, Crete and Corcyra to Sicily, then by Cossyra Isle [1] to their colonies in North Africa, and finally westward along the coast to their colonies in Spain. In addition there were, of course, cross-roads — north and south sea lanes. Four major articles which several Mediterranean countries lacked the Phoenicians first supplied: timber, wheat, oil and wine. To the Greeks the

[1] Modern Pantelleria, Qawṣarah of Arab geographers.

cedar of Lebanon was Phoenician cedar.[1] Later they carried the products of their two leading industries: cloth-making and metal-work. Hard wood was a crying need of alluvial Egypt and Mesopotamia to construct temples and palaces as well as fishing-boats, merchant ships and naval vessels. The coniferous and resinous forests of Lebanon, with their fir, pine, cedar and terebinth trees, provided not only timber but also pitch, and resin, whose traffic accompanied the lumber trade. These ingredients were used for coating ships and preserving them.[2] Oil was used for perfume as well as food. As they extended their market of consumption, the Phoenicians expanded their market of produce until they became the liaison agents distributing the ware of the East in the West and the few products of the West, mostly minerals and earthenware, in the East. The Mediterranean became a Phoenician lake long before it became a Greek or a Roman lake.

Navigation

In their effort to develop sea-borne traffic on an international scale they began the systematic study of navigation. Credited with the discovery of the usefulness of the Pole Star, they became the earliest masters of the art of night sailing — of laying a course by the stars.[3] The Greeks named this star after the Phoenicians. Cedar logs, unsurpassed in durability, were floated down the drainage streams in flood-time to the nearest harbour for constructing ships or for export. Sidon and Tyre received their coniferous timber from Hermon. Phoenician ships from about 1400 B.C. are represented on Egyptian monuments, half-moon in shape, with high stern and bow, two large oars as rudders and two yards across the top of the mast holding a single square sail. The earliest vessels of which we have any representation were impelled both by sails and oars. The boats were broad in the beam so that they could accommodate a large cargo without being long. Phoenician trading vessels and battleships of the later period appear on Assyrian monuments with a high stern, a sharp, pointed ram in front, which could be used in battle, and with a double deck. It was Phoenician shipbuilders who began the practice of placing two or more rowers one above the other. The lower deck had ordinarily two

[1] Theophrastus, Bk. III, ch. 12, § 3; Bk. IX, ch. 2, § 3.
[2] Theophrastus, Bk. IV, ch. 2, §§ 2, 3; cf. Ex. 2:3.
[3] Cf. Strabo, Bk. XVI, ch. 2, § 24

rows of four or five oars each, making sixteen to twenty rowers in all. The number of rowers in later times reached fifty. The upper deck held the passengers. Only one yard was used, and the sail was furled when at anchor or in unfavourable weather. Such was the type borrowed by the early Greeks as evidenced by vase paintings. The same type was presumably built for Solomon by those " shipmen that had knowledge of the sea ",[1]

From Rawlinson's " Phoenicia " (*Longmans Green*)

PHOENICIAN BIREME

A trading vessel or battleship as represented in bas-relief on a palace wall of Sennacherib *ca.* 700 B.C. The rowers, five in a row, sat at two elevations in the lower deck, making twenty rowers in all. The passengers occupied the upper deck. The bow rose perpendicularly from an iron-pointed ram, intended to sink enemy ships

sent by his friend Hiram, king of Tyre, and that docked at Ezion-geber,[2] the seaport of the Israelite kingdom on the Gulf of al-ʿAqabah of the Red Sea.[3] Through this route they exported wood and copper and received in return gold from Ophir and perfume and spices from other parts of Arabia, thereby avoiding passage through the Suez on the Egyptian border. Other land products, such as slaves and horses, were sent to Egypt in exchange for local products. Phoenician merchants in the Delta[4] cities of the Twentieth Dynasty

[1] I K. 9:27. [2] See below, pp. 189-90.

[3] That the Phoenicians had settlements in the Negeb is not generally accepted; Garstang, *Heritage of Solomon*, p. 371; W. F. Albright, *Archaeology and the Religion of Israel* (Baltimore, 1942), pp. 59-60.

[4] " Nile " is thought by some to be of Phoen. derivation; Sem. *nāhal* means to flow.

(1200–1090 B.C.) were especially prominent. In Memphis they seem to have enjoyed in the thirteenth century extraterritorial privileges — a forerunner of modern capitulations.[1]

The Phoenicians were not only the first maritime but the first amphibian nation in history. Their trading stations in the hinterland comprised Edessa and possibly Nisibis (modern Naṣībīn) and connected their Mediterranean ports with their Persian Gulf posts. According to their own tradition, the Phoenicians originally came to the Syrian seaboard from the Persian Gulf, where they had cities bearing the same names of Aradus, Tyre and Sidon.[2] In his commercial chapter (27) Ezekiel gives a graphic description of the land and sea traffic of the Phoenicians in its varied aspects. He lists, among their imports, silver, iron, tin and lead from Spain, slaves and brass vessels from Ionia, linen from Egypt, lambs and goats from Arabia.

Circum-navigation of Africa

The crowning nautical achievement of the Phoenicians was sailing around Africa over two thousand years before the Portuguese navigators usually acclaimed as the first to do so. The feat was accomplished at the direction of Pharaoh Necho (609–593 B.C.) of Dynasty XXVI, who redug the ancient canal connecting the eastern arm of the Nile with the head of the Red Sea. Taking their course from this sea, Phoenician vessels sailed the southern ocean, and on the approach of autumn their sailors landed wherever they happened to find themselves, planted wheat, awaited the crop and again departed. Having thus consumed two years, they in the third rounded the Pillars of Hercules and returned to Egypt. "There they said (what some may believe, though I do not) that in sailing round Libya [Africa] they had the sun on their right hand."[3] This last detail, which "the father of [Greek] history" did not believe, incidentally confirms the authenticity of the story. As ships sail west round the Cape of Good Hope the sun of the southern hemisphere would be on their right

Colonies

Wherever the Phoenicians went there they built. Representing a small people, they could filter into a new place without arousing much suspicion, and possessing no common political life they could without undue strain adapt themselves to any

[1] See below, p. 668. [2] Cf. Strabo, Bk. XVI, ch. 3, § 4.
[3] Herodotus, Bk. IV, ch. 42.

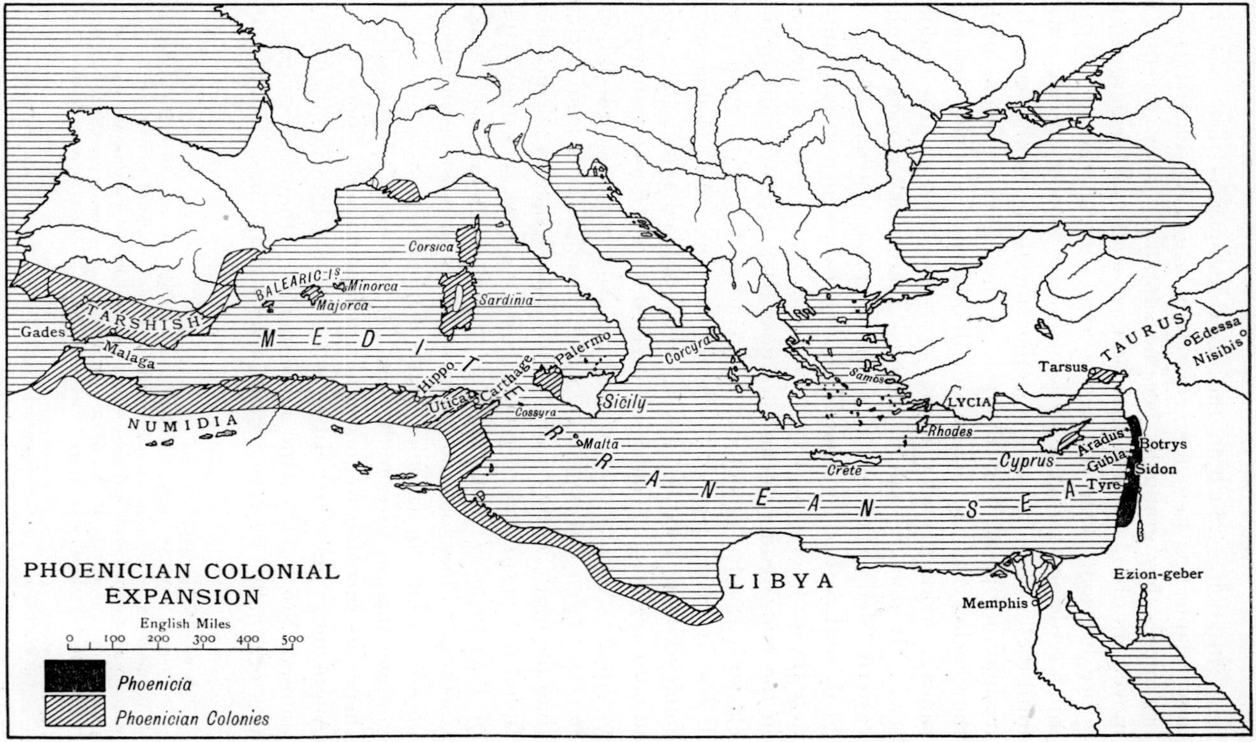
PHOENICIAN COLONIAL EXPANSION
English Miles
0 100 200 300 400 500
Phoenicia
Phoenician Colonies
TARSHISH
Gades
Malaga
BALEARIC IS.
Minorca
Majorca
Corsica
Sardinia
M E D I T E R R A N E A N S E A
Hippo
Utica
Carthage
Palermo
Sicily
Cossyra
Malta
Corcyra
Samos
Rhodes
Crete
LYCIA
Cyprus
Tarsus
TAURUS
Edessa
Nisibis
Aradus
Botrys
Gubla
Sidon
Tyre
Memphis
Ezion-geber
NUMIDIA
LIBYA

new situation — much in the same manner as their modern descendants, the Lebanese emigrants,[1] do. As colonizers and organizers they gradually became supreme. They introduced movement into a world that seemed static and enlarged its entire horizon. One trading factory after another developed into a settlement, and one settlement after another into a colony, until these colonies, linked together and to the mother cities by navigation, spread from the head of the Egyptian Delta, along the Cilician coast, to Greece and all other points of the Mediterranean, making it what its modern name means, " the middle sea ". It may be safely assumed that their colonies in the eastern Mediterranean, including Cyprus, antedate those of Sicily and Sardinia in mid-Mediterranean, which in turn antedate those of north-western Africa and Spain. Their settlement in the mid-Mediterranean isles goes back to the middle of the eleventh century, if not earlier. Gades (Cadiz) in Spain and Utica in that part of North Africa now called Tunis were founded about 1000 B.C.; they are considered among the oldest in those regions. " Gades " is derived from a Phoenician word [2] meaning " wall ", " walled place ". No Phoenician inscriptions have yet been discovered in Sardinia and Cyprus from earlier than the ninth century; the famous Baal-Lebanon [3] dedication, found in Cyprus and once considered the most ancient example of Phoenician writing, belongs to the middle of the eighth. Carthage,[4] illustrious daughter of Tyre and most distinguished of all Phoenician colonies, dates from about 850 B.C. It is younger than its sister to the west, Hippo, once a royal residence (hence its surname Regius) and afterwards the bishopric of St. Augustine. The word Hippo is Libyan. " Libya ", the Greek name of North Africa and subsequently of the whole continent, was originally — Greek legend asserts — the name of the wife

[1] See below, p. 696.

[2] Cognate with Ar. *jidār*. In Berber *agadir* also means wall. The American dollar mark ($), said to be derived from the " pillar " dollar of Emperor Charles V, which was stamped with a design used on early coins of Phoenician Gades, is in reality a modification of P^s, Mexican abbreviation for pesos or piastres; F. Cajori, " Evolution of the Dollar Mark ", *Popular Science Monthly*, vol. lxxxi (1912), pp. 521-30.

[3] G. A. Cooke, *A Text-Book of North-Semitic Inscriptions* (Oxford, 1903), p. 52.

[4] Phoen. *qart ḥadasht*, new town, in contrast to Utica (old town). " Utica " is derived from a stem *ʿātaq*, to be old.

of Poseidon (god of the sea) and mother of Agenor, king of Phoenicia.

The climax of this colonizing enterprise in the western Mediterranean was evidently attained between the middle of the tenth and the middle of the eighth centuries. Its phenomenal success suggests the existence of an earlier stratum of Semitic immigrants into North Africa and perhaps the southern part of the Iberian peninsula. The migration which carried Semites in the third millennium or earlier into Egypt may have continued beyond that land. Vague memory of a tradition that places early Semites in the western Mediterranean regions has been preserved in classical and Arabic writings.[1]

The founding of Gades beyond the Pillars of Hercules (the opposite promontories of the Strait of Gibraltar) introduced the Phoenicians into the Atlantic and resulted in the discovery of the ocean [2] for the ancient world. This discovery ranks among the greatest contributions of Syrian civilization to world progress.[3] It was from the Phoenicians that Homer and Hesiod learned for the first time of the Atlantic. How far the Phoenicians penetrated into the ocean called later by the Arabs " the sea of darkness " is not easy to ascertain. That they reached Cornwall in England in quest of tin has been maintained by some authorities, though there is no early reference to that fact. Herodotus [4] disclaims any special knowledge of the Cassiterides [5] (tin islands) " whence our tin is brought ". These are the Scilly Isles, lying just off the tip of Cornwall. Strabo,[6] who wrote about 7 B.C., asserts that the Cassiterides have tin and lead which the natives barter for pottery, salt and copper utensils and that in former times the Phoenicians alone carried on this

[1] Procopius of Caesarea, *History of the Wars*, Bk. IV, ch. 10, §§ 13-29; al-Idrīsi, *Ṣifat al-Maghrib*, ed. R. Dozy and M. J. de Goeje (Leyden, 1864), p. 57; ibn-Khaldūn, *Kitāb al-'Ibar wa-Dīwān al-Mubtada' w-al-Khabar* (Cairo, 1284), vol. vi, pp. 93-4.

[2] Gr. *ōkeanos*, whose derivation from Semitic *'ūg*, circle (R. Henning, " Die Anfänge des kulturellen und Handelsverkehrs in der Mittelmeer-Welt ", *Historische Zeitschrift*, vol. cxxxix, No. 1, p. 12; H. Lewy, *Die semitischen Fremdwörter im Griechischen*, Berlin, 1895, p. 208) is doubtful.

[3] Arnold J. Toynbee, *A Study of History*, vol. ii (Oxford, 1934), pp. 50, 52, 386.

[4] Bk. III, ch. 115.

[5] Gr. *kassiteros* (tin), whence Ar. *qaṣdīr*, is of Oriental but apparently not Phoen. origin.

[6] Bk. III, ch. 5, § 11.

traffic from Gades, concealing the passage from everyone. Strabo further reports that once when Roman ships followed a Phoenician that they also might find the market, the shipmaster purposely ran his vessel upon a shoal and received from the state the value of the cargo he thus lost — suggesting a virtual monopoly of tin trade and a form of state insurance. Diodorus Siculus,[1] who wrote about three-quarters of a century after Strabo, speaks of tin carried over from Britain to the opposite coast of Gaul and then through the interior into Massilia (modern Marseilles), a Greek colony which may have stood on the site of an earlier Phoenician settlement. The only Phoenician inscription thus far discovered in Britain is probably from the hand of a legionary workman, evidently a Carthaginian,

The American Numismatic Society

A COIN OF GADES

Obverse and reverse of a bronze Phoenician coin of Gades (Cadiz), second century B.C. The types refer to the Tyrian Melkarth (Herakles) and to the famous fisheries

dating from the first century of the Roman occupation.[2] Petrie discovered in ancient Gaza twisted gold ear-rings which he considered of Irish origin and dated 1450 B.C.[3]

In Spain

In Spain Phoenician colonies lay mostly in Tarshish (Tartessus), particularly in the stretch from Carthagena to Gades. These Semitic place names are quite common and occur on coins that are extant. " Tarshish ", which figures in biblical and Assyrian literature, is probably a Phoenician term meaning mine or smelting-place.[4] Tarsus in Cilicia, birthplace

[1] Bk. V, ch. 38, § 4.

[2] Alfred Guillaume, " The Phoenician Graffito in the Holt Collection of the National Museum of Wales ", *Iraq*, vol. vii (1940), pp. 67-9.

[3] Flinders Petrie, *Ancient Gaza*, vol. ii (London, 1932), p. 7; see below, p. 147.

[4] The stem from which it is derived has survived in Ar. *rashsha*, to sprinkle; Albright in *Studies in History of Civilization*, p. 42; cf. Albert Dietrich, *Phönizische Ortsnamen in Spanien* (Leipzig, 1936), p. 32.

of Paul, bore the same name and was likewise a Phoenician colony. The cult of its Baal was practically the same as that of Tyre and Carthage. Carthagena was so named after its mother Carthage in North Africa. "Malaga" [1] means workshop. Strabo [2] mentions a fish saltery in that city which may indicate the type of work that was done there. Gades also was known for salt production. Cordoba (Cordova), originally an Iberian city, was taken over by Phoenicians. Its oldest coins bear Phoenician characters later replaced by Punic. From it, among other Spanish cities, Hannibal's father, Hamilcar Barca, drew troops for his campaign against Rome. Barcelona, farther north, may have had its name connected with Phoenician *bārāq*, lightning, which appears as a surname of Hannibal's father. Through these colonies, a second home was established for Syrian civilization in the western basin of the Mediterranean.

The present capital of Minorca, Mahon, appears first as Mago,[3] originally the name of a Carthaginian general. In the Balearic Islands the Phoenicians maintained posts, but their hold on the islands, whose inhabitants were of the Iberian stock, was not firm. They likewise had posts in Corsica and Sardinia. Palermo in Sicily stands on an ancient Phoenician site.

In Greece Semitic names of places and deities together with numerous legends and myths testify to Phoenician activity. Corinth, probably a Phoenician foundation, is associated in legend with a god of Phoenician origin, Melikertes (Melkarth).[4] Among other Greek islands Samos and Crete figured prominently in Phoenician colonization.[5]

It was to Crete, a centre of civilization before the European mainland became such, that Zeus metamorphosed into a bull carried away, from a mead on the Syrian seashore, Europa, the beautiful daughter of the Phoenician king, Agenor,[6] of whom

[1] Phoen. *melākāh*.
[2] Bk. III, ch. 4. § 2.

[3] Phoen. *magēn*, shield. Eng. "mayonnaise" comes probably from the same word through Fr.

[4] Phoen. *milk-qart*, king of the city, later identified with Hercules. His contests with the twelve hostile beasts of the zodiac are the origin of the twelve labours of the Greek hero.

[5] The derivation of "Samos" from Sem. *shāmash*, sun (Hall, *Ancient History*, p. 523; Autran, *Phéniciens*, p. 5), is doubtful, and so is the derivation of "Crete" from Sem. *kārath*, to cut.

[6] "Phoenix" in *Iliad*, xiv, 1.

he was enamoured. Here he resumed his own form and married her. Minos, celebrated Cretan monarch and legislator, was born from this union, and the name of the mother is still borne by Europe the continent.

To Diodorus [1] the population of Malta, whose name is undoubtedly Semitic,[2] was Phoenician. The island had one of the finest harbours of the Mediterranean; no wonder it was named "place of refuge". Thrace, the region north of Greece, had gold mines which, according to legend, were first worked by Cadmus of Tyre,[3] brother of Europa, whose father had dispatched him in search of his sister. Phoenician miners searched this region for gold as late as the seventh century before Christ. Cadmus is credited, among other things,[4] with the building of Thebes — whose acropolis Cadmea bore his name — and with producing a son Illyrius, whose name was borne by Illyria (roughly modern Albania). The fact is that the proto-Aeolic capital was of Syrian origin and the entire archaic Greek architecture, from which classical forms were derived, is indebted to the same source for its use of columns and capitals.

In Homeric times Phoenician ship cargoes embraced such plants and products as the rose, palm, fig, pomegranate, myrrh, plum and almond, which they disseminated over the whole Mediterranean.[5] The same ships may have been responsible for the introduction from Greece to Syria of laurel, oleander, iris, ivy, mint, narcissus, the Greek names of some of which have been preserved in Semitic tongues. The spice trade was entirely in the hands of Phoenicians who, to guard the secret of their trade routes, spread reports about dangers besetting spice lands and routes. For a long time in the early classical period Syria was believed to produce balm and myrrh. The Arabian origin of the myrrh, whose trade was in Sabaean hands before the Phoenicians, was not established until Alexander's conquest. As a wreath the laurel crowned the poets, and once Daphne the nymph, pursued by her lover Apollo, was meta-

[1] Bk. V, ch. 12, §§ 2-4 [2] From *mālaṭ*, to escape.

[3] Strabo, Bk. VII, ch. 7, § 1; Bk. IX, ch. 2, § 3. "Cadmus" is evidently derived from *qādam* and means newcomer, Easterner.

[4] See below, p. 109.

[5] Albert G. Keller, *Homeric Society* (New York, 1902), pp. 20, 43-4. "Myrrh" is an ancient Semitic term which Greek borrowed.

morphosed into a laurel tree at a spot near Antioch which still bears her name.[1] The balm of Jericho attracted Cleopatra, and she rented gardens there.

Carthage

Though one of the youngest of the African colonies, Carthage was by far the most successful. In the eighth century it was in full competition with the mother country, which began to decline. The decline was accelerated by the wave of Greek colonization in the late eighth and early seventh centuries and by the concurrent Assyrian conquest of Phoenician towns. The extent of Carthaginian trade and the peculiar methods of barter it engendered may be demonstrated by a story in Herodotus,[2] who relates that Carthaginian sailors on the west coast of Africa would unload their merchandise on the beach, withdraw to their ships and kindle a signal fire. The savage natives, seeing the smoke, would come and lay down gold as an equivalent and retire. The Carthaginians disembark again, and if satisfied that the gold left represents a fair price go their way. If not, they wait again in their ships for another attempt on the part of the natives in this dumb bargain. "Neither party (it is said) defrauds the other."

Such was the commercial and political supremacy attained by Carthage that in the sixth century its mighty empire extended from the boundaries of Cyrenaica (modern Libya) to the Pillars of Hercules and embraced the Balearic Islands, Malta, Sardinia and some settlements on the coast of Spain and Gaul. Sidon and Tyre, in the shadow of Egypt and Assyria, had no chance to build an empire but Carthage had. This brought her into conflict with the rising Rome, who contested with her the supremacy of the sea, on which the Carthaginian fleet had such a hold that the Romans were told they could not even wash their hands in its waters without Carthage's permission. A stranded Carthaginian quinquereme, so the story goes, served as a model of which Roman shipbuilders built 130 replicas in sixty days.

In 218 B.C. Hannibal,[3] who as a boy had sworn eternal enmity to Rome, began the enterprise to which he devoted his life by marching against Italy from Spain through the Alps. After fifteen years of successful campaigning on Italian soil, in

[1] See below, p. 254.
[2] Bk. IV, ch. 196.
[3] Phoen. *Ḥanni-baʿal*, grace of Baal.

the course of which Rome itself was attacked, Hannibal was recalled to Africa, where in the following year (202) he was defeated at the decisive battle of Zama, south-west of Carthage. In 196 he fled to Tyre and thence joined Antiochus king of Syria in warring against Carthage's eternal enemies.[1] But he suffered ultimate defeat, and with no further hope of escape committed suicide in Asia Minor in 183, saying: "This will save the Romans the worry of waiting for the death of an old and hated man."

As for Carthage the jealousy aroused by the sight of its rapid recovery and continued prosperity impressed upon the narrow mind of Cato and other influential Romans that "Carthage must be destroyed". For seventeen long days the city was given to flames, until its very site was concealed by a heap of ashes. The plough was then passed over it and the ground was cursed for ever. A foul blot was indelibly marked upon the fair name of the Romans.

[1] See below, p. 243.

CHAPTER X

LITERATURE, RELIGION AND OTHER ASPECTS OF CULTURAL LIFE

SHIPS, like caravans, carry — besides cargoes — intangibles which are equally if not more important to the progress of man. Such intangibles were the varied civilizing influences which Phoenician merchants and colonists exerted over those with whom they came in contact and particularly the Greeks, who became their pupils in navigation and colonization and who borrowed from them in the fields of literature, religion and decorative art. Through Phoenician activity the Mediterranean became a base for multiform cultural impulses which emanated not only from Phoenicia but from Babylonia and Egypt. The Phoenician was the middleman intellectually and spiritually as he was commercially.

The Alphabet

First in significance among the boons conferred upon mankind was the alphabet, which must have been borrowed by the Greeks between 850 and 750 B.C. In fact the invention and dissemination of an alphabetic system is considered by some the greatest gift conferred on humanity by the Syrian civilization. The other two were monotheism [1] and the discovery of the Atlantic Ocean.

The Greeks preserved the Semitic names of the characters and their general form and serial order. In the earliest Greek inscriptions letters ran from right to left as in Phoenician writing. The Greeks acknowledged their borrowing in their story of Cadmus, who is credited with introducing sixteen characters.[2] Stripped of its manifold poetical embellishments, the Cadmus story suggests a recognition of the fact that immigrants from Syria introduced into Greece the alphabet, the art of mining and the worship of Dionysus,[3] the god of wine. The Greeks

[1] See below, pp. 216, 330; above, p. 103.

[2] Herodotus, Bk. V, ch. 58; Pliny, Bk. VIII, ch. 57 (56); Diodorus, Bk. III, ch. 67, § 1; Bk. V, ch. 57, § 5.

[3] Herodotus, Bk. II, ch. 49.

in the sixth century passed on an improved alphabet to the Romans to become the progenitor of most European alphabets. The Aramaeans, who likewise borrowed their alphabet from the Phoenicians, bequeathed it to the Arabs, Indians, Armenians and the rest of the alphabet-writing Easterners.[1] The Phoenician alphabet, consisting of twenty-two symbols, had the great merit of simplicity, bringing the art of writing and reading within the reach of the ordinary man. The South Arabic script may have been derived directly from the Sinaitic, to which the Phoenicians owed the preliminary step.

First to use an exclusively alphabetic and well-developed system of writing and to disseminate it throughout the world, the Phoenicians evidently received the basis for their system from Egyptian hieroglyphic sources through Sinai. The hieroglyphics were originally pictures of the objects they were meant to designate but had developed phonologically forty signs which were consonants. The conservative Egyptians, however, never went as far as using these consonantal signs by themselves. The signs, therefore, remained of little significance until toward the end of the sixteenth century when some Canaanite captive, or workman in the turquoise mines of Sinai, too ignorant to master the complexities of Egyptian hieroglyphic characters, ignored the characters altogether and used the consonantal signs. The scene was modern Sarābīṭ al-Khādim (the pillars of the servant). To the consonantal signs he gave Semitic names and values. He took, for instance, the sign for ox-head — not caring what "ox-head" was in the Egyptian language — and called it by its Semitic name *āleph*. Then, applying the principle of acrophony, he used this sign for the sound *a*. According to this principle the letter is given the initial sound of the name of the object it represents; it is the principle utilized in the old nursery-rhyme: "A is for Archer". The same treatment he accorded to the sign for "house", calling it *bēth* and using it for the sound *b*; to the sign for "hand", calling it *yōdh* and using it for *y*; to the sign for "water", calling it *mēm* and using it for *m*; to the sign for "head", calling it *rēsh* and using it for *r*.[2] Thus did the Sinaitic workman utilize only the alphabetic

[1] See below, p. 169.

[2] Compare table in *Bulletin, American Schools of Oriental Research*, No. 110 (1948), p. 14; David Diringer, *The Alphabet* (New York, 1948), p. 200.

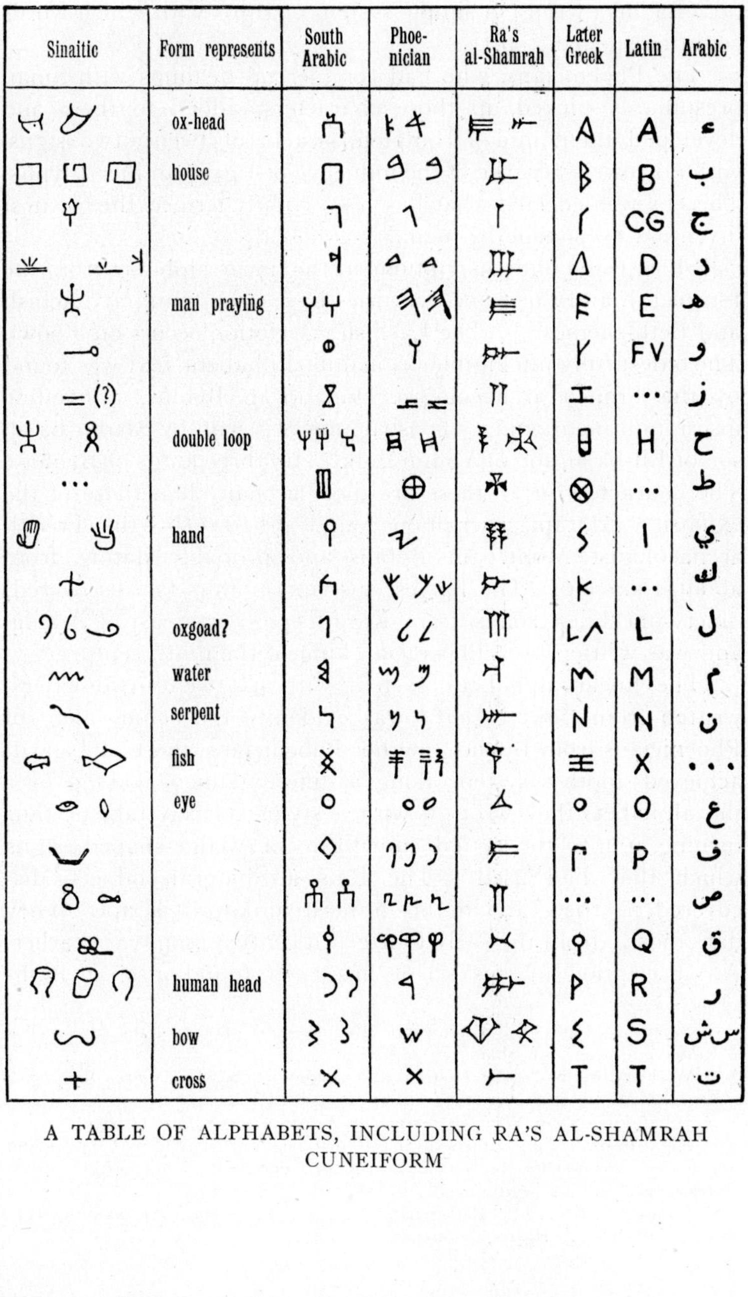
Sinaitic
Form represents
South Arabic
Phoenician
Ra's al-Shamrah
Later Greek
Latin
Arabic
ox-head
house
man praying
double loop
hand
oxgoad?
water
serpent
fish
eye
human head
bow
cross
A B CG D E FV ... H ... I ... L M N X O P ... Q R S T
ء ب ج د ه و ز ح ط ي ك ل م ن ... ع ف ص ق ر س ش ت

A TABLE OF ALPHABETS, INCLUDING RA'S AL-SHAMRAH CUNEIFORM

idea inherent in the Egyptian uni-consonantal signs and compose for his own use a simple system of signs with which words could be spelled.

The Phoenicians, who had commercial dealings with Sinai, presumably picked up those characters, added to them and developed them into a complete system of twenty-two signs, with no vowels because of the influence of Egyptian hieroglyphs. Thereby was effected what has been rightly termed the greatest invention ever made by man.

Phoenician inscriptions

Short Canaanite inscriptions in the linear alphabet from the fourteenth and thirteenth centuries have been found at Lachish and Beth-shemesh.[1] The Lachish inscription occurs on a bowl. The oldest fully intelligible Canaanite alphabetic text was found by the French archaeologist Dunand in Byblus, a five-line inscription mentioning a construction of a wall by Shafaṭ-baʿal, son of Eli-baʿal, son of Yeḥim-milk — all three kings of Byblus.[2] The characters in all these are more archaic than those of the extensive Aḥīrām inscription found in 1923 by the French archaeologist Montet in Byblus and probably dating from about 1000 B.C. The longest inscription thus far discovered, ninety-one lines, comes from Kara Tepe, north-east of Adana, and was written by a Phoenician king of the ninth century.[3]

The linear alphabetic system with its twenty-two letters, written from right to left,[4] was evidently the achievement of Phoenicians from Byblus. Other Phoenicians, those of Ugarit, achieved another system along a different line. Taking over the alphabet, they wrote it with a stylus on clay tablets, thus turning it into the actual cuneiform, or wedge-shaped, signs which they had used.[5] The Ra's al-Shamrah tablets, discovered in 1929, are in this hitherto unknown script. They date mostly from the early fourteenth century, some are earlier. An inscription in this script has been found also at Beth-

[1] Lachish is today Tell al-Duwayr; Beth-shemesh (house of the sun) is Tell al-Rumaylah, near ʿAyn Shams.

[2] W. F. Albright, "Near Eastern Archaeology", *Bulletin, American Schools of Oriental Research*, No. 95 (1944), p. 37.

[3] Julian Obermann, *New Discoveries at Karatepe* (New Haven, 1949).

[4] Right-to-left scripts supposedly have their beginnings as carved scripts and run in that direction for the convenience of the stone carver; left-to-right scripts represent pen-and-ink beginnings.

[5] Johannes Friedrich, "Ras Schamra", *Der alte Orient*, vol. xxxiii (1933), Nos. 1-2, pp. 18-34; Harris, *Grammar*, pp. 11-17.

shemesh. There is reason to believe that the script had wide vogue in the sixteenth and fifteenth centuries.

In addition to these two systems of writing which the Canaanites devised, these people possessed several other more complex scripts of which they invented one. This was the syllabary worked out toward the end of the third millennium, modelled to some extent after the Egyptian and containing about a hundred symbols. This pseudo-hieroglyphic script is represented by inscriptions — all on stone or copper — discovered by

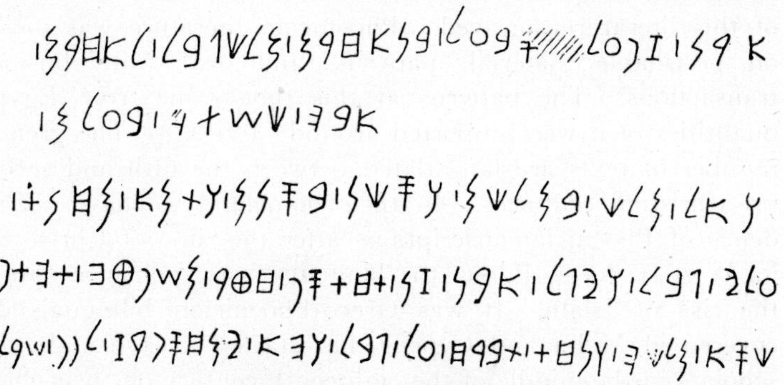

From " Syria ", vol. v (Librairie Orientaliste Paul Geuthner, Paris)

THE AḤĪRĀM INSCRIPTION OF BYBLUS *ca.* 1000 B.C.

The inscription reads: " The coffin which [It]tobaal, son of Aḥīrām, king of Byblus, made for his father as his abode in eternity. And if any king or any governor or any army commander attacks Byblus and exposes this coffin, let his judicial sceptre be broken, let his royal throne be overthrown and let peace flee from Byblus; and as for him let a vagabond [?] efface his inscription! "—*Journal, American Oriental Society*, vol. 67 (1947), pp. 155-6

Dunand in Byblus (1930) and embodying the oldest monument of Phoenician speech. It was displaced in the first centuries of the second millennium by Akkadian cuneiform, the cuneiform in which the Tell al-ʿAmārnah letters were inscribed. The mistakes made by the Canaanite scribes of these letters betray unfamiliarity with the Akkadian language, which they must have learned in school. The style they used leaves no doubt that they were translating their thoughts from Canaanite. Remains of such a scribal school, where scholars could learn the lingua franca of the day — Akkadian — with the aid of glossaries and exercise tables, have been disclosed attached to the temple of Ugarit.

Other than the Tell al-ʿAmārnah tablets, the British archaeologist Woolley discovered in 1937–9 at Tell al-ʿAṭshānah (ancient Alalakh), on the lower Orontes, 300 cuneiform tablets (Akkadian) ranging in date from 1900 to 1200 B.C.[1] Some are astrological and divinatory texts.

Such abundance of scripts from the late third to the late second millenniums leaves no doubt that the age was one of cultural pluralism and cross-fertilization in which Mesopotamian, Egyptian and Syrian scientific and religious ideas freely intermingled and were exchanged. Not much, however, of this literature survived. Phoenician literature was mostly on perishable material, papyrus, and dealt with business transactions. The papyrus at this time came from Egypt; quantities of it were imported around 1100 B.C. The greatest number of texts are late, dated between the fifth and second pre-Christian centuries. In their homeland we have no evidence of Phoenician inscriptions after the time of Christ. In its Western form, Punic, the language was spoken as late as the rise of Islam. It was Greco-Phoenician bilinguals discovered in Malta and Cyprus that started French and other scholars in the middle of the eighteenth century on their efforts at deciphering the language, which culminated in the publication and interpretation of extant texts by the German orientalist Gesenius in 1837.

A late Phoenician literary renaissance attained its height in the sixth century and produced the enigmatic Sanchuniathon of Beirut. His contribution was a collection of mythical poems of his people which were supposedly translated into Greek by his fellow-countryman Philo of Byblus in the early second Christian century.[2] Greek tradition credits Thales of Miletus (d. *ca.* 546), chief of the "seven sages" of Greece, with having learned in Phoenicia what Babylonia and Egypt had to teach.

Fortunately much of the best in Canaanite literature was adopted by the Hebrews and found its way into their sacred writings. This is especially true of the lyric pieces and wise

[1] See below, p. 152.

[2] A considerable fragment of Philo's translation has been preserved by Eusebius, but is considered by modern scholars a forgery by Philo. What purports to be the entire version by Philo was translated into German under the title *Sanchuniathon's phönizische Geschichte* (Lübeck, 1837). "Sanchuniathon" is Phoenician *Sakkonyaton*, "the god Sakkon has given".

sayings, borrowed in Proverbs, the Psalms and the Song of Songs, and the mythological compositions embedded in Genesis and the Prophets. This fact was unknown until the discovery of a forgotten ancient city, Ugarit.

Ugarit

In 1929, as a result of an accidental find in Ra's al-Shamrah [1] by a Syrian peasant, a French expedition began digging the site, which proved to be a mound of superimposed cities. The earliest goes back to the fifth millennium. Around 1400 B.C., when the city enjoyed its heyday, it carried the name Ugarit.[2] It lay a mile inland from its port, now called al-Mīna al-Bayḍā' (the white haven), just across from Cyprus. The city owed its prosperity to the commerce which flowed through it and its port. Its king was then Niqmad (Niqmadda, vengeance of Hadad), whose royal palace had its column bases overlaid with silver. The palace was defended by an imposing square tower, fourteen metres wide, and by a massive revetment.

Most precious among the varied finds which the site yielded were the clay tablets bearing alphabetic script in cuneiform style and found in the temple area. Copied in the early fourteenth century, the originals were composed considerably earlier. The script has thirty characters. The language is a Canaanite dialect. The material is mostly ritual and religious. The find restores an important portion of the long-lost Canaanite literature. One of the most significant poems deals with the yearly struggle between the vegetation deity Aliyan Baal (*ba'al*, lord) and his antagonist Mot (*mōt*, death). Mot first vanquishes Baal, as is appropriate in a land where summer drought puts an end to vegetable life; but with the renewal of the rains in autumn Baal scores his victory over Mot It is possible that this poem was acted as a sacred drama on the Syrian coast centuries before the Greeks, considered the fathers of drama, had conceived of it.

Close parallels and analogies in both language and thought exist between the Ugaritic literature and the Book of Job. Correspondence in vocabulary, thought, metre and literary structure, between it and the Hebrew Psalter, is striking.[3] Parallelism constitutes Ugaritic, as it does Hebrew, poetry.

[1] "The cape of fennel", north of al-Lādhiqīyah.

[2] *Ugārīt*, field, ultimately a Sumerian loan word.

[3] Consult John H. Patton, *Canaanite Parallels in the Book of Psalms* (Baltimore, 1944)

In Ugaritic "rider of the clouds" is an epithet of Baal as it is of God in Hebrew (Ps. 68 : 4). In a Ugaritic text thunder is the voice of Baal; in Job 37 : 2-5 and Psalm 29 : 3-5 it is the voice of Jehovah. This whole Psalm is of clear Canaanite origin. Leviathan is called the "writhing serpent" in both literatures (Is. 27 : 1).[1] Baal slays Leviathan; so does Jehovah. This monster of the sea is a seven-headed creature who reappears centuries later in the Hydra of Hercules. Daniel ("El has judged"), a Ugaritic hero corresponding to the Daniel of the Story of Susanna, "judges the case of the widow, adjudicates the cause of the fatherless",[2] as God does in Psalm 68 : 5, and as the righteous do in Isaiah 1 : 17.

This international emporium of old, in whose art Egyptian and Hittite motifs are evident, in whose homes Amorite then Cypriote and Mycenaean pottery were used and in whose bazaars Hurrian and Hyksos swords were sold, was first destroyed by earthquake and fire about 1365. Again destroyed by the Sea People[3] around 1200, the city disappears from history.

Fertility cult

Prior to the discovery of Ugarit our literary sources for Canaanite religion were meagre. They included Greek writers, some of whom, like Philo of Byblus and Lucian of Samosata (now Sumaysāṭ), were Syrians, but all late and somewhat vague; Old Testament material, which suffered from the hostile attitude of its Hebrew authors; and early Christian fathers, whose knowledge was second-hand. Basic in the Canaanite religion, as indicated by these sources and the recent archaeological discoveries, is the worship of the forces of growth and reproduction on which depends the very existence of an agricultural and stock-raising community in a land of limited and uncertain rainfall. This is true to a large extent of all ancient Semitic religions. The Canaanites undoubtedly borrowed from the cults and rituals of their neighbours in Babylonia and Egypt, just as they borrowed in other cultural fields, and they also lent. The process was reciprocal.

The outstanding features of this Semitic fertility cult are

[1] Cyrus H. Gordon, *The Loves and Wars of Baal and Anat* (Princeton, 1943), p. xii.

[2] Gordon, p. 35; Charles Virolleaud, *La Légende phénicienne de Danel* (Paris, 1936), p. 203.

[3] See below, p. 180.

mourning for the death of the vegetation deity, rites to enable him to overcome his adversary (the god of death and the underworld) and thereby insure enough life-giving rain to produce the new year's crop, and rejoicing at the lamented god's restoration to life. The marriage of the restored god, or Baal, with the goddess of fertility, Ishtar, results in the green that covers the earth in spring. This sacred marriage, sublimated and spiritualized, becomes later the union of Jehovah with his people. The conception of the dying and rising god becomes a vital and cherished part of the Christian tradition.

Associated with the idea of the periodic dying of the vegetation in the summer heat and its revival in spring is the element of the renewed vigour of the victorious sun emerging from the apparent defeat of winter. This was embodied in the early Tammuz [1] myth. The Canaanites called this deity *ādhōn*, meaning lord, which was borrowed by the Greeks and made Adonis. Later he was identified with the Egyptian Osiris. As Adonis he became the most famous of all Syrian deities and his cult was established in Greece in the fifth century. The Phoenicians localized his episode with Ishtar, the Lady of Byblus,[2] at the source of the river in Lebanon now called Nahr Ibrāhīm.[3] Here while hunting the wild boar Tammuz was tusked and borne dying to his distressed mistress. Since then the river has run red at a certain season with his blood. (Modern archaeologists spoil the story by pointing to the red soil washed down by spring floods.[4]) While Tammuz lingered in the underworld, all plant life on earth languished and remained dead until Ishtar penetrated into the nether world and recovered him. Rites commemorating his death developed

[1] Babylonian *dumu-zi*, son of the fresh water, of Sumerian origin. The name has survived in that of the fourth month of the Semitic year, seventh of the modern Arabic calendar, which was dedicated to his worship.

[2] Lucian visited this temple about A.D. 148 and described its rites in *De Dea Syria*, § 6.

[3] After the name of an early Maronite prince, see below, p. 521. The source is now called Afqah, where homage is still paid to the "lady of the place", nominally the Virgin Mary, in the form of lighted lamps in a small alcove below a gnarled fig tree on the branches of which Christian and Shīʿite natives hang strips of their clothing as vows to restore the sick to health.

[4] One version of the myth changes Adonis, whose Phoenician epithet was Neaʿmān, into an anemone, and to this day the anemone is called in Arabic *shaqāʾiq al-Nuʿmān*, the flower stained by the blood of Adonis. "Anemone" came through Greek; *nuʿmān* through Syriac.

at Byblus, five miles north of the mouth of the river, and involved a search for him by the women. The annual feast lasted seven days. Wild with joy on his restoration to life, women devotees sacrificed their honour and men their virility and served in the sanctuary as self-made eunuchs. The pre-nuptial prostitution was later commuted to the symbolic shearing off of the woman's hair. Circumcision, an ancient Semitic practice, began apparently as a sacrifice to the goddess of fertility and furnished a tribal mark. After Christianity it was given up by the Syrians who adopted the new religion.

The cycle of life and death, not being limited to plants, embraced man and resulted in emphasizing the sexual aspect of life. This found expression in sacred prostitution practised in connection with the Ishtar rites not only in Byblus but also in Babylon, Cyprus, Greece, Sicily, Carthage and other places.[1] Certain phases of this cult were evidently borrowed by the Hebrews, who maintained " temple harlots ".[2] Sexual licence was a prominent feature of agricultural festivals among many early communities in both the Old and the New Worlds. The right of the wedding guests to kiss the bride may be considered a vestige of it. The shearing off of the hair is still observed by Christian nuns on their dedication to the Divine Bridegroom.

Gods

The early religion of Canaan and the rest of the Semitic world, being essentially nature worship, had two central deities which were known by varied names but were basically the Father Sky and the Mother Earth. In Ugarit the sky god went by the name of El, the mother goddess by that of Ashirat. El was the supreme deity of the Canaanite-Hebrew world.[3] His surname was Aliyan.[4] As Baal he became localized and served as guardian of a city. Rain and crops were within his control. Festivals humoured and sacrifices propitiated him. Sacrifice was fundamentally a feast shared by the worshipped and the worshipper, a communion. In the lack of any graven image the god was symbolized by a pillar or stone. Moloch or

[1] Herodotus, Bk. I, ch. 199; Strabo, Bk. XVI, ch. 1, § 20; Bk. VI, ch. 2, § 6; Baruch 6:43; Lucian, §§ 22, 43.

[2] Ezek. 8:14; Mic. 1:7; Deut. 23:18.

[3] Hadad, the god of storm and fertility, was the supreme and most colourful deity of the Syrian pantheon. See below, p. 172.

[4] Word unrelated to Heb. *'elyōn*, most high, Gen. 14:18.

Molech,[1] to whom children were sacrificed, was evidently Milkqart (Melkarth), the god of the city — Tyre. Jar burials of infants discovered at sanctuaries confirm the biblical reports about the practice of child sacrifice.[2]

El's consort was Asherah (*athirat*) of Ugarit. Another goddess, Ashtart (*'athtart*) of Ugarit and Tell al-'Amārnah, was the Ishtar of the Assyro-Babylonians. Ashtart was the

From Charles Virolleaud, "La Déesse Anat" (Librairie Orientaliste Paul Geuthner, Paris)

A CLAY TABLET FROM UGARIT

The tablet bears in cuneiform alphabet an invocation, a declaration by Anat and rites in connection with the ascension of Baal

Found by Claude F.-A. Schaeffer, 1931, now in the Louvre

mother goddess. The Hebrews called her Ashtoreth (*'ashtōreth*, plural *'ashtārōth*)[3] and the Greeks Astarte. Taken over by the Greeks and fused with Aphrodite, she became the most celebrated of the fertility goddesses. As Baalat (*ba'alat*, mistress, lady) she became localized and functioned as patroness of a city. Baalat Gubla was such a patroness. The name of

[1] Lev. 18:21; 2 K. 23:10. [2] See above, p. 78.

[3] 1 K. 11:5, 33; 2 K. 23:13. The name occurs in South Arabic as 'Athtar, from a stem "to be rich, to irrigate", applied to a male deity. This is the one divine name that is common to all Semitic peoples.

Ishtar was borne by the local goddesses associated with the Baals at the Canaanite "high places" which seem to have exercised special fascination over the minds of the Hebrews, necessitating repeated denunciation by the Prophets.[1] Elul, the sixth month and the height of summer, was dedicated to this goddess; for it was in this month and through her powers that the ripening of vegetable life, represented by Tammuz, took place. In addition to Baalat, Ishtar bore the title Malkat (queen), recalling the "queen of heaven".[2] A thirteenth century Egyptian inscription found at Beth-shean calls Anat (*'anat*) the "lady of heaven".[3] Anat appears in a Ugarit tablet as a sister of Aliyan Baal and is given the epithet of virgin. Her name has survived in Beth-anath,[4] Beth-anoth[5] and Anathoth.[6] Anat-Ishtar was both a life-giver and a life-destroyer. Love and war were equally prominent as her attributes. Likewise Rashap[7] (flame) was at the same time god of death and of fertility.

Temples

To provide the deity with a domicile was the basic idea in the construction of a temple. Here the god resided in the same sense as any human being did in his own home. Through the temple a point of contact was provided between the divine and the human, enabling the human to establish personal relationship with the divine. The oldest Canaanite temples found go back to the beginning of the third millennium and were located in Jericho and Megiddo. This antique type consisted of a single room with a door on the long side. After the middle of the second millennium the structure becomes more elaborate. The chief features of such a temple,[8] as revealed at Gezer, Beth-shean,[9] Ugarit and other sites, were the rock altar, the sacred pillar, the sacred pole and the subterranean chambers. Of these, the altar, on which the sacrifice was offered, was un-

[1] Judg. 2 : 13; Jer. 32 : 35; 2 K. 23 : 13; 1 Sam. 7 : 3-4.
[2] Jer. 7 : 18; 44 : 17-19, 25.
[3] Burrows, p. 230.
[4] Josh. 19 : 35, modern al-Ba'nah, east of Acre.
[5] Josh. 15 : 59, modern Bayt 'Aynūn, north of Hebron.
[6] 1 Ch. 6 : 60, modern 'Anāta, north-east of Jerusalem.
[7] This word occurs as a personal name in 1 Ch. 7 : 25.
[8] The term used is *hēkallu* (house, palace), a loan word from Sumerian, which has survived in Ar. *haykal*. See below, p. 138.
[9] Baysān, excavated by C. S. Fisher and Alan Rowe; see Rowe, *The Topography and History of Beth-shan* (Philadelphia, 1930); do., *The Four Canaanite Temples of Beth-shan*, pt. 1 (Philadelphia, 1940).

doubtedly the most important. The sacred pillar or stone [1] represented the male deity and may have been of phallic origin. Beside it stood the sacred pole or tree.[2] It represented the evergreen plant in which resided the fertility deity. At Beth-shean the pole stood at the entrance to the inner shrine. The underground chambers were probably utilized for oracular responses. Libation tanks and bowls decorated with serpents, incense bowls and incense stands have been found suggesting practices for which such objects were used.[3] Remains of shrines with platforms on which the worshippers washed their feet before prayer suggest that ablution, an indispensable adjunct to Judaic and Islamic prayer, was not unknown to the Canaanites. Canaanite incense stands were borrowed by Greeks and Etruscans. At Beth-shean a raised cubicle stood at the rear in which perhaps the divine statue was placed, marking the beginning of the "holy of holies".

Veneration of trees, usually oak or pine growing near a spring or the burial-place of a saint, is practised until the present day by Moslems, Christians and Druzes in Syria and Palestine. Rags tied to a sacred tree at Afqah, the source of Nahr Ibrāhīm, can still be seen.[4]

To the Canaanites in general the sacred pillar and pole Idols evidently sufficed and obviated the necessity of making idols. Small images in bronze representing Baal standing with an uplifted right arm brandishing a thunderbolt were in vogue. The goddess was commonly represented naked with arms hanging at the sides or holding the breasts as if providing nourishment. Many such figurines in metal or clay have been found. But they all seem to have been household rather than temple images. They were cherished for their magical efficacy. The educated worshipper considered the statue the abode of the deity; the layman may have considered it itself the deity. The common representation of the Syrian goddess Atargatis [5] in the late second millennium was likewise that of a naked

[1] *maṣṣēbāh*, pl. *maṣṣēbōth* (from stem *nāṣab*, to stand), translated "image", "pillar" in Hos. 3:4; 2 K. 10:27; Gen. 35:14; 2 Sam. 18:18.

[2] *ashērāh*, pl. *ashērīm*, translated "grove" in 1 K. 16:33; 2 K. 23:6-7; Is. 27:9; prohibited in Deut. 12:3; 16:21.

[3] For illustrations see Rowe, *Four Canaanite Temples*, pls. xxii, 20; xli A, 3; lvii A, 3, 4; lxx A, 5.

[4] See above, p. 117, n. 3

[5] See below, p. 173.

From "L'Illustration", No. 4693

THE BAAL OF UGARIT (RA'S AL-SHAMRAH)

With the right hand the god brandishes a club; with the left he holds the stylized thunderbolt. In front of him stands a king of Ugarit whom the deity protects woman with upraised hand holding lily stalks or serpents. Another Syrian goddess, Qadesh, also takes the form of a naked woman standing on a lion. The lion or bull was a symbol of vitality, vigour. Why the serpent should have been chosen as a symbol of fertility is not obvious. This was perhaps because it lived in the bowels of the earth. The ancients were no doubt impressed by its extraordinary ability to cast its skin and rejuvenate its body every year, and to inflict immediate death by its bite. Until the present day a Syrian fellah might hesitate to kill a black snake if found in his home on the assumption that it might be its guardian.

Snake worship was common in ancient Egypt, Crete and other lands of the East. Beth-shean, where strong Egyptian influence is manifest in the four Canaanite temples discovered, was the centre of a snake cult. The earliest of these temples was dedicated to "Mekal, the lord of Beth-shean", from the time of Thutmose III (1501–1447). Mekal, whose name may be connected with Molech, was a form of Rashap of the Canaanites and Amorites. A bowl decorated with a serpent on its exterior has been found in this temple.

"High places"

Aside from the urban temples the Canaanites had local shrines, mostly open-air sanctuaries, on hill-tops. These were the "high places" repeatedly denounced by Old Testament writers.[1] In many cases the shrine was probably nothing more than an altar with its accessory, the sacred stone. In the great "high place" of Gezer remains of infants sacrificed and buried in jars have been found.[2]

Burial customs

The usual procedure was to bury sacrificed children in tapering jars, head first. In Jericho and other places the jars were deposited below house floors.[3] Even in Hebrew days infant burials served in that city as foundation deposits.[4] That the ancestors of the Hebrews, like other Semites, practised this rite may be inferred from the story of Abraham, who felt the impulse to sacrifice his son Isaac, and that of King Mesha of Moab, who actually sacrificed his eldest boy.[5]

In the middle of the second millennium the favoured position for the dead body was full length on the back with

[1] 1 K. 13:2; Jer. 32:35; Hos. 10:8

[2] See above, pp. 24-5, 78.

[3] Cf. above, p. 78.

[4] 1 K. 16:34.

[5] Gen. 22:1-3; 2 K. 3:27.

From Dussaud, Deschamps & Seyrig, " La Syrie " (Paul Geuthner, Paris)

ANTHROPOID SARCOPHAGUS OF ESHMUN-'AZAR, KING OF SIDON

Early third century B.C., now in the Louvre

the head to the north. With the body were often buried a lamp, a jar, a platter and other receptacles of food and drink, attesting to a vague belief that the dead would still enjoy some state of life conceived upon an earthly pattern. Women were interred with their beads and other ornaments, men with their weapons. The huge stone sarcophagus of Aḥīrām, decorated with a funeral procession with wailing women and gift-bearing servants, indicates a desire to preserve the body. Embalming was not practised except in the case of some Canaanite kings under Egyptian influence.

Another Egyptian influence is manifest in royal Phoenician burials in anthropoid sarcophagi. Several such sarcophagi, bearing a human head or even an entire recumbent form on the lid and dating from the sixth to the early third pre-Christian centuries, have been unearthed. One of the most elegant among them is that of Eshmun-ʿazar, son of Tabnith,[1] "king of the two Sidons" as he calls himself, who ruled about half a century after Alexander's conquest. The lid bears one of the longest tomb inscriptions. The main idea expressed is the usual one to prevent disturbance partly by imprecations and partly by the assurance that no treasure is buried with the corpse.[2] The Egyptians were the first outsiders to lord it over Phoenicia; the last before Alexander's conquest were the Persians.

[1] "Eshmun-ʿazar" means Eshmun helps. Eshmun was the principal male deity of Sidon, originally a god of vegetation. His name survives in the ruins of Qabr Shumūn, south-east of Beirut. "Tabnith" is preserved in the name of a village, Kafr Tibnīt, south-east of Sidon; it corresponds to Heb. "Tibni" (1 K. 16:4).

[2] Cooke, pp. 30-40.

CHAPTER XI

INTERNATIONAL RELATIONS: EGYPT

In the third and second millenniums before Christ the major powers of Western Asia were three: Egypt, Babylonia and the Hittites. Three others followed and held the stage till toward the end of the fourth century: the Assyrians, Neo-Babylonians or Chaldaeans, and Persians. The interrelationship, military, commercial and cultural, between the Syrian states and these mighty neighbours forms the main theme of historical events over a period of some three thousand years.

The Old Kingdom

Egypt's contact with the eastern Mediterranean antedates the Phoenician advent in the early third millennium. First commercial, the contact was diversified, intensified and continued until the invasion of the Sea People [1] in the late thirteenth century. With few interruptions, such as the rise of the Hyksos [2] in the eighteenth and seventeenth centuries and the coming of the Khabiru [3] in the fourteenth, Pharaonic domination over the Phoenician seashore lasted from about 2400 B.C. to about 1200 B.C., with the cultural and economic influences outlasting the political. The Egyptian hold on northern Syria and its interior was challenged and interrupted in the fourteenth century by the Hittites.[4]

First among the cities to occupy a central position in Egypto-Syrian relations was Gubla.[5] The Egyptians first knew this city as Kupna, a non-Semitic name which the Phoenicians changed into Gubla after its occupation. Its Semitic name has survived in modern " Jubayl " (little mountain); its Greek name Byblus, which came to mean " papyrus ", " book ", has survived in " Bible ".[6] Long before this city became the port whence papyrus was exported, it was the one from which the coveted

[1] See below, p. 180. [2] See below, p. 146.
[3] See below, p. 160. [4] See below, p. 160.
[5] See above, p. 72. Not to be confused with Gabala (GB'L of Ugaritic inscriptions), modern Jabalah, to the north; also a Canaanite settlement.
[6] See above, p. 72, n. 2.

cedar of Lebanon was shipped to the valley of the Nile. There it was used in building temples, palaces and ships and making coffins and choice furniture. Pharaoh Snefru (*ca.* 2750) imported forty shiploads of cedar for his building operations. The earliest contact between Egypt and Syria of which we have written evidence comes from this Pharaoh's reign. Wine and oils for mummification were also exported from Gubla. In exchange Phoenician cities imported gold, metal-work and writing material (papyrus). Khufu (*ca.* 2720), renowned builder of the largest of the pyramids, incised his name on an alabaster vase to be sent as a gift to the Lady of Gubla. This goddess was identified by the Egyptians with their own Hathor, who thus became for them the mistress of the Syrian lands. In the mortuary temple of Sahure of Dynasty V at Abūṣīr (outside ancient Memphis) there is pictured an expedition to foreign lands showing booty, including olive oil in Canaanite jars.[1] Unis (d. *ca.* 2350), the last king of this dynasty, held Gubla by his fleet. The city may then have been a crown colony.

In the inscriptions of Dynasty VI we begin to read about the "ships of Gubla" in the Mediterranean traffic. From this dynasty we get the first detailed description of land campaigns in Palestine and Syria. These were conducted in the early twenty-third century by Uni, general of Pepi I, whose army "returned in safety" after it had made war on the Asiatic "sand-dwellers" and penetrated north, destroying strongholds and cutting down figs and vines.[2]

Middle Kingdom

The Pharaohs of Dynasty XII (2000–1788), one of the most glorious in Egyptian history, claimed and presumably loosely exercised suzerainty over not only the Phoenician coast but Palestine and a large part of Syria, including Qaṭna.[3] A prince of Ugarit accepted gifts from Senwosret I (1980–1935 B.C.), and a sphinx of Amenemhet III (1849–1801) stood by the entrance of the temple of Baal at that city. The place names on Egyptian lists would indicate that toward the end of Amenemhet's reign Palestine as far east as Gilead, Phoenicia as far north as al-Nahr al-Kabīr valley, Ḥawrān, Damascus and most of al-Biqāʿ were included in the Egyptian empire. From the reign of Senwosret

[1] See above, p. 87.
[2] James H. Breasted, *Ancient Records of Egypt*, vol. i (Chicago, 1906), § 313.
[3] See above, p. 68.

comes the earliest description of social life and organization in Syria-Palestine.[1]

Tale of Sinuhe

The writer was an Egyptian courtier named Sinuhe who, at the accession of this Pharaoh, found it necessary to flee to Syria, where he lived among the Bedouins for many years. At an advanced age he was summoned back to the court of the Pharaoh, where he recorded his memoirs in a poetical form.

At the outset a Bedouin chief on the Egyptian border saved the life of the fugitive by providing him with water and cooked milk and allowing him to stay with his tribe. After sojourning in the south, Sinuhe reached Gubla and then pushed on through Lebanon to the Biqāʿ region, where he went native and identified himself with a tribe whose shaykh's name was Amoritic. The shaykh was urged by his guest to submit to the Egyptian Pharaoh, but displayed no special desire to surrender his independence. Sinuhe married his patron's eldest daughter and was assigned a goodly land with figs and vines and more wine than water. "Plentiful was its honey, abundant its oil, and all fruits were on its trees. There was barley in it and wheat, and countless cattle of all kind."[2] Sinuhe succeeded his father-in-law as head of the tribe, hunted game with his dogs, entertained *à la* Bedouin, gave water to him who was athirst, guided the wayfarer who went astray and took part in the raids. So popular was he that in a duel with a mighty member of the tribe, in which arrows, javelins and axes were freely used, the women shrieked in his behalf and the men shouted encouragement. Homesick and shuddering at the thought of being buried in a strange land and with only a goatskin for wrapping, the exile at last, in response to a decree from Senwosret, put his eldest son in charge of his possessions, left the "sand to its inhabitants and the tree oil to those who know no better ointment" and returned to his homeland, where he could indulge in the luxury of a bath and a real bed.[3]

[1] North Syria was called by the Egyptians Retenu (Rzanu), or Khūru (Kharu). Retenu may be a corruption of some Semitic word; Khūru may be a corruption of Hurrian, biblical Horites; the region between Lebanon and Anti-Lebanon was called Amurru (Amor); the Phoenician plain and Palestine Zahi (Djahi) and the Phoenicians Fenkhu, shipbuilders.

[2] Adolf Erman, *The Literature of the Ancient Egyptians* (London, 1927), p. 19.

[3] Cf. David Paton, *Early Egyptian Records of Travel*, vol. i (Princeton, 1915), text v.

Syria incorporated in the empire

Syria was incorporated in the Egyptian empire at its rise under Ahmose of Dynasty XVIII (d. *ca.* 1546), founder of the New Kingdom. It was this Pharaoh who chased the Hyksos[1] out of Egypt, pursued them into Syria, whence they came, and set his country upon its military and imperialistic career. His successors continued the policy of penetration into Syria-Palestine. Thutmose I traversed the whole land about 1520 without much opposition, reached the upper Euphrates, " the land of two rivers " (Naharin), where he set up a triumphal inscription proclaiming his mighty deeds. The Euphrates, whose water flowed in the opposite direction from that of the Nile, struck the Egyptians as curious. All kinds of reports soon spread about " that inverted water which flows down-stream when really flowing upstream ". The name " inverted water " stuck to the river.[2]

Battle of Megiddo

It was, however, not until Thutmose III (1501–1447), the warrior of ancient Egypt, had undertaken fourteen or more campaigns that the sovereignty of Egypt was finally consolidated and Syria was definitely absorbed in the rising Egyptian empire. The fall of Megiddo[3] in 1479 marks the first and most important campaign. Here the Egyptian army encountered a confederation of 330 princes. The Hyksos, recently driven from Egypt, formed the backbone of the confederation; the prince of Qadesh on the Orontes, its head. The battle was joined beneath the walls of the strongly fortified city. As the Syrian forces retreated before the furious onslaught of the enemy, they found the city gates already barricaded by the inhabitants. Even the prince of Qadesh had to be hauled over the walls by employing clothing as ropes. After a blockade of seven months, the city, " the capture of which was the capture of a thousand cities ", was starved into submission. The enemy princes fell at the feet of the Pharaoh " to beg breath for their nostrils ". The Egyptian troops greedily grabbed an almost incredible amount of booty: 2041 horses, 924 chariots (of which 32 were richly wrought with gold and silver mountings), 1929 bulls, 2000 small cattle, 20,500 other animals, 200 suits of armour and a multitude

[1] See below, p. 149.
[2] Breasted, *Ancient Records*, vol. ii, §§ 73, 478.
[3] The glamour around this name comes from a mysterious verse in Rev. 16 : 16, where it occurs as Armageddon. The Romans stationed troops near it, where there is today a village called Lajjūn (from L. *legio*). Cf. 1 K. 9 : 15.

of valuable weapons. From the royal palace 87 children, 1796 male and female slaves, gold pitchers, articles of furniture and statues were seized. Hostages were provided by the vanquished princes.[1]

The fall of Megiddo sealed the fate of Palestine. Energetic Thutmose marched northward seventy-five miles to the Lebanon region, where he captured three cities and built a fortress. In the course of his fifth campaign he seized Aradus and thereby fastened his hold on the Phoenician plain. In his official war communiqué announcing the capture of this powerful commercial islet city, the Pharaoh uses these words:

> Behold, his majesty overthrew the city of Arvad, with its grain, cutting down all its pleasant trees. Behold, there were found [the products] of all Zahi. Their gardens were filled with their fruit, their wines were found remaining in their presses as water flows, their grain on the terraces [2] —; it was more plentiful than the sand of the shore. The army were overwhelmed with their portions.[3]

Thutmose then lists the tribute, which comprised slaves, horses, cattle, silver dishes, incense, oil, honey, wine, copper, lead, lapis lazuli, green felspar, grain, loaves and fruit and concludes with these words: " Behold, the army of his majesty was drunk and anointed with oil every day as at a feast in Egypt ".[4]

Qadesh

Aradus' northern neighbour Simyra shared in the course of a later campaign the same fate. Qadesh,[5] the main source of the disturbance, was at last captured, but twelve years later Thutmose had to march again against it. Noticing that the Egyptian war chariots were drawn by stallions, the prince of Qadesh resorted to a ruse. He released a mare which galloped straight into their midst and caused such a confusion as to threaten the battle array. Amenemhab, a general and constant companion of Thutmose, saved the day when, sword in hand, he sprang from his chariot and " ripped open her belly, cut off her tail and set it before the king ".[6]

Naharin

The eighth campaign, which netted the Euphrates country,

[1] Breasted, *Ancient Records*, vol. ii, §§ 412-43; George Steindorff and Keith C. Seele, *When Egypt Ruled the East* (Chicago, 1942), pp. 53-6.

[2] See above, p. 86.

[3] Breasted, *Ancient Records*, vol. ii, § 461.

[4] Breasted, *Ancient Records*, vol. ii, § 462.

[5] Tell al-Nabi Mand (mound of the prophet Mand), south of Lake Ḥimṣ; Dussaud, pp. 107-8.

[6] Breasted, *Ancient Records*, vol. ii, § 589.

was one of the greatest of Thutmose's Asiatic wars. The crowning act of this campaign was the erection of a boundary tablet east of the Euphrates, which he probably crossed at Carchemish, and another in the vicinity beside that of his father Thutmose I On his way he plundered the Mitanni land. Advancing down the river, he sacked and destroyed towns, cut down orchards and uprooted growing corn, leaving the land desolate. There may have been more than one campaign against Naharin;[1] in one he built boats of cedar wood in the mountain east of Gubla and transported them on oxcarts all the way to the Euphrates to ferry troops across to Naharin. On his return, while hunting in the marshes west of this river, Thutmose encountered a herd of elephants, one of which would have tusked him to death had it not been for the vigilance of Amenemhab, who instantly struck off its trunk with one blow of his sword.[2]

The adventures of Amenemhab typify a host of others experienced by Egyptian soldiers in Syria. One of them which found its way into the folk tales survived in the story of the capture of Jaffa[3] by another general of Thutmose, Djehuti. The prince of Jaffa was invited by this general to a banquet in the course of which he was wined and killed. The princess was told that her husband had killed Djehuti and was returning with 500 sacks of booty. The city gates were flung wide open. Out of the sacks 500 Egyptian soldiers who were stowed therein pounced and overpowered the garrison. Djehuti's report to the Pharaoh ran as follows:

> Rejoice! your good father Amon has delivered to you the enemy of Jaffa, all his people and his city. Send people to lead them off as captives, in order that you may fill the house of your father Amon-Re, king of the gods, with male and female slaves who will fall under your feet forever and ever.[4]

Thutmose recorded his victories over the walls of his temple at Thebes and gave lists of the names of the cities he conquered. The catalogue of spoils carried away — ivory, ebony, jewelry,

[1] See below, p. 164. [2] Breasted, *Ancient Records*, vol. ii, § 588.

[3] Eg. *yapu*, *iapu*, from Phoen. *yāfi* (fair, beautiful?), whence Heb. *yāfo*, Joppa, modern Yāfa.

[4] C. W. Goodwin in *Transactions of the Society of Biblical Literature*, vol. iii (1874), pp. 340-48; G. Maspero, *Études égyptiennes* (Paris, 1879), vol. i, pp. 53-72; Steindorff and Seele, p. 58.

silver, precious stones, carob wood wrought with gold — bears witness to the wealth of the land and the high culture of its inhabitants. The coastal region must have been thickly populated. In an ode of victory his priests put these words in the mouth of his divine protector:

> Thou hast crossed the waters of the great bend of Naharin,
> in the victory and might which I have decreed unto thee.
> They hear thy battle cry and they creep into their holes;
> I rob their nostrils of the breath of life; I cause the
> terror of thy majesty to pervade their hearts.
>
> . . . . .
>
> I have come to cause thee to trample the chiefs of Djahi [Zahi];
> I prostrate them beneath thy feet throughout the land.[1]

In dealing with conquered Syria, Thutmose introduced the policy of taking over to Egypt the children of native kinglets to be educated in friendship toward Egypt and sent back gradually to replace the old hostile generations.[2] But that did not make much difference. Unable to offer sustained resistance to the Egyptian hosts, the Syrians adopted the tactic of hastening to offer tribute and humble themselves at the approach of the enemy only to discontinue their gifts as soon as he turned his back. For about half a century after the battle of Megiddo, Syria was crossed and recrossed by Egyptian armed forces. The repeated campaigns were necessitated not merely by the desire to subdue rebellious groups but by that of keeping taxes flowing into the treasury. The installation of a new Pharaoh, especially if deemed weaker than his predecessor, served as a signal for a fresh uprising. The country was thus greatly impoverished economically and unable to defend itself militarily against the newly rising powers to the north of it.

Decline of Egyptian control

This was the situation when Amenhotep IV (Ikhnaton, 1375–1358), one of the most fascinating personalities of antiquity, came to the throne. Amenhotep's interest was not in state affairs but in theology.[3] In this he was presumably influenced by his gifted and beautiful wife Nefertiti, supposed by some to be of Syrian origin.[4] The Tell al-ʿAmārnah corre-

[1] Steindorff and Seele, p. 62. [2] Breasted, *Ancient Records*, vol. ii, § 467.

[3] See above, p. 72.

[4] Her world-famous bust, until recently in the Berlin Museum, preserves in its delicate colours an exquisite portrait of the royal lady. It was found in a cache by American troops in 1945.

From Nina M. Davies, " Egyptian Paintings " (University of Chicago Press), pl. lxxviii

TUTANKHAMON (1358–1349 B.C.) SLAYING SYRIAN FOES

From his Theban Tomb, whose discovery in 1922 was one of the sensational events in archaeological annals.

Syrians hampered by heavy clothing are no match for the lightly clad Egyptians. Syrian shields are rectangular; Egyptian shields, slung upon their backs, have rounded tops. The inscription reads: " The good god, son of Amon, valiant and without peer, a lord of might, trampling down hundreds of thousands and laying them prostrate " spondence indicates that before his death Palestine had passed entirely out of Egypt's control. It remained free until the first year of the reign of Seti I (1313–1292) of Dynasty XIX. Ramses II (1292–1225) of this dynasty showed some of the crusading spirit that had characterized its predecessor. His first campaigns extended as far as Beirut. A few miles to the north, at the mouth of Nahr al-Kalb,[1] where the mountain wades in the sea to its knee, he commemorated his feat by cutting in the limestone rock three inscriptions that are now so weathered as to be totally illegible. Thereby he started a series of inscriptions continuing into our time with an Allied tablet in 1942 and a Lebanese one in 1946[2] which has made this rock an open-air museum. Of the six Assyrian inscriptions that of Esarhaddon (671 B.C.) is the only legible one. Then came a Neo-Babylonian inscription by Nebuchadnezzar, a Greek inscription which had been erased, many Latin inscriptions by Caracalla (not the philosopher Marcus Aurelius) and one Arabic. One of the Egyptian panels was smoothed off by the French and a record of their occupation of Lebanon of 1860–61 inscribed on it.[3] Another French inscription was cut by General Gouraud near one in English by General Allenby.

The decline in Egyptian control continued throughout Dynasty XX. From the end of this period we have a vivid story which takes the form of a report submitted to the Pharaoh about 1100 B.C. by his envoy Wenamon, who was sent to Syria to fetch wood for the sacred barge of Amon. The shabby treatment he received at the hands of the prince of Gubla, if historical, proves that no longer could a representative of Egypt command the respect of a Syrian potentate. In reporting his experience, Wenamon says, "I spent nineteen days in his [harbour] and he continually sent to me daily saying, 'Betake thyself away from my harbour'".[4] Despairing of his mission and fearful for his life, Wenamon stood powerless before Zakar-

[1] Dog River, so called from a graven dog which for centuries stood guardian of the defile and gave its name to the river. Legend says its cries on enemy's approach were so loud as to be heard all around. Moslem iconoclasts dumped the image into the river. Australian sappers in 1942 dug up what may be the original dog, a wolf, now in the National Museum, Beirut.

[2] Commemorating the expulsion of foreign troops, mainly French.

[3] Franz H. Weissbach, *Die Denkmäler und Inschriften an der Mündung des Nahr-el-Kelb* (Berlin, 1922)

[4] Breasted, *Ancient Records*, vol. iv, § 569.

Baal, the native ruler. There he would sit upon the shore bewailing his predicament. Silver and gold he had but not the proper credentials. At one time the prince sent him an Egyptian singing girl to comfort him. At last Zakar-Baal's heart is moved with compassion and on his return from the morning rites in the temple, as he " sits in his upper chamber, leaning his back against a window, while the waves of the great Syrian sea beat against the rocks below ", he grants an audience to the haggard and anxious envoy. In the course of the interview the ruler declares, " As for me, I am myself neither thy servant nor am I the servant of him that sent thee. If I cry out to the Lebanon, the heavens open, and the logs lie here on the shore of the sea." [1] Zakar-Baal acknowledges the cultural superiority of Egypt but scouts the idea of overlordship on his domain. Finally, on receiving more money, Zakar-Baal releases the wood.

Syria then, which had been held as a frontier province of Egypt since the close of the Hyksos period in the early sixteenth century, was lost to the empire in the course of the twelfth. Hittites were by that time established in the northern part of the country, Aramaeans in inner Syria, Hebrews in southern Syria and Philistines on the southern coast.

Even when Syria was included in the Egyptian empire, imperial administration aimed on the whole at preserving order, maintaining strong hold on the main highways and exacting tribute. The first two objectives were attained by the use of garrisons, the third by a limited number of resident officials. Egyptian residents in important cities appointed travelling inspectors to make the rounds. The Pharaoh's chief representative in southern Syria had his headquarters at Gaza. Under him were the inspectors concerned with the collection of taxes and the local prefects in charge of garrisons in selected cities. The details of internal administration were in the hands of native chieftains who kept control over their own armed forces.

Syrian influence on Egypt

Marked as was the influence of Egyptian culture on Syria, there are more striking indications of the reverse movement. Syrian influence is manifest in that most sacred of Egyptian stories, the passion of Osiris involving the dismemberment of

[1] Breasted, *Ancient Records*, vol. iv, § 577.

L

his body and its deposit under a tamarisk tree in Gubla.[1] Some think that the mutilated body was deposited in Egypt. The whole Osiris cult may have been derived from the Syrian coast at a very early date.[2] The Canaanite Ḥawrōn, the chief deity of Jabneh,[3] was adopted into the Egyptian temple as early as the days of Amenhotep II (*ca.* 1450–1420) and is reflected in the name of Harmhab, founder of Dynasty XIX (1350 B.C.). That Ashtart was worshipped in the mid-thirteenth century may be inferred from the fact that one of Ramses II's sons bore the name Meri [beloved of] - Astrot. Naukratis, which may have been originally a Phoenician colony, had an Aphrodite-Astarte temple in 688 B.C. The Heracles to whom a temple was dedicated at Kanopus,[4] likewise possibly a Phoenician colony, was undoubtedly Milk-qart.

Syrian girls were more highly prized in Egypt than Egyptian girls in Syria. So many of them were acquired as hostages, slaves or wives when the empire was at its height that a change became noticeable in the facial characteristics of the upper class. The harem of the aristocracy and royalty often included Mitannian, Hittite and Phoenician princesses. The delicate aquiline features of Thutmose IV stand in marked contrast to the heavy-jawed, short-nosed facial type represented by Thutmose I. With the foreign wives came foreign ideas, religious and secular. Fragments of coniferous wood found in predynastic tombs and beams used in the construction of tombs of the First Dynasty reveal importation from Syria at that early date.[5] Later relics in Egypt testify to the abundance and richness of Syrian products in the New Empire period. Syrian workmen produced expensive and decorated weapons, embroidered clothes, elegant vases, furniture and chariots studded with gold and silver. Syrian decorators borrowed from Egypt the lotus, the papyrus and the acanthus, but it was they who elevated the chrysanthemum, the iris and the rose mallow (Ar. *khuṭmi*) to the dignity of ornamental plants. They were also

[1] Plutarch, *De Iside et Osiride*, § 15. "Tamarisk" is Heb. *'ēshel*, Ar. *athl*, ultimately Eg. *'asr*. This tree has been associated with the god of the dead. The tree under which the bones of Saul and his sons were buried (1 Sam. 21 : 33) was tamarisk.

[2] Garstang, *Heritage*, p. 61.

[3] 2 Ch. 26 : 6; Modern Yabneh, 9 miles north of Ashdod. Ḥawrōn was possibly identified with El.

[4] Herodotus, Bk. II, ch. 113.

[5] Cf. above, pp. 126-7.

the first to conceive the idea of putting in metal vases artificial flowers.[1] To transport resin, gum, honey and oil the Syrians utilized jars pointed at the bottom, remains of which have been dug in Egypt and in Gubla. Vases decorated with glaze paint in the North Syrian tradition occur as imports in graves of the first Pharaohs at Abydos. The technique of glaze painting reached Minoan Crete from North Syria.[2] Egyptians rapidly developed a taste for such artistic works, which the fortunes of war or the operation of trade and travel had brought, and started imitating them. In the Saïte renaissance of the seventh century Egyptians borrowed more elements of Phoenician art, which by the following century lost its originality and was eclipsed by the Greek.

The lute appears for the first time in Egypt after the conquests of Thutmose III. The heavy tassels on it are typically Syrian. The lyre appears first with the Semitic Bedouins of Dynasty XII.[3] Syria was probably the source of the lead which became common in Dynasty XVIII.

Four centuries of Egyptian rule were no more sufficient to Egyptianize Syria in ancient times than four centuries of Turkish rule were enough to Turkify it in modern times. Egyptian thought and language hardly impressed the native population. A few Egyptian words have survived in modern Arabic but most of them were transmitted in later times through Greek or Coptic.[4] In Phoenician as in present days many Syrians migrated into the valley of the Nile but few Egyptians reciprocated. Trade relations were mostly in Phoenician hands. The climate of Egypt seems to disqualify people from life in other lands, especially where winter rains and cold spells require special powers of resistance. As the popular saying has it, once you drink from the water of the Nile, you will always want to drink from it

Relations with Mesopotamia: Sumer

Egyptian political control over Syria covered a much longer

[1] Pierre Montet, *Les Reliques de l'art syrien dans l'Égypte du nouvel empire* (Paris, 1937), p. 179.

[2] Childe, *New Light*, pp. 258-9.

[3] See above, between pp. 76-7, fig. of Semite in Egypt playing lute. Flinders Petrie, *Wisdom Literature of the Egyptians* (London, 1940), p. 62.

[4] E.g. *abnūs* through Greek, whence "ebony"; *wāḥah*, oasis, through Coptic; *naḥs*, ill luck, through Coptic, from a word meaning Nubian, black, whence Heb. "Phinehas"; *ṭūb*, also through Coptic. The last Arabic word gave Eng. "adobe" through Sp. Egyptians invented their own brickmaking and their method has not changed since then.

period than Mesopotamian [1] control, but Mesopotamian cultural influence in that land was far greater than Egyptian. Ethnically, linguistically and geographically the Syrians stood closer to the Assyro-Babylonians than to the Egyptians.

Throughout the third pre-Christian millennium the Sumerians, non-Semitic originators of the Euphratean civilization, represented the dominant cultural group of all Western Asia. The cuneiform system of writing which they invented, the religious and spiritual concepts which they evolved and the literature which they developed became, through their Babylonian and Assyrian successors, a part of the heritage of Syria, including Israel. The Babylonian language with its cuneiform characters became the international means of diplomatic and commercial correspondence throughout Western Asia,[2] and the Mesopotamian stories about their gods, including those of creation and the flood, found their way into the Judaeo-Christian literature of Syria.[3] Through Old Testament writers they were transformed into some of the most beautiful literary creations known to man. Not only Sumerian but a large number of Akkadian [4] words were borrowed during this period.[5]

The land of the two rivers formed a hinterland to Syria. Especially did the area of Aleppo serve as a trade route through which passed the mineral ores of Cilicia to the riverine empire. The silver and gold found in the royal tombs of Ur (*ca.* 2700 B.C.) presumably came that way. Gudea (*ca.* 2350), the Sumerian patesi of Lagash, besides gold from Cilicia, obtained cedar from the Amanus. Mesopotamian trading parties in search of the coveted wood discovered the forested heights of the mountains of North Syria even before then.

Babylon

That North Syria was at any time during the second half of

[1] " Mesopotamia " should be limited to the northern region, between the Euphrates and the Tigris, corresponding to the Roman province by that name and to Arabic al-Jazīrah. The southern part, Babylonia, was called by the Arabs al-ʿIrāq. Loosely, however, " Mesopotamia " is applied to the whole territory.

[2] See above, p. 71. [3] See below, pp. 177-8.

[4] The East Semitic dialect of Babylonia and Assyria, so called from Agade (north of Babylon), the Accad of Gen. 10 : 10.

[5] *hēkallu*, temple (see above, p. 120), came directly from Sumerian (*é-gal*, great house) to Canaanite; *kissa'u*, chair, came from Sumerian through Akkadian. Several names of plants and minerals of Assyro-Babylonian origin were introduced through Phoenician and Greek into European languages: carob, cassia, chicory, crocus, cumin, gypsum, hyssop, jasper, mandrake, myrrh, naphtha, nard, saffron, sesame. Ar. *najjār* (carpenter) comes ultimately from Sumero-Akkadian *naggāru* and *lawḥ* (board) from Akk. *lī'u*.

the third millenium under Babylonian rule is now doubted by many scholars. Sargon I (*ca.* 2400 B.C.), the first great figure in Semitic history, "washed his weapons in the sea"[1] and claimed dominion over the cedar mountains, but in his case those mountains were probably the Amanus rather than the Lebanons. His was a raid that carried him into North Syria. His fourth successor, Naram-Sin (*ca.* 2300), who claims rule over the land "up to the cedar forest", may have had in mind the Amanus or mountains east of Assyria.[2] Political and military pressure from the eastern quarters did not begin to tell until the fall of the Hittite and rise of the Assyrian power. Then it became a policy on the part of Mesopotamian rulers to reach out westward in order to seize the Mediterranean termini of the trade routes.

Assyria made her first but premature essay as a world power under Tiglath-pileser I, who in 1094 B.C. raided Syria and proclaimed himself the conqueror of Amurru in its entirety Having penetrated the Taurus into Hittiteland, he claimed the allegiance of Gubla, Aradus, Sidon and other Phoenician cities as the successor of the Hittites in the hegemony of Syria. Gubla may have been still under Zakar-Baal. The invader cut logs of cedar and sent them home for the temple of his gods. He was taken over the "great sea of Amurru" to the mainland at Simyra, killing on the way "a horse of the sea", a dolphin.[3] Several Mesopotamian rulers hunted the wild bull in the Lebanons. Assyria

The trans-Euphratean domain of Tiglath-pileser was soon lost to Aramaean invaders, and his late successor Ashur-nasir-pal (884–859) had to recover it. Following the same route as his predecessors, Ashur-nasir-pal marched against North Syria but then he plunged south, crossed the Orontes, entered Lebanon and descended to the sea without resistance. Here he received what turned out to be the temporary submission of the Phoenician cities. This was the first full-dress invasion of Syria from Mesopotamia; it corresponds to that of Thutmose III of Egypt some six centuries earlier. To Ashur-nasir-pal and his son and successor Shalmaneser III (859–824) was due that military

1 Poebel, *Historical Texts*, pp. 175, 181.
2 Gelb, *Hurrians and Subarians*, pp. 35-7.
3 Luckenbill, *Ancient Records*, vol. i, § 302.

organization which made their country the mistress of Western Asia.

On the battlefield of Qarqar in the Orontes valley Shalmaneser met in 853 an alliance of Syrian states headed by the Aramaean king of Damascus and including Ahab of Israel and representatives of Tyre and other Phoenician city-states.[1] He broke its power. But that the victory was not so decisive as he proclaimed in his inscriptions may be inferred from the fact that he returned again and again intent upon the complete subjugation of Syria-Palestine. It was not until 842 that he received the full submission of the Phoenician cities. In his annals he reports his victory in these words:

> In my eighteenth year of reign, I crossed the Euphrates for the sixteenth time. Hazael of Aram trusted to the mass of his troops. . . . I accomplished his overthrow. . . . To Mount Baʿli-raʾsi, a head (land) of the sea, I marched. My royal image I set up there. At that time I received the tribute of the men of Tyre, Sidon and Jehu, son of Omri.[2]

The empire built by Shalmaneser and his father at the expense of the Syrian and other states fell into decay and was renovated a century later by Tiglath-pileser III[3] and his successor. From 743 to 741 Tiglath-pileser maintained military headquarters at Arpad,[4] whence he sent or led expeditions for the reconquest of Syria. His son Shalmaneser V, according to Syrian annals cited by Josephus,[5] overran Phoenicia and its cities. Sidon, Acre and Tyre on the mainland, eager to free themselves from the financial control and leadership of Tyre on the island, acknowledged the suzerainty of the invader and furnished him with a fleet of sixty ships manned by some eight hundred Phoenician oarsmen. Shalmaneser's fleet was scattered in an engagement with the islanders but enough of his troops were left to maintain a blockade from the shore. The wells within the walls of the island city were sufficient for actual needs and the five years' siege ended in 722 in an honourable treaty.

[1] See below, p. 166.

[2] Luckenbill, *Ancient Records*, vol. i, § 672. The headland referred to is probably that of Carmel, but he was also one of those who left their visiting cards at the Dog River.

[3] "Pul" of 2 K. 15:19; cf. 16:7.

[4] "Arpaddu" of Assyrian inscriptions; mentioned in Is. 10:9; 36:19; Jer. 49:23; modern Tell Arfād, 13 miles north of Aleppo.

[5] *Antiquities*, Bk. IX, ch. 14, § 2.

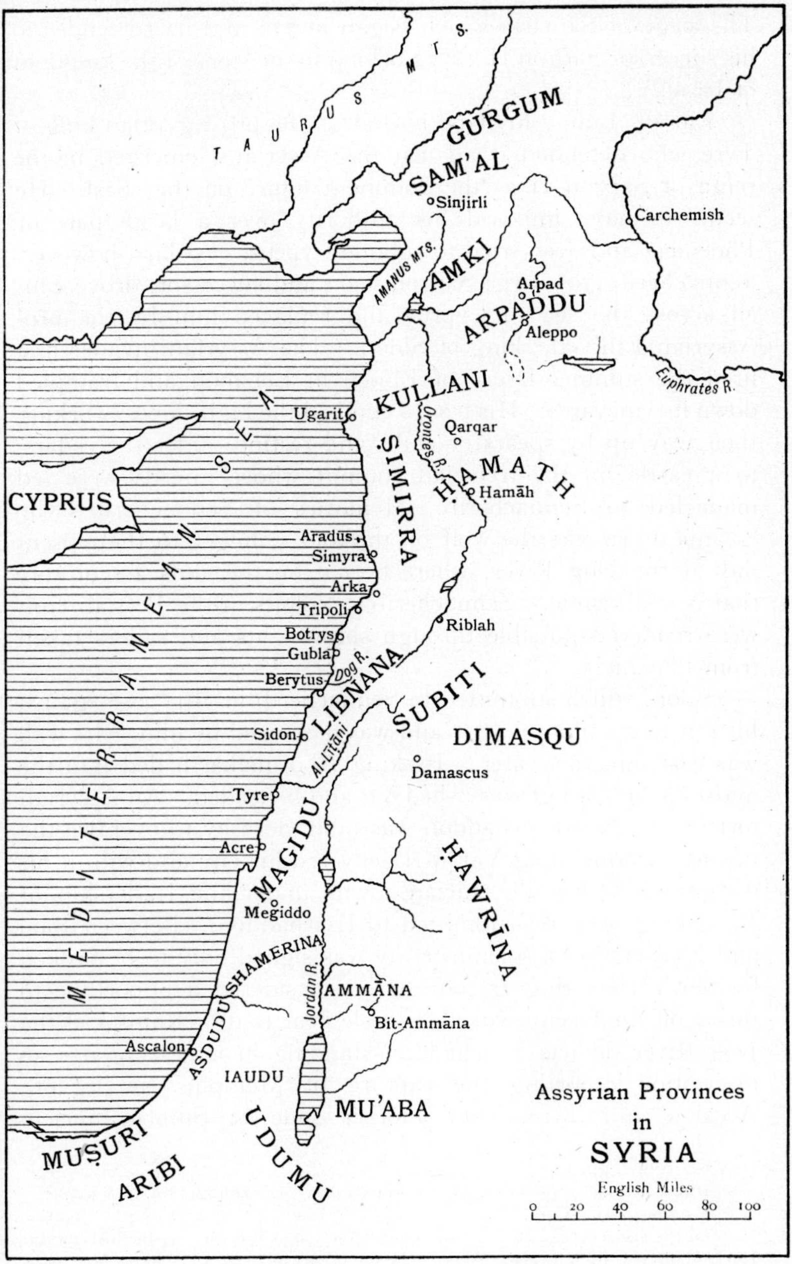

TAURUS MTS.
GURGUM
SAM'AL
Sinjirli
Carchemish
AMANUS MTS.
AMKI
Arpad
ARPADDU
Aleppo
Euphrates R.
KULLANI
Ugarit
Orontes R.
Qarqar
SIMIRRA
HAMATH
Hamāh
CYPRUS
MEDITERRANEAN SEA
Aradus
Simyra
Arka
Tripoli
Riblah
Botrys
Gubla
Dog R.
Berytus
LIBNANA
SUBITI
Sidon
Al-Lītāni
DIMASQU
Damascus
Tyre
MAGIDU
Acre
HAWRĪNA
Megiddo
SHAMERINA
Jordan R.
AMMĀNA
Bit-Ammāna
ASDUDU
Ascalon
IAUDU
MU'ABA
MUṢURI
ARIBI
UDUMU
Assyrian Provinces
in
SYRIA
English Miles
0 20 40 60 80 100

The siege of Samaria which began in 724 and its surrender to his successor Sargon II in 722 belong to the story of the kingdom of Israel.[1]

Elu-eli (Luli, " my God is God "), the pro-Egyptian king of Tyre who defended it against the Assyrians, emerged in the reign of Sargon II as the dominant figure on the coast. He seems to have imposed his authority over a large part of Phoenicia and even tried to subdue Cyprus. At last, however, Sennacherib (705–681), Sargon's son and successor, drove Elu-eli across the sea to Cyprus and replaced him by the pro-Assyrian Ethbaal,[2] king of Sidon. The Assyrian invader first fired the summer house of Elu-eli in Lebanon and trampled down its vineyard. His troops climbed the high slopes, working their way up by spears or clubs and resting under the cedars, to a castle on the tree-clad summit whose guards were led manacled to Sennacherib. Memories of Sennacherib, who " came down like the wolf on the fold ", linger to the present day at the Dog River, where he cut on the cliffs a sculpture that is still visible. Sennacherib's exploits in the Persian Gulf were rendered possible through shipwrights and sailors taken from Phoenicia.[3]

Sidon, which submitted to Sennacherib in 701, rose against his son Esarhaddon in 677 and was destroyed by him. Its wall was cast into the water. Its king Abd-melkarth fled into the midst of the sea but was fished out and beheaded. An Assyrian fort named Kar-Esarhaddon was built close by to overawe the town. Aradus' king Yakin-el delivered his city and with it his daughter. Other Phoenician towns under the leadership of Baal, king of Tyre, submitted to Esarhaddon. Between Baal and Esarhaddon a solemn treaty was signed only to be broken by the Tyrian king as soon as he considered it opportune to throw off the foreign yoke. A stele near that of Ramses at the Dog River depicts Esarhaddon standing in majesty above an inscription reporting the capture of Memphis (in Egypt), Ascalon and Tyre.[4] On another stele in Sinjirli (ancient

[1] See below, pp. 196-7.

[2] Ithbaal, Phoen. *itto-ba'al,* " with him Baal ". Luckenbill, vol. ii, § 309.

[3] See above, p. 99, fig.

[4] Of the six Assyrian steles at the Dog River this is the only legible inscription; Luckenbill, vol. ii, §§ 582-5; Weissbach, pp. 27-30, pls. xi, xii; René Mouterde, *Le Nahr el-Kelb* (Beirut, 1932), p. 18, pl. vi.

RELIEF OF ESARHADDON (*right*) SIDE BY SIDE WITH THAT OF RAMSES II AT THE DOG RIVER

Sham'al), west of 'Ayntāb in northern Syria, he stands holding a rope by which Baal of Tyre and Tirhaka of Egypt are ringed through the nose.[1] The fact is that Tirhaka had never been a captive and the representation must have been meant — like the Axis communiqués of the second world war — for propaganda purposes. Under Esarhaddon and his successor Ashur-bani-pal (668–626) Egypt was conquered and the Assyrian empire, with Nineveh for capital, reached the limit of its expansion.

Chaldaean hegemony

As heirs of the Assyrian empire the Chaldaeans or Neo-Babylonians claimed sway over Syria. But the Phoenician cities were no less restive under the new master than the old. Egypt meantime had shaken off Assyrian rule and began once more to contest with Mesopotamia supremacy over Syria. On the whole, Phoenician cities were more disposed to admit Egyptian than Babylonian dominion.

In 587 Nebuchadnezzar appeared in person in North Syria and established headquarters at Riblah[2] in the Orontes valley, whence he dispatched a portion of his army southward for the reduction of the Phoenician cities and the final conquest of Judah.[3] After a siege of thirteen years ending in 572, Tyre succumbed.[4] In the meantime he warred against Coele-Syria, Moab, Ammon and other parts of the country.[5] With this capture of Tyre the last breath of Phoenician national life was breathed. Greek colonies which had by this time supplanted Phoenician colonies also fell heir to their and their mother cities' maritime activity. Thereby the Phoenician world, active, learned and animated, came to an end; but the Phoenician people kept their individuality down to Alexander's conquest. Neither the new-coming Aramaeans nor the Israelites and Philistines made much of an impression on that individuality.

Cultural penetration

From the Assyro-Babylonian civilization innumerable elements — material, religious and linguistic — were acquired by Syrians and finally passed on through the Greeks to the Western

[1] A. T. Olmstead, *History of Assyria* (New York, 1923), p. 384; cf. Hall, *Ancient History*, p. 499. See below, p. 199.

[2] Represented by a village of the same name, 21 miles south of Ḥimṣ.

[3] See below, pp. 201-2.

[4] Ezek. 29:18; Josephus, *Antiquities*, Bk. X, ch. 11, § 1; Bk. XI, ch. 8, § 4; do., *Apion*, Bk. I, ch. 19.

[5] Josephus, *Antiquities*, Bk. X, ch. 9, § 7. Two steles at the Dog River describe his military and building activities; Weissbach, p. 33.

Europeans. Reference has already been made to the plough, which was invented by the Mesopotamians and spread over the Near East.[1] The employment of the plough led to a greater yield per unit of cultivated land by making possible the application of animal power to agriculture. The wheel was another boon bestowed on the Near East by Mesopotamians. Its appearance was conducive to a fairly elaborate system of travel. Their division of time into a year of twelve months and a week

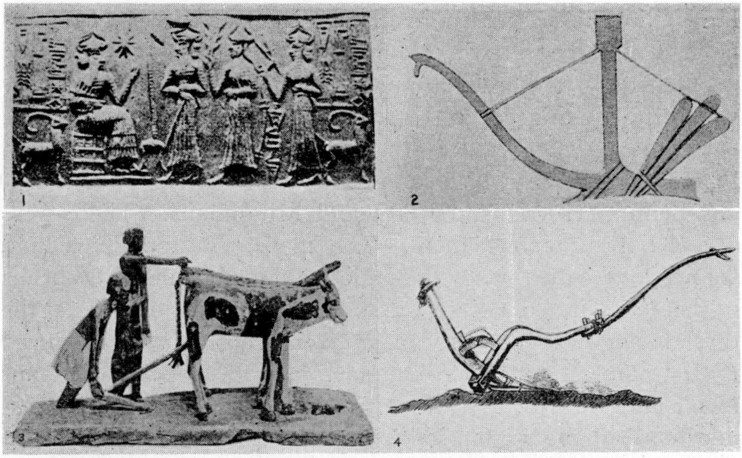

FIG. 1. SUMERIAN PLOUGH. FIG. 2. ASSYRIAN PLOUGH. FIG. 3. EGYPTIAN PLOUGH. FIG. 4. MODERN ARAB PALESTINIAN PLOUGH

They show striking similarity one to the other

of seven days has survived in our reckoning. The first day of the week is called Sunday because it was dedicated by them to the worship of the sun-god; the second is Monday because of its dedication to the moon-god; the last gets its name from Saturn. Our celebration of the Easter holiday still hinges on the lunar calendar of these ancients. With the division of time the Syrians passed on to the Greeks shadow sticks and sundials to measure the flow of hours and a formula for predicting eclipses. Our twelve signs of the zodiac are almost the same as those of Assyria. Many of the existing systems of weights and measures came from the Babylonians

[1] The Eg. word for plough, *epi*, is Sumero-Akkadian *hebi*. See above, p. 17.

through Syrians. A linguistic testimony survives in the word " mina ".

Hyksos Early Egyptian penetration in Syria was interrupted at the beginning of the eighteenth century by the rise to power of a conglomeration of warlike and enigmatic peoples known as Hyksos, who first held sway in Syria and then in Egypt itself. The name goes back to Egyptian *heku shoswet*,[1] meaning " rulers of foreign lands ", but the late Egyptian historian Manetho, the first to use this name, took it to mean " shepherd kings ".[2] First assumed by the Hyksos kings, this title was later transferred to the whole people.

Originally a horde, an unclassified goulash of humanity which the melting-pot of the eastern Mediterranean had spilled over the edge and washed down into Egypt, the Hyksos represented a movement which came to include — besides Semites — non-Semitic Hurrians, Hittites and Mitannians. There were also Khabiru among them. The movement may have had connections with that of the Indo-Iranians or Indo-Europeans in the north, including the Kassites of Mesopotamia. That the crystallizing element was Canaanite or Amorite may be evinced by the names of their earliest rulers as they appear on monuments and scarabs. It was this movement which was responsible for bringing as far south as Palestine a large number of Hittites, Hurrians (Horites) and possibly Jebusites, Perizzites and other non-Semites. The little skeletal evidence available indicates that in this period the earlier Mediterranean type was in part replaced by an Alpine-like type.[3]

Hyksos connection with the Indo-European civilization to the north is attested by their use of the horse, a valued possession shared by the Kassites. Together with the horse which they introduced into Syria and thence into Egypt, the Hyksos brought the chariot into both lands.[4] The horse was not used for riding. The horse-drawn chariot was a war implement. Its appearance must have left the same kind of impression as the tank, poisonous gas or any other " secret weapon " of the first world war. The horse itself terrified the inhabitants, as they had

[1] Steindorff and Seele, p. 24; cf. Robert M. Engberg, *The Hyksos Reconsidered* (Chicago, 1939), pp. 6-7.

[2] Josephus, *Apion*, Bk. I, ch. 14.

[3] Engberg, p. 41.

[4] The Eg. word for chariot is Sem. *markabat*, Ar. *markabah*.

never seen the animal before. No wonder it was accorded by the Hyksos special burial in a private grave or with its owner, as remains in Tell al-ʿAjjūl, ancient Gaza, indicate. In some cases it was evidently offered as sacrifice and its flesh was eaten.[1]

Among other new weapons, the Hyksos brought the curving iron sword and the composite bow which had made its first appearance in Mesopotamia under an Akkadian dynasty in the twenty-fourth century. Their superiority in armament was, moreover, based on their use of bronze, whose trade passed through North Syria. Under them metallurgy was developed in Syria and Egypt to new heights. Jewelry, faïence, ivory work and the glyptic art made marked progress. Carving in bone appears as early as the Stone Age in Syria,[2] but inlaid work was presumably introduced at this time.[3] The early inlays bore simple designs of lines and circles. The practice of inlaying, inserting strips of bone or ivory for decorative purposes in wooden boxes or pieces of furniture, is still a flourishing art in Damascus. New pottery ideas appear with the Hyksos; pottery-making, one of the most successful industries of Palestine, attained its zenith before the close of the period.

In order to provide adequate housing and protecting facilities for their chariotry, which the typical Canaanite fortification could not very well afford, the Hyksos evolved a new type of fortified city. This was represented by a rectangular enclosure about half a mile in length surrounded by high ramparts, massive and sloping, of hard packed earth. For added protection an encircling moat was frequently dug. In Syria, Qaṭna, probably their capital, typifies Hyksos architecture. Qadesh has traces of it. In Carchemish the site shows the earthworks, but the plan is not rectangular. In Palestine the sites of Hazor[4] and of the fortress of Shechem[5] show the Hyksos rectangular plan. Lachish and Sharuhen were also Hyksos cities. Jericho was a Hyksos stronghold

[1] Petrie, *Ancient Gaza*, vol. i, p. 4, pls. viii, ix, lvii; vol. ii, pp. 5, 14; vol. iv, p. 16.

[2] See above, pp. 19-20.

[3] Burrows, p. 190.

[4] "Enclosure", modern Tell al-Qadaḥ, north of the Sea of Galilee.

[5] Al-Balāṭah, outside of modern Nābulus.

from about 1750 to 1600;[1] Beth-shemesh was under Hyksos administration in that period.[2]

In Syria and Egypt the Hyksos imposed a feudal ruling class over the native population. Their society was loosely organized in a kind of feudal state with a concentration of wealth in the hands of an aristocracy consisting in the main of the chariot warriors. The organization was typically militaristic. Their culture in Syria covered the eighteenth and seventeenth centuries.

In Egypt

From Syria the Hyksos filtered gradually into Egypt, where traces of them are noticed as early as 1900 B.C. in the middle of Dynasty XII, but they did not come to power till 1730. In reporting this event, Manetho exclaims:

> A blast of God's displeasure broke upon us. A people of ignoble origin from the east, whose coming was unforeseen, had the audacity to invade our country, which they mastered by main force without difficulty or even a battle. Having overpowered our rulers, they savagely burnt the cities, demolished the temples of the gods and treated the whole native population with the utmost cruelty.[3]

That the Hyksos advent into Egypt was not an unmitigated evil may be inferred from the introduction of the horse and other objects which appear for the first time on Egyptian monuments. The earliest scientific volume that has come down to us dates from seventeenth century Egypt of the Hyksos.[4] The most significant contribution to our knowledge of Egyptian mathematics was compiled in 1580 under the Hyksos.[5] The Hyksos identified their Baal with the Egyptian God Seth and passed on his worship to the Pharaohs of later dynasties, especially the Ramesids, whose ancestry may go back to the Hyksos.[6] They also introduced, among other deities, his sister and consort Anat[7] and identified Astarte with Isis. The settlement of Israel in

[1] Garstang and Garstang, *Story of Jericho*, p. 1.

[2] Elihu Grant, *Rumeileh: Being Ain Shems Excavations*, pt. 3 (Haverford, 1934), p. 11. The name Beth-shemesh (house of the sun) is represented by that of the ruined village 'Ayn Shams (spring of the sun), 20 miles west of Jerusalem on the Jaffa-Hebron road. Near 'Ayn Shams is Tell al-Rumaylah, the site of ancient Beth-shemesh.

[3] Josephus, *Apion*, Bk. I, ch. 14.

[4] James H. Breasted, *The Edwin Smith Surgical Papyrus*, 2 vols. (Chicago, 1930).

[5] T. Eric Peet, *The Rhind Mathematical Papyrus* (London, 1923).

[6] Albright, *From Stone Age*, p. 169.

[7] Cf. above, p. 120.

Egypt and Joseph's rise to power must have taken place in the Hyksos period.

Avaris

The Hyksos Egyptian capital was Avaris[1] in the Delta, whence they extended their rule into Middle Egypt. The first series of Syrian kings there preceded Dynasty XV and bore clear Canaanite or Amorite names: ʻAnat-har, Yaʻqob-har (may Har — the mountain-god — protect). Yaʻqob is definitely biblical Jacob. The kings of Dynasty XV and Dynasty XVI were Hyksos. The most powerful in the fifteenth was Khyan who apparently succeeded, at least for a time, in uniting Syria with Egypt into an extensive empire. His monuments are scattered from Babylonia, where a lion bearing his name has been found, to Crete, where his name appears on an alabaster lid. Almost equally numerous are the monuments of another member of this dynasty, Apophis I. By that time the Hyksos had evidently adopted the Egyptian language and with it the Egyptian names.

After a century and a half of hated Hyksos rule (*ca.* 1730–1580), the war of liberation was seriously begun by a Theban prince, Ahmose I, founder of Dynasty XVIII, who after repeated assaults won the decisive battle of Avaris and chased the foreigners out of the land. Their armed levies withdrew into Syria, where they headed a federation of Semitic princes. Ahmose lost no time in pursuing them. Their first determined stand was made at their southern stronghold Sharuhen.[2] So stubborn was the resistance that the siege was pressed for three years.[3] Ahmose's and his successors' campaigns into Syria inaugurated a new orientation in Egyptian foreign policy which was to endure for years to come. It was Thutmose III (d. 1447) who dealt the fatal blows to Hyksos power in Syria. The Egyptians did their best to obliterate their enemies' monuments; that is one reason why our knowledge of the Hyksos is so defective.

[1] Avaris, the store city built by the Israelites for Ramses II and named after him (Ex. 1 : 11); classical Tanis, medieval Arabic Tinnīs and biblical Zoan (Num. 13 : 22) are different phases of one and the same town. The site is represented today by Ṣān al-Ḥajar, which is reminiscent of its Hebrew name.

[2] Tentatively identified with Tell al-Farʻah in Wādi Ghazzah, north-west of Beer-sheba.

[3] Breasted, *Records*, vol. ii, § 13, and *A History of Egypt* (New York, 1905), p. 227, reads "six years", which makes it longer than any preceding siege in history.

Hurrians

One of the component parts of the Hyksos conglomeration was the Hurrian, a non-Semitic, non-Indo-European people who still belong to the unidentified fringe. Their culture was one of the most vital elements in the late Hyksos and the immediately following periods. Originally from the highlands north-east of the Fertile Crescent, somewhere between Lake Urmiyah and the Zagros, the Hurrians, toward the end of the eighteenth century, invaded northern Mesopotamia, settled in it and thence drifted into North Syria, where they established one of the mighty kingdoms of the Near East The Amorites were already in that part of Syria. Their irruption into the Fertile Crescent may have had some connection with the general movement which carried Indo-Iranians into Persia and India and forced the Kassites from the Zagros to Babylonia

Kingdom of Mitann

It was around 1500 B.C. that the Hurrians succeeded in establishing their kingdom there, called Mitanni, which became so powerful as to extend its rule from the Mediterranean to the highlands of Media, including Assyria. Its capital was Washshukanni; its conjectured site is al-Fakhkhārīyah on the Khābūr, east of Tell al-Ḥalaf and Ḥarrān. Their chief centre in Mesopotamia was Arrapkha (modern Kirkūk), whose suburb Nuzi[1] has been recently excavated. Mitanni was known to the Egyptians as Naharin. It is evidently the same land referred to in the Tell al-ʿAmārnah tablets as Subartu or the "land of the Subarians". The Subarians, another non-Semitic people, must have been among the settlers of the land before the advent of the Hurrians.[2] The Hurrians in Mitanni formed the bulk of the population, but the aristocracy and royalty were Indo-Europeans. In their treaties with their neighbours the Mitannian kings invoked Mithra, Varuna, Indra and other deities worshipped in India. The names of the kings, e.g. Tushratta, are clearly Indo-European.

This Tushratta is the best known of all Mitannian rulers. Several letters of his addressed to Amenhotep III (d. 1375) and Amenhotep IV (d. 1358) have been found in Tell al-ʿAmārnah. They are in Akkadian, the international language of the day, but one letter was written in Hurrian, the official language

[1] More correctly Nuzu, modern Yorgan Tepe, 10 miles east of Kirkūk, the starting-point of the oil pipeline to Haifa and Tripoli.

[2] Gelb, pp. 1-2, 48; see above, p. 68.

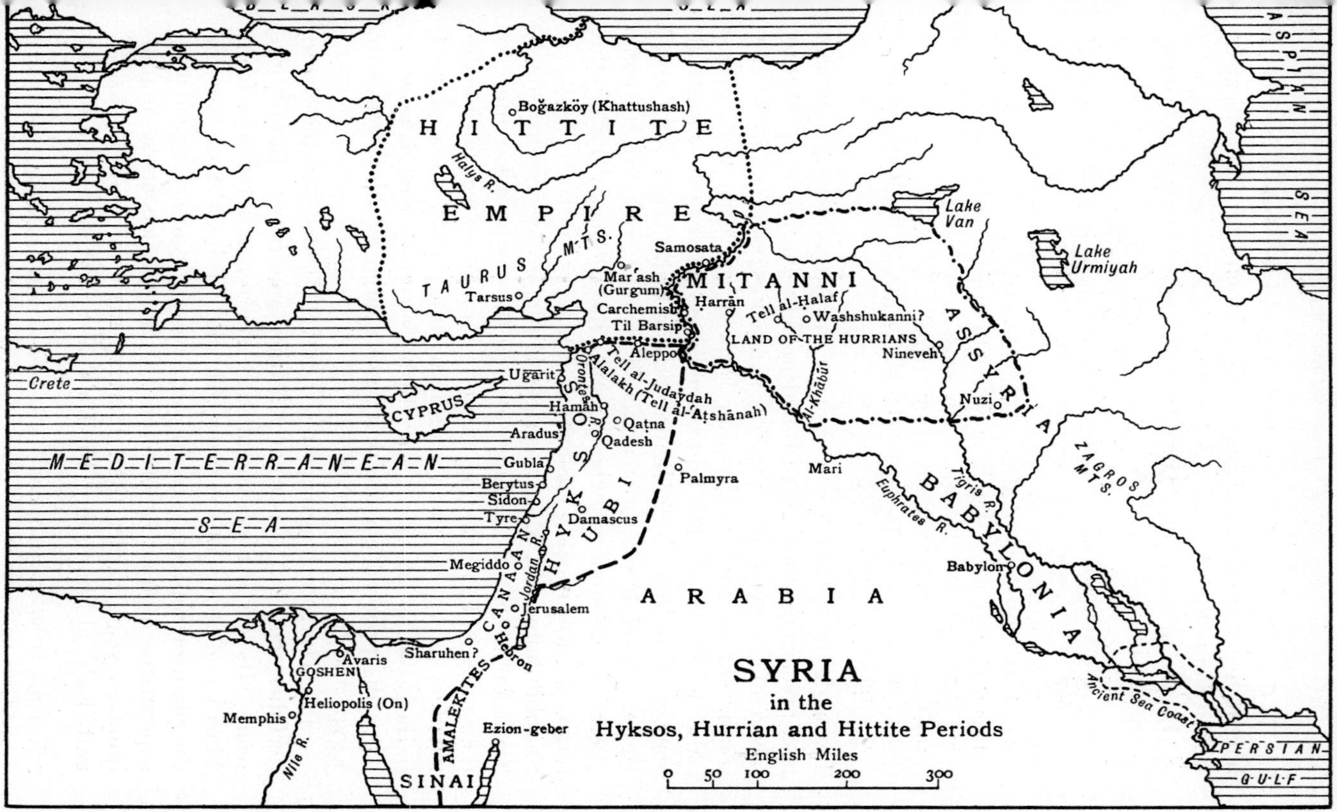

SYRIA
in the
Hyksos, Hurrian and Hittite Periods

inside the state. A sister of Tushratta was in Amenhotep III's harem, and a daughter of his married Amenhotep III and after him Amenhotep IV.

In one of his letters Tushratta addresses himself to Amenhotep III in these words:

> [To] Mimmuria, the great king, king of Egypt, [my bro]ther,
> My son-in-law, who loves me, and whom I lo[ve],
> Thus saith Tushratta, the great king, [thy] father-in-law,
> who loves thee, king of Mitanni, thy brother:
> It is well with me. May it be well with thee! With thy house,
> my sister and thy other wives, thy sons,
> thy chariots, thy horses, thy army,
> thy land and all thy possessions. May peace be multiplied unto thee! [1]

Throughout the fourteenth century the Mitanni kingdom was in a precarious position, hemmed in between the rising Hittite power of the north and the advancing Egyptian empire of the south. From earlier Egyptian records we learn that Thutmose I, Thutmose III and Amenhotep II waged successful wars against Naharin.[2] Before the end of his reign Tushratta, Egypt's loyal friend, was attacked by the great Hittite conqueror Shubbiluliuma, who pursued his conquests during the reign of Mattiwaza, Tushratta's son. In a treaty between Shubbiluliuma and Mattiwaza, the Hittite invader retains North Syria, delimited by the Euphrates on the east and Lebanon on the south. The remaining part of the kingdom was later made tributary to the Assyrian Adad-nirari (1304–1273) and absorbed in the growing Assyrian empire by his successor Shalmaneser I.[3] Thus disappeared a state that once shared world power with Egypt and the Hittite state.

The Hurrian language

The Hurrian language has not yet yielded completely to decipherment, but it is clearly neither Semitic nor Indo-European. Its earliest documents are six religious tablets from Mari [4] and a few others from Alalakh (Tell al-ʿAṭshānah) in the plain of Antioch. In Alalakh the Hurrian settlement was superimposed on an Amorite one. These tablets are some four hundred years earlier than Hurrian material from Boğazköy and Ra's al-Shamrah. In Ra's al-Shamrah a number of

[1] Bezold, No. 8; Mercer, No. 19
[2] See above, pp. 130-31.
[3] Gelb, pp. 76, 80-81.
[4] See above, pp. 65-6.

Hurrian tablets as well as a Sumero-Hurrian dictionary have been found. Qaṭna yielded an inventory of Hurrian personal names. The large number of tablets from fifteenth century Nuzi are written in Akkadian by native Hurrian scribes who here and there used Hurrian words. The meanings of these words have been determined by the Akkadian context. These Nuzi archives, strange as it may seem, throw fresh light upon the way of life practised by the Hebrew Patriarchs. Nuzi marriage contracts, for instance, required the sterile wife to

From Flinders Petrie, "Ancient Gaza" (British School of Egyptian Archaeology).

HYKSOS BUST FOUND IN GAZA, ILLUSTRATING THE HURRIAN FACIAL TYPE

provide her husband with a concubine who would bear him children.[1]

In the course of the fifteenth and fourteenth centuries Hurrians were so widely spread over Syria that the Egyptians began to call Canaan *Khūru*. Remains of their material culture are represented by a characteristic painted pottery with designs in white on a dark background and by a special type of architecture and glyptic art. The Horites of the Old Testament, until recently considered one of the insignificant tribes of old, were none other than the Hurrians. The translation of the name into "cave-dwellers" is now found erroneous. The Hivites were probably identical with the Horites.

Hurrian remains

[1] Cf. Gen. 16 : 2-3.

The Hurrians are the ones supposed to have bequeathed to the Assyrians those physical features which distinguish them from their Semitic cousins to the south, the Babylonians. The so-called Semitic features of the Jews are in reality Hittite-Hurrian. After the Hittite conquest of Mitanni the Hurrians were included under the vague term " Hittite ". In eastern Syria the remnants of the Hurrians were absorbed by the Aramaeans. Near Zaḥlah, in the Lebanon, stands a village named Furzul, which perpetuates the word for iron (*b r ž l*), that occurs in a Ra's al-Shamrah text. Until the present day, according to anthropological researches,[1] the prevailing type among the Lebanese — Maronites and Druzes — is the short-headed brachycephalic one. The same is true of the Nuṣayrīyah in north-western Syria. This is in striking contrast to the long-headed type prevailing among the Bedouins of the Syrian Desert and the North Arabians.[2]

Hittites

The Hittites, whose features on the monuments are like those of the Hurrians, were originally an Anatolian people in the area of the Halys River. They called their land Khatti[3] and their capital (the City of Khatti) Khattushash, modern Boğazköy, ninety miles east of Ankara. The English name comes from Hebrew *Ḥitti*. The site of their earlier capital Kushshar is still unidentified. Around 2000 B.C. the Khattic tribes were overpowered by Indo-European invaders. The admixture of the Anatolian aborigines with the Indo-European conquerors produced the Khattians of Asia Minor. The facial type represented by prominent nose and retreating forehead and chin was that of the aborigines. It still prevails in eastern Anatolia and among the Armenians.

[1] Carl C. Seltzer, *The Racial Characteristics of Syrians and Armenians* (Cambridge, Mass., 1936), pp. 10 *seq.*; do., *Contributions to the Racial Anthropology of the Near East* (Cambridge, 1940), pp. 20-21, 37-50; William M. Shanklin and Nejla Izzeddin, " The Anthropology of the Near East Female ", *American Journal of Physical Anthropology*, vol. xxii (1937), pp. 397 *seq.*; C. U. Ariëns Kappers, " The Anthropology of the Near East ", *Actes du XVIIIe congrès international des orientalistes* (Leyden, 1931), pp. 178-9.

[2] Carleton S. Coon, *The Races of Europe* (New York, 1939), pp. 623-4; William M. Shanklin, " The Anthropology of the Ruwala Bedouins ", *Journal of the Royal Anthropological Institute*, vol. lxv (1935), p. 379; do., " Anthropology of the Akeydat and the Maualy Bedouin ", *American Journal of Physical Anthropology*, vol. xxi (1936), p. 248. Recent research makes cradling at times responsible for short-headedness.

[3] *Kheta* of the Egyptian inscriptions. The word probably means silver.

The old kingdom

The first historical appearance of the Khattians in a major military enterprise took place about 1595, when in a raid their king Murshilish I plundered Babylon and put an end to its first dynasty, that to which Hammurabi belonged. This Murshilish had conquered Ḥalpa (Aleppo) and destroyed it, placing its citizens in captivity and sending Hadad and their other gods as booty to Khattushash, to which he transferred the seat of government from the earlier capital. Aleppo was a centre not only for the cult of Hadad but for a kingdom called Yamkhad which shortly before our period was ruled by Yarīm-Lim, who controlled twenty kinglets.[1] A successor of Murshilish penetrated in the Hyksos land far south into Damasḥunas, which sounds like Damascus.[2] If correct, this would be the first mention of this city in recorded history. The Khattian kings, however, were not able to maintain permanent control of the territory south of the Taurus. That mountain remained the southern frontier of the old kingdom.

The new kingdom

The new kingdom or second empire lasted from about 1450 to 1200 B.C. Its heyday was attained under the mighty Shubbiluliuma (*ca.* 1380–1355). His advance in Mitanni secured for him a firm footing in North Syria and enabled him to wrest from the Pharaohs the territory to a point south of Gubla. By the end of his reign, his empire had become the most powerful state in Western Asia. The Hyksos, Mitannians and Hurrians were all incorporated in a state which may now be termed Hittite. Carchemish became the main stronghold south of the Taurus.

Shubbiluliuma did not depend entirely upon the use of arms. He resorted to stirring up revolt against Egypt in her Asiatic province and to persuading the prince of Ugarit to desert his Pharaonic ally [3] — in all of which he succeeded. He used the Amorite chieftain Abd-Ashirta and his son Aziru as "fifth columnists".[4] With his co-operation Aziru proceeded to capture the coast towns of Phoenicia. At the same time Aziru was writing to Ikhnaton how much he regretted that his duty in resisting the Hittite invasion had deprived him of the pleasure

[1] See above, p. 68, n. 3.

[2] John Garstang, *The Hittite Empire* (London, 1929), p. 3; *Heritage of Solomon*, p. 30.

[3] Knudtzon, No. 45, ll. 22, 30; Mercer, No. 45, ll. 22, 30.

[4] See above, p. 74.

of meeting the Pharaonic envoy. So confused did the issue become that even the Egyptian resident was unable to distinguish friend from foe.

Treaty with Egypt

The struggle for the sovereignty of Syria by the two would-be world powers was resumed when the early Pharaohs of Dynasty XIX tried to retrieve what the late Pharaohs of Dynasty XVIII had not been able to hold. In the famous battle of Qadesh that ensued (*ca.* 1287 B.C.) the victory claimed by Ramses II over his Hittite adversary Muwatallish was not, judging by the results, as brilliant as Ramses proclaimed it to be. Ramses claimed to have vanquished the chief of Kheta, slaughtered all the chiefs of his allies, driven the enemy to the Orontes and "cast them into the water like crocodiles; they fell on their faces, one on top of another, and he slew whomever he desired".[1] The fact is that Ramses barely escaped with his own life when he was lured into an ambuscade and the onslaught of Hittite chariotry dispersed his warriors. He was eventually forced to evacuate North and Central Syria and to sign about 1272 a non-aggression pact with Hattushilish, the brother and second king after Muwatallish. This is the only pact of its kind coming down from ancient times. Its professed object was "to bring peace and good brotherhood between us forever". In it North Syria, including Amurru, was recognized as Hittite; South Syria, including Palestine, was to remain in Egyptian possession.[2] A copy of the original, inscribed on a silver tablet, has been preserved in both Egyptian hieroglyphic and Babylonian cuneiform.

Following a period of decline the Hittite empire fell around 1200 B.C. under the impact of invasions from another direction, the Aegean. Among the invaders the Phrygians evidently played the leading rôle. On the ruins of the Hittite empire there arose in northern Syria petty native kingdoms centring on Carchemish, Aleppo and Ḥamāh. The Assyrians called them Hittite. Their rise coincided with the westward push of the rising Assyrian empire, which continuously threatened their existence. One by one they fell prey to the expanding power from the east. The conquest of Carchemish in 717 by Sargon II marks the end of the last independent Hittite state.

[1] Steindorff and Seele, p. 251; cf. Breasted, *Ancient Records*, vol. iii, § 336.
[2] For full terms consult Breasted, *Ancient Records*, vol. iii, §§ 367-91.

In Palestine

With the dissolution of the empire the term "Hittite" lost its political significance and acquired a new meaning, cultural and ethnic. The Assyrians continued to apply it to the inhabitants of the territories formerly occupied by Hittites, although the vast majority had no ethnic affinity with ancient Anatolian or Indo-European Khattians. Palestine never formed a part of the Hittite empire, but Hittite elements abounded there. The author of one Old Testament document applies the term generally to the non-Semitic natives of the land before the Hebrew conquest. That author claims the existence of a Hittite element among the population of Palestine as early as Abraham's days, and seems to consider Hebron a Hittite town.[1] Esau, we are told, married Hittite wives and the children of Israel intermarried with Hittites.[2] Archaeology bears witness in the form of votive offerings, distinctive seals and weapons to material Hittite influence there in the fourteenth century. There is no doubt that Solomon included Hittite women in his harem.[3] In addressing unfaithful Jerusalem Ezekiel[4] proclaims: "Thy father was an Amorite, and thy mother an Hittite".

Organization

The Hittite kingdom was essentially a feudal aristocracy asserting its power over a heterogeneous mass of ethnic elements. Its military success was due, as in the case of the Hyksos, to the employment of the horse and chariot as its principal arm. The chariot was manned by a driver, a shield bearer and a warrior. The shield was square. In battle array the Hittites also used organized divisions of infantry led by royal princes or local chiefs. The bow, battle-axe, spear and curving sword constituted their offensive weapons.

Language

The Hittite language is mixed, as the Hittite people are, but in general it may be classified as Indo-European or related to that family. The military aristocracy, as in the case of Mitanni, were of Indo-European stock. The two aristocracies may have come from the same origin and spoken the same kind of tongue.

The largest collection of Hittite documents was found in 1906–12 at Boğazköy. They turned out to be the state archives of more than 10,000 clay tablets assembled by their royalty about 1300 B.C. Inscribed in cuneiform script, which

[1] Gen. 23:2-20.
[2] Gen. 26:34; Judg. 3:5-6.
[3] 1 K. 11:1; 2 Sam. 11:3.
[4] 16:3.

was deciphered by a Czech scholar,[1] these tablets constitute our main source of information. The Hittites used the cuneiform script for their daily needs; they used the hieroglyphic script for monumental purposes. The hieroglyphic inscriptions on stone or rock are usually boustrophedon, with lines alternating from left to right and from right to left. In the last few years this script has been deciphered. In Syria the three

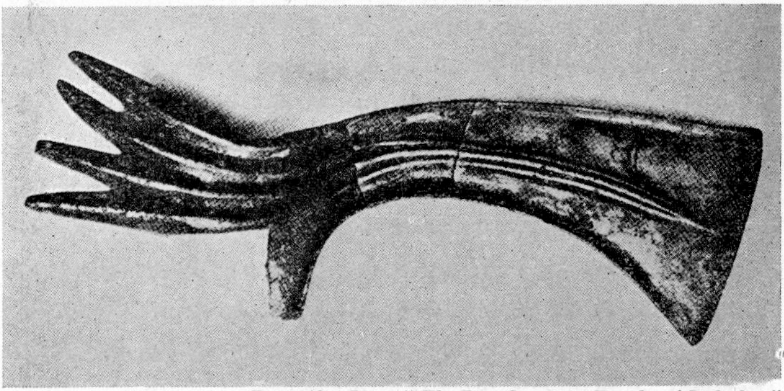

From Alan Rowe, "The Four Canaanite Temples of Beth-shan" (*University Museum, Philadelphia*)

HITTITE AXEHEAD OF THE EARLY FOURTEENTH CENTURY, FOUND AT BETH-SHEAN

The ornamental figures continue in grooves almost to the bit. The knuckles enfold the handle's socket

main centres of their hieroglyphic monuments are Carchemish (Jarābulus), Aleppo and Ḥamāh.[2] From Carchemish twenty-four stone inscriptions are now in the British Museum; from Ḥamāh four are now in the Istanbul museum. Four seals were found at Ra's al-Shamrah.

Hymns, prayers, legends, contracts, letters, form the bulk of extant Hittite literature. A part of their legal code, going back to the middle of the fourteenth century, has been found.[3] The penalties prescribed are much lighter than those of the Semites. The "eye for an eye" legislation is missing and the numerous regulations devoted to agriculture show that it formed the basis of economic life.

Religion

Little is yet known of Hittite religion. Animistic concep-

[1] Friedrich Hrozny; see his *Die Sprache der Hethiter* (Leipzig, 1917); *Hethitische Keilschrifttexte aus Boghazköi* (Leipzig, 1919).

[2] Ignace J. Gelb, *Hittite Hieroglyphic Monuments* (Chicago, 1939), p. 8.

[3] F. Hrozny, *Code hittite provenant de l'Asie Mineure* (Paris, 1922).

The National Museum, Aleppo

THE HITTITE GOD TESHUB, STORM DEITY

Found in 1930 at Tell al-Aḥmar (ancient Til Barsip), south of Carchemish on the Euphrates

The Assyrian beard he wears suggests a twelfth century dating. The solar disk surrounded by the winged moon reveals Egyptian influence. The god holds a three-pronged thunderbolt in his left hand and brandishes a battle-axe in his right. The bull on which he stands is the symbol of might and fertility. Upturned shoes are still worn by mountaineers in Lebanon tions stand out clearly in its primitive form. Springs, rivers, trees and mountains were considered sacred. Among the deities the best known was Teshub, the storm god who was the national deity. He was worshipped by the Mitannians; the city gods were his local manifestations. His Hittite name was Telepinush. He corresponds to the Syrian Hadad. His consort is called Astarte in the Egyptian treaty; her Hittite name is still undetermined, perhaps Ma. She is the Earth Mother, the oldest deity of the conquered people. The Teshub-Astarte cult corresponded to the Syrian Tammuz-Astarte cult which developed in the West into the cult of Adonis and Venus and in Asia Minor (among the Phrygians) into that of Attis and Cybele. The characteristic representation of Teshub is that of a man standing on a bull and holding a thunderbolt. The most powerful female deity was the Sun-Goddess, who became the goddess of war and absorbed certain attributes of the Earth Mother. The garb of the male deity, as seen on the monuments, consists of a short tunic and a conical hat; that of the female consists of a long robe and a high cylindrical hat. Shoes, pointed and turned up at the toes, were a feature common to the dress of both. Human figures were represented in much the same garb but smaller in size. The heavy clothing and upturned shoes suggest origin in a cold, snowy climate.

As the Hittites established contacts with the Syrians, Egyptians and Assyrians, they appropriated foreign gods and goddesses. In the Egyptian treaty "a thousand gods of the male gods and of the female gods" are invoked. The prominence of the female deities in the pantheon and the fact that, when Shubbiluliuma supported Mattiwaza as heir to the throne of Mitanni, he conditioned his support on a monogamous marriage of the Mitannian prince with a princess of Khatti, would seem to suggest that the status of woman among the Hittites was comparatively high with a tendency toward monogamy.

Who were the Khabiru?

As the Hittite army of the ʿAmārnah period was operating from the north in Syria, foreign mercenaries called in the cuneiform inscriptions Khabiru (Khapiru) were overrunning the land farther south.[1] This Akkadian word has been identified by certain scholars with Hebrew ʿ*Ibri* ("Hebrew",

[1] See above, p. 75.

usually rendered " one from the other side ", " a crosser "). In the Nuzi documents of the fifteenth century the Khabiru are characterized as voluntary slaves. In the Egyptian records of about 1300–1150 B.C. the word appears as *ʿEpiru* (with a *p*), which raises a serious question as to the validity of the identification.

In Hittite annals the Khabiru make their first appearance under Murshilish I (*ca.* 1600 B.C.), who hired them. In the Tell al-ʿAmārnah letters [1] the Khabiru co-operate with the rebels against the Pharaohs and in 1367 capture Shakim (Shechem). Six of these letters (Nos. 285-290) were addressed by Abd-Khiba,[2] the vassal of the Pharaoh in Urusalim (Jerusalem),[3] to Ikhnaton expressing loyalty and seeking aid against the threatening Khabiru. Throughout, the Khabiru appear as a nondescript, heterogeneous group recruited, doubtless, from Mesopotamia. There the term is applied first to warriors in the reign of Naram-Sin (*ca.* 2300) of the old Akkadian dynasty. The term recurs in a Mari letter of the eighteenth century and in Nuzi tablets of the fifteenth. Evidently it was not an ethnic term but a general appellation given to groups of nomads, foreigners, bandits ready to join the ranks of any army for pay or for booty.

[1] No. 289.

[2] The first part of his name is Semitic for " slave "; the second is the name of a Hittite-Hurrian goddess.

[3] From Canaanite Yarū-Shalem (let Shalem found). Shalem was a Canaanite god of peace whose name occurs in " Absalom ", " Solomon " and in Phoenician names, and is mentioned in a Ugarit tablet. See Burrows, p. 229.

CHAPTER XII

THE ARAMAEANS: THE THIRD MAJOR SEMITIC PEOPLE

BEFORE the Aramaeans were so named they were nomadic tribes in the North Arabian desert. Like other Bedouins before and after them, they pressed themselves from time to time on the outlying lands of their neighbours in Babylonia and Syria with a view to possessing them. Before the middle of the second pre-Christian millennium these tribes were already settled on the banks of the middle Euphrates. There they developed their nationality and language. Aramaic, it can be assumed, sprang from a West Semitic dialect spoken in north-western Mesopotamia in the first half of the second millennium. Their name "Aramaeans" was not acquired until the days of Tiglath-pileser I (*ca.* 1100 B.C.), when they were settled in the middle Euphrates region as far west as Syria.[1] The Khattian raids in the early sixteenth century into Babylon and North Syria [2] were evidently the events which opened the gates in the face of the Aramaean movement and gave the new settlers from the desert a firm foothold in that region. The destruction of Mitanni by the Hittites a century and a half later further facilitated the Aramaean advent. This Aramaean migration proved to be, after the Amorite and the Canaanite, the third great Semitic movement from the desert.

Early beginnings in Mesopotamia

Several groups formed parts of the Aramaean movement, though not so designated. Besides the Khabiru, noted above, there were the Akhlamu. This designation, meaning "companions", was generic rather than ethnic, and must have been first applied by the Amorites on the Euphrates to a confederation of tribes. The Assyrian Adad-nirari I (*ca.* 1300 B.C.) tells us that his father conquered the hordes of the Akhlamu [3] in upper Mesopotamia. In a letter sent by Hattushilish around

[1] Cf. Emil G. H. Kraeling, *Aram and Israel* (New York, 1918), pp. 20, 22. Etymology of "Aram" (cf. koranic Iram) is uncertain.

[2] See above, p. 155.

[3] Luckenbill, vol. i, § 73.

1275 to a Babylonian king, reference is made to hostile Akhlamu along the Euphrates. Earlier than that we read in an ʿAmārnah letter [1] about Akhlamu in the days of Ikhnaton seizing Syrian townships and lands, evidently with the connivance, if not under the leadership, of disloyal native chiefs. In later records the Akhlamu and Aramaeans are closely associated. Tiglath-pileser I records: "Into the midst of the Ahlamî, Aramaeans, enemies of Ashur, my lord, I marched".[2] These Aramaean tribes lived in the neighbourhood of Carchemish, but later we see Aramaeans as far east as Babylonia, lending a hand to the Kaldu (Chaldaeans, Neo-Babylonians), to whom they were closely related. In other inscriptions Tiglath-pileser and his successors describe their campaigns in the *Māt Arimi*, land of the Aramaeans.[3]

Spread into North Syria

From these and other Assyro-Babylonian records it may be inferred that in the course of the fourteenth and thirteenth centuries a large part of Mesopotamia and North and Central Syria was overrun by Semitic hordes which, with the exception of a few Hittite enclaves like Carchemish, then began to assume Aramaean character. Gradually Amorites, Hurrians and Hittites of the Orontes valley and the region north of it were swamped and absorbed or driven out by the steady pressure of Aramaeans or Aramaeans-to-be. Mount Lebanon hindered this penetration westward and in it Hittite and Amorite communities continued to flourish, while in the maritime plain the Canaanite settlements remained untouched. Damascus, seat of a future Aramaean state, was already peopled by Aramaeans in 1200 B.C. The annals of Ramses III (1198–1167 B.C.) give the Aramaic spelling of the name.[4] Ḥarrān, one of their Mesopotamian centres, must have been occupied before Damascus. Gradually the newcomers assimilated the culture of the Amorites and the Canaanites among whom they settled. But one feature of their culture they retained, language. Unlike the Israelites and the Philistines, who in the late thirteenth

[1] No. 200. [2] Luckenbill, vol. i, § 239.

[3] E. A. Wallis Budge and L. W. King, *Annals of the Kings of Assyria*, vol. i (London, 1902), pp. 134 *seq.*; Luckenbill, vol. i, § 366; vol. ii, § 36.

[4] *Tiramaski*, corresponding to Aram. *Dar* (fortress of) *-Mesheq*; W. Max Müller, *Asien und Europa nach altägyptischen Denkmälern* (Leipzig, 1893), p. 234; Dussaud, p. 292; cf. Sina Schiffer, *Die Aramäer* (Leipzig, 1911), p. 136. In the ʿAmārnah letters the forms it takes are *Dumashqa* (No. 107, l. 28), *Dimashqa* (No. 197, l. 2), *Timashgi* (No. 53, l. 63).

century settled to the south of them, the Aramaeans maintained their original dialect, destined to play a far-reaching rôle in the future life of all Western Asia.

Aramaean states in Mesopotamia

By the end of the thirteenth century both the Aramaean and the Israelite movements had been concluded and the two peoples were contiguously settled in their new homes. The first Aramaean states arose in the middle Euphrates region, the corridor between Mesopotamia and Syria. One of them was called Aram Naharaim,[1] Aram of the Rivers, the rivers being the Euphrates and its tributary al-Khābūr rather than its sister the Tigris. Egyptian " Naharin " is a modification of the same name. The name appears frequently in the cuneiform inscriptions of the late thirteenth century and tends to disappear after the ninth, when the Assyrians had virtually wiped out the Aramaeans of this region.[2] Another Mesopotamian state was Padan [3] Aram. This was not as extensive as Aram Naharaim; it centred on Ḥarrān. In fact the two words are used in the Old Testament synonymously. Situated on a great trade route, Ḥarrān, whose name means " route ", developed into one of the great centres of Aramaean culture. The Hebrew tradition, which never forgot the early Hebrew-Aramaean relationship, brought the Patriarchs from that district before settling them in Palestine. It sent Abraham's messenger back to Ḥarrān in quest of a wife, Rebekah, for Isaac, and dispatched Jacob in person to marry Leah and Rachel.[4] The maternal ancestry of Jacob's children was accordingly Aramaean. In another passage the father of the nation himself was called Aramaean.[5] Genesis, which records the beginning of Hebrew history, is rich in Aramaicisms and Aramaic vocabulary.[6] The forefathers of the Hebrew people presumably spoke Aramaic before settling in Palestine and adopting the local Canaanite dialect.

Aram Damascus

But the most important of the numerous states founded by

[1] " Mesopotamia " in Gen. 24:10; Deut. 23:4; Judg. 3:8.

[2] Cf. Roger T. O'Callaghan, *Aram Naharaim* (Rome, 1948), p. 143.

[3] Corresponding to Arabic *faddān*, the word means field, plain; cf. Abel, *Géographie*, vol. i, p. 245. See Gen. 25:20; 28:5; 31:18.

[4] Gen. 24:4; 29:21 *seq.*

[5] Deut. 26:5 (Authorized Version), where it is translated " Syrian ", see below, pp. 170-71; cf. Josephus, *Antiquities*, Bk. I, ch. 7, § 2.

[6] Gen. 11:28 *seq.*; 12:1 *seq.*; 29:1 *seq.*; 31:21 *seq.*; " Jegartshadutha " (Gen. 31:47), heap of witness, is the earliest citation of an Aramaic phrase in the Bible.

Aramaeans was that which centred first on Zobah and later on Damascus. Established in the late eleventh century, almost contemporaneously with the Hebrew monarchy, this kingdom developed into a major state with its frontiers extended on one

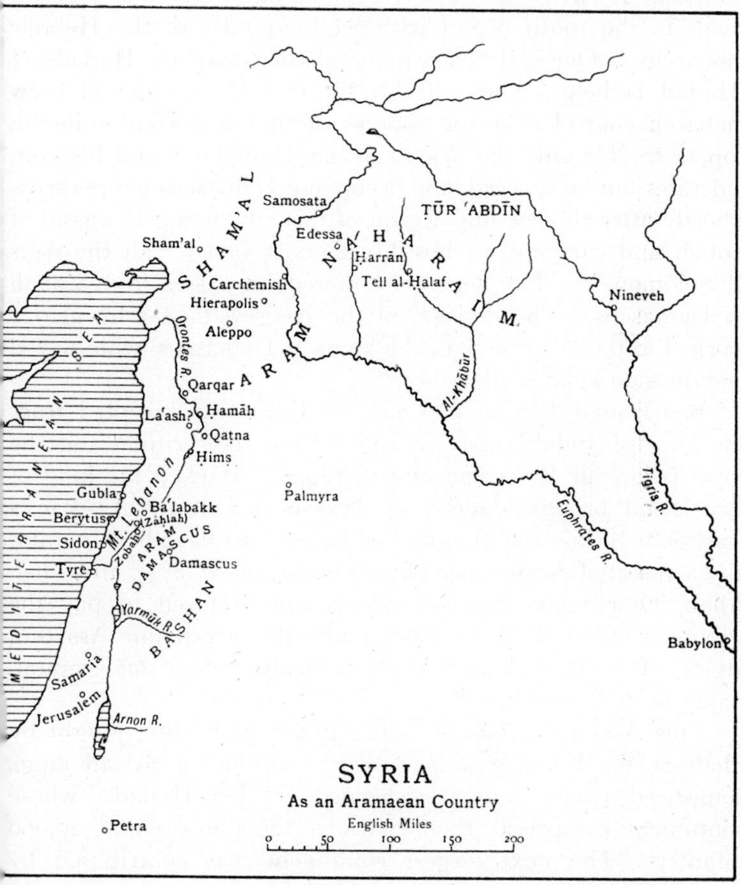

SYRIA
As an Aramaean Country

side to the Euphrates and on the other to the Yarmūk. On the north it was encroaching on Assyrian territory; in the south on Hebrew domain. The hinterland of Syria east of Mount Lebanon, together with North Syria and Bashan, were by about 1000 B.C. firmly under its control. It is this region of Damascus that the Old Testament means when it refers to Aram or Syria. For about two centuries these Aramaeans of

Syria were the formidable foes of the Hebrews.

Zobah was the capital of the kingdom of the same name. The word is derived from *ṣehōbāh*, red, copper. The site conjectured is that of Chalcis, modern ʿAnjar, south of Zaḥlah in the Biqāʿ.[1] The encounters between its kings and their Hebrew rivals to the south began with Saul, founder of the Hebrew monarchy.[2] One of the early monarchs of Zobah was Hadadezer (Hadad is help), whose defeat by David gave the Hebrew monarch control over the sources of that important mineral, copper.[3] Not only did David defeat Hadadezer and his confederates but he succeeded in occupying Damascus temporarily. Shortly after this we find Rezon of this city acting as vassal of Zobah and carrying on hostility against Israel " all the days of Solomon ".[4] The hegemony thereupon passes from Zobah to Damascus. The division of the Hebrew monarchy in 922 worked to the advantage of the kings of Damascus, who played one division against the other.

Ben-Hadad I[5] (*ca.* 879–843) of Damascus accepted from the king of Judah costly treasures from the Temple and the royal palace in Jerusalem and thereupon attacked the king of Israel and brought Gilead in Transjordan under Aramaean control.[6] In fact the kingdom of Israel must have been nominally a vassal of Aram since Omri's last days (*ca.* 875), and when Ahab, Omri's son and successor, either refused to pay the tribute or to join the federation against the threatening Assyrian attack, Ben-Hadad appeared suddenly before his capital, Samaria, to coerce him.[7]

The battle of Qarqar

This Assyrian invasion culminated in the battle fought by Shalmaneser III in 853 B.C.[8] The coalition of Syrian kings comprised twelve and was headed by Ben-Hadad,[9] whose contingent comprised 1200 chariots, 1200 horses and 20,000 infantry. The next largest contingent was contributed by

[1] Abel, vol. i, p. 248; Kraeling, p. 40; Chalcis (Gr. for copper) was later capital of Ituraea (mentioned in Lk. 3:1), an Arab kingdom; see below, pp. 246, 247.

[2] 1 Sam. 14:47.

[3] 1 Ch. 18:8; 2 Sam. 8:8. Berothai mentioned in Samuel is present-day Barītān, south of Baʿlabakk.

[4] 1 K. 11:25.

[5] Heb. for Aram. *bir*, later *bar* (son of) *-Hadad*. Ben-Hadad I and Ben-Hadad II were identical; Albright, " A Votive Stele Erected by Ben-Hadad I of Damascus ", *Bulletin, American Schools Oriental Research*, No. 87 (1942), pp. 26-7.

[6] 1 K. 15:18-20; 2 Ch. 16:2 *seq.*

[7] 1 K. 20:1 *seq.*

[8] See above, p. 140.

[9] " Hadad-ezer " in Luckenbill, vol. i, § 611

Ahab; then came that of the king of Ḥamāh. Several Phoenician city-states offered their quotas. In all, 60,000 troops confronted Shalmaneser at Qarqar on the Orontes and the contest ended in a draw. The Assyrians had many more years to wait before they could subdue Damascus.

A successor of Ben-Hadad, Hazael (God has seen, *ca.* 805), looms as the greatest warrior of Aramaean history. After sustaining two attacks from Shalmaneser, in 842 and 838, he himself took the field against Israel and pushed his domain in Transjordan as far south as the Arnon (al-Mūjib), which flows into the Dead Sea.[1] Jehu (*ca.* 842–814), from whom Shalmaneser exacted tribute, was then king of Israel. So utterly at the mercy of Aram was Israel under Jehu's successor Jehoahaz, that Hazael left him no force but fifty horsemen and ten chariots.[2] With a view to controlling the trade routes with Egypt and Arabia, Hazael pushed his conquests into the coastal plain of Palestine. He then "set his face to go up to Jerusalem" but was bought off by the gold and treasures of the Temple.[3] Enfeebled by Assyrian onslaughts, Hazael's successors could not hold their kingdom's frontiers so far south. Not only were the old frontiers restored by Jeroboam II, who became king of Samaria about 785, but this energetic Israelite took the initiative in attacking Damascus and Ḥamāh. Hazael

The real danger, however, was lurking in another quarter. The Assyrian military machine was once more ready for the march. The opportunity came when in 734 Ahaz, king of Judah, was seriously menaced by Pekah of Israel and Rezin of Damascus, and sought Assyrian intervention.[4] Tiglath-pileser III responded. The sixteen provinces of Damascus with 591 cities were overrun, "destroyed like mounds left by a flood".[5] Among those of the Assyrian tributaries who fought and fell before the walls of Damascus was Panammu II, king of Sham'al (Sinjirli), in the far north. Rezin himself took flight, "like a mouse [? antelope] he entered the gate of his city". There he was shut up "like a bird in a cage". But the siege dragged on. At last in 732 the city was taken. Its king was put to death; the trees of its orchards, the pride of the city in all ages, were cut down, "not one escaped", and its inhabitants

[1] 2 K. 10:32-3. [2] 2 K. 13:7. [3] 2 K. 12:17-18.
[4] 2 K. 16:5 *seq.* [5] Luckenbill, vol. i, § 777.

were deported.[1] Thus came to its end Aram Damascus, and with it Aramaean hegemony was forever ended.

Aramaean merchants

The peaceful penetration of Aramaean commerce and culture surpassed and survived Aramaean political and military penetration. This culture, which attained its height in the ninth and eighth centuries, is but little appreciated today, even in learned circles. No modern Syrians are conscious of their Aramaean ancestry and heritage, though many Lebanese emphasize their Phoenician origins. Aramaean merchants sent their caravans all over the Fertile Crescent, even as far north as the sources of the Tigris. Bronze weights left by them have turned up in the ruins of Nineveh. For centuries they monopolized the internal trade of Syria as their Canaanite cousins and rivals monopolized the maritime trade. Their capital Damascus was the port of the desert as first Gubla, later Sidon and Tyre, were the ports of the sea. The Aramaeans traded in purple from Phoenicia, embroideries, linen, jasper, copper, ebony and ivory from Africa, and in the "product of the seas", perhaps the pearls for which throughout the ages the Persian Gulf has been famous.[2]

Aramaic

Aramaean merchants were responsible for spreading their language, a member of the North-west-Semitic group, early and wide. From the year 731 B.C., in the reign of Tiglath-pileser III, comes the first representation of a scribe recording in Aramaic the plunder taken from a captured city. What he holds in his hands is not a stylus and clay tablet for writing cuneiform but a roll of papyrus and a pen. Presumably he was writing an alphabetic script. By about 500 B.C. Aramaic, once the mercantile language of a Syrian community, became not only the general language of commerce, culture and government throughout the entire Fertile Crescent, but the vernacular of its people. Its triumph over its sisters, including Hebrew, was complete. It became the language of Jesus and his people.[3] The second, if not first-known, reference to Christians is in Aramaic scrawled in Latin characters on the wall of what was apparently a house church at Pompeii, which makes it earlier

[1] Luckenbill, vol. i, § 776; Hugo Winckler, *Keilinschriftliches Textbuch zum Alten Testament*, 3rd ed. (Leipzig, 1909), pp. 31-2; cf. Is. 17 : 1 *seq.*

[2] Olmstead, *History of Palestine*, p. 534.

[3] On Aramaic as the language in which the material of the Gospels was written see Charles C. Torrey, *Our Translated Gospels* (New York, 1936).

than A.D. 79.[1] The ancestor of the most venerable Christian prayer is an Aramaic one called *Qaddīsh* (holy), of which half is repeated virtually word by word. It begins with " Magnified and sanctified be his great name ".[2] The widespread legend of Aḥīqār [3] contains some Assyrian or Babylonian maxims, but is in Aramaic written in the seventh or a later century.

Nor was the penetration of Aramaic confined to the Semitic area. Under Darius the Great (521–486) it was made the official interprovincial language of the Persian government; this rendered it until Alexander's conquest the lingua franca of an empire extending " from India to Ethiopia ". Such a triumph on the part of a language not backed up by imperial power has no parallel in history.

With the spread of Aramaic the Phoenician alphabet, which the Aramaeans were the first to adopt, spread and passed on to other languages in Asia. The Hebrews got their alphabet from Aramaeans between the sixth and fourth centuries. Earlier they used for a time the old Phoenician alphabet. The square characters in which Hebrew Bibles are now printed developed from the Aramaic script. The North Arabians received their alphabet, in which the Koran is written, from the Aramaic used by the Nabataeans. The Armenians, Persians and Indians acquired their alphabet likewise from Aramaean sources; the characters of both Pahlawi and Sanskrit are of Aramaean origin. Buddhist priests from India carried the Sanskrit alphabet into the heart of China and Korea. Thus did the Phoenician characters find their way through Aramaic eastward to the Far East and through Greek westward to the Americas, thereby encircling the entire world.

Inscriptions

The earliest Aramaic inscriptions now known were found in North Syria and date back to the beginning of the ninth century. Among these is a short epigraph from Tell al-Ḥalaf (Gozan).[4] Then comes a newly discovered inscription on a votive stele of

[1] W. R. Newbold, " Five Transliterated Aramaic Inscriptions ", *American Journal of Archaeology*, vol. xxx (1926), pp. 288 *seq*. The other reference is in Acts 11 : 26.

[2] For a Hebrew parallel cf. Ezek. 38 : 23.

[3] First mentioned in Tobit 1 : 21 *seq*., this hero and supposed author of proverbs figures in a number of Hebrew, Syriac, Armenian, Arabic and other stories. Aesop's fables show traces of his influence.

[4] Raymond A. Bowman, " The Old Aramaic Alphabet of Tell Halaf ", *American Journal of Semitic Languages*, vol. lviii (1941), pp. 359-62; cf. Bowman in *Journal of Near Eastern Studies*, vol. vii (1948), p. 71.

about 850 B.C., bearing the name of Ben-Hadad I and found four and a half miles north of Aleppo, which was under the rule of Damascus. The inscription reads:

> The stele which Barhadad, son of Ṭāb-Rammān, son of Khaḍyān, king of Aram, set for his lord Milk-qart, which he vowed to him when he hearkened unto his voice.[1]

Thus the famous inscription of Zakir, king of Ḥamāh and La'ash [2] (*ca.* 775), formerly considered the oldest, is relegated to third position. The Zakir stele was erected by this Aramaean monarch to commemorate his deliverance from an attack of seventeen kings, including those of Damascus, Sham'al and several Phoenician towns.[3]

Other early inscriptions left by Aramaeans come from Sinjirli (Sham'al), their central city in the north. Besides these monumental inscriptions, several dockets and weights bearing Aramaic inscriptions and dating from the eighth pre-Christian century to the fifth have been found. The Aramaic papyri, written by the Jewish colony in Upper Egypt and found in Elephantine (modern Jazīrat Aswān, Uswān), date from about 500 to 400 B.C.

In the course of time the Aramaic language split into two groups, the Eastern occupying the Euphrates valley and represented by Mandaic and Syriac, and the Western represented by biblical Aramaic,[4] the Targums, the dialects of Sham'al and Ḥamāh, Palmyrene and Nabataean. Mandaic was spoken by a Gnostic sect along the Euphrates from the seventh to the ninth Christian centuries. Syriac, the language of Edessa, became with local variations the language of the churches of Syria, Lebanon and Mesopotamia and was used from the third to the thirteenth centuries, when it was displaced by Arabic.[5] As the

[1] Cf. Maurice Dunand, "Stèle araméenne dédiée à Melqart", *Bulletin du Musée de Beyrouth*, vol. iii (1939), pp. 65-76; cf. Albright, p. 26.

[2] Or Lu'ash. Its capital was Hazrek, biblical Hadrach (Zech. 9:1), which lay on the Orontes south of Ḥamāh and west of Qaṭna; Olmstead, *History of Palestine*, p. 407; Dussaud, pp. 144, 236-7.

[3] See H. Pognon, *Inscriptions sémitiques de la Syrie, de la Mésopotamie et de la région de Mossoul* (Paris, 1907), pp. 156 *seq.*

[4] Found in Ezra 4:8-6:18; 7:12-26; Dan. 2:4b–7:28. Aramaic phrases used by Christ are quoted in Mk. 5:41; 7:34. Since in Dan. 2:4 it was put into the mouth of Chaldaeans, Aramaic came to be incorrectly called Chaldee or Chaldaic. What the Chaldaeans or Neo-Babylonians spoke was a dialect of Akkadian.

[5] See below, pp. 545-6.

Aramaean Christians adopted the Edessan dialect and made it the language of the church, of literature and of cultivated intercourse, they became known as Syrians; their earlier name, Aramaean, had acquired in their minds a disagreeable connotation, heathen. It was, therefore, generally avoided and replaced by the Greek terms " Syrian " for the people and " Syriac " for the language. The Greeks, be it remembered, called Aram " Syria ".[1] In the Septuagint and following it the Vulgate the people are often called Syrians and their language Syrian.[2] In modern usage, however, " Syriac " is restricted to the later dialect of Edessa and its development.

Material culture

The Aramaeans adopted the material culture of the people among whom they settled. In North Syria they became the heirs and continuers of the Hittite-Assyrian culture and in Central Syria of that of the Canaanites. Their north-western centre Sham'al [3] presented the aspects of a Hittite city, but its kings mostly bore Aramaean names and left inscriptions in Phoenician characters. This is one of the very few Aramaean cities that have been excavated.

One of its kings, Panammu I, who flourished in the first half of the eighth century, set up for Hadad a colossal statue 9½ feet high in which he represented the deity with a double-horned cap, a curled and rounded beard, inset eyes and arms outstretched in blessing.[4] The inscription below the girdle asserts that the monarch's main concern was the welfare of his people. The land granted him by the gracious gods was " a land of barley, wheat and garlic in which men till the soil and plant vineyards ".[5] A memorial statue of Panammu II (d. 732), erected perhaps on his grave by his son, states, " And in the days of my father Panammu, he installed cupbearers and charioteers ",[6] thus adding to the pomp of the royal court.

This son of Panammu II, Bar-Rakkab, appears hewn in flat relief on a richly carved throne of ebony, ivory and gold

[1] On the etymology of this word see above, p. 58.

[2] Cf. Ezra 4:7; Dan. 2:4.

[3] " North "; modern Sinjirli, a small village rather more than half-way from Antioch to Marʿash, was the chief city of Sam'al.

[4] Found in 1890 at Garjīn, 1½ miles north-east of Sinjirli.

[5] Cooke, p. 161; Arno Poebel, *Das appositionelle Pronomen* (Chicago, 1932), p. 43. Panammu calls himself " king of Ya'udi ", identical with " Judah ".

[6] Cf. Cooke, p. 174; Mark Lidzbarski, *Handbuch der nordsemitischen Epigraphik*, vol. i (Weimar, 1898), p. 443.

scarcely less magnificent than that of his Assyrian suzerain. The throne rests on cedar cones with bulls' heads at the four corners of the seat. Under his feet is a stool of like ornamentation. His long fringed robe and knobbed hat are Hittite; his beard and curls follow the Assyrian style.

Hadad the Thunderer

The deity who received the largest measure of Aramaean worship was the storm-god Hadad, also called Adad, Addu. A god of lightning and thunder, Hadad was beneficent when he sent rain which fructified the earth, maleficent when he sent floods. Among his titles was Rimmon (thunderer).[1] Naaman the Syrian called the god of his master, king of Damascus, by this title.[2] The two are sometimes combined, Hadad-Rimmon. In a relief found at Sinjirli he appears with trident and hammer, emblem of lightning and thunder; at Malatia (Malaṭyah) the sculpture shows him standing on the back of a bull, emblem of creative powers. Hadad's chief sanctuary was at Hierapolis,[3] but he had temples in many other Syrian towns and in Lebanon. A special favourite with the agricultural people of Syria, his cult was later confused with that of the sun; his head was then ornamented with rays, as in Baʿlabakk. In all probability Jupiter Heliopolitanus, of Baʿlabakk, should be identified with Hadad. In Roman times he was metamorphosed into Jupiter Damascenus. In the garden of the Sciarra villa at Rome a small marble altar was found with an inscription dedicated to Hadad of Lebanon.

In his inscription on the Hadad statue, Panammu I instructs his son when offering sacrifice to repeat: "May the soul of Panammu eat with Hadad, may his soul drink with Hadad; let it rejoice in the offering of Hadad",[4] providing an interesting glimpse into the ancient Aramaean idea of the hereafter. The Aramaeans are known to have been in the habit of naming their children "Bar-Hadad", son of Hadad, or son of some other favourite deity. This custom remained popular in Syria until

[1] The Akkadians apparently borrowed this word (etymologically unrelated to rammōn, pomegranate) from the west; the Assyrians pronounced it Ramān, Rammān. *Hadad* may have been derived from a stem surviving in Ar. *hadda*, to break, to crash.

[2] 2 K. 5:18.

[3] Ass. *Nampigi*, Aram. *Nappigu* (later *Mabug*, *Mabbog*, spring; from *nbag*, to spring, to sprout), Gr. *Bambyce*, Greco-Rom. *Hierapolis* (Hieropolis on the coins, sacred city), Ar. *Manbij*.

[4] Cooke, p. 162; Poebel, p. 48.

Christian days and throws interesting light upon the implied relationship between the deity and his worshipper.

Hadad's consort, a goddess of generation, was worshipped in Hierapolis and other Aramaean centres under the name Atargatis.[1] The Greeks and Romans simply called her "the Syrian goddess". A classic description of her cult was left by Lucian,[2] a Syrian from Samosata who was born about A.D. 125 and wrote in Greek. The general features of her cult, as depicted by Lucian, are those of the Semitic mother goddess. On coins from Hierapolis she wears a mural crown and is sometimes accompanied by a lion. Her symbol was composed of the crescent moon in conjunction with the solar disk. She had a temple at Carnion[3] in Gilead. In Palestine, Ascalon, where she was probably identified with Aphrodite, was a centre of her worship. Atargatis

In Seleucid days the worship of Atargatis spread among the Greeks and from them found its way into imperial Rome, where a temple was erected in her name. On Roman monuments she is represented seated on a throne between two lions. Her priests were generally eunuchs who were wont to undertake trips into Greece and Italy to extend her worship by means of prophecies and ecstatic dances and to collect pious alms for her Hierapolitan sanctuary.

A curious type of Atargatis on coins from Hierapolis shows her veiled. Numerous other images of the veiled Atargatis have been found.[4] Women as heavily veiled as any conservative Moslem of today appear on a monumental bas-relief from the temple of Baal in Palmyra and in a fresco from Dura-Europus. Other monuments show the head covered. Evidently the veil was in the ancient East the symbol, the required costume, of a married woman. Assyrian legislation of the mid-second

[1] Gr., from Aram. *'Atār* (*'Attār*) for Ashtart, plus Aram. *'Atāh* (not related to Phrygian *Attis*). Originally two distinct Semitic ones, the cults of 'Atar and 'Atāh, were later amalgamated; S. Ronzevalle, "Les Monnaies de la dynastie de 'Abd-Hadad", *Mélanges de l'Université de Saint-Joseph*, vol. xxiii (1940), No. 1, p. 26.

[2] *De Dea Syria*; tr. Herbert A. Strong, ed. John Garstang, *The Syrian Goddess* (London, 1913); ed. and tr. A. M. Harmon, "The Goddesse of Surrye", in *Lucian*, vol. iv (London, 1925), pp. 337-411. See below, pp. 322-3.

[3] Karnion, Carnain, probably identical with Ashteroth Karnaim (two-horned Ashtaroth) of Gen. 14:5. Present site either Tell 'Ashtara, 11 miles north-west of Dar'a, or more likely Tell al-Ash'ari, 4 miles south of Tell 'Ashtara.

[4] Ronzevalle, pp. 25-6.

millennium before Christ requires the wives and daughters of a free man to veil their heads when out on the street.[1]

Besides the divine couple, Hadad and Atargatis, the Aramaean pantheon comprised an assortment of other deities of secondary rank, some of local character, others borrowed from neighbours. Hadad, El, Rakkab-El, Shamash and Reshuf were the gods who in the inscription of Panammu I gave his hand the sceptre and granted him what he prayed for. *Rakkāb*, charioteer, is an importation into Syria of the Assyrian sun-god. Assyrian *Shamash* was the name of the

From Mélanges de l'Universite Saint-Joseph, vol. xxiii

From H. A. Strong, " The Syrian Goddess ", Ed. J. Garstang

THE VEILED GODDESS ATARGATIS ON A COIN FROM HIERAPOLIS

Dressed in a long robe, the goddess leans on a lion. Her head is covered with a veil reaching to the belt on her back. Her name appears in the abbreviated form *'Atāh*

sun deity worshipped throughout the Semitic world. *Reshūf* is the Phoenician *Rashap*,[2] often represented as an armed soldier. In his inscription, Zakir of Ḥamāh lifts his hands up to Baal-Shamain (lord of heavens) and proclaims: " Whoever effaces the name of Zakir, king of Ḥamāh and Laʿash, from this stele or destroys it from before El Wer, or removes it from its place, or puts forth his hand against it . . . Baal-Shamain and El Wer and Shamash and Sahar and the gods of heaven and the gods of earth . . . shall destroy him." [3] Baal-Shamain is evidently Hadad, but El Wer is not yet identified. Sahar [4]

[1] V. Scheil, *Recueil de lois assyriennes* (Paris, 1921), §§ 41, 42; Morris Jastrow, Jr., " An Assyrian Law Code ", *Journal, American Oriental Society*, vol. xli (1921), pp. 34-8. On the veil in the ancient East, see Morris Jastrow, " Veiling in Ancient Assyria ", *Revue archéologique*, vol. xiv (1921), pp. 209-38; R. de Vaux, " Sur le voile des femmes dans l'orient ancien ", *Revue biblique*, vol. xliv (1935), pp. 397-412.

[2] See above, pp. 77, 20.

[3] Pognon, p. 176; Mark Lidzbarski, *Ephemeris für semitische Epigraphik*, vol. iii (Giessen, 1915), pp. 4, 11.

[4] Ar. *shahr*, month, comes from same stem.

is the moon-god. Ḥarrān was the abode of the moon deity called in Assyrian Sin. On the Taymā'[1] stone, whose Aramaic inscription belongs to the fifth pre-Christian century, his name appears as Shingalla, an Assyrian importation denoting the great Sin. The two other gods cited on this stone are Salm (image, statue), referring probably to the local Baal, and Ashira (Asherah).[2]

[1] Teima, an oasis in northern al-Ḥijāz.

[2] Cooke, pp. 196-7; see above, pp. 119, 121, n. 2.

CHAPTER XIII

THE HEBREW PEOPLE

THE Hebrews were the fourth major Semitic people — after the Amorites, Canaanites and Aramaeans — to settle in Syria. In Amorite days the centre of gravity of Syrian affairs was in the north, in the Syrian Saddle; in Canaanite times it shifted to the littoral; under the Aramaeans it lay in the interior; with the Hebrews it moved to the south, to Palestine.

Hebrew origins

Hebrew entrance into Canaan, as the southern part of Syria was then called, supposedly came in three ill-defined movements. The first migration had its start in Mesopotamia and was roughly contemporaneous with the eighteenth century movement which spread the Hyksos Hurrians over the eastern shore of the Mediterranean.[1] The second was connected with the fourteenth century Aramaeans of the ʻAmārnah age.[2] The third, about which much more is known, was that from Egypt and the south-east under Moses and Joshua in the late thirteenth century.[3] Canaanites formed the bulk of the population when the pioneers from Mesopotamia, the Patriarchs, came. Amorites inhabited the highlands, which were not thickly occupied by a sedentary population, thus giving the newcomers an opportunity to settle. Smaller nationalities occupied out-of-the-way places. With all these the new settlers intermarried. The result was the Hebrew people, with a composite ethnic origin consisting of Semitic, Hurrian, Hittite and other, non-Semitic, elements.

Syria's power to absorb nomadic or quasi-nomadic intruders by encouraging them to become sedentary, and inducing them to relinquish their peculiar source of power — mobility — was once more illustrated in the case of the Hebrews. Coming as wanderers, adventurers, mercenaries, footloose soldiers, the

[1] See above, p. 150. [2] See above, p. 161.
[3] Cf. Theophile J. Meek, *Hebrew Origins* (New York, 1936), pp. 3 *seq.*

future Hebrews gradually settled among the older and more civilized population, learned from them how to till the soil, build homes, practise the arts of peace and, above all, how to read and write. More than that, the Hebrews gave up their old Semitic dialect and adopted the Canaanite one. Phoenician and old Hebrew, as recorded in the Old Testament, are only dialectally distinct. On the whole, the early Hebrews became the heirs of the basic features of Canaanite material culture and the continuers of many Canaanite cults, practices and religious tenets.

The Patriarchal age

Hebrew beginnings in Syria are shrouded in mystery and recorded in legendary and traditional terms. Hebrew tradition, stated in its briefest outline, brings Abraham [1] — their ancestor or ancestral tribe — from Ur in Mesopotamia via Ḥarrān and settles him temporarily near Hebron. His heir Isaac [2] leaves a son Jacob.[3] After sojourning for many years in Padan Aram, Jacob is elected to be the child of promise in preference to his twin brother Esau,[4] and his name is changed to Israel.[5] Esau obtains a second name Edom (red) and his descendants ultimately dispossess the natives of Mount Seir and become known as the Edomites.[6] Esau was thus eliminated from the stream of Hebrew life and thought, just as Ishmael,[7] Abraham's son by the Egyptian concubine Hagar, was earlier eliminated in favour of Isaac. The eleventh of Jacob's twelve sons, Joseph,[8] the elder son of Rachel, is sold to Egypt, where he rises to eminence in state affairs. After a sojourn of many generations in Egypt, Joseph's and his brothers' descendants return to the Land of Promise under the leadership of Moses.

Such is the outline of early Hebrew history as recorded by writers who lived hundreds of years after the events and depended upon hearsay and a long chain of oral transmission.

Not content with beginning their narrative with the ancestor of the Hebrew people, these historians stretched the story of man and sketched it from the beginning of creation. In this they drew their material from Babylonian sources, a fact not realized until after the middle of the last century, when the decipher-

[1] Heb. *abh-rām*, the Father is lofty.
[2] Heb. *yiṣḥāq*, may He [El] smile.
[3] Heb. *ya'qōbh*, may He protect.
[4] See above, p. 164; Gen. 25 : 23, 27-34.
[5] Heb. *yisrĕ-'ēl*, may El rule, or El rules.
[6] Deut. 2 : 4, 12, 22.
[7] Heb. *yishmā'-'ēl*, may El hear.
[8] Heb. *yāsaph*, may He add.

ment of cuneiform inscriptions revealed parallels to the stories of Creation, the Flood and others. In the hands of Hebrew writers, however, these stories were refined, simplified, "moralized" and then expressed in such beautiful form that they became a part of the literary heritage of mankind. As such they never ceased to entertain and instruct generations of readers in all lands and through all languages.

The pre-Patriarchal history as sketched by the Hebrew chroniclers is clearly not history. Even from the Patriarchal narrative the kernel of historical fact is not easy to extract. The Abrahamic story may reflect the earliest migration; the Israelite may reflect the second; the Mosaic is definitely historical.

The Exodus

The real history of the Israelites as a people then begins with the Exodus from Egypt. This epoch-making event took place in the last third of the thirteenth century. In Egypt of the Hyksos, one of the Hebrew tribes — that of Rachel — had found abode and flourished.[1] Their settlement there was in Goshen, by the Hyksos capital Avaris. At last came a Pharaoh who "knew not Joseph",[2] presumably Ramses II (*ca.* 1299–1232). The Exodus took place probably about 1290. A stele of Ramses' son Merenptah at Thebes, dated 1230 B.C., contains the earliest occurrence of the word Israel as the name of a people in Palestine. The reference may have been to Israelites who did not migrate to Egypt.

Leaving Egypt in the early thirteenth century, the Rachel tribesmen lingered many years in Sinai and the neighbourhood of Kadesh-barnea,[3] where they were subjected to untold suffering. That "great and terrible wilderness", whose dangers haunted Hebrew memory for generations, may now be crossed in five hours on a 140-mile asphalt motor highway connecting Egypt with Palestine. In Midian, the southern part of that peninsula, the divine covenant was made. Their leader Moses, whose name sounds like an Egyptian word meaning "son", married the daughter of the Midianite priest, a worshipper of Jehovah,[4] who initiated him to the new cult. This North Arabian deity was a desert god, originally a moon-god whose

[1] See above, pp. 148-9. [2] Ex. 1:8.

[3] Supposedly 'Ayn Qudays of today, 51 miles south of Beer-sheba.

[4] Ex. 3:1; 18:10-12. "Jehovah" is the common English form of the Heb. tetragram Y H W H, *yāhweh*, perhaps imperfect of *hāwāh* (cf. Ar. *hawa*), he causes to be or befall.

abode was a tent and whose ritual comprised feasts and sacrifices from among the herd.[1] Others must have intermarried with Midianites, Kenites [2] and other dwellers of the North Arabian wasteland.

Settlement

Around 1250 B.C. this mixed clan of desert-born nomads appeared from the south-east, the Transjordanian desert, intent upon the occupation of the fertile land. Their number could not have exceeded 6000 or 7000,[3] considering conditions of desert life, scarcity of water and limited supply of food and of space for grazing flocks. The petty kingdoms of Edom, Moab and Ammon, which lay south, east and north-east of the Dead Sea, were by-passed; no attempt was made to subdue them until the time of the monarchy.

In Transjordan the first Hebrew triumph was over the Amorite king of Sihon, followed by that over the giant king Og.[4] In Palestine proper among the first Canaanite walled cities to fall were Lachish (Tell al-Duwayr), Ai [5] and Jericho. Jericho's fall was one of the most spectacular.[6] By Jehovah's authority Joshua burned Jericho with fire "and all that was therein".[7] Megiddo in the north did not succumb until about a hundred years later. Hebrew penetration into Galilee resulted in the temporary conquest of Hazor,[8] capital of a Canaanite kingdom in the north. Hazor had to be reconquered in the days of the Judges.[9] Other important cities like Beth-shean, Jerusalem and Gezer did not fall until about 1000 B.C. or shortly after that.

The so-called Hebrew conquest, nevertheless, was in part military conquest and in part slow and peaceful penetration into the land of "milk and honey". Having secured a foothold in the cultivated land, the newcomers were reinforced by intermarriage with older elements and by adhesion of their kinsmen who had remained in the land and never migrated to

[1] Ex. 3:18; 5:1; Num. 10:35-6.

[2] "Smiths" (Ar. *qayn*, sing.); Judg. 1:16; 4:11; Num. 10:29. Mineral deposits of Sinai and Wādi al-ʿArabah were known to Egyptians and Arabians long before this time.

[3] Cf. Ex. 12:37; Num. 1:21 *seq.*; 2:4 *seq.*

[4] See above, pp. 75-6; Num. 21:21 *seq.*; 21:33 *seq.*

[5] Near modern Dayr Dīwān; Josh. 10:30-31; 8:3 *seq.*

[6] Josh. 6:15 *seq.*

[7] Josh. 6:2, 24.

[8] Tell al-Waqqāṣ or Tell al-Qadaḥ, about 3¾ miles west of Jisr Banāt Yaʿqūb (bridge of Jacob's daughters); Josh. 11:10-13.

[9] Judg. 4:2; 23-4; 1 Sam. 12:9.

Egypt. Thus they rose into a state of predominance. In the minds of their historians the battles naturally loomed high in importance. Not only was the focus in the narrative often on those battles but many events were often telescoped. On the whole the process was one by which the natives were brought within the Hebrew fold by treaty, by conquest or by gradual absorption.

As the land was acquired it was parcelled out among the eleven tribes, leaving the priestly tribe of Levi distributed among the others to minister to their religious needs. As a consequence Judah and Benjamin became domiciled in the hilly country around Jerusalem, and the remaining tribes were established in the more fertile plains to the north.

The Judges

The period of settlement roughly covered the last quarter of the twelfth and the first three-quarters of the eleventh centuries. It coincides with the period called that of the Judges. These Judges were rather national heroes and rulers who spontaneously arose in time of emergency and led their people against neighbouring enemies or foreign oppressors. Deborah, an inspired mother in Israel who with Barak led six tribes to final victory against the Canaanites to the north, was such a Judge; [1] and so was Gideon, who with 300 repulsed the Midianites.[2] Most colourful among the Judges was Samson, whose struggle against the Philistines received layers of embellishment at the hands of imaginative Hebrew story-tellers.[3] The Midianites came as Bedouin raiders using for the first time the domesticated camel.[4] A new weapon of warfare was thereby introduced which proved to be of terrifying effectiveness, especially in long-range raiding.

The Philistines

Most formidable among the rivals for the possession of the land with whom the Hebrews had to contend were the Philistines, one of five groups of the Sea Peoples who came from the Aegean region. Shortly after the Hebrews had conquered the central highlands, the Philistines made themselves masters of the coast land. Obscure movements of peoples in Asia Minor and the Aegean area in the late thirteenth and early twelfth centuries resulted in the dislocation of whole tribes who sought a new abode in less troubled areas. Hordes of migrants, including among others Philistine tribes, turned by land and sea

[1] Judg. 4:4-14.
[2] Judg. 7:15 *seq.*
[3] Judg., chs. 15, 16.
[4] See above, p. 52.

toward Syria and after devastating many of its states, such as Ugarit,[1] reached the Egyptian coast. Here they were checked about 1191 B.C. in a naval and land battle by Ramses III [2] but allowed to settle permanently along the south Syrian coast, which then came to bear the name Philistia. Another group, the Tjeker, settled at Dor under the lee of Carmel, where the Egyptian envoy Wenamon encountered them about two centuries later.[3] The piratical activity in the eastern Mediterranean at Wenamon's time was due to these sea rovers. Before the Philistine incursion other sea rovers from Greece and Asia Minor had come, some via Cyprus, and descended upon the Egyptian coast, when they were repulsed by Merenptah about 1225 B.C

Their five cities

The coast of which the Philistines took permanent possession extended from Gaza to the south of Jaffa. The chief cities in which they installed themselves were Gaza, Ascalon, Ashdod, Ekron and Gath,[4] which retained their Semitic names under the new rule. Gath was their farthest settlement inland, their policy being to keep close by the sea, where they could at once control its ways and utilize the vine-bearing hills behind. Carmel marked the dividing line between their coast country and that of the Phoenicians to the north. With the possible exception of Lydda and Ziklag [5] no colonies were founded by Philistines. From the coastal strip they worked their way inland capturing many Canaanite towns and disarming the populace. The numerous punitive expeditions and severe exactions of successive Pharaohs had impoverished Syria and weakened its resistance to the onslaught of desert hordes as well as sea rovers. Neither Philistines nor Hebrews would have had so much success in gaining a firm foothold in the land, had imperial Egypt been still able to exercise full control over it.

That the Philistines were Europeans is suggested by their

[1] See above, p. 116; Tyre was destroyed shortly afterwards.

[2] Breasted, *Records*, vol. iv, § 403, where the earliest occurrence of the name "Pelest" is found. "Palaeste" was a place name in an Illyrian region, Epirus; G. Bonfante, "Who were the Philistines?", *American Journal of Archaeology*, vol. L (1946), p. 251.

[3] See above, pp. 134-5.

[4] Perhaps Tell ʻAraq al-Manshīyah, 6½ miles west of Bayt Jibrīn (Eleutheropolis).

[5] In the extreme south of Judah, probably to be identified with Tell al-Khuwaylifah, 10 miles east of Tell al-Sharīʻah.

representation on the memorial monument raised by Ramses III. That they came from the Greek islands, particularly Crete,[1] is indicated by the type of pottery they introduced. Having brought their womenfolk along with them, they first kept aloof, constituting a foreign military caste stationed in garrisons and representing an exotic culture. Their five cities were organized into city-states, each under a lord,[2] brought together into a confederacy. Ashdod seems to have held the hegemony. A portrait of a lord with a short beard on the lower lip and plaited side hair, appears on a pottery coffin lid found at Beth-pelet (Khirbat al-Mashāsh), near Beer-sheba, in the most southerly part of Judah.

The second half of the eleventh century saw the zenith of Philistine power. About 1050 B.C. they defeated the Hebrews and captured the Ark, which they took to Ashdod.[3] Around 1020 they were established in garrisons in the hill country itself. During the reign of Saul (d. *ca.* 1004), they exercised control over such an inland town as Beth-shean.[4] This could only mean that the Philistines had then the upper hand over the people of Israel.

What gave the Philistines special advantage over their enemies was their superiority of armour, which depended upon knowledge of smelting and the use of iron for weapons of defence and offence. A snapshot of a metal-clad Philistine warrior has been preserved in the story of Goliath, whose spear's staff was "like a weaver's beam", whose spear's head "weighed six hundred shekels of iron" and whose shield was so heavy as to require the services of a special carrier.[5] Some of the most picturesque military exploits of Hebrew heroes, as in the case of Samson and David, are projected against this background of Philistine might.

Iron

The Philistines exploited their knowledge of smelting and

[1] Caphtor of Amos 9:7; Jer. 47:4.

[2] *seren*, Josh. 13:3; Judg. 3:3; 16:5; 1 Sam. 6:16, one of the few Philistine words surviving. Another word is *kauba'* (helmet), which has survived, through Heb., in Ar. *qub'*, which some take back to Hittite. L. *caput* goes back to same source.

[3] 1 Sam. 5:1. For the relation of the Ark to its Semitic antecedents and parallels — the *qubbah* of pre-Islamic Arabians, the *maḥmil* of the Moslem pilgrimage and the *'uṭfah* of the Bedouins — consult Julian Morgenstern, *The Ark, the Ephod and the "Tent of Meeting"* (Cincinnati, 1945), pp. 1 *seq.*

[4] 1 Sam. 13:3 *seq.*; 31:12.

[5] 1 Sam. 17:7.

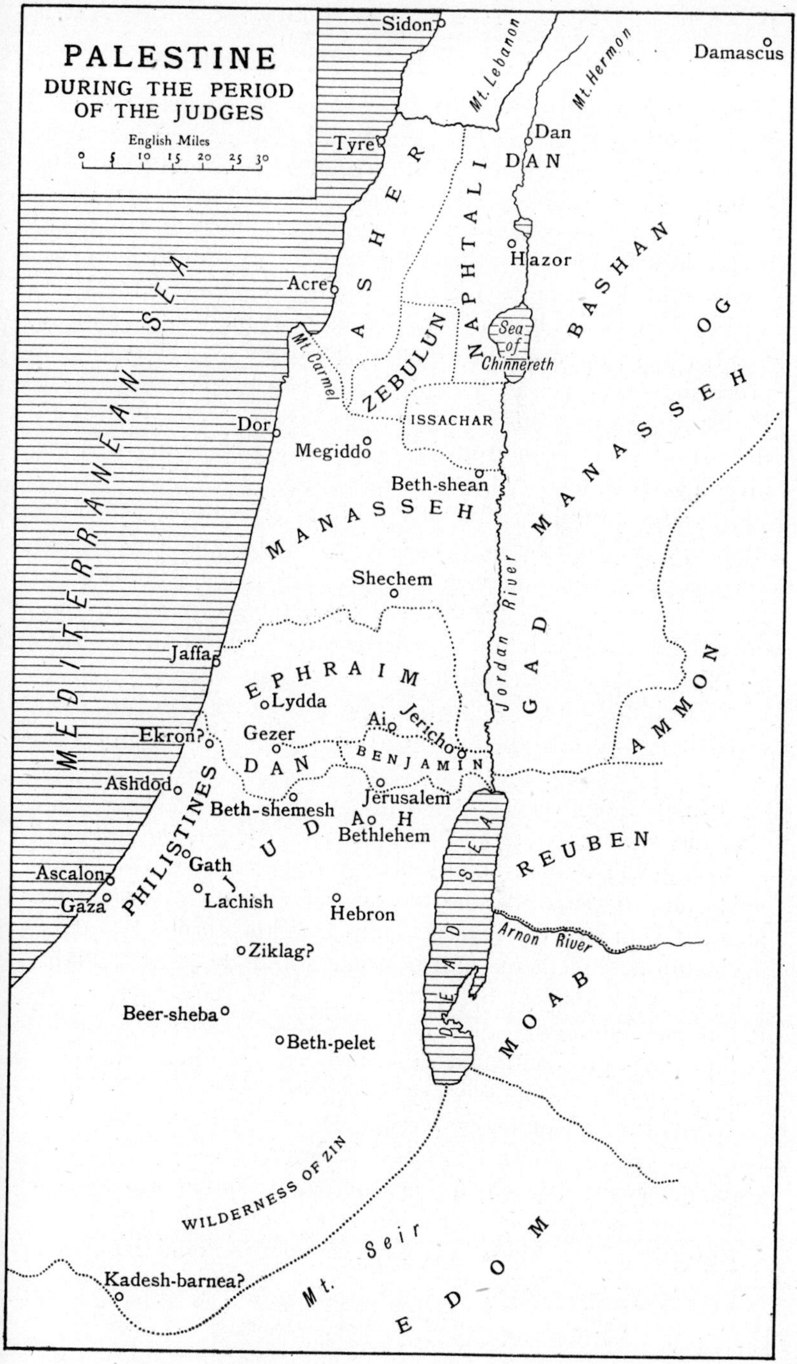
PALESTINE
DURING THE PERIOD
OF THE JUDGES
English Miles
0 5 10 15 20 25 30
MEDITERRANEAN SEA
Sidon
Mt. Lebanon
Mt. Hermon
Damascus
Tyre
Dan
DAN
ASHER
NAPHTALI
Hazor
BASHAN
Acre
Mt. Carmel
ZEBULUN
Sea of Chinnereth
OG
ISSACHAR
MANASSEH
Dor
Megiddo
Beth-shean
MANASSEH
Shechem
Jordan River
GAD
Jaffa
EPHRAIM
Lydda
Ai
Jericho
AMMON
Ekron?
Gezer
DAN
BENJAMIN
Ashdod
PHILISTINES
Jerusalem
Beth-shemesh
JUDAH
Bethlehem
DEAD SEA
REUBEN
Ascalon
Gath
Gaza
Lachish
Hebron
Arnon River
Ziklag?
MOAB
Beer-sheba
Beth-pelet
WILDERNESS OF ZIN
Mt. Seir
EDOM
Kadesh-barnea?

O

employing iron to the point of a monopoly. They required Israelites, with farming implements or cutlery to sharpen, to patronize Philistine smiths.[1] This proved the main handicap in time of war as illustrated by the experience in the reign of Saul.

Prior to the advent of the Philistines, Hittites had made rare use of iron in the early thirteenth century as indicated by the correspondence of Hattushilish, its source being along the shore of the Black Sea. But no common use was made of this metal in Syria until the appearance of the Philistines. The secrets of processing it were as jealously guarded by Hittites as by Philistines. The Canaanites who learned from the Philistines the use of chariots of iron had a decisive advantage over the invading Israelites.[2]

It was not until the time of David (d. *ca.* 960 B.C.), when the Philistine grip on the land was loosened, that the complicated knowledge of smelting iron was acquired by non-Philistines.[3] Besides subduing the Philistines, this Hebrew monarch conquered Edom, which was a rich source of iron ore. Lebanon also had this mineral, which the Phoenicians learned to utilize in their shipbuilding. Thus did the Philistines raise the stage of Syrian culture from that of bronze to a higher one of iron. Herein lay their greatest contribution.

It may, moreover, be assumed that they bequeathed to their Phoenician neighbours and successors a taste for long-distance seafaring which had among its results exploring the Mediterranean, the Red Sea and the eastern Atlantic Beyond that and a few traces of material culture in the form of pottery, agricultural implements and iron adzes and chisels, the Philistines hardly left a relic by which they may be remembered. As a foreign community they had no guarantee of permanency except through continued replenishment of their blood by immigration, an impossibility under the existing conditions. Towards the end of David's reign they tend to disappear as a colony. In due course they were Semitized and assimilated, leaving very little by which their language, religion, architecture and other aspects of their higher life could be determined. Writing in the middle of the fifth century, Nehemiah [4] speaks

[1] 1 Sam. 13:19-22.
[2] Josh. 17:2; Judg. 1:19.
[3] 1 Ch. 22:3.
[4] 4:7; 13:24

not of Philistines but of "Ashdodites" speaking an Ashdodite dialect. "Achish"[1] is one of the very few Philistine proper names that survived. Among their gods Dagon,[2] a god of grain, as the name indicates, was an adaptation from the Canaanite pantheon. His seat of worship was Ashdod; the seat of his partner Astarte was Ascalon. About the architecture of Dagon's temple and the lord's palace at Gaza,[3] and of the other Philistine temples mentioned in the Old Testament, nothing is known.

[1] 1 Sam. 27:2.

[2] Judg. 16:23; 1 Sam. 5:2-7; 1 Ch. 10:10; 1 Macc. 10:84; see above, p. 77.

[3] Judg. 16:23 *seq.*

CHAPTER XIV

THE HEBREW MONARCHY

The united monarchy

RESISTANCE to the Philistines in particular provided the occasion for the creation of the Hebrew monarchy. With the monarchy the history of the Hebrew nation begins. Under it the Hebrews developed pronounced national traits, though they missed the political outlook — a feature of modern nationalism. Of all the ancient Semites the Hebrews were the only ones to develop intense nationalism. Of all the ancient Semites they are the only ones who have maintained their national character and individuality. Religion, of course, greatly contributed to their unification and solidarity.

Their neighbours the Edomites, Moabites and Ammonites had kings; the Philistines had lords who maintained a loose federation; the Phoenicians had city-states, some of which like Byblus, Sidon and Tyre had developed into nations; but the Hebrews thus far had Judges, leaders who arose spontaneously as the occasion demanded. So the elders went to their religious leader Samuel demanding "a king to judge us like all the nations".[1] A man who was head and shoulders taller than any of the people,[2] Saul by name, was anointed first king over them about 1020 B.C. Not only did the inspiration come from outside sources but the monarchy itself in its organization was gradually modelled upon those of the neighbouring realms. In two respects, however, it somewhat differed: the tribal organization was maintained for administrative purposes and the king was to reign according to the dictates of Jehovah as revealed through his holy men.

The first Hebrew monarch was a disappointment, in fact a failure. His character was weak, his temperament melancholy. Like a Bedouin shaykh he lived in a tent in his native Gibeah.[3] His tiny kingdom did not first extend much beyond his own

[1] 1 Sam. 8:5. [2] 1 Sam. 9:2.
[3] Tell al-Fūl, 4 miles north of Jerusalem; 1 Sam. 10:26; 11:4.

tribe Benjamin. His election, nevertheless, was tantamount to a revolt against the Philistine masters. After a protracted struggle the Philistines in the battle of Gilboa [1] slew three of his sons and wounded him so seriously that he committed suicide. After severing his head the victorious enemy affixed his body, together with the bodies of his sons, to the wall of Beth-shean and sent his armour as a trophy to the temple of Ashtart.[2]

David

The real founder of the monarchy was David (*ca.* 1004–*ca.* 960 B.C.), Saul's armour-bearer, who began his royal career under Philistine suzerainty but ultimately succeeded not only in achieving full independence but also in extending the limits of the kingdom beyond any ever reached before or after. David inaugurated a series of campaigns which lifted the Philistine yoke from Hebrew necks, brought Edom, Moab and Ammon under his rule and what is more amazing, netted him Aramaean Hollow Syria, presumably as far as the borders of the state of Ḥamāh.[3] His victorious army trod the streets of Damascus. The kingdom established by David was the most powerful native state that Palestine ever produced.[4] His conquest of Edom brought under his control the great trade route between Syria and Arabia. We hear of no kingdoms in this small country or its two northerly neighbours, Moab and Ammon, prior to the thirteenth pre-Christian century. In the preceding century offshoots from the Aramaeans and some Khabiru evidently settled in this region, which since the twentieth century had been the roaming ground of nomads. All remains of the pre-twentieth century civilization must have been destroyed by the Hyksos and the Aramaeans. Modern exploration has failed to reveal any sizable town in the Transjordanian area throughout all this long period.

With his kingdom consolidated, its boundaries well rounded and its neighbours subdued, David effected temporary unity among his people. The official census he took, one of the

[1] Jabal Fuqūʿah, the north-east spur of Mount Ephraim forming the watershed between the Kishon basin and the Jordan valley. The name of the modern village Jalbūn suggests the ancient name.

[2] 1 Sam. 31 : 1-10; 1 Ch. 10 : 1-10; cf. 2 Sam. 1 : 6-10.

[3] 2 Sam., chs. 8, 10, 12 : 26-31; cf. Num. 34 : 7; see above, p. 166.

[4] Since it did not include the entire coast, this does not discredit the first part of George Adam Smith's statement (*Historical Geography*, p. 58): "Palestine has never belonged to one nation, and probably never will".

earliest in recorded history, must have yielded a figure of perhaps some six or seven hundred thousand.[1] For his capital he chose the Jebusite stronghold Jerusalem, which he had wrested from the hands of its native Jebusites. The choice was a happy one. The city lay outside the original tribal settlements, almost on the border between the northern and the southern parts of the kingdom and commanded one of the most important inland routes, that which ran north and south along the spine of the west Jordan valley. Yet it was easy to defend. Here David established his royal residence, a palace built with stone and with cedar from Lebanon by Tyrian masons and carpenters sent by his Phoenician friend King Hiram (981–947 B.C.).[2] Tyrian-Israelite amity was based on mutual interest: Tyre was poor in farm products, Israel lacked sea-borne commerce. In addition to his palace David erected a national sanctuary for Yahweh at the new capital, thus establishing Yahwism as the official religion of the united state. To the Hebrews he became the ideal king.

Under David, "the man of war", Hebrew literature, one of the richest and noblest legacies of the Ancient East, had its beginnings. The *mazkīr* (remembrancer), whose official duty was that of recording important events and keeping royal annals, makes his appearance.[3] The script was borrowed from the Phoenicians.[4] Presumably priests began later to prepare parallel books of official records. From such records the history of the early monarchy was drawn and in part incorporated in the Old Testament. The historian of the period, whoever he was, presents his material in a vivid and completely objective way. He describes David not only as a king but as a man and writes only as a contemporary could write. His first two chapters of 1 Kings are the first piece of Hebrew prose; his biography of David in 2 Samuel, chapters 9 to 20, is a masterpiece of historical composition. No such history was ever written before. This unknown historian, the earliest in time, seems strangely modern. Collections of poetical works were also begun under David, himself no minor poet. In fact so deep was the impression his poetical and musical talent left that posterity ascribed to him the composition of numerous

[1] Cf. 2 Sam. 24: 9; 1 Ch. 21: 5.
[2] 2 Sam. 5: 11.
[3] 2 Sam. 2: 16; 2 K. 18: 18, 37.
[4] See above, pp. 110, 169.

psalms so timeless and universal in their human appeal that they are still used for inspiration and spiritual uplift.

Solomon in all his glory

David was succeeded by his son Solomon (*ca.* 960–*ca.* 925 B.C.), under whom the Hebrew monarchy reached dazzling heights of glamour and pageantry. Solomon's mercantile and industrial enterprises, his extensive mining activity, building operations and lavish scale of living find no parallel in Hebrew royal annals. Amidst these scenes of animated activity he lived the life of an autocratic, voluptuous monarch in a court that was a replica of that of Egypt or Assyria. His reign brought the Hebrews more fully into the stream of Oriental life and civilization.

Solomon's palace, like that of his father, was built by Phoenician architects using cedars from Lebanon. The palace took thirteen years to build. So rich in cedar columns was the royal quarter that it became known as the " house of the forest of Lebanon ".[1]

Of more national importance was the temple he built. The site is conjecturally the one covered today by the Dome of the Rock. Originally designed as a royal chapel, an appanage to the palace, the Temple of Solomon took only seven years to build and later became the public place of Hebrew worship. Again the architects and builders were Tyrians using the cedar of Lebanon. To this end 30,000 of his subjects were levied to work in relays, one month in Lebanon with Hiram's men and two months at home pursuing their usual work.[2] The cut lumber was carried to the sea, transported as rafts to Jaffa and then conveyed to Jerusalem. The decoration of the Temple was inspired by the contemporary Canaanite motifs. Its ritual and sacrifices reflected Canaanite practice. The Temple slaves were Canaanites. Even the name *hêkāl* (temple) was borrowed from Canaanite vocabulary.[3]

Ezion-geber

The building operations of Solomon included fortifications, barracks and store-houses. His recently excavated stables at Megiddo, where his chariotry was housed, show stalls in double rows which could accommodate 450 horses, some of which were procured from Egypt and Cilicia.[4] With the aid of his Phoenician friend King Hiram he built a fleet of ships for Red Sea trade.

[1] 1 K. 7 : 2.
[2] 1 K. 5 : 13.
[3] See above, p. 138, n. 5.
[4] Cf. 1 K. 10 : 26, 28-9.

The base of the fleet was Ezion-geber,[1] subsequently renamed Elath, Aila in Roman times. From this seaport Solomon's fleet under Tyrian officers undertook naval expeditions around the coast of Arabia and East Africa.[2] The main object was to import frankincense, algum, ivory, gold and precious stones. Copper and iron refined at Ezion-geber formed the chief export article shipped by sea or sent by caravan to Arabia in exchange for imported commodities from there and from India. Edom and the entire section (now called al-ʿArabah) of Solomon's domain between the Dead Sea and the Gulf of al-ʿAqabah were rich in copper and iron. This made Solomon's seaport a mining and smelting centre. The native Kenites [3] must have been the ones who first introduced the Edomites, Solomon's men, to the arts of mining and metallurgy. Caravans coming from Arabia and laden with spices from that country were subjected to toll as they passed through Solomon's domain.

Legend and romance have conspired to transmit Solomon's name down through the ages as synonymous with might, splendour and wisdom. Even the jinn [4] did his bidding on land and in the air. The magnificence of his court attracted a South Arabian queen, Bilqīs of Moslem tradition. The ruling dynasty of Abyssinia claims descent from this union; its present representative includes among his official titles "lion of Judah". On "Solomon the wise" many proverbs have been fathered, some of which found their way into the canon.

The historical record fails to support this thesis. The kingdom inherited by Solomon was much larger than that bequeathed by him. Philistia acknowledged Pharaonic sovereignty. The Canaanite fortress Gezer was reduced by the Pharaoh whose daughter Solomon espoused and was handed over as a dowry for his daughter. This princess was one of a harem of 700 wives and 300 concubines.[5] Under the influence

[1] Tell al-Khulayfi at the head of the Gulf of al-ʿAqabah, excavated in 1938; Nelson Glueck, "The First Campaign at Tell el-Kheleifeh", *Bulletin, American Schools of Oriental Research*, No. 72 (1938), pp. 3-18. Today al-ʿAqabah is included in Transjordan (Jordan) but is still claimed by ibn-Suʿūd.

[2] 1 K. 9:27-8; 10:11; 2 Ch. 9:10.

[3] See above, p. 179, n. 2. It appears that by Moses' time they had become largely incorporated with the Midianites.

[4] Ar. *jinn*, in English confused with "genie", "genius", goes back to an Aramaic word meaning hidden.

[5] 1 K. 11:3.

of his harem he erected "high places" near Jerusalem for the worship of the deities of Sidon, Moab and Ammon.[1] Toward the end of his reign the Aramaean Rezon freed himself and his domain.[2] Before that the Edomite prince Hadad, whom David had chased from his province where he liquidated every male, returned to plague Solomon.[3] For his public works Solomon employed compulsory labour. In this unwise measure and in his lavish expenditure lay a prime cause of the popular discontent which under his successor led to the division of the kingdom.

The divided monarchy

Heretofore two separate peoples, Israel and Judah were brought into temporary union by David and Solomon. The economies of the two peoples were different. The northern people were agricultural, living on wheat, olives, vines and other produce of their fertile land; those of the south were in the main pastoral, living in highlands good for sheep and other flocks. Ephraim and the other northern tribes were more openly exposed to Canaanite influence. Their preference in worship seems to have been for Elohim (plural of El), whom they adored with solar rites and ritual derived from the older Canaanite cult. Judah and Benjamin in the south evidently preferred Jehovah, whose dwelling was the Temple of Jerusalem and whose worship was simpler. The immediate cause of the schism, however, was economic.

When upon Solomon's death, about 925 B.C., an assembly of the representatives of the twelve tribes met at Shechem to anoint his son Rehoboam king, the question was raised as to whether or not he was ready to pledge himself to lighten the burden of taxation. The answer of the sixteen-year-old lad was rash: "My father hath chastised you with whips, but I will chastise you with scorpions".[4] Thereupon the ten tribes refused to acknowledge Rehoboam and proceeded to elect Jeroboam of Ephraim, the spokesman of the assembly, as their king. These ten tribes constituted the kingdom of Israel, whose capital was first Shechem, then Tirzah and later Samaria. The two remaining tribes, Judah and Benjamin, who remained steadfast in their allegiance to Rehoboam, constituted the kingdom of Judah, with Jerusalem for capital.

The two kingdoms became rivals, at times enemies. They both had many ups and downs. The balance of power inclined

[1] I K. 11:5-8. [2] See above, p. 166. [3] I K. 11:14-22. [4] I K. 12:11.

now to Israel and now to Judah. The tendency to internal disintegration was illustrated by the frequent dynastic changes in Israel, which witnessed nineteen kings in its two centuries of existence, and by the repeated revolts and intrigues in both states. Such were the internal forces that finally brought about their undoing. Hebrews, like other Syrians, never took to heart the exclamation of their minstrel: "How good and how pleasant it is for brethren to dwell together in unity!"[1]

The kingdom of Israel

Most distinguished among the early monarchs of Israel was Omri (*ca.* 885–874), whose name (*ʿOmri*) indicates Arabian, very likely Nabataean, descent. His great monument was the city of Samaria,[2] which he founded and fortified and to which he transferred the seat of government from Tirzah.[3] In the new capital he built a palace which was enlarged and beautified by his son and successor Ahab. This is "the ivory house",[4] in which modern excavation revealed furnishings of ivory inlay much of which had evidently been covered with gold leaf. In that period the main school of ivory carvers flourished to the north, in Syria, where rich houses had cedar-lined rooms inlaid with ivory panels. David's and Solomon's palaces in Jerusalem probably had such cedar-lined rooms. The royal palace of Samaria is the only example of an Old Testament palace identified. Such was the impression left by Omri on his contemporaries that for a century after the extirpation of his dynasty, Assyrian annals continued to refer to Samaria as the "House of Ḥumri".

Ahab (*ca.* 874–852) lived on friendly terms with his neighbours but had difficulties at home. As an ally of Damascus he took a leading part in the indecisive battle of Qarqar.[5] He married Jezebel, forceful daughter of Ethbaal, king of Tyre and Sidon, who completely dominated her husband and attempted to impose the cult of the Tyrian Baal upon Israel.[6] This led to

[1] Ps. 133:1.

[2] Modern Sabasṭiyah, from Gr. Sebastos (august), the new name given to the town in honour of Augustus by Herod the Great when he rebuilt it in 27 B.C.; see below, p. 283.

[3] 1 K. 16:24. Samaria lay 6 miles north-west of Shechem. Site of Tirzah still unidentified; see "Tirzah", in John D. Davis, *The Westminster Dictionary of the Bible*, rev. Henry S. Gehman (Philadelphia, 1944); Abel, vol. ii, p. 485.

[4] 1 K. 22:39; Amos 3:15; 6:4; J. W. Crowfoot and Grace M. Crowfoot, *Early Ivories from Samaria* (London, 1938), pp. 1-6.

[5] See above, pp. 166-7.

[6] 1 K. 16:31; Josephus, *Antiquities*, Bk. IX, ch. 6, § 6.

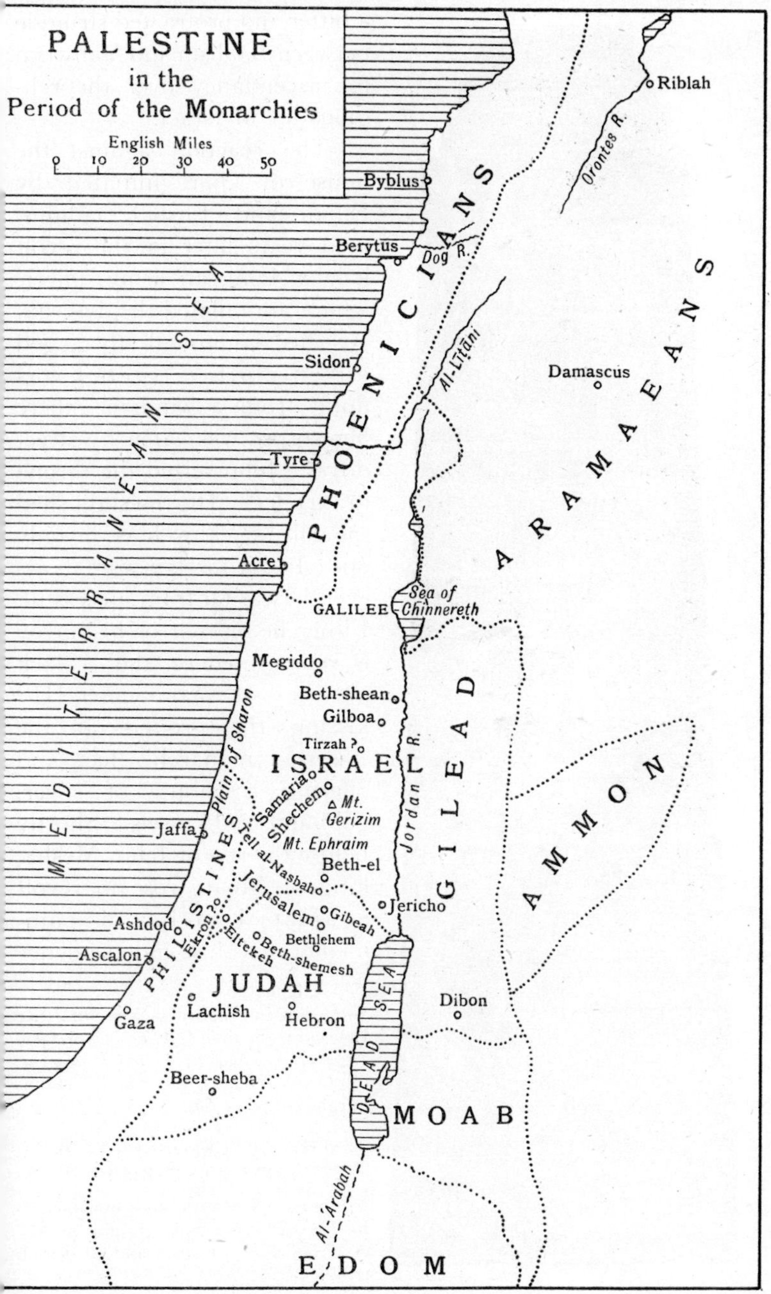
English Miles
0 10 20 30 40 50
MEDITERRANEAN SEA
PHOENICIANS
ARAMAEANS
Riblah
Orontes R.
Byblus
Berytus
Dog R.
Al-Lītāni
Sidon
Damascus
Tyre
Acre
GALILEE
Sea of Chinnereth
Megiddo
Beth-shean
Gilboa
Tirzah ?
ISRAEL
Jordan R.
GILEAD
AMMON
Plain of Sharon
Samaria
Shechem
Mt. Gerizim
Mt. Ephraim
Jaffa
Tell al-Nasbah
Beth-el
PHILISTINES
Jerusalem
Gibeah
Jericho
Ashdod
Ekron ?
Elteķeh
Bethlehem
Beth-shemesh
Ascalon
JUDAH
DEAD SEA
Lachish
Hebron
Dibon
Gaza
Beer-sheba
MOAB
Al-'Arabah
EDOM

PALESTINE in the Period of the Monarchies

British Museum

a bitter and protracted struggle between Baalism and Yahwism for ascendancy over the religious life of Israel.

The reaction against the house of Omri initiated by Elijah and Elishah culminated years later in the revolt led by Jehu, an army officer, which annihilated the dynasty. By his command the aged queen-mother Jezebel was flung from a window; there her corpse was eaten by street dogs.[1] Jehu seized the throne in 842 B.C. He re-established the cult of Yahweh as the only one. In his foreign wars, however, he was far from successful. Either he himself or his envoy is represented on the "black obelisk" of Shalmaneser III[2] kissing the ground at the Assyrian monarch's feet and offering a tribute of silver, gold and lead vessels. Shortly before the rise of Jehu, Mesha, king of Moab, rose in revolt against Israel and commemorated his independence

[1] 2 K. 9:33-5.

[2] Now in the British Museum. See Eberhard Schrader, *The Cuneiform Inscriptions and the Old Testament*, tr. O. W. Whitehouse, vol. i (Edinburgh, 1885), p. 199.

THE BLACK OBELISK OF SHALMANESER III

Jehu (*ca.* 842 B.C.), king of Israel, or his envoy kisses the ground at the Assyrian monarch's feet and offers rich tribute

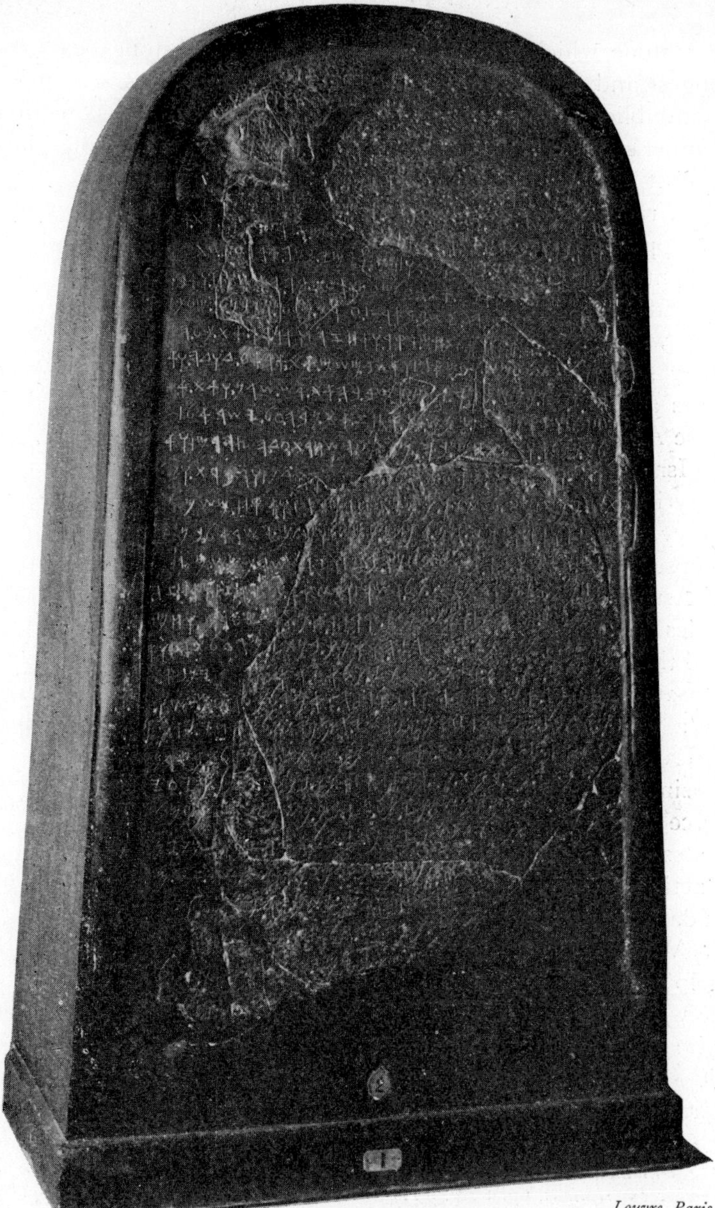

Louvre, Paris

MOABITE STONE COMMEMORATING THE VICTORY OF MESHA, KING OF MOAB, OVER ISRAEL

Erected shortly before 842 B.C.

in a stone which he set up at Dibon.[1] This stone bears the longest and one of the earliest Hebrew inscriptions. It differs from biblical Hebrew only dialectally. At about the same time another successful revolt, that of the Edomites, was taking place against Judah, showing the weakness of both states.

A rather unexpected manifestation of new strength makes its appearance under Jeroboam II (*ca.* 785–745), third in descent from Jehu. In his reign the northern boundary was pushed far at the expense of Aram.[2] Remains of the double wall with which he refortified Samaria have been unearthed. They show a thickness of thirty-three feet in places. What gives added distinction to his reign is the fact that toward its close Amos prophesied at Beth-el.[3]

Israel was able to enjoy a breathing spell mainly because Assyria was for the time being not in a position to pursue her policy of aggression. Imperial Egypt was likewise in a state of eclipse. With the rise of Tiglath-pileser III (747–727), restorer of Assyria's imperial power, the situation was changed. In a series of swift campaigns he reduced Damascus, Gilead, Galilee and the Plain of Sharon and made Assyrian provinces of them.[4] Unsatisfied with the old procedure of leaving the native ruler as a vassal, Tiglath-pileser inaugurated the policy of sending viceroys from Assyria to rule over the conquered territories.[5] Rezin, last king of Damascus, and Pekah of Israel had tried to force Ahaz of Jerusalem into line to form a confederacy of states against the common foe.[6] Israel was reduced to a fraction of its old self. Samaria paid a heavy tribute as did Judah and their neighbours Philistia, Ammon, Moab and Edom.

Israel's end

When a few years later Hoshea king of Israel, expecting help from Egypt, refused to continue the payment of tribute, he was attacked by Shalmaneser V, Tiglath-pileser's successor, who besieged the city for three years, so strong were its fortifications.[7] It yielded in 722 to 721 to his successor Sargon II, who carried away the cream of Israel's young manhood, 27,280

[1] Dhībān in Transjordan. The stone is now in the Louvre. Cooke, *North-Semitic Inscriptions*, pp. 1 *seq.* The characters are strictly Phoenician.

[2] 2 K. 14 : 25. See above, p. 167.

[3] " House of God ", Luz of the Canaanites ; its ruins, Baytīn, lie about 11 miles north of Jerusalem.

[4] 2 K. 15 : 29.

[5] Luckenbill, *Records*, vol. i, §§ 803, 805, 806, 809.

[6] See above, p. 167

[7] 2 K. 17 : 4.

persons, into captivity in Media.[1] The kingdom of Israel was forever destroyed. Those deported formed but a fraction of the 400,000 or so who constituted the population of the northern kingdom west of the Jordan. The "lost ten tribes" were never lost Those of them who were deported were generally assimilated. Search for them and claims of descent from them by certain groups in Great Britain and the United States are ludicrous. The twelfth century traveller Benjamin of Tudela showed better historical judgment when he wrote that the Jewish congregation in the mountains of Nīshāpūr in eastern Persia are descendants of the original exiles.[2]

The Samaritans

To the policy of deportation — transplanting those who constituted a thorn in Assyria's side — Sargon and his successors added that of colonization. To replace those Israelites carried into captivity, they brought tribes from Babylonia, Elam, Syria and Arabia and settled them in Samaria and its territory.[3] The new immigrants intermingled with the Israelites to form the Samaritans. Their religious beliefs were also combined with the worship of Jehovah.[4] The final rift between the two communities took place around 432 B.C., after Ezra and Nehemiah had returned from the exile, advocated racial purity and chased from Jerusalem a grandson of the high priest for marrying the daughter of the Samaritan governor.[5] The expelled young man evidently became the priest of the Samaritans and a rival temple was built for him on Mount Gerizim. At that time the Jewish canon consisted of the Pentateuch only. Therefore this part of the Old Testament has ever remained the only sacred book of the Samaritans. They transmit it in a variety of archaic Hebrew characters. To them Gerizim, not Zion, is the true sanctuary.

Antipathy between Jews and Samaritans increased as the years rolled on. Intermarriage has never been permissible. One of the most interesting dialogues of Christ was with a Samaritan woman who was surprised that he as a Jew would

[1] 2 K. 17 : 6; Schrader, vol. i, p. 264; Julius Oppert in *Records of the Past*, vol. vii (London, 1876), p. 28.

[2] *The Itinerary of Rabbi Benjamin of Tudela*, ed. A. Asher (London, 1840), p. 83; tr., p. 129.

[3] Luckenbill, vol. ii, §§ 17, 118; 2 K. 17 : 24. Samaria takes its name probably from Shemer (guard, watcher, 1 K. 16 : 24).

[4] 2 K. 17 : 25-33.

[5] Neh. 13 : 28; cf. Josephus, *Antiquities*, Bk. XI, ch. 7, § 2; ch. 8, §§ 2, 4; see below, p. 246.

ask a drink of her.[1] In one of his most beautiful parables Christ chose a despised Samaritan as the hero of a story in which he played a noble part.[2] During the persecution of Antiochus Epiphanes (175–164 B.C.), the Samaritans suffered equally with the Jews [3] in spite of their seeming willingness to compromise and dedicate their temple on Mount Gerizim to Zeus.[4]

Like a fossil this community has survived through the ages until the present day. It is represented now by about two hundred individuals living in Nābulus, ancient Shechem. In the Middle Ages Samaritan congregations flourished in Gaza, Cairo, Damascus and other towns. Arabic is their language today. On Passover tourists who happen to be in Nābulus may still see them sacrifice the Paschal lamb.

The kingdom of Judah

The throne of Judah witnessed as many kings as those of Israel, nineteen, but the southern kingdom outlived the northern by about a century and a third. Noteworthy among the early political events was the invasion by an Egyptian Pharaoh. Taking advantage of the division of the kingdom, Shishonk (biblical Shishak), a Libyan who established Dynasty XXII, penetrated the land (*ca.* 920), destroyed cities, sacked Jerusalem and carried off as booty all the treasures of the Temple and the palace.[5] Rehoboam was in no position to repel the invasion. A daughter of this Pharaoh married Jeroboam; a daughter of his predecessor had married Solomon.

In the eighth century Judah no less than Israel profited by the lull in the Assyrian and Egyptian imperial aggressiveness. The long reign of Uzziah (sometimes called Azariah, *ca.* 782–*ca.* 751) marks an upward trend in the kingdom's fortunes. He reorganized the army, repaired the fortifications of Jerusalem, won victories over Philistines and Arabians and received tribute from the Ammonites and other foes.[6] His interests transcended military affairs. He promoted agriculture by digging cisterns and protected his flocks in the wilderness by building towers which exist to this day, identified by dated potsherds.[7]

Hezekiah

The removal of Israel from the way in 721 exposed Judah to more direct attacks from Assyria. A few years after that, early in the reign of Hezekiah (721–693), it became a tributary.

[1] John 4:9. [2] Lk. 10:30-37. [3] 2 Macc. 5:23; see below, pp. 244, 246.
[4] 2 Macc. 6:2; Josephus, *Antiquities*, Bk. XII, ch. 5, § 5.
[5] Eg. Shishonk. 1 K. 14:25-6; Breasted, *Records*, vol. iv, §§ 709 *seq.*
[6] 2 Ch. 26:6-8. [7] 2 Ch. 26:9-10.

Incited by Egypt and heedless of Isaiah's warning, Hezekiah embarked upon a policy of defiance and entered into an alliance with the Philistine cities and other neighbouring states. In anticipation of a siege he dug a 1700-foot conduit through the rock to insure a supply of water to his capital.[1] This is the Siloam tunnel, on the wall of which a six-line Hebrew inscription was incidentally discovered, indicating that the digging was undertaken from both ends and with remarkable precision: "While yet [the miners were lifting up] the pick one toward another and while there were yet three cubits to be [bored, there was heard] the voice of each calling to the other, for there was a split in the rock".[2]

Consequently a series of campaigns and punitive expeditions were conducted by the energetic Sargon and his successor Sennacherib (705–681) against Phoenicia, the Philistine cities and Judah culminating in the siege of Jerusalem in 701. After capturing Sidon and Acre and receiving the submission of envoys from Ashdod, Ammon, Moab and Edom, Sennacherib proceeded along the Philistine coast, reducing Jaffa and other cities as far south as Ascalon and the Egyptian border. Then he turned east and captured Lachish. Tyre and Ekron[3] held out. Hearing that the Egyptian army was advancing north and deeming it unwise to leave so mighty a stronghold as Jerusalem in his rear, the Assyrian invader sent a detachment to Jerusalem and himself marched with the rest southward. At Eltekeh[4] he joined battle with the combined Egyptian and Ethiopian forces, led by the twenty-year-old Tirhakah (Taharqa), and repulsed their advance. But before he could turn his full force against Jerusalem "the angel of the Lord went out, and smote it"[5] destroying "185,000" in one night. This must have been the bubonic plague, the same that afflicted the Napoleonic army in that region in 1799[6] and that has often harassed the Moslem pilgrims.

Jerusalem did not fall but the countryside was laid waste. Isaiah and the king evidently believed that Jehovah would

[1] 2 K. 20:20; 2 Ch. 32:2.

[2] Cooke, *North-Semitic Inscriptions*, p. 15. The characters do not differ much from those of the Moabite Stone.

[3] Represented today by 'Aqīr, 6 miles west of Gezer.

[4] Probably Khirbat al-Muqanna', about 6 miles south-east of 'Aqīr.

[5] 2 K. 19:35; Herodotus, Bk. II, ch. 141.

[6] See below, p. 690.

under all conditions protect his city.[1] Hezekiah was permitted to retain his throne but he had to pay the arrears of tribute and, after Sennacherib's return to Nineveh, to send his own daughters as well as other palace women and rich treasures. Sennacherib boastfully sums up his achievement in the following words:

As for Hezekiah, the Jew, who had not submitted to my yoke, 46 of his strong, walled cities and the cities of their environs, which were numberless I besieged, I captured, I plundered, as booty I counted them. Him, like a caged bird, in Jerusalem, his royal city, I shut up. . . . That Hezekiah, — the terrifying splendor of my royalty overcame him.[2]

The "200,150 men" whom he claims to have "carried off" must refer to the estimated population in Judah whom he regarded as spoil.

Josiah's reforms

Judah was left in a weakened and reduced condition as a result of this invasion. In the first three-quarters of the seventh century it continued as a submissive vassal of mighty Nineveh, paying tribute regularly. No sooner, however, did it sense weakness on the Tigris than it began to bestir itself. That is what happened under Josiah, who had come to the throne about 638, when eight years old. In his reign the kingdom expanded northward in an attempt to reunite Israel with Judah. The fall of Nineveh in 612 into the hands of the Neo-Babylonians (Chaldaeans) encouraged Egypt to push once more the frontiers of its empire into North Syria. Accordingly Pharaoh Necho advanced at the head of his army northward along the coast. Josiah, who apparently considered himself a vassal of Assyria's heir, Neo-Babylonia, marched to oppose the Egyptian advance and was mortally wounded (*ca.* 608) by an arrow on the memorable battlefield of Megiddo.[3]

Josiah won immortal fame as a religious reformer. In 621 as repairs were being made in the Temple a copy of a book was found which must have been Deuteronomy or the significant part of it. That book was evidently lost sight of during the periods of apostasy and persecution, particularly that of Manasseh (693–639),[4] Hezekiah's son. The reading of the

[1] 2 K. 19:6-7, 20.

[2] Luckenbill, vol. ii, § 312; cf. Schrader, vol. i, pp. 286, 297; J. M. Rodwell in *Records of the Past*, vol. vii (London, 1876), p. 62.

[3] 2 K. 23:29-30; 2 Ch. 35:20-24; cf. Herodotus, Bk. II, ch. 159.

[4] 2 K. 21:16; 2 Ch. 33:9.

book so deeply affected the king and his people that they covenanted to worship Yahweh, and Yahweh only, burned the vessels of Baal and of the deified heavenly bodies that were in the Temple, destroyed the adjoining houses of sodomites and demolished the "high places" throughout Judah and even Israel.[1]

Last days of Judah

Judah after this vacillated between the policy of submission to the new power on the Euphrates and that of alliance with the old one on the Nile. Josiah's son Jehoiakim (608–597) chose the latter course.[2] Originally an appointee to the throne by Necho, he defied Nebuchadnezzar, whose father Nabopolassar had headed the successful revolution which, with the aid of the Medes, had destroyed Nineveh and founded the Neo-Babylonian empire. Nebuchadnezzar, while still a general in his father's army, had given a demonstration of his military ability by crushingly defeating Necho at Carchemish in 605 and wresting from Egypt all her Asiatic possessions.[3] This was the turning-point of the age. The long-drawn struggle for supremacy in Western Asia was finally settled. Babylon under the Chaldaeans was to be the dominant and undisputed power in that area's affairs.

Jehoiakim was no match for Nebuchadnezzar, whose army entered Jerusalem in 597 and bound the rebel king with chains to carry him to Babylon.[4] But he either died or was murdered and his body was cast off beyond the gates of Jerusalem. Jeremiah, who wrote a roll against Jehoiakim which the king had cut up with a penknife and committed to the flames,[5] had prophesied that Jehoiakim would be buried "with the burial of an ass".[6] Nebuchadnezzar's inscription at the Dog River dates from shortly before this event and duplicates his inscription on a rock at Wādi Barissa (Brissa), west of Riblah, where Nebuchadnezzar in one place stands before a cedar tree and in another wards off a springing lion.[7]

The son and successor Jehoiachin was no wiser than the father. He occupied the throne three months in 597, when Nebuchadnezzar appeared in person at the gates of his capital.

[1] 2 K. 23 : 1-25; 2 Ch. 34 : 29 to 35 : 18.
[2] 2 K. 23 : 34; 2 Ch. 36 : 4 *seq.*
[3] 2 K. 24 : 7.
[4] 2 Ch. 36 : 6.
[5] Jer. 36 : 21-3.
[6] Jer. 22 : 19; cf. Josephus, *Antiquities*, Bk. X, ch. 6, § 3.
[7] 2 K. 24 : 8-16; 2 Ch. 36 : 9-10; Dussaud, *Topographie*, p. 95; see above, pp. 134, 144.

After a brief siege the city surrendered. The youthful Jehoiachin with his wives, mother, officials, 7000 of his soldiers and 1000 of his skilful artisans was carried off to Babylon. Ezekiel was among the religious leaders taken captives. Jehoiachin's uncle Zedekiah, a son of Josiah, was appointed king by Nebuchadnezzar.

Fall of Jerusalem

The twenty-one-year-old Zedekiah (597–586) remained professedly loyal to Nebuchadnezzar for a number of years, after which he yielded to the chronic temptation and struck for independence. In this he responded to the urge of his nationalist leaders and as usual counted on Egyptian aid. Exasperated, Nebuchadnezzar dispatched an army intent upon the destruction of Jerusalem, which was put under siege. The siege was temporarily raised on the approach of an Egyptian expeditionary force under Hophra [1] but was soon pressed again. After a year and a half the garrison was exhausted and the city walls were breached in 586. Under cover of night its king stole away with his men of war but was pursued and overtaken in the plain of Jericho. Brought to Nebuchadnezzar's headquarters at Riblah,[2] he saw his sons slain before his eyes, which were then put out so that the tragic sight would be the last one registered through them. The blind monarch was then fettered and carried to Babylon.[3] As for Jerusalem, it was destroyed with its Temple. The leading inhabitants of the city and the country, estimated at 50,000, were carried into captivity. Only a miserable remnant was left behind. Almost every important town in Judah was laid waste [4] and so remained for centuries. By 582 Nebuchadnezzar had completed the reconquest of Judah's neighbours with the exception of Tyre which held out under siege till 572.[5] Its king and defender was Ethbaal III, who in 574 gave way to Baal II. A faint revolt by Tyre in 564 was easily dealt with. All Syria was now secure in Chaldaean hands.

1 "Apries" of Herodotus, Bk. II, ch. 161; Diodorus, Bk. I, ch. 68.

2 See above, p. 144.

3 2 K. 25:1-7; 2 Ch. 36:11-20; Jer. ch. 39; 52:4-11, 27.

4 Jer. 39:8-10; 52:12-30; 2 Ch. 36:17-21; Josephus, *Antiquities*, Bk. X, 11; *Apion*, Bk. I, ch. 21.

5 See above, p. 144.

CHAPTER XV

ASPECTS OF CULTURAL AND SPIRITUAL LIFE: MONOTHEISM

IN their early career in Palestine the Hebrews followed the culture pattern of the Near East as exemplified by the Canaanites. Canaan imparted to Israel its language and its alphabet, as we learned before.[1] As the Israelites became domiciled in their new abode, they forsook their old Semitic dialect in favour of that of the people among whom they settled. Since their dialect was only a spoken one, they had to wait until they acquired the art of writing from their neighbours before they could produce a literature.

Canaan taught Israel farming. The Hebrews entered the land as Bedouins. Their passage from the pastoral to the agricultural stage was effected after their settlement. In the hill country of Judah many of their descendants continued to pursue the pastoral way of life, but in the fertile plain to the north agriculture became the chief source of livelihood.

Borrowed ritual

With farming and through intermarriage the Hebrews acquired from the Canaanites those religious ideas and practices considered essential for fertility and for insuring good crops. This meant taking over, almost wholesale, a body of old rites and ceremonies including wooden poles,[2] "high places", serpent worship [3] and the golden calf.[4] The belief that the proper way to worship was to sacrifice an animal and to offer at the sanctuary gifts from the products of field and flock was universal among the peoples of Syria and Mesopotamia. David's dance before the Ark [5] was a reflex of a Canaanite fertility dance. Its relics persist in the ritualistic rhythmic movements of modern dervishes.

The ritual prohibitions in the Pentateuch imply that before they were prohibited those practices were adopted by the

[1] Pp. 79, 164, 169.
[2] *ashērāhs*; see above, pp. 120 *seq.*
[3] See above, pp. 121 *seq.*; 2 K. 18:4.
[4] 1 K. 12:28-9; 2 Ch. 13:8.
[5] 2 Sam. 6:14.

Hebrews from their neighbours and later considered by the leaders as inconsistent with the tendencies of the Hebrew religion. The taboo against seething a kid in its mother's milk [1] seemed strange and was wrongly explained until the Ugarit literature revealed that this was practised there.

The acknowledgment of Yahweh as the supreme deity by right of conquest did not preclude considering the local deities as controllers of the productivity of the land. Yahweh's jurisdiction was over the state; affairs of ordinary life — agriculture, trade — were not his primary concern. At times, especially in the northern part of the kingdom, Jehovah acquired many attributes of Baal which made him lord of heaven, sender of rain, controller of storms. Hebrew parents often named their first-born after Yahweh, but the younger after Baal. The proportion of Hebrew names compounded with Baal increases steadily through the early period. Saul names his son Esh-baal (the man of Baal); Jonathan, Merib-baal (Baal contends); and David, Beeliada (Baal knows).[2] Yahweh had such a rival in this Canaanite deity that in the time of Ahab and Jezebel [3] there were only 7000 who had not bent knees to Baal, a number, however, which seems to have gratified Elijah.

Art

The Canaanite origin of Hebrew religious art and architecture is unmistakable. The Temple of Solomon, the only religious monumental structure of the ancient Hebrews, was not only built by Tyrian architects but modelled after a Canaanite sanctuary. Its decoration followed Canaanite models. The royal palace of Jerusalem was also the product of Phoenician craftsmanship.[4] The two cherubs, in the form of human-headed animals guarding the tree of life, represent an ancient Semitic motif. Our conception of the cherub as a tiny winged boy goes back through Renaissance art ultimately not to the Assyrian winged bull, as supposed by some, but to the Syrian winged sphinx or winged lion with human head. The veil of the Tabernacle and the walls of Solomon's Temple were decorated with cherubim. The Israelites conceived of their God as standing or enthroned on a cherub.[5]

The ritual of the Temple called forth musical performance.[6]

[1] Ex. 23:19; 34:26.

[2] 1 Ch. 8:33-4; 9:39-40; 14:7.

[3] See above, pp. 192, 194; 1 K. 19:18.

[4] See above, p. 189.

[5] 2 Sam. 22:11; Ps. 18:10.

[6] 1 Ch. 25.

Its first musicians and singers were Canaanite in personnel or in training. When David initiated and Solomon developed Hebrew sacred music, there was no pattern to follow but the Canaanite. Even the musical guilds of later Israel delighted in tracing their origin to families with Canaanite names.[1] A sketch of a woman from Megiddo playing the harp proves that that instrument was known in Palestine a couple of thousand

1

2

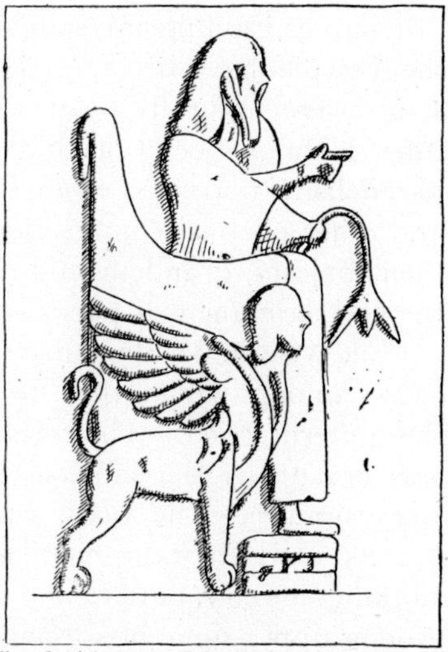

From " The Biblical Archaeologist ", vol. i (American Schools of Oriental Research)

FIG. 1. A CHERUB OF RAPHAEL, FROM HIS SISTINE MADONNA. FIG. 2. A CHERUB OF PHOENICIAN TIMES, SUPPORTING THE THRONE OF KING AḤĪRĀM OF BYBLUS

years before David. The author of Genesis [2] acknowledges the antiquity of the musical instruments of his people by crediting an early descendant of Cain with being " the father of all such as handle the harp and organ ". Once acquired, the instruments were naturally used for profane as well as sacred music.

Foremost among the percussion instruments of the Israelites stood the hand drum, to which there are many biblical references.[3] The wind instruments were represented by the pipe or

[1] Albright, *Archaeology and the Religion of Israel*, pp. 14, 126-7.
[2] 4:21.
[3] Ex. 15:20; Judg. 11:34; 1 Sam. 18:6; Ps. 68:25.

flute and the trumpet. The pipe was a simple reed, single or double, of the type still used by Syrian shepherds. The trumpet, shofar, was made from the horn of a ram or goat and is still in current use in Hebrew synagogues.[1] Among the stringed instruments the lyre became a favourite. We have no idea about the tunes played on those instruments.

With the music went songs. One of the earliest preserved is the song of Deborah celebrating an Israelite victory over Canaanites.[2] Pilgrim songs of ascent, used on the way to the Temple, have become incorporated in many Psalms.[3] The songs were naturally poetic compositions. Parallelism constitutes Hebrew poetry as it does the poetry of Ugarit.[4] It is parallelism, borrowed from Canaanites, that gives the Psalms and other poetical compositions of the Old Testament much of their majesty, grandeur and rhythmic cadence. Almost half of the Old Testament is poetical in structure.

Domestic affairs

Likewise in secular affairs Hebrews copied the manners of those among whom they became domiciled and with whom they intermarried. Their general view of life and of after-life was practically the same as that of Canaan. Burial customs were similar. The body was laid in a tomb together with objects used in daily life, such as dishes and jars.[5] Their clothing, jewelry, pottery and crafts followed Canaanite fashions. A long upper tunic of special character was worn by kings and prophets and later adopted by women. The linen wrapping was also worn by the better class and consisted of rectangular pieces of thin linen.[6]

Spinning and weaving were home industries generally conducted for personal consumption. The Hebrew wise man includes in his description of the good wife that " she seeketh wool, and flax, and worketh willingly with her hands ".[7] The many loom weights found in Kirjath-sepher [8] and the fragments of wooden looms and dying vats found at Lachish indicate the existence of professionals who produced for public consumption.[9] Both cities were early Canaanite centres. In no art other than

[1] See Curt Sachs, *The History of Musical Instruments* (New York, 1940), pp. 110-12.

[2] Judg. ch. 5.

[3] Ps. 120-34.

[4] See above, p. 115.

[5] See above, pp. 123-7.

[6] Cf. above, pp. 91-2.

[7] Prov. 31 : 13.

[8] " City of books ", modern Tell Bayt Mirsim, 13 miles south-west of Hebron.

[9] Consult Barrois, *Manuel*, vol. i, pp. 482-7.

gem cutting did Hebrew craftsmen excel. Seals from the period of monarchy reveal a high degree of proficiency in that art. Biblical references to families of scribes and of weavers and to sons of goldsmiths [1] suggest some kind of loose organizations, corresponding to guilds, which united members of the same profession for mutual economic and social or religious benefit.[2]

Linen cloth was made from native flax. This ancient plant flourished very early along the eastern Mediterranean and in Egypt. It grew in the plain of Jericho before the occupation by Hebrews.[3] The common flax has practically vanished from Palestine, but wild flowers belonging to the flax family still colour the spring landscape of Syria and Lebanon.[4] Cotton was introduced after linen, but wool was used long before. Home-grown and home-woven wool provided the everyday garment of the prosperous middle class.

The Gezer calendar [5] of the mid-tenth century mentions — besides flax — wheat, olives and grapes. The land promised by Jehovah was " a land of wheat, and barley, and vines, and fig trees, and pomegranates ; a land of oil olive, and honey ".[6] Wheat stood high in importance among the cereals. Enemy raids were often directed against the threshing floors,[7] as they still are. Small millstones for grinding flour have been excavated in many sites. The ovens found at Beth-shemesh indicate that certain bread-making customs have been continued into the present day where *tannūrs* are used.[8] The remains of presses for oil and for wine are quite common.[9] Olive pits have been found in such quantities at Lachish as to indicate that this industry was a major one in the period of the monarchy. The Hebrews adopted the Canaanite lamp [10] which burned with olive oil and used it exclusively for about seven centuries. The earliest foreign lamp, an importation from Mesopotamia of about 500 B.C., was found at Beth-shemesh

[1] 1 Ch. 2 : 55 ; 4 : 21 ; Neh. 3 : 8, 31 ; cf. Amos 7 : 14 ; see above, p. 86.

[2] See above, pp. 86-7.

[3] Josh. 2 : 6.

[4] George E. Post, *Flora of Syria, Palestine and Sinai* (Beirut [1896]), pp. 181-184.

[5] See above, pp. 91-2.

[6] Deut. 8 : 8.

[7] 1 Sam. 23 : 1.

[8] Elihu Grant, *Rumeileh*, p. 49 ; do., *The People of Palestine* (Philadelphia, 1921), pp. 78 *seq.* ; see above, p. 148, n. 2.

[9] For illustrations consult Elihu Grant, *Ain Shems Excavations*, pt. 1 (Haverford, 1931), pp. 27, 78 ; *Rumeileh*, pl. vii.

[10] See above, p. 86.

and showed improvement in having a handle on the side and a cover at the top with a hole for the wick. A jar in the form of a conical hive found at Tell al-Naṣbah illustrates the practice of bee-keeping.[1] Biblical references to onions, garlic, beans, lentils, cucumbers, coriander and other vegetables and cereals indicate that the eating habits of the Hebrews did not differ much from those of their neighbours.[2] Peas and lentils were prized for pottage.[3]

The grape-vine and its products figured prominently in Hebrew ritual and economics. The plant itself signified fertility.[4] Wine was used as an offering in the Temple.[5] In art vines and grapes figured on mosaics and sculptures of early synagogues and burial-places. The pomegranate also was used in decoration and its juice was favoured as a cooling drink.[6]

Among flowers the lily[7] was regarded as the choicest. It figured in the Temple decoration and later on coins. The Song of Solomon abounds in references to this and other plants. The term may have been applied extensively to include the anemone and the daisy, which still spread in spring a carpet of gorgeous colour over the Syrian landscape. Christ must have had one of these in mind when he said it was more gaily attired than "Solomon in all his glory".[8]

Coinage

Coined or stamped money was not introduced into Palestine until the fifth pre-Christian century. Before the introduction of coinage the Babylonian system based on the shekel as a unit of weight was used.[9] When business transactions were not carried out by barter, they were conducted by means of the balance. Weights of various sorts modelled on the shekel system have been discovered in various sites.

In the early fifth century Athenian silver money, which had become almost an international currency, found its way into the Near East and was imitated in Palestine and Arabia.[10] The

[1] Burrows, p. 172. Tell al-Naṣbah, about 8 miles north of Jerusalem and 2 miles south of al-Bīrah, has been identified by many scholars with Mizpah (1 K. 15:22; 1 Sam. 7:5-16); see "Mizpah", *Westminster Dictionary*.

[2] Num. 11:5; 2 Sam. 17:28; Ezek. 4:9; Is. 1:8; Ex. 16:31; Num. 11:7.

[3] Gen. 25:30.

[4] Num. 15:5.

[5] Lev. 23:13; Num. 15:5 *seq*.

[6] Song 8:2.

[7] *shōshannāh*, whence Susanna; Song 2:1-2, 16; 4:5; 6:3.

[8] Matt. 6:28.

[9] See above, pp. 87-8.

[10] Hitti, *History of the Arabs*, pp. 57-8.

earliest Hebrew coin yet found belongs to the mid-fifth century and was perhaps struck by Nehemiah.

Religious teachers

If the Hebrew contribution to world progress did not lie in the field of art, politics or economics, wherein did it then lie? It lay in one field only, religion. It was the religious contribution that made the Hebrews the ethical and moral teachers of mankind. Their entire genius manifests itself in the Old Testament.

No equally remarkable or significant piece of literature has

From "A Hebrew Shekel of the Fifth Century", by Dr. A. Reifenberg ("Palestine Exploration Quarterly", vol. 75)

A HEBREW SHEKEL OF THE FIFTH PRE-CHRISTIAN CENTURY, THE OLDEST HEBREW COIN KNOWN

The obverse has a bearded head wearing a fillet. The reverse shows a female head, perhaps that of Aphrodite-Ashtart, wearing an ear-ring which at the same time represents the Hebrew letter *ʿayin*, which is the last letter of the inscription below: BQʿ (*beqaʿ*), one-half

come down to us from pre-Christian antiquity. More than a piece of literature, the Old Testament is the monument of a civilization. Other literary relics of ancient civilizations, after lying dead for countless generations, have been handed down to us through modern excavation; this one was transmitted by uninterrupted tradition. Throughout the ages the Old Testament has ever remained a dynamic force in the lives of men and women. The material itself passed through many processes — selection, elimination, editing — before it assumed its final form. A certain unity pervades it throughout. There was never a time in which this material was not made the object of intensive study.

Artists, poets and writers in ancient, medieval and modern times have never ceased to draw inspiration from biblical themes. Almost all civilized tongues bear the stamp of biblical allusions and biblical ideology.

A variety of teachers, besides historians, contributed to the authorship of the Old Testament. There was first of all the lawgiver, personified in Moses, who spoke as the mouthpiece of Jehovah. The Mosaic law, as given by God through Moses,[1] had its counterpart in the Hammurabi laws, which though more than half a millennium older reflect a higher stage, industrial and commercial, as opposed to the pastoral and agricultural stage of the Hebrews. In the Hammurabi code the slave is freed in the fourth year;[2] in the Mosaic code in the seventh year.[3] In Hammurabi the restitution ranges from two to three fold;[4] in the covenant, four to five.[5] Smiting a parent is punished in Hammurabi by mutilation;[6] in Moses, by death.[7] Hammurabi inflicts punishment on bribed judges;[8] Moses only forbids bribery.[9] Both systems codify existing practices and incorporate the Bedouin element of blood revenge according to the "eye for an eye" principle,[10] which marks a higher step than the earlier practice of unlimited revenge. Both Hammurabi and Moses receive their codes from on high, one from Shamash and the other from Jehovah; but the moral element in the Mosaic code as embodied in the Decalogue is unequalled in any other code. No one but Christ has ever been able to improve on those Ten Commandments. In them prohibition goes beyond the realm of action into thought and involves covetousness.

Another Hebrew teacher was the priest, *kōhēn*, who taught the law but performed more than taught. The priest officiated at the altar and in other rites, thus functioning as a mediator between man and God. Priests formed a distinct class among the nations of antiquity, and in the case of the Hebrews priesthood was hereditary in the family of Aaron and restricted to it.[11]

[1] Ex. 20:19-22; Matt. 15:4.

[2] Robert W. Rogers, "The Code of Hammurabi", in *Cuneiform Parallels to the Old Testament* (New York, 1912), § 117.

[3] Ex. 21:2; Deut. 15:12.

[4] Rogers, §§ 120, 124.

[5] Ex. 22:1.

[6] § 195.

[7] Ex. 21:15.

[8] § 5.

[9] Ex. 23:8; Deut. 16:18-19.

[10] Ex. 21:24; Deut. 19:21; Lev. 24:20; Hammurabi, §§ 196, 197, 200.

[11] Ex. 28:1; Num. 16:40.

Still another teacher was the wise man. The Hebrew sage addressed himself to the individual rather than to the community and his message was the achievement of success rather than winning the favour of the deity. Unlike law, wisdom proceeded from man; it was the product of his own observation and experience. The great books of Hebrew wisdom are Job, Proverbs and Ecclesiastes, and the greatest among them — indeed, among any books of wisdom literature — is undoubtedly Job.

The author of Job was not only an unequalled wise man but an unsurpassed poet also. Hebrew poetry, like all other poetry, represented utterance born of strong feeling and cast into a particular form.[1] The lyric poet was the commonest in Israel. As a minstrel he sought by his triumphal odes to celebrate the deliverance wrought by Jehovah; as a psalmist he expressed the emotions of a penitent suing for mercy or expressing joy for forgiveness,[2] or those of a weak man crying out in distress or praising God for succour.[3] The poet was also a teacher in Israel.

The prophets

Especially significant among the teachers was the prophet. By "prophet" is meant here not one who foretells future events but one who speaks for another, in this case God. This is the etymological meaning of the term.[4] It is with the prophets that the Hebrew religion begins.

Prophetism arose as a protest against Baalism and other alien cults. On the positive side its object was to uphold the religion of Jehovah. The prophets were the champions of Jehovah. Starting from this as a base, the prophets of Israel worked their way into a lofty and sublime realm of spiritual thinking. They in effect produced a new religion, a monotheistic one, centring on one and only one supreme and universal deity. This one God, the prophets taught, was an ethical, righteous being. More than that, he expects his followers to be ethical and righteous like him. Such a deity rejoices not in sacrifice but in ethical living. Conduct rather than cult interests him. An exclusive ethical monotheism was the cardinal principle in this prophetic teaching.

[1] See above, p. 206. [2] Ps. 51; 32. [3] Ps. 3; 38; 23.

[4] The Hebrew word for prophet, *nābī'*, is Arabic in form and means announcer. The stem is an ancient Semitic one occurring in Akkadian *nabu*, to call.

Amidst a world all of whose religions consisted of a series of acts and observances, the correct performance of which was considered essential for the securing of the god's favour or the averting of his anger, stood these new teachers with a novel interpretation of God, man and their interrelationship. Their objective was not the salvation of the soul [1] but the development of the individual and the preservation of society. They became the exponents of social justice. No religious teachers of Babylon, Khatti or Greece made such an attempt at associating morality with religion or considering the rules of social conduct as divine ordinances. The moral element in the Book of the Dead and other pieces of Egyptian literature is very faint indeed in comparison. Christ built on the foundation of prophetic, rather than legal or priestly, Hebraism. Muḥammad continued on the joint structure. It is no exaggeration then to claim that Hebrew prophetism "ushered in the greatest movement in the spiritual history of mankind".[2]

Not only did prophetic thinking produce a new concept of the nature of God and His attributes and of man's relation to God and to man, but it produced a new type of literature, strophic, rhythmic and effective. A great deal of its oral effect is, of course, lost through translation. The mass of prophetic literature made its appearance between 750 and 550 B.C.

The Babylonians, the Assyrians, the Egyptians, the Greeks at their best achieved henotheism, a belief in one god as supreme though not to the exclusion of belief in other gods. In worship they attained monolatry, worship of but one deity, although more than one was recognized as co-existent. That some prayed to Marduk, Aton [3] or Apollo as though for the time being no other god existed does not make them monotheists. Monotheism is a militant, aggressive system of belief that denies not only the jurisdiction of other deities in limited fields but the very existence of any other deities. Its god cannot be tribal or national; he has to be international, universal. Henotheism

[1] Of the ancient peoples only the Egyptians had an elaborate scheme of life after death. Sheol, the Hebrew abode of the dead, was vague and undefined, with no official plan. The righteous and the wicked went to it, but particularly the wicked, and passed a dull inactive existence. See Gen. 37:35; 1 Sam. 2:6; Ps. 9:17; 6:5; 31:17; Ecc. 9:10; Is. 14:9; cf. Is. 26:19; Dan. 12:2.

[2] Julius A. Bewer, *The Literature of the Old Testament in its Historical Development* (New York, 1926), p. 87.

[3] See above, p. 72, n. 5.

is an intermediary step between polytheism and monotheism.

Moses was a henotheist, and so was David. To them Jehovah was god of the Hebrews only. His jurisdiction was over the land of Israel.[1] This intimate connection between god and land was not peculiarly Hebraic; it was recognized by their contemporaries. It was not until the dawn of the prophetic period that the Hebrew Jehovah, who started his career as a tribal deity rejoicing in the infliction of cruel measures upon the Egyptian oppressors of his people and then became a national deity authorizing the extermination of Amorites and Canaanites [2] and ordering the slaughter of hundreds of his rival's priests,[3] was raised into a unique position as the only deity throughout the world and as one endowed with love, righteousness, mercy and forgiveness. How this evolution took place is not easy to explain. According to the antique system of reasoning when a tribe or a people succeeds in conquering another it is proof positive that the god of the conqueror is more powerful; automatically the conquered people accept him. The Hebrew prophets did not follow that line of reasoning. While the Assyrian armies were subjecting Jehovah's people, his prophets were teaching that Jehovah was simply using Ashur as an instrument of punishment against his own people because they had transgressed. Thus was defeat turned into victory and Jehovah's position was not only maintained but raised a notch higher to a supreme and unique position of universality.

Amos, the first monotheist

That a shepherd and dresser of sycamore trees from an insignificant village in Judah and the neighbouring wilderness should be the first in the history of thought to conceive of God in terms of oneness and universality seems incredible. This was Amos of Tekoa,[4] who proclaimed his message about 750 B.C. Amos was a speaking, not a writing, prophet; so was Muḥammad. Maybe he was illiterate. He expounded his thesis in the kingdom of the north under Jeroboam II, whose conquests had brought new riches and new luxuries to the Israelite society.[5] Amos was the first to look upon Jehovah as god of peoples other than the Israelites [6] and as a god of

[1] Deut. 28:64.

[2] Josh. 10:8-42; see above, p. 179.

[3] 1 K. 18:36-40; cf. Deut. 13:13-17; 17:2-5.

[4] The name still lingers in Khirbat Taqūʿ, Taqūʿah, a ruined village 6 miles south of Bethlehem.

[5] See above, p. 196.

[6] Amos 9:5-7.

social righteousness. These are the words he put into the mouth of Yahweh (chapter 5):

21 I hate, I despise your feast days,
And I will not smell in your solemn assemblies.
22 Though ye offer me burnt offerings and your meat offerings,
I will not accept them;
Neither will I regard the peace offerings of your fat beasts.
23 Take thou away from me the noise of thy songs;
For I will not hear the melody of thy viols.
24 But let judgment run down as waters,
And righteousness as a mighty stream.[1]

Isaiah and the holiness of God

Isaiah, who started on his prophetic career about 738, thought like Amos in terms of theoretical monotheism. To him the rival gods were worthless, created by man.[2] He advanced the thinking of his age by emphasizing the holiness of God, bringing out His perfection as contrasted with man's imperfection: "Holy, holy, holy, is the Lord of hosts: the whole earth is full of his glory".[3] Living in a turbulent age which saw the destruction of Samaria by Sargon (722 B.C.) and the attack on Jerusalem by Sennacherib (701 B.C.), Isaiah stood head and shoulders above his contemporaries and furnished a shining example of the type of patriotism which shrinks from no sacrifice because inspired by an unfailing faith in a holy god. For three years he went naked and barefoot to illustrate the kind of treatment the Egyptian and Ethiopian captives would receive at the hands of the Assyrians.[4] Isaiah was, moreover, a Messianic prophet who with the eye of faith saw a vision of universal peace, under a "Prince of Peace" with world-wide dominion, an era in which swords will be beaten into ploughshares and wolves will dwell with lambs.[5] He preached a "new deal" which twenty-six hundred years of progress have not been able to realize. Second Isaiah, author of chapters 40 to 55, was also a monotheist.

Jeremiah and the new covenant

Unlike Amos and Isaiah, Jeremiah was a writing prophet.[6] His ministry (626–586 B.C.) was one of long suffering. His is perhaps the noblest character in the whole Old Testament. He witnessed Nebuchadnezzar attack Jerusalem in 597 and

[1] Passages set in poetic form are quoted from the Westminster Study Edition.
[2] Is. 2:8, 18; 10:10.
[3] Is. 6:3.
[4] Is. 20:3.
[5] Is. 9:6-7; 2:2-4; 11:1-9.
[6] See above, p. 201.

devastate it in 586. Like Amos and Second Isaiah he was a monotheist, but his monotheism was more thoroughgoing and practical. In unmistakable terms he pronounced all other deities vanities, man-made, figments of imagination.[1] Like Isaiah he envisioned a Utopia in which judgment and justice would be executed.[2]

But the crown of Jeremiah's book is in chapters 30 to 33, considered by some as embodying the noblest conceptions of Old Testament thinking. Herein Jehovah enters into a new covenant with his people, one involving inwardness and inscribed not on stone tables as in the case of their fathers, but on human hearts.[3] Jesus in the Last Supper appropriated the new covenant idea and the author of the Epistle to the Hebrews quoted the original reference to it.[4] In the same connection Jeremiah enunciates the doctrine of individual responsibility as opposed to the earlier one of "the fathers have eaten a sour grape, and the children's teeth are set on edge",[5] marking a stage of moral sensitiveness unattained in our own day by some European nations as judged by their conduct in the second world war.

Other prophetic contributions

Other Hebrew prophets made their contribution. Hosea, a native of the northern kingdom, who flourished between 745 and 735 B.C., from a tragic experience in his domestic life, worked out the sublime idea that God is love.[6] His wife, who bore him three children, proved unfaithful but still he loved her; so did Jehovah love Israel the unfaithful. Micah (fl. 730–722), a contemporary of Isaiah and spokesman of the poor whom he saw suffering from oppression and perversion of justice, also saw a vision of better things to come.[7] As exponent of social righteousness, his words are immortal (chapter 6):

6 Wherewith shall I come before the Lord,
  And bow myself before the high God?
Shall I come before him with burnt offerings,
  With calves of a year old?
7 Will the Lord be pleased with thousands of rams,
  Or with ten thousands of rivers of oil?
Shall I give my first-born for my transgression,
  The fruit of my body for the sin of my soul?

[1] Jer. 5:7; 14:22; 10:10-12; 16:17-21.
[2] Jer. 23:5.
[3] Jer. 31:31-4; 32:40.
[4] Matt. 26:28; Lk. 22:20; Heb. 10:16-17.
[5] Jer. 31:29-30; cf. Ezek. 18:2-4.
[6] Hos. 14:4.
[7] Mic. 4:1-8.

8 He hath showed thee, O man, what is good;
And what doth the Lord require of thee,
But to do justly, and to love mercy,
And to walk humbly with thy God?

In his great chapter (18) on individual responsibility Ezekiel, a contemporary of Jeremiah, showed sensitiveness to ethical ideals that the Christian nations of the twentieth century failed to show in their wars. In the utterances of the Hebrew prophets a level was reached that has never been surpassed except by those of Christ and perhaps Paul. Islam, third among the great monotheistic religions of the world, adopted the ethical monotheism of Judaism and Christianity. Zoroastrianism shared some of the salient features of these two early religions. With monotheism, in its Judaic and Christian aspects, the third of the major feats of the ancient Syrian civilization was achieved.[1]

[1] See above, p. 109; below, p. 330. Consult Toynbee, *Study of History*, vol. ii. pp. 75-7. Toynbee makes both the Arabic and Iranic civilizations "affiliated" to the Syrian, which was a sort of parent. He considers the 'Abbāsid caliphate a re-integration of the Syriac universal state (vol. i, pp. 67-8) interrupted by the intrusion of Hellenism.

CHAPTER XVI

UNDER PERSIAN RULE — FROM THE SEMITIC ERA TO THE INDO-EUROPEAN

Neo-Babylonian suzerainty

THE destruction of mighty Nineveh in 612 B.C. by the Neo-Babylonian Nabopolassar and the Median Cyaxares, followed by the annihilation in 609 of the remnant of the Assyrian army, which fell back on Ḥarrān, by the Neo-Babylonian forces, raised the question as to whether new Babylon or old Egypt should fall heir to the eastern Mediterranean area. The decision was not long delayed. The overwhelming defeat administered at Carchemish in 605 by the general Nebuchadnezzar, Nabopolassar's son, to Pharaoh Necho [1] left no doubt as to where the supremacy over that area would lie. Hophra, heedless of the experience of his predecessor Necho, dared challenge that supremacy and met the same fate on the battlefield in Palestine.[2] The new masters of Syria, also called Chaldaeans, were Semites, cousins of the Assyro-Babylonians but probably members of a later migration which had some connection with the Aramaeans.[3]

Meantime another question was raised in the minds of the nations that had lain for centuries under the heel of the greatest military power the world had yet known. Had the time come for them to enjoy once more their freedom? The destruction of Jerusalem by Nebuchadnezzar (605–562) in 586 and the reduction of Tyre in 572 after a thirteen-year siege [4] gave the final answer. Greater Syria for the next forty-eight years was again to be ruled from Mesopotamia.

The fall of new Babylon

The end of that rule came in 538 B.C., when a new people farther east, the Persians, rose under Cyrus and attacked their neighbour Babylon. Cyrus had united the Medes and the Persians, originally cousins, under one sceptre and overthrown Croesus and his kingdom of Lydia in the distant part of Asia

[1] See above, p. 201.
[2] See above, p. 202.
[3] See above, pp. 162, 170, n. 4.
[4] See above, pp. 144, 202.

Minor.[1] Babylon was then under Nabonidus (556–538), "the antiquarian king" whose interest in relics of the past had carried him so far as to populate his capital with ancient images of gods of other cities to the disgust of his priests and the disaffection of his subjects. Strangely enough he made his residence for some time a distant oasis in northern al-Ḥijāz, Taymā' (Teima), and left the affairs of the state in the incompetent hands of his son Belshazzar.[2] The crown prince was more interested in having a good time in the royal palace sumptuously built by Nebuchadnezzar than in taking measures to keep the fortifications of his capital in good repair. On that palace wall the writing was clear to all those with vision: "Thy kingdom is divided, and given to the Medes and Persians".[3]

A new world power: the Persians

The blow fell on Babylon in 539 B.C. but the citadel and royal palace held out until March 538. Thereupon the whole Babylonian empire, including Syria-Palestine, acknowledged the new Persian rule. The capture of Babylon signalized more than the destruction of an empire. Then and there one era, the Semitic, ended; another era, the Indo-European, began. The days of Semitic empires were gone, not to return for more than a thousand years. And when they returned, they did so under the auspices of fresh representatives, the Arabians, who had played no important rôle in ancient international affairs. The Persians, who ushered in the Indo-European era, belonged to the Indo-Iranian branch of the family. In their mastery over the Semitic world they were succeeded by Macedonians, Romans and Byzantines, all of whom were Indo-Europeans.

The petty states of Syria and Palestine now became part of a great empire, one of the largest of antiquity. Within a quarter of a century after its birth this empire was to comprise the whole civilized world from Egypt and the Ionian cities in Asia Minor to the Panjāb in India and then to begin casting covetous eyes across the Hellespont into the only civilized part of Europe. The far-flung parts of the empire were brought

[1] This is the Croesus of the simile "rich as Croesus". He had consulted two oracles before opening hostilities and was assured "he would destroy a great empire", which turned out to be his; Herodotus, Bk. I, ch. 53.

[2] Sidney Smith, *Babylonian Historical Texts* (London, 1924), pp. 76 *seq.*; Raymond P. Dougherty, *Nabonidus and Belshazzar* (New Haven, 1929), pp. 105 *seq.* "Belshazzar" comes from Akkadian *Bēl-shar-uṣur*, "Baal protect the king".

[3] Dan. 5:28.

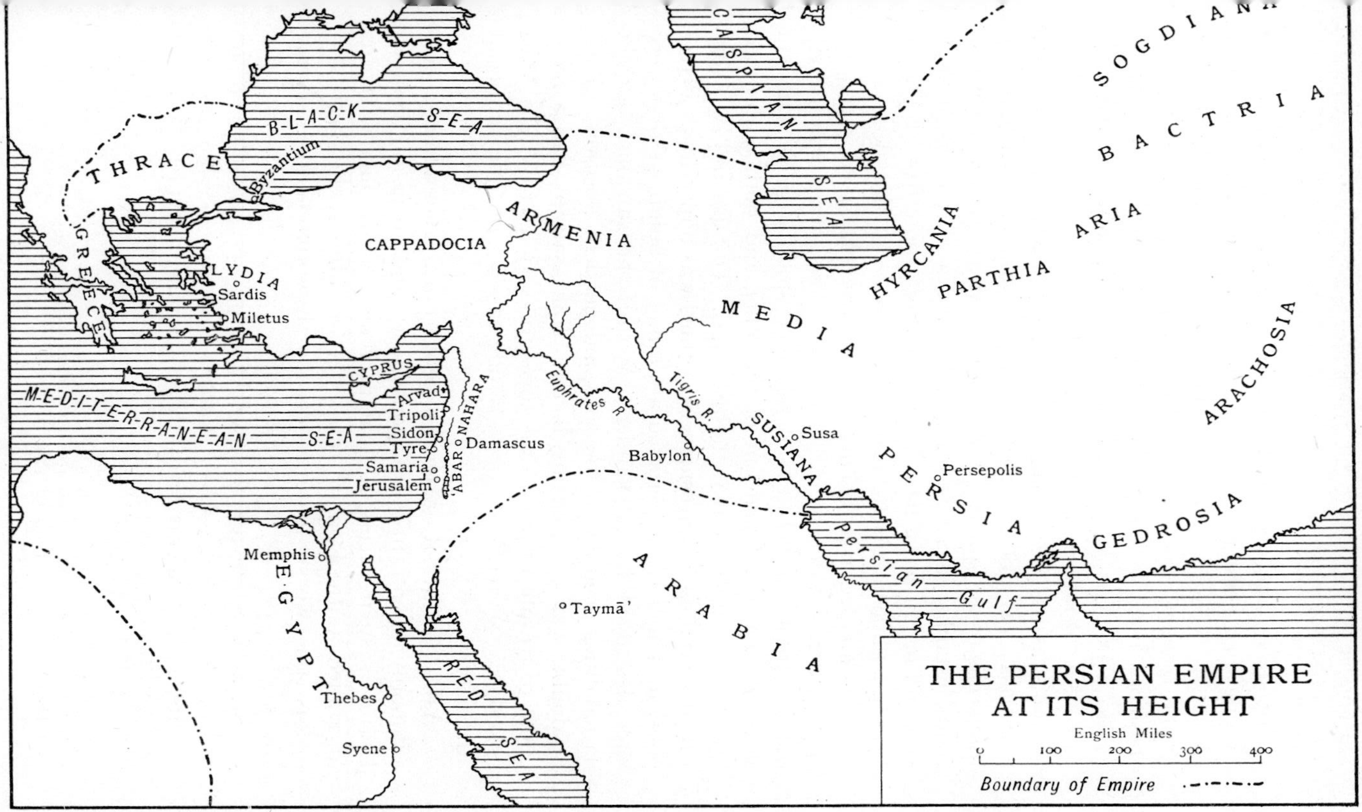

THE PERSIAN EMPIRE AT ITS HEIGHT

together by better roads than had ever existed, by a uniform stamped coinage and by an official language, Aramaic. Side by side with Persian, Aramaic, which had enjoyed a long vogue as the speech of commerce, now became the official language of the western provinces. All edicts and records designed for these provinces were furnished with an official Aramaic version.[1] Under Pax Persica the Phoenician cities began to flourish again as centres of international trade.

The organization of the empire

The task of organizing the colossal empire devolved upon Darius I (521–486), one of the ablest and most enlightened monarchs of antiquity. It was Darius who built and improved roads, established a postal system, introduced reforms in taxation and organized a fleet to provide a sea route from Egypt to Persia. Phoenicians formed the backbone of this fleet. The land he divided into twenty-three provinces, called satrapies, each under a governor called satrap. The satrap was a civil, not a military, governor. Beside him stood a general and a secretary, each independent of the other and both authorized to communicate directly with the capital. To Susa and Babylon, which served as royal residences, a third was now added, Persepolis, in which Darius erected a number of buildings that were later destroyed by Alexander. Within the satrapies subject nationalities occupied a tolerably independent position. This, no doubt, was a stabilizing factor. Each satrapy had a fixed quota of tribute to pay to the royal treasury. Travelling commissioners served as "eyes and ears" for the imperial authority.

As an imperial system of government combining local autonomy, centralized responsibility and over-all control, Darius' system excels all that preceded it. In fact it stands unrivalled until Roman times. It combines the best and avoids the worst features of the Egyptian and Assyrian systems.[2]

Syria-Palestine together with Cyprus were included in the fifth province, the ʿAbar Nahara[3] satrapy. They paid a tribute of 350 talents,[4] a rather light one. Cyprus still had several Phoenician colonies.

[1] See above, pp. 169, 170, n. 4.
[2] See above, p. 135.
[3] "Across the river" (Euphrates); see Ezra 6:6, 8, 13.
[4] Herodotus, Bk. III, ch. 91.

When Cyrus entered Babylon in 539–538, he encountered there a Jewish colony which owed its origin to the deportees of Nebuchadnezzar in 597 and 586. It is not difficult to assume that members of this colony had facilitated his subjugation of the city. The Persian conqueror immediately issued an edict to the effect that those who wished to return to their fatherland and rebuild the Temple could do so.[1] He evidently figured that a Jewish community in Palestine which owes its existence to his beneficence would form an effective counterbalance to the pro-Egyptian faction which always figured in Palestinian affairs. Here then is a reversal of the Assyro-Chaldaean policy of deporting subject peoples. Cyrus was hailed as the divinely appointed saviour.[2] The restoration

Exactly how many Jews embraced the opportunity thus offered is not possible to ascertain. The figure 42,360 given by Ezra and Nehemiah seems too high when compared with the total deportees (58,000) and does not tally with the breakdown in the detailed lists preceding the summary.[3] The response to the invitation must have come largely from dissatisfied elements and from those who had struck no root in the new soil. To the nostalgia felt by many, their poet gave expression in touching, never-dying words (Ps. 137):

By the rivers [canals] of Babylon,
There we sat down, yea, we wept,
When we remembered Zion.
2 We hanged our harps
Upon the willows in the midst thereof.
3 For there they that carried us away captive required of us a song;
And they that wasted us required of us mirth, saying,
Sing us one of the songs of Zion.
4 How shall we sing the Lord's song
In a strange land?
5 If I forget thee, O Jerusalem,
Let my right hand forget her cunning.
6 If I do not remember thee,
Let my tongue cleave to the roof of my mouth;
If I prefer not Jerusalem
Above my chief joy.

[1] Ezra 6:3-5.
[2] Is. 44:28; 45:1.
[3] Ezra 2:64; Neh. 7:66; see above, p. 202.

Many other exiles no doubt heeded Jeremiah's advice (chapter 29):

5 Build ye houses, and dwell in them; and plant gardens, and eat the fruit of them.
6 Take ye wives, and beget sons and daughters; and take wives for your sons, and give your daughters to husbands, that they may bear sons and daughters; that ye may be increased there, and not diminished.
7 And seek the peace of the city whither I have caused you to be carried away captives, and pray unto the Lord for it: for in the peace thereof shall ye have peace.

The prosperous among the exiles preferred to remain, as may be inferred by the frequent occurrence of Hebrew names in the business documents of the period, some compounded with the names of Babylonian deities. Their principal settlement there was on the Chebar,[1] the Kabaru ("the great one") of the Babylonians. This great canal of the Euphrates lay south-east of Babylon. Those who remained and resisted assimilation were the first members of what became known as the Diaspora. One potent factor which held the Jews together in their dispersion was their unique religion.

The leader of the restored Jews[2] was Zerubbabel,[3] a descendant of King Jehoiachin. Zerubbabel brought back the Temple treasures looted by Nebuchadnezzar and became for a time the recognized governor of the restored community. After many difficulties the rebuilding of the Temple was completed about 515 B.C. under Darius. The project was carried out at the expense of the state.

Following the precedent established by Cyrus, Artaxerxes I (465–424) authorized the return of two subsequent groups of exiles, one under the leadership of Nehemiah and the other under that of Ezra. Nehemiah was a twenty-one-year-old cup-bearer in the royal court and presumably a eunuch. He arrived

[1] Ezek. 1:1, 3; 3:3, 23.

[2] The term Jew, originally meaning a member of the tribe or the kingdom of Judah (from which word it is derived), was later applied to anyone of the Hebrew people who returned from captivity, and finally to all members of this people throughout the world. "Israel" designates a descendant of Israel, i.e. Jacob; "Hebrew" (see above, pp. 160-61) is a still more comprehensive term and includes the Israelites.

[3] From Akkadian *zēru-babīli*, "the seed of Babylon"; also called "Sheshbazzar", Ezra 1:8, 11; 5:14, "Zerobabel" in Matt. 1:12. See Neh. 12:1-9.

in Jerusalem about 444 B.C. with the express purpose of rebuilding the city walls. This he accomplished in the face of opposition from neighbours, such as Sanballat [1] governor of Samaria, Gashmu [2] an Arabian chief, and even from local Jewish notables. Nehemiah ruled over his people under Persian suzerainty from 444 to 432 B.C. The state was a theocracy as under Zerubbabel.

Before Nehemiah, according to the biblical tradition [3] accepted by a growing number of scholars, Ezra, the priest and scribe, had returned to Jerusalem and laboured under royal authorization to effect reform in the people's religion. While he worked for purity of faith he also worked for purity of blood. His racial programme went so far as compelling divorce of non-Judaean wives and declaring their children illegitimate.[4] In this he outdid Nehemiah, who was satisfied with cursing such husbands, smiting them, plucking off their hair and making them promise under oath not to do it again.[5] In one case Nehemiah chased the guilty husband from the country.[6]

Under Zerubbabel and Nehemiah the Jews enjoyed a privileged autonomy. But in their time the Hebrew language had ceased to be the vernacular not only in the land of exile but also in Judah.[7] Aramaic had replaced it. Hebrew was retained as the sacred tongue. Aramaic was used by the Jews in their official correspondence.[8] With its death Hebrew left a rich legacy of vocabulary in most civilized tongues. Some of the commonest proper names in English, John, Joseph, Paul, Mary, are of Hebrew origin.

While the Persians were encouraging the Jews to rebuild their old homeland, they were drawing upon Phoenician resources to enlarge the empire. The invasion of Egypt by Cyrus' son Cambyses (529–522) was accomplished with the aid of Phoenician ships and resulted in adding Egypt as far as In Phoenicia

[1] Assyrian *sin-ubal-lit*, " Sin gives life ", presumably a descendant of someone brought by the Assyrian kings to replace those deported from Samaria. He is the one whose daughter married the grandson of the high priest; see above, p. 197.

[2] Perhaps a descendant of an Arabian tribe, such as the Tamud (koranic Thamūd), whom Sargon deported to Palestine; see above, p. 197.

[3] Ezra 7 : 1 *seq*.

[4] Ezra 10 : 3-5, 10 *seq*.

[5] Neh. 13 : 25.

[6] See above, p. 197.

[7] Neh. 13 : 24.

[8] Ezra 4 : 7; see above, p. 168.

Nubia to the empire of Persia. To supply water for the land troops crossing the desert between Palestine and Egypt camels were hired from Arabians. Cambyses died somewhere in Syria while returning from Egypt.[1]

The Phoenician fleet also formed the core of the Persian navy in its attack on Greece under Xerxes (486–465).[2] The Phoenicians evidently welcomed an opportunity to deal a blow to their ancient maritime rivals and furnished 207 ships. In digging the canal through the isthmus to avoid the storms around Mount Athos, Phoenician engineering skill showed its excellence.[3] In the naval battle of Salamis (480) the entire fleet was destroyed.[4]

The struggle with Hellas was started by Xerxes' father Darius, whose army was defeated at Marathon in 490. To Darius the Greeks were a nation of barbarians and sea pirates, a source of constant trouble to the coasts of Asia Minor in his domain. The level of culture represented by Darius was certainly not lower than that of his contemporary Greeks. He and his immediate successors were followers of Zoroaster, who saw life as a ceaseless struggle between the forces of good, of light, personified in Ahura Mazda, and the forces of evil, of darkness, personified in Ahriman. The ethical precepts of Zoroastrianism were then lower only than those of Judaism. To the Greeks, as interpreted by their poets and historians, the war was one between liberty and Oriental despotism. The fields of Marathon and Thermopylae were soon clothed with honour and glory; those who laid their lives thereon were raised to the rank of national and immortal heroes. To the world at large the Perso-Greek episode was the first phase in a conflict between East and West, a conflict that was continued by Alexander, Pompey, Muʿāwiyah, Ṣaladin (Ṣalāḥ-al-Dīn), down to Napoleon and Allenby.

Tripoli, Phoenician capital

Damascus was the chief city of Syria under the Persians.[5] In Phoenicia four cities, Aradus, Byblus, Sidon and Tyre, were

[1] Josephus, *Antiquities*, Bk. XI, ch. 2, § 2, makes Damascus the scene of his death; Herodotus, Bk. III, ch. 64, makes it "Agbatana"; Pliny, Bk. V, ch. 19, makes it Ecbatana on the promontory of Carmel.

[2] Herodotus, Bk. VII, ch. 96.

[3] Herodotus, Bk. VII, ch. 23.

[4] Herodotus, Bk. VIII, chs. 86, 89-90, 96.

[5] Strabo, Bk. XVI, ch. 2, § 20.

allowed local autonomy and the right to rule respectively over four miniature states. In the fourth century these Phoenician city-states were federated with one another and a newly created city, Tripoli, was made the seat of the federal institutions. Originally consisting of three separate settlements with different names for representatives of Tyre, Sidon and Aradus, the city of Tripoli coalesced into one in the first year of the reign of Artaxerxes III (Ochus, 359–338) and was called "Athar'" or the like, as the name appears on a native coin of 189–188 B.C. The Greeks called it Tripolis (Ar. Ṭarābulus).[1] As the meeting-place of the Phoenician common assembly the triple city functioned as a capital for Phoenicia.[2] The assembly had annual meetings in which some three hundred delegates participated. At these meetings the natives were treated by the Persian officials with such arrogance that they finally resolved to break away. The Phoenicians must have sensed by the middle of the fourth century that the Persian sun was on the way to its setting.

Sidon in ashes

The rebellion against this Artaxerxes started in the Sidon section of Tripoli and spread thence until it involved the whole Phoenician coast. As usual the encouragement came from Egypt. The centre of the rebellion soon shifted to Sidon itself under King Tennes. The Sidonians cut down the trees in the royal park in or near their city, set on fire the hay stored for the use of the Persian cavalry, secured mercenaries, triremes, arms and provisions and made ready for the ensuing struggle. In 351 Artaxerxes set out from Babylon with an army of 300,000 footmen and 30,000 horsemen.[3] While he was on the march, his satraps of Syria and Cilicia who were trying to suppress the rebellion were being chased from Phoenicia. Nine leading Phoenician cities expelled the Persians and declared themselves independent. Hearing news of the advance of Artaxerxes in person at the head of a mighty host, Tennes lost heart, fled and betrayed his city to the approaching enemy. Its people, however, resolved to die as free men. In their hour of desperation they burned all ships in the harbour, lest some citizen might be tempted to escape, and shut themselves in their homes while the

[1] George F. Hill, *Catalogue of the Greek Coins of Phoenicia* (London, 1910), § 48.

[2] Strabo, Bk. XVI, ch. 2, § 15; Pliny, *Natural History*, Bk. V, ch. 20.

[3] Diodorus, Bk. XVI, ch. 40, § 6.

raging fire devoured them and their possessions.[1] More than 40,000 are said to have thus perished. The few who were taken prisoners were carried away into Babylon.[2] The entire city, once the mistress of the Mediterranean, went down in ashes and deprived the learned world of its records. This is the second time in which Sidon was wiped out of existence; the first was at the hands of Esarhaddon in 677.[3] Warned by the tragic fate of Sidon the rest of the Phoenician cities capitulated.

Cultural aspects

Little is known of the development and modification of Syrian culture under the impact of Persian domination; in fact the whole history of Syria during this period is one of the most obscure in the entire career of that land. Our sources of information are limited to a few coins, scattered inscriptions and Hebrew and classical writings. The Hebrew sources come to an abrupt stop around 400 B.C. Archaeology has but little to offer. It is nevertheless certain that Syrian civilization continued to be a complete Semitic syncretism with the dominant note furnished by the Aramaean-Phoenician culture as in the Neo-Babylonian age.

If the Aḥiqār story was first composed in the Persian period,[4] it could be taken as an index of the type of literature then cultivated. It is the wisdom type. Then there is the Persian influence on Judaism which, strange as it may seem, does not manifest itself until later, in the second pre-Christian century. The form it takes is a tendency toward dualism involving the evolution of a personal antagonist to the one God. This dualistic conception is carried over into the New Testament, where it takes the form of the opposition of the principle of wrong to that of right, of darkness to light. The Jewish progressive organization of an angelic hierarchy and the growth of a belief in the last judgment with its reward and punishment after death can also be traced to Iranian stimulation. The idea of the last judgment as presented in the Book of Enoch (41 : 1), involving the weighing of the actions of man by a balance, betrays Persian influence, though the balance itself goes back to earlier Babylonian and Egyptian sources. Daniel's con-

[1] Diodorus, Bk. XVI, chs. 43-5; Frederick C. Eiselen, *Sidon* (New York, 1907), pp. 75-7.

[2] Sidney Smith, p. 149; A. T. Olmstead, *History of the Persian Empire* (Chicago, 1948), pp. 436-7.

[3] See above, p. 142.

[4] Cf. above, p. 169.

ception of the last day (7 : 9-12) is not Iranian. Only a few ancient Persian loan words found their way into Hebrew and Aramaic. " Paradise " came from Persian through Hebrew and Greek.[1]

In architecture the only noteworthy remains are a palace and a sanctuary found in Tell al-Duwayr (Lachish). The palace can definitely be dated to the middle of the fifth century by a fragment of red Attic ware. Presumably a Persian residency, it had round tile drains and other appurtenances of comfort. Statues recently found in the ruins of a Persian

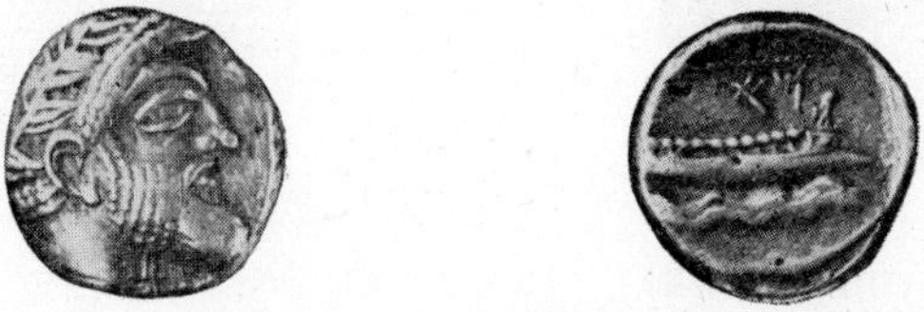

The American Numismatic Society

A COIN OF ARADUS

Obverse and reverse of a silver stater of Aradus, early fourth century B.C. The head is that of a male deity, laureate, hair and whiskers dotted. The reverse shows a galley with figurehead on prow and an inscription probably signifying " from (or of) Aradus "

official's palace in Sidon (351 B.C.) follow the style of statues in the capital Persepolis; but the numerous marble anthropoid sarcophagi found in Sidon[2] indicate that by the fourth century Attic sculpture was firmly established in the land. In that century the Attic drachma had become standard; in the preceding century it had gained wide currency.[3] In those two centuries Greek earthenware found an extensive market throughout the eastern Mediterranean lands. Native pottery manifests definite decline throughout the Persian period, due in part to the intrusion of Greek products. On the whole it may be said that by the fifth century Greece, which in the seventh century was on the receiving end of the cultural line from the standpoint of Phoenicia, had reversed its position and shifted to the giving end. In the sixth there was something of

[1] Originally meaning " garden " (Ecc. 2 : 5; Song 4 : 13) the term developed to mean " heavenly abode of the blessed " (Lk. 23 : 43). Ar. *firdaws* came through Aramaic.

[2] See above, p. 125. On the " sarcophagus of Alexander " see below, p. 235.

[3] See above, p. 208.

a balance between the giving and the receiving processes. In that century Greek trading settlements make their appearance in the Syrian land. Their number steadily increases thereafter. For at least a century before the conquest of Alexander the coastal cities were sprinkled with Greek merchants and craftsmen.

The American Numismatic Society

DOUBLE SHEKEL COIN OF SIDON, *ca.* 384–370 B.C.

Obverse shows war galley with oars and double ruddery; below double zigzag line of waves. Reverse shows the king of Persia in a car drawn by four (?) pacing horses, driven by a charioteer who leans forward. The king raises his right hand. Behind the car an Egyptian figure, wearing crown of Upper Egypt and waistcloth, holds in right hand a sceptre with animal's head

PART III

THE GRECO-ROMAN PERIOD

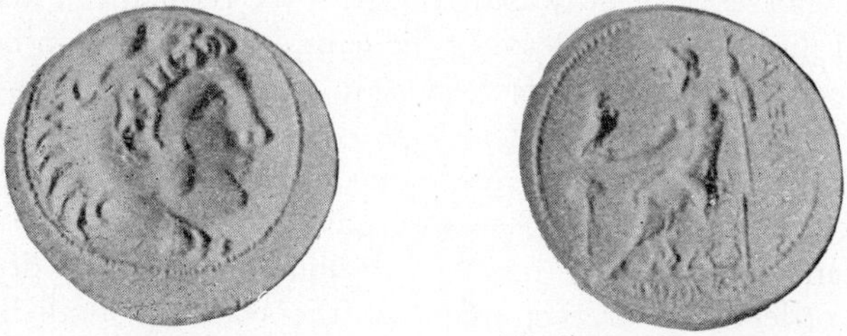

The American Numismatic Society

A COIN OF ARADUS

Obverse and reverse of a tetradrachm of Alexander struck at Aradus in 234 B.C. The date is inscribed on the reverse in Phoenician characters and in the era of Aradus

CHAPTER XVII

ALEXANDER AND HIS SUCCESSORS, THE SELEUCIDS

PLANS to " liberate " the Greek cities in Asia Minor held by Persia and incidentally repay the visit paid Greece by Darius and Xerxes were projected by Philip of Macedon but executed by his more energetic and illustrious son Alexander. Philip had raised Macedon to the headship of the Greek states when an assassin's dagger cut short his life.

Battle of Issus

Starting in the spring of 334 B.C. at the head of 30,00 to 40,000 men, the twenty-year-old Alexander crossed the Hellespont, swept through Asia Minor — then a part of the Persian empire — and as he emerged from the Cilician Gates [1] and lowlands, encountered Darius III (336–330) with a motley host of over two hundred thousand. All people of Asia, according to a late Oriental historian,[2] " were persuaded that the Macedonians would not so much as come to a battle with the Persians on account of their multitude ". In the battle that followed at

[1] See above, p. 60.

[2] Josephus, *Antiquities*, Bk. XI, ch. 8, § 3.

Issus [1] (333), a narrow defile where the numerical superiority of the Persian army could be of no account, victory was easy. Darius, who watched the battle from a gorgeous chariot drawn by four horses abreast, was driven with the remnant of his army in wild flight eastward leaving the camp and his harem behind. The royal harem were treated with chivalrous courtesy. In commemoration of the victory the city Iskandarūnah (Alexandretta), that still bears his name, was founded on the site. The echoes of the decisive victory gave new glory to the Greek name and filled Persian hearts with doubts if not with dread.

Tyre resists

In order to insure command of the sea and of all lines of communication behind him, Alexander pushed south instead of pursuing the fugitive foe. He dispatched his general Parmenio with a detachment of cavalry up the Orontes valley to occupy Damascus, Persian headquarters in Syria. The victory at Issus laid the whole country at his feet He himself followed the coastal route. Marathus,[2] Aradus, Byblus, Sidon surrendered. Only Tyre, the queen city of the Phoenician coast, which had defied Sennacherib, Esarhaddon and Nebuchadnezzar, dared shut its gates in the face of the invader Alexander built a mole half a mile long and 200 feet wide from the mainland to the two-mile-long island. The unhappy city expected aid from her sisters to the north; instead, their triremes were put at the disposal of the invader. She also expected aid from her distant daughter Carthage, to which Tyre had sent her old men, women and children for refuge. But she was again disappointed. After a siege of seven months by sea and by land Alexander received Tyre's submission, hanged about 2000 of its people and sold some 30,000 into slavery. In this he followed the common practice in war. His victory he celebrated by games, rites and a sacrifice in the temple of the city god Milk-qart, whom he identified with Hercules.[3]

In Tyre's opposition to Alexander's advance, history records the last flare of Phoenician national spirit. The ancient tradition

[1] Arrian, *Anabasis Alexandri*, Bk. II, chs. 9-13; Polybius, *Historiarum libri*, Bk. XII, chs. 17-22; Diodorus, Bk. XVII, ch. 33. For full description of the battle of Issus consult W. W. Tarn, "Alexander", *Cambridge Ancient History*, vol. vi (Cambridge, 1927), pp. 366-9.

[2] See above, p. 65, n. 2.

[3] Arrian, Bk. II, chs. 18-24; Diodorus, Bk. XVII, chs. 41-6. Quintus Curtius, *De rebus gestis Alexandri Magni*, Bk. IV, ch. 2; see above, p. 105, n. 7.

was broken forever; the old spirit never reasserted itself.

While still besieging Tyre Alexander received a message from Darius offering partition of the empire, of which all west of the Euphrates would go to Alexander together with money and the hand of Darius' daughter. Parmenio advised in favour of the bargain, adding he would readily accept if he were Alexander. "So would I," retorted Alexander, "if I were Parmenio." [1]

Heedless of Tyre's experience, Gaza, once chief among the five Philistine cities, offered a resistance equally heroic but not equally long. After two months' siege its garrison, which comprised many Arabians, was overpowered and annihilated; its eunuch commander was dragged around the city walls lashed to the back of Alexander's chariots. The population was sold into slavery. Alexander was slightly wounded here as he was at Issus.[2] Enormous stores of spices were captured here, for the city was the chief Mediterranean depot for the products of Arabia and adjacent lands. By the capture of Gaza another nail was driven into the coffin of Persian supremacy in the Mediterranean.

Egypt reduced

The way now lay open to Egypt. Its conquest would complete the neutralization of the Persian fleet. The Egyptians willingly exchanged masters. When there Alexander paid a visit to Ammon (later identified with Jupiter) in the oasis now called Sīwah in the Libyan desert, some 200 miles from the Egyptian border, and was hailed as son of the god by the priest. He also laid the foundation of the city that still bears his name. Both acts were pregnant with a significance for the future far beyond what the actor could have foreseen. The association between the idea of divinity and that of the monarchy was introduced into the Greco-Roman world and eventually established itself there. Divine kingship, a normal institution in the ancient Orient, had no trace in Europe before the age of Alexander and his successors. Alexandria in due course rose to eminence as a seat of Hellenistic culture, an Oriental successor of Athens. In the Roman period it ranked second to Rome. As a contribution to history the founding of this seaport at the north-western extremity of the

[1] Plutarch, "Alexander", in *Vitae*.
[2] Arrian, Bk. II, ch. 27; Curtius, Bk. IV, ch. 6.

Delta was of greater significance than the mere conquest of Egypt.

The decisive battle near Arbela

In the spring of 331 the dashing conqueror returned to Syria, where he halted long enough to chastise the Samaritans for having assassinated his deputy and to celebrate again, with splendour and pomp, games and rites at the temple of Tyre.[1] That he visited Jerusalem on the way down to Egypt and personally received its submission is doubtful.[2] The route he took now was through Coele-Syria and the Orontes valley striking the Euphrates at Thapsacus.[3] Near by he ordered the foundation of a city which was probably completed by his general Seleucus Nicator and given his name Nicephorium.[4] Traversing Mesopotamia north-easterly, he forded the Tigris above the site of Nineveh. On the plain between that site and Arbela farther east the last army raised by an Achæmenean, the dynasty which produced Cyrus the Great and Darius the Great, was shattered. Darius III himself escaped.[5] Babylon, the central seat of government, whose walls stood 300 feet high, was Alexander's next objective. Its native priests and Persian officials welcomed the newcomer with wreaths and gifts. Enormous treasures were seized. But they paled into insignificance before the fabulous riches which the Persian emperors had amassed in their spring residence Susa and which were the next to be seized. From Susa the march was continued in winter over the high, rugged mountains into Persepolis. The city was stripped of its treasures, and the royal palace erected by Darius was set to flames. The destruction of the Greek temples by Xerxes in Athens was avenged.[6]

Out of the valley of Persepolis in the spring of 330 a swift marching column headed by Alexander faced north. Its objective was Ecbatana (ancient capital of Media, modern Hamadhān), where Darius had fled. As the column approached, Darius was transfixed by two conspirators in his camp. Alexander was allowed to become master of the corpse, which he

[1] Arrian, Bk. III, chs. 1-4.

[2] Cf. Josephus, Bk. XI, ch. 8, §§ 3-5; Olmstead, *History of the Persian Empire*, p. 507, n. 11.

[3] See above, p. 60.

[4] Modern al-Raqqah. Pliny, Bk. V, ch. 21, Bk. VI, ch. 30; cf. A. H. M. Jones *Cities of the Eastern Roman Provinces* (Oxford, 1937), p. 216.

[5] Arrian, Bk. III, chs. 14-15.

[6] Arrian, Bk. III, chs. 16-18; Diodorus, Bk. XVII, ch. 7.

sent to Persepolis for royal burial. The Macedonian now considered himself the legitimate successor of the last Persian monarch.

As if he had not yet had enough, Alexander penetrated eastward, made a raid across the Jaxartes [1] and then plunged southward through Kābul into the Panjāb in north-western

From William Robert Rogers, "History of Ancient Persia" by courtesy of Charles Scribner's Sons

THE "SARCOPHAGUS OF ALEXANDER"

Found in Sidon, now in Istanbul, this late fourth century B.C. sarcophagus very likely represents battles between the Persians and the great Macedonian, but all ancient tradition points to Egypt as the final resting-place of the conqueror. It may have been the work of the Phoenician governor of Sidon

India. In the course of the Indian campaign his tired army and generals began to murmur. Some mutinied. It was the year 326. Alexander returned to Babylon, where he gave himself up to drinking and carousing. He died of fever in the palace of Nebuchadnezzar in June 323, before he was fully thirty-three years old, leaving behind him a singular record of physical courage and endurance, impulsive energy and fervid

[1] Modern Sīr Darya, Ar. Sayḥūn, an adaptation of Pison of Gen. 2 : 11.

imagination. His name became that of the hero of various cycles of romance, embroidered with all kinds of fantastic exaggerations. Daniel (8 : 5, 21) has a clear reference to him, and in the Koran (18 : 82 *seq.*) Iskandar dhu-al-Qarnayn (the two-horned) seems to be invested with a divine commission.

Fusion of East and West

Perhaps the greatest contribution rendered by Alexander to history consisted in the provision of an opportunity for the fusion of Greek and Oriental ideas and institutions. The process of cultural osmosis had its start before his days [1] but his conquests accelerated and facilitated it. He himself set an example in fusing Greek and Asiatic blood by marrying princess Roxana of Bactria (Balkh) and two others from the royal Persian house at Susa. He encouraged his officers and soldiers to follow his precedent. On state occasions Alexander donned Oriental garb. He " began to indulge in the soft and effeminate manners of the Persians and to imitate the luxury of the Asiatic Kings ".[2] Unlike Xerxes he tried to join Europe and Asia " not with rafts and timbers and senseless bonds but by the ties of lawful love and chaste nuptials and by community of offspring ".[3] That was a significant moment in history when at a banquet attended by 9000 Macedonians and Persians on the banks of the Tigris, Alexander prayed for a union of hearts and a joint commonwealth.[4] Before him prophets had transcended in their imagination the boundaries of nationality and envisaged, however imperfectly, a brotherhood of man; but here was the first great man of affairs who dreamt of a society with no barrier between Greek and barbarian and who wrought for its realization. That resplendent hope which the Phoenician philosopher Zeno [5] later embodied in his *Republic* has never quite left men since.

The planting of cities, upwards of seventy we are told, was another means of implementing his considered policy of bringing East and West closer together. These cities served the triple purpose of providing settlements for his discharged warriors, forming a chain of military posts on the lines of communication and creating centres for radiating Hellenic cultural influence. Alexander must have been an apt student of his teacher

[1] See above, pp. 227-8.
[2] Diodorus, Bk. VII, ch. 8.
[3] Plutarch, *De Alexandri Magni fortuna aut virtute*, Bk. I, ch. 7.
[4] Arrian, Bk. VII, ch. 11, § 9.
[5] See below, p. 255.

Aristotle, for, we are told, he kept a copy of Homer's *Iliad*, corrected by Aristotle, with his dagger under his pillow. In a letter from Asia to his teacher he allegedly wrote, " For my part, I assure you, I had rather excel others in the knowledge of what is excellent than in the extent of my power and my dominion ".[1] Greek language soon became the language of learning. Three centuries later when Christ delivered his message and it was rendered into Greek it became available to the whole civilized world.[2]

The break-up of the empire

The hastily assembled far-flung Macedonian empire fell to pieces at the death of its founder. His generals scrambled for its choicest bits. The scramble involved bloody and protracted wars. Out of the chaos four generals emerge at the head of four states: Ptolemy in Egypt, Seleucus in the satrapy of Babylonia, Antigonus in Asia Minor and Antipater in Macedonia. " The great horn was broken; and for it came up four notable ones, toward the four winds of heaven ".[3] Of the four Ptolemy was the most astute, but Seleucus was certainly the ablest.

Seleucus, founder of the Syrian monarchy

Seleucus I (312–280 B.C.), surnamed Nicator (victor), first distinguished himself in the Indian campaign under Alexander. At the partition of the empire he did not hold Syria-Palestine, which went with Asia Minor. In 312 B.C. Ptolemy, with the aid of Seleucus, defeated Antigonus at Gaza and added Palestine to his Egyptian territory. There it remained for over a century with few interruptions. In the same year Seleucus recovered Babylon, which he had lost, and after taking part in another victory over Antigonus at Ipsus (in Great Phrygia, 301 B.C.), he obtained possession of the whole eastern part of Asia Minor as well as Syria from the Euphrates to the Mediterranean.[4] Antioch, which he built on the Orontes and named in honour of his father, then became the seat of government for Syria. The year 312, however, is reckoned as marking the birth of the Syrian monarchy and as the starting-point of the Seleucid era.[5] " Kings of Syria " appear for the first time. The establishment of a standard calendar for the entire Near East was, next to colonization, the greatest Seleucid achievement. Meantime

[1] Plutarch, " Alexander ", in *Vitae*.
[2] See below, pp. 335, 369.
[3] Dan. 8:8.
[4] Appian, *Syrius*, § 55.
[5] The Syrians and Jews called it the Greek era; 1 Macc. 1:10. The year began Oct. 1 and is even now in limited use in Syria; cf. Richard A. Parker and Waldo H. Dubberstein. *Babylonian Chronology* (Chicago, 1942), p. 18.

Ptolemy had pushed the boundary of his kingdom to a line north of Aradus and south of Emesa. This line receded considerably to the south of Beirut and Damascus about 250 B.C., advancing again to the north of Aradus twenty-five years later.

Eastward Seleucus extended the frontier of his Syrian

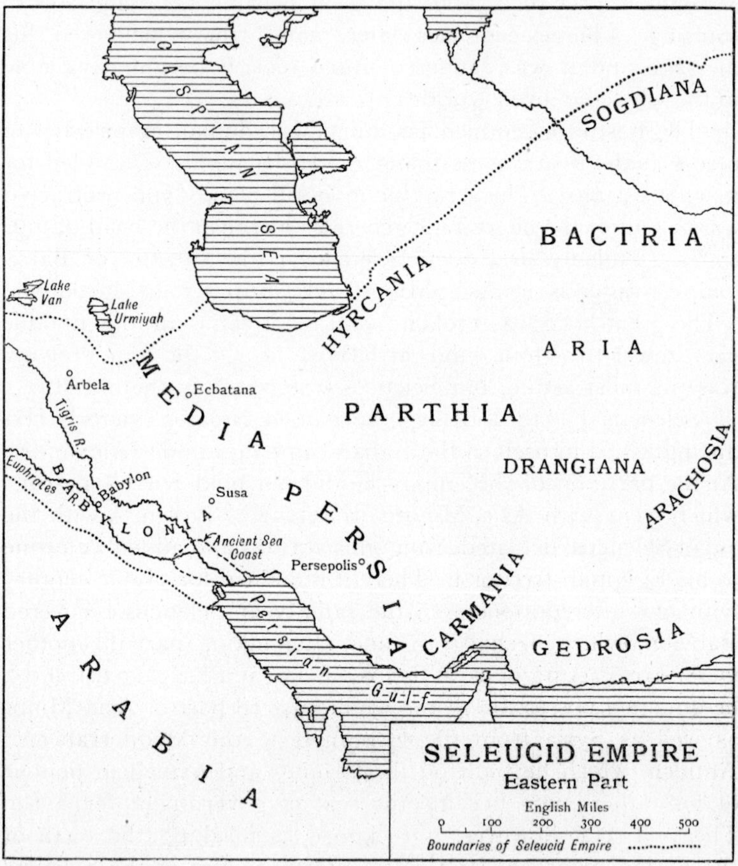

monarchy to include Persia as far as the Oxus in the north and the Indus in the south. The kingdom of Syria then nearly coincided with the Asiatic part of Alexander's empire. His was then by far the most extensive and powerful of all those which arose on the ruins of the dominions of Alexander. Not satisfied he crossed the Hellespont at the end of 281 intent upon the addition of Macedonia, whose throne was left vacant by the death of another one of Alexander's generals, Lysimachus, to his vast domain. There he was assassinated.

In pursuit of the policy of Hellenization projected by Alexander, Seleucus founded no less than sixteen cities bearing the name of his father Antiochus, nine bearing his name, five that of his mother Laodicea and three that of his Bactrian wife Apama.[1] The Seleucia[2] (modern Salūqiyah) built to guard the mouth of the Orontes and as a seaport to Antioch was either his or one of his immediate successors' foundation. His body was removed and buried in it and he was worshipped there as a deity.[3] It then became the burial place of the dynasty. Of the Laodiceas that on the Syrian coast, Arabicized al-Lādhiqīyah (Latakia), is still flourishing and has the best harbour on the coast. Apamea on the Orontes (Afāmiyah of Arab geographers) is now a small village Qalʿat al-Maḍīq (castle of the straits). It developed into a great centre in the Syrian kingdom and housed the army, the war treasury and a national stud of 30,000 mares and 300 stallions.[4] It served as a depot where war elephants were bred and trained. Of the Antiochias the capital was, of course, the most important one.

The empire built by Seleucus I was all but lost under his almost immediate successors. During the reign of his great-grandson Seleucus II Callinicus (246–226), Ptolemy Euergetes invaded Syria, occupied Antioch and carried his arms unopposed to the Euphrates. But domestic disturbances necessitated his return home, giving Seleucus a chance to recover his lost provinces. Meantime the Parthians availed themselves of the disordered state of the Syrian kingdom to throw off its yoke. Arsaces, king of Parthia,[5] defeated Seleucus in a battle shortly after 240 B.C., which marks the real birth of the Parthian dynasty.[6] The king of Pergamum was also busy extending

[1] Appian, § 57.

[2] Often called, especially on coins, Seleucia Pieria, to distinguish it from other towns of the same name. Pieria, originally name of a region in Macedonia, was given to a district on the northern coast of Syria and the right bank of the Orontes. The city was located 5 miles north of the Orontes to take advantage of an easily fortified place and to avoid silted shallows and had in 219 B.C. a population of 30,000.

[3] Appian, § 63.

[4] Strabo, Bk. XVI, ch. 2, § 10.

[5] Part of a satrapy south-east of the Caspian Sea. The Parthians were of Scythian origin.

[6] An earlier battle of 250 was later celebrated as the beginning of Parthian independence; cf. Edwyn R. Bevan, *The House of Seleucus* (London, 1902), vol. i, p. 285.

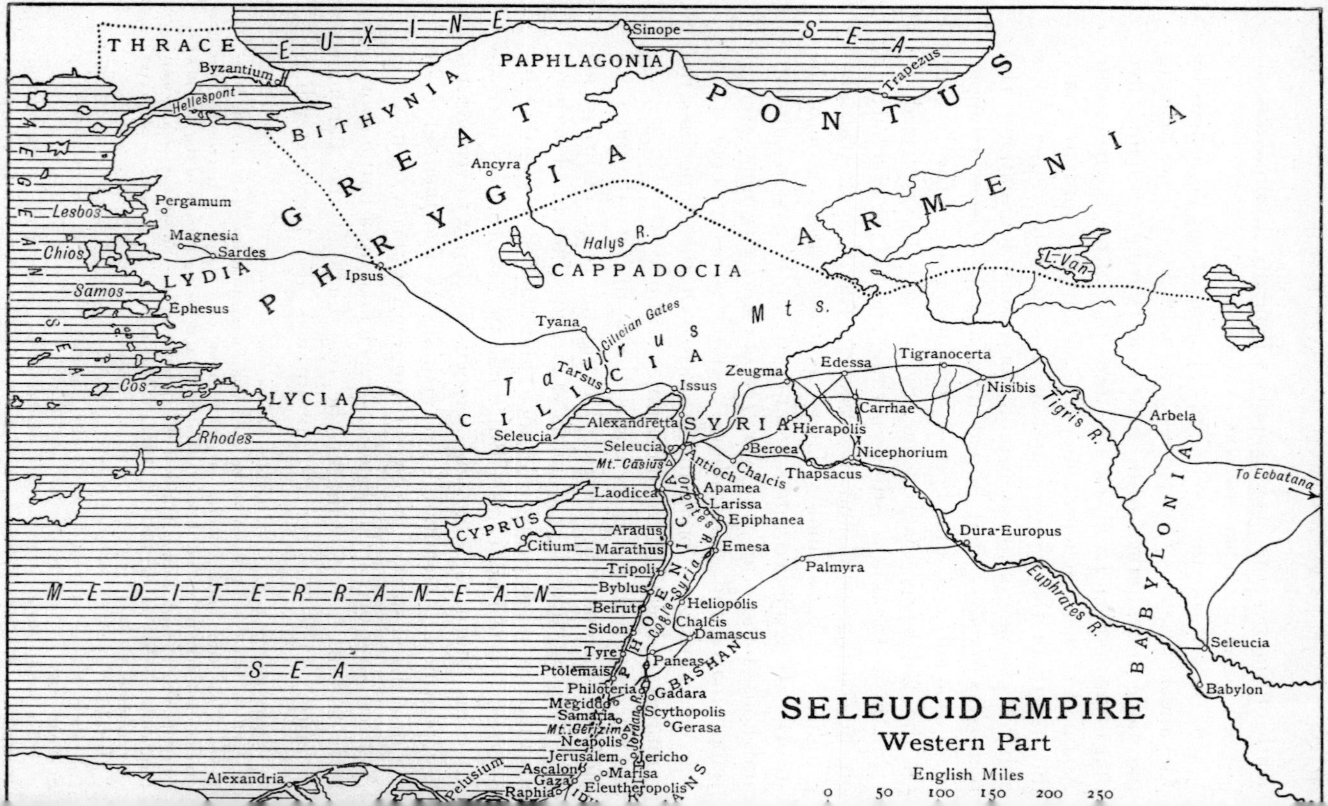

SELEUCID EMPIRE
Western Part

his authority over the greater part of Asia Minor.

At the accession of Antiochus III (223–187) [1] the Seleucid kingdom had lost much of its territory and brilliance. Antiochus resolved to save the situation. At the head of his troops he first marched eastward to reconquer the Iranian territory. Success was his. His army crossed the Hindu Kush, descended the Kābul valley, plunged south and stood at the door of India. For the second time those distant peoples were treated to the sight of a Macedonian army. On his return to Babylon he, as Alexander had done before him, took note of Arabia. The need for its spices and other tropical products and the importance of its intermediary position, from the standpoint of waterways, between the western and the eastern flanks of the empire, were weighty considerations. A trip with his fleet from the Tigris along its forbidden coasts, however, sufficed to convince Antiochus of the futility of any plans for the permanent occupation of such a desert peninsula. So he returned (204 B.C.) to Seleucia-on-the-Tigris, capital of the eastern satrapies.

Antiochus then directed his attention to the southern enemy, Ptolemy. Earlier, in 217, he had made an attempt to restore

[1] The tree below shows the genealogical relationship of the members of the Seleucid house:

1. Seleucus I Nicator (312–280 B.C.)
2. Antiochus I Soter (280–261)
3. Antiochus II Theos (261–246)
4. Seleucus II Callinicus (246–226)
   - 5. Seleucus III Ceraunus (226–223)
   - 6. Antiochus III the Great (223–187)
     - 7. Seleucus IV Philopator (187–175)
       - 10. Demetrius I Soter (162–150)
     - 8. Antiochus IV Epiphanes (175–164)
       - 9. Antiochus V Eupator (164–162)
       - * * * * * 11. Alexander I Balas (150–146)

Note.—Starred line indicates pretended father and son relationship. For the remaining monarchs see below, p. 250, n. 1. Cf. Parker and Dubberstein, pp. 19 *seq.*; Neilson C. Debevoise, *A Political History of Parthia* (Chicago, 1938), pp. 70-71.

the amputated parts of Syria but failed on the battlefield of the frontier town Raphia,[1] but now in 198 his effort was successful. At Paneas,[2] where Antiochus defeated the Egyptian forces, the

Atlas photo

ANTIOCHUS III THE GREAT

From a Bust in the Louvre

Syrian army, as at Raphia, used elephants of which the monarch had brought back a fresh supply from India.[3] By twenty years of incessant fighting Antiochus had won back almost all that

[1] Tell Rifaḥ, south of Gaza.

[2] The sources of the Jordan were marked by a precinct dedicated to a deity in whom the Greeks recognized their god Pan. When a city was afterwards built there it was named Paneas, Arabic Bāniyās, Caesarea Philippi of the Gospels. Philip the tetrarch rebuilt or enlarged it and named it Caesarea in honour of Tiberius; Bevan, vol. ii, p. 37; Dussaud, *Topographie*, pp. 390-91.

[3] Polybius, Bk. XVI, chs. 18 *seq.*

his father and grandfather had lost and with it he won the epithet of Great.

At this time an embassy from Rome appeared in his court to warn him to keep hands off Egypt. This is the first communication we hear of between Rome and Antioch and marks a new era in ancient international affairs. It was then that Hannibal sought asylum in Syria and urged Antiochus to invade

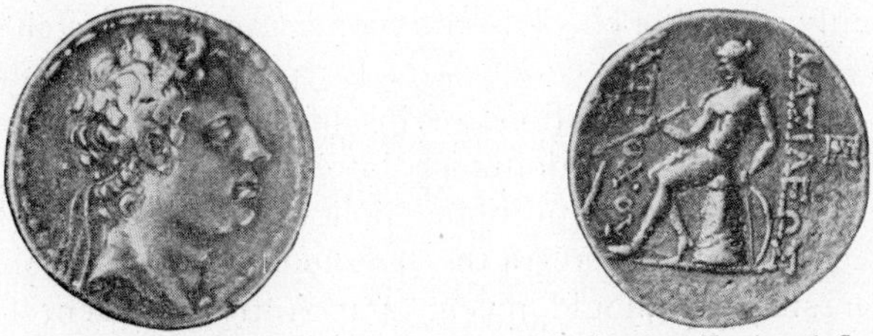

The American Numismatic Society

A TETRADRACHM OF ANTIOCHUS IV

Struck in Tyre 175–164 B.C. Obverse shows the diademed head of the monarch; reverse shows Apollo seated on omphalos holding an arrow in his right hand. The inscription reads BASILEUS [King] ANTIOCHUS

Italy.[1] Antiochus was not fully conscious of the might of the new giant looming in the west. He ventured to strike a blow for Greece, where the Romans were penetrating, and there he met defeat at their hands at Thermopylae (191 B.C.).[2] In the following year he suffered another defeat from the Romans near Magnesia, in western Asia Minor, and in 188 was forced to cede to them all his dominions beyond the Taurus and pay a heavy war indemnity.[3] Asia Minor with its land trade routes and direct access to Greek civilization was forever lost. In the hour of greatest triumph since its foundation, the house of Seleucus received a terrific blow

The ignominious peace and heavy tribute left Syria in a feeble condition, but not too feeble to resume before long an aggressive rôle. Learning that Egypt was preparing an expedition to regain Coele-Syria — the bone of contention — Antiochus IV (175–164) struck first by land and sea, crushingly defeated in 169 B.C. the Egyptian army at the frontier fortress

[1] Livy, *Historiarum*, Bk. XXIV, chs. 43, 60.
[2] Appian, §§ 18-20.
[3] Polybius, Bk. XXI, chs. 16-17; Livy, Bk. XXVII, ch. 45

called Pelusium[1] and captured the king himself, Ptolemy Philometor. Soon Lower Egypt was entirely in Antiochus' hands. Only Alexandria refused to submit, and it was for the first time in its existence subjected to a siege. The siege was soon raised, however, under pressure from Rome, to whom Antiochus was still paying instalments of the war indemnity.[2] The Syrian conqueror evacuated the land and returned home.

The Maccabean revolt

While Rome might circumscribe Antiochus' military activity, it certainly could not check his missionary activity as a champion of Hellenism. By the conquest of Egypt the king satisfied one of the two ruling ambitions of his life, the second being the welding together of his dominion into a cultural unity. In this he was following the traditional policy of the Seleucid house, which considered Hellenism the common denominator on which all their subjects should meet; but Antiochus went too far. He even proclaimed himself Theos Epiphanes (God manifest) and associated himself in this capacity with Zeus Olympius. Not being jealous, the gods of the Syrians conceded their followers the privilege of worshipping the king; but the case was different with the god of the Jews.

In Jerusalem the aristocracy, the rich and the modernized Jews had thus far responded to the outside stimuli by adopting the Greek language and customs and were now ready to collaborate. They had no objection to being called Antiochians.[3] Greek dress became fashionable among the young and the Greek gymnasium made its appearance. Counting on their co-operation, Antiochus encouraged the identification of Jehovah with Zeus and set an altar in the Temple for the Greek deity. That was "the abomination that maketh desolate" of Daniel (11 : 31). This Temple he had on his way back from Egypt stripped of all its treasures. Later he laid his hands on the riches of nearly all other sanctuaries in Syria. He needed the money to satisfy his many whims and fancies.[4]

Though bearing a Greek name, the Zeus Olympius of Antiochus was as much the Oriental Baal as he was the Occidental Zeus. With semi-Semitic attributes, he was worshipped in quasi-Semitic temples and represented with semi-

[1] Ar. al-Farmā'; Polybius, Bk. XXVIII, ch. 18.

[2] Livy, Bk. XLVII, ch. 11; Polybius, Bk. XXIX, ch. 2; Josephus, *Antiquities*, Bk. XII, ch. 5, § 2.

[3] 2 Macc. 4 : 9.

[4] Polybius, Bk. XXVI, ch. 1; Livy, Bk. XLI, ch. 20.

Semitic dress.[1] The fundamentalists and the nationalists among the Jews were nevertheless united in their determined opposition. The revolt broke out in Judaea [2] in 168 B.C. under the leadership of Judas, son of a humble priest named Mattathias of the Hasmonaean (Asmonean) family. Judas afterwards assumed the title Maccabeus.[3] The uprising was directed first more against the upper class, who exploited the masses, than against the central government. Judas with his brothers organized guerilla bands which operated in the hills and avoided pitched battles with the royal forces. There were pietists (*ḥasīdīm*) among those opposed to Antiochus who would not profane the Sabbath by striking a blow and were easily butchered.[4] This is one of the earliest cases of religious martyrdom in recorded history. Through the efforts of the Maccabean brothers Jerusalem was captured, the Temple was cleansed and the daily sacrifice restored. In celebration of this event the feast of Hanukkah (dedication) was instituted and has since been kept annually.

A Jewish commonwealth

Though of a religious character at the outset, the movement developed into a national revolt aimed at liberating the land. The clash was not only with the Syrian forces but also between nationalist fundamentalists who were unwavering in their devotion to Hebraism and adherents to the new culture who constituted the Hellenistic or Reform party. In both conflicts the victory was on the Maccabean side. Judas' brother Simon was elected in 141 B.C. high priest and ruler. The Seleucid Demetrius II Nicator granted the Jews under Simon independence.[5] Simon began to coin money. Jerusalem started a new era; documents were hereafter dated: "In the first year of Simon the high priest, the governor".[6] A new Jewish commonwealth was born, to live until the advent of the Romans eighty years later.

[1] M. Rostovtzeff, *The Social and Economic History of the Hellenistic World* (Oxford, 1941), p. 704.

[2] A geographical term first used by Ezra 5 : 8 to designate a province of the Persian empire.

[3] 1 Macc. 2 : 4; Josephus, *Antiquities*, Bk. XII, ch. 6, § 1. Origin and meaning of the term uncertain, perhaps from Heb. *maqqebeth*, hammer, in allusion to the crushing blows inflicted on the enemy.

[4] 1 Macc. 1 : 62-3; 2 : 38.

[5] Josephus, *Antiquities*, Bk. XIII, ch. 6, § 7; 1 Macc. 13 : 34 *seq.*

[6] 1 Macc. 13 : 42.

The Maccabean Jews, triumphant, became more narrowly nationalistic than the Jews of old. They fought their Hellenizing brothers as well as non-Jews. John Hyrcanus I (135–105), who succeeded his father Simon, attacked the Samaritans, who had succumbed to the Antiochene scheme, and demolished their city with its temple.[1] Before that he forced the Idumaeans, who had by this time penetrated into southern Judaea, to be circumcized and Judaized (*ca.* 126 B.C.).[2] Under the early Maccabees the Jewish commonwealth was theocratic. John inscribed on his coins " John the High Priest ", but his son Aristobulus (105–103) assumed the title of king or, in the words of Josephus, " put a diadem on his head ".[3] He and all the later kings of the dynasty bore Greek as well as Hebrew names. After the time of his successor Alexander Jannaeus (103–76), under whom the territory under Maccabean control reached its maximum extent, Greek legends become common on coins alongside the Hebrew. The Galilee which we know in the Gospels was Aristobulus' creation. For long inhabited by non-Jewish peoples [4] and now by Ituraeans (a community of Arabian stock but Aramaic speech), Galilee was offered the choice between expulsion or circumcision. The majority preferred circumcision.[5] Of the people, therefore, among whom Christ laboured and from whom He drew His apostles, many were of non-Jewish origin and pronounced Hebrew with an accent. They were looked upon as lower than the old Jews and incapable of producing a prophet.[6] The practice followed by Hyrcanus and his son established a precedent which was followed by others of the Hasmonaean house in dealing with cities or peoples they conquered: a choice between Judaism and destruction.[7]

Last convulsions of the Seleucid kingdom

Not only Jews were pressing in where Seleucid power was giving way, but also neighbouring Arabian tribes, particularly the Nabataeans on the southern fringe of the empire. Farther

[1] See above, p. 198; Josephus, *Antiquities*, Bk. XIII, ch. 4, §§ 2-3.

[2] 1 Macc. 4:29; 5:65; Josephus, *Antiquities*, Bk. XIII, ch. 9, § 1. " Idumaea " was the Greek form for Edom.

[3] *Antiquities*, Bk. XIII, ch. 11, § 1.

[4] Is. 9:1; 1 Macc. 5:15; Matt. 4:15.

[5] Josephus, *Antiquities*, Bk. XIII, ch. 11, § 3.

[6] Mk. 14:70; Lk. 22:59; Acts 2:7; John 1:46; 7:41, 52; Bevan, vol. ii, p. 256.

[7] Josephus, *Antiquities*, Bk. XIII, ch. 15, § 4.

east Parthia, Bactria and adjoining lands were reasserting their independence. About 130 B.C. an Arab dynasty in Edessa makes its debut with nominal dependence on Parthia and with most of its kings named Abgar. Another Arab tribe succeeds in making its shaykhs rulers of a new state centring on Emesa and only nominally dependent on the Seleucids. Another native state, of Ituraeans, firmly established itself in Coele-Syria with Chalcis for capital. The successors of Antiochus IV were on the whole incompetent. Under them the Seleucid house, which for generations had stood before the world as the imperial house of the East, was progressively losing prestige, power and dignity. The entire century after Epiphanes presents a confused picture of native revolts, internal dissension, family quarrels and gradual loss of territory. The empire which once stretched from the lower Mediterranean and the Aegean to Turkestan and India now shrank into a local state in North Syria.

Among the Arabians the Nabataeans, who about 312 B.C. had driven the Edomites from the region of Petra, were now becoming a considerable power. Around 85 B.C. Coele-Syria was wrested by Nabataeans from Seleucid hands, and Damascus put herself under their protection to escape the worse fate of falling into the hands of the Ituraean dynast.[1] The Ituraeans were then overrunning the coast between Sidon and Theouprosopon[2] and devastating the fields of Byblus and Beirut. Other Phoenician cities were then regaining their local freedom. Of the cities on the seaboard between Phoenicia and Egypt, only a few like Ascalon were spared to nurse the seeds of Hellenic life. The rest, like Gaza where Hellenic culture had flourished, stood in desolate ruins — monuments of the vengeance of the Jews.[3]

During this period of Seleucid decline all the eastern provinces of the empire were lost. By 130 B.C. the Parthians had extended their empire over the territory from the Euphrates to the Indus and from the Oxus to the Indian Ocean. On the west the progress of Parthian arms was checked by the Armenian

[1] Josephus, *Antiquities*, Bk. XIII, ch. 15, § 2; *War*, Bk. I, ch. 4, § 8; see below, p. 378. The Ituraeans are the Jetur of Gen. 25:15; 1 Ch. 1:31.

[2] Phoen. *P'ne-El* (Penuel, god's visage), the precipitous headland now called Ra's al-Shaqʿah, wrongly given as Shaqqa in Abel, vol. ii, pp. 4, 117; Baedeker, *Palestine and Syria* (Leipzig, 1912), p. 338. Strabo, Bk. XVI, ch. 2, §§ 15, 18.

[3] Bevan, vol. ii, p. 264.

Director of Antiquities of Syria

A FUNERARY OR COMMEMORATIVE MONUMENT ON MOUNT HIRMIL, NEAR ḤIMṢ, ERECTED PROBABLY BY ONE OF THE NATIVE RULERS OF EMESA IN THE LATE HELLENISTIC PERIOD

The building displays a mixture of Greek and Oriental elements both in architecture and sculptural decoration. In the hunting scene animals and weapons are shown but not the hunters themselves. The monument was recently partially restored king Tigranes (Dikran) and his father-in-law Mithradates [1] the Great of Pontus. Under Tigranes the Armenian kingdom reached the height of its power.

This ambitious monarch had overrun Mesopotamia, held by the Parthians, and by 83 B.C. was overrunning North Syria and Cilicia,[2] which was still under the Seleucids and whose population was akin to the Aramaeans. The two Syrian princes who then called themselves kings, Philip I Philadelphus and Antiochus X Eusebes,[3] are no more heard of. Tigranes built a new royal city Tigranocerta [4] in the upper Tigris region and assumed the title "king of kings". Worn out with the civil broils and dynastic feuds the Syrians were in no mood to offer resistance. Even the Greek cities welcomed an opportunity to enjoy normal life again. All acquiesced with relief in the new rule. In their southward push the arms of Tigranes reached Acre, now Ptolemais, which he occupied about 69 B.C. The Jewish kingdom was thereby threatened. Palestine could be used as a stepping-stone for the occupation of Egypt, on which Rome had her eye, especially at this juncture when the Ptolemaic house was tottering.

The Romans annex Syria

While Tigranes was expanding his domain at the expense of the Parthians and the Syrians, his father-in-law and ally Mithradates was carving an empire for himself at the expense of Asia Minor and the Romans.[5] At last the Roman legions caught up with him and drove him out of the land. He sought asylum with Tigranes, who refused to deliver him. Rome declared war and Tigranes was forced to withdraw his garrisons from Syria (69 B.C.). The district of Antioch was then reoccupied by a Seleucid prince Antiochus XIII Asiaticus, and his claim was acknowledged by Rome.[6] His rule was contested by Philip II. These two were the last to wear the royal diadem

[1] Less correctly "Mithridates", derived from Per. *mithras*, sun, and probably means "sun-given". The kingdom of Pontus, on the south-east shore of the Black Sea to the north of Armenia, was originally a satrapy of the Persian empire and won its independence at its fall. Its kings claimed descent from an early Persian monarch.

[2] Appian, § 48.

[3] See below, p. 250, n. 1.

[4] Strabo, Bk. XI, ch. 12, § 4; ch. 14, § 15. Exact site undetermined, perhaps Mayyāfarīqīn.

[5] Strabo, Bk. XII, ch. 3, § 1.

[6] Appian, § 49.

of the Seleucids.[1] Shortly after that Mithradates managed to recover the throne he had lost. This time Pompey moved against him, occupied Pontus and put him to flight. Rome's greatest enemy in Asia Minor was thus removed from the way. Tigranes then sued for peace, resigning all claims to Syria and Asia Minor. This was the year 64 B.C., a landmark in Syrian history. Palestine was occupied the following year.[2] Pompey decreed that Syria be ruled directly by a Roman proconsul.[3] An old order came to an end; a new one, Roman, began.

[1] Table of Seleucid kings, some of whom were competitive pretenders (see above, p. 241, n. 1):

12. Demetrius II Nicator (son of Demetrius I) 146–138, 128–125 B.C.
13. Antiochus VI Theos (son of Alexander I) 144–142.
14. Tryphon (usurper) 142–137.
15. Antiochus VII Sidetes (son of Demetrius I) 137–128.
16. Alexander II Zabinas (son of a merchant) 128–122.
17. Seleucus V (son of Demetrius II) 125.
18. Antiochus VIII Grypus (son of Demetrius II) 125–96.
19. Antiochus IX Cyzicenus (son of Sidetes) 112–96.

In the last thirty-two years of confusion Syria was parcelled out among several rulers:

Seleucus VI Epiphanes (son of Grypus) 96–93; Antiochus X Eusebes (son of Cyzicenus) 94–92 at Antioch; Antiochus XI Epiphanes (son of Grypus) 95–94; Philip I Philadelphus (son of Grypus) 92–83; Demetrius III Theos (son of Grypus) 95–88; Antiochus XII Dionysus (son of Grypus) 88–84; Antiochus XIII Asiaticus (son of Eusebes) 69–65; Philip II (son of Philip I) 68–64; 83–69 interregnum.

[2] Josephus, *Antiquities*, Bk. XIV, ch. 4.

[3] See below, p. 281.

CHAPTER XVIII

THE HELLENISTIC AGE

THE introduction of Hellenism into Western Asia, as we learned before,[1] preceded Alexander's conquests; its advance was facilitated by them and then accelerated and intensified by the Seleucid programme. The result of this interpenetration of Greek and Semitic cultures was the synthetic civilization known as Hellenism in contradistinction to the Hellenic or purely Greek. Hellenism, the chief phenomenon of the Seleucid period, rose to supremacy not only in Syria but throughout Western Asia and Egypt. Sandwiched in time between two Semitic layers — the lower being Aramaic and the upper Arabic — Hellenism survived in Syria for a thousand years, until the Moslem conquests.

Greek settlements

The nursery of this eclectic Greek culture which extended mostly over non-Greeks was the series of cities planted by Alexander and his successors. The planters chose the sites with care, in strategic spots, at the cardinal points of intercourse and along river valleys. The colonies were cities of Greek speech and constitution. In them, it was evident, a Greek population could survive, whereas it could not if scattered in different native communities. The colonists were primarily Greek and Macedonian soldiers and mercenaries settled by royal decree. Wives were supplied partly from the native stock. Civilians gradually thronged to these settlements attracted by hopes of advantage or driven from their old homes by political or economic forces. In time half-breeds and natives who had put on the externals of Hellenism were added to the colonial population, which then came to comprise traders, artists, scholars and slaves.

First among the centres for the diffusion of Greek culture stood the capital Antioch. It was built about 300 B.C. on the left bank of the Orontes, some twenty miles from the sea, in

[1] Above, p. 197.

a beautiful valley. Under the Seleucids it became the chief political city of all Asia. As a centre of Greek culture it was surpassed by Alexandria, Constantinople and perhaps one or two other Greek colonies. Seleucia, Laodicea and Apamea came next. A number of rhetoricians and philosophers in the last two pre-Christian centuries — none, with the exception of Posidonius, of first rank — flourished in these towns.

While the Seleucids were engaged in planting Greek cities north of the Lebanon, the Ptolemies were doing the same south of it. The Macedonian rulers of Egypt, however, were less missionary-minded than those of Syria. Among their foundations was Philoteria [1] on the Sea of Galilee, named after Philotera, sister of Ptolemy II Philadelphus. Pella [2] in what later became the Decapolis [3] may have been founded by Alexander himself. It was so named after the capital of Macedonia. Another member of the Decapolis, Gerasa,[4] was founded as a Hellenistic city probably by Antiochus IV and designated Antioch on the Chrysorrhoas.[5] Several other cities like Arethusa (al-Rastan, on the Orontes south of Ḥamāh) and Cyrrhus (Qūrus, north of Aleppo) proclaim their Macedonian origin by their names.[6] In many cases native hamlets or fortresses were transformed into Greco-Macedonian cities.[7]

The Greek cities were built according to a preconceived form and provided with theatres, baths, gymnasiums, forums and other institutions in which the individual expressed himself as a member of society. In them the political formation of the Greek city-state was maintained with ample provision for the self-realization of the citizen as an integral part of the community. In all this the new settlements differed from the old Semitic ones, which were usually built around a fortress, a spring or a shrine as a nucleus,[8] but grew according to no plan

[1] Probably Khirbat Karak, on the southern point of Lake Tiberias; Abel, vol. ii, p. 131; cf. Dussaud, *Topographie*, p. 22; Polybius, Bk. V, ch. 70.

[2] Cf. Appian, § 57. Ar. Fiḥl or Faḥl.

[3] Mk. 5:20; see below, p. 281.

[4] Now Jarash, of ancient Semitic but uncertain etymology. See below, p. 318.

[5] A stream which arose from springs in the vicinity. See Carl H. Kraeling, *Gerasa, City of the Decapolis* (New Haven, 1938), pp. 27 *seq.*

[6] Arethusa was the nymph of a famous well in a Greek island; Cyrrhus was a city of Macedonia in the vicinity of Pella.

[7] See below, pp. 316-17.

[8] See above, p. 82.

and had no channels in which the democratic way of life found expression. Syria had more cities now than ever before.

Cities re-colonized

Under both Seleucids and Ptolemies not only were new foundations laid but old towns with Semitic names were re-colonized and renamed. Acre became Ptolemais under Ptolemy II Philadelphus (285–247 B.C.). In honour of the same king Rabbath-Ammon [1] was called Philadelphia. Beth-shean (modern Baysān) was named Scythopolis.[2] In the north Berytus became Laodicea in the second century and Ḥamāh acquired the name Epiphania in honour of Antiochus IV. Neighbouring Shayzar changed its appellation to Larissa after a city in Thessaly. Edessa had a Macedonian namesake. Its transformation to the Macedonian colony of Antiochia Callirrhoe is attributed to Alexander himself. It was rebuilt by Antiochus IV and called Antioch.[3] Nisibis (now Naṣībīn), through which the highway of communication between Syria and the lands beyond the Tigris ran, was built, according to an inscription, by Nicator. In the recolonized cities the native element was allowed to retain its place to a larger degree than was usual in the new settlements. The superimposed Greek or Macedonian city often went native.

It is interesting to note that most of the cities that were thus recolonized and renamed in due course shed their Greek nomenclature and with it the thin veneer of Hellenization, reasserted their Semitic character and restored their Semitic names by which they are today known. Beroea is today Ḥalab (Aleppo); Chalcis in Coele-Syria is ʻAnjar (contraction of ʻAyn al-Jarr) and Eleutheropolis is Bayt Jibrīn.[4] The only exception is Tripoli. Shechem, which was rebuilt by the Emperor Titus and named Neapolis (new town), is today Nābulus. Likewise most districts, mountains and rivers which assumed Greek names are now known by their Semitic names.

Many of the artistic, architectural and other cultural elements, however, introduced by the Greek and Macedonian

[1] Modern ʻAmmān (capital of Transjordan), which echoes the ancient name.

[2] So called from the Scythians whose swarms about 627 B.C. ravaged Syria to the border of Egypt. See Herodotus, Bk. I, ch. 105; Jer. 6:23. This village was in later times the sole relic of their invasion.

[3] Pliny, Bk. V, ch. 21; Polybius, Bk. V, ch. 51. The earliest form of its name is Aram. Urhai, which has survived in Ar. al-Ruhā', corrupted into Tur. Urfa

[4] Or Jibrīl, on the Gaza-Jerusalem road. See below, p. 414, n. 3.

settlers survived. They make themselves manifest in the Roman period. The destruction of the Hellenistic kingdom did by no means entail the destruction of its Hellenistic culture. The arch and vault were known before but the Corinthian capital steadily gained. The theatres and gymnasiums erected by members of the Herodian family under the Romans were in the Hellenistic tradition.[1] In fact the bulk of the Hellenistic remains in Syria belong to the Roman period.

Degrees of Hellenization

Different parts of Syria responded in differing measure to Greek stimuli. In the north not only cities but other places were named after those of the motherland. Native deities, too, were identified with Greek gods and rechristened. Baal became Zeus. Indo-European legends and myths were domesticated in the new land. Four miles south of Antioch lay its pleasure garden Daphne, where the nymph by the same name, pursued by Apollo when charmed by her beauty, was metamorphosed into a laurel tree. The original scene was in Thessaly. To the sanctuary of Apollo in Daphne, which stood amidst a laurel grove with abundant water [2] and was invested with the right of asylum, Antiochians and pilgrims flocked from all over Syria, making it a centre of licentiousness. On the whole, North Syria became a " new Macedonia ", where the invasive Greek element made itself thoroughly at home.

Next came the Phoenician cities. These, be it remembered, had had contacts with the Greek world going back to the eleventh century if not earlier.[3] The fact that they by this time had lost their nationalistic spirit contributed to the ease with which the Greco-Syrian synthesis was accomplished. Tyre, Sidon, Aradus, Laodicea-Berytus (as Beirut was sometimes called), Marathus, had no hesitancy in striking coins bearing Greek legends alongside Phoenician ones. The Hellenism that struck root in Phoenician Syria became more vigorous, more productive than that of Aramaean Syria. At this time an educated Phoenician must have felt somewhat at home in a city of Greece, and a Greek must have felt the same in a Phoenician seaport. In Sidon and Tyre, no less than in Antioch and Laodicea, Greek philosophy and literature were assiduously

[1] See below, pp. 283, 309.

[2] Hence the Arabic name Bayt al-Mā' (the home of water). Strabo, Bk. XVI, ch. 3, § 6.

[3] See above, pp. 97-8, 102 *seq.*, 116

cultivated. Some of the distinguished Greek-writing authors of the last two pre-Christian centuries were natives of these two Phoenician towns. One of them, Zeno of Sidon, was the teacher of his namesake Zeno of Citium, Cyprus (333–261 B.C.), founder of the Stoic school of philosophy, the greatest creation of the age. Citium was itself a Phoenician colony and its distinguished

The American Numismatic Society

A COIN OF BEIRUT

Obverse and reverse of a bronze coin of Berytus, second century B.C. On the obverse is a bust of Tyche with turreted crown; on the reverse, Baal-Beroth in a car drawn by four hippocampi. The inscription is in Phoenician and Greek

son was to his contemporaries a Phoenician. Zeno, "the noblest man of his age",[1] went to Athens and began to teach in the Painted Porch (*stoa poikile*) in 302. He was a friend of Alexander's general Antigonus but kept clear of politics. The decree accompanying the honours voted to him by Athens after his death ended with these words: "He made his life a pattern to all, for he followed his own teaching". In a sepulchral epigram someone wrote about Zeno:

> And if thy native country was Phoenicia,
> What need to slight thee? Came not Cadmus thence,
> Who gave to Greece her books and art of writing?[2]

Another Phoenician head of a philosophical school in Athens was Diodorus the Peripatetic of Tyre, who was still active in 110 B.C. and was mentioned by Cicero.[3] One of his ethical maxims was that the greatest good consists in a combination of virtue with the absence of pain, a formula that suggests an attempted reconciliation between Stoic and Epicurean viewpoints.

A more renowned Syrian eclectic was Antiochus of Ascalon,

[1] W. W. Tarn, *Hellenistic Civilisation*, 2nd ed. (London, 1930), p. 295.

[2] Diogenes Laertius, *Lives of Eminent Philosophers*, tr. R. D. Hicks (London, 1925), Bk. VII, § 30; cf. *The Greek Anthology*, ed. and tr. W. R. Paton (New York, 1927), Bk. VII, § 117.

[3] *De Oratore*, Bk. I, ch. 11.

who tried to unite the views of the Platonists and those of the Stoics. Besides his Syrian academy, Antiochus founded one at Alexandria and another at Athens. Cicero[1] attended his Athenian academy six months and speaks of him in affectionate and respectful terms. Plutarch[2] characterizes him as "a persuasive man and powerful speaker". In describing Ascalon, Strabo[3] mentions Antiochus' birth as a mark of distinction for the city.

Persistence of Aramaic

Greek language and culture naturally acquired special glamour from their association with the conquering people. The absolute superiority of Greek literature and civilization was recognized as incontestable on both sides. The fact remains that the Hellenic East was but an artificial creation. In its midst Baalism and Judaism kept their old traditions. More than that, local cults were adopted in a Hellenized form by the Seleucids, most of whom showed respect to the local gods. In looking for a site for his projected harbour city Seleucus I sacrificed to Zeus of Mount Casius, the native god of storm and thunder, who sent an eagle to show him where to found it.[4] Seleucus' wife rebuilt the temple of Atargatis at Bambyce-Hierapolis, where the cult of the Semitic goddess continued to flourish.[5] The mysteries of Byblus began to be associated with Aphrodite and Adonis, but that does not so much imply the Hellenization of the Orient as it does the Orientalizing of the Hellenic world.[6] Aramaic persisted throughout as the vernacular of the people, who at core remained Semitic in their way of life. As late as the third century after Christ Palmyra used Aramaic side by side with Greek as the official language; Dura-Europus also used both Aramaic and Greek in its inscriptions. The Greek colonists gradually became more affected by Semitic life than the natives by Greek life. Some of the late Seleucid kings acquired Aramaic nicknames. Alexander I (150–146) was known as Balas and Alexander II (128–122), who was not of Seleucid stock, as Zabinas.[7] In Aramaic Syria

1 *Brutus*, Bk. XCI, § 315.

2 "Lucullus", in *Vitae*, ch. 42.

3 Bk. XVI, ch. 2, § 29.

4 Malalas, *Chronographia*, ed. L. Dindorf (Bonn, 1831), p. 199, ll. 2 *seq.*

5 Lucian, § 17; see above, p. 173.

6 See above, p. 117.

7 "Balas" is evidently *ba'lā*, an abbreviation of some compound name in which Ba'l, the name of the deity, figured. "Zabinas" is *zĕbina*, "bought", "the bought one". The name occurs in Ezra 10:43 and must have originally meant bought from God.

and Jewish Palestine the native culture in general more than held its own; it gave more than it received.

The educated Syrians, no doubt, studied Greek and wrote in it. But there is no reason to believe that they used it at home except in the case of those who were brought up in Greek colonies. The population of the recolonized cities was presumably bilingual. The countryside, of course, fully retained its old speech and its customs and manner of living. The bulk of the people were no more Grecized than modern Syrians were Frenchified. What the introduction of Hellenism did was to disrupt the purely Semitic political and intellectual structure and to open the door for subsequent Romanizing influences. A thousand years had to pass before a reintegration was possible.

Literary activity

Aramaic literature of Seleucid Syria has left no remains. Nor have any Aramaic inscriptions of this period been discovered. Before the Muses of Hellas native literary activity shrank with a sense of inferiority to almost nothing. But there is no doubt that many writers of the age who bore Greek names and wrote in that language were of Syrian origin. In the first decades of the twentieth century several dissertations and other works appeared in French bearing Frenchified names of Lebanese authors which are almost impossible to recognize as Arabic. It is also safe to assume that some Aramaic pieces of literature were written but did not survive. Certain Hebrew works would have met the same fate had they not had the good fortune of finding a Greek translator and being accepted among the Apocrypha. One of our main sources of knowledge of this era, 1 Maccabees, was evidently written between 105 and 63 B.C. and translated into Greek from a Hebrew original. In the pseudepigraphical Book of Enoch, originally written in Hebrew or Aramaic about the same time but surviving in its entirety only in Ethiopic, immortality, hitherto for the righteous only, is extended to all men and accompanied with the ideas of reward and punishment. Here is an expression of perhaps the greatest thought of the time.[1] One of the problems treated by Enoch, that of the unrighteous flourishing, greatly exercised Jewish as well as Greek minds. Two Hebrew works of the Seleucid era worked their way into the canon, Ecclesiastes, written about 200 B.C. by an aristocratic Hellenized Jew, and Daniel, com-

[1] See above, p. 226.

posed in the second pre-Christian century. Of the two Ecclesiastes has much the closer affinity with Greek thought.

No part of the Seleucid empire developed into a real centre of artistic, literary or scientific creativeness. The kings were never munificent patrons of learning; nor were the Ptolemies, with the exception of Ptolemy I, founder of the world-renowned library and museum of Alexandria. Libraries were established in the capitals, and Antioch had one. Considering the improvement in communication, the spread of a common civilization and the prevalence of a common speech, learning would have flourished more had it received royal encouragement. The only name worth mentioning in the eastern provinces is that of Seleucus of Seleucia-on-the-Tigris, originally a Chaldaean, who lived sometime in the second pre-Christian century and maintained that the sun was the centre of the universe. In this he followed the hypothesis of Aristarchus [1] and tried to find proofs for it. Seleucus advanced scientifically correct views on the connection between the tides and the moon which were quoted by the Syrian Posidonius.[2]

Posidonius the historian

Hellenistic Syria produced a couple of historian geographers, a few astronomers, a limited number of poets none of whom was of first rank, and a remarkable number of philosophers mainly of the Stoic school. Almost all belonged to the second or early first century before Christ. Stoicism from the outset established close connection with the Semitic conception of life and remained throughout its career congenial to the Semitized Greeks as well as to the Hellenized Semites. In its stress on brotherhood and a world state, virtue and ethical living, and in considering all that had to do with the body — strength and weakness, health and sickness, wealth and poverty — as a matter of indifference, this philosophy was in a sense a precursor of Christianity. Foremost among the Syrian writers was Posidonius of Apamea, Stoic philosopher, historian and natural scientist, whose most influential work was a continuation of the history of Polybius that became a source for Livy, Strabo, Plutarch and others and thus contributed to the important task of education of the early Romans and paving the way for the glory of the Augustan age. Posidonius was born about 135 B.C., studied in Athens and after

[1] Of Samos, flourished in Alexandria, 280–264 B.C.

[2] Strabo, Bk. III, ch. 5, § 9.

travelling in Italy, Gaul, Spain and Sicily settled as the head of the Stoic school in Rhodes, where he died in 51 B.C. Such was his fame that Pompey on his return from Syria stopped at Rhodes to attend his lectures. Arriving at the home of the philosopher, the great Roman general forbade his lictor to knock at the door, as was usual, and paid further homage by lowering the fasces.[1] Cicero [2] says that he too attended the lectures of Posidonius. His was the last great intellect Hellenism, untouched by Rome, produced. The following excerpts from his writings illustrate the high life of Syrian towns and describe some natural products:

There were many clubs in which they amused themselves continuously, using the gymnasia as baths, anointing themselves with expensive oil and unguents, and using the *schools*, for so they called the dining-halls of the members, as if they were their own houses, stuffing themselves there for the greater part of the day with wines and food, and even carrying off much besides, amidst the sound of noisy lyres, which made whole cities ring with the uproar.[3]

Arabia and Syria also produce the persea, and what is called the pistachio. This bears a grapelike fruit with white shell, and of a long shape, so as to resemble a tear. They press against one another like vine-clusters; the inside is pale green, less well-flavoured than pine-cones but more fragrant.[4]

Greco-Syrian poets

Though not strikingly original, Greco-Syrian poetry is marked with versatility, appreciation of natural beauty, richness in imagery and colour and a keen sense of the ludicrous. Many of the poets were adept in the art of improvisation and the composition of epigrams. Antipater of Sidon, formerly of Tyre, who flourished at the beginning of the first pre-Christian century, employed the epigram chiefly for dedications and epitaphs. The following hortatory epigram recalls his residence in a Phoenician seaport:

'Tis time the ship speed on; the ocean's breast
No darkling storm with billowy furrows cleaves;
Beneath the roof the swallow forms her nest,
And o'er the meadows laugh the tender leaves.

[1] Cicero, *Tusculanarum disputationum*, Bk. II, ch. 25; Pliny, Bk. VII, ch. 31.
[2] Cicero, *De Natura Deorum*, Bk. I, ch. 3.
[3] E. S. Bouchier, *Syria as a Roman Province* (Oxford, 1916), p. 202; cf. Athenaeus, *The Deipnosophists*, ed. and tr. Charles B. Gulick (London, 1933), Bk. XII, § 527.
[4] Bouchier, p. 202; Athenaeus, Bk. XIV, § 649; see below, pp. 274-5.

Draw in your dripping moorings, sailors all,
And drag the buried anchors from the sands;
Haul up well-woven canvas at my call,
So Bacchus' son, the harbour's lord, commands.[1]

Antipater was Epicurean in his philosophy:

Men learned in the stars say I am short-lived. I am, Seleucus,[2] but I care not. There is one road down to Hades for all, and if mine is quicker, I shall see Minos [3] all the sooner. Let us drink, for this is very truth, that wine is a horse for the road, while foot-travellers take a by-path to Hades.[4]

Another Epicurean philosopher and epigrammatic poet was Philodemus, who was born in the early first pre-Christian century at Gadara,[5] a Macedonian colony planted among the semi-nomads of Transjordan on a bold headland overlooking the gorge of the Hieromax (Yarmūk) and the southern end of the Sea of Galilee. Philodemus settled in Rome at the time of Cicero, who praises him warmly. Most of his surviving epigrams are of a light and amatory character bearing out Cicero's statement concerning the licentiousness of his matter and the elegance of his manner.[6] Here is a specimen:

I fell in love with Demo of Paphos — nothing surprising in that: and again with Demo of Samos — well that was not so remarkable: and thirdly with Demo of Naxos — then the matter ceased to be a joke: and in the fourth place with Demo of Argos. The Fates themselves seem to have christened me Philodeme [" lover of the people "]; as I always feel ardent desire for some Demo.[7]

Meleager

The most interesting poet of an unpoetic age was probably Meleager of Gadara. Meleager was Syrian by nationality, probably spoke Aramaic at home and knew Phoenician as well as Greek. Like most Syrian writers of the age he sought his fortune outside his native town. At the age of twenty (*ca.* 115 B.C.) he migrated to Tyre, of whose inner life we gain a

[1] Bouchier, pp. 193-4; cf. *Greek Anthology*, Bk. X, § 2.

[2] The reference is evidently to Seleucus the Chaldaean, who was also an astrologer.

[3] King and legislator of Crete who after his death became one of the judges of the shades of Hades.

[4] *Greek Anthology*, Bk. XI, § 23.

[5] Josephus, *Antiquities*, Bk. XVII, ch. 11, § 4; site is near modern Umm Qays. The Gadarenes are mentioned in Mk. 5:1; Lk. 8:26, 37.

[6] *In Pisonem*, chs. 28, 29.

[7] *Greek Anthology*, Bk. V, § 115.

glimpse from his epigrams. The life of the town must have been voluptuous. Singers and harpers were popular and drink common. The harem of the better class lived in seclusion and were attended while in the streets. Later Meleager moved to the isle of Cos, where he compiled an anthology, *Garland*, of select poems by earlier writers, each one of whom he compared in a poem of his to some beautiful flower or graceful tree.[1] In another striking short poem he describes a garland of seven boys he himself knew at Tyre and compared to the sweet lily, scented white violet, rose, vine, blossom, golden-tressed saffron, sprig of thyme and evergreen olive shoot. This garland was offered by Love to Aphrodite.[2] Following are two sepulchral epigrams by Meleager:

Island Tyre was my nurse, and Gadara, which is Attic, but lies in Syria, gave birth to me. From Eucrates I sprung, Meleager, who first by the help of the Muses ran abreast of the Graces of Menippus.[3] If I am a Syrian, what wonder? Stranger, we dwell in one country, the world; one Chaos gave birth to all mortals.[4]

Go noiselessly by, stranger; the old man sleeps among the pious dead, wrapped in the slumber that is the lot of all. This is Meleager, the son of Eucrates, who linked sweet tearful Love and the Muses with the Graces. Heavenborn Tyre and Gadara's holy soil reared him to manhood, and beloved Cos of the Meropes tended his old age. If you are a Syrian, Salam! if you are a Phoenician, Naidius![5] if you are a Greek, Chaire! (Hail) and say the same yourself.[6]

[1] *Greek Anthology*, Bk. IV, § 1.

[2] *Greek Anthology*, Bk. XII, § 256.

[3] A satirist, also of Gadara, who flourished about 280 B.C. Originally a slave and afterwards an adherent of the Cynic school of philosophy, he treated the follies of mankind, especially of philosophers, in a sarcastic tone. His satire was much used by Lucian. Menippus has been called the father of *feuilleton* literature. His artistic prose, with occasional intermingling of passages in verse, is reminiscent of al-Ḥarīri's *Maqāmāt*.

[4] *Greek Anthology*, Bk. VII, § 417.

[5] This Phoenician word for "hail" looks like the first person plural imperfect of *yādhāh*, to give thanks, with the Greek suffix.

[6] *Greek Anthology*, Bk. VII, § 419.

CHAPTER XIX

SELEUCID INSTITUTIONS

The royalty

THE political institutions of the Seleucid realm were a strange mixture of Greco-Macedonian and Syro-Persian elements, among which the latter predominated. At the head of the state stood the king with absolute power. In fact he was the state. All authority stemmed from him. He appointed and dismissed officials at his pleasure. His rule was personal and dynastic based on the right of conquest and succession. He was surrounded by a divine halo, a heritage from Alexander and the Oriental monarchs. The divine descent of the founder of the house was proclaimed early in his career by an oracle and was generally accepted. It became a part of the royal style under his successors. The native non-Greek population maintained an attitude which may best be described as passive acquiescence.

The régime of the palace, with its display of crimson and gold and the conspicuousness of its chamberlains and eunuchs, was more Oriental than Occidental. On state occasions the monarch wore on his head a diadem, symbol of his royalty. The diadem as seen on the coins was a narrow gold ribbon.[1] The signet ring also served as emblem of royalty.[2] Seleucus used an engraved anchor for his ring for reasons that remain obscure;[3] the anchor also figures on Seleucid coins and weights. The royal dress remained the old national garb of Macedonia but glorified and made of purple. The purple robe was associated with royalty and high priesthood.[4]

The regal banquets were marked with splendours. Gold and silver plates, choice wines, stringed instruments and odours of myrrh and other Oriental perfumes played their part. Posidonius[5] has left us snapshots of the brilliant receptions held in

[1] See above, p. 243. [2] I Macc. 6:15. [3] Appian, § 56.
[4] I Macc. 10:20; 11:58; Polybius, Bk. XXVI, ch. 1; see above, p. 95.
[5] Athenaeus, Bk. XII, ch. 540.

celebration of the games at Daphne by Antiochus VII Sidetes [1] (137–128 B.C.). The royal host would let each feaster carry home enough uncarved meat of land and sea animals to fill a cart, besides quantities of honey cakes and wreaths of myrrh and frankincense with matted fillets of gold " as long as a man ". Antiochus VIII Grypus (hook-nosed, 125–96 B.C.) on such occasions would distribute to the diners live geese, hares and

Director of Antiquities, Beirut

A SQUARE LEAD-WEIGHT BEARING THE FIGURE OF AN ANCHOR AND THE NAME OF ANTIOCHUS VIII GRYPUS (125–96 B.C.)

Found in Antioch, now in the National Museum, Beirut

gazelles together with gold wreaths, silver vessels, slaves, horses and camels. After mounting his camel, each man would drink a toast and accept the camel and everything upon it as well as the attending slave. Besides feasting the chief royal recreation comprised hunting and horsemanship.

Around the monarch the court was grouped. The language (The court) of the court was undoubtedly Greek. It is improbable that the Seleucid king knew the language of any of his native subjects. When young, several of the royal princes sought their education

[1] So nicknamed from Side in Pamphylia, where he was brought up.

in Athens or Rome. The highest office in the court was that of "minister for affairs", a continuation of the Persian office of vizir. The hierarchy included the head of the royal chancery, the finance minister, the financial secretary, the quartermaster and the chief physician. In the provinces the officials were satraps, district governors, secretaries and overseers of taxes. The ministry of finance was an especially favoured office.[1]

The Macedonian nobility, uprooted from its ancestral soil and grafted with the new nobility consisting of officials whom the king's favour elevated, was in no position to act as a check on the imperial power. The women of the palace sometimes quarrelled and intrigued for power. The Seleucids and Ptolemies, with the possible exception of the first generation of Alexander's successors, were monogamous but kept mistresses. Antiochus IV invested his mistress with royal power over Tarsus and another city in Cilicia, to the disgust of their people.[2] Members of both houses practised sister marriage, as the Pharaohs and Persian kings had done. Members of the royal family and of the official corps had a plethora of slaves. Hellenistic society everywhere was poor in machines, rich in slaves.[3]

Army

Both army and navy were the king's. The Seleucid army was influential in state affairs. Seleucus I considered it expedient to secure its consent when he arranged for the strange marriage of his son and successor Antiochus I to his stepmother, and for appointing him over certain provinces.[4] The army in its early stages consisted of all Macedonians and Greeks in the realm and provided a principal means by which men could rise to power. Its headquarters were in Apamea [5] but a camp stood in Antioch for the royal guard. At the battle of Raphia in 217 [6] the army of Antiochus III consisted of 20,000 European settlers, supported by 10,000 picked men of many nationalities, 10,000 Arabian and other tribesmen and a number of mercenaries swelling the whole to 62,000 foot and 6000 horse.[7] The cavalry ranked higher and received more pay than the infantry.

The nucleus of the army was the phalanx. Recruited mainly

1 Consult Appian, § 45.

2 2 Macc. 4 : 30.

3 For further details on the court and its life consult E. Bikerman, *Institutions séleucides* (Paris, 1938), pp. 31-50.

4 Appian, § 61.

5 See above, p. 239.

6 See above, pp. 241-2.

7 Polybius, Bk. V, ch. 79.

from Greek and Macedonian settlers, it varied in number. At the battle of Magnesia in 190 B.C. it numbered 16,000.[1] The phalanx was armed with swords and huge spears, twenty-one feet long, and protected with helmets and shields. The national weapon of the Greeks and Macedonians was the spear, not the sword, and so remained. The missile shooters consisted of archers, slingers and javelineers drawn from the non-Hellenic element of the population. The artillery of the Hellenistic kings, including catapults, opened a new chapter in the history of siegecraft and provoked a corresponding improvement in the art of city fortification. In the battle of Raphia 2000 Persian and Kurdish bowmen and slingers took part. In that of Magnesia a squadron of about a thousand Median cavalry and a royal squadron of a thousand horsemen, mostly Syrians, participated. In front of the cavalry Arabian archers on dromedaries carried slender swords four cubits long that they might be able to reach the enemy from so great a height.[2]

War elephants

The camel and horse as instruments of warfare had been known in Western Asia for centuries, but the elephant was a new feature of the Seleucid army. This animal became a Seleucid emblem, as indicated by the coins. In the elephant depot at Apamea [3] training was evidently conducted by Indians. The Syrian kings alone could procure elephants from India. The Egyptian kings used African elephants. In 273 B.C. the governor of Bactria sent twenty elephants to Antiochus III, who used them against Egypt.[4] In Magnesia and Raphia Indian and African elephants met on the battlefield and the Indian won, but they on both occasions outnumbered the African and the deduction that they were stronger may not be justified.[5] At Raphia Antiochus employed 102 elephants.[6] In the battle of Ipsus (301 B.C.) Seleucus I used 480 of them, a fact which was largely responsible for the victory which netted him the province of Asia. In all there were about 500 in the Seleucid depot.[7]

In the battle array an Indian mahout bestrode the neck of the elephant which carried a wooden tower with four fighting

1 See above, p. 243; Appian, § 32.

2 Livy, Bk. XXXVII, ch. 40; cf. Appian, § 32.

3 See above, p. 239.

4 Sidney Smith, p. 156.

5 Livy, Bk. XXXVII, ch. 39, § 13; Polybius, Bk. V, ch. 84.

6 Polybius, Bk. V, ch. 79.

7 Strabo, Bk. XVI, ch. 2, § 10.

men.[1] So awe-inspiring must have been the sight of these fighting beasts that the Jew who reported their performance in one of the Maccabean battles saw their backs covered with towers each holding two and thirty strong men.[2] The same reporter states that the animals were provoked to fighting by showing them " the blood of grapes and mulberries ".[3]

On the battlefield the elephant corps was commanded by a special officer.[4] He used the animals not only to fight the enemy animals, as in Raphia, but also as a screen against the cavalry, as in Ipsus. This was evidently the primary use to which the Seleucids put their animals. They also used them to break into a fortified position. In this respect the elephant was the tank of antiquity.[5] In their attack on infantry elephants were deadly enemies of troops encountering them for the first time, but their effectiveness was lost vis-à-vis experienced infantry.

In 163 B.C., learning that there were many war elephants in Syria, the Romans sent a mission to destroy them. The destruction of these tame and rare beasts so infuriated a native of Laodicea that he stabbed to death the chief of the mission while he was anointing himself in the gymnasium of that city.[6] Shortly after that one of the Seleucids got possession of the elephants of a Ptolemy, which he lost to a rival. That is the last we hear of them. The years between the death of Alexander and that event constitute the only period in history in which this animal played an important part in Western warfare.

The fleet

The same Roman mission which destroyed the war elephants was charged with burning the Seleucid fleet, which had been increased beyond the number allowed to Antiochus III in the peace treaty. While the fleet played no decisive rôle in any of the recorded battles, yet it must have had enough nuisance value to necessitate inclusion in the treaty of a clause limiting the number of its units and confining its sphere of activity to Asiatic waters. A small part of it was evidently maintained in the Persian Gulf.[7] On the whole the function of the navy was to co-operate with the active army and to protect the military

[1] Livy, Bk. XXXVII, ch. 40.
[2] 1 Macc. 6:37.
[3] 1 Macc. 6:34.
[4] Appian, § 33.
[5] W. W. Tarn, *Hellenistic Military and Naval Developments* (Cambridge, 1930), p. 95.
[6] Appian, § 46.
[7] Polybius, Bk. XIII, ch. 9, § 5.

transports. It was no doubt manned mostly by Phoenicians.

The unit was the quinquereme, which by this time had replaced the less powerful trireme and was probably invented in Phoenicia or Cyprus shortly before Alexander's time.[1] The quinquereme was rowed by a single row of oars with five men to each oar. A deck stretched over the rowers' heads. The ship carried troops who, in the second pre-Christian century, were protected by light wooden turrets placed on deck. The ship itself could be used for ramming, a practice in which the Phoenicians excelled.

Government of the provinces

The unity of the Seleucid empire found expression in the uniformity of its military organization and in the administrative system of the provinces inherited in large part from the Persians. Of the local provincial government not much is known, but it is evident that the old governmental machinery was maintained. The administrative division kept its Persian name, satrapy. Appian,[2] who claimed that under Seleucus I the empire had as many as seventy-two satrapies, must have confused some of the satrapies' subdivisions with the satrapies themselves. According to Posidonius[3] Syria had eight satrapies, four in the thickly populated north, "Seleucis", and four in the south, "Coele-Syria". The northern provinces clustered around the four colonies: Antioch, Seleucia, Apamea and Laodicea. It seems that Damascus and Lebanon went with Phoenicia to form the first South Syrian satrapy; Samaria and Galilee went with the coast to form the second; Transjordan and Idumaea formed the remaining two. Judaea was for most of the time, as noted above, a tributary priest-state under Seleucid suzerainty.

The satrapy was divided for administrative purposes into districts entrusted to subordinate governors. The arrangement of these subdivisions is difficult to determine and perhaps fluctuated from time to time. The royal mint was, of course, in Antioch, but provincial mints existed in Tyre, Sidon, Aradus and other important cities.

Cities

The Greco-Macedonian colonies were in general organized according to the old Hellenic idea of the self-governing city-state. The Grecized cities likewise formed such city-states. They were required to pay taxes and obey occasional royal ordinances but allowed to administer their internal affairs. The

[1] Tarn, p. 132. [2] § 62. [3] Strabo, Bk. XVI, ch. 2, § 4.

more favoured among them were even allowed to control neighbouring territories. The people of Antioch voted as members of a Hellenic community and possibly also in the imperial assembly of the army. The architectural characteristic of a Hellenistic city was its straight streets, intersecting at right angles, which cut it up into blocks that made it appear from an overlooking spot like a chessboard. The general pattern was that of a Greek city, with a public square (an agora) somewhere in the centre to which the temples opened. The agora of Dura-Europus was 28,079 square yards. Its streets varied from 18 to 24 feet in width, with the main street 36 feet wide.[1] Unfortunately, other than Dura-Europus, no Seleucid city has thus far been fully excavated.[2] The "ethnic" city, on the other hand, differed in its appearance as it differed in its policy. In it the indigenous element of the population continued to live in the traditional way.

Taxes

The native peasantry lived in villages that maintained their status and way of life unmindful of dynastic changes. The land they cultivated was mostly the king's or some landowner's and they were bought and sold with it. Their position was that of serfs. They no doubt paid their taxes in kind.

The Seleucids continued the practice immemorial in Western Asia of collecting tithes, one-tenth of the harvest. From sporadic references it would seem that the tax was imposed not on the individual but on the community.[3] A large part of it was paid in kind in the name of the city, people or tribe by the chief or high priest. Our knowledge about the different taxes, their amounts and manner of assessment is far from being perfect, but there is no doubt that much was determined by ancient tradition and adapted to the immediate economic conditions.

In addition to the tribute and revenues from land, which were quite high in Judaea, there were the royal taxes, which comprised poll tax, crown tax[4] and salt tax. In his charter to Jerusalem of about 200 B.C. Antiochus III discharged the city

[1] M. T. Rostovtzeff *et al.*, *The Excavations at Dura-Europos*, vol. ix (New Haven, 1944), pp. 23, 25.

[2] For a plan of Dura, see Rostovtzeff, *Caravan Cities*, tr. D. and T. Talbot Rice (Oxford, 1932), p. 154.

[3] 1 Macc. 10:29-30; Josephus, *Antiquities*, Bk. XIII, ch. 4, § 9.

[4] The term indicates that the Jews were wont to present to the Syrian kings crowns of gold and later their value.

from taxes for three years and after that for a third of them.[1] Half a century later, when there were two rival Seleucid kings, a rather common occurrence in that age, both of them were ready to offer any price for Jewish support. One of the two, Demetrius I Soter, in 152 B.C. offered in a letter to Jonathan the high priest exemption for the Jews from the greater part of the tribute and taxes hitherto paid including poll tax, tax upon salt and the value of the crowns together with the third part of the product of the fields and the half of the fruits of the trees which usually went to the king. He also offered freedom to Jerusalem from the customary tithe.[2] The salt tax mentioned by both Antiochus and Demetrius suggests that the salt-pits were considered the property of the crown. Mines, quarries, forests and fisheries were also probably owned and operated by the kings. In his charter Antiochus authorizes the Jews to draw wood tax free from Lebanon for rebuilding their Temple and other structures.[3]

[1] Josephus, *Antiquities*, Bk. XII, ch. 3, § 3.
[2] Josephus, Bk. XIII, ch. 2, § 3; 1 Macc. 10: 29-30.
[3] For further information on this subject consult, Bikerman, pp. 106-32, Rostovtzeff, *Social and Economic History*, pp. 440 *seq*.

CHAPTER XX

TRADE AND INDUSTRY

SYRIA was the backbone of the Seleucid empire, Antioch its political head, Seleucia its commercial capital, Apamea its military headquarters, Seleucia-on-the-Tigris the capital of its eastern wing and Sardes the capital of its western wing. To join these different parts of the empire and different commercial and political centres by convenient and safe roads was a chief concern of the early Seleucid kings. Whenever a new colony was built, care was taken to connect it with the existing highways and local roads, to which the Hellenistic kings of Syria and Egypt added new ones. The added facility of communication and the fact that the Hellenistic world, even when broken up, had a certain uniformity of general culture, including a common speech and similar coinage, gave special impetus to trade. The colonizing activity itself was accompanied by an outburst of Greek commercial and industrial activity which brought merchants, business men and artisans.

Seleucid policy

The trade of Syria on both the domestic and foreign levels was of great consequence to the kingdom and to its population. The Seleucid policy seems to have been first to attract to their country Arabian, Indian and Central Asiatic merchandise for local consumption and for transit, and secondly to promote Syrian commercial relations with the West, especially the Greco-Roman world. In bidding for transit trade Egypt was the rival of Syria. The unceasing military conflicts between the Seleucids and the Ptolemies, therefore, had economic as well as political bases.

India

The products of India could come by sea to depots in al-Yaman (Arabia Felix), there to become part of the Arabian trade [1] and then proceed by caravan to Petra [2] and the Ptolemaic

[1] For more on South Arabian trade consult Hitti, *History of the Arabs*, pp. 44-8.

[2] See below, pp. 376 *seq*.

territory, or they could go by sea along the western coast of the Persian Gulf, through Gerrha and up the Tigris to Seleucia. Supplemented by the overland caravan trade which this Seleucia gathered, the accumulated commodities moved westward either up the Euphrates and through Dura-Europus on to Antioch or by the old way east of the Tigris, crossing at what the Arabs called Jazīrat ibn-ʿUmar and then sweeping west to Nisibis, on to Edessa and thence to Antioch or Damascus. This made Seleucia-on-the-Tigris the clearing house of the eastern trade, an inheritor of ancient Babylon and a predecessor of medieval Baghdād. Throughout the third pre-Christian century this eastern trade route through Seleucia-on-the-Tigris remained popular, but in the troubled period of the late second and early first centuries the trans-desert route through Palmyra became more convenient, especially because the Palmyrene tribes were then in a position to guarantee safety and water supply. The short cut through the oasis city of Palmyra remained in frequent use for about four centuries.[1]

Caravans starting from Egypt, Petra or the Philistine coast could follow the coastal route all the way to Laodicea and thence connect with Seleucia and Antioch or they could switch off from Megiddo or Tyre to Damascus, following the great ancient international highway.[2] Those starting from Aradus or Marathus could likewise either follow the coastal route northward or turn off eastward to Emesa and Apamea. Seleucia or its neighbour Antioch on the then navigable Orontes was the Syrian meeting-place of all such caravans.

In their heyday the Seleucids were also undisputed masters of the "silk route", penetrating the Iranian plateau and Central Asia from distant Mongolia, in so far as it was in use in those days. A large part of that route passed through the Seleucid domain. The Far Eastern products joined the Indian and western Arabian products in Mesopotamia and moved westward either through Nisibis and Edessa or through Dura-Europus.

Dura-Europus

The main highways were, under the Seleucids, guarded by chains of strong and prosperous colonies which at the same time provided adequate resting-places for the caravaneers and

[1] See below, pp. 389-90. [2] See above, pp. 60, 63.

relay centres for their camels. Dura-Europus [1] was such a colony. Founded around 300 B.C. by Seleucus I on the desert road half-way between the capitals of Syria and Mesopotamia, this colony soon developed from a strong fortress to an important emporium. It stood in a position of great natural strength on a rocky plateau overhanging the Euphrates and flanked by two deep ravines. The city reached its height as a caravan centre under the Parthians. The Romans used it as a stronghold on the Euphratean frontier of the empire. It was captured and destroyed by the Sasanians shortly after A.D. 256, whereupon it reverted to the desert. Its ruins, known today as al-Ṣāliḥīyah, were not known to the learned world until a British officer in 1920 hit upon some interesting frescoes while engaged in digging trenches.[2] So imposing have the ruins of Dura turned out to be that it has been called the "Pompeii of the East".

Gerrha

The most important commercial centre on the Persian Gulf was Gerrha.[3] This Arabian city was in practical control of the western shore of the Persian Gulf and of the great caravan roads of that part of Arabia. One of these roads went south and connected Gerrha with al-Yaman and the other shot west through the desert into Taymā' and on into Petra. By sea, too, the main connection between India and the Seleucid empire was through Gerrha. The little we know about this commercial centre and its merchants comes entirely from classical sources; [4] but Pliny's [5] remark that the towers of the city were built of square blocks of salt is difficult to explain. There is no evidence from these sources that the Gerrheans were ever subject to the Seleucids. Antiochus III stopped there on his way back from his eastern campaign and the Gerrheans honoured him with the gift of 500 talents of silver, 1000 talents of frankincense and 200 talents of oil of myrrh or cinnamon.[6]

Through the Gerrheans as middlemen the Seleucids evidently received their chief supply of Arabian merchandise,

1 Akkadian *dūru* means circuit, wall (cf. Dan. 3:1); "Europus" was added to the name in commemoration of the Macedonian birthplace of Seleucus I.

2 Rostovtzeff, *Caravan Cities*, p. 153.

3 Probably modern al-'Uqayr, Bedouin pronunciation 'Ujayr.

4 Strabo, Bk. XVI, ch. 3, § 3; Diodorus, Bk. III, ch. 42.

5 Bk. VI, ch. 32.

6 Polybius, Bk. XIII, ch. 9; see above, p. 241.

especially in the period when southern Syria was a part of the Ptolemaic domain. The merchandise consisted of myrrh, frankincense and other aromatics. Frankincense was in great demand throughout the Seleucid empire as no worship, Greek, Jewish or other Semitic, could be complete without it. It smoked on every altar throughout the Hellenistic world, as it did later in the Christian world. Cinnamon was another highly prized tropical product. It was in reality a product of India but the Greeks thought it was Arabian. A fair amount of Indian goods received in Seleucid lands passed through Gerrhean hands.

Trade with the West

Arabian, Indian and Central Asian commodities shipped to Syria were partly consumed locally and partly re-exported westward. The Seleucid trade with the West followed land as well as sea routes and contributed no small share to the prosperity of Syria. It consisted of agricultural and industrial products of Syria as well as of goods in transit from lands east of it. An important element in the Syrian trade was slave traffic. Traffic in slaves among the Hellenistic states and with foreign countries was most active at this time, with the Seleucids more interested in it than the Ptolemies. War supplied the slave market with prisoners, and piracy supplied it with victims of kidnapping. Throughout the third and second centuries a steady influx of slaves into the Greek cities of the west moved from Syria and neighbouring lands. The demand for slaves was at least as great as the modern demand for domestic servants. Besides, the labour in mines, building operations and public works was almost entirely furnished by slaves. Temples also owned and trafficked in this human commodity.

New Phoenician colonies

On the sea route Rhodes was for a time the leading commercial power. Another island, Delos, seat of a great sanctuary in honour of Apollo which was one of the most famous religious foundations of antiquity, rose after the fall of Corinth in 146 B.C. to eminence as a centre of an extensive transit trade. Berytus had special trade relations with this Aegean island. Destroyed in 140 B.C. by Tryphon, a contestant for the Seleucid throne, Berytus — judging by the evidence of coins [1] — soon recovered and possessed enough vitality to establish a colony in this Aegean island. The colony was dedicated to Poseidon, the

[1] *Catalogue of Greek Coins of Phoenicia*, p. liii; cf. Strabo, Bk. XVI, ch. 2, § 19.

patron god of Berytus. It owned a temple with ancillary blocks and porticoes for displaying Phoenician ware. In the commercial, social and religious activities of Delos, the Berytians occupied a position second only to that of the Italians.

The stimulation given to the colonizing and commercial activity of Phoenician cities under the Seleucids and Ptolemies resulted in founding more than one colony. Phoenician merchants followed in the wake of Alexander's terrible march through distant Gedrosia. The Sidonians at Shechem who in the Maccabean uprising asked leave to convert the Samaritan temple on Mount Gerizim to a temple for Jupiter were presumably Hellenized Phoenicians.[1] Sidon had another colony, Marisa,[2] farther south, in Idumaea. Marisa was a flourishing commercial city in the Ptolemaic period. It was one of those Idumaean cities whose males submitted to circumcision rather than exile under John Hyrcanus.[3]

In this commercial renaissance of Syria under the Seleucids, the Jews seem to have played no more conspicuous a part than in any earlier period. In the words of their historian and spokesman Josephus (*ca.* A.D. 37–100), " We neither inhabit a maritime country nor delight in commerce, nor in such intercourse with other men as arises from it ".[4]

Agricultural products

Syria developed in the last Hellenistic age into an important agricultural-horticultural country. The upward curve began under the Ptolemies in Coele-Syria, Phoenicia and Palestine. The early produce of grain (barley and wheat), grapes and other fruits, wines and vegetables[5] was now increased by improved methods and under the urge of greater demands. A wider market for unguents for which native flowers were used was now created. The lively intercourse with neighbouring foreign lands resulted in the exchange of agricultural products and the introduction of new plants.

Egyptian beans, lentils, mustard, gourds and other typically Egyptian plants were presumably introduced into southern Syria under the Ptolemies.[6] The pistachio tree, originally

[1] Josephus, *Antiquities*, Bk. XII, ch. 5, § 4; see above, pp. 198, 246.

[2] Perhaps " head place ", cf. biblical Maresha, 2 Ch. 11 : 8; 14 : 9, 10; identified with Tell Sandaḥanna, 1 mile south of Bayt Jibrīn. [3] See above, p. 246.

[4] *Antiquities*, Bk. I, § 12. [5] See above, pp. 26, 48, 85-6.

[6] F. M. Heichelheim, " Roman Syria ", *An Economic Survey of Ancient Rome*, ed. Tenney Frank (Baltimore, 1934), vol. iv, p. 130; Rostovtzeff, *Social and Economic History*, p. 1165.

Persian as the name indicates,[1] was also evidently introduced into Syria at this time. From this country the plant and with it the name found their way into Greek, Latin and Italian.[2] The course followed by other Persian trees, such as the apricot, peach and cherry, seems strangely enough to have been the reverse. They make their appearance in Italy before the Hellenistic East. Of oranges and lemons, also Persian in provenance, there is no record in Hellenistic times. Cotton, though known from earliest times in Egypt and India and introduced into Assyria about 700 B.C.,[3] was never cultivated on a large scale in Seleucid Syria. It was more of a curiosity. Native silk was produced from the wild silkworm of Western Asia [4] but real Chinese silk was imported after 115 B.C. Sugar and rice were imported from India. Pliny [5] refers casually to a vain attempt on the part of Seleucus (I ?) to acclimatize Indian amomum [6] and nard, "those most delicate of perfumes". In the same connection Pliny speaks of the cinnamon shrub as not having sufficient strength to acclimatize itself in the vicinity of Syria.

Under the Ptolemies the wine and oil industry became more lively. These two products together with olives, bread and fish formed a substantial part of the diet of the people. In Hellenistic times the lumber industry was no less flourishing than in Pharaonic days. Treeless Egypt drew on the cedars of Lebanon, always a royal domain, and on the oaks of Bashan. The exploitation of Syria's and Lebanon's forests was the privilege of the sovereigns under the Seleucids as it was under the Persians, the Assyrians and the Phoenicians.[7] The Sea of Galilee supplied scented bushes [8] and Jericho had a monopoly of balsam.[9] Industry

The textile industry, which goes back to Phoenician and pre-Phoenician days, maintained its primacy. Syrian manufacturers continued to use the same skill and technique but varied the designs to suit the tastes of a varied clientele. The

[1] Per. *pistah*, the nut. [2] See below, p. 294. [3] See above, p. 91.
[4] See above, p. 92. [5] Bk. XVI, ch. 59.
[6] The name of this aromatic shrub from which the Greeks and Romans prepared a costly fragrant balsam is originally Indic coming through South Arabic. The name is now applied to ginger and cardamom.
[7] Under the Romans and probably under the Phoenicians the sovereign monopoly included cypress, pine, fir and juniper.
[8] Strabo, Bk. XVI, ch. 2, § 16; cf. Polybius, Bk. V, ch. 45, § 10.
[9] Josephus, *Antiquities*, Bk. XV, ch. 4, § 2; Strabo, Bk. XVI, ch. 2, § 41.

Syrian wool industry was especially large. Purple-dyed stuffs remained in great demand. Woollen cloth imported into Mongolia about the beginning of the Christian era suggests a Hellenistic Syrian tradition.[1]

In pottery and glassware, a specialty of the Near East from time immemorial, Syria upheld its ancient reputation. The Greek pottery which subsequent to Alexander's conquest flooded the

Louvre, Paris

A BEAUTIFUL RED-GLAZED GRECO-SYRIAN BOWL

The lower part is adorned with stylized leaves of acanthus and another type of leaf alternating. Between them are rich but leafless scrolls. The upper part has groups of Bacchic figures separated from each other by scrolls

Near Eastern market was soon imitated by Syrians and produced locally. Especially popular at first was black-glazed pottery, later superseded by a type of red ware with a fine brilliant glaze which was introduced in the second century. Fragments of Attic and Rhodian stamped jars are strewn all over the land. The glass of Sidon and Tyre was highly prized and greatly desired. Down to the Roman period these cities supplied the world with its best glass.[2] Excellent sand for glass production was found near Sidon. These two and other Phoenician cities manufactured and exported vessels of cast glass before they invented blown glass. This epoch-making invention must have

[1] Rostovtzeff, p. 1223.

[2] Consult Strabo, Bk. XVI, ch. 2, § 25; Pliny, Bk. V, ch. 17.

taken place late in the first pre-Christian century.[1]

In the Hellenistic age clay tablets give way as writing material to parchment or papyrus rolls. From the second century on parchment was Pergamum's monopoly; the term itself means belonging to Pergamum. Alexandria supplied the world with papyrus. From Egypt this writing material was introduced into Syria-Palestine; occasional references to papyrus growing there are not lacking.[2] Probably the process of making papyrus involved removing the rind of the plant, cutting the stem longitudinally into thin strips, laying them vertically upon a board and overlaying them crosswise with another set of strips. The whole was then moistened with water, to which glue was perhaps added, and dried in the sun. The sheets could be used singly or pasted as rolls.[3] From Phoenicia the material was introduced into Greece, where it was in general use in the sixth century.

The art of metalwork took long strides forward at this time. Antiochus Epiphanes often eluded court attendants in order to visit the silversmiths' and goldsmiths' workshops and discuss technical matters with the moulders and other craftsmen.[4] Silver was supplied by Nabataean Arabia, whence also came gold, and by the Taurus Mountains. Iron came from the Taurus Mountains and from southern Palestine, particularly Idumaea, and the Lebanon in the neighbourhood of Berytus.[5] For economic purposes this metal was undoubtedly the most valuable. The Ptolemies may have also exploited the copper, iron and other mines of the Lebanon range. The exploitation continued into Roman times.[6] Pearls, unknown in the West before Alexander's days, now became highly valued as ornaments.

Coinage

In all the Hellenistic monarchies the coinage of money [7] was promoted as an instrument for developing trade. Money as a medium of exchange was gradually adopted in place of time-honoured barter. With money came royal weights, issued in

[1] Rostovtzeff, p. 698.

[2] Pliny, Bk. XIII, ch. 22.

[3] The ancient Semitic word for roll has survived in Ar. *majallah*, now used for magazine. "Papyrus", whence "paper", goes back to an Egyptian word related to "Pharaoh". The Pharaohs evidently monopolized the industry.

[4] Polybius, Bk. XXVI, ch. 1.

[5] Cf. above, p. 35; below, pp. 571, 656.

[6] Consult Heichelheim, pp. 156-7.

[7] For specimens consult above, pp. 243, 255. Cf. above, p. 254.

Antioch and Seleucia.[1] Different weights and measures were allowed in the different provinces, even cities, within the realm.

Manifestations of luxury

With the increase of trade and its implementation with money and official weights and with the improvement and progress of agriculture Seleucid Syria enjoyed a period of comparative prosperity. History has preserved reports which give an idea of the size of the fortunes accumulated by the magnates of the age. For instance Hermias, prime minister of Antiochus the Great, around 200 B.C. was able to advance the pay of the entire royal army from his own funds.[2] Another case was that of Dionysius, a " friend " (assistant) of Antiochus Epiphanes. At the celebration of the Daphne games, we are told, he had 1000 slaves marching in the procession carrying silver vessels, none of which weighed less than a thousand drachmae. Then came 600 royal pages bearing vessels of gold and 200 women who sprinkled scented oil from gold pitchers. Close upon these in the procession came 80 women seated in litters with gold supports and 500 women in litters with silver supports.[3] Epiphanes himself wishing to outdo the Roman triumphs celebrated the Daphne games by a display of gold and silverware which was nothing less than fabulous. In the parade marched 3000 Cilicians wearing gold crowns; 10,000 Macedonians with gold shields, 5000 with bronze shields and 5000 with silver shields; the majority of 3000 citizen soldiers wore gold cheek-coverings and gold crowns; the rest had cheek-coverings of silver.[4]

Population

The standard of living throughout the land must have been very high in the early first century judging by the testimony of Posidonius. " All the people of Syria, because of the great plenty which their land afforded, were relieved of any distress regarding the necessaries of life ".[5] With the rise in the standard of living it may be fair to assume an increase in population part of which was due to colonization under the founder of the dynasty and his early successors. The trend upward continued to the Roman period. Strabo[6] (*ca.* 63 B.C.–*ca.* A.D. 24) makes Antioch " not much inferior in riches and magnitude to Seleucia-

1 See above, p. 263, fig.

2 Polybius, Bk. V, ch. 50, § 2.

3 Athenaeus, Bk. V, ch. 195.

4 Athenaeus, Bk. V, ch. 194.

5 Athenaeus, Bk. V, ch. 210; consult above, p. 259.

6 Bk. XVI, ch. 2, § 5.

on-the-Tigris and Alexandria in Egypt". In Pliny's time, shortly after Strabo's, Seleucia's population was reportedly 600,000.[1] Under Augustus Caesar, Alexandria had about the same population. In the Roman period preceding the Empire it is estimated that the population of Syria ranged from five to six million of whom two million lived in Palestine.[2]

[1] Pliny, Bk. VI, ch. 30.

[2] Julius Beloch, *Die Bevölkerung der griechish-römischen Welt* (Leipzig, 1886), pp. 242 *seq*; cf. below, pp. 292, 484.

CHAPTER XXI

SYRIA AS A ROMAN PROVINCE: THE PRE-EMPIRE PERIOD

THE progress of Roman arms in Western Asia, commencing on the battlefield of Magnesia in 190 B.C.,[1] moved in a crescendo to the conquest of Syria by Pompey in 64 B.C.[2] The annexation of Syria found that country in a state of chaos into which the spineless late Seleucid rule had reduced it. Arab chiefs were in control of towns in the north. Nabataeans and Jews had encroached upon the Hellenistic domain in the south. Robber chiefs held many Phoenician coast towns as pirate bases.[3] Mountainous Lebanon provided the geographical conditions necessary for their protection as did Cilicia, the acropolis of piracy in the eastern Mediterranean. In Cilicia's rugged and remote recesses the pirates built rock castles to conceal their families and treasures for security and to provide asylum for themselves in time of danger.[4] As long as trade with Mesopotamia and lands farther east was more profitable the temptation to embark upon a career of piracy and robbery was not so strong, but now with the prevailing Seleucid anarchy and the disorganization of the hinterland trade by successive Armenian and Parthian conquests, the situation was changed. Indeed, one of the Seleucid kings, Tryphon (142–137 B.C.), himself originally a slave, actually encouraged piracy in Cilicia and used it as a means for strengthening his hold on the throne.[5]

The pirates were the robbers of the sea highways, which in the case of the eastern Mediterranean were well defined and much frequented. Before the advent of Pompey they had organized themselves into an international sea power which embraced in its activity the whole eastern Mediterranean basin, causing a scarcity of provisions for Rome, which relied on over-

[1] See above, p. 243. [2] See above, p. 250. [3] See above, p. 37.

[4] Theodor Mommsen, *History of Rome*, tr. William P. Dickson (New York 1894), vol. iv, pp. 58, 143.

[5] Mommsen, vol. iii, p. 87; vol. iv, p. 59.

seas trade for its grain supply. Though Pompey had supposedly exterminated the pirates from that whole region before the annexation of Syria,[1] some of them still flourished there even in the days of his successor.[2]

All geographical and traditional Syria was incorporated by Pompey in 64 B.C. under one title Provincia Syria. The kingdom of Syria gave way to the province of Syria, with Antioch as capital, while Cilicia was made a province by itself. Arab dynasts were allowed to remain with their authority restricted to their original domains and paid annual tribute. The Nabataean king, however, kept Damascus for a lump sum of money. Judaea was left a subject state within the framework of the province of Syria; [3] but the cities with a Greek constitution which the Jews had added to their domain were restored to their former status and granted internal freedom under provincial governors. Ten of these cities then formed a league known as the Decapolis [4] to which other cities were added later. With the exception of Scythopolis (Baysān) they all lay east of the Jordan. Antioch, Seleucia, Gaza and other colonies were also given autonomy and placed under provincial governors.

The Syrian province was considered of such focal importance in the Asiatic possessions as to be put under the direct rule of a Roman proconsul with power to levy troops and engage in war.[5] Some of the most prominent Roman officials were put in charge. The first was Gabinius (57–55 B.C.), Pompey's able legate, who further reduced the power of the Jewish monarchy by depriving the high priest Hyrcanus II, grandson of Aristobulus,[6] of his royal rank, subjecting the people to heavy taxation and dividing the state into five small cantons, each under a council or Sanhedrin. Gabinius rebuilt a number of Greco-Syrian cities which had been destroyed by the Maccabees, such as Samaria, Scythopolis, Dora and Gaza.[7] Proconsuls

Gabinius was succeeded by Crassus, member of the first triumvirate, which comprised also Pompey and Julius Caesar. A man of insatiable avarice, Crassus immediately upon his arrival in 54 B.C. made Syria a base of military operations

[1] Mommsen, vol. iv, pp. 142-6.
[2] Dio (Cassius), *Historia Romana*, Bk. XXXIX, ch. 56.
[3] Josephus, *Antiquities*, Bk. XIV, ch. 4, § 4.
[4] See above, p. 252.
[5] See above, p. 250; Appian, § 51.
[6] See above, p. 246.
[7] Josephus, *Antiquities*, Bk. XIV, ch. 5, § 3.

against Parthia, whose capital was Ctesiphon and whose wealth was considered inexhaustible. With the successive elimination of Pontus and Armenia and the acquisition of Syria, Rome came into direct contact with Parthia. In his second campaign in the spring of 53 Crassus was betrayed by his Arab ally Abgar [1] of Edessa and there in the Syrian Desert, thirty miles south of Carrhae (Ḥarrān), his army was cut to pieces and he himself was slain. Crassus' head and right hand were severed and sent to the Parthian king in Seleucia-on-the-Tigris, who is said to have poured molten gold down the dead man's throat saying, " Sate thyself now with that of which in life thou wert so greedy ".[2]

Crassus' able quaestor (state treasurer) Cassius, afterwards one of Caesar's murderers, succeeded his chief. Realizing that the crushing defeat south of Carrhae put all Syria in jeopardy, Cassius hastened to prepare for the coming invasion, which did not materialize until the year 51. At the head of two legions the proconsul took his stand in Antioch ready to offer a determined resistance. Sensing a lengthy siege, the Parthians retired along the Orontes and ultimately withdrew from all Syria.[3] The incursion, however, left its effect in the revival of several local dynasts many of whom favoured the Parthians.

The civil war in Rome and the unstable condition of the whole Roman state threw Syria once more into a state of confusion. In the course of his march against a son of Mithradates the Great, who, taking advantage of the war between Pompey and Caesar, had reinstated himself as king of Pontus, Caesar stopped in Syria (47 B.C.) and conferred privileges on several of its cities. In the division of the Roman world by the second triumvirate, of which Octavian (later Augustus) was a member, Mark Antony was given the East, including Syria and Egypt. His rule of four years (40–36 B.C.) brought neither stability nor peace. He lived voluptuously with Cleopatra and neglected affairs of state. The great Parthian inroad of 40–38 B.C. dislodged the Romans from the entire province with the exception of Tyre.[4] It was with difficulty that at length order

[1] " Abgarus " of Latin sources, " Ariamnes " of Plutarch, " Crassus ", ch. 21, in *Vitae*.

[2] Cf. Dio, Bk. XL, ch. 27; Plutarch, " Crassus ", ch. 33.

[3] Dio, Bk. XL, ch. 29.

[4] Bouchier, p. 29.

was restored. Antony went so far as to grant a large part of Phoenicia and Coele-Syria to his Egyptian inamorata and to inaugurate a son of his by her, Ptolemy by name, as titular sovereign of Syria. The boy had Seleucid blood in him through intermarriage between the two dynasties of Egypt and Syria. After the celebrated naval battle of Actium (31 B.C.), in which Octavian vanquished Antony and Cleopatra, the future Roman emperor passed through Palestine and Syria and was welcomed by the provincials, who longed for a stable government. This victory left Octavian the sole ruler of the Roman world. Four years later he received from the senate the title of Augustus (venerated, exalted) and began his rule as emperor. A new chapter in the history of the world begins.

In the days of Herod the king

When Antony was charged with the affairs of the East he discarded the Maccabean in favour of the Herodian family. The founder of this family was a shrewd Idumaean politician, nominally a Jew,[1] who was granted Roman citizenship and appointed procurator (fiscal agent) of Judaea by Julius Caesar when visiting Syria.[2] Antipater became the real power behind the weak Hyrcanus. Antipater's son Herod took for his second wife a granddaughter of Hyrcanus II, thus uniting the two families.[3] In the year 37 B.C. this Herod, later known as the Great, took Jerusalem and established his authority as king, which by the grace of Rome he was able to wield for thirty-three years.

Herod promoted Roman against national interest. He succeeded where Antiochus Epiphanes had failed in forcibly making of Judaea a passable imitation of a Hellenistic realm. He launched a public works project which literally altered the face of the country. In Jerusalem he built a hippodrome, a theatre and an amphitheatre and held public games, all of which were inconsistent with Judaism. In addition he rebuilt the Temple. Samaria was his favourite residence. This city he adorned with buildings and renamed Sebaste[4] in honour of Augustus Caesar. Remains of his buildings have been excavated. To please further his imperial patron he rebuilt Straton's Tower (Turris Stratonis) on the coast and named it

[1] See above, p. 246.
[2] Josephus, *Antiquities*, Bk. XIV, ch. 8, §§ 3, 5.
[3] Josephus, *Antiquities*, Bk. XV, ch. 6, § 4.
[4] Gr. *sebastos* means *augustus* in Latin; see above, p. 192, n. 2.

Caesarea,[1] destined to become the capital of Roman Palestine. At his court flourished Nicolaus of Damascus, who as philosopher and historian excelled Posidonius. Nicolaus, who knew Augustus personally, composed a universal history of which the section on Herod survives in substance in Josephus.[2]

Herod married ten wives, butchered some of them and other members of his family and mercilessly crushed opposition to his despotic rule. He died in the year 4 B.C., a year or two after the birth of Christ as fixed by scholars (6–4 B.C.). In his altered will he bequeathed his kingdom to his son Archelaus,[3] who competed with his brother Herod Antipas for the throne and received a large portion of the kingdom, but with the title only of ethnarch.[4] Herod Antipas received the tetrarchy of Galilee.[5] He was the one who built Tiberias, naming it after Tiberius Caesar.[6] Like his father and other Herods, Herod Antipas was double-faced: Jew at home, Hellenist abroad. On the deposition of Archelaus (A.D. 6), Judaea was placed under the direct rule of Roman governors or procurators, of whom the fifth was Pontius Pilate.[7]

Roman Hellenism

Hellenism of the Roman brand, which had its start in 64 B.C., lasted until A.D. 323 when Constantine the Great shifted his capital from Rome to Byzantium, thereby inaugurating a new era in the history of the Mediterranean lands.[8] Roman civilization itself, be it remembered, was an heir and beneficiary as well as continuer of the earlier Greek civilization. In fact, of all the Mediterranean peoples the Romans, as Indo-Europeans, were the only ones who proved capable of accepting more than the outward show of the civilization of their Greek kinsmen.[9] To the bulk of the Semitic and Hamitic populations of Western Asia and North Africa that civilization remained an alien imposition.

By the first pre-Christian century a harmonization of Latin

[1] Josephus, *Antiquities*, Bk. XV, ch. 9, § 6; Pliny, Bk. V, ch. 14; Strabo, Bk. XVI, ch. 2, § 27. The Straton after whom the tower was named may have been the king of Sidon at its conquest by Alexander.

[2] Fragments of Nicolaus' works were edited by Ludwig Dindorf, *Historici Graeci minores*, vol. i (Leipzig, 1870), pp. 1-153.

[3] Josephus, *Antiquities*, Bk. XVII, ch. 8, § 1.

[4] " Ruler of a people "; Josephus, Bk. XVII, ch. 11, § 4.

[5] Lk. 3:1.

[6] Josephus, Bk. XVIII, ch. 2, § 3.

[7] See below, p. 287.

[8] See below, p. 349.

[9] M. Cary and T. J. Haarhoff, *Life and Thought in the Greek and Roman World* (London, 1940), p. vi.

and Greek civilizations had been achieved. A compromise was made in favour of the Greek tongue, which remained a lingua franca in the East as it was before; but Latin became the official language of the administration. The Greeks were weak on the political and organizational side, and that was exactly where the Romans were strong. The Romans were rather poor in the artistic and philosophic field, where the Greeks were rich. Thus did Hellenism, strengthened and enriched under the Roman aegis, continue its onward march in Syria. Thanks to Roman protection it remained secure from "barbarian" peril Syrian Greek city life, with its characteristic political forms, round of festivities, amusements and intellectual exercise, moved on as before. Such local dynasties as were suffered by the mighty Romans to exist — the Herods of Judaea, the Aretas of Petra [1] and the Odenathus of Palmyra [2] — all had a Greek complexion.

Under the provincial system of Roman rule the native communities suffered but little restriction in the exercise of their autonomy. They retained their own religion, language and customs. The Romans took upon themselves the responsibility for their protection. This was done by means of Italian troops. In lieu of military service tribute was exacted from the native population. The Roman governors, who exercised general supervision over domestic affairs, were normally appointed for a short period and received no pay except what they could exact by dubious methods and farming out taxes.

[1] See below, p. 377.

[2] See below, pp. 391 *seq.*

CHAPTER XXII

UNDER THE EARLY ROMAN EMPERORS

Provincial government

WHEN Rome rose to world power, the centre of political history for the first time shifted from Asia into Europe where, except for the period of the caliphate, it has since remained. But imperial Rome had but one pattern before it which it could imitate in its government of the Western Asiatic provinces: the Seleucid. It was therefore only natural that the Roman emperors should be guided by the same general principles and keep the same governmental form as those that prevailed under the Hellenistic kings whom they superseded.

Owing to its location as a frontier province bordering on the only serious rival and formidable foe of Rome — Parthia, Syria was constituted an imperial province of which the emperor himself was the titular proconsul. As such it was placed under a legate,[1] always of consular rank, whose term of office lasted from three to five years. Its governorship, along with that of Gaul, was the most honourable and highly prized that the empire could confer.[2] Syria in the East, like Gaul in the West, was a central seat of military control. The governor was assisted by an adequate staff among whom the procurators stood high as collectors of state revenue. The collection was made either directly or through tax farming. Under the legate's control was a strong military force of four legions, consisting in the early empire almost entirely of Italian troops. The legate of Syria was responsible for the security of Roman possessions throughout Western Asia. One of the early legates was Quirinius,[3] who was appointed by Augustus and took census

[1] Cf. Lk. 2:2.

[2] For a list of governors consult Gustave A. Harrer, *Studies in the History of the Roman Province of Syria* (Princeton, 1915), pp. 11-65.

[3] "Cyrenius" of Lk. 2:2. From Josephus, *Antiquities*, Bk. XVIII, ch. 1, § 1; Bk. XVII, ch. 5, § 2, however, it is learned that Quirinius was made governor of Syria about A.D. 5. The man under whose governorship Christ was born was Quintilius Varus, who was appointed in 6 B.C. His predecessor was Sentius Saturninus (9–6 B.C.). For more on Quirinius consult Tacitus, *Annales*, Bk. III, ch. 22; Suetonius, *Vitae Duodecim Caesarum*, Bk. III, ch. 49.

of the Jews. Pontius Pilate was in reality procurator of Judaea (A.D. 24–37) but was intrusted by Tiberius [1] with its entire administration under the legates of Syria, one of whom, Vitellius, dismissed him for his ill-treatment of the Samaritans.[2]

Local government

The local communities lived under a variety of governments. The Greco-Macedonian colonies kept their own magistrates under whom were a senate and a popular assembly. The ancient Greek city-state remained the organization type. The Phoenician city-states likewise retained their traditional oligarchical systems, to which a Greek colouring had been by this time added. The Aramaean communities of the interior continued in control of their internal affairs as before. The Arabs subsisted under more than one system. In Emesa the government was that of priest-kings.[3] In Chalcis, too, farther south in Coele-Syria, a native ruled. Both of these small princely houses maintained their rule until toward the end of the first Christian century. On the desert frontier, where the nomadic or semi-nomadic way of life was still the rule, the tribe was the social unit and the patriarchal form of administration was maintained. In Judaea the high priest, no longer a king,[4] acted as head of the community and was nominated by the Jewish aristocracy. Throughout, Rome displayed a remarkable degree of toleration in the face of such diversity.

Behind this diversity of organization and control was a measure of ethnic and cultural similarity far beyond anything

[1] A genealogical table of the Julian-Claudian line:

1. Augustus (adopted son of Julius Caesar) (27 B.C.–A.D. 14)

2. Tiberius (A.D. 14–37)

Germanicus

3. Gaius (Caligula, great-grandson of Augustus through his daughter Julia) (37–41)

4. Claudius (41–54)

5. Nero (54–68)

Note.—Broken line indicates adoptive relationship.

[2] Lk. 3 : 1; Josephus, *Antiquities*, Bk. XVIII, ch. 4, §§ 1, 2; ch. 6, § 5; *War*, Bk. II, ch. 9, § 2; Tacitus, Bk. XV, ch. 44.

[3] See above, p. 247.

[4] See above, p. 281.

that prevailed before. All Syrians were by this time fully Semitized, speaking one tongue, Aramaic, and the educated among them writing one language, Greek. The Phoenicians, who had acquired a thicker veneer of Hellenism than their eastern neighbours and kinsmen[1], the Aramaeans, lost their hold in the first Christian century on their mother tongue, which remained current till a much later time in their African colonies. The Jews, who by this time were not confined to Judaea but had settlements in all the large Syrian towns, kept Hebrew as a sacred tongue.[2] Of the Arabs the Ituraeans, powerful in North Palestine, and the Idumaeans, nominally Judaized and settled in the south-western part of Palestine, were tending to adopt Aramaic. Those of them who were not yet settled no doubt clung to their Arabic. Farther south the Nabataeans, who of the Arabs had the closest contact with the Romans, persisted in their Arabic speech but adopted Aramaic for their inscriptions.[3] On the whole the picture presented quite a contrast to the ethnic and cultural anarchy of, say, the ʿAmārnah period.

A Greco-Macedonian element was sprinkled all over Syrian cities, being thickest in the Seleucid colonies — such as Antioch, Seleucia, Apamea and Laodicea — and in the seats of trade, such as the Phoenician and Philistine cities on the coast and Damascus and Palmyra in the interior. These settlers were descendants of Macedonian and Greek veterans, merchants, craftsmen and adventurers who for political or other reasons had sought their fortunes in the Orient. The Romans planted but few colonies. They had a settlement of veterans in Beirut under Augustus and another in Baʿlabakk, both destined to become vital foci of Roman culture.[4] The Latin-speaking colonists were far outnumbered by the Greek-speaking ones; many of them already knew Greek and could communicate with the natives and the other colonists through that tongue. Moreover, unlike the Greeks, the Romans kept somewhat aloof, unmindful of the culture of the provincials whom they ruled. The chief Roman interest in Syria was to use it as a base against the enemy and to exploit its resources. The Syrians manifested but little interest in the Roman military campaigns except when their own safety was threatened.

[1] See above, pp. 114, 254-5.
[2] See above, p. 257.
[3] See below, pp. 383-4.
[4] See below, pp. 309-10.

The performance of Roman administration in such a province as Syria, which had a civilization as high as the Roman though differing in character, was not as successful or brilliant as in such half-civilized provinces as Spain or Gaul. In Syria the Greek settlements, Phoenician cities and Judaean towns, with their developed social, intellectual and economic life and with their schools of art, philosophy and literature, found but little to borrow from Rome. To them Latin literature remained a sealed book.[1] But the case of the Arabians and the Aramaeo-Arabs was different. Among them, east of Anti-Lebanon and of settled Transjordan, Roman colonies were set up, each starting with a nucleus of Italian settlers, around which others were grouped, and developing into special communities. This was made possible after Trajan in A.D. 106 had annexed Transjordan as well as Ḥawrān, which was once under Nabataean rule but later transferred by Augustus to Herod. In 105 Trajan had reduced Petra.[2] Arabia Petraea was then incorporated into the Roman Empire under the name Provincia Arabia. With Syria as the focus of Roman power in the Near East, Roman administration established a chain of posts along the fringe of the desert to protect the more settled and civilized areas. The forts were often garrisoned with auxiliaries recruited from friendly tribes. The transversal road from east to west, connecting the cities of the Tigris and the Euphrates with those of the Mediterranean and passing through Palmyra, cut through this territory. A great longitudinal road crossed it, the Via Maris of the Romans, the King's Highway of the Bible.[3] This road ran from Damascus through Ḥawrān to Gilead, Moab and on southward to join the Arabian caravan route. Going back to the late second millennium B.C. this principal road of Transjordan was paved by Trajan and used as the military road of the legions, later of the Moslem pilgrims.[4] The new facilities promoted a tendency toward a settled life on the part of nomadic or semi-nomadic communities. Urbanization was a cardinal point in Roman policy.

Roman contribution

[1] Bouchier, p. 5.

[2] See below, pp. 381-2.

[3] Gen. 14:1-5; Num. 20:17; 21:22. For more on Roman roads consult Peter Thomsen, "Die römischen Meilensteine der Provinzen Syria, Arabia und Palaestina", *Zeitschrift des deutschen Palästina-Vereins*, vol. xl (1917), pp. 1 *seq.*; Christina P. Grant, *The Syrian Desert* (London, 1937), pp. 62-5.

[4] Since its reconstruction in recent years by the Transjordan government, the road has become King 'Abdullāh's Road.

In brief it may be claimed that the chief service which Roman administration rendered the Syrian province was immunity from civil disturbances and protection against external enemies. Incidentally it opened up a wider market, a world market, before it.

Syria at its height

In the first century of imperial rule (*ca.* 30 B.C. to A.D. 70) Syrian recovery from the depression into which it had sunk as a result of foreign and civil wars was rapid and sure. The province found itself an integral part of an empire that stretched from the Atlantic and the North Sea to the Euphrates and from the Rhine and the Danube to the Sahara. Under the shelter of imperial arms order and Pax Romana prevailed. Security from brigandage and piracy was established. Parthian and Arabian incursions were checked. Strategic passes, like the Cilician, were well guarded. A network of roads, an outstanding achievement of administrative and engineering skill, knit all parts of the empire into a relatively compact unit. Several of the milestones which marked the well-kept, well-drained Syrian roads are still preserved. Augustus instituted a postal service which brought the central government into closer contact with its provincial agents. Trade was stimulated. The curve of prosperity tended upward again. After A.D. 70 the entire Roman state enjoyed a long period of immunity from serious civil disturbances.[1] From A.D. 96 to 180 it was fortunate in having an unbroken succession of worthy emperors beginning with Nerva and ending with Marcus Aurelius. Theirs is designated "the age of the good emperors".[2] No great state was better governed than the

[1] Cf. below, p. 339.

[2] Genealogical table of the five good emperors:

12. Nerva (96–98)
¦
13. Trajan (98–117)
¦
14. Hadrian (117–38)
¦
15. Antoninus Pius (138–61)
¦
16. Marcus Aurelius (161–80)

Note.—Broken line indicates foster father and adopted son relationship. A genealogical table of the Antonines:

15. Antoninus Pius (138–61)

16. Marcus Aurelius (161–80) | 17. Lucius Verus (161–80)

18. Commodus (180–92)

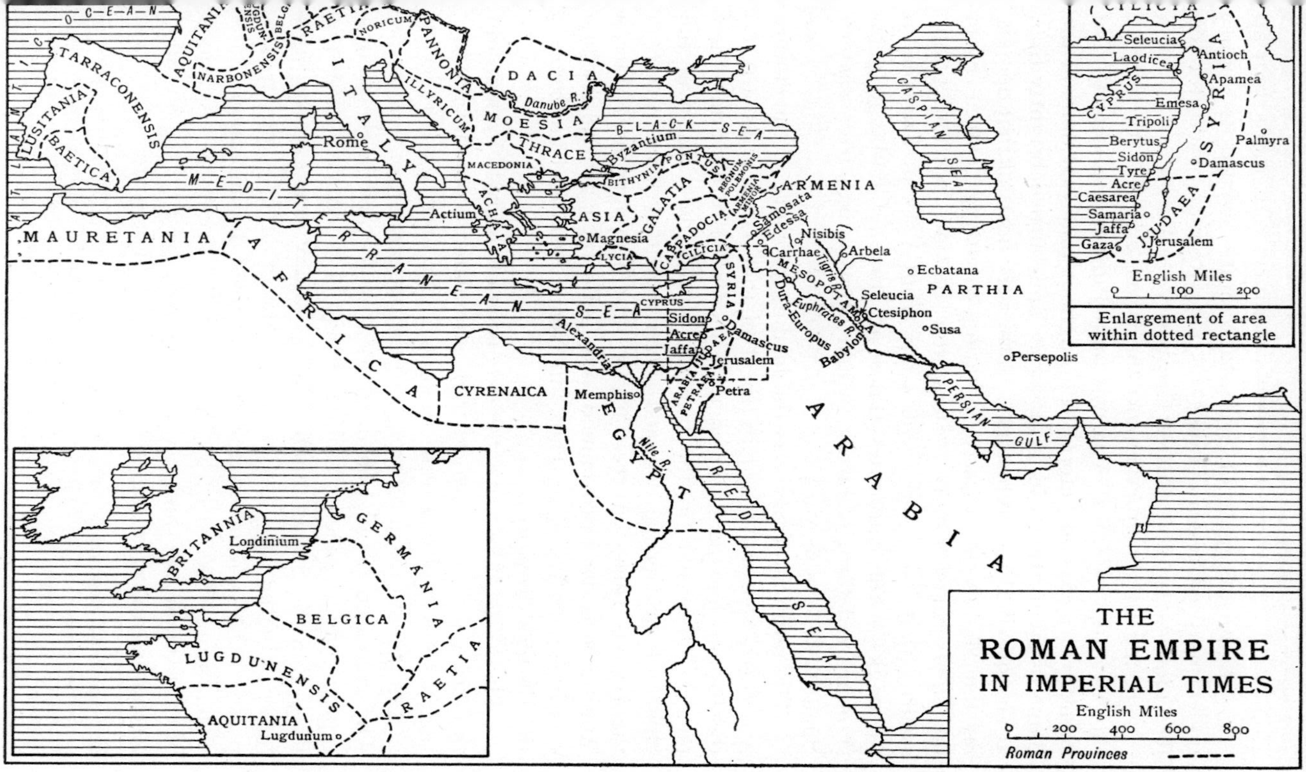
THE
ROMAN EMPIRE
IN IMPERIAL TIMES
English Miles
0 200 400 600 800
Roman Provinces
Enlargement of area within dotted rectangle
English Miles
0 100 200
ATLANTIC OCEAN
TARRACONENSIS
LUSITANIA
BAETICA
AQUITANIA
NARBONENSIS
RAETIA
NORICUM
PANNONIA
ILLYRICUM
DACIA
Danube R.
MOESIA
THRACE
MACEDONIA
ACHAIA
Actium
ITALY
Rome
MEDITERRANEAN SEA
MAURETANIA
AFRICA
CYRENAICA
EGYPT
Alexandria
Memphis
Nile R.
BLACK SEA
Byzantium
BITHYNIA
PONTUS
REGNUM POLEMONIS
ARMENIA MINOR
ASIA
Magnesia
LYCIA
GALATIA
CAPPADOCIA
CILICIA
CYPRUS
SYRIA
Sidon
Acre
Jaffa
JUDAEA
Jerusalem
Damascus
ARABIA PETRAEA
Petra
ARMENIA
Samosata
Edessa
Nisibis
Carrhae
Arbela
MESOPOTAMIA
Tigris R.
Euphrates R.
Dura-Europus
Babylon
Seleucia
Ctesiphon
Ecbatana
PARTHIA
Susa
Persepolis
CASPIAN SEA
PERSIAN GULF
ARABIA
RED SEA
BRITANNIA
Londinium
GERMANIA
BELGICA
LUGDUNENSIS
AQUITANIA
Lugdunum
RAETIA
CILICIA
Seleucia
Laodicea
Antioch
Apamea
Emesa
Tripoli
Berytus
Sidon
Tyre
Acre
Caesarea
Samaria
Jaffa
Gaza
Jerusalem
Damascus
Palmyra
CYPRUS
SYRIA
JUDAEA

Roman in the second Christian century.[1] Under Hadrian (117–38), an ex-legate of Syria, the empire reached its height; under his predecessor Trajan (98–117) Roman Syria attained its widest extent and greatest prosperity.[2]

During that century almost the whole civilized world from the Atlantic to Central Asia was united under one sceptre. No such empire existed before. Throughout that vast domain the flame of civilization was held higher and burned brighter than at any previous age in history. In the very heart of that domain lay the Mediterranean as a radiating, vitalizing centre. Syria lay on its eastern shore. Such were the facilities and public security that one could travel safely from York in England to the banks of the Euphrates almost any time. One language, a standardized form of Greek, would carry a man from eastern Spain to the Indus valley.

The position of Syria as the leading province of the empire was further strengthened by the fact that as early as A.D. 69 the Roman legions stationed in it succeeded in elevating their general Vespasian to the imperial throne over his rival the choice of the German legions. Over a century later (A.D. 175) the legions there on receiving a false rumour that Marcus Aurelius was dead proclaimed as emperor their general Avidius Cassius,[3] a native of Cyrrhus [4] in North Syria and governor of the Eastern provinces.

Economic productivity

The sense of security, the extension of the road system and the creation of a new world trade stimulated economic production beyond anything hitherto known. Prosperity was reflected in a higher standard of living and the appearance of new towns The increased population of greater Syria must in the second century have reached the all-time high of 7,000,000.[5] It is not likely that the Syrian population has at any time exceeded this figure. In the case of Coele-Syria the great productivity was partly due to another factor, the effective administration of the water supply furnished by the Orontes. Technical inventions of the Roman age included an improved plough, the so-called Archimedean screw and the watermill.[6] The water wheel was

[1] Cary and Haarhoff, p. 82. [2] Bouchier, p. 40. [3] Harrer, pp. 35-6.

[4] On the slopes of the Taurus north-east of Antioch, see below, p. 521.

[5] Cf. Heichelheim, pp. 158-9; Henri Lammens, *La Syrie, précis historique* (Beirut, 1921), vol. i, p. 11; Beloch, pp. 245 *seq.*; cf. above, p. 279, below, p. 484.

[6] See above, p. 40.

also improved. That whole valley, now partly a desert, must have been a seat of intensive cultivation.[1] Remains of oil presses abound east of Ḥimṣ, where no trees of any kind grow today. Apamea, which in the census of Quirinius under Augustus numbered 117,000 free inhabitants,[2] is now desolate. Even Transjordan, now mostly desert, was to Josephus [3] a land abounding in crops and with plains producing all varieties of trees such as dates, grapes and olives. The fertility of the northern continuation of Transjordan, Ḥawrān (Auranitis and Trachonitis), was proverbial. It was transformed under the aegis of the Romans from a country of shepherds and semi-nomads into one of cities and villages. The entire region was made dependent on the use of reservoirs in which the irregular but sometimes heavy rainfall was collected. Lying on the threshold of the desert Ḥawrān, with its capital Bostra,[4] was the first to be settled and cultivated by desert tribesmen. Under Trajan the city was enlarged, fortified and given the name Nova Trajana Bostra. It was an important junction of caravan roads leading to Damascus, the Mediterranean, the Red Sea and the Persian Gulf. After Diocletian (284–305) it became the capital of the province of Arabia. The degree of prosperity attained by this region under the Romans was never approached even under the Umayyads, whose capital was Damascus.[5]

Agriculture

From sporadic passages in Strabo (d. *ca.* A.D. 24), Pliny (d. 79), Athenaeus (fl. 228) and other Latin authors the impression of general prosperity in Syrian agriculture is gained. The forest-crowned summits of lofty Lebanon presented the same aspect as before; many writers include the mountain among the well-known lumber regions. It may be assumed that the system of wild tree protection and methodical felling was applied at least to the cedars. Pliny [6] enumerates among the trees of Syria the date, pistachio, fig, cedar, juniper, terebinth and sumac. In the first Christian century several Syrian trees were introduced into Italy. Vitellius, the legate under Tiberius,

[1] Theodor Mommsen, *The Provinces of the Roman Empire*, tr. William P. Dickson (London, 1909), vol. ii, p. 136.
[2] *Ephemeris epigraphica*, vol. iv (Berlin, 1881), p. 538.
[3] *War*, Bk. III, ch. 3, § 3.
[4] Bosora of 1 Macc. 5 : 26, 28, Eski Shām (old Damascus) of the Turks, Buṣra of the present day.
[5] Cf. Yāqūt, *Mu'jam al-Buldān*, vol. ii, p. 358.
[6] Bk. XIII, chs. 10-13.

is credited with the introduction of several varieties of figs and the pistachio to his country seat at Alba Longa.[1] The Nicolaän dates, thus called from Nicolaus of Damascus,[2] who when visiting Rome with Herod the Great made Augustus a present of the finest fruit of the date palm, were sweet as honey and of such size that "four of them, placed end to end, will make a cubit in length".[3] In the cultivation of the vine and other fruit plants use was made of water machines and presses and of advanced methods in manuring.[4] The Damascus plum tree was introduced into Italy long before Pliny; the jujube tree was introduced not long before his time.[5] Of the oil-bearing trees Pliny [6] refers to one that grows spontaneously in the maritime parts of Syria whose produce has a sweet flavour and is employed for medicinal purposes, evidently a terebinthine.

Grain constituted the principal nourishment. In addition to the staple cereals rice, which requires artificial irrigation, was cultivated spasmodically along the coast.[7] The commonest adjunct to cereal food was a leaf vegetable. Meat was not in regular demand except among the rich. Of the legumes lentils, beans, kidney beans, chick-peas, vetch and lupin were widely cultivated. Lupin was more popular for cattle. Bulbous plants, such as onions, leeks and garlic, were especially relished by the poor. Of the spices coriander, mustard, anise, cumin, ginger [8] and mint flourished in Syria.[9] The sources mention the mushroom of Jerusalem, the garlic of Heliopolis and the onion of Ascalon.[10] Ascalon also produced henna, which was highly valued. Syrian cabbage was popular. On enumerating the varieties of radish, a plant native to Syria, Pliny [11] considers the Syrian, which had recently been introduced into Italy, the very best. In the judgment of this Roman authority on natural

[1] Pliny, Bk. XV, chs. 21, 24; Athenaeus, Bk. XI, § 500; see above, pp. 259, 274-5.

[2] See above, p. 284.

[3] Pliny, Bk. XIII, ch. 9; Athenaeus, Bk. XIV, ch. 22.

[4] Cf. Matt. 21:33.

[5] Bk. XIII, ch. 10; XV, chs. 12, 14; see below, pp. 297-8.

[6] Bk. XV, ch. 8; XXIII, ch. 50.

[7] Strabo, Bk. XV, ch. 1, § 18. See above, pp. 274-5.

[8] See below, p. 619.

[9] Ex. 16:31; Num. 11:7; Matt. 13:31; Mk. 4:31; Matt. 23:23; Is. 28:25, 27.

[10] Strabo, Bk. XVI, ch. 2, § 29; Pliny, Bk. XIX, ch. 32; see below, p. 618, n. 3.

[11] Bk. XIX, ch. 26.

history the lilies of Antioch and Laodicea were the most esteemed.[1] Papyrus was grown and used for writing material.[2] Flax, hemp and cotton continued to grow all over Western Asia.[3] The liquorice root still grows wild near the marshes and on river banks around Antioch.

Syrian gardening was a pleasant feature of ancient Roman civilization. It goes back to early Semitic beginnings which grew out of the widespread fruit, flower and herb cultivation which depended solely upon summer irrigation. The Semitic Paradise was but a garden which the Lord God planted eastward in Eden.[4] It was modelled after the earthly gardens in the artificially irrigated lands from Palestine to Persia. Given an impetus under Persian rule, Semitic gardening technique was perfected under the Romans. It was applied not only on a private but also on a public scale, as exemplified in the sacred groves and temple grounds. Daphne, whose temple and grove were dedicated to Apollo, was one of the beauty spots in the Roman world; it attracted imperial pilgrims and visitors.[5] The flowery retreats which attended the Mediterranean civilization and were represented in Antioch, Damascus and Jerusalem became a prototype of the pleasure gardens that worked their way into Rome and later into Granada.[6] Until today water is handled as an artistic motif in the flowing jets (sing. *nafūrah*) emitting a veil-like spray in the courtyards of Damascus. Gardening

The production of dyes in the textile manufacturing districts of Sidon and Tyre seems to have continued under the Romans. Phoenician purple was held everywhere in high esteem. In Strabo's[7] time the great number of dyeing works in Tyre rendered the city "unpleasant as a place of residence". Pliny[8] states that the leaves of the sumac were used for tanning leather;[9] they are still used today. Syria and Egypt were the main sources of linen goods for the empire and among the best sources of leather. Industry was literally a process of "manufacture"; that is, production by hand. With no experimentation and no machinery it remained virtually static. Several Syrian plants provided medicinal and aromatic products for the Industry

[1] Bk. XXI, ch. 11. [2] See above, p. 277. [3] See above, pp. 91, 275.
[4] Gen. 2:8. For the etymology of "Paradise" see above, p. 227.
[5] See below, pp. 303-5. [6] Hitti, *History of the Arabs*, pp. 528-9.
[7] Bk. XVI, ch. 2, § 23. [8] Bk. XIII, ch. 13.
[9] The New Testament has a reference to a tanner in Jaffa, Acts 9:43; 10:6.

domestic as well as foreign market.[1] Syrian wines enjoyed well-deserved popularity throughout the whole ancient world.[2] Antioch, Byblus,[3] Tripoli, Berytus, Tyre, Lebanon, Ḥawrān, Ascalon and Gaza produced wine. The wine of Apamea was said to be well adapted for mixing with honey.[4] The wine of Galilee is cited in the New Testament.[5]

First among the mineral resources was asphalt or bitumen, found in large quantities in the region of the Dead Sea (Lake Asphaltites) and to a lesser extent in the vicinity of Sidon.[6] Syrian cinnabar and orpiment were used for painting; orpiment was of gold colour.[7] One of the uses to which amber was put by women was the making of spindles' whorls.[8] The alabaster of Damascus was whiter than other varieties.[9] Gypsum was prepared in Syria evidently by the same process by which plaster of Paris is prepared today.[10] Stone quarries existed near Antioch,[11] which also had chalk quarries as had Heliopolis. Copper was mined in Mount Lebanon and southern Palestine, in the vicinity of Jericho, Beirut and the sources of the Jordan.[12] Most of the mines of the Near East were controlled by the government and worked by slaves. Statuary was also produced. When the Emperor Caligula (37–41) ordered a colossal imperial effigy set up in the Temple of Jerusalem, his Syrian legate applied to an artificer of Sidon.[13] Men of each profession — merchants, shipowners, shopkeepers, artisans — formed associations for mutual protection and benefit. Palmyra had a guild of goldsmiths and silversmiths[14] and Gerasa had one of potters. The imperial armament factories established by the Emperor Diocletian (d. 313) in Antioch, Damascus and Edessa must have been outgrowths of earlier firms.[15]

Trade

Commerce, especially in its foreign and inter-provincial aspects, provided the main source of wealth. The richest cities of the Roman Near East were the commercial cities, such as

1 See below, p. 297.
2 Strabo, Bk. XV, ch. 3, § 22.
3 Athenaeus, Bk. I, ch. 29, § a.
4 Pliny, Bk. XIV, ch. 9.
5 John 2 : 3. Cf. Josephus, *War*, Bk. III, ch. X, § 8.
6 Pliny, Bk. XXV, ch. 51; Strabo, Bk. XVI, ch. 2, § 42, where the Dead Sea is wrongly called "Lake Sirbonis". See above, p. 40.
7 Pliny, Bk. XXX, ch. 22.
8 Pliny, Bk. XXXVII, ch. 2.
9 Pliny, Bk. XXXVI, ch. 12.
10 Pliny, Bk. XXXVI, ch. 59.
11 Libanius, *Orationes*, No. 11, § 25.
12 Cf. above, p. 277.
13 Philo (Judaeus), *Opera*, ed. Leopold Cohn and Paul Wendland (Berlin, 1915) vol. vi, ch. 31, §§ 220-22.
14 See below, p. 390.
15 Malalas, p. 307, ll. 20 *seq.*

Petra, Palmyra, Gerasa and the Phoenician coast towns. Industrialists and landowners stood next to merchants in opulence.

By and large the traders were natives of the land. The Roman trader (*negotiator*, *mercator*), a novel phenomenon in the history of the Levant, makes his debut subsequent to the annexation of Syria by Pompey. He is either Italian or Greek-Italian and settles first in Antioch. By the time of Augustus he reaches Petra. In the course of the first Christian century, however, he retreats before his shrewd and more experienced Syrian rival and under the attraction of new markets in the West until he virtually disappears from the market.[1] Commerce remained as individualistic as industry. Companies or partnerships were rare. Trade in slaves continued to flourish. Insolvent debtors forfeited their persons to their creditors, and professional slave traders seized unwary adults, kidnapped infants and bought unwanted ones.

From H. B. Walters, "Catalogue of Bronzes in the British Museum"

BRONZE STATUETTE OF A DONKEY WITH PANNIERS

The donkey, with head raised and legs stiff, is braying

Syrian traffic reached its peak in those golden days of Roman rule when the caravan cities of Petra, Gerasa, Bostra, Palmyra and Dura-Europus were flourishing centres of trade. The maritime routes were then enriched by Trajan's restoration of the canal which connected the Nile with the extreme north-west arm of the Red Sea and which was first dug by the ancient Pharaohs. The Phoenician cities exported dates and "the finest wheat flour".[2] The frankincense exported from Syria [3] was in reality of South Arabian origin.[4] Products of the medicinal and aromatic plants of Western Asia were exported to the entire Roman world. Perfumes and drugs produced in that region enjoyed world-wide vogue. Latin sources make frequent reference to Syrian styrax, silphium, *magydaris* and nard. Wines,

[1] M. Rostovtzeff, *The Social and Economic History of the Roman Empire* (Oxford, 1926), pp. 158-9.

[2] Athenaeus, Bk. I, ch. 28, § a.

[3] Athenaeus, Bk. I, ch. 27, § f.

[4] See above, pp. 272-3; Hitti, *History of the Arabs*, pp. 47-8

various oils, dried fruits and unguents were exported in quantities. Vessels bearing the signature of a certain Ennion of Sidon, the most renowned Syrian glassmaker of the first Christian century, have been found in Egypt, Cyprus, Italy and southern Russia.[1] His workshops must have had an office in Rome. Another Sidonian glass manufacturer maintained a branch office as far away as Cologne. The best workers in bronze in the middle of the first Christian century likewise flourished in Sidon.[2] Remains of Syrian weavers' products — cheap linen and woollen goods, purple-dyed silks — have been found in several places outside of Syria.

Syrian imports comprised pottery from Greece and Italy, dried fish from Egypt and Spain, papyrus from Egypt, myrrh and incense from South Arabia, spices and jewels from India and silk from China. 'Akka was an important centre for the fish trade. Among the seaboard population marine animals formed a large part of the popular diet. Papyrus was used for ships' ropes as well as for writing purposes.

[1] Heichelheim, p. 189; Rostovtzeff, p. 540, n. 43. [2] Cf. above, p. 296.

CHAPTER XXIII

CITY AND COUNTRY LIFE

THE general aspect of country life in Roman Syria did not radically differ from the earlier pattern. The land was studded with thousands of villages inhabited mostly by peasants who lived on the produce of the vineyards or farms. No traces of serfdom can be found among these villages; nor is there record of the presence of public slaves doing menial labour. Police duty was probably the responsibility of the city in whose territory the village lay. There is no clear record of a village spending money for education, public health or charity.[1] Some of the land surrounding a village may have been held in common, constituting a source of revenue to the village. Villages were occasionally owned by private individuals. The villages

The type of the common man was the peasant or his fellow-villager who worked as carpenter, blacksmith, shoemaker or shopkeeper. These villages were as little affected by the Romanizing process as they were by the Hellenizing process. The villagers, especially those far removed from urban centres, tenaciously clung to their traditional ways of life. The script and contents of the inscriptions found at al-Ṣafa — the volcanic region some one hundred miles south-east of Damascus — which date from the first three Christian centuries reveal the persistence of ancient rites and customs.[2]

Above the peasantry stood a native aristocracy. Its component parts were large landowners and proprietors of flocks of sheep and goats domiciled in neighbouring towns. The members of this class were also leaders in religious affairs. The caravan cities, coastal towns and Greco-Roman colonies housed the rich merchants and industrialists as well as the government officials. In the cities slavery created a "white-collar" class, too proud The well-to-do

[1] George M. Harper, Jr., *Village Administration in the Roman Province of Syria* (Princeton, 1928), p. 57.

[2] René Dussaud and Frédéric Macler, *Mission dans les régions désertiques de la Syrie Moyenne* (Paris, 1903), pp. 54 *seq.*; see below, p. 403, n. 3.

to work. Some masters made good use of their leisure in the service of city or state, others in the service of the Muses, but the majority developed into a " gentleman " class addicted to sports, amusements and social functions. The climatic conditions and traditional concepts of life, however, made for temperate habits; and the sense of family loyalty, a most precious element in the legacy of the patriarchal age, never lost its hold upon the people; it is still a living force today.

Social conditions

The country women went then, as they still go today, unveiled. The city women wore veils which either formed only a

From M. Rostovtzeff, " Excavations at Dura-Europos " (*Yale University Press*)

THE GREAT SOUTH THEATRE AT GERASA (JARASH)

Built in the reign of Domitian, end of first century

headdress or were brought round the head and down the shoulders like a hood, something like the modern system of veiling.[1] Statues of women exhibit occasional tattooing, often on the chest, a custom that still persists.

Since Roman law never recognized anything but monogamy, polygamy could not have been prevalent in the settled parts of Roman Syria. Circumcision, an early Semitic practice,[2] evidently began to fall into disuse as a result of contact with Indo-Europeans [3] and was finally abandoned under the influence of Christianity.

[1] See above, pp. 173-4. [2] See above, p. 118. [3] Herodotus, Bk. II, ch. 104.

In the Hellenized or Romanized cities and in the coastal towns the amusements were those of the ordinary Greco-Roman type—wrestling, chariot racing, musical competition and theatrical performances. Dromedary racing was popular in the regions bordering the desert. Hunting was a favourite among the well-to-do. Monuments show scenes in which bears, antelopes, gazelles and wild boars are hunted by archers or mounted lancers. Hounds were sometimes used. The institution of *thermae*, a combination of gymnasium and hot bath which made its emergence in Seleucid Syria, subsisted in the Roman period.

Louvre, Paris

TERRACOTTA STATUETTE REPRESENTING TWO GIRL MUSICIANS ON CAMEL-BACK

Seated under a canopy fastened to a richly draped saddle, one girl plays the drum, the other the double flute. The girls are apparently taking part in a religious procession organized by some temple. Such a scene was probably familiar to the Syrians in Roman times

From the early empire the Syrian began to be associated in the Roman mind with music, dancing, circus playing and other forms of entertaining. Jockeys from Laodicea, actors from Berytus, circus players from Tyre, ballet dancers from Caesarea, flute players from Heliopolis, musicians from Gaza and wrestlers from Ascalon figure in Latin literature. Professional Syrian performers organized regular troupes, went from place to place and were available for hire in banquets and on festal occasions. Rome must have patronized many such troupes, some of which came from Antioch. The Roman satirist Juvenal[1] (*ca.* A.D. 60–140) exclaims in an angry mood: "The Syrian Orontes has long since poured its water into the Tiber, bringing with it its lingo and its manners, its flutes and its slanting harp strings". Romans spoke of the Syrian *ambubaia*[2] as in modern times people spoke of the Parisian coquette. According to a report in Athenaeus,[3] Phoenicia "rings from one end to the other with indecent songs". After his Parthian campaign (A.D. 166) the dissolute Emperor Verus took time to amuse and enjoy himself at Laodicea and Daphne and returned to his capital with a train of Syrian musicians, actors, buffoons and other entertainers who sensibly affected the taste of the time.[4]

Antioch and Daphne

The palm for luxurious and dissolute living goes to Antioch with its suburb Daphne. Nowhere else in Roman Syria does the enjoyment of life seem to have been the goal and the duties of life the side issue as in this North Syrian spot. Antioch was allowed by Pompey to retain the privilege of autonomy which it possessed under the Seleucids. For the support it gave his rival, Septimius Severus degraded it after his victory at Issus (194) from the rank of metropolis and made it a "village" of Laodicea. His successor Caracalla made it a colony.[5] Julius Caesar bestowed on it, among other works, a theatre and an amphitheatre. Herod the Great contributed a road and a colonnade.[6] Caligula, Trajan and Hadrian added baths. Antoninus Pius paved its main street with granite from Egypt. Commodus (177–92) reorganized its periodic Olympian games. In the days of Josephus[7] it was the third largest city of the empire (after Rome and Alexandria). Lamps illuminated its paved streets and public squares after nightfall. In contrast to other cities this was one "where the brightness of the lights at night commonly equals the resplendence

[1] *Satura*, No. 3, ll. 62-5. [2] From Syriac *ambūbō*, fife. [3] Bk. XV, § 697c.

[4] Mommsen, vol. ii, p. 132; Bouchier, p. 17.

[5] Glanville Downey, "The Political Status of Roman Antioch", *Berytus*, vol. vi (1939–40), pp. 1 *seq.* For the privileges of cities and colonies see A. H. M. Jones, *The Greek City* (Oxford, 1940), pp. 132 *seq.*

[6] Josephus, *Antiquities*, Bk. XIV, ch. 5, § 3; *War*, Bk. I, ch. 21, § 11.

[7] *War*, Bk. III, ch. 2, § 4; George Haddad, *Aspects of Social Life in Antioch in the Roman-Hellenistic Period* (Chicago, 1949), pp. 70-73.

From " Antioch on-the-Orontes ", ed. G. W. Elderkin (Dept. Art and Archaeology of Princeton University)

SYMPOSIUM OF HERACLES AND DIONYSUS, END OF FIRST CHRISTIAN CENTURY MOSAIC FROM ANTIOCH

Heracles and Dionysus are engaged in a drinking contest. At the extreme left is a female flute player. Heracles drains a cup. He wears a garland of ivy leaves, as do others in the group. That he is losing in the contest is clear. Dionysus tips his cup to show that not a drop remains. The victory of the god of wine is acclaimed by the youthful protégé in front of him and the attendant behind him. Mosaics then played a decorative part comparable to that of rugs and tapestry in our day.

Now in Art Museum, Worcester, Mass.

of day".[1] In a panegyric on his home town the late Antiochene rhetorician Libanius[2] (314–*ca.* 393) refers to this feature: "Other lights take the place of the sun's light, lamps which leave the Egyptian festival of illumination far behind; and with us night is distinguished from day only by the difference of lighting". There is no such record as to any other city of antiquity. After describing the springs of Daphne and the aqueduct thence to Antioch, Libanius[3] boasts:

> In the public baths every stream has the proportions of a river; in the private baths several have the like. . . . As many as are the dwelling houses, so many are also the running waters, nay there are even in individual houses often several; and the majority of the workshops have also the same advantage. Therefore we have no fighting at the public wells as to who shall come first to draw — an evil under which so many considerable towns suffer, when there is a violent crowding round the wells and outcry over broken jars. With us the public fountains flow for ornament since every one has water within his doors. And this water is so clear that the pail appears empty, and so pleasant that it invites us to drink.

The road between Antioch and Daphne — a distance of five miles — was bordered by parks, fountains, villas and splendid structures appropriate to the gay procession that thronged from the city gate to the scene of consecrated pleasure. Ten miles in circumference, Daphne itself was a pleasure garden — "the purest gift of the queen of nymphs", in Libanius' words. The place was world renowned for its flowing, gushing waters, its shady paths, its beautiful laurel trees (for which it was named) and for its tall cypresses, all dedicated to Apollo.[4] Even the Christian emperors in later days spared those trees. The law forbidding their cutting was still in force in the sixth century.[5] In the sacred grove was a stream whose water for reasons unknown was periodically troubled. The attendant priests were at the same time affected with ecstasy and answered inquiries. This oracle of Daphne was consulted even by emperors. The Apollo and Diana temple, originally built by Seleucus, possessed the right of asylum.[6] It had rows of columns on two sides and walls bright with marble. A colossal statue of Apollo reaching

[1] Ammianus Marcellinus, *Rerum gestarum*, Bk. XIV, ch. 1, § 9.
[2] *Orationes*, No. 11, § 267.
[3] *Orationes*, No. 11, §§ 244-5.
[4] See above, p. 295.
[5] Procopius, Bk. II, ch. 14, § 5.
[6] Strabo, Bk. XVI, ch. 2, § 6; 2 Macc. 4:33.

almost to the ceiling stood in it. Early emperors who made the pilgrimage to Daphne encamped in tents. Diocletian (284–305) built a palace in it that was beautified by Theodosius (378–95). Hadrian, who was legate of Syria and received in Antioch the news of his elevation to the throne, presented several buildings to Antioch and a theatre to Daphne. The aqueducts which supplied both towns with water were repaired or enlarged by

From Dussaud, Deschamps and Seyrig, " *La Syrie* " (*Paul Geuthner, Paris*)

THE ROMAN AQUEDUCT OF ANTIOCH BRINGING THE WATER FROM DAPHNE

him. Several other buildings adorned Daphne. " No city in all the empire excelled it in the splendour and magnificence of its public structures." [1] Its main street, two miles long, with a covered colonnade on both sides and a broad carriage road in the middle, ran through the middle of the city parallel to the Orontes.[2]

Since Seleucid days Daphne had been the scene of the greatest celebration of games in Syria.[3] A wealthy Antiochene senator who accompanied Augustus on his return to Rome

[1] Mommsen, *Provinces*, vol. ii, p. 129.

[2] G. Downey, " Imperial Building Records in Malalas ", *Byzantinische Zeitschrift*, vol. xxxviii (1938), p. 308.

[3] See above, p. 278.

willed his fortune to the establishment of a thirty-day Daphnean festival — the Olympian games — with dances, dramatic performances, chariot races, athletic and gladiatorial contests. Early in the third century the duration was extended to forty-five days. Women participated in some of these performances, and the festival, as might be expected, was the scene of many moral irregularities. Daphne became proverbial for its dissoluteness.

Proud, turbulent and satirical, the Antiochians were noted for their mastery of the art of ridicule. They evidently could not forget that theirs was once a royal city and stood ready to side with any pretender whom the Syrian army put up. With the emperors who sojourned in their city they invariably quarrelled. Hadrian withdrew from the city the right of coinage, Marcus Aurelius the right of assembly; Septimius Severus transferred the primacy of Syria to Laodicea, where it temporarily remained. For a time Antioch, as noted above, was made dependent on Laodicea. Emperors bestowed titles and rights upon a city as a reward for good behaviour; they withdrew these privileges as a punishment for disloyalty. Severus ordained the partition of Syria into a northern province — called Coele-Syria — which was allowed two legions, and a southern — called Syro-Phoenicia — which was allowed one legion. Antioch's later trouble with Julian, who spent the winter of 362 there preparatory to his Persian campaign, started when he tried to regulate the price of drinks and dancing. The senators were running the "black market". The majority of the people were then Christians, but the emperor was not and had tried to restore paganism. They ridiculed him as a dwarf displaying a billy-goat's beard.[1] They themselves kept clean shaved even when old. Long before him Trajan had made Antioch the headquarters of the Parthian campaigns which closed his life. While wintering there in A.D. 115, when the emperor narrowly escaped destruction, the city suffered one of the most violent earthquakes on record. "Even Mt. Casius itself was so shaken that its peaks seemed to lean over and break off and to be falling upon the very city."[2] The second great calamity that befell the city was its capture in A.D. 260 by the Persian Shāpūr I (Sapor). On that occasion the

[1] Ammianus Marcellinus, Bk. XXII, ch. 14, § 3.
[2] Dio, Bk. LXVIII, ch. 25, § 6. See above, p. 40.

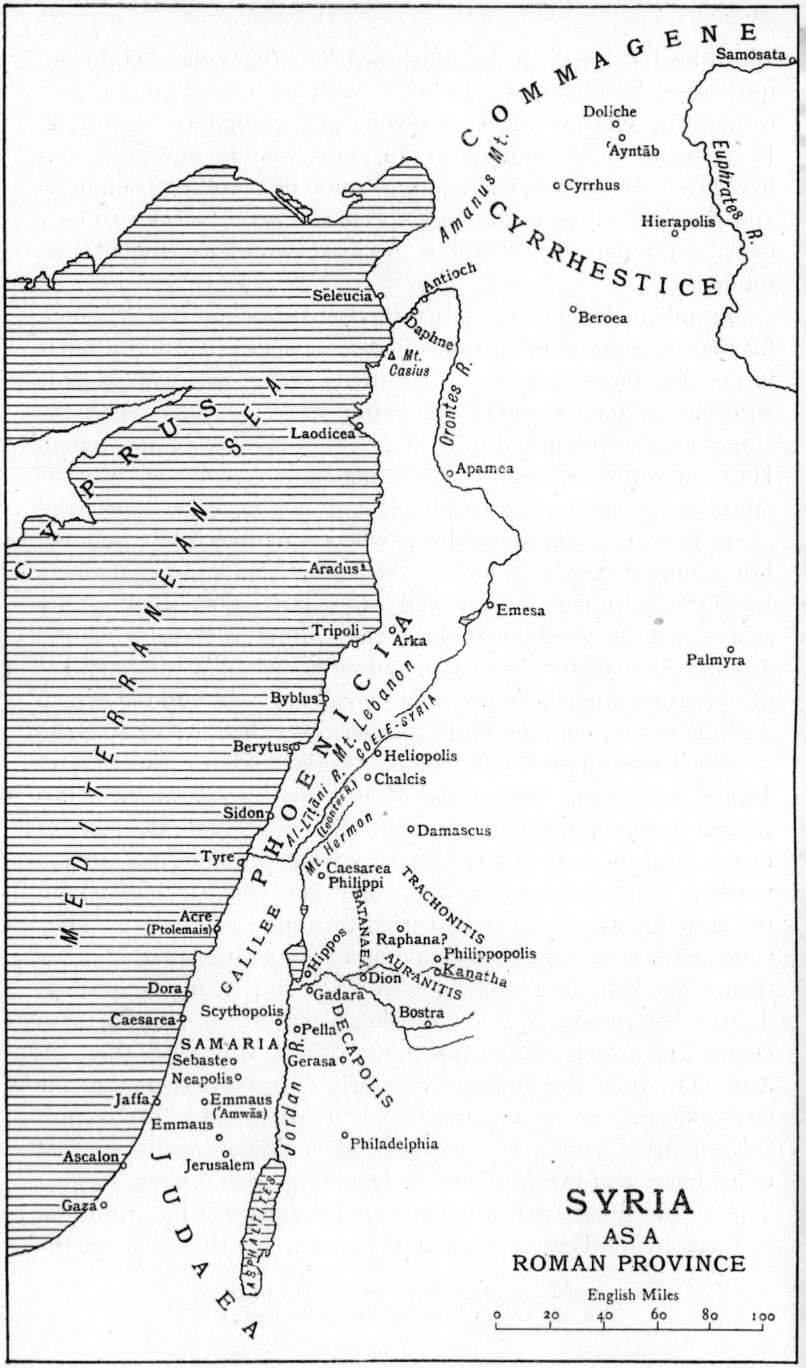

COMMAGENE
Samosata
Doliche
Ayntāb
Euphrates R.
Cyrrhus
Hierapolis
Amanus Mt.
CYRRHESTICE
Antioch
Seleucia
Beroea
Daphne
Mt. Casius
Orontes R.
CYPRUS
MEDITERRANEAN SEA
Laodicea
Apamea
Aradus
Emesa
Tripoli
Arka
Palmyra
PHOENICIA
Mt. Lebanon
Byblus
COELE-SYRIA
Berytus
Heliopolis
Al-Līṭāni R.
(Leontes R.)
Chalcis
Sidon
Mt. Hermon
Damascus
Tyre
Caesarea Philippi
TRACHONITIS
Acre (Ptolemais)
BATANAEA
GALILEE
Raphana?
Hippos
Philippopolis
AURANITIS
Kanatha
Dion
Dora
Gadara
Scythopolis
Bostra
Caesarea
Pella
DECAPOLIS
SAMARIA
Sebaste
Jordan R.
Gerasa
Neapolis
Jaffa
Emmaus ('Amwās)
Emmaus
Philadelphia
Ascalon
Jerusalem
ASPHALTITES
Gaza
JUDAEA
SYRIA
AS A
ROMAN PROVINCE
English Miles
0 20 40 60 80 100

citizens were absorbed in the enjoyment of a theatrical performance when the wife of the actor suddenly cried, "Is it a dream, or are the Persians here?" whereupon all the people turned their heads about and saw the arrows being showered upon them.[1] The city was set on fire and many of its inhabitants butchered without the loss of a single Persian.

Antioch's rival to the south, Laodicea, was also a favourite pleasure resort frequented by dignitaries. In the early first Christian century the gently sloping hills overhanging the city were all covered with vines almost to their summits. The vineyards extended eastward nearly to Apamea and the wines were exported from Laodicea's excellent harbour to Alexandria.[2] Herod the Great (d. 4 B.C.), who inaugurated the royal Jewish policy of bestowing favours on the colonies as a means of currying imperial favour, furnished Laodicea among other cities with an aqueduct,[3] a large fragment of which is still to be seen. Laodicea and Apamea

Laodicea's sister colony inland, Apamea, had boasted since Seleucid days royal parks full of game and a neighbourhood rich in pasturage. Its temple housed a famous oracle, probably the one who foretold the greatness of Julia Domna, mother of the Syrian imperial dynasty,[4] and encouraged the designs of her husband Septimius Severus on the throne. Severus visited the town again as an emperor. Dedications to the Baal of Apamea have been found as far west as Vaison in southern France, where an altar was set up to "Baal the director of fortune".[5] Certain sons of Apamea achieved distinction in the Byzantine and Christian periods.[6]

South of Apamea on the Orontes lay Emesa (Ḥimṣ), which retained its native rule of priest-kings throughout the Roman period. Other cities ruled by native aristocracies were Damascus, Palmyra and Edessa. Each of these was the centre of a petty state; the Palmyrene state grew into a formidable one.[7] The Emesene nobility like the Palmyrene and the Damascene achieved for a time inclusion in the imperial nobility and consequent participation in the administration of the empire even before two of its members captured the imperial throne.[8] The founder of the Emesene house was a man with the Latinized Emesa

1 Ammianus, Bk. XXIII, ch. 5, § 3.
2 Strabo, Bk. XVI, ch. 2, § 9.
3 Josephus, *War*, Bk. I, ch. 21, § 11.
4 See below, pp. 340 *seq.*
5 *Philologus*, vol. xxxi (1872), p. 362.
6 See below, pp. 321, 324.
7 See below, pp. 393 *seq.*
8 See below, pp. 340 *seq.*

name Sampsigeramus,[1] whose descendants were dethroned by Domitian (81–96). A scion of the family, however, reappeared under Valerian and in A.D. 258 led the militia of his town against the Parthians,[2] as did the Abgars of Edessa and the kings of Palmyra on various occasions. Emesa's temple of Baal achieved distinction in elevating one of its young priests, Bassianus, to the throne of the Caesars under the name Elagabalus (218–22), after the name of the Emesene deity.[3] On the coins of this emperor the city is called metropolis, on those of his predecessor Caracalla, colony. It was Caracalla who made it the capital of Phoenicia Libanesia.[4]

Damascus

Throughout the Seleucid and Roman periods Damascus, former and future capital of Syria,[5] was overshadowed by Antioch and eclipsed by some of the coastal towns. It was given but scanty notice by the classical authors. In Strabo's [6] days the territory of Damascus was still liable to incursions from robbers, one of whose caves in the hills of Trachonitis to the south could shelter 4000 of them. These brigands were also likely to assail caravans from Arabia Felix. Damascus' territory was so extensive as to involve it under Tiberius in a boundary dispute with Sidon.[7] For prosperity it depended upon its trade and irrigated gardens as well as income from its territory. Its status was evidently improved in the second century. Hadrian raised the city to the rank of a metropolis (chief city) and Alexander Severus (222–35) conferred on it colonial rights. Under Diocletian it became the seat of an arsenal,[8] a presage of the skill of its inhabitants in forging arms. Her merchant sons carried her Semitic deity Hadad Rammanu,[9] under the designation Jupiter Damascenus, as far west as Italy. A priest of Jupiter Optimus Maximus Damascenus sat on the local senate of Puteoli, now Pozzuoli, the seaport.[10]

Berytus

Of the maritime cities Berytus was the only one to play a

[1] Wrongly rendered "Sampsikeramus" in Strabo, Bk. XVI, ch. 2, § 10; cf. Rostovtzeff, *Social and Economic History*, p. 248. The name sounds like Aramaic for "may the sun-god strengthen". Art. "Sampsigeramus", Pauly-Wissowa, *Real-Encyclopädie der classischen Altertumswissenschaft*.

[2] Malalas, p. 296.

[3] "Elagabal" sounds like Arabic *Ilāh al-jabal*, "the god of the mountain"; Art. "Elagabal", Pauly-Wissowa; see below, pp. 343-4.

[4] Malalas, p. 296.

[5] See above, pp. 164-5, 224; below, pp. 469 *seq*.

[6] Bk. XVI, ch. 2, § 20.

[7] Josephus, *Antiquities*, Bk. XVIII, ch. 6, § 3.

[8] See above, p. 296.

[9] See above, p. 172.

[10] *Corpus Inscriptionum Latinarum*, vol. x (Berlin, 1883), No. 1576.

significant rôle in other than commercial, industrial activity. Sidon was granted colonial rights by Elagabalus. Tyre acquired metropolitan rights under Hadrian and was raised to the rank of colony by Septimius Severus as a reward for its attachment to his cause during the contest for imperial power with Niger, who was favoured by Berytus. But Berytus was one of the earliest Roman colonies in Syria, having received the honorific but cumbersome designation Colonia Julia Augusta Felix from Augustus after his daughter.[1] Under this emperor its harbour was improved by a double mole in crescent form with towers at each end from which a chain could be stretched so as to block the entrance of undesirable ships.[2] As the seat of a detachment of Legion III Gallica since Augustus' days, Berytus became a garrison town and its inhabitants supplied auxiliaries when needed by the legate.[3] Very early it became an isle of Romanism in a sea of Hellenism. Jewish kings eager to ingratiate themselves with Roman emperors by bestowing gifts on the colonies made it the recipient of many material favours. Agrippa I (A.D. 41–4), grandson of Herod the Great, erected in Berytus a theatre supreme in sumptuousness and elegance, an amphitheatre, a bath and porticoes — all at lavish expense.[4] The inaugural festival was celebrated with musical performances and an exhibition of some seven hundred pairs of gladiators. To add to the excitement of the exercises a number of criminals were introduced into the arena and the gladiators set upon them and destroyed them. A few years later Titus celebrated the birthday of his father Vespasian by the exhibition of similar spectacles, but in this case the victims were captive Jews.[5] Agrippa II (d. 100) made Berytus his favourite residence, endowed its annual spectacles and set up in it many statues. Its theatrical entertainments and circus games were still in vogue in the fourth century.

The city distinguished itself in another sphere of activity. As seat of the most renowned provincial school of Roman law it became and remained for the rest of the whole period of the empire a mecca for the legal minds of the entire East.[6] Poseidon

[1] Consult Pliny, Bk. V, ch. 17, § 20.

[2] Cf. below, p. 446.

[3] Josephus, *Antiquities*, Bk. XVII, ch. 10, § 9.

[4] Josephus, *Antiquities*, Bk. XIX, ch. 7, § 5.

[5] Josephus, *War*, Bk. VII, ch. 3, § 1; ch. 5, § 1

[6] See below, pp. 325 *seq*.

(Neptune), the city's patron god, was represented on the coins holding a trident or drawn by sea-horses.

Heliopolis

Berytus had a sister colony in Coele-Syria, Heliopolis. This Greek name (city of the sun), imposed by the Seleucids when its Baal was definitely identified with the sun, was retained under the Romans. The ancient Semitic name, which may have meant the Baal of al-Biqāʿ,[1] rather than the city of Baal, reasserted itself and survives in Arabic Baʿlabakk (colloquial Baʿalbak). The city was made a colony by Augustus, who planted in it a garrison from the same legions as those used in colonizing Berytus. On the coins of his reign it is entitled Colonia Julia Augusta Heliopolis. But the city remained less

The American Numismatic Society

A COIN OF BEIRUT

Obverse and reverse of a bronze coin of Berytus, first century B.C. Poseidon (as Baal-Beroth) is represented on both obverse and reverse; on the latter he is driving a team of hippocampi

Roman than Berytus, less Greek than Antioch and more Semitic than either.

The flute players of Heliopolis like the musicians of Antioch were popular all over the empire. Their services were in demand not only in connection with festive occasions but also with the ritual of the temples. The women of the city were noted for their beauty, a boon bestowed on them by the Syrian goddess who haunted the neighbouring slopes of Lebanon,[2] and the men for their eloquence, an inspiration from the Muses of their mountain district. But the world-wide fame of the city rested on its great temple.

Originally dedicated to the worship of the Syrian god Hadad,[3] the temple must have gone back to pre-Seleucid days. Its oracle acquired great repute even before it was rebuilt and

[1] See above, p. 39.

[2] "Expositio", in C. Müller, *Geographi Graeci minores*, vol. ii (Paris, 1861), p. 518.

[3] See above, p. 172.

enlarged by the Roman emperors. Before embarking on his second campaign against Parthia (A.D. 116), Trajan first tested the oracle by submitting a blank sheet of paper in a sealed wrapper. In response he received a similar blank reply and thus conceived a high idea of the prescience of the oracle.[1] He then proceeded with his consultation in earnest. The response was symbolically conveyed by a bundle of wood wrapped in a cloth. His death in 117 in Cilicia, whence his bones were transmitted to Rome, gave a perfect but belated interpretation to the oracular performance.

The elaborate enlargement of the Heliopolitan temple was initiated by Antoninus Pius (138–61)[2] and progressed slowly

The American Numismatic Society

A COIN OF SEPTIMIUS SEVERUS

Obverse and reverse of a bronze coin of Heliopolis (Baʿlabakk) struck in the name of Septimius Severus *ca.* A.D. 211. The reverse displays a front and side view of the temple of Jupiter Heliopolitanus

until the time of Caracalla (211–17) and other emperors of the Syrian dynasty who completed the structure, making it one of the wonders of the world. The temple appears for the first time on the reverse of the coins of Septimius Severus. Caracalla and his Syrian mother Julia Domna inscribed "Heliopolis" as a legend on their coins. Vows in honour of these two are still partially legible in Latin on the pedestal of the portico of the great temple, where the inscription states that the brazen pillars had been dedicated and the capitals gilded in their honour by a member of the legion.[3] The temple's name also occurs on the coins of Philip the Arab (A.D 243–79).[4]

The temple housed a gold statue of the deity, whose local representation depicted him as a beardless youth in the garb of

[1] Macrobius, *Saturnalium*, Bk. I, ch. 23, §§ 14-16.
[2] Malalas, p. 280, where Antoninus is credited with building the entire temple.
[3] *Corpus Inscriptionum Latinarum*, vol. iii, No. 138.
[4] See below, pp. 345-6.

a charioteer holding in his right hand a whip and in his left thunderbolts and ears of grain.[1] On certain annual festivals this statue was borne on the shoulders of prominent Heliopolitans who prepared themselves for the solemnities by shaving the head and vowing abstinence and chastity. At this temple also were reverenced black conical stones, one of which was transferred by Elagabalus to a temple in Rome.[2] A fair was held in the city on this occasion. The temple made Heliopolis for centuries the most conspicuous city in the region of Libanus and second to Antioch in the province of Syria. Under the appellation Jupiter Heliopolitanus, whose full title was Jupiter Optimus Maximus Heliopolitanus, this ancient Semitic deity was carried by merchants and veterans to many lands in the West.

From O. Puchstein and T. von Lupke, "Ba'albek" (Berlin)

JUPITER OPTIMUS MAXIMUS HELIOPOLITANUS, BA'LABAKK

The ruins of the temple of Heliopolis[3] surpass any others bequeathed from Roman days, not excluding those of Rome itself. The Moslems who converted the temple area into a citadel ascribed its construction to Solomon; for who else but he who controlled the jinn could have raised

[1] Macrobius, Bk. I, ch. 23, §§ 11-13.

[2] Consult above, pp. 118, 123; below, pp. 385, 429, 452.

[3] Excavated by O. Puchstein beginning 1902; see his *Erster und zweiter Jahresbericht über die Ausgrabungen in Baalbek* (Berlin, 1902, 1903); do., *Führer durch die Ruinen von Ba'albek* (Berlin, 1905); consult Theodore Wiegand, *Baalbek*, 3 vols. of text, 1 of illustrations (Leipzig, 1921–5).

such a structure? Despite the work of earthquakes and Mongols enough is left to impress all beholders. Within the area of the acropolis lie the ruins of two temples, that of Jupiter-Hadad and that of his consort Atargatis (Ashtart), commonly attributed to Bacchus,[1] with their extensions. Of the two the Atargatis temple is younger, smaller and better preserved. Indeed it is the best preserved and most richly ornamented ancient building

From O. Puchstein and T. von Lupke, "Ba'albek"

THE TEMPLE OF (BACCHUS) ATARGATIS FROM THE NORTH-WEST

in all Syria. The shrine of Jupiter-Hadad is surrounded by a peristyle of large columns of yellow stone with Corinthian capitals and a frieze above. Of these columns six hold themselves proudly erect to this day, facing the Lebanon in majestic grandeur. In fact these are the chief remains of the entire temple of Jupiter-Hadad. Each column consists of three blocks and rises to a height of 62 feet, being $7\frac{1}{2}$ feet in diameter.

[1] Hermann Thiersch, "Zu den Tempeln und zur Basilika von Baalbek", *Nachrichten von der Gesellschaft der Wissenschaften zu Göttingen*, Philologisch-historische Klasse (Berlin, 1926), pp. 1 *seq.*; do., "Le Temple de la déesse à Ba'albek", *Revue biblique*, vol. xxxv (1926), p. 461.

Porphyry columns, originally from Egypt, were taken from Baʿlabakk by Justinian and used in building Santa Sophia (Aya

From O. Puchstein and T. von Lupke, "Baʿalbek"

THE SIX COLUMNS OF THE TEMPLE OF JUPITER IN BAʿLABAKK

Sofya). One of them, broken en route, displays the attaching bracelets.

The great court in which stood the altar is roughly 340 feet square. It was surrounded by a peristyle of forty-eight columns. On its west side a basilica with three apses was erected in the sixth century but commonly ascribed to Constantine or Theodosius of the fourth.[1] The whole temple complex, still visible at a great distance, rests on an artificial terrace formed by a huge understructure of vaults. The north-west side of the wall of enclosure consists of enormous blocks which may have been designed to insure stability for the building in case of earthquakes. Three of these blocks, 20 feet from the ground, are roughly 62 × 14 × 11 feet each. It is estimated that there is enough material in each block to build a square house with walls 1 foot thick, a frontage of 60 feet and a height of 40 feet. A

1 2

From O. Puchstein and T. von Lupke, "Ba'albek"

FIG. 1. CORNICE OF THE TEMPLE OF JUPITER
FIG. 2. ARCHITRAVE OF THE COLONNADE IN THE GREAT COURT

sister block is still lying in the quarry on the outskirts of the town.

Aside from the huge size of the stone blocks in the walls and the colossal magnitude of the pillars, it is the wealth of detail in ornamentation and the figure work in the friezes that constitute a feature of the surviving group of buildings. The decorations comprise wheat and poppies (emblems of life and death), winged genii lifting a veil and cupids with bows and arrows or mounted on dragons and dolphins. Vines and garlands adorn the doorsteps. Geometrical figures, interspersed with foliage, and busts of emperors or deities, cover the ceiling. The portals of the temple of Atargatis are especially rich in foliage and fine figure work.

[1] Thiersch, pp. 20 *seq.*

Some 300 yards from the acropolis is a circular temple of the late imperial age attributed to Venus or Fortuna (goddess of fate). Its medieval transformation into a chapel dedicated to St. Barbara insured its preservation. It stands in the midst of the present town.

South Syria

Cities of a variety of types existed side by side in South Syria. There were the old Philistine cities along the coast — Gaza and its suburb Anthedon,[1] Ascalon, Jaffa and Acre — all of which by this time had become Hellenized. Jaffa, according to Strabo,[2] was a notorious haunt for robber chiefs. Then came the Jewish foundations of the Herodian family: Caesarea on the sea, Sebaste, Tiberias [3] and Caesarea Philippi.[4] These were followed by a few Roman colonies, one of which was Neapolis (new town), Shechem of the Old Testament.[5] In the course of the Jewish war the Jews of this city, then called Scythopolis, turned against their own people and sided with the Romans, two of whose legions spent a winter there.[6] The city was subsequently laid waste by the insurgent Jews.[7] After the war Vespasian, whose praenomen was Flavius, rebuilt the city, which was then named in his honour Flavia Neapolis. The name persists in present-day Nābulus. Neapolis was the birthplace of Justin Martyr,[8] an early Father of the Church credited with the opening of the first Christian school at Rome, where he is said to have been scourged to death about A.D. 165.

Vespasian built another city, Emmaus, in which he located 800 veterans.[9] This is the Emmaus of Luke (24:13), seven miles north-west of Jerusalem on the Roman road [10] and should be distinguished from Emmaus, now ʿAmwās, twenty miles north-west of Jerusalem.[11] In the Ḥawrān district Philippopolis provides an example of the elevation of a village to the rank of a city. Originally an insignificant village in the neighbourhood of Bostra, Philippopolis was exalted into a city in A.D. 244 by

[1] Its name was changed by Herod to Grippias; Josephus, *Antiquities*, Bk. XIII, ch. 13, § 3. Pliny, Bk. V, ch. 14, wrongly places it inland. The ancient name survives in Khirbat Tida; Abel, vol. ii, p. 200.

[2] Bk. XVI, ch. 2, § 28.

[3] See above, p. 284.

[4] See above, p. 242, n. 2.

[5] See above, p. 198.

[6] Josephus, *War*, Bk. II, ch. 18, §§ 3-4.

[7] Josephus, *War*, Bk. II, ch. 18, § 1.

[8] See below, p. 336.

[9] Josephus, *War*, Bk. VII, ch. 66.

[10] Either present-day Kubaybah or its neighbour Qalūniyah (*colonia*).

[11] 1 Macc. 3:40; 9:50; Josephus, *War*, Bk. II, ch. 20, § 4.

Philip the Arab, who was born in it. That year marked his accession to the throne of the Caesars. The city was also augmented by a new element, Italian colonists, and became itself a Roman colony. It is the Shahbah of Arab geographers.[1]

In the interior the league of "ten cities", the Decapolis continued in existence. Pliny [2] enumerates the cities and refers to the "region of Decapolis", which evidently began where

From Carl H. Kraeling, "Gerasa, City of the Decapolis" (Yale University Press)

THE ROMAN TRIUMPHAL ARCH OF GERASA

End of second or early third century

Esdraelon opened into the Jordan valley and expanded eastward. The region was dominated by these cities, whose number varied from time to time. Ptolemy lists Beth-shean, Pella,[3] Dion,[4] Gerasa,[5] Philadelphia,[6] Gadara, Raphana,[7] Kanatha (Canatha),[8] Hippos [9] and Damascus. Other towns were later

[1] Yāqūt, vol. iii, p. 339; Dussaud, *Topographie*, p. 368; Abel, vol. ii, p. 184.

[2] Bk. V, ch. 16.

[3] See above, p. 252; below, p. 414.

[4] After a Macedonian town; present-day Tell al-Ash'ari, between Hippos and Kanatha east of Lake Tiberias; Abel, vol. ii, p. 306.

[5] See above, p. 252.

[6] Rabbath Ammon, present-day 'Ammān; see above, p. 253.

[7] Al-Rāfah in Ḥawrān.

[8] Qanawāt, south-east of Raphana.

[9] Qal'at al-Ḥiṣn on the east side of Lake Tiberias.

added, swelling the number to eighteen. Under the Romans Beth-shean, which lay on the west side of the Jordan, held the primacy over her sisters, all of which lay to the east of the Jordan.[1] Basilides the Younger, a philosopher and teacher of Marcus Aurelius, was born in Beth-shean. Another distinguished city of the Decapolis was Gerasa,[2] now Jarash, thirty-seven miles south-east of Lake Tiberias and thirty-two miles south-east of Gadara. Its recent excavation reveals the Greek plan of the city with theatres, temples, stadium, forum and colonnades, most of which date from the late first or second Christian century. The imposing ruins, like those of Petra, Palmyra and Heliopolis, are among the most conspicuous from Roman Syria. Multitudes from the Decapolis followed Jesus in his early ministry.[3]

[1] Rowe, *Topography and History of Beth-Shan*, p. 46.

[2] See above, p. 252.

[3] Matt. 4 : 25.

CHAPTER XXIV

INTELLECTUAL ACTIVITY

ROMAN SYRIA, which distinguished itself in the domain of entertainment and produced the heroes of the circus and theatre,[1] fell short of its neighbour Egypt — with its Alexandrian library and school — in intellectual performance. As was to be expected, several of the early literary productions were stories of lovers, robbers, soothsayers and travellers that proved to be of no permanent value. With the exception of that of Probus, the Latin philologist and critic of Berytus, hardly any Syrian contribution to Latin literature was of special significance. Antioch, the richest and largest city of Roman Asia and the third greatest in the empire, offers no prominent author's name.

Marcus Valerius Probus flourished in the second half of the first Christian century. He began his career as a soldier but later devoted his entire attention to the study of the classical literature of Rome. There he settled and produced critical versions of Vergil, Horace and other major poets. He thereby laid the foundation for the classicism of the later imperial period and was ranked among the greatest Latin philologists.[2]

The Syrian contribution to Greek literature was much more significant. Our principal authority for the history of Syria under the early empire is a Greek work by a Jewish historian. This was Josephus, born at Jerusalem about A.D. 37, author of *Antiquities of the Jews* and *The Jewish War*.[3] Josephus claimed descent through his mother from the Maccabees. As a young man he went to Rome to plead before Nero the cause of some priests of his co-religionists, and on his return he became a general in the Jewish army in its revolt against Roman suzerainty. He History

[1] See above, pp. 301-2.

[2] Cf. "Probus", *Harper's Dictionary of Classical Literature and Antiquities*, ed. Harry T. Peck (New York, 1897).

[3] Josephus' works have been translated by William Whiston, new ed., 2 vols. (London, 1897) and revised by A. R. Shilleto, 5 vols. (London, 1890–1900); also edited and translated by H. St. J. Thackeray *et al.*, 7 vols. (London, 1926–43).

was taken prisoner but Vespasian spared his life. Henceforth Josephus attached himself to the family of Vespasian and returned with Titus to Rome. There he assumed the name of Flavius as a dependant of the Flavians and composed the existing works. His *Antiquities* draws heavily upon the Old Testament in sketching the entire history of the Jews and deals in great detail with the later Maccabean and the Herodian reigns. *The Jewish War*, which was written originally in Aramaic, gives a detailed account of the fatal struggle with Rome of which he had been an eye-witness. The account is coloured by the author's desire to gratify his imperial patrons.

Other than Josephus there is hardly a notable name in Syrian historiography. Little is known of Philo of Byblus (*ca.* A.D. 61–141), the grammarian and author of a work on Phoenician religion, fragments of which have been preserved in Eusebius.[1] Equally unknown is Menander of Laodicea, a rhetorician who lived later (third century) and worked out some Phoenician chronicles. In the second half of the second century lived another somewhat mysterious writer Jamblichus (Iamblichus), who wrote a Babylonian history. As a young man he was taken by an Armenian king into his court and became familiar with the Babylonian language and Persian magic.[2] Jamblichus says about himself that he was a Syrian on both his father's and mother's sides. He did not become acquainted with Greek until a later period in his life. In addition to his history Jamblichus composed a love story in Greek which if not the earliest was at least one of the first productions of this kind in Greek literature.

Geography

In the field of geography the most notable contribution was made by Marinus of Tyre, who flourished in the mid-second century. Marinus was the first to substitute maps mathematically drawn according to latitude and longitude for those merely based on itineraries. By assigning each geographical place its latitude and longitude Marinus helped end the uncertainty that had hitherto prevailed respecting their relative positions. He thus became the founder of scientific geography. Ptolemy[3] quotes him and even admits that he bases his entire work on that of Marinus.

[1] See above, p. 114.

[2] Mommsen, vol. ii p. 124.

[3] *Geography*, Bk. I, ch. 6.

Only one other worker in the scientific field arrests our attention, Archigenes the physician of Apamea. Archigenes practised in Rome under Trajan in the early second century. He is cited several times by Juvenal,[1] from which it appears that he was a favourite practitioner among the fashionable class in the capital, especially for mental diseases. Archigenes wrote a treatise on the pulse which was the subject of a commentary by Galen, and he left a number of disciples who for years maintained a respectable rank in the profession.

Rhetoricians

A fellow-townsman of Marinus, Adrianus, was a rhetorician and philosopher. Rhetoric was then the branch of literary profession most in favour. Theoretically a rhetorician was the one to plead in court and to teach the art of pleading. Practically he was a lecturer who went from place to place displaying his ability as a speaker before educated audiences. Rhetoricians declaimed without conviction on a wide range of topics. Adrianus migrated from Tyre to Athens, where he held the chair of rhetoric. In his inaugural address to the Athenians "he dilated not on their wisdom but on his own, for he began by announcing: 'Once again letters have come from Phoenicia'".[2] As professor he performed his duties with great ostentation, wore expensive clothes, bedecked himself with gems and rode to his lectures in a carriage with silver-mounted bridles. The students referred to him as the Phoenician and some would try to imitate his accent. When in Athens Adrianus met Marcus Aurelius, who on his return to the capital invited Adrianus to his court. Adrianus was glad to quit Athens, where he had been tried and acquitted for the murder of a sophist who had insulted him. The emperor honoured the rhetorician with his friendship; he even condescended to set the thesis of a declamation for him. Aurelius' successor, Commodus, appointed him his private secretary.

A pupil of Adrianus who like him received imperial consideration was Antipater of Hierapolis. In his orations, both extempore and written, Antipater showed no superiority over his contemporaries, but in the art of letter writing he excelled. That was why Severus chose him for private secretary.[3] He

[1] *Satura*, No. 6, l. 236; No. 13, l. 98; No. 14, l. 252.

[2] Philostratus and Eunapius, *The Lives of the Sophists*, ed. and tr. Wilmer C. Wright (London, 1922), p. 227.

[3] Philostratus and Eunapius, p. 269.

also appointed him preceptor for his two sons Caracalla and Geta, and when later (A.D. 212) Caracalla assassinated his own brother, Antipater wrote him a chiding letter lamenting that Caracalla now had " but one eye left and one hand " and that those whom the preceptor had taught " to take up arms for one another " had now " taken them against one another ".[1] Severus had raised Antipater to the consular dignity and made him prefect of Bithynia. There he showed himself too ready with the sword and was dismissed. He retired to his native town, where he is said to have died of voluntary starvation.

A more engaging literary figure of the Antonine age was also a North Syrian, Lucian of Samosata, capital of Commagene. Lucian was born about A.D. 125. After practising law in Antioch and working as a " ghost writer " for speech makers there, he adopted the profession of a travelling lecturer and toured Asia Minor, Macedonia, Greece, Italy and Gaul. In Gaul he temporarily occupied the chair of philosophy in a town with Greek culture before his return to his native land.

Lucian was a Syrian, as he took pains to point out in view of contemporary ethnic ignorance. Aramaic was his mother tongue; but, like all cultured Syrians of the day, he was Greek educated. In an age when facilities for travel were greater than at any time till within the last hundred years or so, he familiarized himself with the most advanced regions of the empire. To the Syrian wanderlust he added Syrian versatility and fertility of imagination. Of the eighty-two works that have come down to us under his name, some of which are undoubtedly spurious, the most important are his *Dialogues*. His *A True Story*[2] is a lineal ancestor of *Sindbad the Sailor*, *Gulliver's Travels* and other progeny. His *The Syrian Goddess*[3] is our most important authority on the religion of Roman Syria in his time.

Lucian's distinction in the history of letters lies in the fact that he was the first to employ dialogue between the dead as a vehicle of comedy and satire. In this he was imitated by de Fontenelle,[4] Lord Lyttelton[5] and other moderns. Lucian uses

[1] Philostratus and Eunapius, p. 271.

[2] Ed. and tr. A. M. Harmon in *Lucian*, vol. i (London, 1913), pp. 248-357.

[3] See above, p. 173.

[4] Bernard le Bovier de Fontenelle; see his *Nouveaux Dialogues des morts* (Paris, 1683).

[5] George Lyttelton; see his *Dialogues of the Dead* (London, 1760).

ridicule not only intensively but also extensively. Olympian deities, Greek philosophers, Roman aristocrats, religious fanatics, travellers, ill-balanced enthusiasts, all are in turn the victims of his caricature. Not even Homer, Hesiod or Herodotus receive any veneration from his pen. His destruction, however, is not followed by construction. The hero of his *Icaro-Menippus*, disgusted with the disputes and pretensions of the philosophers, resolves on a visit to the stars to determine the measure of correctness in philosophic theories. By the mechanical aid of a pair of wings Menippus first alights at the moon, whence he surveys the squabbles and passions of men. Thence he proceeds to Olympus and is presented to Zeus himself. Here he witnesses the manner in which prayers are received in heaven. They ascend by enormous holes and become audible to Zeus on removing the huge covers. Zeus turns out to be a partial judge, influenced by the size of the reward promised. Nevertheless, he pronounces judgment against the philosophers and threatens to destroy them all in four days.

At an advanced age Lucian was appointed, perhaps by Commodus, procurator of Egypt, where presumably he died toward the close of the century.

Philosophy

In the domain of philosophy, particularly of the Neo-Platonic type, Syrian thinkers rendered no small contribution. This was in line with the Seleucid Syrian tradition.[1] Strabo [2] was impressed by the distinguished philosophers in his time who were natives of Sidon and mentions two as fellow-students. At an earlier date the atomistic theory is said to have been formulated in that city. Tyre also kept up its philosophic reputation. Strabo [3] cites a Stoic philosopher among its natives by the name of Antipater. He is evidently the same Antipater described by Pliny [4] as a poet and reported as attacked with fever every year on his birthday. A better-known Tyrian philosopher was Maximus, who travelled extensively, visited Rome more than once and there resided in the time of Commodus. That he was a teacher of Marcus Aurelius has been disputed. Maximus was a sophist and rhetorician, rather than an original thinker. Like other Platonists he opposed God to matter and made demons play an intermediary rôle between God and man. In his forty-one sur-

[1] See above, pp. 254-6, 258-9.

[2] Bk. XVI, ch. 2, § 24.

[3] *Loc. cit.*

[4] Bk. VII, ch. 52.

viving dissertations [1] he freely uses similes and poetical excerpts.

Tyre was far outstripped by Apamea as a philosophic centre. In the Antonine age, probably under Marcus Aurelius, one of its sons, Numenius, became the real founder of Neo-Platonism. Plotinus, the Greek philosopher of Egypt, credited with that distinction, was properly accused of basing his teachings on those of this Apamean and of "strutting around in his feathers".[2] Numenius acquired his Greek education possibly at Alexandria. He sojourned in Athens and probably returned to Apamea to close his life. He was quoted on one hand by Porphyry, Jamblichus and other heathen philosophers and on the other by Clement of Alexandria, Origen and other Christian Fathers. He knew the Greek and Egyptian mysteries, but it was his knowledge of the Old Testament that distinguishes his writings from those of other philosophers. To him Moses was "the prophet" as Homer was "the poet". Plato was the "Greek Moses". He considered God as a cosmic triunity comprising three divinities: Father, Creator and Creature (the world).[3]

In the third century Apamea became the seat of a Neo-Platonic school of some importance founded by Aemelius under the patronage of Queen Zenobia of Palmyra.[4] Aemelius was an admirer and intellectual kinsman of Numenius. He was a pupil of Plotinus, the first to systematize the Neo-Platonic doctrine, and a master of Porphyry, one of the great Syrian votaries of Neo-Platonism.

Porphyry was born in 233 in Batanaea.[5] He was educated at Tyre and later at Athens, where his teacher Longinus [6] changed his Semitic name *Melik* (king) to the Greek *Porphyrios* (clad in royal purple).[7] The fame of Plotinus attracted him to Rome, where for six years he specialized on Neo-Platonism. He continued to reside and teach in Rome, where he died about 301. While there he edited the master's *Enneads*; but for Porphyry, Plotinus might now be little more than a name.

[1] Ed. (Gr. and L.) Fred. Dübner, *Theophrasti Characteres* (Paris, 1877), pp. 1-177; for a critical study of Maximus consult Karl Meiser, *Studien zu Maximos Tyrios* (Munich, 1909).

[2] Kenneth S. Guthrie, *Numenius of Apamea: The Father of Neo-Platonism* (London, 1917), p. 96.

[3] Guthrie, p. 38.

[4] See below, p. 399.

[5] Southern district of Ḥawrān. The name is the Greek form of the ancient Bashan; Smith, *Historical Geography*, p. 542; it is still traceable in al-Bathanīyah. For more on Batanaea consult Dussaud, *Topographie*, pp. 323 *seq.*

[6] See below, p. 399.

[7] Philostratus and Eunapius, p. 355.

Porphyry was a prolific author in philosophy, grammar, rhetoric, mathematics, psychology, music and vegetarianism. He was the savant among the Neo-Platonists. In his teachings he ascribed reason to animals but did not extend the migration of human souls to their bodies. For the purification of the soul he demanded, more than Plotinus, certain ascetic practices, such as celibacy, abstinence from meat and absence from shows and amusements.[1] Most of his works, including a treatise against Christians, were publicly burned in 448 under Theodosius II.

A pupil of Porphyry and follower of Plotinus was Jamblichus[2] (Iamblichus) of Chalcis, Coele-Syria. Jamblichus deviated from the practice of his learned countrymen and resided in Syria throughout his life, making every year a trip to the hot springs of Gadara.[3] He died about A.D. 330. The admiration he enjoyed among his contemporaries[4] is not shared by modern scholars, who maintain that he established his reputation by magic and wonder working. By his pupils and later Neo-Platonists he was deified; *theios* became his usual epithet. With his speculation in theology he united speculation in numbers to which, after the pattern of Neo-Pythagoreanism, he ascribed a higher value than to scientific mathematics.[5] In his cosmology he shares with his school the doctrine of the eternity of the world. In his psychology he attempts more than Porphyry to keep for the soul her medial position between infra-human and superhuman beings, and he differs from Porphyry in not ascribing reason to animals.

The law school of Berytus

If Apamea made her mark in philosophy, Berytus made hers in jurisprudence, thanks to the school of Roman civil law which flourished in it from the early third to the mid-sixth century. Founded perhaps by Septimius Severus[6] (193–211) — who was commemorated in Berytus by a temple and a statue — and promoted by his successor of the Syrian dynasty, this school was

[1] Consult Eduard Zeller, *Die Philosophie der Griechen*, 3rd. ed. (Leipzig, 1881), vol. iii, pt. 2, pp. 636-77.

[2] Perhaps a descendant of the historian cited above, p. 320.

[3] Mentioned in classical writings and the Talmud, these mineral springs (al-Ḥammah) are today fully exploited. Abel, vol. i, pp. 154, 458; vol. ii, p. 19.

[4] Philostratus and Eunapius, p. 363.

[5] Zeller, p. 700.

[6] Cf. Paul Collinet, *Histoire de l'École de Droit de Beyrouth* (Paris, 1925), pp. 16-25; Henri Lammens, *La Vie universitaire à Beyrouth sous les Romains et le Bas Empire* (Cairo, 1921), p. 4.

not only the earliest renowned academy of its kind but one of the longest lived. A creation of Rome, it became and remained a creative intellectual centre in the Roman Empire. Other provincial schools existed later in Alexandria, Athens and other places but Berytus held the primacy throughout. Alexandria and Athens were more Greek than Roman; Berytus was more Roman than Greek. Besides, Berytus was more fortunate in attracting a galaxy of brilliant students and professors who made of the academy a university and spread its fame far and wide. Legal training was then a prerequisite for holding a government office.

Papinian

The two names which shed lustre on the academy and which have been immortalized in the Justinian Code were those of Papinian and Ulpian. Justinian styled Berytus "the mother and nurse of the laws". Papinian (Aemilius Papinianus) was evidently a native of Emesa. There is reason to think that he made his legal debut as a teacher at Berytus before he was invited by Septimius Severus, husband of Julia Domna of whom Papinian was a kinsman, to become his counsellor at Rome. After dismissing Papinian from office, Caracalla murdered his own brother Geta (A.D. 212) and ordered Papinian to be beheaded. He only rebuked the executioner for using an axe instead of a sword.[1] The reason for the execution is not clear; but it is not difficult to see that such a tyrant could not tolerate the existence of so stern a monitor and so honest a man. Though he was only thirty-seven years old when executed, no Roman jurist bequeathed a richer heritage. No less than 595 excerpts from his writings were incorporated in Justinian's *Digest*, one of whose compilers, Anatolius, was another professor of law at Berytus. Papinian's *Responsa* formed part of the third year's course of study in the law schools. A great sixteenth century commentator[2] considers Papinian the first of all lawyers who have been or are to be, and declares that no one ever surpassed him in legal knowledge and no one will ever equal him. Papinian's erudition guided by intellectual honesty and integrity of character have made him the model of a true lawyer.

Ulpian

Papinian had a rival in his fellow-countryman and successor Ulpian. Ulpian (Domitius Ulpianus) was a native of Tyre and

[1] Dio, Bk. LXXVIII, ch. 1, § 1; ch. 4, § 1.

[2] Cujacius, *Opera*, vol. iv (Naples, 1722), cols. 3 B, 4 A-B.

taught in its northern neighbour Berytus. From his chair there he was called to the capital city of the civilized world to assist Papinian in the government of the empire in the name of the Syrian Caesars. Caracalla's successor Elagabalus, who became emperor in 218, deprived Ulpian of his functions, but Alexander Severus on his accession in 222 reinstated him as imperial adviser. In this capacity he introduced judicial and other reforms which were not palatable to certain parties. In 228 he perished by the hands of soldiers who forced their way at night into the imperial palace, to which he had run for refuge, and killed him in the presence of the emperor and the emperor's mother.[1]

Ulpian lived longer and contributed more extensively than Papinian. The compilers of the *Digest* excerpted from his works about twenty-five hundred extracts, forming altogether one-third of the whole body. In the Theodosian Code compiled in 438 for the Eastern Roman Empire all the writings of Ulpian and Papinian are pronounced authority for the judge. Ulpian's style is easier and more perspicuous than Papinian's. Through the copious extracts from their writings both jurists exercised abiding influence on the systems of Europe.

Until the early fifth century Latin was the language of instruction in Berytus.[2] Then Greek was substituted. By that time Berytus had been drawn politically and intellectually from the orbit of Rome into that of Constantinople. Certain pieces of Syrian literature, written in barbarous Greek in the early Roman imperial period, however, have had a more enduring and wholesome influence than all the Greek and Latin classics put together. These were the Gospels and other early Christian writings.

[1] Dio, Bk. LXXX, ch. 1, §§ 1-3.

[2] For student life in Berytus see below, pp. 360-61.

CHAPTER XXV

THE RISE OF CHRISTIANITY

In or about 4 B.C.[1] was born he who split history into two eras. The limelight was then on Rome, mistress of the world, and on the resplendent throne just set up by the august Caesar. That a carpenter's son in a remote province of the empire should gather some followers around him, teach, preach, heal and be crucified for his convictions was of no concern to the historian. A younger contemporary historian, co-religionist and fellow-countryman of Jesus devotes to this " wise man " and " doer of wonderful works ", as he describes him, a brief paragraph which closes with this remark : " And the tribe of Christians, so named from him, are not extinct at this day ".[2] The only Latin historian who mentions " Christus " [3] remarks in a casual way that he " had undergone the death penalty in the reign of Tiberius, by sentence of the procurator Pontius Pilatus ".[4] This was in A.D. 28 or 29.[5] Those, however, who were closest to Jesus in Galilee and Judaea and knew him best became convinced that he was not an ordinary man but the Son of God. They readily changed their lives and, like him, did not hesitate to lay them down for their convictions. Some of them took pains to record the teachings and doings of their master. Hence the Gospels, our primary source for the life of Christ. That seemingly negligible new faith of a few Jewish peasants in a minor dependency of the great and highly civilized Roman Empire was destined to persist long after the empire, apparently stable and permanent, had fallen and passed into memory. It

[1] See above, p. 284.

[2] Josephus, *Antiquities*, Bk. XVIII, ch. 3, § 3. The passage is considered spurious by some critics.

[3] Translation of Heb. *māshīah* (anointed, Messiah), used as title of Jewish kings and hence of the promised future king. " Jesus " is Hellenized form of Joshua, developed from Jehoshua, Heb. *yehōshua'* (Jehovah is salvation).

[4] Tacitus, Bk. XV, ch. 44.

[5] Lactantius, *De mortibus persecutorum*, Bk. II, fixes a date that corresponds to March 23, 29.

outlived every other philosophy and creed of Rome and Greece.

No extraordinary event in Christ's life — virgin birth, astral association, miracle performance, crucifixion, descent to the underworld, reappearance, exaltation to heaven — lacks its parallel in earlier Near Eastern religious experience. Hardly a teaching of his was not anticipated by Hebrew prophets [1] or early Semitic teachers. But nowhere can one find such a concentration of noble thoughts and such emphasis on lofty ideas, and at no time can one discover a character who so completely practised what he taught. Even the Golden Rule has an Assyrian parallel from the seventh pre-Christian century: "As for him who doeth evil to thee, requite him with good".[2] Other sayings in the Gospels perpetuate older Aramaic, Hebraic or Canaanite formulas. The Christmas message (Lk. 2 : 14) repeats the message of Aliyan Baal to ʻAnat: [3]

> Remove war from the earth!
> Do away with passion!
> Pour out peace over the earth,
> Loving consideration over the fields! [4]

The keynote of the new message was love, love of God and love of man. One love implied the other. God Himself is love. Through love the Christians reduced mankind to one family, all under one fatherhood. Thus a universal ideal was set by primitive Christianity against the provincial ideal that prevailed everywhere. The Greeks and Romans thought of humanity in terms of nationality. The Syrian Christians were the first to give the world an effective world outlook. Their appraisal of the world was not that of an asset to be treasured but of a liability. Their society had no worldly ambition. Throughout, the emphasis was on the duty of unselfish devotion to God and service to man, inward spirituality instead of ritualism and ceremony.

None of the Hellenistic creeds had love as its basic philosophy. Only Stoicism strove in that direction. None taught that a redeeming deity was seeking even the lowest of mankind. None had a vital message for the poor and the outcast, the

[1] See above, p. 212.

[2] Samuel H. Langdon, *Babylonian Wisdom* (London, 1923), p. 90, l. 6.

[3] See above, p. 120.

[4] Albrecht Goetze, "Peace on Earth", *Bulletin*, *American Schools of Oriental Research*, No. 93 (1944), p. 20.

publican and the sinner. Hardly any heathen religion touched the inner springs of conduct and life. They were all concerned primarily with ritual. None established as effective an association between religion and morality or paid as much heed to the after-life.

Christianity intimately related ethical living to religion. Charity then became an act of faith rather than an act of justice. For the maltreated and the unfortunate the new faith sought compensation in the hope of a future life. The next world would offer the delights denied by this world to the righteous. The Greeks and Romans accorded immortality only to him who was the benefactor of his people or who was initiated in some mystery religion.

Thus in its ideology, ethics, eschatology and dogmatic certainty the new religion was evidently able to satisfy spiritual, intellectual and social demands which enlightened people everywhere must have been making, but unsuccessfully, on their traditional religions. Then in its organization as an institution the church developed techniques that far surpassed anything the other religions had developed. Slowly but surely this Syrian religion worked its way into a position of spiritual predominance. Through it Syrian culture consummated its third and greatest contribution to world progress.[1] The civilized world does not always appreciate that it was in the Christian literature of Syria that its highest idealism had its primary expression.

Its progress

The rate of progress made by Christianity was slow at the beginning. Until the end of the first century Christianity must have looked to the average Roman citizen like an obscure Jewish sect, another one of the many philosophies that were spreading from the Near East. The nucleus of the early Christian assemblies was Jewish. The Emperor Domitian executed a cousin of his on a charge of atheism connected with Judaism,[2] implying, no doubt, Christianity. Not until the time of Trajan [3] was national attention drawn to the potentialities of the new religion. As Christianity issued its challenge to the older religions, both Greek and Latin writers fought the newcomer. To these writers the old faiths were associated with the past glories of national history. To the Romans in general they were symbols of imperial power. Besides, certain features of the new religion

[1] See above, pp. 109, 216. [2] Dio, Bk. LXVII, ch. 14. [3] See below, p. 332.

seemed alien to the Greco-Roman mind. The gap was finally bridged through the efforts of Paul and early Christian Fathers. By Hellenizing Christianity these early writers adapted it for world expansion. Paul knew Greek and Greek philosophy. He used philosophic expressions and terms and adopted points of view from the mystery religions. Thanks to the lead he gave, a reconciliation was effected between the Christian religion and Greek culture. Christianity was Hellenized before it became palatable to the Greco-Romans. Their national cults, it must be admitted, were tending in the direction of monotheism. The increase in travel and intercourse served to undermine loyalty to a host of local deities and to substitute a limited number of gods with a wider range of operation. The replacement of the republic by the monarchic system of government tended in the same direction. When one owes allegiance to one supreme ruler on earth, he finds it more natural to establish allegiance to one supreme ruler on high. All these circumstances worked in favour of Christianity; but before its triumph was assured, its devotees had to go through the fire of persecution.

Persecution

As polytheists the Greeks and Romans were on the whole tolerant in their attitude toward professors of other faiths. Indeed, they even went so far as to add continually new recruits to their pantheons. Even in the capital of the empire they tolerated the strange Egyptian worship and the Jewish rites and permitted the performance of dramas not only in Latin and Greek but in Hebrew, Phoenician and Aramaic. In religion their policy was "live and let live". As monotheists the Christians could not compromise and were aggressive in their quest of new converts. Their early communities refrained from participation in the religious and public functions of their towns. Such an uncompromising attitude toward all heathen practices, coupled with an unceasing effort to win recruits, was bound to end in a clash.

The first severe persecution was under Nero, occasioned by an accidental conflagration which in A.D. 64 destroyed the centre of Rome. The angry populace explained the fire as another of their emperor's mad pranks. Terrified, Nero sought to shift the blame on the Christians in the capital and ordered their wholesale destruction.[1] Though local this persecution was

[1] Tacitus, *Annales*, Bk. XV, ch. 44

followed by sporadic outbreaks against Christians in the provinces.[1] About A.D. 68 Paul was condemned to death in Rome as a Christian in accordance with the Neronian decree.[2] Peter evidently also suffered martyrdom [3] in Rome by crucifixion about the time of Paul's martyrdom by the sword.[4] Many others no doubt lost their lives. The fact that Christians held themselves aloof from other communities aroused suspicion and gossip against them. They provided the mob with a convenient scapegoat whenever an untoward happening befell the town or community. Provincial governors often visited punishment on their Christian subjects for membership in what they considered secret societies.

The second severe persecution took place in A.D. 95 under Domitian. It was likewise local and directed particularly against the Jews with whom the Christians were still often confused by the Romans. Among those tried during this persecution were grandsons of Judas, brother of Christ, who were acquitted as "simple folk".[5] In 112 Trajan decreed that Christians who refused to pay homage to the gods of the state and to the emperor when challenged in court were to be punished as traitors. Of the state cults the worship of the emperor was the most vigorous and widespread. Established by Augustus it became a visible expression of loyalty to the throne. Trajan's decree made the Christians for the next two centuries virtual outlaws; on several occasions they were systematically sought and punished. In the third century as the empire began its downward course and the Christian church became secure in its upward march, the rulers sought to stamp out Christianity as a means of restoring the prestige of the state. In 250–51 Decius renewed the punishment of all those in the realm who refused to perform public acts of worship to the gods of the state. In 257–8 Valerian not only required Christians to offer sacrifice publicly but forbade their reunions. Some, at least openly, abjured their faith.

Diocletian was the author of the great persecution of the fourth century. His edict of February 303 decreed that their churches be razed, their books burned and all those of them

[1] Cf. 1 Pet. 4:13-19.
[2] Cf. 2 Tim. 4:6-8.
[3] John 12:18-19.
[4] Lactantius, Bk. II.
[5] Eusebius, *Historia ecclesiastica*, Bk. III, ch. 20, §§ 1-4.

in civil and military offices be dismissed. All kinds of penalties, short of execution, were ordered; but even that was practised and on a large scale. Coming from one who had openly favoured the Christians, this edict was a surprise. Diocletian's wife and daughter were supposedly Christians.[1] Evidently the security and prosperity that Christians enjoyed throughout the land aroused jealousy among the high officials and the heathen priesthood who filled the emperor's head with reports of alleged conspiracies and seditions. For ten years the persecution raged with unmitigated fury. Malicious ingenuity was strained to devise new means of torture. Eusebius [2] speaks of Christians in Arabia butchered with the axe and in Antioch roasted on gridirons. He also reports cases of women who threw themselves into the Orontes to escape rape. So many were those thus destroyed throughout the empire that the imperial executioners at last erected a triumphal column bearing the boastful inscription that they had extinguished the Christian name and superstition and restored the worship of the gods to its former purity and splendour. A few years later, Christianity was adopted under Constantine as the official religion of the state. Diocletian's was the last persecution under the empire of Rome.

Mystery religions

When Christianity made its bid for world dominance, it had for rivals other religions of Oriental origin, chief among which were the mystery cults. Originally vegetation deities, several mystery gods were by this time fully Hellenized and adopted by the Greeks and Romans. One of the earliest among such deities was Dionysus,[3] a wine god and a spirit of plant life in general. Pre-eminent among the female deities was the Egyptian Isis, whose cult was admitted by Caligula (*ca.* A.D. 40) among the official Roman cults. So popular did Isis worship become that in the first two Christian centuries it spread all over the empire. The goddess' representation as nursing the infant god Horus became a model for the Christian Madonna.

Youngest and most popular among the new mystery religions was that of Mithras, originally a Persian sun-god. Beginning as a Zoroastrian cult, Mithraism by the third Christian century had found great favour, especially among Roman soldiers. To them the robust character of this religion, which pictured life as a constant struggle between a beneficent deity

[1] Lactantius, Bk. XV. [2] Bk. VIII, ch. 12, §§ 1, 2. [3] See above, p. 109.

and an evil power, held special appeal. For a time it looked like a toss-up between Christ and Mithras.

One feature of mystery religions was their secret character. Participation was restricted to those who were initiated. The rite of initiation culminated in imparting the knowledge that the one thus privileged was saved. Salvation was sought by personal union with a divine saviour who had himself experienced life and death.

Another feature of mystery religions was a freer exercise of personal emotion than the state and family cults would allow.[1] Lacking the recognized authority of official creeds, the mystery religions resorted to new devices in order to win proselytes. Their ceremonies often had a "revivalistic", even orgiastic, element. Moreover, these religions promised a blissful state for those who went through the necessary probation. After death the initiated rose to the sphere of the divine and dwelt with the gods. In this and their theory of salvation these religions bore close resemblance to the Christian one and presented an appeal to which the Greco-Roman cults could furnish no adequate counter-attraction.

Gnostic sects and mystery cults belonged to the same religious type. In both groups the central idea was *gnosis*, high knowledge, spiritual enlightenment, offered to the elect whereby the soul might be delivered from its condition of bondage. Christian tradition makes Simon the sorcerer (Acts 8 : 9 *seq.*) the originator of the Gnostic movement.

In Syria itself Christ had several rivals in the first two centuries. Most powerful among these was Hadad Rammanu, metamorphosed in the Hellenistic period into Zeus (or Jupiter) of Damascus, of Heliopolis and of Hierapolis. His worship spread all over the empire.[2] His consort Atargatis was a rival of Isis and of the Virgin. Another Zeus or Jupiter was that of Doliche,[3] who lived "where the iron grew". Originally the Hittite deity Teshub,[4] Jupiter Dolichenus succeeded in spreading his worship throughout the empire in the track of the Roman

[1] Franz Cumont, *Les Religions orientales dans le paganisme romain*, 4th ed. (Paris, 1929), pp. 24 *seq.*

[2] See above, pp. 172, 308, 312.

[3] 'Ayntāb (Gaziantep); Dussaud, *Topographie*, p. 472; Franz Cumont, *Études syriennes* (Paris, 1917), pp. 173 *seq.*

[4] See above, pp. 158-60.

sword. As in the case of other Oriental religions soldiers, slaves and merchants transported his cults to most of the European countries. His original devotees were ironsmiths, the best in Asia west of China. Wherever they found iron there the broken-up community of this deity set up their forges and practised their inherited techniques. Their god travelled with them. "The Roman might conquer the Syrians; but the Roman gods had in their own home yielded the field to those of Syria".[1]

Centres of Syrian Christianity

Organized Syrian Christianity had its first headquarters in Antioch.[2] The church of Antioch became in a special sense the mother of the churches established in gentile lands. From it Paul and other early propagators of the Christian faith set out on their missionary campaigns; to it they returned to report. After the destruction of its rival Jerusalem by the Romans in A.D. 70,[3] Antioch became the sole capital of Christendom. It exercised for some time a certain measure of jurisdiction over at least neighbouring sees. Its bishop in the fourth century was called metropolitan (archbishop). More than thirty councils of bishops (synods) were held in the city, the first of which was convened in 269.[4] Antioch gave its name to a school of theology whose most brilliant representative was John Chrysostom (d. 407).[5] In opposition to the emotional, mystical trend in religion the school stressed the human element and centred attention on the historical Christ. The language of the school was clearly Greek.

From apostolic times both Greek and Aramaic were used in the worship. After Antioch's rise to a position of leadership in the Greek-speaking part of Syria, Edessa began to rise to a corresponding position in the Aramaic (Syriac)-speaking world. This city was the earliest seat of Christianity in Mesopotamia.[6] It was also the cradle of Syriac literature. The chief versions of the Syriac Bible were probably made in it late in the second century.[7] In the fourth and fifth centuries Christological controversies split Syrian Christianity into a number of divisions.[8]

Church Fathers

Christianity owes no small measure of its success in expansion to a succession of authors, known as the Church Fathers, who expounded and expanded the doctrines of the church. The

[1] Mommsen, *Provinces*, vol. ii, p. 123.
[2] See below, pp. 365, 373.
[3] See below, p. 339.
[4] Eusebius, Bk. VII, ch. 29.
[5] See below, pp. 356-8.
[6] See below, pp. 369-70.
[7] See below, p. 369.
[8] See below, pp. 370-72.

earliest six are designated Apostolic Fathers because during a part of their lives they were contemporary with the Apostles. One of these was a Syrian, Ignatius, " the second after Peter to succeed to the bishopric of Antioch ".[1] Tradition relates that when Trajan visited Antioch in 107 this prelate conducted himself with such boldness in the imperial presence that he was sent to Rome to be executed in the amphitheatre by the fury of wild beasts. Of his various works seven genuine epistles remain.

Of the Ante-Nicene Fathers (A.D. 15–325), two prominent men had Syrian connections, Justin (the) Martyr and Origen.[2] Justin was born in Neapolis (Nābulus) about A.D. 100, but not of Samaritan parents. A zealous student of Platonic philosophy, he was eventually converted to Christianity as a result of a dialogue with a meek and venerable old man he met on the shore. The old man recommended the study of the Hebrew prophets and Christ. Justin was often referred to as the philosopher. He incorporated elements of the Platonic and Stoic philosophies into the Christian theology and fought Gnostic teaching. A Gnostic Christian contemporary of his, Marcion, distinguished between the God of the Old Testament and the God of the New Testament, and taught that Christ suffered only in appearance. From Rome the Marcionite heresy spread into Antioch and the rest of Syria.

Addressing the Emperor Antoninus Pius, Justin had the audacity to declare: " So far as we are concerned we are convinced that we can suffer evil from no one unless we be convicted of being evil doers or proven to be men of base lives. As for you, kill us you can; hurt us you cannot." [3] Justin is credited with opening the first Christian school in Rome. There he was scourged and beheaded, perhaps under Marcus Aurelius, for refusing to offer sacrifice to the gods. He was canonized by the Western as well as the Eastern Church. His legendary grave at Tyre is still pointed out as that of the great magician Ūriyānus.

[1] Eusebius, Bk. III, ch. 36.
[2] Taught in Caesarea, died at Tyre, 253.
[3] Justin, *Apologia*, I, § 2.

CHAPTER XXVI

SYRIANIZING VERSUS ROMANIZING

THE penetration of Christianity into the farthest parts of the Roman Empire and its final triumph over all Greco-Roman cults and Oriental rivals was but one phase of the Syrianizing process that was going on, the religious phase. The other phases were economic, social and political. Meantime, Romanizing processes were operating in the opposite direction.

Romanization through citizenship

Romanization decreased as distance from Rome increased. In Syria there were too few Italian residents to act as foci for Latin culture. Those were mostly government officials who collected taxes, decided important lawsuits, attended games and festivals but continued to be treated as outsiders. But from the outset the emperors bestowed on native residents of such colonies as Berytus and Heliopolis Roman citizenship, which gave them a favoured position among the provincials. By grant or treaty other cities which were not colonies received citizenship or special privileges. Tyre, for instance, even enjoyed exemption from ordinary taxes. " Divide and rule " was an ancient Roman political technique applied to prevent the different cities or communities from clubbing together against Rome.

The policy of extending the Roman franchise to non-Italians was accelerated when Trajan, a native of Spain, was elevated to the throne of the Caesars. It reached its culmination in A.D. 212, when Caracalla issued his famous edict bestowing full citizenship on practically all free residents of the provinces. Henceforth any Syrian became *ipso facto* a Roman citizen and if qualified could hold the highest position in the state. In practice, however, the advantages were limited to social prestige and to certain economic benefits. The cry of Paul, " I am a Roman citizen ",[1] " I appeal unto Caesar " [2] must have been reiterated by many a Syrian in those days. This, however, does not mean that the Syrians ceased to feel themselves Syrians. Hellenic civiliza-

[1] Cf. Acts 22 : 27.

[2] Acts 25 : 11.

tion under the Roman aegis was on the right way toward the solution of the knotty problem of moulding a mass of different nationalities into a quasi-whole in the field of intellect and politics. The forgotten dream of Alexander — a partnership of victors and vanquished — seemed partially realized.[1]

Through military service

From the beginning the Romans used non-Italians as auxiliaries. Gradually the legions themselves came to consist largely of natives. Members of the military force became automatically Roman citizens. Syrian soldiers in Roman units were stationed in various parts of the empire. When the third legion went to help establish Vespasian in Italy, its men saluted the rising sun "according to the Syrian custom".[2] The legion stationed in Numidia had a large proportion of Syrian veterans from Apamea, Damascus, Tripoli, Berytus, Sidon and Tyre. Latin was the language of the army, and those of the Syrians who served in the western provinces showed by their inscriptions on their return that they could use it. Some of them adopted Roman names or at least praenomina.

Latin was also the official language of the magistrates. The imperial edicts were issued in Latin but carried a Greek translation.[3] Most of the local calendars gave way to the Roman one and the Roman system of weights and measures was generally adopted.

Jewish resistance

Of the numerous Syrian communities the Jewish was the one that least responded to Romanizing stimuli. The aristocracy was already Hellenized. The Sadducees, who represented the aristocratic party and monopolized the offices, received support from Rome. The Pharisees, who represented the commonalty, adhered to strict orthodoxy and aimed at liberation. In ideology the Pharisees reach back to the Hasidim of the Maccabean age.[4]

Because of the strict monotheism of their religion the Jews had been treated since Pompey's[5] days as a privileged community. Under the emperors they were exempt from military service and the obligation of the imperial cult. They were not required to participate in the sacrificial worship of the Roman ruler. As they maintained their policy of exclusiveness and isolationism, they nourished their national feeling. This led to

[1] See above, p. 236.
[2] Tacitus, *Historiae*, Bk. III, ch. 24
[3] Josephus, *Antiquities*, Bk. XIV, ch. 12, § 5.
[4] See above, p. 245.
[5] See above, p. 281.

clashes which broadened into a national rebellion in A.D. 66–70 under Nero and in 132–4 under Hadrian. These two rebellions resulted in the final breach between Jews and Christians and in enduring disaster to the Jewish society.

Titus destroys Jerusalem

The suppression of the first rebellion was entrusted by Nero to his general Vespasian,[1] who in 67–8 reduced the open country and isolated fortresses.[2] Jaffa was among the cities destroyed. The Roman army numbered 50,000 and met little resistance. As Vespasian was about to besiege Jerusalem, Nero died and he was elevated to the throne. The completion of the military task was entrusted to his son Titus, who pressed the siege against Jerusalem for five months ending in September 70. An idea of the tragic fate of the besieged may be gained from a description of a pact of mutual self-destruction as the Roman soldiers were storming the city. After destroying their own wives and children, everyone of them laid himself down, threw his arms around the butchered members of his family and offered his neck to the stroke of him who by lot executed that melancholy duty. The description comes from the pen of a historian who himself took part in this war: [3]

> Husbands tenderly embraced their wives, and took their children into their arms, and clung to their parting kisses with tears in their eyes; but at the same time they carried out what they had resolved on, as if doing it with the hands of strangers, making their anticipation of the miseries they would suffer, if they fell into the hands of their enemies, their comfort for the necessity of this. . . . Miserable men indeed were they for the necessity they were in, to whom to slay their wives and children with their own hands seemed the lightest evil before them! [4]

The city was destroyed. The Temple was burned. This was the ornate temple built by Herod [5] on successive structures on the same site. So completely was the work done by Titus that the people forgot whether the Temple stood on the east or the west hill of Jerusalem. All attempts to reconstruct it from biblical description alone have failed. It is estimated that a

[1] Dio, Bk. LXIII, ch. 22, § 1.
[2] Josephus, *War*, Bk. II, ch. 18, §§ 1, 3-4.
[3] See above, pp. 319-20.
[4] Josephus, *War*, Bk. VII, ch. 9, § 1. The quotation is from the revised translation of A. R. Shilleto (London, 1890). Cf. Dio, Bk. LXV, ch. 6, § 3.
[5] See above, p. 283.

million Jews perished in this war. Many of the captives were forced to fight each other or against wild beasts in an amphitheatre.[1] The remnants were denied access to their capital. In fact it was no more their capital. Judaea as a political state ceased to be. The Jews henceforth became what they remained until today, a homeless people. A Roman chapter in the history of the Diaspora was added to the Assyrian and Chaldaean ones.

The seven-branched candlestick was snatched by a Roman soldier from the burning Temple and carried in the triumphal procession which graced Titus' return to the imperial capital.[2] To this day a soldier holds it aloft on the arch erected near the Forum to commemorate the great victory. As for Judaism it decayed with the decay of its devotees. Its narrow national basis and certain features of its ritual were not favourable to its expansion. All attempts of Jewish scholars, beginning with Philo of Alexandria (fl. A.D. 40), to commend it to Greco-Roman mentality resulted in failure.

One last throe of death was experienced when the Jewish banner of revolt was unfurled by a mysterious leader, Simon Bar Kokba [3] (Kochba), in A.D 132–5. Hadrian crushed the rebellion and turned Jerusalem into a Roman colony as Aelia Capitolina.[4] Aelius was his first name. He replaced the old Temple by one dedicated to Jupiter Capitolinus. Dio [5] estimates that the number of villages destroyed was nine hundred and eighty-five and of the people slain five hundred and eighty thousand.

Syrian dynasty at Rome

The gates of Syrian influence at Rome were opened wide when toward the end of the second century the husband of a lady from Emesa succeeded in enthroning himself in the seat of the Caesars. She was Julia Domna, daughter of a priest of Elagabal [6] at Emesa. The husband was Septimius Severus, commander of a legion in Syria. The marriage took place about A.D. 187.

[1] See above, p. 309.

[2] See above, p. 189.

[3] Aramaic for "son of the star", with probable reference to Num. 24: 17. After his defeat the Jews called him Bar Koziba, "son of lies".

[4] Eusebius, Bk. IV, ch. 5; cf. Dio, Bk. LXIX, ch. 12, where the erection of the Roman colony is made the cause, rather than the result, of the war.

[5] Bk. LXIX, ch. 14, § 1.

[6] On etymology of this word see above, p. 308, n. 3.

Septimius was born in Leptis (modern Labdah in Tripoli), a Phoenician colony in Africa. He was the only Roman emperor in history who hailed from that continent. Latin to him was a foreign tongue, which he spoke with an accent all his life. His language was Punic, not radically different from Aramaic, the language of his wife. Septimius elevated himself to the throne in 193,[1] and by a spurious and posthumous adoption he affiliated himself through Marcus Aurelius to the Antonines.

W. F. Mansell

PORTRAIT BUST OF JULIA DOMNA SHOWING HER WAVY HAIR

The queen is described as of great beauty, intellectual power and political and literary ability. She received the title of Augusta and collaborated with her husband in the conduct of the affairs of the state. The chief counsellor was her relative, the eminent jurisconsult Papinian.[2] On the death of her husband on the battlefield in Britain (A.D. 211) she did not cease to wield control over her two sons Caracalla and Geta, who succeeded their father as co-emperors.

Caracalla's real name was Bassianus, after that of his maternal grandfather. This nickname he acquired from a kind of Gallic cloak which he introduced.[3] He was himself born in Lyons, Gaul. The two brothers bore toward each other from infancy the most inveterate hatred. Now Caracalla, the elder of the two, sought to make himself sole ruler, and to this end he had his brother Geta assassinated in his mother's arms in her own apartment, to which Geta had been invited under pretence of an attempt at reconciliation. Julia herself received a wound

[1] For his contest with Niger and other rivals consult Herodian, *Historiarum*, Bk. III, chs. 1 *seq.*

[2] See above, p. 326.

[3] Dio, Bk. LXXIX, ch. 3, § 3.

in her hand trying to shield her son.[1] That was in 112, the year in which Caracalla extended Roman citizenship to all free provincials. He was then twenty-three years old, one year the senior of his brother. Thereafter the wretched empress-mother " was doomed to weep over the death of one of her sons, and over the life of the other ".[2]

Having started on a career of bloodshed, Caracalla did not know where to stop. All those considered partisans of his brother and others were slaughtered, some twenty thousand in all. Among the victims was Papinian, who had adorned the court of his father. Caracalla ruled by the sword and admired Hannibal, statues of whom he set up in different places.[3] He demanded of the senate that he himself be enrolled among the gods. A contemporary historian has this appreciation of Caracalla:

Antoninus belonged to three races; and he possessed none of their virtues at all, but combined in himself all their vices; the fickleness, cowardice, and recklessness of Gaul were his, the harshness and cruelty of Africa, and the craftiness of Syria, whence he was sprung on his mother's side.[4]

Amidst this orgy his mother stood helpless. She dared not even shed a tear over her murdered son. Caracalla put her in charge of his correspondence and the state papers and her salon included, besides Papinian and his successor Ulpian, the biographer of Greek historians, Diogenes Laertius,[5] the historian and government official Dio Cassius and the sophist Philostratus, the works of all three of whom have been referred to in this history. The great Greek physician Galen was also a member of this circle which centred on the charm and versatility of a Syrian lady of low origin. Her father's Latin name Bassianus meant low; while hers, Domna, meant lady, mistress. Such display of feminine traits was rare among real Roman matrons.

1 Dio, Bk. LXXVIII, ch. 2, §§ 3-4.

2 Edward Gibbon, *The History of the Decline and Fall of the Roman Empire*, ed. J. B. Bury, vol. i (London, 1898), p. 141.

3 On his contribution to the great temple in Heliopolis see above, p. 311.

4 Dio, Bk. LXXVIII, ch. 6, § 1. The quotation is from the translation of Ernest Cary (London, 1927), vol. ix, p. 291. Modern critical scholars believe Dio painted Caracalla black chiefly because he did not kowtow to the senate, although the senate then was quite incompetent.

5 So called from Laertes in Cilicia, mentioned by Strabo, Bk. XIV, ch. 5, § 3. Exact site still undetermined.

Julia is represented by several historians as of loose morals, but Dio reports no scandals.

When the news of her son's murder by the instigation of Macrinus at Edessa (A.D. 217) came to her, Julia chanced to be in Antioch. Macrinus was the prefect of the praetorians and became his successor. She attempted suicide by starvation not because of grief over her hated son but because she could not countenance retirement to private life after "she had hoped to become sole ruler and make herself the equal of Semiramis and Nitocris,[1] inasmuch as she came in a sense from the same parts as they".[2] Her repeated attempts to commit suicide were at last successful and her body was taken to Rome for burial.

Julia Domna's work was carried on by her younger and abler sister Julia Maesa.[3] Maesa was born at Emesa, and after the marriage of her sister moved to Rome. There she lived at the court until the assassination of her nephew Caracalla. Endowed with remarkable force and political sagacity and possessed of great wealth, she plotted successfully for the overthrow of Macrinus and the enthroning of her grandson Elagabalus.[4] Her husband was a rich Roman who held the chief command in several provinces and rose to the consulship in A.D. 209. Elagabalus' father was a Syrian from Apamea, but the boy is stated to have been born at Emesa, where he inherited the priesthood. The Syrian army supported the fourteen-year-old great-nephew

[1] For the deeds ascribed to these ladies by the ancients consult Herodotus, Bk. I, chs. 184-6.

[2] Dio, Bk. LXXIX, ch. 23, § 3.

[3] Fem. of Maesius, an ancient Roman name.

[4] His original name was Bassianus after his great-grandfather. Following is the genealogical table of the Syrian dynasty:

Julius Bassianus of Emesa

. Septimius Severus + Julia Domna (A.D. 193–211) — Julia Maesa + Julius Avitus

Caracalla (211–17) — 2. Geta (211–12)

Varius Avitus + Julia Soaemis (Suḥaymah ?) — Julia Mamaea + Gessius Marcianus

. Elagabalus (218–22) — 4. Alexander Severus (222–35)

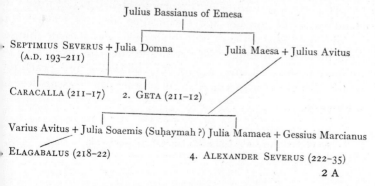

of Domna and Macrinus was defeated and killed at Antioch in A.D. 218.

The Syrian un-god installed in Rome

The priest-emperor entered Rome triumphantly with the sacred black stone of Emesa in his chariot. This was the emblem of his Emesene Baal, the sun-god whose name he bore. It was originally enshrined in the magnificent temple of Emesa, which was ornamented with gold, silver and jewels [1] and which enjoyed a general right of asylum. The worship of the Syrian deity now became supreme in the Roman world. The ritual introduced along with it was most gorgeous, attended by costly sacrifices on altars loaded with perfumes over which rich wines were poured to mingle with the blood of the victims. To his many titles the emperor added a new one, "the most exalted priest of the unconquered Sun-God Elagabalus". As for his rule it was but a continuation of that of his cousin — a series of acts of debauchery and extravagant folly. His grandmother conducted the government, and when she sensed the imminence of his downfall she persuaded him to adopt her other grandson Alexander Severus [2] and nominate him his successor. In A.D. 122 Elagabalus was murdered by the praetorians, and Alexander succeeded.

Alexander was then a lad, thirteen years old. His father was a Syrian of rank, native of Arka (ʻArqah).[3] His mother, a widow like her sister, was proclaimed Augusta and exercised the power of a regent. Alexander was the last and best of this Syrian dynasty. He restored to their original homes the religious curiosities and sacred stones which his predecessor had installed in Rome, forbade the worship of himself while alive and set up in his private oratory busts of Zoroaster, Abraham and Christ. His mother attended the lectures of the theologian Origen. He put down court luxury, lightened taxes, raised the standard of the coinage and encouraged art and science; but he did not have enough self-reliance to emancipate himself from maternal tutelage. Nor could he curb the licence of the military caste. In one mutiny his counsellor and praetorian prefect Ulpian was sacrificed. In another Dio Cassius lost his command.

[1] Herodian, Bk. V, ch. 5.

[2] Original name Alexianus Bassianus; Herodian, Bk. V, ch. 5.

[3] Dio, Bk. LXXIX, ch. 30, § 3. On ʻArqah see above, p. 71, n. 4.

In 233 Alexander celebrated at Rome a triumph over the Persians, from whom he had recovered Mesopotamia. A revival of nationalism was now bestirring these people under a new leader Artaxerxes, founder of the Sāsānid dynasty (A.D. 227) on the ruins of the Parthian.[1] Called to face an invasion in Gaul by German tribes, Alexander lost his life in 235 in a mutiny in which his mother too was slain.

Philip the Arab

About a decade later Rome saw another Syrian enthroned, Philip the Arab. Born in a small village in Ḥawrān,[2] Philip

The American Numismatic Society

A COIN OF PHILIP THE ARAB

Obverse and reverse of a bronze coin of Heliopolis (Baʿlabakk) struck in the name of Philip the Arab, A.D. 244–9. The reverse presents a front and side view of the temple of Jupiter Heliopolitanus

was a praetorian prefect when his predecessor fighting the Persians was murdered and he was hailed by the soldiers as his successor. The choice was ratified by the senate in 244. This Syrian emperor did not render his name odious by any tyrannical abuse of power, but the recollection of the foul means he used to accomplish the ruin of his beloved predecessor was never forgotten. His campaigns against tribes on the lower Danube gained for him the title of Germanicus Maximus. It fell to the lot of this Arab Syrian to preside in A.D. 248 at the ceremonies commemorating the thousandth birthday of the Eternal City. The games and other events were conducted with great splendour. The emperor was considered pro-Christian, if not fully Christian, and certain letters are said to have been addressed by Origen to him and to the empress.[3] Even so, he left no impress on the church, and historians unite in making Constantine the first Christian emperor. In 249 he suffered the same fate that befell

[1] Dio, Bk. LXXX, ch. 3, §§ 1-4; Herodian, Bk. VI, ch. 2.

[2] See above, pp. 316-17.

[3] Eusebius, Bk. VI, chs. 34, 36, 39.

many other emperors of this period, violent death at the hands of mutinous troops. His successor is said to have imported lions from Africa and let them loose in the Syrian Desert to the discomfort of its unruly denizens.

Economic penetration

Syrian economic penetration in the Latin provinces was manifest in the number of settlements whose history can be

Director of Antiquities, Beirut

BAS-RELIEF OF A STONE SARCOPHAGUS SHOWING A SAILING MERCHANT SHIP

In the waves are seen leaping dolphins and fish. Though carved in the second Christian century the ship retains the main features of an ancient Phoenician one. Now in the National Museum, Beirut

traced from the beginning to the end of the empire. Especiall[y] in the second and third centuries was a veritable colonization o[f] the Mediterranean world undertaken by the *Syri*, a term applie[d] to all those from its eastern part. Syrian ships dotted the se[a] as in earlier days. The old Phoenician traits of energy, adaptability, love of lucrative trade and ability to make bargains an[d] close large and small deals were reactivated. " Among all th races of the Empire the most active in these mercantile ventures were the Syrians."[1]

Syrian settlements, with their economic, social and religious features, spread all along the coasts of the Mediterranean and followed inland the commercial highways and the courses of the great rivers. Among the islands Delos [2] and Sicily were seats of strong Syrian colonies. Of the Italian ports Naples and Ostia were especially favoured. By way of the Danube Syrian merchants reached Pannonia; by way of the Rhone, Lyons. In Spain, Syrian business men had centres but in Gaul they were especially active. A late second century rescript discovered in Lebanon is addressed to sailors who had charge of the transportation of wheat.[3] A bilingual epitaph of the third century found in Gaul mentions a Syrian merchant from Kanatha [4] who owned two factories in the Rhone basin, where he imported goods from Aquitania.[5] His name was Thayyim (or Julian), son of Saʿd.

As importers Syrian merchants monopolized a great deal of the trade of the Latin provinces with the Levant; as bankers they had no rivals. Wines, spices, grain, glassware, fabrics and jewelry were their chief commodities. Some of these commodities served as models which native manufacturers and artisans gradually learned to imitate. Wherever Syrian merchants settled, there they established their temples. The Baal of Gaza was worshipped in Ostia; that of Berytus, in places as far as Spain. The god of Berytus went by the name Baal Marqod [6] (Balmarcodes, the god of the dances) and his shrine has been found at Dayr al-Qalʿah (crowning a hill overlooking the city), some of the columns of which were recently used for building the Maronite cathedral in Beirut. In Puteoli [7] stood altars on which two golden camels were offered by a worshipper to the Nabataean deity Dusares (Dūshara).[8] Other

[1] Arthur E. R. Boak, *A History of Rome to 565 A.D.*, rev. ed. (New York, 1930), p. 319.

[2] See above, p. 274.

[3] J. P. Waltzing, *Étude historique sur les corporations professionnelles chez les Romains* (Louvain, 1899), vol. iii, No. 1961.

[4] See above, p. 317.

[5] Cumont, *Les Religions orientales dans le paganisme romain*, 4th ed., p. 100.

[6] From the stem *rāqad*, to dance. Consult Georgius Kaibel, *Epigrammata Graeca* (Berlin, 1878), No. 835; Louis Jalabert, "Inscriptions grecques et latines", *Mélanges de la faculté orientale* (Beirut, 1906), vol. i, pp. 181-8.

[7] See above, p. 308.

[8] For the ruins of his temple at Sīʿ, Ḥawrān, consult Howard C. Butler, *Syria*, Div. II, Sec. A (Leyden, 1919), pp. 385-90.

worshippers in this city offered a dedication to Jupiter of Heliopolis. While such dedications in the West are chiefly in Latin, one from Palmyrene settlers in Rome is in Aramaic addressed to the gods of Tadmur.[1]

As carriers of the Christian religion Syrian merchants, colonists, soldiers and slaves were no less enthusiastic than as carriers of pagan cults. Their influence on its development in the West was manifest in the direction of asceticism, monasticism and a more emotional form of worship. Devotion to the cross and its adoption as a religious emblem were other Christian elements introduced by Syrians into Europe. In Rome their colony was strong enough to furnish the church with a number of popes.[2]

[1] *Corpus Inscriptionum Latinarum*, vol. vi (Berlin, 1876), No. 710.

[2] Louis Bréhier, *Les Origines du crucifix dans l'art religieux* [3rd ed.] (Paris, 1908), pp. 50, 54-5, 59; see below, p. 484.

CHAPTER XXVII

BYZANTINE SYRIA

THE third century, in which Syrian religious and economic penetration made its way through the Latin provinces at an accelerated pace, witnessed the end of one phase of the Greco-Latin civilization and the initiation of another. The somewhat uniform type of culture which had hitherto characterized the empire was being disrupted. Its material basis was being undermined by protracted civil wars and repeated foreign invasions. Its tottering intellectual and spiritual pillars were subjected to the onslaught of new waves of Christian ideas. The change was henceforth rapid and complete. A new cultural stage, the Byzantine, product of the union of Christianity and pagan Hellenism, was replacing the old. It had a Christian Greco-Oriental colour. Its centre was Constantinople.

The later Roman Empire

This city owes its name to Constantine, co-emperor in 306 and sole emperor from 324 to 337. Founded by him on the site of ancient Byzantium, where Europe meets Asia, it was dedicated as the new capital on May 11, 330. Its strategic geographic position gave it military and economic advantages and all these factors united to make the new city the natural centre about which the Eastern world could readily cluster. Soon the "New Rome" on the Bosphorus eclipsed the old Rome on the Tiber.

Constantinople, the new capital

The shift itself indicates a recognition of the preponderance of the Eastern half of the empire. Those provinces were now the richest in wealth and natural resources. The whole empire fronted in that direction. The major civilized state with which Rome was in constant antagonism, Persia, lay in the East. The centre of gravity in world affairs was again moving eastward.

Prior to his foundation of a new capital for the state Constantine gave recognition to a new official religion. In his edict of Milan, issued in 313, he accorded complete toleration to the Christians in his domain.[1] In 325 he convened an ecumenical

Christianity, the new religion

[1] Eusebius, Bk. X, ch. 5.

council of all the bishops of the empire at Nicaea in Bithynia, Asia Minor. This was the first congress of its kind. In it Arianism [1] was condemned and the Christian faith was definitely codified in the Nicene Creed.

The story of Constantine's adoption of Christianity is probably legendary. It relates that on his march in 312 against Rome, he beheld in the sky a brilliant cross with a Greek inscription proclaiming: " By this conquer ".[2] So much at least is certain: Constantine employed the cross as the imperial standard and with it advanced to victory against his competitor Maxentius.[3] Whether Constantine's conversion was one of convenience or of conviction is of no historical consequence. The fact remains that under him Christianity, once an exotic and obscure cult, now became the official religion of the empire. If Greece had conquered the mind of the Romans, Syria now conquered their souls.

By this time the most influential men in the empire had become followers of Christ, though the majority of the population, including Constantine's foes, were still pagan. Discipline, organization, wealth and the driving power were on the side of the minority. Constantine's mother Helena was a devout Christian. She undertook a pilgrimage to Jerusalem, where tradition credits her with the discovery of the true cross on the spot where the Church of the Holy Sepulchre now stands. There Constantine erected the first Christian church. The cult of the holy places introduced by the emperor and his mother accelerated the Christianizing of Syria.

These two events in the reign of Constantine — the transference of the capital from Rome to Constantinople and the official recognition of Christianity — mark out that reign as one of the most conspicuous landmarks in the history of Europe. They justify his title the Great. Christian in doctrine, Greek in language and Eastern in its orientation the new empire inaugurated by Constantine was to endure, with many vicissitudes,

[1] An attempt to determine the relation of the Persons of the Trinity on a basis of distinction and subordination, maintaining that the Son is of a nature similar to — not the same as — the Father. Its tendency was toward the denial of the divinity of Christ. The founder was Arius, who flourished at this time at Alexandria. Arian missionaries converted the Goths, Lombards and other Germanic tribes. Consult Sozomenus, *Historia ecclesiastica*, Bk. I, chs. 20, 21.

[2] Cf. Sozomenus, Bk. I, ch. 5.

[3] Cf. Lactantius, ch. 44; Eusebius, Bk. IX, ch. 9, § 2.

for about eleven centuries and a quarter. From the seventh century on it served as a bulwark against Islam. Finally, in 1453, it succumbed under the onrush of the new champions of that religion, the Ottoman Turks.

For a few years after the establishment of Constantinople the external and theoretical continuity of the empire was maintained. In practice, however, the two halves of the empire were separated more than once and ruled by different emperors. The final division came in 395 when Theodosius the Great died and his two sons Honorius and Arcadius succeeded, one over the West and the other over the East. Theodosius (379–95) was the last emperor of the united empire. Thenceforth there was a Roman Empire of the East, whose fortunes rose as those of its sister in the West declined. At last, in 476, Rome fell in consequence of the invasions of Germanic tribes. Theodosius won the title Great for his valiant stand against the Goths and for his support of orthodox Christianity. All the successors of Constantine, with the single exception of Julian (361 – 3), professed the Christian faith.

Adminis-trative divisions

Syria at the end of the fourth century was divided into several districts. Its northern part retained the name Syria and was split into two: Syria Prima, with Antioch as metropolis and Seleucia, Laodicea, Gabala (Jabalah),[1] Beroea (Aleppo) and Chalcis ad Belum as chief towns; and Syria Secunda, having Apamea for its chief centre and Epiphania (Ḥamāh), Arethusa (al-Rastan) and Larissa (Shayzar) as dependent towns. Phoenicia was likewise split into two: Phoenicia Prima, whose metropolis was Tyre and chief towns were Ptolemais (Acre), Sidon, Berytus, Byblus, Botrys, Tripoli, Arka and Aradus; and Phoenicia Secunda or Phoenicia ad Libanum, having Damascus for its capital and embracing the cities of Emesa, Heliopolis and Palmyra. The first Phoenicia was the historic, maritime one; the second was an inland district with cities that never before belonged to either Phoenicia or Lebanon. Palestine was split into three: Palaestina Prima, whose chief city was Caesarea and which comprehended Jerusalem, Neapolis (Nābulus), Joppa (Jaffa), Gaza, Ascalon and others; Palaestina Secunda, with Scythopolis (Baysān) for its capital and Gadara and Tiberias as chief towns; Palaestina Tertia, whose chief city was Petra and

[1] See above, p. 126, n. 5.

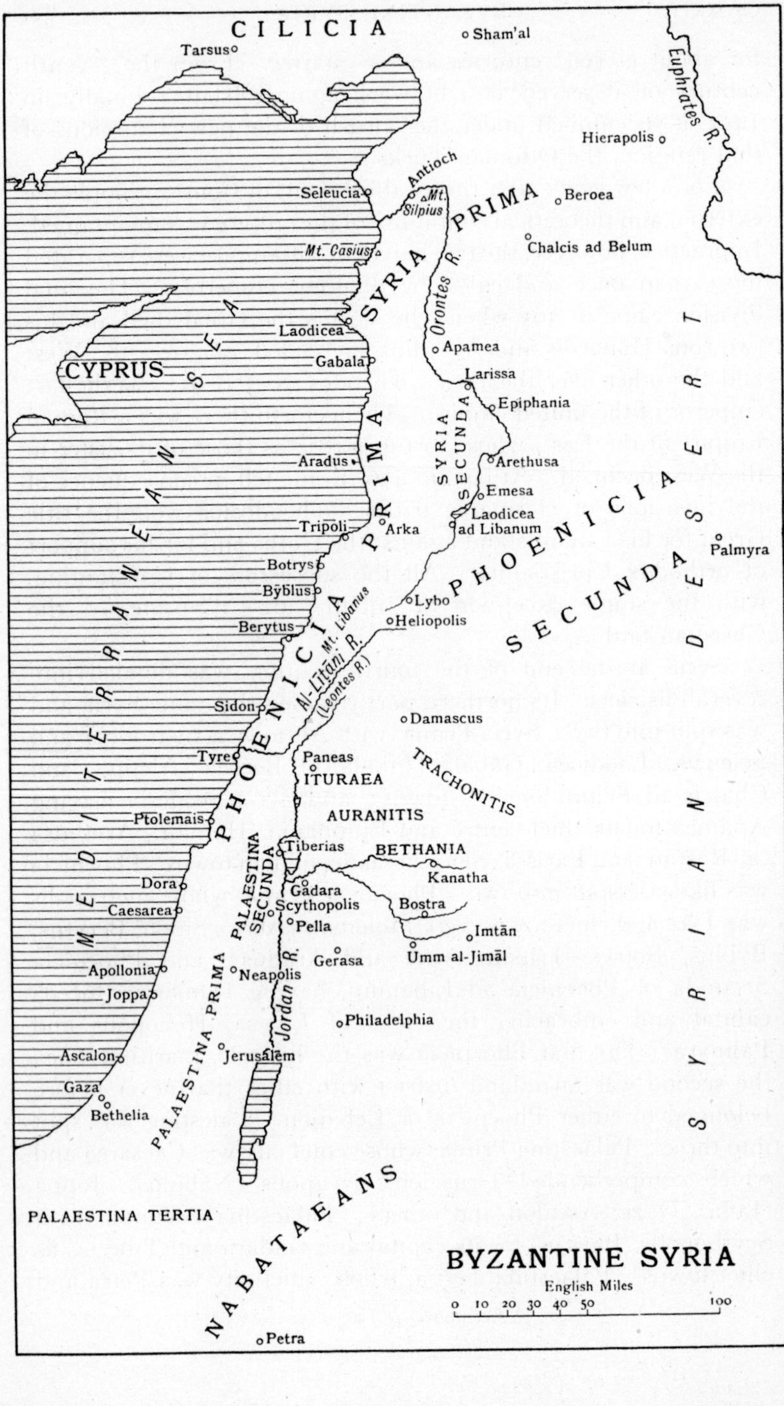
CILICIA
Tarsus
Sham'al
Euphrates R.
Hierapolis
Antioch
Mt. Silpius
Seleucia
Beroea
SYRIA PRIMA
Chalcis ad Belum
Mt. Casius
Orontes R.
MEDITERRANEAN SEA
Laodicea
Gabala
CYPRUS
Apamea
Larissa
Epiphania
PRIMA
SYRIA SECUNDA
Aradus
Arethusa
Emesa
Laodicea ad Libanum
Tripoli
Arka
Palmyra
Botrys
Byblus
PHOENICIA
Lybo
Heliopolis
Mt. Libanus
Berytus
Al-Līṭānī R.
(Leontes R.)
SECUNDA
SYRIAN DESERT
Sidon
PHOENICIA
Damascus
Tyre
Paneas
ITURAEA
TRACHONITIS
AURANITIS
Ptolemais
PALAESTINA SECUNDA
Tiberias
BETHANIA
Kanatha
Dora
Gadara
Scythopolis
Bostra
Caesarea
Pella
Imtān
Umm al-Jimāl
Gerasa
Apollonia
Neapolis
Jordan R.
Joppa
PALAESTINA PRIMA
Philadelphia
Ascalon
Jerusalem
Gaza
Bethelia
PALAESTINA TERTIA
NABATAEANS
Petra
BYZANTINE SYRIA
English Miles
0 10 20 30 40 50 100

which was formed out of the former province of Arabia.

Trade

The division of the empire and the fragmentation of its Syrian province does not seem to have affected the domestic and foreign trade relations of Syria adversely. In the Byzantine period as in the earlier one Mediterranean trade was almost entirely in Syrian and Greek hands.[1] St. Jerome describes Syrian merchants as traversing the entire Roman world in the fourth century, prompted by their love of lucrative trade and defying all dangers.[2] Their settlements did not cease to flourish throughout the Mediterranean world. They could be found among other commercial centres in Rome, Naples, Carthage, Marseille and Bordeaux. They imported wines from Ascalon and Gaza, purple from Caesarea, woven fabrics from Tyre and Berytus, pistachios and sword blades from Damascus and embroidered stuffs from several towns. Embroidery was especially in demand for ecclesiastical use.

An old commodity which now assumed new importance was silk, whose entire trade was controlled by Syrians. Tradition asserts that the eggs of silkworms from China were first introduced in bamboo tubes to Constantinople in the mid-sixth century (under Justinian) by monks, apparently Nestorians.[3] But there is reason to believe that Syrians had some acquaintance, through wild silkworms, with sericulture long before this time.[4] The Chinese silk textures found their way via Petra into some Phoenician port, where they had to undergo the process of dyeing and of weaving, perhaps re-weaving before being rendered acceptable to the Roman market. Thus had the silk industry in Syria become linked with the purple industry. Both soon became a Byzantine state monopoly.

From Arabia and India, Syria continued to import spices and other tropical products. In exchange Syria exported to these lands — as well as to China — glass, enamelled work and fine stuffs. We hear of a Syrian merchant in China as early as the third Christian century.[5]

As in the case of the modern Syrian emigrants, those of the

[1] J. B. Bury, *History of the Later Roman Empire* (London, 1923), vol. ii, p. 316.

[2] Cumont, *Religions orientales*, p. 100.

[3] Procopius, Bk. VIII, ch. 17, §§ 1-8; Bouchier, p. 162.

[4] F. Hirth, *China and the Roman Empire* (Leipzig, 1885, reprinted in China, 1939), pp. 255-6; cf. above, pp. 92, 275. Consult Robert S. Lopez, " Silk Industry in the Byzantine Empire ", *Speculum*, vol. xx (1945), pp. 1-42.

[5] Hirth, p. 306.

Byzantine age as a rule became indefinitely domiciled in their lands of adoption. A few returned home accompanied with their foreign wives. Above the door of a mosque of a village now called Imtān[1] on the borders of the Syrian Desert, stands a Greek inscription, originally a Greek epitaph of the mid-fourth century, in memory of a Gallic wife from Rouen who died "far from her native land".[2] The colony in Orleans felt so much at home that when in 585 King Gontrand entered the city they were among those who received him singing his praises "in the language of the Syrians, the Latins and the Jews".[3] The Paris colony under the Merovingians, about 591, was influential enough to elect one of its members, a merchant by the name of Eusebius, bishop over the city, and to control the ecclesiastical offices.[4]

Emigrant artisans

The majority of Syrian emigrants were business men but some were slaves, soldiers, monks or artists. Syrian architects and sculptors at home were instrumental in the development of the late Hellenistic styles, usually termed Byzantine. As early as the second century architects from the Eastern provinces were employed in Rome.[5] The engineer who built for Trajan the bridge over the Danube during the second Dacian campaign was a Damascene, Apollodorus. He is the one who later designed, in commemoration of his patron's victories, the forum of Trajan at Rome, with the temple, library and still-existing columns. The motif of mounting a statue on a colossal column was characteristically North Syrian.

It is probable that artistic craftsmen from Syria were summoned to embellish the new capital, Ravenna, to which Honorius (395–423) removed his court to escape the dangers of the Germanic invasions. They remained there to teach their craft to native artists. They introduced their mosaic and other decorative motifs. In the fifth century Ravenna became the artistic capital of North Italy. Its school of art and architecture has been described as "half-Syrian".[6] After Ravenna Venice became the representative of Eastern culture on Italian soil. The city of Ravenna itself was also characterized as half-

[1] Mothana (al-Muthanna), south-east of Ṣalkhad in Ḥawrān; Dussaud, *Topographie*, p. 355.

[2] *Revue archéologique*, vol. xxxix (1901), pp. 375-6.

[3] Gregory of Tours, *Historiae Francorum*, Bk. VIII, ch. 1.

[4] Gregory, Bk. X, ch. 26.

[5] Pliny, *Epistulae ad Traianum*, No. 40.

[6] O. M. Dalton, *Byzantine Art and Architecture* (Oxford, 1911), pp. 8, 77.

Syrian. Syrian bishops were installed in it. A visitor from Gaul, to whom the Syrians must have been familiar figures in southern France, noted the presence of a Syrian who " chants the Psalms ".[1] There must have been many such deacons and monks.

Literature and education

Confusion marked the intellectual life of Byzantine Syria in its early period. Polemics between Christian and non-Christian Greek and Latin writers were carried on for years after Constantine's profession of the Christian faith. Neo-Platonism, whose most flourishing period covered the third century and the first decades of the fourth and whose two chief exponents were the Syrian Porphyry and Iamblichus,[2] was far from being dead. Church Fathers were inching their way to the front as leaders of thought. Sophists and rhetoricians were retreating though not quite disappearing.

Libanius

Most voluminous among the Syrian rhetoricians of the fourth century was Libanius (314–*ca.* 393), a native of Antioch whose name suggests some Lebanese connection. After receiving his education at Antioch and Athens, Libanius set up a school of rhetoric at the new imperial capital. He also taught in Nicaea and Nicomedia, and at the age of forty returned to his native town, where for forty years he remained active as orator, teacher and statesman, honoured with the friendship of high officials and emperors.

Libanius never bothered to study Latin,[3] despised Christianity as an enemy of true culture and saw no good except in Hellenism. He was disappointed and pained when his most promising pupil in Antioch, the future Chrysostom, renounced the gods of Greece in favour of Christ.[4] Another student of his was Basil the Great (329–79), who studied under Libanius at either Constantinople or Antioch and later became bishop of Caesarea in Cappadocia and a champion of orthodoxy against Arianism. Libanius' old age was saddened by bodily suffering caused by his being struck by lightning and by the decline of pagan learning which followed the lamented death, in 363, of his imperial admirer and patron Julian.

Libanius' extant writings, largely letters and orations, give us a vivid picture of the times and places in which he lived.[5]

[1] Sidonius Apollinaris, *Epistulae*, Bk. I, No. 8.
[2] See above, pp. 324-5.
[3] *Epistulae*, No. 923, cf. No. 956.
[4] Cf. Sozomenus, Bk. VIII, ch. 2.
[5] Quoted above, p. 303.

They also open before us a small window through which we may gain a glimpse of the educational methods of the day. At Antioch courses extended over the winter and spring months; summer was taken up with festive activities. Classes began early and lasted till noon. Some students were as young as sixteen. Higher education was in the hands of rhetoricians. As professors the rhetoricians were elected in the cities by the local senate, in the small towns by the communities at large. The rhetors taught, declaimed by way of example and were responsible for the discipline. In Antioch they were organized into three corporations, each with its own president. For their services the rhetors received pay from the cities and from the students. Greek classics formed the core of the curriculum. Latin was patronized only by those intent upon a government career. Logic was emphasized. Aristotle enjoyed a renaissance consequent upon his rediscovery by Porphyry.

Ammianus Marcellus

One of the correspondents of Libanius was Ammianus Marcellus (*ca.* 330–401), also an Antiochian. Born of a noble Greek family, Ammianus joined the army at an early age and attained high commands in a long and honourable career in Mesopotamia and Gaul. Late in life he wrote in Latin a continuation of Tacitus, of which only a part survives. In it he pays more than the usual attention to racial and personal character and to social institutions. Ammianus may be regarded as the last ancient writer in Latin really deserving the name of historian. In his attitude toward Christianity he was more tolerant than Libanius. Like Libanius he took infinite pride in his native city and country. Antioch was " without a rival, so rich in imported and domestic commodities "; [1] Phoenicia, " lying at the foot of Mount Libanus ", was " a region full of charm and beauty "; [2] Palestine was one " abounding in cultivated and well kept lands "; [3] and Roman Arabia, " a land producing a rich variety of wares and studded with strong castles and fortresses ", embraced among its great cities " Bostra, Gerasa and Philadelphia [ʿAmmān], all strongly defended by mighty walls ".[4]

John Chrysostom

Thanks to the productivity of such authors as Libanius and

[1] Bk. XIV, ch. 8, § 7. [2] Bk. XIV, ch. 8, § 9. [3] Bk. XIV, ch. 8, § 11.

[4] Bk. XIV, ch. 8, § 13. The works of Ammianus have been edited and translated by John C. Rolfe, *Ammianus Marcellinus*, 3 vols. (London and Cambridge, Mass. 1935–8).

Ammianus, Antioch became the intellectual capital of North Syria. Both Arius and Nestorius [1] were educated in it. Lustre was added to it by the brilliant achievement of Christian orators and authors, chief among whom was John Chrysostom (347–407).

John was educated for the bar but soon forsook it for an ascetic life on a mount near the city. Could this have been the rugged Mount Silpius — rising to the south of Antioch — where a dim light has been kept in a grotto burning through the ages by the local community commemorating a Moslem saint? [2] His eloquent preaching in his native town was marked by a denunciation of laxity in morals and luxury in living. The rich were condemned for acquiring their riches by violence, deceit, monopoly and usury, and for their attitude of indifference to the cause of the under-privileged and poor.[3] His was a social message in an age of ecclesiasticism and theology. So celebrated for his talents as a preacher did he become, that he was chosen in 398 patriarch of Constantinople.[4] There he sold for the benefit of the needy the treasures collected by his predecessor and pursued the same line of preaching. He insisted that the infidelity of the husband was no less of an evil than that of the wife. He began "sweeping the stairs from the top".

Such uncompromising insistence on moral and social reform was sure to bring him into conflict with the court. One of the potent enemies he made was the high-spirited Eudoxia, wife of Arcadius, whom John compared in a sermon to Herodias and to the setting up of whose statue near the great church he objected.[5] Twice was he banished from the capital. Throughout he sustained himself with fortitude until his death on his way to exile at the extreme boundary of the empire, near the Caucasus. Forced to make long marches and exposed to the sun and the rains, he broke down and died on the way [6] His body was later translated to Constantinople and buried with great pomp. His fame as the greatest preacher of the early Church won him posthumously the epithet "the golden mouth". His sermons,

[1] See below, p. 371.
[2] Ḥabīb al-Najjār.
[3] Sozomenus, Bk. VIII, ch. 2.
[4] Sozomenus, Bk. VIII, chs. 3, 5.
[5] Sozomenus, Bk. VIII, chs. 16, 20; Palladius, *Dialogus de vita S. Joannis Chrysostomi*, Bk. VIII.
[6] Sozomenus, Bk. VIII, ch. 28; Palladius, Bk. XI.

full of more eloquence than learning, throw some light on the social life of his time.[1] He remains for all time one of the most remarkable teachers of Christian ethics that the church has produced.[2]

Eusebius

Another distinguished Church Father of the age was Eusebius (264–*ca.* 349), bishop of Caesarea in Palestine, the first great Church historian. Eusebius was born in Palestine, probably in Caesarea itself, and educated at Antioch. In common with many contemporary bishops he at first espoused the cause of Arius; but at the historic Council of Nicaea, where Constantine assigned Eusebius the high office of opening the session, Eusebius condemned the heresiarch. He delivered a panegyrical oration in honour of the emperor and sat at his right hand. Throughout his life Eusebius remained an intimate friend and ardent admirer of Constantine. Eusebius was one of the most learned men of the age. He produced several historical works, one of which, *Ecclesiastical History*, has been cited above.[3] In it he narrates in detail the rise of Christianity and its relation to the empire.

Another historian of Caesarean birth was Procopius [4] (d. *ca.* 563), principal historian for the eventful reign of Justinian (527–565). As a young man Procopius in 527 was appointed private secretary and legal adviser of the Roman general Belisarius [5] and hence accompanied him in all his campaigns in Asia, Africa and Italy. Justinian made him senator. At times Procopius writes as a Christian, at others as a devotee of the gods of Greece. What gives authority to the information in his history is that it is derived partly from oral testimony and largely from his own experience.

Several Christian notables are associated with southern Syria though not of Syrian nativity. Pre-eminent among these was St. Jerome (345–420). Jerome's ascetic temperament led

[1] For a complete edition of his works consult *Patrologia Graeca*, ed. J.-P. Migne, vols. xlvii-lxiv (Paris, 1862–3); for a translation of his homilies and letters, *The Nicene and Post-Nicene Fathers of the Christian Church*, ed. Philip Schaff, ser. 1, vols. ix-xiv (New York, 1889–90).

[2] His portrait in mosaic, hidden in the plaster wherewith the Turks covered it with other portraits centuries ago, was found on the wall of Santa Sophia in 1946.

[3] Pp. 332, n. 5, 335, n. 4, 336, n. 1, etc.

[4] Cited above, pp. 103, n. 1, etc. His works have been edited and translated by H. B. Dewing, *Procopius*, 7 vols. (London and Cambridge, Mass., 1914–40).

[5] See below, p. 372.

him in 386 to a monastery in Bethlehem and thence to the Syrian Desert, where he spent five years of solitary life among the hermits. He was later instrumental in introducing monastic life into the West. A more significant contribution perhaps was his translation of the Bible into Latin, the Vulgate, which has ever since been used as the standard for the services in the Roman Catholic Church.

Gaza

Other than Caesarea, Gaza was the only southern city which kept its intellectual fire in this age. Jerusalem was still suffering from the havoc wrought by the Romans. Sozomen (Sozomenus), the Greek ecclesiastical historian of the fifth century, was a native of a village Bethelia or Bethel, outside of Gaza. His parents were Christians and his writings show intimate familiarity with that city and its environs. He dedicated his history to Theodosius II (408–50). But the city owed its fame chiefly to the school of rhetoric which flourished about A.D. 500. The school drew its inspiration from Alexandria and occasionally exchanged teachers and students with Caesarea and other learned centres. A few of its professors were Neo-Platonists, but the majority styled themselves Christian sophists. Their productions included biblical commentaries and treatises against the Hellenes or Gentiles. On the whole the cities of the southern coast were less addicted to ecclesiastical controversy than Antioch and other cities of the north.

Berytus as a scientific centre

Of all the cities of Byzantine Syria, Berytus was the only one which vied with Antioch for intellectual leadership. This was due to the fact that it housed the academy of law,[1] a science that was more assiduously cultivated than any other in the Byzantine period.

This institution reached its greatest development in the fifth century, when it attracted some of the finest young minds in the Byzantine Empire. The Constantinople school, founded in 425, offered no competition. The curriculum comprised science, geometry, rhetoric, Greek and Latin. It covered four years but Justinian, who ascended the throne in 527, added a fifth year. Students were exempt from military service until twenty-five years old. Many of the Christian bishops, saints and martyrs made their academic debut at Berytus.

The earliest allusion to the academy in the ecclesiastical

[1] See above, pp. 325-6.

writings occurs in an oration by Gregory Thaumaturgus[1] (wonder worker) delivered about A.D. 240. Gregory came from Cappadocia to study first at Berytus and then at Caesarea in Palestine, where he was converted to Christianity by his teacher Origen. Another distinguished student was Pamphilus, himself a native of Berytus and later bishop of this Caesarea, where he suffered martyrdom under Galerius in 309. Pamphilus counted among his pupils the distinguished historian Eusebius. So great was the student's reverence for the teacher that Eusebius added to his own name Pamphilus. Gregory of Nazianzus (in Cappadocia), future bishop of Constantinople and saint, quit Athens about 356 in favour of Berytus in pursuit of his legal study. Even more famous was Severus, Jacobite patriarch of Antioch (512–18), whose biography was written by his fellow-student Zacharias of Gaza.[2]

Student life

Interesting details of university life in such a cosmopolitan city as Berytus, lying on the confines of the East and the West, are preserved in Severus' biography. The entering students were evidently received by the older ones with ridicule, though not with actual ill-treatment,[3] in order to test their power of self-control — a sort of "freshman hazing" like that which has prevailed in American universities. Zacharias arrived in Berytus in the autumn of 487 or 488, one year after Severus. Like all freshmen he was nervous when he first attended the class of the distinguished professor Leontius, but was well received by Severus and the older students. At the close of the exercises Zacharias, who was deeply religious, went to pray in the Church of the Resurrection. After that he met Severus by the harbour and pleaded with him to attend church daily after the lectures, to avoid horse races and theatres and to abstain from drink and gambling, in which other students indulged. The future patriarch, who accompanied by slaves came to college from a rich family, assured his young friend that he was a law student and not a monk, but promised to do what he could.

All class exercises were suspended Saturday afternoon and Sunday.[4] The evenings were free to enable the student to repeat

[1] *The Works of Gregory Thaumaturgus, Dionysius of Alexandria, and Archelaus*, tr. S. D. F. Salmond (Edinburgh, 1871), pp. 49-50.

[2] Edited in Syriac (Greek original lost) and translated as *Vie de Sévère* by M.-A. Kugener, in *Patrologia Orientalis*, vol. ii (Paris, 1907), pp. 1-115.

[3] Zacharias, p. 47.

[4] Zacharias, p. 52.

the work done in the daytime. Zacharias organized a Christian society which met every evening in the Church of the Resurrection to study the works of Basil, Chrysostom and other Fathers. The cosmopolitan membership of the society indicates the large number of foreign students. The president was one Evagrius of Samosata, formerly a student at Antioch, where he was wounded in a disturbance. Evagrius fasted daily. He indulged in the luxury of a bath once a year on Easter eve.[1] Touched by these examples of asceticism, Severus began to abstain from meat.

In the meantime another student society was organized to promote interest in occultism. An Armenian, a Thessalonian, a Syrian from Heliopolis and an Egyptian from Thebes were the leading spirits. The Egyptian was enamoured of a woman who did not reciprocate his affections. It was consequently agreed that sacrifice of the Egyptian's black slave would influence the demons and produce the coveted results.[2] As the rite was being performed in the circus at midnight, it was suddenly interrupted by passers-by. The frightened Negro escaped and reported his master. Search was made for the magic books, which were at last found stuffed in the lower part of the student's chair and were committed to the flames. They were found full of strange names and pictures of demons, some attributed to Zoroaster. Further investigation revealed that even Professor Leonitus was implicated in similar illicit practices. A court of inquiry, consisting of clergy and municipal officials, found Leonitus, together with others, guilty. Their books were burned and some of the accused fled the city.

Berytus' trouble with magic did not end there. A party of vagrant magicians arrived in the city and undertook in collaboration with a student from Asia Minor and the connivance of two priests to excavate in the tombs of a church where they promised to unearth treasures hidden by Darius. To evoke the demons the help of the censer and other silver church objects was necessary. The ceremony was cut short by an earthquake and the priests were punished; one of them by confinement in a monastery.[3]

Between 551 and 555 a series of earthquakes almost pulverized the cities of the Phoenician coast. Berytus had suffered a shock in 349 which partially destroyed it but evidently did not

[1] Zacharias, p. 56. [2] Zacharias, p. 58. [3] Zacharias, pp. 70-73.

arrest the progress of its university. This time, however, it was different. The city "most beautiful, hitherto the ornament of Phoenicia, was then deprived of its beauty. Its famous masterpieces of architecture were thrown down, almost none were left standing. Only the foundations were spared. A large number of its inhabitants, native and foreign, perished under the ruins."[1] The university professors moved to Sidon, where they offered their courses pending the reconstruction of their city and university. Just before dedication of the new university buildings in 560 another calamity befell them, fire broke out and devoured every one of them. We hear no more of the university.

[1] Agathias, *Historiarum*, Bk. II, § 15.

CHAPTER XXVIII

AN ECCLESIASTICAL AGE

BYZANTINE Syria presents a different aspect from Roman Syria. It was on the whole a Christian land. In fact this is the only period in which Syria has been a fully Christian country. Sandwiched in between the pagan Roman and the Arab Moslem, the Byzantine period was therefore unique in Syrian annals.

Not only was the country Christian but the age was an ecclesiastical age. The Church was its greatest institution ; the saints were its most revered heroes. From the fourth to the sixth centuries monks, priests, bishops,[1] nuns, anchorites, flourished as never before and as never after. Church buildings, chapels, basilicas, monasteries, all with a new style of architecture involving domes, bell towers and prominent crucifixes, dotted the land. Hermit caves [2] were enlarged or created. Pillars were erected on which stylites curiously enough lived and died. Pilgrimage boomed. Vows and prayers at tombs of saints were considered more efficacious than visits to physicians. Byzantine architectural remains and religious relics are today more numerous than those of all other ages together.

Monasticism

Monasticism was a favoured way of life. Its ideals of celibacy, poverty and obedience held wide appeal. With the decline of population, the waning of prosperity and the civil disturbances that marked the Roman period in the third and fourth centuries went a loss of confidence and faith in secular institutions. Christianity presented something supernatural and ultra-mundane, including a belief in spiritual values worth renouncing this world for and dying for.

[1] A Syriac manuscript lists 19 bishops from Palestine, 10 from Phoenicia, 22 from Coele-Syria and 6 from Arabia (Bostra, Philadelphia, etc.) who attended the Council of Nicaea ; B. H. Cowper, *Syriac Miscellanies* (Edinburgh, 1861), pp. 9-10. Bishops evidently had not as yet attained the distinction which definitely separated them from presbyters.

[2] See above, p. 38.

As a system monasticism sprang from the Christian practice of asceticism. Its founder was an Egyptian, St. Anthony, who retired to the desert and died between A.D. 356 and 362. From Egypt the new style of Christian life soon spread into

From Robin Fedden, "Syria" (Robert Hale, Ltd.)

THE SO-CALLED BAPTISTERY OF QAL'AT SAM'ĀN

Built between 480 and 490, the convent of St. Simeon Stylites was one of the grandest and largest of the Christian monuments of the early centuries

southern Syria, where Hilarion of Gaza, a disciple of Anthony, pioneered the way. In the late fourth century colonies of hermits made their appearance around Antioch. Ephraim (d. *ca.* 373) was one of the founders of Syrian monasticism. In the following century the first of the stylites, Saint Simeon (d. 459), made his

From M. I. Rostovtzeff, " The Excavations at Dura-Europos " (Yale University Press)

MOSES AND THE BURNING BUSH, A MURAL IN THE SYNAGOGUE AT DURA-EUROPOS

This third century synagogue has the oldest representations of Jewish biblical art; now in the National Museum, Damascus debut in the north of the country. The pillar on which he perched is still shown, amidst the ruins of a magnificent church (Qalʿat Samʿān), to tourists. This strange form of monastic life survived as late as the fifteenth century. The lives of the early monks of Egypt and South Syria became the admired prototype for all Christendom. "Hermit" comes from a Greek word meaning desert.

Church buildings

The Christian Church grew out of small circles of disciples who proclaimed their leader Saviour and Messiah. The first circle to be designated Christian was that of Antioch.[1] The Apostles began their preaching at synagogues; their converts were either Jews or gentile frequenters of synagogues. The nucleus of the first Christian assemblies was, therefore, largely Jewish. It must then have been difficult to distinguish the nascent Christian from the established Jewish community.

The earliest Christian places of worship were presumably private homes where informal meetings were held or synagogues. When these places of worship were formalized into churches they had only the synagogue for model. The Jewish synagogue was a local substitute for the Temple after its destruction. The synagogue represented a new and revolutionary means of worship, one that excluded initiation by mysteries and propitiation by sacrifice. As such it became the prototype of both church and mosque.

The oldest remains of a Palestinian synagogue date from the first Christian century.[2] At Dura-Europus the earliest synagogue was a private house transformed about A.D. 200. A mid-third century synagogue there was provided with a door for women and special benches for their use. Its murals are unique in synagogue art; they depict scenes from the careers of Jewish patriarchs and monarchs.[3] At the same city are remains of a church of about A.D. 232, older than any known church in Palestine.[4] In fact this is the earliest Christian church ever unearthed. From the days of Constantine some traces have

[1] See above, p. 335.

[2] E. L. Sukenik, *Ancient Synagogues in Palestine and Greece* (London, 1934), pp. 8, 69.

[3] Rostovtzeff *et al.*, *Excavations at Dura-Europos*, vol. vi, pp. 309-96; Sukenik, pp. 82-5.

[4] Rostovtzeff *et al.*, *Excavations at Dura-Europos*, pp. 238-88; J. W. Crowfoot, *Early Churches in Palestine* (London, 1941), pp. 1 *seq.*

been left to this day in the Holy Sepulchre and in the Church of the Nativity. The present structure of the Church of Nativity

From Ludwig Preiss and Paul Rohrbach, "Palestine and Transjordania" (Sheldon Press)

THE CHURCH OF THE HOLY SEPULCHRE

was erected by Justinian. Most of the churches of Gerasa belong to the sixth century though some include work of the fourth and fifth centuries. One of them was a synagogue rebuilt as a church. In later centuries churches were rebuilt as mosques.

From these and other remains the conclusion may be drawn that church and synagogue were architecturally related. Both of them in the Byzantine period represented the basilica type. The synagogue was oriented Jerusalem-ward; the church was oriented eastward. Their art was likewise closely related.

From Ludwig Preiss and Paul Rohrbach, "*Palestine and Transjordania*" (*Sheldon Press*)

THE CHURCH OF THE HOLY NATIVITY

The primitive type of Christian church was an elongated room, favoured because of its simplicity and relation to the prevailing type of structure. The one-nave church of Umm al-Jimāl (A.D. 344), south of Buṣra in Ḥawrān, illustrates this type.[1] The Syrian basilica of the fourth and fifth centuries consisted of a transverse nave to which were attached, on the east, three apses, or rather a central apse flanked by two side chambers. The plan had its roots in the pre-Christian model of building. Remains of a chapel in a sixth-century monastery excavated at Scythopolis (Baysān) show no side aisles. There

[1] Howard C. Butler, *Early Churches in Syria*, pt. 1 (Princeton, 1929), p. 19.

was a horseshoe apse at the east end. The altar doubtless stood in the entrance to the apse.[1] In the hall of the monastery was found a calendar mosaic throughout which the prevailing colours are the blue-black of polished basalt and a variety of shades of red and light brown on a whitish background.

Christian art

Traces of early Christian art reveal its indebtedness to Jewish art. The church drew upon the synagogue for its symbolism. In its earliest representations the figure of Jesus is depicted with a rod, presumably that with which Moses struck the rock. The figure of Jesus on the catacombs is clearly one adapted by Christians from representations of Moses. Though Syria was, in the opinion of certain scholars, the fount of Christian art,[2] Christian iconography in its gradual development drew upon Hellenistic formulas for divinities, poets and orators. It varied in time and place until some definite individualization and standardization was attained in the fourth and fifth centuries.

A most popular subject of early Christian artists is that of the Good Shepherd. It appears, among other biblical figures, on the wall of the Dura-Europus church. The shepherd is usually portrayed carrying on his shoulder a lamb. The shepherd idea is very old in Semitic thought. In the prologue to his code of laws Hammurabi calls himself " the shepherd "[3] of his people. The earliest figures of the shepherd are those of a beardless youth in a short sleeveless tunic, the type familiar in Greco-Roman art. The Greek motif itself, however, goes back to Near Eastern origins. A ninth pre-Christian century relief from Sham'al, North Syria, and an eighth from Dur Sharrukin, near Nineveh, show figures with gazelles on their shoulders, each with the head of the animal facing in the same direction as that of the man. The gazelle was probably meant for sacrifice.

In architecture, painting, sculpture and other fields of ornamental art the Syrian of Byzantine days sought new ways of expression independent of the Greco-Roman models which

[1] G. M. Fitzgerald, *A Sixth Century Monastery at Beth-Shan* (Philadelphia, 1939), p. 3.

[2] On this consult Joseph Strzygowski, *Orient oder Rom* (Leipzig, 1901); do., *Origin of Christian Church Art* (Oxford, 1923), pp. 1-16; do., *L'Ancien Art chrétien de Syrie* (Paris, 1936), pp. xlvi-lii.

[3] Robert W. Rogers, *Cuneiform Parallels to the Old Testament* (New York, 1912), p. 399.

From G. M. Fitzgerald, "A Sixth Century Monastery at Beth-Shan" (University Museum, Philadelphia)

CALENDAR MOSAIC IN THE HALL OF A SIXTH CENTURY MONASTERY AT BAYSĀN (From a drawing)

The centre holds two half-length figures bearing torches, representing the sun and the moon. The sun is crowned with golden rays, the moon with a crescent. The twelve full-length figures around the centre represent the twelve months. At the foot of each the name of the month in Latin and the number of days in Greek are inscribed. On the whole, the representation follows the traditional Byzantine pattern. The feet of January are shod, referring to cold. February carries over his shoulder a rake with two prongs. March is represented by a warrior, booted and leaning on a shield. April carries a goat and a basket. May carries flowers in the folds of his cloak. June holds a bunch of fruit, July a sheaf of corn. August is destroyed. September with knife and basket represents the vintage. October, traditionally a fowler, and November, a sower, are not clear. December is represented as the sower

From M. I. Rostovtzeff, "The Excavations at Dura-Europos" (Yale University Press)

GOOD SHEPHERD, A PAINTING IN THE CHRISTIAN CHAPEL AT DURA-EUROPUS

The shepherd is depicted in frontal view, standing behind his flock of seventeen rams huddled ether. On his shoulders he carries a huge ram. The rams are of the fat-tailed variety with long, ving horns. Near the shepherd are a number of trees which probably indicate Paradise

since Alexander's conquest had inspired artistic production. The native art aimed resolutely at realism. It gradually freed itself from the use of nude models and the conventional forms and paved the way for Christian medieval art as well as for Moslem art.

Aramaic revived

Linguistically the Christian Church in Syria developed along two lines: Greek on the coast and in the Hellenized cities, Syriac in the interior.[1] The Syriac-using Church had its start as early as the second century. With the spread of Christianity in the third century Syriac asserted itself against Greek. In the Byzantine period revulsion from Greek and reversion to Aramaic signalized the new awakening among the Syrians. The revived interest in the ancient Semitic tongue was an index of a revival of national consciousness.

Always polyglots, the Syrians interested in the bar studied Latin; those addicted to philosophy took up Greek; but the rest, especially those outside of the cosmopolitan centres, stuck to the native idiom. Byzantine officials in the interior had to use interpreters. Even in Antioch Chrysostom[2] complains that his audience could not understand his Greek sermons and that the priests heard nothing but vulgar Syriac.

Edessa

The Syriac literature extant is almost entirely Christian, but comprises also handbooks of science and philosophy translated from Greek. Its first great centre, away from the Greek-speaking cities, was Edessa, the Athens of the Aramaic world, where Syriac was first used for literary purposes. The school of Edessa flourished until 488–9, when it was totally destroyed by the order of the Emperor Zeno. The professors then moved to Nisibis, which became heir of Edessa as a Syro-Greek centre of learning. The Edessan Church, established toward the end of the second century, found itself in the succeeding centuries out of harmony with the Greek traditions of Antioch and the West. It used its own biblical versions, first in the form of the Diatessaron and later in that of the Peshitta (simple version).[3] The Peshitta has since remained the standard Syriac version.

The first great theologian of the Syrian Church was Ephraim Syrus (the Syrian, *ca.* 306–*ca.* 373), who was also a sacred poet

[1] For the distinction between Aramaic and Syriac see above, pp. 170-71.
[2] Joannes Chrysostomus, *Opera omnia*, vol. ii (Paris, 1837), p. 222.
[3] See above, p. 335.

and was instrumental in introducing monasticism.[1] Ephraim was born at Nisibis and came to Edessa, where he founded or reorganized a seminary which became the great university of the Syrians. Before him lived Bardesanes[2] (A.D. 155–223), also an Edessan, who had laid the foundation of Syrian hymnology and introduced music into that Church but is reckoned by some as a Gnostic.

Religious schisms

Opposition to Christian thought as represented by Byzantium and Antioch resulted in schisms, "heresies" from the orthodox viewpoint. As in the case of language these schisms were to a certain extent an expression of the national awakening. After a submergence of centuries under a wave of Greek culture the Syrian spirit was at last asserting itself. The Syrians as a people were no more Grecized now than they were Romanized before. Their alienation from their Byzantine rulers was due not only to ideological but to political and economic causes. The Byzantines were more autocratic in their rule and more oppressive in their taxation. They disarmed the natives and had but little regard for their feelings. Even in matters religious they displayed less tolerance than their pagan predecessors.

Theological controversy was the breath of life among the intelligentsia of the fourth and fifth centuries. It centred on the nature of Christ and kindred topics which no longer agitate Christian minds. The result was innumerable heresies and schools of thought, some of which reflect the exercise of Aristotelian logic and the application of Neo-Platonic principles. Meanwhile, cults akin to Zoroastrianism and to Buddhism were raising their heads amidst Christian communities. Chrysostom[3] refers to a group in Antioch who believed in transmigration of souls and wore yellow robes. Most dangerous among the new religions spreading from the East was Manichaeism, founded by Mani about A.D. 246 Mani suffered crucifixion for his belief.[4] His religion, which combined Christian, Buddhist and Zoroastrian tenets in one syncretistic system, spread in the Byzantine

[1] See above, p. 363. For a selection of his hymns and homilies consult *Nicene and Post-Nicene Fathers*, ser. 2, vol. xiii (New York, 1898), pp. 119-341.

[2] Syr. *bar* (son of) *Daiṣān* (name of a stream in Edessa); mentioned by Eusebius, Bk. IV, ch. 30, and by Arab writers beginning with al-Nadīm, *al-Fihrist*, ed. Gustav Flügel (Leipzig, 1872), pp. 338-9.

[3] *Opera omnia*, vol. iv, p. 53.

[4] *Fihrist*, pp. 327-38, has preserved one of the earliest extensive accounts of Mani and his system.

age from Persia to Spain. Its "errors" aroused the Syrian Fathers as no other errors did.

Apollinaris

The protagonists of the so-called heresies were of Syrian nativity or education. The series began with the fourth century Arius, whose system was condemned in the Council of Nicaea [1] but retained great importance, both theological and political. As a reaction against Arianism, with its emphasis on the humanity of Christ, Apollinaris, bishop of Laodicea (d. *ca.* 390), affirmed that while Christ had a true human body and a true human soul (that part of man common to him and the animal), the Logos or Word occupied in Him the place of the spirit, which is the highest part of man. In his reasoning Apollinaris was clearly using the Neo-Platonic doctrine that human nature is the composite of three elements — a body, a soul (that activates) and a spirit (that makes man reasonable and distinct from animals). Apollinarism links Arianism and Nestorianism by opposing the one and paving the way for the other.

The Nestorian Church

Nestorius [2] was born in eastern Cilicia and lived in a monastery near Antioch. In 428 he was elevated to the bishopric of Constantinople at the suggestion of the Emperor Theodosius II, who thereby hoped to bring from Antioch a second Chrysostom. In 431, however, he was condemned by the Council of Ephesus. The objectionable view he held was that in Jesus a divine person (the Logos) and a human person were joined in perfect harmony of action but not in the unity of a single individual. Nestorius had many followers who constitute the real Nestorians.

The so-called Nestorians of Persia came later. More properly they constituted the East Church, or, as it proudly calls itself, the Church of the East. This Church had existed from the Apostolic Age; it still has surviving representatives today. Cut off from the Roman Empire its adherents evolved their local doctrines and ritual. They count Nestorius among the Greek, not the Syrian, Fathers. True, some of the writers of this Church have used decidedly Nestorian language, but the liturgical and synodical vocabulary of the Church as a whole is remarkably free from it. This is the Church which in later times had sufficient vitality to send missionaries as far as India and China.[3]

The Jacobite Church

Next to Nestorianism, Monophysitism was the greatest schism the Oriental Church suffered. Strictly, the Monophy-

[1] See above, pp. 349-50. [2] See above, p. 357. [3] See below, pp. 518, 519, fig.

sites were those who did not accept the doctrine of the two natures (divine and human) in the one person of Jesus, formulated by the Council of Chalcedon (A.D. 451). They took for watchword " the one nature of the incarnate Word of God ". In other words, the Monophysites maintained that the human and the divine in Christ constituted but one composite nature. Hence their name.[1]

In the late fifth and early sixth centuries Monophysitism won to its doctrine the major part of North Syria and fell heir to Apollinarism in the south. Its success was due largely to the propagandist zeal of a Syrian monk Barsauma, bishop of Nisibis (*ca.* 484–96), and to the personality of Severus, patriarch of Antioch (512–18).[2] Simeon the Stylite, it is contended by Monophysites, held their theological view. The Ghassānids [3] and other Syrian Arabs espoused the same doctrine. The Monophysite Church in Syria was organized by Jacob Bardaeus,[4] who was ordained bishop of Edessa about 541 and died in 578. In consequence the Syrian Monophysites came to be called Jacobites. The western part of the Syrian Church thus became entirely separated from the eastern.

From Syria the Monophysite doctrine spread into Armenia to the north and Egypt to the south. Armenians and Copts to this day adhere to the Monophysite theology. In Syria and Mesopotamia the number of its adherents has been on the decrease ever since Islam became the dominant power in those lands.

The Persian peril

In the Byzantine age not only Syria but Egypt and Mesopotamia became conscious anew of their ancient traditions. Under the aggressive Sāsānid dynasty neighbouring Persia began to dispute with Byzantium mastery over the Orient. The first incursion (527–32) was checked by Justinian's able general Belisarius. Procopius of Caesarea, the historian of this war, accompanied Belisarius as an adviser.[5] This incursion, however, was but a forerunner of the impending peril.

In 540 the Persians appeared again under Chosroes I Anūsharwān (531–79). At the head of 30,000 men this energetic

[1] Gr. *monos*, single, + *physis*, nature.

[2] See above, pp. 360-61.

[3] See below, p. 403.

[4] Ar. Ya'qūb al-Barda'i, " he with the saddlecloth ", or " he who manufactures saddles ".

[5] Procopius, Bk. I, ch. 12, § 24; see above, p. 358.

monarch descended upon Syria by way of Hierapolis (Manbij) and set fire to Aleppo, which could not raise the heavy tribute imposed.[1] This was 4000 lbs. of silver, double the amount by the payment of which Hierapolis had purchased immunity. Thence Chosroes proceeded to Antioch, which was but poorly garrisoned. A reinforcement of 6000 soldiers from Lebanese Phoenicia,[2] the region of Emesa, proved no match for the Persian invader. The strength of the Roman army was at this time in the West, where Justinian was attempting to re-assemble the ancient Roman Empire. The city was sacked. Its cathderal was stripped of its gold and silver treasures and of its splendid marbles. The whole town was completely destroyed. Its inhabitants were carried away as captives.[3] For them the conqueror built, near his capital Ctesiphon, a new city which he proudly named Antioch of Chosroes.

The career of the city as an intellectual centre thus after eight centuries came to an end. In its last days Antioch was a prominent Christian city, ranking with Constantinople and Alexandria as a patriarchal see. Ten ecclesiastical councils were held in it between A.D. 252 and 380. The estimate of Chrysostom [4] that its Christian congregation numbered a hundred thousand apparently ignored the slaves and the children. In the catastrophic earthquake of 526 its native and contemporary historian Malalas [5] reports the destruction of 250,000 Antiochians.[6] The economic consequences of the Persian sack and of this earthquake and that of 528 were disastrous.

From Antioch Chosroes moved on to Apamea, another flourishing Christian centre. Its church claimed the possession of a piece of the true cross, one cubit in length, reverently preserved in a jewelled casket.[7] Guarded by special priests, the precious relic was displayed once a year, when the whole population worshipped in its presence. Its casket, together with all the gold and silver in the town, was collected to satisfy the greedy invader; but the relic itself was spared. For him it was devoid of value. When one of the citizens accused a Persian soldier of

[1] Procopius, Bk. II, ch. 7, §§ 1-13.
[2] See above, p. 351.
[3] Procopius, Bk. II, ch. 9, §§ 14-18.
[4] *Opera omnia*, vol. vii, p. 914.
[5] Syr. Malala, orator.
[6] For more on population consult Bury, *History of the Later Roman Empire*, vol. i, p. 88.
[7] Procopius, Bk. II, ch. 11.

having entered his home and violated his maiden daughter, Chosroes directed that the adulterer be impaled in the camp.[1] The natives ascribed the deliverance of the city from destruction to the efficacy of the holy relic.

Chalcis, near Aleppo, was the next victim. It purchased its safety by a sum of gold. Chosroes' campaign of extortion was then continued in the provinces east of the Euphrates.

In 542 a truce was concluded and thereafter renewed several times until 562, in which a fifty-year treaty was signed binding Justinian to pay tribute to the "great king" and to refrain from any religious propaganda in Persian territory. In the early seventh century hostilities were renewed, but their story belongs to a later chapter, that of the rise of the Moslem Arab state.[2]

[1] Procopius, Bk. II, ch. 11, §§ 36-8.

[2] See below, p. 409.

CHAPTER XXIX

PRE-ISLAMIC SYRO-ARAB STATES

BEFORE the emergence of Islam and its spread northward Syria witnessed the rise and fall of three Arab states on its periphery: the Nabataean in the south, the Palmyrene in the north and the Ghassānid in between. The three shared certain common features in their successive careers. They owed their origin to the domestication of nomadic or wandering tribes and their prosperity to transit trade. Each allied itself for some time as a buffer state with one of the two world powers — Rome and Persia — and received subsidy therefrom. The Nabataean and the Palmyrene nationalities were finally destroyed by Rome, the Ghassānid by Byzantium and Persia.

1. The Nabataeans

The Nabataeans appear first in the early sixth pre-Christian century as nomadic tribes in the desert east of what is today termed Transjordan. This land had been since the beginning of the thirteenth century the home of the petty kingdoms of Edom and Moab in the south, Ammon and Gilead in the north — all Canaanite and Aramaean.[1] Prior to the thirteenth century Edom and Moab, as judged by archaeological remains, were not occupied — their history a blank back to the nineteenth century. From the twenty-third century to the nineteenth, when they evidently succumbed to desert attacks, they had been heavily settled. At times, as under the Judges and David, Hebrew military might and religion were able to penetrate into these lands, but the Hebrew monotheistic faith was never able to cross the Jordan in full force or to establish a foothold south of it.[2] It is these people who were later incorporated into the Nabataean federation, together with the Thamūd [3] and the Liḥyān [4] tribes in northern al-Ḥijāz.

From herders to tillers

In the fourth century before Christ the Nabataeans were still

[1] See above, p. 193, map. [2] See above, pp. 191, 194, 196, 246.

[3] Mentioned in the Koran, 7 : 71 ; 11 : 64, 71.

[4] Closely related to Thamūd. See Pliny, Bk. VI, ch. 32, § 156 ; ch. 33, § 165.

nomads, living in tents, speaking Arabic, abhorring wine an uninterested in agriculture. In the following century the abandoned the pastoral in favour of the sedentary way of lif and engaged in agriculture and trade. By the end of the secon century they had evolved into a highly organized, culturall advanced, progressive and opulent society.[1] Theirs was anothe case illustrating the ever-recurring theme of ancient Nea Eastern history — the theme of herders becoming tillers an then traders in lands of deficient resources but of favourabl location for caravan commerce that made up for natura deficiency.

The first fixed date in Nabataean history is 312 B.C., whe they succeeded in repulsing the attacks of two expeditions fron Syria against their "Rock" under one of Alexander's suc cessors, Antigonus.[2] Their metropolis, which had started as mountain fortress and had become a caravan station at th junction of trade routes for incense and spice traffic, was the already strongly fortified. This rocky shelter, Petra, was befor Nabataean days a city of refuge for the Edomites, who ha wrested it from the hands of Horites (Hurrians, children of Seir) Carved in the bosom of a sandstone rock displaying all th rainbow colours, the Nabataean capital presented a uniqu combination of art and nature.

From tillers to traders

The word Petra, Greek for "rock", is a translation o Hebrew Selaʿ.[3] The Arabic correspondent is al-Raqīm.[4] Umn al-Biyārah in Wādi Mūsa (the valley of Moses) is the moder name of the site From their capital the Nabataeans extende their authority and with it their settlements to the neighbourin northern region, where old Edomite and Moabite cities wer rebuilt by them, new posts to guard the caravans were erecte and fresh stations for exploiting the mineral resources wer established.[5] Theirs was the only town between the Jorda and al-Ḥijāz which had not only abundant but invitingly pur water. Besides, the city was impregnable on three sides, east, west and south. From the end of the fourth century on, Petra

[1] Consult Strabo, Bk. XVI, ch. 4, §§ 22, 26; Diodorus, Bk. III, ch. 43, § 4.

[2] Diodorus, Bk. II, ch. 48, §§ 6-7; Bk. XIX (ch. 6), § 94; above, p. 237.

[3] Mentioned in Is. 16:1; 42:11; 2 K. 14:7. Cf. 2 Ch. 25:12; Jer. 49:16 Ob. 3:4.

[4] Koran 18:8; Yāqūt, vol. i, pp. 91, 728; vol. ii, pp. 125, 804; cf. Josephus *Antiquities*, Bk. IV, ch. 4, § 7; ch. 7, § 1.

[5] See above, pp. 190, 296.

became a key city on the caravan route, linking spice-producing South Arabia with the consuming and marketing centres in the north. It commanded the routes to the port of Gaza in the west, to Buṣra and Damascus in the north, to Aila [1] on the Red Sea, and to the Persian Gulf across the desert.[2] In it the relays of camels were provided.

Not satisfied with the water of their springs, Nabataean hydraulic engineers became adept in extracting subterranean water and in husbanding and conserving the little rain water that fell. They seem to have inherited that magic rod which had enabled an earlier Semitic wanderer in that territory, Moses, to bring water out of the dry rock.[3] Thus were they able to take more bites from the desert and convert them into sown lands than any other Arabian people before or after.

Little is heard of Nabataea in the third century while its settlers were developing their potentialities. Early in the second it emerges as a force to be reckoned with in Near Eastern politics. In the period of its emergence it fell under Ptolemaic influence. With the year 169 B.C. a series of definitely known Nabataean kings is inaugurated.

The monarchy

First on the list was Ḥārithath (al-Ḥārith, 169 B.C.), "Aretas the king of the Arabians".[4] The name was borne by many kings of Nabataea and later by the royalty of Ghassān. Ḥārithath was a contemporary of the founder of the Maccabean family. The two houses started as natural allies against the Seleucid kings of Syria.[5] Later they became rivals. Ḥārithath II ("Erotimus",[6] *ca.* 110–96 B.C.), founder of the dynasty, rushed in 96 B.C. to the aid of Gaza, besieged by the Maccabean Alexander Jannaeus. About 90 B.C. a successor of Ḥārithath II, 'Obīdath ('Ubaydah, Obodas I), won over Jannaeus[7] a significant victory. The battle was fought on the eastern shore of the Sea of Galilee and opened the way for the occupation of south-eastern Syria, present-day Ḥawrān and Jabal al-Durūz. Taking advantage of the decline of their Seleucid and Ptolemaic neighbours, 'Obīdath and his successor Ḥārithath III (*ca.* 87–62) pushed the Arabian frontier northward. Rome had not yet appeared on the Oriental scene.

[1] See above, p. 190; below, p. 383.
[2] Cf. Pliny, *Natural History*, Bk. VI, ch. 32, § 145.
[3] Ex. 17:6.
[4] 2 Macc. 5:8.
[5] 1 Macc. 5:24-7; 9:35.
[6] Dussaud and Macler, *Mission*, p. 70.
[7] See above, p. 246.

This Ḥārithath was the real founder of Nabataean power. He repeatedly defeated the Judaean army and laid siege to Jerusalem. In response to an invitation from Damascus he installed himself in 85 B.C. as the ruler of that Seleucid city and of the rich plain that went with it, Coele-Syria. The invitation was prompted by Damascene hatred for the Ituraean tetrarch of Chalcis (ʿAnjar), who aspired to the Syrian throne.[1] Twelve years later Ḥārithath repulsed an attack from Pompey,[2] who dreamed of extending the Roman frontier as far as the Red Sea, and loomed as the most powerful potentate of Syria. This was the first direct contact with Rome.

While with one hand Ḥārithath pushed back the Roman arms, with the other he opened the door wide for Greco-Roman influences. He brought his kingdom within the full orbit of Hellenistic civilization and earned the title of Philhellene. He was the first to strike Nabataean coinage, for which he adopted the Ptolemaic standard. Into his capital he imported Syrian-Greek artisans who may have carved for him the beautiful façade, now called al-Khaznah (the treasury), originally designed as a tomb for himself. The theatre was also probably built in his days.[3] Petra then began to take on the aspects of a typically Hellenistic city, with a beautiful main street and several religious and public buildings. From this time on Nabataea assumes the rôle of " client ", ally to Rome. Māliku (Mālik, Malchus I, *ca.* 50–28 B.C.) was requested by Julius Caesar in the year 47 to provide cavalry for his Alexandrian war. His successor ʿObīdath III [4] (*ca.* 28–9 B.C.) encouraged Aelius Gallus, prefect of Egypt under Augustus Caesar, to undertake in the year 24 the ill-fated expedition against Arabia Felix and promised him wholehearted co-operation. Strabo, a friend of Gallus, blames the entire failure on the perfidy of the guide, " Syllaeus the minister of the Nabataeans ".[5] When ʿObīdath's successor Ḥārithath IV assumed the kingship without asking the per-

[1] See above, p. 247.

[2] Josephus, *Antiquities*, Bk. XIV, ch. 5, § 1; *War*, Bk. I, ch. 8, § 1.

[3] See Rudolf E. Brünnow and Alfred v. Domaszewski, *Die Provincia Arabia*, vol. i (Strasbourg, 1904), pp. 250-61; Gustaf Dalman, *Petra und seine Felsheiligtümer* (Leipzig, 1908), pp. 183-8.

[4] The ruined city of ʿAbdah (Oboda) north-west of Petra owes its name to this or some other ʿObīdath; Abel, vol. ii, p. 400.

[5] Bk. XVI, ch. 4, § 23; Hitti, *History of the Arabs*, p. 46; cf. A. Kammerer, *Pétra et la Nabatène* (Paris, 1929), p. 199.

From R. E. Brünnow and A. v. Domaszewski, " Die Provincia Arabia "
(Karl J. Trübner, Strasbourg)

AL-KHAZNAH, THE MOST BEAUTIFUL MONUMENTAL FAÇADE OF PETRA

Probably designed as a tomb for Ḥārithath III (*ca.* 87–62 B.C.)

mission of Augustus, he nearly lost his throne in consequence.

The kingdom at its height

Under the long and prosperous rule of Ḥārithath IV (9 B.C.–A.D. 40) the kingdom attained its height. The process of Romanization was continued by him. It was an ethnarch of this king who endeavoured to arrest Paul at Damascus.[1] Herod the tetrarch, son of Herod the Great, married a daughter of this Ḥārithath and was bold enough to divorce her in favour of an entertainer who was the prime mover in the murder of John the Baptist.[2] The resentful father waged a successful war against the Jewish king.[3] The "high places" still standing in Petra[4] and the fine tombs represented by those of al-Ḥijr (Madā'in Ṣāliḥ) in al-Ḥijāz may date from his reign. Al-Ḥijr was a Thamūd centre.[5]

At its height the kingdom included southern Palestine and Transjordan, south-eastern Syria and northern Arabia. The Syrian part, however, was widely separated from the Transjordanian part by the territory of the Decapolis union.[6] The two parts were held together by Wādi al-Sirḥān. This desert rift on the eastern frontier of Transjordan was utilized as a great highway leading from the heart of Arabia to Syria and bypassing the Decapolis.[7] It may be assumed that meanwhile subterranean springs were tapped and caravanserais, watch-towers, fortresses and police posts were established along this route as along the Wādi al-ʿArabah route, the rift passing by Petra and connecting the Jordan valley with the Gulf of al-ʿAqabah. Such measures were necessary as a protection against Bedouin raids. The Wādi al-ʿArabah route branched off at the Dead Sea eastward into Palestine and westward into Transjordan, where it connected with the royal highway[8] bisecting the fertile part of the plateau. Through these two Wādis as corridors Nabataean wares flowed in time of peace and arms in time of war.

The last monarchs

Beyond a few facts gleaned from native inscriptions, coins and classical writings not much is known about the last rulers

[1] 2 Cor. 11 : 32. [2] Matt. 14 : 6-11.

[3] Josephus, *Antiquities*, Bk. XVIII, ch. 5, §§ 1-2.

[4] Alexander B. W. Kennedy, *Petra: Its History and Monuments* (London, 1925), figs. 42, 53, 57, 156.

[5] Koran, 15 : 80. [6] See above, p. 317.

[7] Nelson Glueck, *Explorations in Eastern Palestine, III* (New Haven, 1939), pp. 144-5.

[8] See above, p. 289.

of Nabataea. Beginning with the reign of ʿObīdath III [1] (*ca.* 28–9 B.C.), coins display the effigy of the queen together with the king. The jugate busts of the royal couple continued henceforth to appear until the overthrow of the monarchy. An inscription on a statue of this ʿObīdath calls him " divine ", [2] showing that Nabataeans deified their kings after death. On the coins of Māliku II (A.D. 40–75), son of Ḥārithath IV, the queen is designated " sister of the king ",[3] indicating that following the Pharaonic and Ptolemaic practice some queens were sister-wives of the reigning monarchs. The inscription on ʿObīdath's statue suggests that one of the wives of Ḥārithath IV

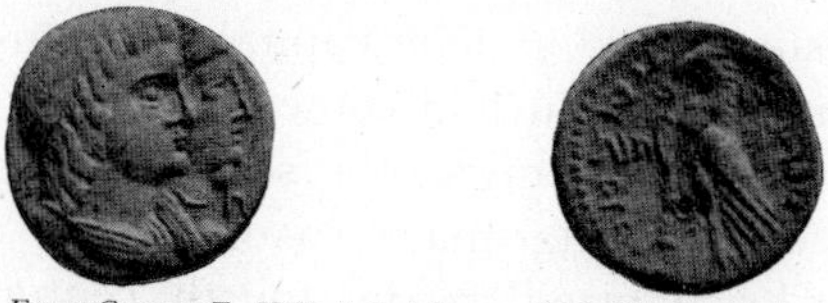

From George F. Hill, " Catalogue of the Greek Coins of Arabia, Mesopotamia and Persia " (British Museum)

DRACHMA OF ʿOBĪDATH III (*ca.* 28–9 B.C.), KING OF THE NABATAEANS

Obverse shows the jugate busts of the king and queen. The king wears long hair and is diademed. The queen wears a stephane and a necklace. Reverse shows an eagle standing left. Nabataean inscription

was also his sister. It was this Māliku who about A.D. 67 sent 1000 horse and 5000 foot to the assistance of Titus in his attack on Jerusalem.[4] During his reign Damascus passed into Roman hands, probably under Nero.

To Māliku's son and successor Rabbil II (Rabel, *ca.* 71–105), last of the Nabataean kings, inscriptions found in Ḥawrān refer, ironically as it may seem, as the one " who brought life and deliverance to his people ".[5] Some of his coins indicate that he ruled for a time with his mother. What precisely transpired in that fateful year 105–6 which resulted in the overthrow of this border Syro-Arab state and its annexation by imperial Rome is

[1] Obodas II in Cooke, p. 216. For complete lists of kings and discrepancies in numbering and dating cf. Kammerer, pp. 176-7; Cooke, p. 216; René Dussaud and Frédéric Macler, *Voyage archéologique au Ṣafâ et dans le Djebel ed-Drûz* (Paris, 1901), p. 172; Dussaud and Macler, *Mission*, pp. 69-90.

[2] Cooke, p. 244.

[3] Kammerer, p. 254.

[4] Josephus, *War*, Bk. III, ch. 4, § 2.

[5] Cooke, p. 255; Dussaud and Macler, *Voyage*, pp. 166-7; Kammerer, pp. 255-6.

not determined. Rome had already absorbed all the petty kingdoms of Syria and Palestine and was getting ready to measure swords with that great Asiatic power, Parthia. No semi-independent power could be tolerated in between. All intermediary states must come within the full embrace of the empire. Perhaps at the end of Rabbil's reign the Romans simply refused to acknowledge his successor, and the move of Trajan's legate in Syria, Cornelius Palma, against Petra was enough to crush any resistance.[1] In the following year Nabataea became a part of the Roman province of Arabia, with Buṣra as the leading city and later as the capital.[2] Arabia Petraea was no more.

Its picturesque and opulent capital was pushed into the limbo of history, whence it had come. The east-to-west trade route shifted north to Palmyra, the south-to-north moved east to where the Moslem pilgrimage road and the modern Ḥijāz railway lie. Christianized in the fourth century, Petra was Islamized in the seventh and following centuries. Immediately after his appointment as king in 1100 Baldwin I occupied the stronghold city, which was held until the decisive victory of Ṣalāḥ-al-Dīn in 1189. Derelict it remained until its ruins were discovered in 1812 to the learned world by the Swiss explorer Burckhardt.[3]

Commercial and industrial contacrs

Petran commercial radiation penetrated to some of the farthest points of the then civilized world. It left epigraphical traces scattered from Puteoli, for a time port of Rome, to Gerrha[4] on the Persian Gulf. Other Nabataean records have been found in Miletus, Rhodes, the eastern Delta of the Nile, Upper Egypt and the mouth of the Euphrates. The mutilated inscription of Puteoli, now in the museum of Naples, dates from A.D. 5 and dedicates some object for the life of King Ḥārithath IV in a recently restored sanctuary, which had been built some fifty years before.[5] Chinese records testify to Nabataean business enterprise.[6]

Myrrh, spices and frankincense from South Arabia, rich

[1] Dio, Bk. LXVIII, ch. 14, § 5.

[2] See above, p. 293.

[3] John L. Burckhardt, *Travels in Syria and the Holy Land* (London, 1822), pp. 418-34.

[4] See above, pp. 272-3.

[5] *Corpus Inscriptionum Semiticarum*, pars II, tom. i (Paris, 1889), No. 158.

[6] See above, p. 353.

silk fabrics from Damascus and Gaza, henna from Ascalon, glassware and purple from Sidon and Tyre and pearls from the Persian Gulf constituted the principal commodities. The native produce of Nabataea comprised gold, silver and sesame oil, which they used instead of olive oil.[1] Asphalt and other remunerative minerals were probably exploited from the eastern shore of the Dead Sea. In exchange raw silk was imported from China. Chinese silk as a material had been known in Syria since Seleucid days,[2] and raw silk was already being woven in Sidon in the first Christian century. Greek and Roman imports were brought in Attic jars, sherds of which can still be found around Petra and Aila.[3] Aila was one of the links in the chain of caravan stations. Buṣra and Ṣalkhad were other links. These and other cities were used as depots for arms and wares. Native troops were reinforced by Nabataean colonists. A recently discovered site, Jabal Ramm, twenty-five miles east of Aila, draws added interest from the fact of its identification with Iram of the Koran.[4] Nabataeans protected the caravan routes, imposed taxes on goods in transit and for some time exercised a sort of monopoly. Strabo found them "so much inclined to acquire possessions that they publicly fine anyone who has diminished his possessions and also confer honours on anyone who has increased them".[5]

Cultural aspects

Arabic in speech, Aramaic in writing, Semitic in religion, Greco-Roman in art and architecture, the Nabataean culture was synthetic, superficially Hellenic but basically Arabian, and so it remained.

Strabo, Josephus and Diodorus were right in calling the Nabataeans Arabians. Their personal names, the names of their gods and the Arabicisms in their Aramaic inscriptions leave no doubt that their native speech was a North Arabic dialect. In the Puteoli inscription, cited above, the name ʿAli, of later Islamic vogue, occurs for the first time in literature.[6] In

[1] Strabo, Bk. XVI, ch. 4, § 26; above, p. 277. [2] See above, pp. 275, 298.

[3] Ancient Elath (see above, p. 190), now al-ʿAqabah, so called since Aḥmad ibn-Ṭūlūn (see below, p. 557) built a fortress on the site.

[4] M.-R. Savignac and G. Horsfield, "Le Temple de Ramm", *Revue biblique*, vol. xliv (1935), pp. 245-78; Harold W. Glidden, "Koranic Iram, Legendary and Historical", *Bulletin, American Schools of Oriental Research*; No. 73 (1939), pp. 13-15.

[5] Bk. XVI, ch. 4, § 26.

[6] For another Puteoli inscription see above, p. 347.

another, Ḥabīb and Sa'īd, still popular Arabic names, are mentioned.[1] Such Arabic words as *qabr* (tomb) and *ghayr* (other than) occur in several inscriptions. In a late inscription (A.D. 268) so many pure Arabic words are used that the entire text approaches the Arabic.[2]

Lingua franca of the age, Aramaic was used by Nabataeans as it was used by their northern neighbours.[3] There were, be it remembered, no Arabic letters then. The message the Nabataeans wrote in 312 B.C. to Antigonus was in "Syriac characters".[4] Aramaic was the only language they could use on their monuments and coins. The Nabataean script gradually differentiated itself from the Aramaic, and about the middle of the first pre-Christian century assumed its distinctive character and became standardized.

It may be assumed that Nabataean merchants were to some extent bilingual, if not polyglot, just as the merchants of Cairo and Beirut are today. Some of them must have had control over not only Arabic and Aramaic but Greek and, to a less extent, Latin.

What gives added significance to Nabataean characters is the fact that the Arabic alphabet is directly descended from them, as an epigraphic study of the early Arabic inscriptions clearly indicates. The oldest Arabic text extant is that of al-Namārah in eastern Ḥawrān, A.D. 328, inscribed in Nabataean characters.[5] The cursive script in which Arabic was written is as old as the Kufic, ascribed to al-Kūfah in Mesopotamia. Moslem tradition disagrees with the epigraphic evidence and wrongly points to Mesopotamia as the first home of true Arabic writing.

Religion

Nabataean religion was of the common Semitic type based on agricultural fertility rites. It preserved elements of the old worship associated with "high places"[6] and standing stones.

At the head of the pantheon stood Dūshara (dhu-al-Shara,

[1] *Corpus Inscriptionum Semiticarum*, pp. 260, 242.

[2] Jaussen and Savignac, *Mission archéologique en Arabie* (Paris, 1909), pp. 172-6.

[3] See above, pp. 168-9, 170-71, 220. For more on the language of the Nabataeans consult J. Cantineau, *Le Nabatéen*, 2 vols. (Paris, 1930–32).

[4] Diodorus, Bk. XIX (ch. 6), § 96.

[5] Cantineau, vol. i, p. 22.

[6] See above, p. 123.

Dusares),[1] a sun deity worshipped under the form of an obelisk or an unhewn four-cornered black stone. The ruins of a Nabataean shrine at Khirbat al-Tannūr, south-east of the Dead Sea, built perhaps in the first pre-Christian century, have preserved a simple box-like shrine resembling a ka'bah.[2]

Associated with Dūshara was Allāt, chief goddess of Arabia. She was a moon-goddess. Other Nabataean goddesses cited in

From G. A. Cooke, "North Semitic Inscriptions" (Clarendon Press)

A NABATAEAN SEPULCHRAL INSCRIPTION OF A.D. 26, FOUND IN AL-ḤIJR (MADĀ'IN ṢĀLIḤ)

Nabataean characters are parents of the Arabic alphabet

the inscriptions were Manāh and al-'Uzza, of koranic fame. Hubal also figures in the inscriptions. The Aramaean goddess Atargatis was represented at Khirbat al-Tannūr as the goddess of grain, foliage, fruit and fish.[3] Several divinities of this place correspond to those of Palmyra, Dura-Europus, Hierapolis and Heliopolis. Serpent worship formed a part of the religion.

Little is known about the ceremonies connected with Nabataean worship. Strabo's description of a royal banquet in

[1] "The owner of Shara", a place name; consult W. H. Waddington, *Inscriptions grecques et latines de la Syrie* (Paris, 1870), pp. 478-9. The cretaceous mountain towering north-east of Petra is still called Shara (Sharra in *The Quarterly of the Department of Antiquities in Palestine*, vol. vii (1938), pl. i). The word probably means *ḥima*, temenos, sacred precinct; Dalman, p. 49.

[2] M. E. Kirk, "An Outline of the Ancient Cultural History of Transjordan", *Palestine Exploration Fund Quarterly* (1944), p. 196.

[3] Nelson Glueck, *The Other Side of the Jordan* (New Haven, 1940), pp. 180-86; Kirk, p. 196.

which " no one drinks more than eleven cupfuls, each time using a different golden cup " [1] sounds more like a ritual ceremony. The old-time sobriety [2] must have given way under the impact of " modern civilization ". Ritual is also suggested by the report from the same source that " they eat common meals in groups of thirteen persons, each group being attended by two girl singers ". As the luxuries and the Hellenistic way of conduct were adopted, the deities changed their old Semitic names and put on Roman guise. Dūshara became Dionysus.

The delineation of Nabataean national character in Strabo [3] and Diodorus,[4] our two best authorities, is doubtless in exaggerated colours but must have an element of truth. The general picture is that of a sensible, acquisitive, orderly, democratic people absorbed in trade and agriculture. The society had few slaves and no paupers. The members kept such state of peace with one another that they refrained from prosecution. The king was so democratic that he often rendered an account of his kingship to the popular assembly. So absorbed were the people in matters pertaining to this life that they had the same regard for the dead as for dung.

On one side Nabataean influence reached north into Hebrew lands, on the other south into Arabia proper. Omri, king of Israel and founder of Samaria, where he was buried about 874 B.C., was presumably a Nabataean.[5] About a century later Amaziah, king of Judah, deemed the Edomite gods of Petra so powerful as to necessitate setting them up in the Temple of Jerusalem to be worshipped as the equals of Jehovah.[6] Judging by his name, Gashmu, opponent of the wall-building project for Jerusalem, was a Thamūd Nabataean.[7] The " wise men from the east " [8] were possibly Arabians from the Nabataean desert rather than Magi from Persia.[9] Justin Martyr [10] and other Church Fathers drew this inference from the nature of the gifts offered. The Arabians of the day of Pentecost [11] were in all

[1] Bk. XVI, ch. 4, § 26.
[2] See above, p. 376.
[3] Bk. XVI, ch. 4, §§ 21, 26-7.
[4] Bk. XIX (ch. 6), §§ 94-7.
[5] 1 K. 16 : 24; above, p. 192.
[6] 2 K. 14 : 7; 2 Ch. 25 : 14.
[7] See above, p. 223.
[8] Matt. 2 : 1.
[9] Cf. Ernst E. Herzfeld, *Archeological History of Iran* (London, 1935), pp. 64-66.
[10] " Dialogue with Trypho ", *Ante-Nicene Christian Library*, vol. ii (Edinburgh, 1867), pp. 195-6.
[11] Acts 2 :11.

probability Nabataeans, and the Arabia in which Paul found a place of retreat [1] was undoubtedly some desert tract in that region.

Further research would probably reveal a larger measure of Nabataean influence over infant Christianity and Islam than

From " Quarterly of Dept. of Antiquities in Palestine ", vol. vii (Oxford)

FAÇADE OF A TEMPLE IN PETRA

This vast façade was carved into the mountain mass

hitherto realized. Koranic *ḥanīf*,[2] applied to contemporaries of Muḥammad who held some vague monotheistic ideas, is of Aramaic Nabataean origin.

Art and architecture

The Nabataeans were responsible for a new type of architecture involving temples, tombs and other structures carved in the living rock. The vaulted type of chamber is characteristic. In decorative motif they may have originated the stucco variety, which was passed on from them to Mesopotamia and Persia.[3]

In their sculpture as in their religion the people of Petra show close affinity with those of the cities of the desert fringe, such as Palmyra and Dura-Europus.

[1] Gal. 1 : 17.

[2] Sūr. 2 : 129; 3 : 6; 4 : 124; Hitti, *History of the Arabs*, p. 108.

[3] Neilson C. Debevoise, " Origin of Decorative Stucco ", *American Journal of Archaeology*, vol. xlv (1941), p. 60.

Inspired by Greek models, Nabataean artisans introduced a new type of pottery which stands out among the finest produced in that region.[1] Remains of cups, saucers, dishes, jugs and bowls are of amazing egg-shell thinness and attest superior workmanship. They reveal all varieties: plain, painted and rouletted. The clay used is reddish buff, the designs usually stylized floral or leaf patterns. The prevalence of grapes and vine-leaves in ceramic and architectural decoration is another indication that the earlier abstinence from wine was no longer practised. Archaeologists of the American School of Oriental Research at Jerusalem have through sherds identified some five hundred Nabataean sites between al-ʿAqabah and the northern edge of the Dead Sea.[2] "In art, architecture, and engineering, perhaps in literature, certainly in ceramics, the Nabataeans were one of the most gifted people in history."[3] Conductors of caravans which functioned as arteries in the trade of the Ancient East, architects of a city unique in the history of man's handiwork, builders of dams and cisterns where no water today exists, the Nabataeans are represented now by the lowly Ḥuwayṭāt Bedouins, who still rove where their ancestors once flourished and pitch their tents outside of their "rose-red city half as old as time".

2. The Palmyrenes

As the sun of Petra began to set, that of Palmyra, another caravan city, began to rise. A copious spring of drinkable though sulphurous water in the heart of the Syrian Desert gave birth to an oasis nucleated by a hamlet. The settlers were a few Arabian tribes. A new orientation in world empires and a shift in international trade routes raised the hamlet to a dazzling position of affluence and power among the cities of antiquity.

Tadmur

The natives called their settlement Tadmor. Under this form it appears first around 1800 B.C. and reappears in a later Assyrian record according to which Tiglath-pileser I (*ca.* 1100 B.C.) pursued his Bedouin adversaries to this desert refuge.[4] Josephus says the Syrians pronounced the name Thadamora.[5] The ancient Semitic form survives in the Arabic Tadmur. The

[1] Kirk, p. 195; Glueck, pp. 173-4.
[2] Glueck, p. 173.
[3] Glueck, pp. 159-60.
[4] Julius Lewy, "Les Textes paléo-assyriens", *Revue de l'histoire des religions*, vol. cx (1934), pp. 40-41; P. Dhorme, "Palmyre dans les textes assyriennes", *Revue biblique*, vol. xxxiii (1924), pp. 106-8; cf. Luckenbill, vol. i, §§ 287, 308.
[5] *Antiquities*, Bk. VIII, ch. 6, § 1.

Hebrew chronicler (2 Ch. 8 : 4) who reports that Solomon built "Tadmor" either intended to aggrandize Solomon and his kingdom or confused the name with Tamar in Idumaea, which owes its foundation to the Hebrew monarch.[1] The Greek name Palmyra denotes a city of palms, corresponding to Hebrew *tāmār*. The etymology of *tadmōr* is uncertain.[2] Remembering the Jewish tradition and impressed by the magnitude and magnificence of the ruins, Moslem story-tellers ascribed the building to the jinn commandeered by Solomon.

Centre of trans-desert trade

The expansion of the Parthian empire into the Euphrates region in the mid-second pre-Christian century created a new situation in the Near East.[3] So did the annexation of Syria by Rome about three-quarters of a century later. Between these two world empires stood Palmyra. Its isolated location in the heart of the desert put it outside the reach of the Roman legions as well as the Parthian cavalry. Its merchants benefited by its unique position as the main halting-place on the trans-desert crossing of the north-to-south and east-to-west routes.[4] Its politicians shrewdly exploited its strategic situation between the two great rival powers and, by siding one time with Rome and another with Parthia, kept the balance of power and profited by neutrality. By playing one adversary against the other, they maintained the independence of their city as a buffer state

Palmyrene chiefs secured safe-conducts for passing caravans from desert shaykhs; guides led those caravans through the barren region; mounted archers protected them against Bedouin raids; and the city imposed heavy duty on each article of merchandise as it passed through its gates. The commodities comprised some of the necessities and many of the luxuries of the contemporary world. They did not differ much from those which passed through Petra: wool, purple, silk, glassware, perfumes, aromatics, olive oil, dried figs, nuts, cheese and wine.[5] Pieces of Chinese silk have been found in a tomb of A.D. 83.[6] The greater part of the Mediterranean trade with Persia, India

[1] Ezek. 47 : 19; 48 : 28; cf. 1 K. 9 : 18.

[2] Perhaps related to Syr. *tedmortâ*, to marvel at; W. F. Albright, "The North-Canaanite Poems of Al'êyân Ba'al and the Gracious Gods", *Journal, Palestine Oriental Society*, vol. xiv (1934), p. 130, n. 149.

[3] See above, pp. 238, 247-8.

[4] See above, p. 271.

[5] Cf. J.-B. Chabot, *Choix d'inscriptions de Palmyre* (Paris, 1922), pp. 26-30.

[6] R. Pfister, *Textiles de Palmyre* (Paris, 1934), pp. 39 *seq.*, 62.

and China was then handled by Palmyrenes.[1] Indicative of the high esteem in which merchant citizens were held are inscriptions of the mid-third Christian century proclaiming the setting up by the "council of people" of statues for the "chief of the caravan" and the "chief of the market".[2] Native industry flourished alongside commerce. An inscription of A.D. 258 proves the existence of an influential "guild of smiths who work in gold and silver".[3] That agriculture was not entirely neglected may be indicated by the recent excavation of a dam, one-fourth of a mile long, built between two hills to catch and use water for irrigation. The result was the growth of Palmyra into one of the richest cities of the Near East.

Gradually its mud huts were replaced by limestone houses. Wide streets were laid out, with the main one leading to the sanctuary of Bel. The streets were lined with colonnades, and the city assumed the aspect of a prosperous Greco-Roman town with an agora and a theatre. Its wealth was enough to excite the cupidity of Mark Antony, who in 41 B.C. ordered a cavalry raid against it. All that the Palmyrenes did was to vacate their city and flee with their valuables across the Euphrates.[4] This was the first recorded contact between Rome and Palmyra.

A vassal of Rome

It was not easy for the desert city to preserve full sovereignty in face of the growing ascendancy of the empire on its west. By the start of the Christian era Palmyra must have acknowledged the suzerainty of Rome, judging by imperial decrees of A.D. 17–19, under Tiberius, regarding its customs duties, but never surrendered its independence. About the same time the city apparently received a resident representative of Rome and allowed one of her citizens, Alexandros, to undertake a mission on behalf of Rome to Sampsigeramus of Ḥimṣ.[5] Trajan incorporated it in the province he created in 106 and Hadrian on his visit in 130 granted it the name Hadriana Palmyra[6] as a vassal of Rome. Palmyra's dependent cities also became Roman vassals. At the beginning of the third century Palmyra received colonial rights from Septimius Severus or some other emperor of the Syrian dynasty in Rome. On the coins of Caracalla the city

[1] Harald Ingholt, "Tomb in the Syrian Desert", *Asia*, vol. xli (1941), p. 506; Grant, *Syrian Desert*, pp. 55, 61, 64.

[2] Cooke, pp. 274, 279.

[3] Cooke, p. 286.

[4] Appian, *De bellis civilibus*, Bk. V, § 9.

[5] Mentioned above, p. 308.

[6] Cooke, p. 322.

is called *colonia*. As such it was exempted from customs duty. It was but natural for the Severi to favour Palmyra. Consoles once decorated with effigies of Julia Maesa and other members of the family [1] have been found in the agora excavated in 1939.[2] As vassals of Rome Palmyra and her satellites entered upon a fresh period of prosperity lasting for over a century and a half. Roman roads connected Palmyra with Damascus, capital of inland Syria, with the cities of the Euphrates [3] and with the frontier forts protecting the limes. Recent surveys from the air reveal remains of such forts from the Tigris through Syria and Transjordan as far as the Red Sea.[4] Prominent Palmyrene citizens began to add Roman names to their own. The city itself took on a new appellation. One family had "Septimius" prefixed to its Semitic name, indicating its receipt of citizenship under Severus and probably in recognition of services rendered in the struggle against Parthia.

First among the cities dependent on Palmyra was Dura-Europus. This city was used as a fortress to protect Palmyra's growing commerce. Remains have been found in it with frescoes representing Palmyrene soldiers. Another important annex of Palmyra was Resapha, later called Sergiopolis, after its native Saint Sergius. A soldier martyred about 305 in the reign of Diocletian, Sergius remained for a long time the favourite saint of the Syrian Church and his city became an important place of pilgrimage and a bishop's see.[5] In the form Raṣappa this city is mentioned in an Assyrian inscription of the late ninth pre-Christian century [6] and is identical with Rezeph (glowing coal), destroyed by Sennacherib.[7] The city, Arabicized al-Ruṣāfah, was destined to play a more important rôle as the favourite summer resort of the Umayyad caliphs.[8]

The family of Udaynath

The family with Septimius prefixed to its name rose in the

[1] See above, p. 343.
[2] Jean Starcky, *Palmyre, guide archéologique* (Beirut, 1941), p. 48.
[3] Alois Musil, *Arabia Deserta* (New York, 1927), pp. 514-16; do., *Palmyrena* (New York, 1928), pp. 237-46.
[4] Antoine Poidebard, *La Trace de Rome dans le désert de Syrie* (Paris, 1934); Aurel Stein, "Surveys on the Roman Frontier in 'Iraq and Trans-Jordan", *Geographical Journal*, vol. xcv (1940), pp. 428-38.
[5] Ptolemy, Bk. V, ch. 15, § 24; Procopius, Bk. II, ch. 5, § 29. Musil, *Palmyrena*, pp. 260-68, 299-326. See above, pp. 332-3.
[6] Winckler, *Keilinschriftliches Textbuch*, p. 77; cf. Dussaud, *Topographie*, pp. 253 *seq.*
[7] 2 K. 19: 12; Is. 37: 12.
[8] Cf. below, p. 510.

mid-third century to a position of leadership in Palmyra. A statue erected in 251 in honour of its head, Septimius Ḥayrān, son of Udaynath, calls him " the illustrious senator and chief (*ras*) of Tadmor ".[1] Apparently he was the first Palmyrene to add the title of chief to his Roman rank as a senator. His father appears in the inscriptions as simply a senator, a rank conferred on him presumably when in 230 or 231 Alexander Severus visited Palmyra in connection with the Persian wars. This Ḥayrān was probably the father of the famous Udaynath (Grecized Odenathus, cf. Arabic *udhaynah*, a little ear).[2] Judging by the personal names, the family was of Arab origin. A Greek historian calls this Udaynath " ruler of the Saracens ".[3] Members of the family were the executive branch of the government which was vested in the council of the people. Meritorious persons were honoured by this council.

It was not until the time of Ḥayrān that Palmyra began to play a conspicuous part in international affairs. By then a new and energetic dynasty had replaced the old Parthian. This was the Sāsānid, whose career lasted from A.D. 227 to the rise of Islam.[4] In 260 the Sāsānid army under Shāpūr I achieved the distinction of inflicting such a shameful defeat on the Roman legions near Edessa that their emperor Valerian fell into the hands of the enemy. Valerian had bestowed two years earlier the consular rank on Udaynath.[5] Subsequent Persian depredations extended to northern Syria and resulted in the sack of Antioch and other cities.[6] At this juncture Udaynath rushed with a sizable army of Syrians and Arab bands to the rescue of Valerian. He defeated the Persians on the banks of the Euphrates, pursued them to the very walls of their capital, Persepolis, and captured some of the royal harem, but was unable to recover the imprisoned emperor.[7] Valerian died in captivity and his skin was stuffed and hung in one of the temples.

Udaynath's loyalty to the new emperor Gallienus was rewarded in 262 when the Palmyrene chief was granted the title

[1] Chabot, p. 55; de Vogüé, *Inscriptions sémitiques* (Paris, 1868–77), p. 24; Cooke, p. 285; cf. Daniel Schlumberger in *Bulletin d'études orientales, l'Institut français de Damas*, vol. ix (1943), pp. 41-2, 53 *seq*.

[2] Zosimus, *Historia nova*, Bk. I, § 39. Cf. G. Ryckmans, *Les Noms propres sud-sémitiques*, vol. i (Louvain, 1934), p. 41.

[3] Procopius, Bk. II, ch. 5, § 6.

[4] See above, p. 345.

[5] Cooke, p. 286.

[6] See above, pp. 530-6.

[7] Pollio in *Scriptores historiae Augustae*, Bk. XXIV, ch. 15.

of *dux Orientis*, which made him a sort of vice-emperor over the eastern part of the empire. The empire was then in a feeble and confused state, with the whole barbarian world falling upon it in Europe as well as Asia. In the zenith of his success Udaynath was murdered together with his heir under mysterious conditions (266 or 267) while celebrating a festive occasion in Ḥimṣ. His own nephew was implicated in the conspiracy, devised possibly by Rome. Of hardy and athletic physique Udaynath was able to endure hardships and excelled in those pastimes and virtues prized highly by Arabs. His munificence manifested itself in elaborate and spectacular banquets, in patronizing religious festivals and in gifts of oil for public baths.

Zenobia

As a historical figure, however, he was eclipsed by his ambitious and beautiful widow, who ruled after him in the name of her minor son Wahab-Allāth (the gift of al-Lāt, translated Athenodorus).[1] Zenobia, Bath-Zabbay of the Palmyrene inscriptions ("daughter of the gift"), the semi-legendary al-Zabbā' of Arabic sources, was like her husband of hardy but agile frame, devoted to hunting and riding. Brunette in complexion, with pearly teeth and large flashing eyes, she conducted herself with regal dignity and pomp in a resplendent court modelled after that of the Chosroes. Her entourage greeted her with Persian prostration. On state occasions she wore a purple robe fringed with gems and clasped with a buckle at the waist, leaving one of her arms bare to the shoulder. She rode, helmet on head, in a carriage shining with precious stones. She claimed relationship with her Egyptian counterpart, Cleopatra, patronized Greek learning and herself spoke Aramaic and Greek and some Latin.[2] She even compiled a history of the East. Her court's chief intellectual ornament was the philosopher Longinus.

But Zenobia was much more ambitious and effective as a ruler than Cleopatra. Under her the Palmyrene state assumed the proportions of a real empire, extending over Syria, part of Asia Minor and northern Arabia. In 270 her general Zabda marched at the head of reportedly 70,000 troops into Egypt, dispossessed a usurper and established a garrison in Alexandria. Coins were first struck in this city displaying the head of Wahab

[1] Vopiscus in *Scriptores*, Bk. XXIII, ch. 13; Bk. XXVI, ch. 38.
[2] Bouchier, pp. 144-5.

beside that of Aurelian. In the following year (271) Alexandrian coins were issued minus the head of Aurelian. By that time Zenobia had reached the conclusion that she was powerful enough to declare her son fully independent. He assumed the title of " king of kings ". On Alexandrian and Antiochian coins he is also styled Augustus and she Augusta. Syrian milestones give the names of the emperor and Zenobia Augusta.

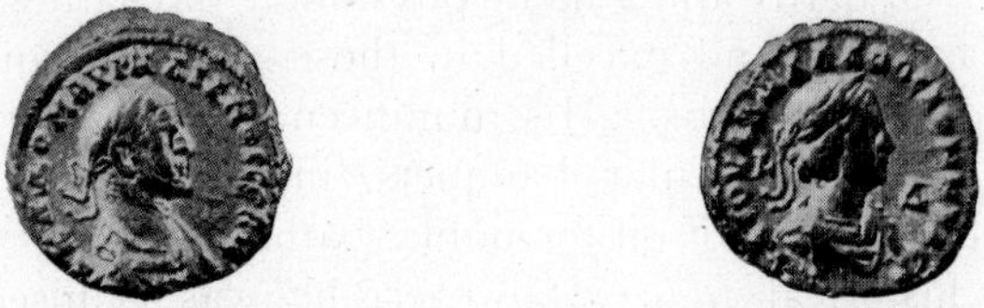

The American Numismatic Society

A COIN OF WAHAB-ALLĀTH

Obverse and reverse of a billon coin of Wahab-Allāth and Aurelian struck at Alexandria A.D. 270. The reverse bears the name of the Palmyrene king in Greek characters

On a high column of the grand colonnade in Palmyra a statue of the queen was set in August 271 bearing the still legible Greek and Palmyrene inscriptions :

> To their Lady Septimia Zenobia, the most illustrious and pious queen, the excellent Septimii Zabda,[1] commander-in-chief, and Zabbay,[2] commandant of the place, in the month of August of the year 582.[3]

Near by stood another statue bearing only a Palmyrene inscription :

> Statue of Septimius Udaynath, king of kings and restorer of all the Orient, which was erected to their lord by the excellent Zabda, commander-in-chief, and Zabbay, chief of the army of Tadmor in the month of August of the year 582.[4]

Forestalling action on the part of Rome, the two Palmyrene generals, Zabda and Zabbay, penetrated deep into Asia Minor.

[1] Cf. Zabad, 1 Ch. 7 : 21 ; a South Arabic word, " he (God) has given " ; Ryckmans, vol. i, p. 83. North Arabic *Wahab* has same meaning.

[2] Probably a contraction of *Zabday*, a form of *Zabad*. Ezra 10 : 28 ; Neh. 3 : 20.

[3] Of the Seleucid era, beginning Oct. 1, 312 B.C. (see above, p. 237) ; J. Cantineau, *Inventaire des inscriptions de Palmyre*, fasc. i (1930), p. 27.

[4] Starcky, p. 49 ; cf. Chabot, p. 56 ; de Vogüé, pp. 28-9 ; Cooke, pp. 290-93 ; Cantineau, fasc. i, p. 25.

They stationed garrisons as far west as Ancyra (Ankara); even Chalcedon, opposite Byzantium, felt the presence of their troops.[1] Thus did the queen of the desert carve for herself and her son at the expense of Rome an empire, albeit abortive, that anticipated by four centuries that of the Umayyads.

Last days of Palmyra

At last the Roman emperor bestirred himself. This was Aurelian (270–75), whose vigorous arm restored order to the empire after a period of disturbance marked by invasions from Franks, Alemanni and Goths as well as Persians. Early in 272 Aurelian reduced the Palmyrene garrisons in Asia Minor and then proceeded against Syria. Antioch, which together with Seleucia was pro-Roman, offered but feeble resistance; Ḥimṣ, whose people harboured jealousy because of the primacy claimed by Palmyra, was occupied after some resistance. Zenobia and Zabda, whose heavy cavalry was outmanœuvred by the light cavalry and infantry of Aurelian, retired to Palmyra.[2] The desert way to the capital was now open before the invading enemy. Aurelian took time to set up in Ḥimṣ new shrines to the sun-god of Elagabalus,[3] and on his return to Rome built a special temple for him in which Syrian rites were practised.

Aurelian laid siege to Palmyra. His troops were reinforced by Egyptians, but Zenobia received no aid, not even from Persia. The besiegers were pelted with stones, darts and fire-balls. The queen first rejected the mild terms of surrender offered by Aurelian but then realized she was fighting a losing battle and sought safety in flight on a dromedary by night. Pursuing horsemen overtook her when attempting to cross the Euphrates.[4] Her son had already fallen defending his city. Palmyra had no choice but to surrender. The conqueror despoiled it of its rich fabrics and precious ornaments, some of which were taken to embellish the new sun temple at Rome. The populace was punished only to the extent of the imposition of a fine and a Roman governor with a body of archers.

Among other royal advisers Longinus paid for his life at Ḥimṣ for the encouragement he had given the queen to throw off Roman tutelage. On reaching the Hellespont on his way back home (late 272), Aurelian heard of a fresh uprising in

[1] Mommsen, *Provinces of the Roman Empire*, vol. ii, p. 107.
[2] Zosimus, Bk. I, § 52.
[3] See above, p. 344.
[4] Vopiscus in *Scriptores*, Bk. XXVI, ch. 28

Palmyra resulting in the murder of his governor and the overpowering of its garrison.[1] He rushed back, took the city by surprise, destroyed it and put its inhabitants to the sword. The Bel temple was spared. Zenobia was taken to Rome with one son.[2] Loaded with jewels and led by golden chains, she was made to grace the triumphal entry of Aurelian into his capital in 274. She was presented with a villa near Tibur (Tivoli), where she spent the remaining years of her life. There she remarried, probably a Roman, and left children.[3]

Palmyra fell into insignificance, except for short periods of restoration under Diocletian (284–305) and Justinian (527–65) and gradually it drifted into obscurity; despite an occasional reference as the seat of a bishopric, as its people relaxed their grip on the desert, the desert overcame them. This has always been the case. In modern times the whole populace was housed inside the remains of the old temple, a ghost of its ancient self, overlooking the magnificent ruins of their ancestors' home. In 1929 the French made the people evacuate the place and build a village outside. A military airport and barracks for the *méharistes* (camel corps) were also built.

Monumental ruins

The remains of Palmyra stand today as the most imposing sight in the desert. They attract and fascinate lovers of antiquity from all over the world. The temple of Bel, standing on a raised terrace, has been converted into a sort of museum. In it figures of women, veiled and participating in a religious ceremony, have been found.[4] In front of the temple stood the monumental arch, which opened to the grand colonnade. This avenue of columns, 1240 yards in length, formed the main axis of the town with minor streets branching off from it. Of its 375 or more columns, each 55 feet high, about 150 are wholly or partly extant. Most of them are of rosy white limestone with Corinthian capitals. A few are of granite speckled with blue, indicating Egyptian (Uswān) origin. To the columns were attached consoles decorated with statues erected in honour of meritorious citizens, a peculiarity of Palmyrene architecture. Palmyrene busts as a rule are frontal, not profile, show wide open eyes and bear an inscription above the shoulder. The royalty and aristocracy appear dressed in Greek garb, the

[1] Zosimus, Bk. I, § 6.
[2] Zosimus, Bk. I ,§ 59.
[3] Pollio in *Scriptores*, Bk. XXIV, ch. 27.
[4] Cf. above, p. 74, coin.

PALMYRA: THE COLONNADE AND TRIUMPHAL ARCH

commonalty in Parthian.[1] A cupbearer has been found wearing Parthian costume and another figure with a Roman toga.

Equally peculiar are the tombs, or "houses of eternity" — to use a Palmyrene expression.[2] They rise outside the city like

From Chabot, " Inscriptions de Palmyre " (Imprimerie Nationale, Paris)

A PALMYRENE FATHER AND THREE CHILDREN, *ca.* A.D. 170

The father, beardless and with uncovered head, holds a vase in his left hand and a bunch of dates or bananas in his right. His son, between the two daughters, holds a bird in his left hand and a cluster of grapes in his right. The two girls wear veils which do not cover the face. The inscription near the left arm of the man gives his name: Zabdibōl, son of Moqīmu, son of Nūrbēl, son of Zabda, son of ʿAbday, [son of Zabdi]bōl. The names of the children from right to left are: Tadmōr, his daughter; Moqīmu, his son; Aliyat, his daughter

lofty towers, comprising chambers in stories and adorned inside with colours and the sculptured portraits of the deceased. Dura-Europus has a few tomb towers.

The frescoes of Palmyra[3] and Dura are of special signifi-

[1] For illustrations consult Henri Seyrig, *Antiquités syriennes*, ser. 2 (Paris, 1938), pp. 51 *seq.*

[2] Harald Ingholt, " Five Dated Tombs from Palmyra ", *Berytus*, vol. ii (1935), pp. 60, 109.

[3] Consult Harald Ingholt, " Quelques Fresques récemment découvertes à Palmyre ", *Acta Archaeologica*, vol. iii (1932), pp. 1-20.

cance for the history of art. They serve to bridge the gap between the ancient Semitic art of Assyro-Babylonia and Phoenicia and early Christian art. Through them may be traced the beginnings of Oriental influences over Greco-Roman paintings, thus preparing the way for the advent of Byzantine art.

Language

The Palmyrene was a peculiar culture, a blend of Syrian, Greek and Persian elements. The original inhabitants were doubtless Arabian tribes who adopted in their speech and writing the prevalent Aramaic tongue. The bulk of the population remained Arab though mixed with Aramaeans. Native inscriptions do not date earlier than 9 B.C., when the city was on the way to becoming an outstanding trade post. Originally the cursive of the Aramaic-writing people of Seleucid Syria of the first pre-Christian century, the Palmyrene script did not develop any radical differences. Public acts were set up in both Greek and Aramaic. The Greek duplication has facilitated the reading of the Aramaic. Palmyra gave Hungary one inscription and Great Britain another. The British inscription was left by a Palmyrene who married a British wife and made a representation of her. Palmyrene archers were employed by Romans in places as distant as Morocco and Britain.

The dialect spoken by the Palmyrenes belonged to Western Aramaic rather than to Eastern Aramaic (that of Edessa). It was virtually the same as that used in Syria, Nabataea and Egypt, not different from the one spoken by Christ. The cultured class, no doubt, spoke Greek as well as Aramaic. Arabic was presumably understood by men in business and used by some Palmyrenes as a vernacular.

Longinus

Other than Dionysius Cassius Longinus (213–73) Palmyra boasted no man of high intellectual calibre. Probably a native of Ḥimṣ, Longinus studied first in Alexandria and then in Athens, where he had as a pupil the celebrated Porphyry.[1] His mother was Syrian and he knew Syriac.[2] A contemporary of Longinus was Aemelius of Apamea.[3] In an age of rhetorical phrase-makers and fanciful quibblers this Palmyrene philosopher stands solitary. So extensive was his knowledge that he

[1] See above, p. 324.
[2] Vopiscus in *Scriptores*, Bk. XXVI, ch. 30.
[3] See above, p. 324.

was styled by a contemporary as " a living library and a walking museum ".[1] It was Longinus who taught Zenobia Greek literature and then became her adviser. Unfortunately only fragments and quotations from his works survive.[2] They show that he remained a pagan, though not hostile to Judaism or Christianity. His execution at the hands of Aurelian he bore with a firmness and cheerfulness worthy of a Socrates.[3]

Palmyrene gods

The Palmyrene pantheon comprised an assortment of deities from Syria, Arabia, Persia and Babylon, some of whom bore additional Latin names. In essence the religion did not differ from that of North Syria and its desert. Bel dominated the scene. He was not exactly a solar but a cosmic god of Babylonian origin, corresponding to Marduk. He presided over the destinies of man and had charge of the celestial gods. The great temple was dedicated to him. He was later identified with Zeus. Another temple in Palmyra was dedicated to Baal-Shamīn (the lord of heavens).[4] He, like Bel, had a temple in Dura, where he is cited in a votive inscription of A.D. 32.[5] Several altars have been found in Palmyra dedicated to Shamash (Samas, sun). This solar deity is sometimes represented on one side of Bel with the lunar deity on the other. ʿAgli-bōl (the calf of Bōl) was the name of the moon-god.[6] In certain figures he appears with a crescent over his shoulders.[7] Yarkhi-bōl, judging by the first part of his name, must have also been a lunar god; but he was the one who rendered oracles, a correspondent of Apollo. Malak-bel (the angel of Bel) was the messenger god, analogous to Hermes. An interesting altar has been found dedicated to " the anonymous god, the good and compassionate ".[8]

The inscriptions comprise several religious dedications to

[1] Philostratus and Eunapius, p. 355.

[2] Whether the Longinus, author of *On the Sublime*, which still figures in English university curricula, is this man or not is still uncertain.

[3] Zosimus, Bk. I, § 56.

[4] Cf. above, p. 174. Consult Chabot, p. 43; Henri Seyrig, " Antiquités syriennes ", *Syria*, vol. xiv (1933), pp. 246 *seq.*

[5] Du Mesnil du Buisson, *Inventaire des inscriptions palmyréniennes de Doura-Europos* (Paris, 1939), pp. 13-14; Chabot, pp. 43, 73-5; Rostovtzeff *et al.*, *Excavations at Dura-Europos*, vols. vii-viii, pp. 299 *seq.*, pl. xxxvii.

[6] Chabot, pp. 71-3; Cooke, pp. 269, 301-2; de Vogüé, p. 93.

[7] Chabot, p. 65.

[8] Harald Ingholt, " Inscriptions and Sculptures from Palmyra ", *Berytus*, vol. iii (1936), p. 92; cf. Acts 17 : 23.

Arṣu [1] and ʿAzīzu,[2] whose names indicate Arabian origin. The two are styled "the good and remunerating gods".[3] ʿAzīzu was also worshipped in Edessa and in Ḥawrān, the land of the Ghassānids. Allath, whose name formed a part of that of the last king of Palmyra, was the chief Arabian goddess.[4] She was also worshipped in the land of the Ghassānids. Another goddess in the Palmyrene pantheon was ʿAthar-ʿatheh (Atargatis), the Aramaean divinity, the chief centre of whose cult was at Hierapolis.[5] An altar erected by a Nabataean in Palmyra (A.D. 132) was dedicated to the Nabataean deity Shayʿ-al-Qawm (he who accompanies, protects, the people), evidently the special patron of caravans. The divinity is styled he "who does not drink wine".[6]

3. The Ghassānids

About the same time in which the Palmyrene state was passing away, a South Arabian tribe, so tradition asserts, was working its way into Ḥawrān. These were the banu-Ghassān, whose departure from al-Yaman was blamed on an early bursting of the Ma'rib dam.[7] In Ḥawrān they encountered earlier Arab settlers, the Ḍajāʿim of the Salīḥ tribe, whom they replaced as masters of the territory under Roman suzerainty. In the course of the fourth century the Ghassānids were Christianized.[8] The founder of their dynasty was one Jafnah ibn-ʿAmr Muzayqiyā', whose date is uncertain. In fact the whole history of the Jafnid dynasty is obscure. In Arabic chronicles the number of sovereigns varies from eleven to thirty-two; [9] in Byzantine histories the main point of interest is contact with Constantinople. Only the last five monarchs, whose reigns

[1] Raḍu of the Safaitic inscriptions, meaning favour, grace. See above, p. 299; below, p. 403, n. 3.

[2] Ar. *ʿazīz*, mighty; see *Berytus*, vol. iii (1936), pl. xxiv, 2.

[3] Chabot, p. 69.

[4] Koran 53: 19.

[5] Cooke, p. 268. See above, pp. 121, 173.

[6] Consult Chabot, pp. 67-8; Cooke, pp. 304-5.

[7] Hitti, *History of the Arabs*, pp. 64-5.

[8] Certain Christian families living today in Syria and Lebanon, e.g. the Maʿlūfs and the ʿAṭīyahs, trace their descent to the Ghassānids.

[9] Ibn-Qutaybah, *al-Maʿārif*, ed. F. Wüstenfeld (Göttingen, 1850), pp. 314-16; al-Masʿūdi, *Murūj al-Dhahab*, ed. and tr. C. B. de Meynard and P. de Courteille, vol. iii (Paris, 1864), pp. 217-21; Ḥamzah al-Iṣfahāni, *Ta'rīkh Sini Mulūk al-Arḍ w-al-Anbiyā'*, ed. Gottwaldt (Leipzig, 1844), pp. 115-22; abu-al-Fidā', *Ta'rīkh* (Constantinople, 1286), vol. i, pp. 76-7; cf. Th. Nöldeke, *Die Ghassânischen Fürsten aus dem Hause Gafna's* (Berlin, 1887), pp. 52-60; tr. Pendali José and Costi K. Zurayk, *The Princes of Ghassān from the House of Gafna* (Beirut, 1933), pp. 57-67.

cover the century preceding the birth of Islam, are fairly well known.

Al-Ḥārith ibn-Jabalah

First and greatest among these was al-Ḥārith ibn-Jabalah [1] (*ca.* 529–69), who makes his debut in 528 battling against the Lakhmid al-Mundhir III [2] of al-Ḥīrah. The Lakhmids, likewise of South Arabian origin, were domiciled along the western border of the Persian empire and used as a buffer state in the same way as the Ghassānids were used by the Byzantine. In recognition of his services the Emperor Justinian in the following year appointed al-Ḥārith lord over all the Arab tribes of Syria with the titles of phylarch and patricius, the highest next to that of the emperor himself. The Arabs rendered the titles as *malik*, king. The kings of Ghassān may have considered themselves successors of the kings of Nabataea.

Loyal to the Byzantine crown, al-Ḥārith continued his struggle against the Lakhmids, contributed to the suppression of the Samaritan rebellion and fought in the Byzantine army under Belisarius in Mesopotamia.[3] In 544 a son of his was taken prisoner by al-Mundhir and sacrificed to al-ʿUzza, Aphrodite's counterpart.[4] Ten years later in a decisive battle near Qinnasrīn (Chalcis), al-Ḥārith avenged himself by killing his Lakhmid adversary. This is probably the battle celebrated in Arabic histories as that of Ḥalīmah, after al-Ḥārith's daughter who is said to have with her own hands anointed her father's warriors with perfume prior to their engagement in the battle.[5] In 563 al-Ḥārith visited Justinian's court, where as an imposing Bedouin shaykh he left a lasting impression on the courtiers,[6] not unlike that left by the Suʿūdi Arabian princes in the course of their recent visits to the United States. Years after the event whenever the chamberlains wanted to quiet down Justinian's nephew and successor the moronic Justin, they would simply

[1] Sometimes referred to as al-Ḥārith II in distinction from his grandfather al-Ḥārith ibn-Thaʿlabah, a great-grandson of Jafnah. Arab historians call him al-Aʿraj, the lame.

[2] Alamoundaros of Greek historians; Alamoundaras in Procopius, Bk. I, ch. 17, § 47, where al-Ḥārith's name is rendered Arethas, son of Gabalas.

[3] Procopius, Bk. II, ch. 16, § 5; Malalas, ed. Dindorf, p. 435; see above, pp. 358, 372.

[4] Procopius, Bk. II, ch. 28, § 13.

[5] Ibn-al-Athīr, *al-Kāmil fi al-Taʾrīkh*, ed. C. J. Tornberg, vol. i (Leyden, 1871), p. 400; ibn-Qutaybah, pp. 314-15; cf. abu-al-Fidāʾ, vol. i, p. 84.

[6] Theophanes, *Chronographia*, ed. C. de Boor (Leipzig, 1883), p. 240.

shout: "Hush! Else we call al-Ḥārith".[1]

While in Constantinople al-Ḥārith secured the appointment of Yaʿqūb al-Bardaʿi [2] of Edessa as prelate of the Syrian Monophysite Church. During his and his son's reigns the new doctrine spread all over Syria. Jacob is said to have ordained a hundred thousand priests and installed eighty-nine bishops in that country. The kingdom then reached its height from near Petra to al-Ruṣāfah north of Palmyra and comprised al-Balqā', al-Ṣafa [3] and Ḥarrān. Buṣra, whose cathedral was built in 512, became the ecclesiastical capital of the region and stood preeminent as a trading centre. Moslem tradition made Muḥammad with his caravan pass through it to learn much of what he knew about Christianity. As for the political capital of the Jafnids it was evidently first a movable camp, after which it was fixed at al-Jābiyah [4] in the Jawlān and for some time at Jilliq [5] in southern Ḥawrān.

Al-Mundhir

Al-Ḥārith was succeeded by his son al-Mundhir (Alamoundaros, *ca.* 569–82) at about the same time in which Muḥammad was born. The son followed in the footsteps of the father. He promoted the cause of Monophysitism and battled against the Lakhmid vassals of Persia. His zeal for the rite considered unorthodox by Byzantium, however, alienated him from Justin, who even suspected his political loyalty. The emperor thereupon wrote a letter to his governor in Syria ordering him to dispose of al-Mundhir, but the secretary mistakenly addressed it to the victim himself instead of the letter intended for him in which he was politely requested by the emperor to visit the governor for consultation. After a period of alienation reconciliation was effected and the venerable phylarch with his two

[1] John of Ephesus, *Ecclesiastical History*, ed. William Cureton (Oxford, 1853), p. 151; tr. R. Payne Smith (Oxford, 1860), p. 174.

[2] See above, p. 372.

[3] This volcanic region (see above, p. 299) was occupied before this time by Arabs who left some six thousand inscriptions and monuments with figures of mounted lancers hunting gazelles The inscriptions mention Ythʿ (none other than Heb. Yēshûaʿ, Aram. Yeshûʿ, Ar. Yasūʿ, Jesus), Allāt and Allāh and according to the accepted view represent, with the Liḥyānite and Thamūdic scripts, a northward extension of South Arabic; F. V. Winnett, *A Study of the Lihyanite and Thamudic Inscriptions* (Toronto, 1937), pp. 53-4; René Dussaud, *Les Arabes en Syrie avant l'Islam* (Paris, 1907), pp. 66-7, 151.

[4] Dussaud, *Topographie*, pp. 332-3. The western gate of Damascus is still known by this name.

[5] Perhaps al-Kiswah, 10 miles south of Damascus; Dussaud, *Topographie*, pp. 317-18; Leone Caetani, *Annali dell' Islām*, vol. iii (Milan, 1910), p. 928.

sons visited Constantinople (580) and was received with great honour by the new emperor Tiberius II. The emperor even replaced the diadem on al-Mundhir's head with a crown. In the same year al-Mundhir burned the Lakhmid capital al-Ḥīrah.[1] Two years later, while attending the dedication of a church at Ḥūwārīn in response to an invitation from the governor of Syria, he was apprehended and sent with his wife and three children to Constantinople and thence to Sicily. The annual subsidy to the Jafnids was then cut off and all friendly relations terminated.

Anarchy

Under the leadership of al-Nuʿmān, al-Mundhir's eldest son, several raids were directed from the desert against Roman Syria. Finally al-Nuʿmān was himself tricked (*ca.* 584), as his father before him, and carried to Constantinople. The Ghassānid nationality was thereby broken up. The kingdom was split into several sections, each with a prince or princeling of its own. Some princes allied themselves with Persia; others maintained their independence; still others remained on the side of Byzantium. At this point the Greek chroniclers lose all interest in the subject; the Arab chronicles remain confused. Anarchy prevailed until Persia conquered Syria in 611–14.

Fourteen years later, when Heraclius drove the Persians out of the country, he possibly restored the old dynasty. In the war of the Moslem conquest the tribes of the former state of Ghassān were reported fighting on the Byzantine side.[2] The last Ghassānid prince, Jabalah ibn-al-Ayham, fought in 636 against the Moslem invaders in the decisive battle of the Yarmūk,[3] but later adopted Islam. In the course of his first pilgrimage, we are told, a Bedouin stepped on his cloak and was slapped by him. The caliph decreed that the prince should either submit to a similar blow from the Bedouin or pay a fine, and Jabalah renounced the new faith and retired to Byzantium.[4]

The grandeur of the Ghassānid court

The glowing splendour of the Jafnid court has been immortalized in the anthologies of several pre-Islamic poets who found in its princes munificent patrons. One of these bards was

[1] Cf. al-Ṭabari, *Taʾrīkh al-Rusul w-al-Mulūk*, ed. M. J. de Goeje, vol. i (Leyden, 1879–81), p. 1021; abu-al-Faraj al-Iṣbahāni, *al-Aghāni*, vol. ii (Būlāq, 1285), p. 27.

[2] See below, p. 414.

[3] Al-Balādhuri, *Futūḥ al-Buldān*, ed. M. J. de Goeje (Leyden, 1866), p. 136; tr. Philip K. Hitti, *Origins of the Islamic State* (New York, 1915), pp. 208-9.

[4] Ibn-ʿAbd-Rabbihi, *al-ʿIqd al-Farīd* (Cairo, 1302), vol. i, pp. 140-41; cf. ibn-Qutaybah, p. 316.

the celebrated al-Nābighah al-Dhubyāni. After falling out with the Lakhmids, al-Nābighah won the good graces of the Ghassānids and was showered with their largess, while reciprocating by singing their praises. In an oft-quoted verse he extols their military prowess:

> No fault is theirs — save that their swords
> Are dull from striking hostile hosts.[1]

Another poet, the Medinese Ḥassān ibn-Thābit, before becoming poet laureate of the Prophet, spent happy days in the court of the Ghassānids, with whom he claimed kinship. From a description ascribed to him in *al-Aghāni*,[2] we catch a glimpse of the luxurious surroundings of Jabalah ibn-al-Ayham:

> There I saw ten female singers, of whom five were singing in Greek to the music of lutes and five chanting airs of the people of al-Ḥīrah. . . . There were also Arab singers who had come from Mecca and elsewhere. Whenever he sat to drink wine he had spread under him a mattress of myrtle, jasmine and other varieties of sweet-smelling flowers. Ambergris and musk were offered in vessels of gold and silver (it was the real musk that was offered in those silver vessels). In winter aloes-wood was burned for his comfort; in summer ice was used. He and his courtiers wore in the hot season specially made light robes, and in the cold season white heavy furs or the like. And by Allah, never was I once in his company but he bestowed on me the robe he was wearing that day.[3]

When this Jabalah embraced Islam and made his ceremonial entry with his courtiers into Medina, he is said to have worn the ancestral crown adorned with two pearls which once formed ear-rings for al-Ḥārith ibn-Jabalah's mother.[4] These pearls, each the size of a pigeon's egg, became proverbial in Arabic literature.[5]

Such reports, though exaggerated, imply a flourishing

[1] Al-Nābighah al-Dhubyāni, *Dīwān*, ed. M. Hartwig Derembourg (Paris, 1869), p. 78; cf. Charles J. Lyall, *Translations of Ancient Arabian Poetry* (New York, 1930), p. 96.

[2] Vol. xvi, p. 15. Though apocryphal the description is doubtless based on the poet's odes; cf. his *Dīwān*, ed. Hartwig Hirschfeld (Leyden, 1910), pp. 16-17, 45, 55; *'Iqd*, vol. i, p. 142.

[3] Cf. Reynold A. Nicholson, *A Literary History of the Arabs*, 2nd ed. (Cambridge, 1930), p. 53.

[4] Called in *Aghāni*, vol. xiv, p. 4, " Māriyah ", which under Aramaic influence may have been a title equivalent to lady, rather than a personal name. This lady's name may have been Māwiyah as in *Aghāni*, vol. xvi, p. 103.

[5] Al-Maydāni, *Majma' al-Amthāl* (Cairo, 1310), vol. i, p. 156.

economic condition. The Ghassānids must have mastered the technique necessary for the full utilization of rain water and exploitation of underground sources, a technique which was acquired by Syrians in the Roman period and lost thereafter. The remains of some three hundred towns and villages on the eastern and southern slopes of Ḥawrān testify to this fact.[1] What is more significant, however, is the fact that the Ghassānids, like their Nabataean predecessors, mediated certain vital elements of Syrian culture to their original kinsmen in Arabia, particularly al-Ḥijāz — future cradle of Islam. The Nabataeans transmitted those letters which made the writing of the Koran possible.[2] The Ghassānids before passing away passed on Christian ideas which with other ideas germinated into Islam.[3] Thus did Syrian culture provide Islam with the germ of creative power as it had provided Judaism and Christianity before it. Moreover, these border Syrian states of Arabian origin, last among which was the Ghassānid, paved the way in a sense for the ensuing conquest of Syria by Arabians under the banner of Islam. They served as a pre-view of the gigantic show soon to come.

[1] See above, p. 43.

[2] See above, p. 384.

[3] The tradition about Muḥammad cited above (p. 403) at least has that much truth in it.

PART IV

THE ARAB ERA

CHAPTER XXX

SYRIA IN THE EMBRACE OF ISLAM

On the eve of Islam

TWO episodes of late ancient times stand out in significance: the migration of the Teutonic tribes which resulted in the destruction of the Roman Empire in the West, and the eruption of the Moslem Arabian tribes which annihilated the empire of the Persians and stripped the Byzantine of its fairest provinces. Of the two the Arabian episode was the more phenomenal. At the time of its occurrence Persia and Byzantium were the only two world powers; the Arabians were nobody. Who living then could have guessed that such a happening was within the realm of possibility?

In 628, after six years of war with several reverses, Heraclius, whose ancestral home was Edessa (al-Ruhā') in North Syria, succeeded in recovering Syria, which had passed into Persian hands. Chosroes II had swept over the country (611–14) carrying plunder and destruction wherever he passed. He pillaged Damascus and decimated its people by murder and captivity. The Church of the Holy Sepulchre he left in ruins; its treasures, including the true cross, he carried off as booty. On September 14, 629, the triumphant Byzantine emperor restored this cross to Jerusalem [1] and was hailed deliverer of Christendom and restorer of the unity of the Eastern Empire.

Preliminary raids

Meantime a band of 3000 Arabians was carrying a raid into a town east of the southern end of the Dead Sea called Mu'tah.[2] The leader was Zayd ibn-Ḥārith, adopted son of Muḥammad. The object was ostensibly to avenge the murder, by a Ghassānid, of an emissary sent by the Prophet to Buṣra, actually to gain for the new converts rich booty including the coveted Mashrafīyah swords manufactured in that neighbourhood.[3] The policy of

[1] The occasion is still celebrated with bonfires by the Christians of Lebanon.

[2] In Transjordan, two hours' journey south of al-Karak; visited by Alois Musil; see his *Arabia Petraea*, vol. i (Vienna, 1907), p. 152.

[3] Consult Yāqūt, vol. iv, p. 536; M. J. de Goeje, *Mémoire sur la conquête de la Syrie* (Leyden, 1900), p. 5.

attacking border countries thus inaugurated by Muḥammad was calculated to make the new religion popular among the believers. Zayd fell on the battlefield. The remnant of his army was led back to Medina by young Khālid ibn-al-Walīd,[1] soon to become the champion of militant Islam. To the natives the attack on Mu'tah was but another of the frequent Bedouin raids to which they had long been accustomed. In reality it was the first shot in a struggle that was not to cease until Byzantium itself had surrendered and the name of the Arabian Prophet substituted for that of Christ on its cathedrals.

In the following year (630) Muḥammad led in person an expedition against the oasis of Tabūk [2] in northern al-Ḥijāz, whence he opened negotiations with neighbouring settlements which led to their submission. The people were granted security and the right to retain their property and profess their religion on condition that they paid an annual tribute. First among those settlements was Aylah (Aila) at the head of the Gulf of al-ʿAqabah,[3] whose population was Christian. South of it on the gulf stood Maqna,[4] with a Jewish population mostly engaged in weaving and fishing. Another was Adhruḥ, with a population of about a hundred families, which lay between Petra and Maʿān. An hour's journey to the north of Adhruḥ, on the ancient Roman road from Buṣra to the Red Sea, lay al-Jarbā', whose people were also Christians. The site later played a part in the Crusades. These were the only places in Syria with which Islam established contact in the lifetime of the Prophet. The terms of their capitulation [5] are suggestive of what was to come. The attempt on these settlements in southern Syria by Muḥammad was but a rehearsal for what was to follow under his successors.

The year after the death of the Prophet, the stage was set for

[1] Ṭabari, vol. i, p. 1610; cf. Theophanes, p. 336; J. Wellhausen, *Skizzen und Vorarbeiten*, vol. vi (Berlin, 1899), p. 52.

[2] On the pilgrimage road and now the railroad between Damascus and Medina. Al-Wāqidi, *al-Maghāzi*, ed. A. von Kremer (Calcutta, 1855–6), pp. 425-6; Yāqūt, vol. i, pp. 824-5; Balādhuri, p. 59; tr., p. 92; Caetani, vol. ii, pp. 238 *seq.* For a description of the modern village consult Jaussen and Savignac, pp. 57-64; Alois Musil, *The Northern Ḥeǧâz* (New York, 1926), pp. 234-7, 318-19.

[3] See above, p. 190; Caetani, vol. ii, pp. 253-5.

[4] Yāqūt, vol. iv, p. 610. For a modern description of this oasis consult Musil, *Northern Ḥeǧâz*, pp. 114-16, 312.

[5] Balādhuri, pp. 59-60; tr., pp. 92-4.

a full-dress invasion of neighbouring lands. Arabia had just concluded its so-called wars of apostasy [1] and was consolidated and unified under the leadership of one man, the first caliph abu-Bakr (632–4). The momentum acquired in these internal wars had to seek new outlets, especially since the new religion had supposedly converted its adherents into one brotherhood. The martial spirit of the tribes, to whom raids [2] were a sort of national sport from time immemorial, could not but assert itself in some form after Islam. Then there was the expectation of collaboration on the part of the Arabian tribes domiciled in southern Syria. These tribes, such as the Judhām and Quḍāʿah,[3] were by this time Christianized but not satisfied. The annual subsidy which for years they had been receiving for guarding the frontiers had recently been suspended by Heraclius as a measure of economy.[4] The forts along that southern border had also been neglected and stripped of their garrisons to enable concentration in the north in face of the Persian danger. Syria was the nearest arena.

The invasion begins

To it three detachments were led in 633 by ʿAmr ibn-al-ʿAṣ, Yazīd ibn-abi-Sufyān and Shuraḥbīl ibn-Ḥasanah.[5] ʿAmr, future hero of the Egyptian campaign, was to be the commander-in-chief in case of unified operation. The standard-bearer in Yazīd's army was his brother Muʿāwiyah, future founder of the Umayyad dynasty in Damascus. The route followed by Yazīd and Shuraḥbīl was the much-frequented Tabūk-Maʿān one, that by ʿAmr was the coast route via Aylah. The detachments were later augmented from about 3000 to some 7500 each. Abu-ʿUbaydah ibn-al-Jarrāḥ, who later became generalissimo, probably came at the head of one of the reinforcements.

The first engagement took place at Wādi al-ʿArabah,[6] the great depression south of the Dead Sea. There Sergius, patrician of Palestine with headquarters at Caesarea, suffered a defeat at the hands of Yazīd. His retreating army was overtaken at Dāthin,

[1] *riddah*; Hitti, *History of the Arabs*, pp. 140-42; C. H. Becker in *The Cambridge Medieval History* (New York, 1913), vol. ii, pp. 334-6.

[2] *ghazw*, whence English razzia.

[3] The Saliḥ (above, p. 401) were a clan of Quḍāʿah. The ʿĀmilah were at this time settled a little farther north, whence they later spread into southern Lebanon, still called Jabal (mountain of) ʿĀmil—ʿĀmilah in abu-al-Fidā', *Taqwīm*, p. 228.

[4] Theophanes, p. 335.

[5] Balādhuri, pp. 107-8; tr., p. 165; de Goeje, pp. 21-4.

[6] See above, p. 36 map.

near Gaza, and almost annihilated (February 4, 634).[1] Sergius himself lost his life. The way was now temporarily clear. Yazīd and ʿAmr raided the entire southern part of Palestine. Even Caesarea was threatened. Jerusalem was cut off from the sea.[2]

Khālid's perilous crossing

On receiving the news Heraclius, who was still in Emesa (Ḥimṣ), where reportedly he had received a message from the Prophet summoning him to Islam, hastened to organize and dispatch a fresh army under his brother Theodorus. Meantime Khālid ibn-al-Walīd received orders from abu-Bakr to rush from al-ʿIrāq to the reinforcement of the army on the Syrian front. The raid on al-ʿIrāq began shortly before that on Syria, but Syria being closer to al-Ḥijāz was of greater concern.

Khālid probably started his perilous march across the desert from al-Ḥīrah, which with other places had capitulated to him. The track he followed was presumably the south-westward one leading to Dūmat[3] al-Jandal (modern al-Jawf), midway between the two countries. Once in Dūmah he could have continued through Baṭn al-Sirr (Wādi al-Sirḥān) to Buṣra, eastern gateway of Syria; but forts lay on the way. He, therefore, followed the north-western route to Qurāqir (Qulbān Qarāqir) on the eastern boundary of the Baṭn. Thence he pushed northward to Suwa,[4] a journey of five days in almost waterless desert. Water for the troops, who numbered five to eight hundred, was carried in bags; but for the horses the paunches of camels served as reservoirs. This camel water could also be used by men in case of emergency. The horses were led alongside and intended for use only at the time of the encounter. The guide, one Rāfiʿ ibn-ʿUmayr of the Ṭayyiʾ tribe, was at one point so dazzled by the rays of the sun that he could not spot the expected sign for underground water. So he besought the troops to look for a box-thorn (*ʿawsaj*) and as they dug near it, they struck damp soil with water. Thus was the

[1] Yāqūt, vol. ii, pp. 514-15; Balādhuri, p. 109; tr., pp. 167-8; de Goeje, pp. 31-4; Caetani, vol. ii, pp. 1141-54.

[2] The Arabic records of the war of conquest, compiled two to three centuries after the events, are confused in chronology, fact and evaluation. The reconstruction followed here is based on Caetani, de Goeje, Wellhausen, Becker and other modern critical scholars.

[3] Mentioned in Gen. 25:14; Is. 21:11.

[4] Near modern Sabʿ Biyār (seven wells), north-east of Damascus.

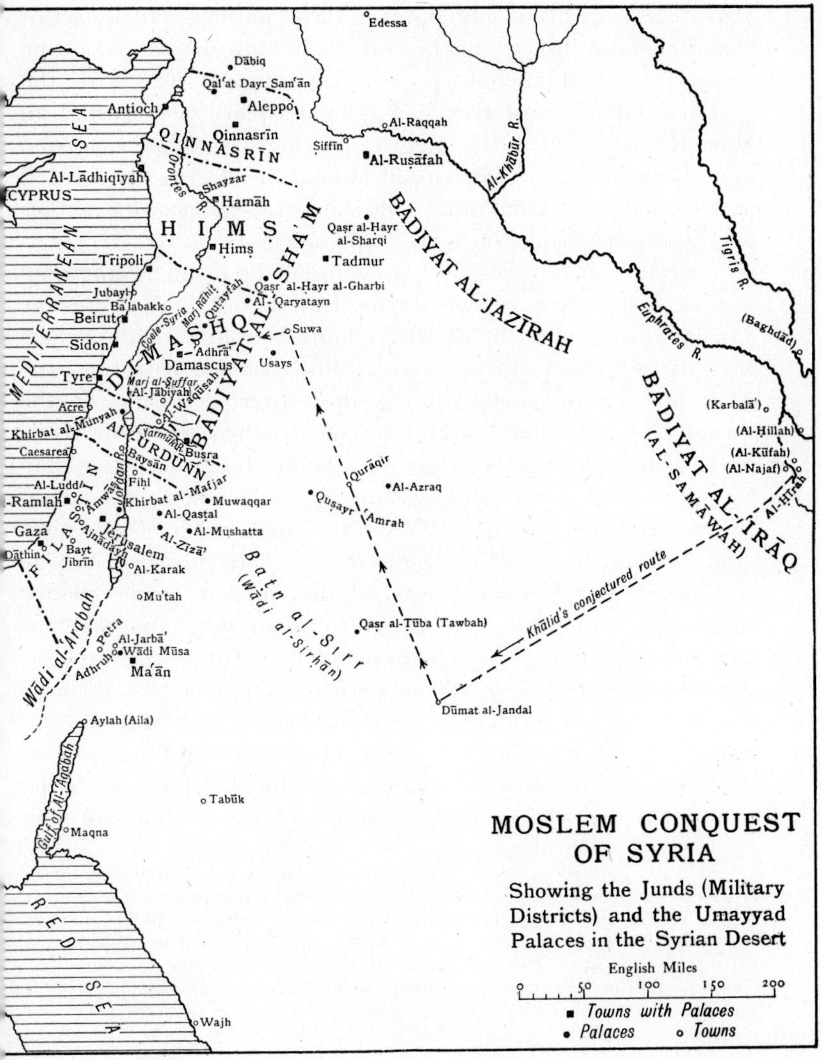

MOSLEM CONQUEST OF SYRIA

Showing the Junds (Military Districts) and the Umayyad Palaces in the Syrian Desert

army saved and an unparalleled feat in the desert saga achieved.[1]

With dramatic suddenness Khālid made his appearance (April 24, 634), after only eighteen days' journey, north-east of Damascus and directly in the rear of the improvised Byzantine army. His first encounter, a successful one, was with the Christian Ghassānid forces on Easter at a place near 'Adhrā' in Marj Rāhiṭ.[2] Shrewd strategist that he was, Khālid pressed southward through Transjordan aiming at effecting a junction with the harassed army of his fellow-generals; desire for neither self-aggrandizement nor booty could sidetrack him.

Damascus surrenders

The combined forces, perhaps with Khālid in chief command, won a bloody victory at Ajnādayn[3] (July 30, 634). All Palestine now lay open before the invader. For six months random raids were carried on in all directions. Buṣra yielded with but little resistance. Fiḥl,[4] commanding the eastern crossing of the Jordan, followed suit; so did Baysān on the other side of the river. The new Byzantine general Baanes fared no better than his predecessor. A month later the Byzantine army was again encountered and routed at Marj al-Ṣuffar,[5] whence it sought safety behind the walls of Damascus. Khālid pursued it. He laid siege to the future capital of the Moslem empire which simply meant that he endeavoured to isolate it, as the Arabians had not yet acquired the technique of the siege or implements. After six months the city surrendered (September 635) through treachery. The negotiators were the bishop and Manṣūr ibn-Sarjūn, grandfather of St. John the Damascene and high official in the finance department of the government. The traditional report that the city was conquered half by force (*'anwatan*) and

[1] Khālid's itinerary in Arabic sources presents many historical and geographical problems; cf. Balādhuri, pp. 110-12; tr., pp. 169-72; Ṭabari, vol. i, pp. 2111-13, 2121-4; ibn-al-Athīr, vol. ii, pp. 312-13; al-Ya'qūbi, *Ta'rīkh*, ed. M. Th. Houtsma (Leyden, 1883), vol. ii, pp. 150-51; ibn-'Asākir, *al-Ta'rīkh al-Kabīr* (Damascus), vol. i, p. 130; al-Baṣri, *Futūḥ al-Sha'm*, ed. W. N. Lees (Calcutta, 1854), pp. 63-5. The itinerary conjectured here is based on Musil, *Arabia Deserta*, pp. 553-73; Caetani, vol. ii, pp. 1220-36.

[2] A plain 15 miles from Damascus. Balādhuri, p. 112; tr., p. 172; Yāqūt, vol. iv, p. 1016.

[3] This otherwise unknown place should perhaps be emended to Jannābatayn, between al-Ramlah and Bayt Jibrīn (Eleutheropolis) on the Gaza-Jerusalem road. Caetani, vol. iii, pp. 176-87; Wellhausen, *Skizzen*, vol. vi, pp. 57-8; Dussaud, *Topographie*, p. 318.

[4] Or Faḥl, Gr. Pella, Bi-hi-lim of the 'Amārnah tablets (above, p. 71), now Kkirbat Faḥil. Caetani, vol. iii, pp. 187-211; Abel, vol. ii, pp. 34, 405.

[5] A plain 20 miles south of Damascus.

half by capitulation (*ṣulḥan*) has all the earmarks of being a late one intended to justify the partition of the cathedral by the Umayyads.[1] The terms of surrender embodied the same principles as those exacted by the Prophet[2] and established a precedent for dealing with other Syrian towns:

In the name of Allah, the compassionate, the merciful. This is what Khālid ibn-al-Walīd would grant to the inhabitants of Damascus if he enters therein: he promises to give them security for their lives, property and churches. Their city wall shall not be demolished, neither shall any Moslem be quartered in their houses. Thereunto we give to them the pact of Allah and the protection of His Prophet, the caliphs and the believers. So long as they pay the poll tax, nothing but good shall befall them.[3]

With the fall of the Syrian metropolis, total victory was assured. Before the end of the year abu-ʿUbaydah had occupied Ḥimṣ. All neighbouring towns — Baʿlabakk, Ḥimṣ, Ḥamāh — opened their gates. In some cases, as that of Shayzar,[4] "The people went out to meet him accompanied by players on the tambourines and singers and bowed down before him". Only Jerusalem, Caesarea and certain coastal towns held out in expectation of aid from Heraclius.

Heraclius did not intend to disappoint them. Having mustered from the vicinity of Antioch and Aleppo an army of some fifty thousand, mostly Armenian and Arab mercenaries, he put it again under the command of his brother Theodorus assisted by Baanes.[5] Realizing the superiority of this army in numbers, Arabian generalship immediately relinquished Ḥimṣ, even Damascus and other strategic towns, and concentrated about 2500 men at the valley of the Yarmūk,[6] whence retreat to the desert would be assured if forced. Heraclius' army took the Coele-Syria-Transjordan route. After a period of skirmishing, in the course of which Baanes was declared emperor by the troops, the battle was joined. The locale was at the juncture of the Yarmūk with its tributary al-Ruqqād near al-Wāqūṣah (modern al-Yāqūṣah). The climax came on a hot day (August,

[1] Caetani, vol. iii, pp. 359-92. See below, pp. 513-15.
[2] See above, p. 410.
[3] Balādhuri, p. 121; tr., p. 187.
[4] Larissa, modern Sayjar, on the Orontes, 15 miles north-west of Ḥamāh. See below, pp. 621-2.
[5] Theophanes, p. 337; Ṭabari, vol. i, p. 2125.
[6] Hieromax, now Sharīʿat al-Manādhirah (after a Bedouin tribe; Abel, vol. i, p. 171), tributary of the Jordan; not to be confused with Jarmuth of Josh. 10: 3, modern Khirbat Yarmūk, near Ajnādayn.

20, 636) with a dust storm before which the Arabians were at a decided advantage. The Byzantine troops were manœuvred into a tight position between the two streams. On the west the bridge of al-Ruqqād was occupied by the Arabians; on the east the line of communication was also cut off. All chances of retreat were thus nullified. The chants and prayers of the priests and the use of the crosses were of no avail.[1] Before the onslaught of the sons of the desert Armenian and Syro-Arab mercenaries could not hold their own. Some were slaughtered then and there. Others were driven relentlessly into the river. Still others deserted and were caught and annihilated on the other side. Theodorus was one of the victims. The fate of Syria was sealed. Even Heraclius admitted it. "Farewell, O Syria", were his last words, "and what an excellent country this is for the enemy!"[2]

In the autumn of the same year a contingent, probably under abu-ʿUbayadah, reoccupied Damascus. All other cities previously occupied now received the conqueror with open arms. "We like your rule and justice", declared the natives of Ḥimṣ, "far better than the state of tyranny and oppression under which we have been living."[3] Farther north Aleppo and Antioch were soon reduced. Only Qinnasrīn put up some resistance. Finally the Taurus Mountains, natural boundary of Syria, put a stop to the uninterrupted advance of Arabian arms.

Jerusalem and Caesarea reduced

Other generals were operating with equal success in the interior and along the coast. Shuraḥbīl reduced Acre and Tyre.[4] Yazīd and his brother Muʿāwiyah acquired Sidon, Beirut, Jubayl and Tripoli.[5] In the south Jerusalem and Caesarea (Qaysārīyah), both Hellenized, persisted in their resistance. Jerusalem held out against ʿAmr till 638, when its people stipulated that ʿUmar, who was then visiting in al-Jābiyah, receive the capitulation in person.[6] The problem of Caesarea was complicated by the fact that the city was accessible to naval aid. At last it fell in 640, after seven years of intermittent attacks climaxed by a

[1] Ibn-ʿAsākir, vol. i, p. 163; Baṣri, p. 197.

[2] Balādhuri, p. 137; tr., p. 210; cf. Ṭabari, vol. i, pp. 2395-6.

[3] Balādhuri, p. 137; tr., p. 211. Almost the same sentiments were attributed to the natives of Fiḥl; Baṣri, p. 97.

[4] Balādhuri, p. 116; tr., p. 179; de Goeje, p. 133.

[5] Balādhuri, p. 126; tr., p. 194; Caetani, vol. iii, p. 801.

[6] Ṭabari, vol. i, pp. 2402 *seq.*; Balādhuri, pp. 138-9; tr., pp. 213-14; Yaʿqūbi, vol. ii, pp. 167-8; de Goeje, pp. 152 *seq.*

siege conducted by Muʿāwiyah.[1] The treachery of a Jew inside its walls contributed to the final fall. In those seven years (633–40) the entire country from south to north was subdued.

"Easy conquest"

This "easy conquest"[2] of a strategic province of the Byzantine empire is not difficult to explain. The military structure of that empire had been as effectively undermined by the Persian incursions of the early seventh century as the spiritual unity of its society had been disrupted by the Monophysite schism of the middle fifth. Heraclius' last minute effort (638) to bridge the religious gap by offering a compromise was as fruitless as earlier ones. The compromise was devised by his patriarch Sergius, a Syrian of Jacobite lineage, and aimed at glossing over the controversial issue of the nature of Christ and emphasizing his one will (*thelēma*). The new formula satisfied neither the Byzantine orthodox nor the Syrian dissenters. In fact it resulted in the creation of a new sect, the Monothelites, who maintained that Christ had but one will, the divine. The bulk of the Syrians held on to their Church. To them it was more than a religious institution; it was an expression of a submerged, semi-articulate feeling of nationality.

At no time since Alexander's conquest, as we learned before,[3] did the people of Syria, as a people, lose their national character, their native tongue, their Semitic religion, and identify themselves wholeheartedly with the Greco-Roman way of life. At its thickest Hellenistic culture was only skin-deep, affecting a crust of intelligentsia in urban settlements. The bulk of the population must throughout that millennium have considered the rulers aliens. The alienation between rulers and ruled was no doubt aggravated by misrule and high taxation. To the masses of seventh century Syria the Moslem Arabians must have appeared closer ethnically, linguistically and perhaps religiously than the hated Byzantine masters.

The administrator replaces the warrior

Now that all Syria is conquered, the general must give way to the administrator. Khālid, whose brilliant military record in Arabia, al-ʿIrāq and Syria had entitled him to the appellation "the sword of Allah", was replaced on orders from the Caliph

[1] Balādhuri, pp. 140-42; tr., pp. 215-19; de Goeje, pp. 166-9; Caetani, vol. iv, pp. 156-63.

[2] Balādhuri, p. 16, l. 18, p. 126, ll. 13, 19; tr., p. 179, l. 17, p. 193, l. 22, p. 194, l. 7.

[3] Above, pp. 254, 256-7, 281, 287-8.

'Umar by abu-'Ubaydah, distinguished Companion of the Prophet, and member of the triumvirate which had monopolized Islamic authority.[1] The two other members were abu-Bakr and 'Umar. 'Umar had succeeded abu-Bakr as caliph shortly after the battle of Ajnādayn in 634 and evidently harboured ill feeling against Khālid, but did not entrust the supreme command to his friend abu-'Ubaydah until after the Yarmūk battle. Khālid withdrew from public life to Ḥimṣ. There he died in oblivion (642) to live in tradition as a miracle worker. His shrine and mosque were built in 1908 in Turkish style. His wife Faḍā' was buried with him.

When in 638 'Umar visited the Moslem camp in al-Jābiyah to solemnize the conquest and determine the status of the conquered, he not only confirmed abu-'Ubaydah in his position as generalissimo but appointed him governor-general and vice-regent. The aged caliph's entry into Jerusalem riding on a camel and wearing shabby raiment did not leave a favourable impression.[2] He was received by the patriarch and "honey-tongued defender of the church" Sophronius, who is said to have turned to an attendant and remarked in Greek,[3] "Truly this is the abomination of desolation spoken of by Daniel the Prophet as standing in the holy place".[4]

Significance of the conquest

The conquest of Syria transcended local and temporary considerations. It gave the nascent power of Islam prestige before the world and confidence in itself.

With Syria as a base an Arab army under 'Iyāḍ ibn-Ghanm operated north-east and between 639 and 646 subjugated all Mesopotamia.[5] The way was thence open to north-west Persia and lands beyond; full advantage was taken thereof. Another army under 'Amr and other veterans of the Syrian campaign operated south-westward and between 640 and 646 subdued Egypt.[6] From Egypt operations were easily continued with the

[1] H. Lammens, "Le Triumvirat Aboû Bakr, 'Omar et Aboû 'Obaidah" *Mélanges de la faculté orientale*, vol. iv (Beirut, 1910), pp. 113 *seq.*

[2] De Goeje, p. 157; cf. Ṭabari, vol. i, p. 2407.

[3] Theophanes, p. 339; Constantine Porphyrogenitus, "De administrando imperio" in J.-P. Migne, *Patrologia Graeca*, vol. cxiii (Paris, 1864), col. 109. Sophronius was probably of Maronite origin.

[4] Dan. 9:27; 11:31; 12:1; quoted in Matt. 24:15; Mk. 13:14. The reference in Dan. is to Antiochus Epiphanes; see above, p. 244.

[5] Balādhuri, pp. 172 *seq.*; tr., pp. 269 *seq.*; Ṭabari, vol. i, pp. 2505-8.

[6] Hitti, *History of the Arabs*, pp. 160 *seq.* The same term *ghazw*, formerly used for petty tribal raids, was used for the national Moslem campaigns.

collaboration of Syrians into north-west Africa and ultimately into Spain. From northern Syria, Asia Minor was vulnerable to attacks which were carried on intermittently for almost a century.

Interpretation of the Islamic conquests

All these conquests, however, belong to the category of systematic campaigning rather than the casual raiding to which the earlier conquests belonged.[1] The initial campaigns into al-ʿIrāq and Syria were not the result of purposeful and far-sighted planning. Neither abu-Bakr nor ʿUmar, under whom most of these victories were achieved, held a war council, worked out a strategy or even dreamed — at least in the initial stages — of ever establishing a permanent foothold in the conquered territories. But the logic of events forced such an outcome. The armies were first not allowed to settle in cities; a camp near al-Jābiyah served as initial capital. In fact there is reason to believe that some of the early operations, like Khālid's campaign into al-ʿIrāq, may have been undertaken not only without caliphal orders but perhaps against them.

Nor should the Moslem conquests be viewed as primarily or mainly religious crusades. The classical interpretation of Moslem historians follows the theological interpretation by the Hebrews of their national history and by the medieval Christians of the expansion of the Church; it makes the movement predominantly religious and providentially determined. In reality the Arabian Islamic expansion had underlying economic causes.[2] This economic aspect did not fully escape the attention of judicious Arab historians like al-Balādhuri,[3] who declares that, in recruiting for the Syrian campaign, abu-Bakr "wrote to the people of Mecca, al-Ṭā'if, al-Yaman and all the Arabians in Najd and al-Ḥijāz summoning them to a holy war and arousing their desire for it and for the booty to be got from the Greeks".

Viewed in its proper perspective the Islamic expansion was one in a series of migrations, "waves", which carried a surplus population from a barren peninsula to a bordering fertile region with a more abundant life. In fact it was the last stage in the age-long process of infiltration which had begun with the Babylonians some four thousand years before.[4] The Islamic move-

[1] Hitti, *History of the Arabs*, pp. 160, 167-8.

[2] Worked out by Caetani, vol. ii, pp. 831-61, followed by Becker, Lammens and other modern critical scholars.

[3] P. 107; tr., p. 165.

[4] Consult above, pp. 62, 64.

ment, however, did possess one distinctive feature — religious impulse. Combined with the economic, this made the movement irresistible and carried it far beyond the confines of any preceding one. Islam admittedly provided a battle cry, a slogan comparable to that provided by " democracy " in the first and second world wars. More than that it served as a cohesive agency cementing tribes and heterogeneous masses never united before. But while the desire to spread the new faith or go to Paradise may have been the motivating force in the lives of some of the Bedouin warriors, the desire for the comforts and luxuries of settled life in the Fertile Crescent was the driving force in the case of many of them.

A corresponding and equally discredited hypothesis held by Christians portrays the Arabian Moslems as going around with the offer of the Koran in one hand and the sword in the other. In the case of *ahl al-kitāb* (people of the Book),[1] there was a third choice offered — tribute. " Make war . . . upon such of those to whom the Book has been given until they pay tribute offered on the back of their hands,[2] in a state of humiliation ".[3] It is important to remember that from the conquerors' point of view tribute was more desirable. Once a non-Moslem professes Islam tribute should no more be paid.

In historical significance the Moslem conquests of the first century rank with those of Alexander. The two stand out as the principal landmarks in the political and cultural history of the ancient Near East. For a thousand years after Alexander's conquest the civilized life of Syria and its neighbouring lands was oriented westward, across the sea; now the orientation changed eastward, across the desert. The last links with Rome and Byzantium were severed; new ones with Mecca and Medina were forged. Strictly the orientation was a reversion to an old type, for the Arab Moslem civilization did not introduce many original elements. It was rather a revivification of the ancient Semitic culture.[4] Thus viewed Hellenism becomes an intrusive phenomenon between two cognate layers.

In about a decade the Moslem conquests changed the face of

[1] See below, p. 422, n. 3.

[2] *'an yadin*, differently rendered ' out of hand ", " readily ", " by right of subjection ".

[3] Sūr. 9 : 29.

[4] Consult Hitti, *History of the Arabs*, pp. 174-5.

the Near East; in about a century they changed the face of the civilized world — something more than Alexander's conquests could claim. Far from being peripheral, the victories of Islam proved to be a decisive factor in the evolution of medieval society. They changed *mare nostrum* to a Moslem lake. Contact by sea between East and West was thus broken. This, coupled with the occupation of the eastern, the western and the southern shores of the Mediterranean, created a new world, that in which Charlemagne (768–814) and his contemporaries lived. Thereby ancient times ended and the Middle Ages began.[1]

[1] This is the thesis of Henri Pirenne, *Mahomet et Charlemagne*, 7th ed. (Brussels, 1935); do., *Histoire de l'Europe* (Paris, 1936), pp. 18-24.

CHAPTER XXXI

ARAB ADMINISTRATION

HOW to administer the new domain was the next question. The Arabians awoke after the intoxication of the great victory to find themselves confronted with a new and colossal problem for which they were ill prepared. There was nothing in their past experience on which they could draw. Clearly the laws of their primitive Medinese society were not adequate and those of their new Islamic society were not applicable, as the conquered people were not yet Moslems.

'Umar's covenant

'Umar was the first man to address himself to this problem. On the "day of al-Jābiyah", as it is called, a three-week conference was held in which he and his generals took up the question. What exactly transpired there is not known. Nor does anybody precisely know the terms of the so-called covenant (*'ahd*) of 'Umar.[1] Different versions [2] have been handed down and they all clearly contain enactments that belong to later times. 'Umar could not have legislated for situations that had not yet risen.

It may be assumed, however, that certain principles in the covenant represent 'Umar's policy. First among these was that Arabian Moslems in conquered lands should constitute a sort of religio-military aristocracy, keeping their blood pure and unmixed, living aloof and abstaining from holding or cultivating any landed property. The conquered peoples were given a new status, that of *dhimmis* (or *ahl al-dhimmah*),[3] people of the covenant or obligation. As Dhimmis they were subject to a tribute which comprised both land-tax (later *kharāj*) and poll-

[1] A. S. Tritton, *The Caliphs and their Non-Muslim Subjects* (Oxford, 1930), p. 12.

[2] Consult ibn-'Asākir, vol. i, pp. 178-80, pp. 150-51; al-Ibshīhi, *al-Mustaṭraf* (Cairo, 1314), vol. i, p. 99.

[3] Originally meant to apply only to the "people of the Book", i.e. Jews, Christians and Ṣābians (of Mesopotamia), the term was later widened to include Zoroastrians and others.

tax (later *jizyah*) but enjoyed the protection of Islam and were exempt from military duty. Only a Moslem could draw his sword in defence of the land of Islam. Thus was established the principle of inequality between victor and vanquished as a permanent basis of policy.

Another principle said to have been enunciated by 'Umar was that moveable property and prisoners won as booty constituted *ghanīmah* and belonged to the warriors as hitherto, but not the land. The land belonged to the Moslem community and, with all moneys received from subjects, constituted *fay'*. Those who cultivated *fay'* lands continued to pay land-tax even with the adoption of Islam.

The tax legislation traditionally ascribed to the initiative of 'Umar is clearly the result of years of practice. The first caliphs and provincial governors could not have devised and imposed a system of taxation and finance administration; it was easier for them to continue in Allah's name the system of Byzantine provincial government already established in Syria and Egypt. In the Moslem empire tribute varied from place to place according to the nature of the soil and the previously prevailing system (Byzantine or Persian) and not according to whether the Moslem acquisition of the land was by capitulation (*ṣulḥan*) or by force (*'anwatan*). This explanation of tax variation on the basis of the type of conquest, which is the one ordinarily given in Arabic sources,[1] is clearly a late legal fiction. Even the distinction between *jizyah* as poll-tax and *kharāj* (from Gr. *chorēgia* or Aramaic) as land-tax could not have arisen at so early a date as that of 'Umar. The two terms must have been used in that early period interchangeably, both meaning tribute in general. In the Koran (9: 29) *jizyah* occurs only once and in no legal sense; *kharāj* likewise occurs once (23: 74) and in a sense different from land-tax. In fact no differentiation between the terms *jizyah* and *kharāj* was made till late Umayyad days.

Poll-tax was an index of lower status and was exacted in a lump sum. It was generally four dinars[2] for the well-to-do, two

[1] Al-Māwardi, *al-Aḥkām al-Sulṭānīyah*, ed. M. Enger (Bonn, 1853), pp. 253-6; abu-Yūsuf, *Kitāb al-Kharāj* (Cairo, 1346), p. 46; Balādhuri, pp. 120-21; tr., pp. 186-7.

[2] Ar. *dīnār*, from Gr.-Latin *denarius*; the unit of gold currency in the caliphate, weighing approximately 4 grams. In 'Umar's time the dinar was equivalent to 10 dirhams, later 12.

for the middle-class and one for the poor. Women, children, beggars, the aged and the diseased were exempt except when with independent income. Land-tax was paid in instalments and in kind from the cattle and the produce of the land, but never in the form of pigs, dead animals or wine, the use of which was prohibited in the Koran. In addition the subject people were liable to special exactions in support of Moslem armed forces.

Military districts

At the Jābiyah conference, Syria was divided for administrative purposes into four military districts (sing. *jund*), corresponding to Byzantine provinces found at the time of the conquest. These were Dimashq (Damascus), Ḥimṣ, al-Urdunn (Jordan) and Filasṭīn (Palestine). The Urdunn covered Galilee and extended eastward to the desert. Filasṭīn comprised the region south of the plain of Esdraelon (Marj ibn-ʿĀmir). Later the Caliph Yazīd, Muʿāwiyah's son, formed a new district, Qinnasrīn, detached from Ḥimṣ and embracing Anṭākiyah (Antioch), Manbij (Hierapolis) and al-Jazīrah (Mesopotamia).[1] The Caliph ʿAbd-al-Malik separated al-Jazīrah and made it a district by itself. The camp at al-Jābiyah was, for the time being, maintained as capital. Other military camps soon grew near Ḥimṣ, ʿAmwās,[2] Ṭabarīyah [3] (for the Urdunn district) and al-Ludd (Lydda, for Filasṭīn). Later al-Ramlah replaced al-Ludd.

To these camps the Arabian soldiers, soon to become the new citizenry of the conquered province, brought their families; many of their wives or concubines were no doubt captured native women. As warriors and defenders (*muqātilah*) they enjoyed rights and privileges which later immigrants from Arabia could not enjoy. At their head stood the commander-in-chief and governor-general who combined in his person all the executive, judiciary and military functions. The governmental framework of the Byzantine system was preserved; even the local officials who did not withdraw from the country at the time of conquest were left in their positions. The Arabians had no trained personnel to replace such officials. Besides, their paramount interest was to keep the captured province under

[1] Yāqūt, vol. i, p. 136; Balādhuri, pp. 131-2; tr., pp. 302-3; cf. Yaʿqūbi, vol. ii, p. 176; consult p. 413, map.

[2] Or ʿAmawās, ancient Emmaus; Lk. 24: 13.

[3] Tiberias, modern Ṭabarayyah.

control and to collect the taxes due from its people.[1] In its primitive stage the Arabian provincial government, whether in Syria, Egypt or al-ʿIrāq, was purely military with a financial end in view.

The plague of ʿAmwās

Before the year of the Jābiyah conference (639) was over, a terrible plague, which had its start at ʿAmwās, spread and played havoc among the troops. Some 20,000 of them are said to have thus perished. The commander-in-chief himself, abu-ʿUbaydah,[2] was carried off, as was his successor Yazīd.[3] ʿUmar thereupon appointed Yazīd's younger brother Muʿāwiyah. This was in the year 640. For twenty years after this Muʿāwiyah dominates the scene in Syria as its governor; for twenty more he dominates the world of Islam as its caliph. When Syria under him became the seat of the caliphate, it entered upon an era of leadership and pre-eminence which lasted for almost a century.

Muʿāwiyah as governor

The policies initiated by Muʿāwiyah the governor were themselves pursued by Muʿāwiyah the caliph and resulted in giving him a permanent and prominent niche in the Arab hall of fame. He made the starting-point of his policy the cultivation of his new Syrian subjects, who were still Christians, as well as the Arab tribes, such as the Ghassānids, who were domiciled in the country since pre-Islamic days and were Christianized. Many of these tribes were of South Arabian origin as opposed to the new emigrants, who were North Arabians. For wife Muʿāwiyah chose a Jacobite Christian, Maysūn, daughter of Baḥdal of the Kalb, a South Arabian tribe. She retained her religion and became the mother of Yazīd. Both his personal physician and his court poet were also Christians.[4] For financial controller of the state Muʿāwiyah retained Manṣūr ibn-Sarjūn.[5] Arab chronicles dilate on the sense of loyalty which the Syrians cherished toward their new chief consequent upon his enlightened and tolerant policy.[6]

[1] J. Wellhausen, *Das arabische Reich und sein Sturz* (Berlin, 1902), pp. 18, 20-21; tr. Margaret G. Weir, *The Arab Kingdom and its Fall* (Calcutta, 1927), pp. 28, 32.

[2] His memory, like that of other early Moslem conquerors, lives today as that of a saint.

[3] Yaʿqūbi, vol. ii, p. 172; Ṭabari, vol. i, pp. 2516-20; ibn-ʿAsākir, vol. i, pp. 175-7.

[4] See below, pp. 439, 494, 497.

[5] Mentioned above, p. 414.

[6] Ṭabari, vol. i, pp. 3409-10; Masʿūdi, vol. v, pp. 80, 104; cf. *ʿIqd*, vol. i, p. 207, l. 31.

Muʿāwiyah then proceeded to organize the province on a stable basis. The raw material which constituted the Arab army he now whipped into the first ordered, disciplined military force in Islam. Its archaic tribal organization, a relic of patriarchal days, was abolished. There was no interference from Medina especially since the new caliph ʿUthmān (644–56), ʿUmar's successor, was a relative of Muʿāwiyah, both being members of the aristocratic Umayyad branch of the Quraysh. Muḥammad belonged to another clan of the same tribe. The army was kept in fit condition by seasonal raids into the "land of the Romans" (*bilād al-Rūm*, Asia Minor).

First navy built

For the defence of a province bordering on the sea, Muʿāwiyah realized that a body of disciplined, loyal troops did not suffice. In Acre he found fully equipped Byzantine shipyards.[1] These he now put into such use that this arsenal became second only to that of Alexandria. The forests of Lebanon were still there ready to provide the necessary wood for construction. Later Umayyads transferred the dockyards to Tyre.[2] The new Moslem fleet was doubtless manned by Greco-Syrians, who had a long seafaring tradition.

From Acre the first naval expedition was conducted in 649 against Cyprus (Qubrus), which pointed like a dagger against the heart of Syria. So close was the island, wrote Muʿāwiyah to the Caliph ʿUthmān, that people in Syria "could hear the dogs of the Greeks bark and their roosters crow".[3] The expedition received the half-hearted assent of ʿUthmān, who stipulated that Muʿāwiyah take his wife along as evidence of the proximity of the island and the contemplated ease of its subjugation.[4] This expedition made Muʿāwiyah the first admiral [5] in Arab annals. ʿUthmān's predecessor, ʿUmar, had flatly refused to authorize this naval campaign, as he had also done in the case of Africa. His instructions to ʿAmr ibn-al-ʿĀṣ indicate the terror that a man of the desert instinctively feels toward the sea: "Let no water intervene between me and thee, and camp not in any place which

[1] Ar. *dār al-ṣināʿah*, whence "arsenal". Balādhuri, p. 117; tr., p. 180.

[2] Balādhuri, pp. 117-18; tr., p. 181; Guy Le Strange, *Palestine under the Moslems* (Boston, 1890), p. 342.

[3] Ṭabari, vol. i, pp. 2820-21.

[4] Balādhuri, pp. 152-3; tr., pp. 235-6.

[5] This word, from Ar. *amīr al*-[*baḥr*], commander of the sea, was not introduced into European languages until the Arab-Spanish period, when it was confused with L. *admirabilis*, admirable.

I cannot reach riding on my mount ".[1]

The first naval expedition in the history of Islam netted Cyprus; the second (654) reached Rhodes (Rūdis). Two years later the remains of its colossus, the statue of Apollo which rose to a height of a hundred and twenty feet and was considered one of the seven wonders of the ancient world, were sold for old metal to a junk dealer who reportedly employed nine hundred camels to carry them away. In the year 655 the Syrian fleet under Busr ibn-abi-Arṭāh, in conjunction with the Egyptian fleet, encountered the Byzantine navy commanded by the Emperor Constans II (Heraclius' son) at Phoenix (modern Finike) on the Lycian coast. This marked the first great naval victory of Islam. Arabic chroniclers named the battle dhu (or dhāt)-al-Ṣawāri (that of the masts),[2] either because the place was rich in cypress trees or because of the large number of masts of the many boats engaged. By tying each Arab ship to a Byzantine one the Arabs converted the sea fight into a hand-to-hand encounter, to which they were accustomed. This battle did for the Byzantine naval forces what the Yarmūk had done for their land forces, virtually annihilated them.[3] The historian al-Ṭabari [4] asserts that the water of the sea was saturated with blood.

The Byzantine fleet almost annihilated

Muʿāwiyah, however, could not take full advantage of these exploits by his admirals and generals. Domestic disturbances leading to civil war were convulsing the Moslem world. In 658 or 659 he even found it expedient to purchase a truce from Constans II at the price of a yearly tribute mentioned by Theophanes [5] and referred to in passing by al-Balādhuri.[6] But the tribute was soon repudiated and hostilities were pressed against the eternal enemy to the north by land and by sea.

[1] Yaʿqūbi, vol. ii, p. 180; cf. ibn-al-Ṭiqṭaqa, *al-Fakhri*, ed. H. Derenbourg (Paris, 1894–5), p. 114.

[2] Ibn-ʿAbd-al-Ḥakam, *Futūḥ Miṣr wa-Akhbāruha*, ed. Charles C. Torrey (Leyden, 1920), pp. 189-90; Ṭabari, vol. i, pp. 2865, 2927.

[3] Theophanes, pp. 332, 345-6.

[4] Vol. i, p. 868. [5] P. 347. [6] P. 159, l. 1; tr., p. 245.

CHAPTER XXXII

THE ORTHODOX CALIPHATE

On June 16, 656, Islam witnessed the first murder of a caliph[1] by Moslem hands. This was 'Uthmān, third among the four orthodox (*rāshidūn*) caliphs, so called because all four were closely related to and associated with the Prophet, and in the conduct of state affairs largely tried to act in accordance with his behests and precedent. The awe inspired by Muḥammad's personality and behaviour was still a dominant force in their lives. All of them but 'Uthmān were early believers. Medina was their capital.

Orthodox Caliphs

1.	Abu-Bakr	632–4
2.	'Umar	634–44
3.	'Uthmān	644–56
4.	'Ali	656–61

None of these caliphs passed the caliphate on to his son; none founded a dynasty. Each was elected by a process termed *bay'ah* (sale), whereby the leaders of the people and shaykhs of tribes would literally or figuratively take the hand of the candidate as a token of homage.

A patriarchal period

The orthodox caliphs lived in patriarchal simplicity but achieved on a grand scale. Abu-Bakr, who was Muḥammad's father-in-law and three years his senior, conquered and pacified Arabia and by the sterling qualities of his character won the title al-Ṣiddīq (veracious). 'Umar had to his credit the fixing of the year of the *hijrah* (Hegira, 622) as the commencement of the Moslem era, the supervision of the conquest of large portions of the then known world, the institution of the state register

[1] Ar. *khalīfah*, successor, successor to Muḥammad in all but his prophetic function. As the last (" seal ") of the prophets Muḥammad could have no successor. The caliphal office is therefore purely secular. With no priesthood and no hierarchy Islam could have no correspondent to the pope at its head. The contrary and utterly false notion was not given wide currency until the late eighteenth century. See Hitti, *History of the Arabs*, pp. 185-6.

(*dīwān*) [1] and the organization of the government of captured provinces. Struck down by the poisoned dagger of a Christian Persian slave,[2] he left a name that has lived in tradition as the greatest in early Islam after Muḥammad's.

'Uthmān introduced a discordant element into an otherwise harmonious series. He was a member of the Umayyad aristocracy of Quraysh which held out until Mecca fell into Muḥammad's hands in 629–30, two short years before his death. As custodians of the Ka'bah, which by attracting pilgrims was an important source of income, the Umayyads had much more at stake than other converts. In 'Uthmān's reign the compilation and canonization of the Koran was accomplished. Thereby was the word of Allah given an unalterable form, which it has preserved until the present. In his reign the conquest of Persia, Ādharbayjān and a part of Armenia was completed. But 'Uthmān's record was not free from blemish. He appointed a foster brother of his, who was one of the ten proscribed by Muḥammad at the conquest of Mecca, governor over Egypt; a half-brother, who had spat in Muḥammad's face over al-Kūfah; a cousin,[3] over the important financial bureau of the state register. The caliph himself accepted presents from his governors or their partisans; one came to him in the form of a beautiful maid from al-Baṣrah. Charges of nepotism and irregularity were circulated, and feelings of dissatisfaction were fanned by three aspirants to the caliphate. All three were Qurayshites. 'Ali stood first among them.[4]

'Ali's case

'Ali had from the outset a devoted following which religiously maintained that he and no one else should have succeeded Muḥammad in 632. By virtue of his being first cousin [5] of the Prophet, second or third believer in him, husband of his only surviving daughter (Fāṭimah) and father of the two (al-Ḥasan and al-Ḥusayn) who were the only descendants of Muḥammad,

[1] This public register of state receipts and expenditures was evidently borrowed from the Persian system as the word itself (Persian *dīwān*) indicates; *Fakhri*, p. 116; Māwardi, pp. 343-4; Hitti, *History of the Arabs*, p. 172.

[2] Ṭabari, vol. i, pp. 272-3; Ya'qūbi, vol. ii, p. 183.

[3] Marwān ibn-al-Ḥakam, a future Umayyad caliph; see below, p. 446, table.

[4] The other two were Ṭalḥah ibn-'Ubaydullāh and al-Zubayr ibn-al-'Awwām, early converts and Companions of the Prophet and counted among the ten to whom he had promised Paradise (*mubashsharah*).

[5] The subjoined tree shows the genealogical relationship between 'Ali, 'Uthmān, Mu'āwiyah and Muḥammad: [*contd. on p.* 430

ʿAli — so his partisans argued — was entitled to first consideration. More than that these partisans (*shīʿah*) of ʿAli held that elevation to the highest office in Islam could not have been left to the whims and predilections of an electorate, that it was something for which Allah and Muḥammad must have made provision and that ʿAli was the one designated for that office by them. This would make ʿAli the only legitimate successor to Muḥammad and relegate his predecessors to the position of usurpers. After ʿAli, these legitimists maintained, his descendants were entitled to the successorship by the right of heredity.

The ʿAlids organized a strong party in al-Kūfah. There the uprising against ʿUthmān had its inception. Thence it spread to Egypt, which sent some five hundred rebels to Medina. This was in April 655. The aged caliph was shut in his residence and as he read the copy of the Koran [1] which he had once canonized, one of the insurgents, son of his friend, abu-Bakr, laid the first violent hand on him ʿAli was then (June 24, 656) and there proclaimed caliph.

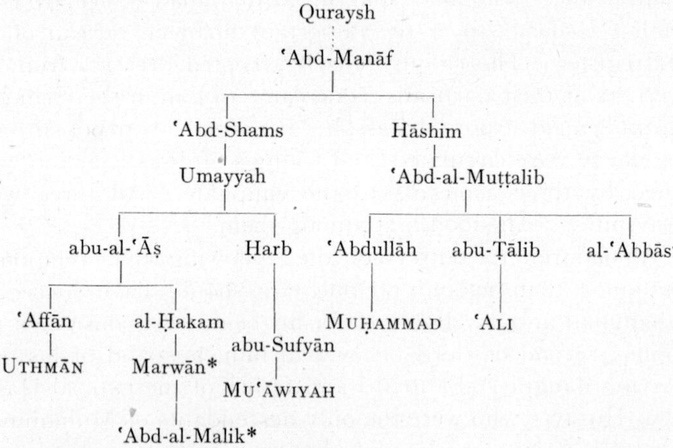

* Members of the Umayyad caliphate.
† Father of the founder of the ʿAbbāsid caliphate.

[1] Different cities claim the honour of having preserved this copy with ʿUthmān's blood staining the page on which this verse occurs: " And if they believe even as ye believe, then are they rightly guided. But if they turn away, then are they in schism, and Allah will suffice (as a protection) for thee against them. And He is the hearer, the knower " (2 : 131). A mosque in al-Baṣrah claimed the copy when ibn-Baṭṭūṭah visited it about 1326; see his *Tuḥfat al-Nuẓẓar fi Gharāʾib al-Amṣār wa-ʿAjāʾib al-Asfār*, ed. and tr. C. Defrémery and B. R. Sanguinetti, vol. ii (Paris, 1894), pp. 10-11.

The caliphate of ʿAli was beset with trouble from beginning to end. The first problem was how to dispose of the two remaining claimants, Ṭalḥah and al-Zubayr, who with their followers in al-Ḥijāz and al-ʿIrāq had refused to recognize his succession. The dissidents' position was reinforced when ʿĀ'ishah, favourite wife of the Prophet, joined their ranks. ʿĀ'ishah harboured a lifelong grudge against ʿAli; for when she once in her youthful days loitered behind her husband's caravan, ʿAli cast doubt upon her fidelity, necessitating intervention in her favour by Allah through a revelation.[1] The battle was joined December 9, 656, outside of al-Baṣrah and was styled "the battle of the camel", after the camel on which ʿĀ'ishah rode. Both rivals of ʿAli fell.[2] ʿĀ'ishah was captured and treated with the consideration befitting "the mother of the believers". Thus came to an end the first civil war in Islam. ʿAli established himself in his new capital al-Kūfah as the seemingly undisputed caliph. The second civil war, however, was not far off.

'Ali's caliphate

Only one provincial governor denied the new caliph the usual oath of fealty. That was Muʿāwiyah. The governor of Syria and kinsman of ʿUthmān now came out as the avenger of the martyred caliph. Dramatically he exhibited in the Damascus mosque the blood-stained shirt of ʿUthmān and the fingers chopped from the hands of his wife Nā'ilah, originally like Muʿāwiyah's wife a Syro-Arab of the Kalb tribe, as she tried to defend her husband.[3] Carefully keeping his own interests under cover Muʿāwiyah publicly confronted ʿAli with this dilemma: punish the assassins or accept the position of an accomplice. Punishing the culprits was something ʿAli neither would nor could do. But the issue at bottom transcended personalities. It involved the question as to whether al-ʿIrāq or Syria, al-Kūfah or Damascus, should head the Islamic world. Medina clearly was out of the race. The far-flung conquests had shifted the centre of gravity to the north and relegated the former capital to a marginal position.

Muʿāwiyah enters the arena

On the plain of Ṣiffīn [4] the two armies — that of al-ʿIrāq led

The second civil war

[1] Sūr. 24: 11-20. [2] Ṭabari, vol. i, pp. 3218 *seq.* [3] *Fakhri*, pp. 125, 137.

[4] South of al-Raqqah on the west bank of the Euphrates; "Sapphin" in Theophanes, p. 347. Ṭabari, vol. i, pp. 3256 *seq.*; Yaʿqūbi, vol. ii, pp. 218 *seq.*; al-Dīnawari, *al-Akhbār al-Ṭiwāl*, ed. Vladimir Guirgass (Leyden, 1888), pp. 178 *seq.*

by ʿAli and that of Syria led by Muʿāwiyah — at last met. After weeks of skirmishing the battle was joined on July 26, 657. ʿAli's forces were on the point of achieving complete victory after three days of bloody fighting when lo and behold manuscripts of the Koran, fastened to lances, were lifted high in the air. The gesture, contrived by the shrewd and wily ʿAmr ibn-al-ʿĀṣ, Muʿāwiyah's lieutenant, was interpreted as meaning an appeal from the decision of arms to the decision of the Koran — whatever that might mean. Hostilities stopped. ʿAli, pious and simple-hearted, accepted Muʿāwiyah's proposal to arbitrate "according to the word of Allah" and thus spare Moslem blood.[1]

Arbitration

For the arbitration ʿAli appointed as his personal representative abu-Mūsa al-Ashʿari, a man of undoubted piety but of dubious loyalty to the ʿAlid cause. Muʿāwiyah matched him with ʿAmr ibn-al-ʿĀṣ, one of "the four Arabian political geniuses (*duhāt*) of Islam".[2] Muʿāwiyah himself was counted among the four.[3] The two arbiters (sing. *ḥakam*), each accompanied by four hundred witnesses, held a public session in January 659 at Adhruḥ, on the main caravan route between Damascus and Medina.

The classical view is that the two umpires privately agreed to depose both principals, thus clearing the way for a "dark horse"; but after abu-Mūsa, as the elder of the two, had stood up and publicly declared the caliphate of his chief null and void, ʿAmr stood up and confirmed his chief, thus double-crossing his associate.[4] Modern critical scholars, however, are inclined to believe that what really happened was that both referees deposed both principals, which meant practically that ʿAli was the one deposed, as Muʿāwiyah was not yet a caliph.[5] Of course the fact of the arbitration itself had raised Muʿāwiyah's position to the level of that of ʿAli, or lowered ʿAli's position to the level of Muʿāwiyah's; but the sentence of the judges deprived ʿAli of

[1] For the arbitration document consult Dīnawari, pp. 206-8.

[2] Masʿūdi, vol. iv, p. 391; ibn-Ḥajar, *al-Iṣābah fi Tamyīz al-Ṣaḥābah*, vol. v (Cairo, 1907), p. 3.

[3] For the other two see below, p. 436.

[4] Cf. *Fakhri*, pp. 127-30; Yaʿqūbi, vol. ii, pp. 220-22; Ṭabari, vol. i, pp. 3340-3360; Masʿūdi, vol. iv, pp. 392-402.

[5] H. Lammens, "Études sur le règne du calife Omaiyade Moʿawia Ier", *Mélanges de la faculté orientale*, vol. ii (1907), pp. 17-32; Wellhausen, pp. 57-9; tr., pp. 89-93; Caetani, vol. x, pp. 6-76.

a real office and Muʿāwiyah of a fictitious claim which he had not yet dared publicly assert. In fact not until two years after the arbitration did Muʿāwiyah proclaim himself caliph; by that time ʿAli was dead.

Early on January 24, 661, as ʿAli was on his way to the mosque at al-Kūfah, he was struck on the forehead with a poisoned dagger wielded by a Khārijite. The Khārijites (seceders) were alienated followers of ʿAli who adopted as slogan *la ḥukma illa lillāh* [1] and turned to be his deadly enemies. Their organization constituted the first sect in Islam. The murderer, though, was actuated by purely personal motives.[2] The lonely spot outside of al-Kūfah where ʿAli was interred was kept secret throughout the Umayyad and early ʿAbbāsid periods until Hārūn al-Rashīd in 791 fell upon it by chance.[3] This is the present Mashhad [4] (shrine of) ʿAli in al-Najaf, one of the great centres of pilgrimage in Islam and the greatest in al-Shīʿah.

ʿAli dead proved to be more influential than ʿAli living. To his Shīʿite partisans he soon became the patron saint, the *wali* (friend and vice-regent) of Allah. Deficient in the traits that make a politician, he was rich in those that, from the Arab point of view, constitute a perfect man. Eloquent in speech, sage in counsel, valiant in battle, true to his friends, magnanimous to his foes, tradition raised him to the position of paragon of Moslem chivalry (*futūwah*). Enough proverbs, orations, wise sayings, verses and anecdotes have clustered around his name to make another Solomon of him. The sabre he wielded, dhu-al-Faqār (cleaver of vertebrae), supposedly the one first used by Muḥammad on the memorable battlefield of Badr,[5] has been immortalized in an oft-quoted verse: *La sayfa illa dhu-l-Faqā —ri wa-la fatan illa ʿAli* (no sword can match dhu-al-Faqār and no youth can compare with ʿAli). The youth (*fityān*) move-

[1] *Fakhri*, p. 130; cf. Koran 12:70.

[2] Al-Mubarrad, *al-Kāmil*, ed. William Wright (London, 1864), pp. 548-51.

[3] For the earliest detailed account of the tomb consult ibn-Ḥawqal, p. 163.

[4] Ar. *mashhad* means place of a *shāhid*, one who bears witness to the oneness of God but not necessarily by dying for it as a *shahīd*, martyr. As an architectural term it replaces Syr. *shahdē*. Ar. *maqām*, literally place of standing or sojourn, technically means a commemorative monument over a spot where once a holy man stopped. It corresponds to Heb. *māqōm* (Gen. 28:11). Loosely it is used interchangeably with *mashhad*.

[5] On this battle consult Hitti, *History of the Arabs*, pp. 116-17.

ment in Islam, which developed later along lines parallel to those of the medieval orders of chivalry, took ʿAli for its model. Many dervish fraternities have likewise considered him their ideal exemplar and patron. To most of his partisans he has remained through the ages infallible ; to the extremists (*ghulāh*) among them he even became the incarnation of the deity.[1]

[1] See below, pp. 577-8, 586, 610.

CHAPTER XXXIII

MUʿĀWIYAH ESTABLISHES THE UMAYYAD CALIPHATE

EARLY in 661 [1] Muʿāwiyah was proclaimed caliph at Īliyā' (Jerusalem), but he chose Damascus for capital. Jerusalem was closer to the Bedouins and Arabians than the ancient capital of the Aramaeans and the recent seat of the provincial Byzantine government. The seaports were open to naval attack. Medina and al-Kūfah had the desert for a background.

The anti-caliph out of the way

His first problem was to get rid of the claimants to the caliphate, pacify the empire and consolidate it. In this he was fortunate in having the collaboration of a group of lieutenants the like of which Islam thereafter seldom produced. His right-hand man, ʿAmr, had already (658) wrested Egypt from ʿAlid rulers, which made him the double conqueror of that land, and was now holding it in Muʿāwiyah's name.[2] This he continued to do until his death in 663.[3] Al-Ḥijāz was naturally lukewarm in its loyalty to the new caliph. Mecca and Medina never forgot that the Umayyads were late believers and that their belief was one of convenience rather than conviction. But for the time being the cradle of Islam gave no serious trouble. Al-ʿIrāq openly and immediately declared for al-Ḥasan, eldest son of ʿAli and Fāṭimah. To its people he was the one and only legitimate successor of his assassinated father. In the course of a swift campaign (661) Muʿāwiyah secured from the claimant definite renunciation of all claims. Al-Ḥasan, as a matter of fact, was more at home in the harem than in the court. In consideration of a handsome subsidy, the amount of which he himself fixed, he abdicated in favour of Muʿāwiyah and retired to a life of ease and luxury in Medina. The subsidy was for life

[1] Shawwāl, A.H. 41 in Masʿūdi, vol. v, p. 14; A.H. 40 in Ṭabari, vol. ii, p. 4, and Yaʿqūbi, vol. ii, p. 256.

[2] Ibn-al-Athīr, vol. iii, pp. 295 *seq.*

[3] Yaʿqūbi, vol. ii, pp. 262-3; Ṭabari, vol. i, pp. 3401-11.

and consisted of five million dirhams [1] from the Kūfah state treasury and the revenue of a Persian district, plus a two-million-dirham pension for his younger brother al-Ḥusayn.[2] About eight years later al-Ḥasan died in Medina, aged forty-five, after having made and unmade no less than a hundred marriages, which earned him the title *miṭlāq* (great divorcer). He was evidently consumptive, but his death was possibly caused by poisoning [3] connected with some harem intrigue; his followers blamed it on Muʿāwiyah and raised al-Ḥasan to the rank of a *shahīd* (martyr), in fact the " *sayyid* (lord) of all martyrs ".

Al-ʿIrāq temporarily pacified

Over jealous, humiliated and turbulent al-Kūfah Muʿāwiyah appointed (661) al-Mughīrah ibn-Shuʿbah, a native of al-Ṭā'if in al-Ḥijāz who had been dismissed by the Caliph ʿUmar from the governorship of al-Baṣrah because of lax morality.[4] Al-Mughīrah was described as " one who if shut behind seven doors his cunning would find a way to burst all the locks ". In the confusion following ʿAli's assassination, he had forged a diploma of appointment from Muʿāwiyah over the annual pilgrimage to al-Ḥijāz. As governor he pitted Khārijite against Shīʿite and Shīʿite against Khārijite, suppressed ʿAlid opposition and established Umayyad prestige in his domain. Thereby he won his place among the four political geniuses of Islam.[5]

Al-Mughīrah was succeeded by his protégé Ziyād ibn-Abīh, the fourth political genius. Ziyād had unfurled the ʿAlid flag in Persia but, recognizing in him a man of unusual ability, Muʿāwiyah by a bold and shameless stroke accorded him official acknowledgment as half brother, son of his father abu-Sufyān and a prostitute in al-Ṭā'if.[6] Because of the doubt which clouded the identity of his father, he was nicknamed ibn-Abīh (son of his father). Ziyād's appointment over al-Kūfah was extended to include, besides al-ʿIrāq, Persia and the dependent

[1] From Per. *diram*, from Gr. *drachme*, the unit of silver coinage in the Arab monetary system. It was generally $\frac{1}{10}$ or $\frac{1}{12}$ of a dinar (see above, p. 425, n. 1), but its real value varied greatly.

[2] Ṭabari, vol. i, p. 3; Dīnawari, p. 231; ibn-Ḥajar, vol. ii, pp. 12-13.

[3] Yaʿqūbi, vol. ii, p. 266.

[4] Balādhuri, pp. 256, 344-5; tr., p. 410; ibn-al-Athīr, *Usd al-Ghābah*, vol. iv (Cairo, 1286), p. 407.

[5] See above, p. 432.

[6] This legitimization (*istilḥāq*) is reported in Masʿūdi, vol. v, pp. 20-22; Ṭabari, vol. ii, pp. 69-70; ibn-ʿAsākir, vol. v, pp. 409-10.

parts of Arabia. This made him viceroy over the eastern half of the empire. With an open eye on all happenings in this vast domain, sharp ear close to the ground and firm hand on the sword, the illegitimate son of abu-Sufyān held the turbulent realm within the Sufyānid orbit. The problem of troublesome Arabians and Bedouins from al-Baṣrah and al-Kūfah he solved by transplanting 50,000 of them to eastern Persia.[1]

Second wave of conquests

With the territory of Islam temporarily pacified Muʿāwiyah's extraordinary energies sought new outlets in the form of campaigns into foreign territory by land and sea. The naval campaigns were entirely against the Byzantines.[2] Muʿāwiyah's conquests constitute the second wave of Moslem expansion after an interruption by the two civil wars,[3] the first wave having been initiated by abu-Bakr and having culminated under ʿUmar.

On land the expansion under Muʿāwiyah took two courses, one eastward and the other westward. Al-Baṣrah of Ziyād served as headquarters of the eastern campaigns, which resulted in completing the subjugation of Khurāsān (663–71), crossing the Oxus [4] and raiding Bukhāra in far-away Turkestan (674).[5] Marw (Merv), Balkh, Harāt (Herat) and other cities which developed into brilliant centres of Islamic culture were captured. The army returned to al-Baṣrah laden with booty from the wandering Turkish tribes of Transoxiana. The first contact between Arabs and Turks, destined to play a major rôle in later Islam, was established.

The hero of westward expansion was ʿUqbah ibn-Nāfiʿ, whose mother was a sister of ʿAmr's mother, conqueror and governor of Egypt.[6] In 663 ʿUqbah was appointed by his cousin over Ifrīqīyah (now Ifrīqiyah).[7] There he established (670) al-Qayrawān [8] as a military base against the Berbers. The new camp was built partly with material taken from the ruins of

[1] Balādhuri, p. 410; Ṭabari, vol. ii, pp. 81, 155-6. For earlier cases of transplantation in the Near East consult above, pp. 196-7, 202.

[2] To be treated in the next chapter.

[3] See above, pp. 430, 431.

[4] See below, pp. 458 *seq.*

[5] Yaʿqūbi, vol. ii, p. 258; Balādhuri, pp. 409-10; Ṭabari, vol. ii, pp. 166 *seq.*

[6] Ibn-Khaldūn, *Kitāb al-ʿIbar*, vol. iii, pp. 10-11.

[7] Africa Minor, Tunis, modern Tunisia; corruption of Latin Africa. The name was borrowed by the Arabs from the Romans and given to the eastern part of Barbary, the word Maghrib being reserved for the western part.

[8] From Per. *kārwān*, whence English caravan. For ʿUqbah's campaigns consult ibn-ʿAbd-al-Ḥakam, pp. 171, 194-9.

near-by Carthage, of which it became a Moslem successor. As the Berbers were Islamized, they were pressed into the Arab army and served as relays for its further conquests in North Africa and later in Spain. With their aid ʿUqbah chased the Byzantines out of a large part of North Africa. The place where he fell in battle (683) is still known after him as Sīdi (Sayyidi, my lord) ʿUqbah, a few miles south-east of Biskra in Algeria,[1] where his tomb stands as a national shrine. Brilliant as it was, ʿUqbah's military advance in Algeria, like that of his contemporary in Central Asia, was of no lasting significance, because it was not followed up by occupation. Here as in Transoxiana the work had to be done over again.[2]

Other achievements

These campaigns, colossal as they were, did not make the commander-in-chief neglect domestic affairs. The financial administration of the state was left in the hands of the capable and experienced Sarjūnids, of whom St. John was a descendant.[3] Such was the revenue that Muʿāwiyah could double the pay of the soldiers, strengthen the Syrian frontier fortresses against the northern enemy, undertake projects of agriculture and irrigation in al-Ḥijāz — the province least favoured by nature — and appease through subsidy ʿAlids and Hāshimites. The Hāshimites included the ʿAbbāsids, who were closer of kin to the Prophet than the Umayyads. This technique of "reconciling the hearts" (*ta'līf al-qulūb*)[4] was introduced by the Prophet himself. In Syria Muʿāwiyah instituted a bureau of registry and laid the basis of a postal service (*barīd*).[5]

Throughout his undertakings, peaceful or military, he was sustained by the unflinching loyalty of his Syrian subjects, natives and Arabian immigrants. The Syro-Arabs were mostly of Yamanite, not Ḥijāzite, origin and, as we learned before, had been Christianized. His wife Maysūn was one of them, but he is said to have divorced her because of poems attributed to her in which she expressed her yearning for the desert and her preference for a different type of a husband:

A tent with rustling breezes cool
  Delights me more than palace high,
And more the cloak of simple wool
  Than robes in which I learned to sigh.

[1] Ibn-al-Athīr *Kāmil*, vol. iv, p. 91.
[2] See below, pp. 458 *seq*.
[3] See above, p. 425.
[4] Consult Koran 9:60.
[5] *Fakhri*, p. 148. Cf. below, p. 474.

The crust I ate beside my tent
 Was more than this fine bread to me;
The wind's voice where the hill-path went
 Was more than tambourine can be.[1]

His Christian physician ibn-Uthāl he appointed financial administrator over the district of Ḥimṣ — an unprecedented appointment for a Christian in Moslem annals.[2] His poet laureate, al-Akhṭal,[3] belonged to the Christian tribe of Taghlib. Maronites and Jacobites brought their religious disputes before Mu'āwiyah.[4] In Edessa he reportedly rebuilt a Christian church that had been demolished by an earthquake.[5] By such acts of tolerance and magnanimity Mu'āwiyah fastened his hold upon the hearts of the Syrians and firmly established the hegemony of their country in the Moslem empire.

But perhaps his most prominent quality was what his Arab biographers term *ḥilm*,[6] that *finesse politique* which made him unerring in doing the right thing at the right time. This supreme statesmanship he himself defined in these words: "I apply not my sword, where my lash suffices; nor my lash, where my tongue is enough. And even if there be one hair binding me to my fellowmen, I do not let it break. When they pull, I loosen; and if they loosen, I pull."[7] The letter he sent to al-Ḥasan inducing him to abdicate further illustrates this trait: "I admit that because of thy blood relationship thou art more entitled to this high office than myself. And if I were sure of thy greater ability to fulfil the duties involved, I would unhesitatingly swear allegiance to thee. Now then, ask what thou wilt." Enclosed was a blank already signed by Mu'āwiyah.[8] This *ḥilm* made his personal relations with his contemporaries frank and friendly. His opponents would call him the bastard's brother and express their devotion to 'Ali even in his presence, and his friends would tease him about his name, which meant "a barking bitch", and

[1] Nicholson, *A Literary History of the Arabs*, p. 195; abu-al-Fidā', vol. i, p. 203.
[2] Ya'qūbi, vol. ii, p. 265; Wellhausen, p. 85, considers the report fictitious.
[3] See below, p. 494.
[4] Wellhausen, p. 84. This is the first mention of Maronites in Arab history.
[5] Theophanes, p. 356.
[6] *Fakhri*, p. 145; *'Iqd*, vol. ii, p. 304; Mas'ūdi, vol. v, p. 40; Lammens in *Mélanges*, vol. i, pp. 66-108.
[7] Ya'qūbi, vol. ii, p. 283; *'Iqd*, vol. i, p. 10.
[8] Ṭabari, vol. ii, p. 5.

about his huge buttocks. His family name was a diminutive of *amah*, bondwoman.

A crown prince nominated

In 679,[1] six months before his death (April 680) at the age of eighty, Mu'āwiyah nominated his son Yazīd as his successor, an unprecedented procedure in Islam. Yazīd had been brought up by his mother partly in the *bādiyah* (desert), more particularly Palmyrena, where her Christian tribe roamed.[2] In the capital he also associated with Christians and counted among his boon companions St. John, when still a layman, and the poet al-Akhṭal. In the desert the youthful prince became habituated to the chase, rough riding and hard life; in the city, to wine-bibbing and verse-making. Al-Bādiyah from this time on became the open-air school to which the young royal princes of the dynasty resorted for vacationing, acquiring the pure Arabic[3] — unadulterated with Aramaicisms — and incidentally escaping the recurring city plagues. That the caliph had had in mind for some time the nomination of his son may be inferred from his sending him as early as 668 against Constantinople,[4] where Yazīd's success served to dispel any doubts that the puritans might have entertained regarding his qualifications. And now Mu'āwiyah, after being sure of the capital, summoned deputations from the provinces and took from them the oath of allegiance (*bay'ah*) to his favourite son. Unsympathetic 'Irāqis were cajoled, coerced or bribed.[5]

This master stroke was a landmark in Islamic history. It introduced the hereditary principle,[6] which was followed thereafter by the leading Moslem dynasties. It established a precedent enabling the reigning caliph to proclaim as his successor him among his sons or kinsmen whom he considered competent and to exact for him an anticipatory oath of allegiance. The designation of a crown prince tended to promote stability and continuity and discourage ambitious aspirants to the throne.

Mu'āwiyah the model king

Despite his unparalleled contributions to the cause of the Arabs and Islam, Mu'āwiyah was no favourite with the Arab Moslem historians. Nor were his "tyrannical" lieutenants.

[1] Mas'ūdi, vol. v, pp. 69-73; cf. Ṭabari, vol. ii, pp. 174-7, and ibn-al-Athīr, vol. iii, pp. 416-17, where the date is made three years earlier.

[2] Lammens in *Mélanges*, vol. iii, pp. 189-226.

[3] *'Iqd*, vol. i, p. 293, l. 30.

[4] See below, p. 444.

[5] *'Iqd*, vol. ii, pp. 306-9; ibn-'Asākir, vol. iv, pp. 327-8.

[6] For succession in the orthodox caliphate see above, p. 428.

The explanation is not difficult to find. Most of those writers were Shīʿites or members of the ʿIrāqi-Persian and Medinese schools.[1] As historians they reflect the puritanical attitude which resented the fact that he was the man who secularized Islam and transformed the *khilāfat al-nubūʾah* (the prophetic, i.e. theocratic, caliphate) into a *mulk* [2] (a temporal sovereignty). Muʿāwiyah, they emphasized, was the first *malik* (king) in Islam, a title so abhorrent to Arabians that they applied it almost exclusively to non-Arab potentates. He is blamed for several profane innovations, including the *maqṣūrah*,[3] a sort of bower inside the mosque reserved for the exclusive use of the caliph, the delivering of the Friday noon sermon (*khuṭbah*) while seated,[4] and the use of a royal throne (*sarīr al-mulk*).[5] The fact remains that such was the example of energy, tolerance and astuteness he set before his successors that while many of them tried to emulate it [6] few came near succeeding.

[1] Of the Syrian school only one major representative, ibn-ʿAsākir of Damascus (1105-76), has survived.

[2] Ibn-Khaldūn, *Muqaddamah* (Cairo), pp. 169 *seq.*; Yaʿqūbi, vol. ii, p. 257.

[3] Yaʿqūbi, vol. ii, p. 265; Dīnawari, p. 229; Ṭabari, vol. ii, p. 70, l. 20; Mubarrad, p. 552. The bower was built as a protection after an unsuccessful attempt on the life of the caliph while praying.

[4] Ibn-al-ʿIbri, *Mukhtaṣar al-Duwal*, ed. Anṭūn al-Ṣāliḥāni (Beirut, 1890), p. 188. Muʿāwiyah's excuse was that he had become in his late years excessively corpulent and pot-bellied.

[5] Ibn-Khaldūn, *Muqaddamah*, p. 217; al-Qalqashandi, *Ṣubḥ al-Aʿsha*, vol. iv (Cairo, 1914), p. 6.

[6] Masʿūdi, vol. v, p. 78. Muʿāwiyah's tomb in the cemetery of [al-] Bāb al-Ṣaghīr at Damascus is still visited.

CHAPTER XXXIV

HOSTILE RELATIONS WITH THE BYZANTINES

Syrian marches

IN the Umayyad period, as in the ʿAbbāsid down to about the middle of the twelfth century, the frontier between Arab and Byzantine lands was formed by the great ranges of the Taurus and Anti-Taurus. As the two hostile states stood face to face across this line, they first sought to keep each other off by turning the intervening stretch of land into a desolate terrain. Muʿāwiyah contributed to the creation of this unclaimed waste zone.[1] Later Umayyads pursued a different policy aiming at establishing a footing there by rebuilding as fortresses abandoned or destroyed towns and building new ones. Thus grew a cordon of Moslem fortifications stretching from Tarsus in Cilicia to Malaṭyah (Malaṭīyah, Melitene) by the upper Euphrates and including Adhanah, al-Maṣṣīṣah (Mopsuesta) and Marʿash (Germanicia). These units were strategically situated at the intersections of military roads or the entrances of narrow passes. The term *ʿawāṣim* (defences) was rightly applied to them. The same term was used in a narrow sense for only the inner, the southern, line of fortresses in contradistinction to the outer, the northern, called *thughūr*.[2] The *thughūr* zone stretched across the Syrian and Mesopotamian marches. The part guarding Syria was styled *al-thughūr al-Shaʾmīyah*; that guarding Mesopotamia *al-thughūr al-Jazīrīyah*.[3]

Under the ʿAbbāsids the *thughūr* zone shrank to the limits of the area extending from Awlās on the Mediterranean, past Tarsus to Sumaysāṭ (Samosata) on the Euphrates.[4] As the city commanding the southern entrance of the celebrated pass across the Taurus known as the Cilician Gates, Tarsus served as a base

[1] Balādhuri, pp. 164-5; called *ḍawāḥi*, outer land, in Ṭabari, vol. ii, p. 1317, and ibn-al-Athīr, vol. iv, p. 250.

[2] Pl. of *thaghr*, fissure, opening. Cf. Guy Le Strange, *The Lands of the Eastern Caliphate* (Cambridge, 1930), p. 128.

[3] Balādhuri, pp. 183 *seq.*, 163 *seq.*

[4] Iṣṭakhri, pp. 67-8.

for the major military campaigns against the territory of the Romans. In it a good-sized army of horse and foot was stationed. A less-frequented path across the Taurus led from Marʿash to Abulustayn [1] and was called Darb al-Ḥadath. All these strongholds changed hands again and again as the tide of war ebbed or flowed. Under the Umayyads and ʿAbbāsids almost every foot was contested repeatedly and fiercely. It was a real "no man's land". Its soil was soaked with more blood than perhaps any other piece of land in Asia.

In Muʿāwiyah's time as well as that of ʿAbd-al-Malik and other successors a greater campaign in summer (*ṣā'ifah*) and a smaller one in winter (*shātiyah*) [2] were undertaken year by year as a matter of routine. The campaigns served as a training school. The objective, as in the case of the traditional Bedouin raids, was booty, though the dim spectacle of Byzantium may have beckoned from beyond in the distant background. Constantinople lay four hundred and fifty miles from Tarsus in a direct line. At no time did the Arabs establish a firm foothold in Asia Minor. Their main military energy followed the line of least resistance and was directed eastward and westward. The lofty ranges of the Taurus and Anti-Taurus seem to have been eternally fixed by nature as the boundary line. Then there was the climate of Anatolia, too rigorous for the sons of the desert. The Arabic language froze on the southern slopes of those ranges. No part of Asia Minor ever became Arabic speaking. Since earliest times, those of the Hittites, its basic population has been non-Semitic.

Constantinople reached

The recurring raids into Asia Minor did at last reach the capital. That was in 668,[3] only thirty-six years after Muḥammad's death. It was then for the first time that eyes of Arab warriors opened to see the mighty and proud city on the Bosphorus. The leader was Faḍālah ibn-ʿUbayd al-Anṣāri.[4] The army wintered in Chalcedon (the Asiatic suburb of Constantinople), where it suffered severely from want of provisions and

[1] Yāqūt, vol. i, pp. 93-4; cf. Le Strange, p. 133. The Byzantine name was Ablastha, the Greek Arabissus, late Arabic al-Bustān (cf. below, p. 552, n. 6).

[2] Balādhuri, p. 163, l. 1.

[3] Ibn-al-Athīr, vol. iii, p. 381; Ṭabari, vol. ii, pp. 86, 111, cf. p. 27, where a report about an earlier naval attack on Constantinople by Busr ibn-abi-Arṭāh is questioned.

[4] Of the *anṣār*, helpers; technically the believers of Medina who received and assisted the Prophet after his migration from Mecca in 622.

from smallpox and other diseases.[1] Muʿāwiyah sent, in the spring of 669, his pleasure-loving son Yazīd, much against his will, with reinforcements.[2] Yazīd and Faḍālah laid siege to Constantinople with its high triple wall. The fleet no doubt supported this enterprise. But the siege was raised that summer; Byzantium had found a new and energetic emperor, Constantine IV (668–85).

In the legendary account of this siege Yazīd distinguished himself for bravery and fortitude. He thereby earned the title *fata al-ʿArab* (the champion of the Arabs). As the pendulum of victory swung from one side to the other, alternate shouts of jubilation were heard from two Byzantine tents — so the *Aghāni*[3] reports. One was occupied by the daughter of the king of the Rūm (Romans); the other by the daughter of the ex-king of Ghassān, Jabalah ibn-al-Ayham.[4] The prospect of seizing the Arab princess spurred Yazīd to extraordinary activity. But Yazīd's legendary fame was eclipsed by that of the aged abu-Ayyūb al-Anṣāri, once the standard-bearer of the Prophet and his first host in Medina at the time of the hijrah.[5] In the course of the siege abu-Ayyūb died of dysentery. His tomb outside the city walls soon became for the Christian Greeks a shrine where prayer was considered especially efficacious for bringing rain in time of drought.[6] In later times when Constantinople was besieged by other Moslems, Ottoman Turks, the tomb was miraculously discovered by rays of light — reminiscent of the discovery of the "holy lance" at Antioch by the first Crusaders.[7] A mosque was built on the site; and the Medinese gentleman became a saint for three nations.

Second siege of Constantinople

Twice did Muʿāwiyah stretch his mighty arm across the territory of the Romans into the capital itself The second time was five years after the first. This was the so-called seven years' war (674–80), waged mainly between the two fleets in the Bosphorus and the Sea of Marmora. What made such a long operation possible was the early occupation of the peninsula

[1] *Aghāni*, vol. xvi, p. 33; al-Nuwayri, *Nihāyat al-Arab fi Funūn al-Adab* (Cairo, 1925), vol. iv, p. 91.

[2] Lammens in *Mélanges*, vol. iii, pp. 306-12; J. Wellhausen, "Die Kämpfe der Araber mit den Romäern in der Zeit der Umaijiden", *Nachrichten von der Königlichen Gesellschaft der Wissenschaften zu Göttingen, philologisch-historische Classe* (Göttingen, 1902), pp. 423 *seq.*

[3] Vol. xvi, p. 33.

[4] See above, p. 404.

[5] Balādhuri, p. 5.

[6] Ibn-al-Athīr, vol. iii, p. 382.

[7] See below, pp. 592-3.

projecting from Asia Minor into Marmora and styled Cyzicus by the Greeks and "the isle of Arwād" by the Arabs.[1] Cyzicus served as winter headquarters for the invading army and a base for spring and summer attacks. Arab and Byzantine accounts of these campaigns do not tally and are in themselves badly confused. The city was saved supposedly by the use of Greek fire, a newly invented highly combustible compound which would burn even on or under water. The inventor was a Syrian refugee from Damascus named Callinicus. This was perhaps the first time this "secret weapon" was used. The Byzantines kept its formula unrevealed for several centuries after which the Arabs acquired it; but it has since been lost. Greek accounts dilate on the disastrous effects of this fire on enemy ships. What was left of the Arab fleet was wrecked on the return journey,[2] necessitated by the death of Muʻāwiyah.

To this period also belong several naval attacks on islands in the Aegean and eastern Mediterranean waters. Cyprus was already secure in the Moslem fold. Rhodes, which had been pillaged by Muʻāwiyah's fleet as early as 654,[3] was temporarily occupied in 672.[4] Two years later Crete (Iqrīṭish) was treated to the same operation. Sicily (Ṣiqillīyah), destined to become later a flourishing appanage of the Arab Aghlabid dynasty which conquered it from Africa, was also reached about 664 and repeatedly attacked thereafter.[5] Under a successor of Muʻāwiyah, Sulaymān, Rhodes was again temporarily occupied (717–18).

Last Umayyad attack on Constantinople

For thirty-five years after Muʻāwiyah's death lull characterized the hostile relations between Arabs and Byzantines. His son's short reign (680–83) was occupied by domestic disturbances,[6] and his grandson Muʻāwiyah II's reign lasted only three months. This Muʻāwiyah was a weak and sickly youth, and Yazīd was no worthy successor of his father — what genius' son is? It was not until Sulaymān (715–17), a member of the Marwānid branch of the Umayyad family,[7] that expeditions

[1] Theophanes, pp. 353-4; Ṭabari, vol. ii, p. 163; ibn-al-Athīr, vol. iii, p. 413; Balādhuri, p. 236.

[2] Theophanes, pp. 353 *seq.*

[3] See above, p. 427.

[4] Balādhuri, p. 236; cf. Ṭabari, vol. ii, p. 157.

[5] Balādhuri, p. 235.

[6] See below, pp. 450-52.

[7] The subjoined tree shows the relation between the Sufyānid and the Marwānid branches of the family:

[*contd. on p.* 446

were resumed. A current *ḥadīth* (saying attributed to the Prophet) claimed that the caliph to conquer Constantinople would bear the name of a prophet. Sulaymān (Arabic for Solomon, whom the Moslems considered a prophet) took the *ḥadīth* to refer to himself. No sooner, therefore, had he been installed than he began to expedite the equipment and departure of the expedition which his great brother al-Walīd had started. Another brother, Maslamah, late in 715 led the expedition through Asia Minor. The land forces were supported by sea forces. Neither met initial success. While the fleet was in Cilicia on its way, Byzantine sailors landed on the Syrian coast and burned al-Lādhiqīyah. In Phrygia Amorium (Amorion, ʿAmmūrīyah, modern Assar Qalʿah) was passed by after an unsuccessful siege. Farther west, however, Pergamum and Sardis were taken. Finally the Dardanelles were crossed at Abydos and on August 25, 716, Constantinople was blockaded on the land side and two weeks later on the sea side. The Arab armada anchored by the walls of the city along the coast of Marmora and the Bosphorus. Entrance to the Golden Horn was barred by a chain, the first historical reference to such a barrier.

Of all the Arab attacks on the capital this was unquestionably the most threatening and the best recorded. The besiegers received aid from the Egyptian fleet. They used naphtha and siege artillery.[1] But the city was fortunate in having for defender Emperor Leo[2] the Isaurian (717–40), a soldier of humble Syrian origin from Marʿash, who was probably born a subject of the caliph and knew Arabic as perfectly as Greek.[3]

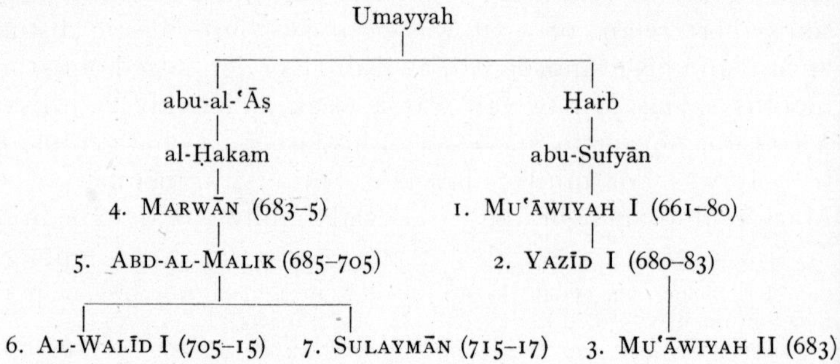

[1] *Al-ʿUyūn w-al-Ḥadāʾiq*, ed. de Goeje (Leyden, 1871), pt. 3, p. 24.
[2] Ilyūn of Arabic sources; Ṭabari, vol. ii, p. 1315.
[3] *ʿUyūn*, pt. 3, p. 25.

While the besieged were hard pressed, the besiegers were equally harassed. Pestilence, Greek fire, scarcity of provisions and attacks from Bulgars wrought havoc among them.[1] The rigours of an unusually severe winter added its share. But Maslamah stubbornly persisted. Neither such hardships nor the death of the caliph [2] seemed to deter him. But the order of the new caliph, 'Umar ibn-'Abd-al-'Azīz (717-20), he had to heed. The army withdrew in a pitiful state. The fleet, or what was left of it, was wrecked by a tempest on its way back; out of the 1800 vessels, if Theophanes' figures [3] are credible, only five survived to reach port in Syria. The Arab armada was gone. The Syrian founder of the Isaurian dynasty was hailed the saviour of Christian Europe from Moslem Arabs.

Only on one other occasion after this did an Arab host reach Constantinople; but that was not under the Umayyads. The leader was the 'Abbāsid Hārūn al-Rashīd, when still a crown prince, and the date was 782.[4] Hārūn encamped at Scutari (Chrysopolis) and exacted tribute from the Empress Irene.[5] The "city of Constantine" was no more to witness a Moslem invader at its gate until about seven centuries thence, when a new ethnic element, the Central Asian Turks, had adopted the religion of the Arabs and became its world champions.

Though a failure in itself the determined and energetic campaign by Maslamah fired the imagination of Moslem reporters and left many a legendary souvenir. Maslamah may have built a mosque at Abydos,[6] where he encamped, and dug a fountain that became known by his name; but that he was the first to erect a mosque in Constantinople,[7] stipulate the erection

[1] Consult Theophanes, pp. 386-99; ibn-al-Athīr, vol. v, pp. 17-19.

[2] Sulaymān died at Dābiq, the base of military operations against Asia Minor, which he had taken an oath not to leave until Constantinople was captured; Ṭabari, vol. ii, pp. 1315-16, 1336.

[3] Pp. 395, 399.

[4] Balādhuri, p. 168.

[5] Ṭabari, vol. iii, pp. 503-5; ibn-al-Athīr, vol. vi, 44-5. See below, p. 540.

[6] Ar. Abdus, corrupted into Andus in Yāqūt, vol. i, p. 374, and in ibn-al-Faqīh, *al-Buldān*, ed. M. J. de Goeje (Leyden, 1885), p. 104, l. 1, and into Andalus in Mas'ūdi, vol. ii, p. 317; cf. ibn-Khurdādhbih, *al-Masālik w-al-Mamālik*, ed. de Goeje (Leyden, 1889), p. 104.

[7] Ibn-al-Athīr, vol. x, p. 18; al-Dimashqi, *Nukhbat al-Dahr fi 'Ajā'ib al-Barr w-al-Baḥr*, ed. A. F. Mehren (Saint Petersburg, 1865), p. 227. Ibn-Taghri-Birdi, *al-Nujūm al-Zāhirah fi Mulūk Miṣr w-al-Qāhirah*, ed. W. Popper, vol. ii, pt. 2 (Berkeley, 1909-12), p. 40, ll. 12-13, claims that a Faṭimid *khuṭbah* (Friday noon sermon) was pronounced in this mosque. Consult ibn-al-Qalānisi, *Dhayl Ta'rīkh Dimashq*, ed. H. F. Amedroz (Beirut, 1908), p. 68, ll. 27-8.

of a special house for Arab prisoners near the imperial court and enter on horseback into Santa Sophia is pure fiction. The Syrian geographer al-Maqdisi [1] enthusiastically writes in 985: "When Maslamah ibn-'Abd-al-Malik invaded the land of the Romans and penetrated into their territory, he stipulated that the Byzantine dog should erect by his own palace in the Hippodrome (*maydān*) a special building [2] to be occupied by [Moslem] notables and noblemen when taken captives". The chief of Maslamah's guard, 'Abdullāh al-Baṭṭāl, stood next to Maslamah in legendary distinction. He won the title of champion of Islam. Killed in a later campaign (740),[3] he became a Turkish national hero under the title Sayyid Ghāzi (lord conqueror). At his grave in Eski-Shehr (medieval Dorylaeum) a Baktāshi *takīyah* (monastery) has risen. Local Greek Christians likewise canonized him. His was another instance of "an illustrious Moslem for whom Christians have raised a statue in one of their churches".[4]

Mardaites in Lebanon

An earlier and less spectacular campaign of Maslamah was directed against an obscure semi-independent people who occupied the rugged regions of North Syria. From their fastnesses in the Amanus (al-Lukkām) and the Taurus, these Mardaites (Maradah [5]), as they were called, had furnished recruits and irregular troops to the Byzantines and proved a thorn in the side of the Arabs. They were also called Jurājimah (Jarājimah) after their chief city al-Jurjūmah in the Amanus.[6] Entrenched on the Arab-Byzantine border they formed a "brass wall" [7] in defence of Asia Minor. Christians they were, but whether Monothelites or Monophysites is undetermined. As rebels, adventurers and warriors they offered their services to the highest bidder. When the Arab Moslems seized Antioch, the Jurājimah agreed to serve as scouts and guardians of the passes in their neighbourhood.[8] About 666 the Byzantine emperor dispatched bands of them, with his cavalry and regular

[1] *Aḥsan al-Taqāsīm*, p. 147.

[2] Known as al-Balāṭ, mentioned in Yāqūt, vol. i, p. 709, as being in use at the time of Sayf-al-Dawlah al-Ḥamdāni (944–67, see below, p. 564). *Balāṭ* is a loan word through Syriac from Latin or Greek *platea, palatium*.

[3] Ṭabari, vol. ii, p. 1716.

[4] Mas'ūdi, vol. viii, p. 74.

[5] From an ancient Semitic stem *mrd*, to rebel, to resist. Cf. Dīnawari, p. 130 l. 3, where *mard* is erroneously made Persian for "man".

[6] Yāqūt, vol. ii, p. 55; Balādhuri, p. 159.

[7] Theophanes, p. 364.

[8] Balādhuri, p. 159.

troops, which penetrated into the heart of Lebanon and occupied its chief strategic points as far as Palestine. Mount Lebanon then must have been very sparsely populated [1] and thickly wooded; only the part bordering on the maritime plain was fairly settled. Around these Mardaites as nucleus, fugitives and malcontents gathered. In northern Lebanon they were fused with the Maronites.[2] At that time Muʿāwiyah had his hands full with ʿAlid and other domestic problems and agreed to the payment of a heavy annual tribute to the emperor in consideration of his withdrawal of support from this internal enemy, to whom the caliph also agreed to pay a tax. Mountainous warfare, be it remembered, was never palatable to the Arabs. Ibn-Khaldūn's [3] observation that Arab facile domination is limited to plain lands is not without historic justification.

Evidently to counteract these Jurājimah Muʿāwiyah in 669 transported fresh people from al-ʿIrāq to the maritime coast and Antioch.[4] Earlier (662 or 663) he had transplanted many from Persia to replace the Greeks who left after the Moslem conquest and as a measure of protection against Byzantine naval raids. The Persians were settled in Sidon, Beirut, Jubayl, Tripoli, ʿArqah, Baʿlabakk and other towns.[5]

The Jurājimah caused as much trouble to the early Marwānids as they had done to the Sufyānids. Around 689 ʿAbd-al-Malik accepted the terms of Justinian II and agreed to pay a thousand dinars weekly to the Jurājimah. The emperor had loosed fresh bands of these highlanders on Syria. Thereby ʿAbd-al-Malik followed "the precedent established by Muʿāwiyah" [6]

At last in the days of ʿAbd-al-Malik's son al-Walīd (705–15) it was resolved to put an end to this Mardaite peril. Maslamah attacked the troublesome people in their own headquarters and demolished their capital al-Jurjūmah. Some perished, others migrated to Anatolia, and of those who remained some joined the Syrian army and fought under the banner of Islam. In the days of Yazīd II they co-operated in suppressing rebellions in al-ʿIrāq.[7]

[1] Cf. above, p. 82. [2] See below, pp. 521-2. [3] *Muqaddamah*, p. 125.
[4] Balādhuri, p. 162. [5] Yaʿqūbi, p. 327; Balādhuri, p. 148.
[6] Balādhuri, p. 160, l. 8; do. *Ansāb al-Ashrāf*, ed. S. D. F. Goitein, vol. v (Jerusalem, 1936), p. 300.
[7] For more on the Mardaites consult Lammens in *Mélanges*, vol. i, pp. 14-22; do. *Tasrīḥ al-Abṣār fi Ma Yaḥtawi Lubnān min al-Āthār*, vol. ii (Beirut, 1914), pp. 41-8.

CHAPTER XXXV

DOMESTIC DISTURBANCES: SHĪʿITES, MEDINESE, PERSIANS

The tragedy of al-Husayn

As long as the rule of powerful Muʿāwiyah lasted, no ʿAlids dared dispute his authority in an overt act; but the accession of frivolous Yazīd (680) was an invitation to secession. In response to urgent and reiterated appeals from ʿIrāqis, al-Ḥusayn, younger son of ʿAli and Fāṭimah, now declared himself the legitimate caliph after his elder brother and father.[1] At the head of a weak escort of devoted followers and relatives, including his harem, al-Ḥusayn, who had hitherto resisted the solicitations of his ʿIrāqi partisans and lived in retirement in Medina, set out from Mecca for al-Kūfah. ʿUbaydullāh, son of Ziyād whom Muʿāwiyah had found convenient to acknowledge as brother,[2] was now his father's successor in the governorship of al-ʿIrāq. Having received advance news of al-Ḥusayn's move, ʿUbaydullāh planted outposts on all roads leading from al-Ḥijāz to al-ʿIrāq. In Karbalā', twenty-five miles north-west of al-Kūfah, ʿUbaydullāh's cavalry patrol closed in on the pretender and when he refused to surrender, ʿUmar, son of Saʿd ibn-abi-Waqqāṣ, famous conqueror of al-ʿIrāq and founder of al-Kūfah, attacked with his 4000 men. Al-Ḥusayn was slaughtered, his band of 200 was cut down.[3] The head of the Prophet's grandson was sent to Yazīd in Damascus. The caliph turned it over to al-Ḥusayn's sister and son, who had accompanied it to the capital, and it was buried in Karbalā'.[4]

The day on which al-Ḥusayn fell, Muḥarram 10, A.H. 61 (October 10, 680), has since become a national day for mourning in Shīʿah Islam. Annually a passion play is enacted on this "tenth day" (*ʿāshūrā'*) portraying the "heroic" struggle and tragic suffering of the martyred leader (*imām*). The more

[1] *Fakhri*, p. 59; Dīnawari, pp. 243-4.
[2] See above, p. 436.
[3] Cf. Yaʿqūbi, vol. ii, p. 289; Masʿūdi, vol. v, p. 143.
[4] Ibn-Ḥajar, vol. ii, p. 17; ibn-ʿAsākir, vol. iv, pp. 332-5; ibn-al-Athīr, vol. iv pp. 67-75; Dīnawari, pp. 264, 267.

violent of the Persian mourners would, until recent times, walk in the streets almost naked with blood gushing from wounds inflicted on their bodies by themselves as acts of love, anguish and mortification. The names of Yazīd, 'Ubaydullāh and 'Umar have ever since been held accursed by all Shī'ites, to whom Karbalā' became the holiest place in the world. Pilgrimage to it is still considered more meritorious than to Mecca. In it Shī'ism was born. Al-Ḥusayn's blood, even more than 'Ali's, proved to be the seed of the new "church". From then on leadership and successorship in 'Ali's progeny became as fundamental a dogma in Shī'ite creed as that of the prophethood of Muḥammad in Sunnite Islam.[1] The "day (*yawm*) of Karbalā'" and "vengeance for al-Ḥusayn" became the battle cry of the Shī'ite camp, a camp that never ceased its activity even after it had made its contribution to the undermining of the Umayyad throne.

Another pretender

The elimination of al-Ḥusayn did not end the struggle for the caliphate, as it was a three-cornered struggle. 'Abdullāh ibn-al-Zubayr, whose father had fruitlessly disputed the caliphate with 'Ali,[2] now came out openly against Yazīd. In fact, he was one of those who had encouraged al-Ḥusayn in his perilous adventure,[3] and now al-Ḥijāz proclaimed him commander of the believers (*amīr al-mu'minīn*). Quick to act, Yazīd dispatched against the Medinese dissidents a disciplinary force in which many Christian Syrians served. The leader was the one-eyed Muslim ibn-'Uqbah, whose old age necessitated his carriage in a litter.[4] The battle was joined August 26, 683, and won by the Syrians. That for three days unchecked Damascene soldiery pillaged the city of the Prophet[5] is apocryphal. Ibn-al-Zubayr took refuge in Mecca, whose soil was considered inviolable, and Muslim pursued him.[6] *En route* the Syrian general died and was succeeded by al-Ḥuṣayn ibn-Mumayr al-Sakūni, one of whose arrows had pierced the mouth of al-Ḥusayn at Karbalā' as he was drinking.[7] Al-Ḥuṣayn had no scruples in directing his catapults against the Ḥaram (holy mosque).[8] The Ka'bah itself caught fire and was burned to

[1] See below, p. 502.
[2] See above, p. 431.
[3] Mas'ūdi, vol. v, p. 131; Dīnawari, pp. 256-7.
[4] Not related to 'Uqbah, above, p. 437.
[5] Dīnawari, pp. 274-5.
[6] *Ansāb*, vol. iv B, p. 40.
[7] Ṭabari, vol. i, p. 2220; Ya'qūbi, vol. ii, p. 299; Dīnawari, p. 269.
[8] *Ansāb*, vol. iv B, pp. 47-9.

the ground. The Black Stone, a fetish of pre-Islam and the holiest relic of Islam, was split in three.[1] The house of Allah looked " like the torn bosoms of mourning women ".[2] Meantime Yazīd had died and the operations which had begun September 24, 683, were suspended on November 27.

The death of Yazīd and the sudden withdrawal of Syrian troops from Arabian soil improved ibn-al-Zubayr's chances. He was thereupon proclaimed caliph not only in his home al-Ḥijāz but in al-ʿIrāq, South Arabia and even parts of Syria. Over al-ʿIrāq he appointed as his representative his brother Muṣʿab.[3] In Syria he appointed as provisional regent al-Ḍaḥḥāk ibn-Qays al-Fihri, leader of the Qaysite (North Arabian) party, which had always been anti-Umayyad.[4] The Yamanites (South Arabians), who included the Kalbites, rallied to the support of the aged legitimate caliph Marwān ibn-al-Ḥakam [5] and inflicted a crushing defeat on al-Ḍaḥḥāk and his party. This was on July 684 at Marj Rāhiṭ, a plain north-east of Damascus.[6] Rāhiṭ was another Ṣiffīn for the Umayyads. It marked the end of the third civil war in Islam which, like the second between Muʿāwiyah and ʿAli, was a dynastic war.[7] As for the internal feud between the Qays, representing the new emigrants from North Arabia, and the Kalb, staunch supporters of the Umayyad cause, it lingered and finally precipitated the fall of the Umayyad dynasty. The Qaysi and Yamani parties figured even in the modern politics of Lebanon and Syria.[8]

The crushing of the anti-Umayyad party in Syria amputated the limb but the head was still animate in al-Ḥijāz. There the anti-caliphate of ibn-al-Zubayr continued to exist until Marwān's son and successor ʿAbd-al-Malik sent against it his iron-handed general al-Ḥajjāj ibn-Yūsuf, formerly a schoolmaster in al-Ṭāʾif. Al-Ḥajjāj belonged to the same tribe, Thaqīf, to which al-Mughīrah belonged.[9] He was then thirty-one years old. His army had reportedly 20,000 men.[10] For six and a half months beginning March 25, 692, al-Ḥajjāj pressed the siege against

[1] Yaʿqūbi, vol. ii, pp. 309-11; *Ansāb*, vol. iv B, pp. 52, 55. For a Nabataean black stone and kaʿbah see above, p. 385.

[2] Ṭabari, vol. ii, p. 427.

[3] Yaʿqūbi, vol. ii, p. 314.

[4] See above, p. 425.

[5] Cited above, pp. 429, n. 3, 446, table.

[6] *ʿIqd*, vol. ii, pp. 320-21; Masʿūdi, vol. v, p. 201; *Ansāb*, vol. v, pp. 136 *seq.* See above, p. 414.

[7] See above, pp. 431-2.

[8] See below, pp. 686-7.

[9] See above, p. 436.

[10] Yaʿqūbi, vol. ii, p. 318.

Mecca. He had no more hesitancy than al-Ḥuṣayn in using his catapults effectively against the Holy City. Inspired by the heroic exhortations of his mother Asmā', daughter of abu-Bakr and sister of 'Ā'ishah, ibn-al-Zubayr fought valiantly but hopelessly.[1] At last he was slain. His head was sent to Damascus. His body, after hanging upside down on a cross, was delivered to his mother.[2] This is the first recorded crucifixion in Islam.

With the death of ibn-al-Zubayr the last champion of primitive Islam passed away. 'Uthmān was avenged. The Anṣār's (supporters') power was forever broken. The new orientation in Islam was secure; the ascendancy of the political over the religious in state authority was complete. Henceforth Mecca and Medina take back seats, and the history of Arabia begins to deal more with the effect of the outer world on the peninsula and less with the effect of the peninsula on the outer world. The mother "island" had spent itself.

Al-Ḥajjāj, energetic viceroy

'Abd-al-Malik committed to al-Ḥajjāj the government of al-Ḥijāz. This he held for a couple of years in the course of which he pacified not only that region but al-Yaman and even al-Yamāmah in the east. In 694 he was called to an equally, if not more, difficult task in the government of al-'Irāq.

Al-'Irāq was still a seething cauldron of discontent. Its people were "men of schism and hypocrisy".[3] In addition to Zubayrites and regular Shī'ites there were Khārijites [4] and those of the 'Alids who after al-Ḥusayn's death had proclaimed a half-brother of his, Muḥammad ibn-al-Ḥanafīyah, as their imām and *mahdi*.[5] This Muḥammad was a son of 'Ali and was so called after his mother. Especially troublesome were the Khārijites. They kept the east in constant turmoil. From al-'Irāq they spread into Persia, split into several fanatic, theocratic sects, overran al-Ahwāz and Karmān, took al-Rayy, besieged Iṣbahān and ravaged wherever they went. In Persia their movement

[1] Ṭabari, vol. ii, pp. 845-8.

[2] Ya'qūbi, vol. ii, pp. 319-20; Dīnawari, p. 321; *Aghāni*, vol. xiii, p. 43; *Ansāb*, vol. v. pp. 368-9.

[3] Mas'ūdi, vol. v, p. 295; Ya'qūbi, vol. ii, p. 326.

[4] See above, p. 433. For their tenets of belief consult al-Baghdādi, *Mukhtaṣar al-Farq bayn al-Firaq*, ed. Philip K. Hitti (Cairo, 1924), pp. 65-94.

[5] The divinely guided one. In Shī'ite circles the *mahdi* came to mean some forthcoming leader who would restore true Islam, conquer the world and, Messiah-like, usher in a period of peace and prosperity before the end of all things; Hitti, *History of the Arabs*, p. 441.

allied itself with the rising of the *mawāli*,[1] clients, against the Arabian masters. These were Persians who had accepted Islam on the assumption that it equalized all those within its fold and were now disappointed and disillusioned.

No sooner had al-Ḥajjāj received his appointment than he set out from Medina with a small mounted escort, crossed the desert by forced marches and arrived at al-Kūfah disguised and unannounced. It was early dawn, time of prayer. Accompanied by only twelve cameleers and with his bow on his shoulder and sword on his side, he entered the mosque, removed the heavy turban which veiled his stern features and delivered a fiery oration that has ever since formed one of the most favoured and dramatic themes in Arabic literature:

> " I am he who scattereth darkness and climbeth summits.
> As I lift the turban from my face, ye will know me."
>
> O people of al-Kūfah. Certain am I that I see heads ripe for cutting, and verily I am the man to do it. Methinks I see blood flowing between the turbans and the beards. . . . Verily the commander of the believers has ordered me to distribute among you the military stipends and enroll you under al-Muhallab ibn-abi-Ṣufrah[2] against the enemy. He of you who in three days after receiving his allowance does not depart, I swear by Allah that I will decapitate him.[3]

Saying this, al-Ḥajjāj commanded the caliph's rescript to be read aloud. It opened with: " In the name of God, the merciful, the compassionate. From the slave of God ʿAbd-al-Malik, the commander of the believers, to those of al-Kūfah who are Moslems. Peace be unto you ! " But there was no response. " Stop ", shouted al-Ḥajjāj in anger to the reader. " Has it come to such a pass that ye respond not to the greeting of the commander of the believers ? By Allah I will teach you soon to mend your ways. Begin again, young man." The reader did and when he repeated the caliphal salutation not one of the terrified congregation failed to join in the loyal

[1] Pl. of *mawla*, a non-Arab embracing Islam and affiliating himself with an Arabian tribe. His ill-defined rank placed him below the Moslem Arabians. See below, pp. 474, 485.

[2] This was the general who early in Muʿāwiyah's days (664–5) had undertaken a campaign as far as India and raided Kābul and Multān; cf. above, pp. 474, 485. Al-Ḥajjāj was his son-in-law.

[3] Mubarrad, pp. 215-16; cf. Yaʿqūbi, vol. ii, p. 326; Masʿūdi, vol. v, p. 294. The verse introducing the oration was a quotation from an earlier poet.

response: "And peace be unto the commander of the believers!"[1]

The new viceroy who had laid down the teacher's rod and taken up the warrior's sword was as good as his word. No neck proved too high for him to reach, no head too strong to crush. His task was to establish the ascendancy of the state over all elements within its framework — cost what it may. This he did. Human lives to the number of 120,000 are said to have been sacrificed by him; 50,000 men and 30,000 women were found held in prison at his death.[2] These undoubtedly exaggerated figures with the equally exaggerated reports about the tyranny of this Arab Nero, his blood-thirstiness, gluttony and impiety indicate that what the historians — mostly Shī'ites or Sunnites of the 'Abbāsid régime — have left us is a caricature rather than a portrayal of the man.

Reading between the lines, one can detect a number of constructive administrative achievements to the credit of al-Ḥajjāj. He dug old canals and opened new ones. He built a new capital Wāsiṭ (medial), so called from its half-way position between the two key cities of al-'Irāq — al-Baṣrah and al-Kūfah.[3] He introduced regulations to reform currency, taxes and measures.[4] The corruption of the Koran with which he was charged was evidently limited to a slight critical revision and to the introduction of orthographical signs designed to prevent incorrect reading of the sacred text.[5] Justifiable or not the repressive measures he took restored order in al-Kūfah and al-Baṣrah, hotbeds of discontent and opposition. The state authority was likewise firmly established along the eastern coast of Arabia, including hitherto independent 'Umān. His vice-royalty embraced also Persia. Here his general al-Muhallab practically eliminated that sect of the Khārijites most dangerous to Moslem unity, al-Azraqis. These got their name from their first leader, Nāfi' ibn-al-Azraq (the blue one), whose teaching went as far as considering all non-Khārijites — even if Moslems — infidels, whose blood with their wives' and

[1] Mubarrad, p. 216.
[2] Ibn-al-'Ibri, p. 195; cf. Mas'ūdi, vol. v, p. 382; do., *al-Tanbīh w-al-Ishrāf*, ed. M. J. de Goeje (Leyden, 1893), p. 318; Ṭabari, vol. ii, p. 1123.
[3] Ibn-Khallikān, *Wafayāt al-A'yān* (Cairo, 1299), vol. i, p. 221; al-Dhahabi, *Duwal al-Islām* (Ḥaydarābād, 1337), vol. i, p. 42; Ṭabari, vol. ii, p. 1125.
[4] See below, pp. 474.
[5] See below, p. 476.

children's was lawful.[1] By this time the Azraqis had, under the leadership of Qaṭar ibn-al-Fujā'ah, acquired mastery over Karmān,[2] Fāris and other eastern provinces. Beyond Persia al-Ḥajjāj's generals penetrated into the valley of the Indus, as we shall see in the next chapter. In his capital al-Ḥajjāj depended upon the faithful support of his garrison of Syrian troops, in whom his confidence — like his loyalty to the Umayyad house — knew no bound.

[1] Al-Shahrastāni, *al-Milal w-al-Niḥal*, ed. William Cureton (London, 1846), pp. 89-90; Baghdādi, pp. 72-6; Ṭabari, vol. ii, pp. 1003 *seq.*

[2] Or Kirmān, Yāqūt, vol. iv, p. 263; ibn-Khallikān, vol. ii, pp. 184-5.

CHAPTER XXXVI

THE GLORY THAT WAS DAMASCUS

DURING the reigns of ʿAbd-al-Malik and his four sons [1] the Umayyad dynasty in Damascus reached the meridian of its power and glory. Under al-Walīd (705–15) and his brother Hishām (724–43) the Islamic empire attained its greatest expansion, from the shores of the Atlantic and the Pyrenees to the Indus and the confines of China — an extent greater than that of the Roman empire at its height. At no time before or after did the Arab empire reach such dimensions. It was in this period of glory that the final and definite subjugation of Transoxiana, the reconquest and pacification of North Africa and the acquisition of the Iberian peninsula were accomplished. To this era also belong the nationalization or Arabicization of the state administration, the introduction of the first purely Arab coinage, the development of a system of postal service and the erection of such monuments of architecture as the Dome of the Rock in Jerusalem, the holiest sanctuary in Islam after those of Mecca and Medina.

The acquisition of Syria, al-ʿIrāq, Persia and Egypt under ʿUmar and ʿUthmān brought to an end the first stage in the history of Moslem conquest. The extension of the Moslem frontier under Muʿāwiyah to Khurāsān and Central Asia in

[1] The subjoined tree shows the genealogical relationship of the Marwānid branch of the Umayyad dynasty:

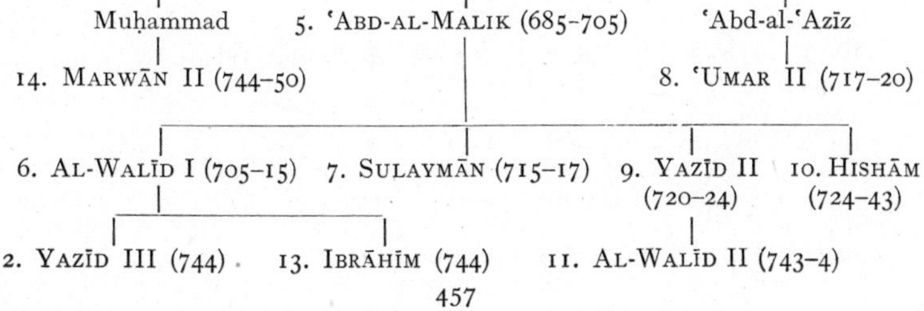

the east and to Ifrīqiyah in the west marked the second stage.[1] The definitive reduction of Transoxiana and the Indus valley under ʿAbd-al-Malik and his immediate successors signalize the third stage.

Subjugation of Transoxiana

It was the generals of al-Ḥajjāj who brought about the final reduction of the regions now called Turkestan, Afghanistan, Baluchistan and the Panjāb. One of these was ʿAbd-al-Raḥmān ibn-Muḥammad ibn-al-Ashʿath, governor of Sijistān and scion of the old royal family of Kindah in Central Arabia. His sister had married a son of al-Ḥajjāj. In 699–700 ʿAbd-al-Raḥmān marched against the *Zunbīl*,[2] Turkish (Iranian?) king of Kābul (Afghanistan), who had refused to pay the customary tribute. The dynasties and armies of these and other kingdoms in Central Asia were Turkish, but the subjects were mostly Iranians. So magnificently equipped was ʿAbd-al-Raḥmān's army that it was styled "the army of peacocks". ʿAbd-al-Raḥmān's successful campaign was cut short by his rebellion against al-Ḥajjāj, which resulted in the downfall of the general. In 704 he threw himself from the top of a tower and was killed,[3] one of the rare recorded cases of suicide in Islam.

The exploits of ʿAbd-al-Raḥmān pale before those of Qutaybah ibn-Muslim al-Bāhili, who in 704 on the recommendation of al-Ḥajjāj was appointed governor over Khurāsān, which he held as a subordinate of the viceroy.[4] From his capital Marw Qutaybah in a decade conducted a series of brilliant military campaigns into the lands "beyond the river" (*ma warāʾ al-nahr*). The river was the Oxus,[5] which until then had formed the traditional, though not historical, boundary line between "Īrān and Tūrān", i.e. between the Persian- and the Turkish-speaking peoples. In this period, the caliphate of al-Walīd, a permanent Moslem foothold was established there. Qutaybah's army comprised 40,000 Arab troops from al-Baṣrah, 7000 from al-Kūfah and 7000 clients.[6] In his first campaign

[1] See above, pp. 437-8.

[2] Wellhausen, *Reich*, p. 144, n. 3; less correctly Rutbīl, Ṭabari, vol. ii, pp. 1042 *seq.*; *Tanbīh*, p. 314.

[3] Ṭabari, vol. ii, p. 1135.

[4] Ibn-Khallikān, vol. ii, p. 180; Masʿūdi, vol. viii, p. 321.

[5] Modern Āmu Darya, Ar. and Per. Jayḥūn, adaptation of Gihon of Gen. 2 : 13. Sayḥūn for its sister river, Jaxartes, modern Sīr Darya, is an adaptation of Pison of Gen. 2 : 11.

[6] Balādhuri, p. 423; Ṭabari, vol. ii, pp. 1290-91.

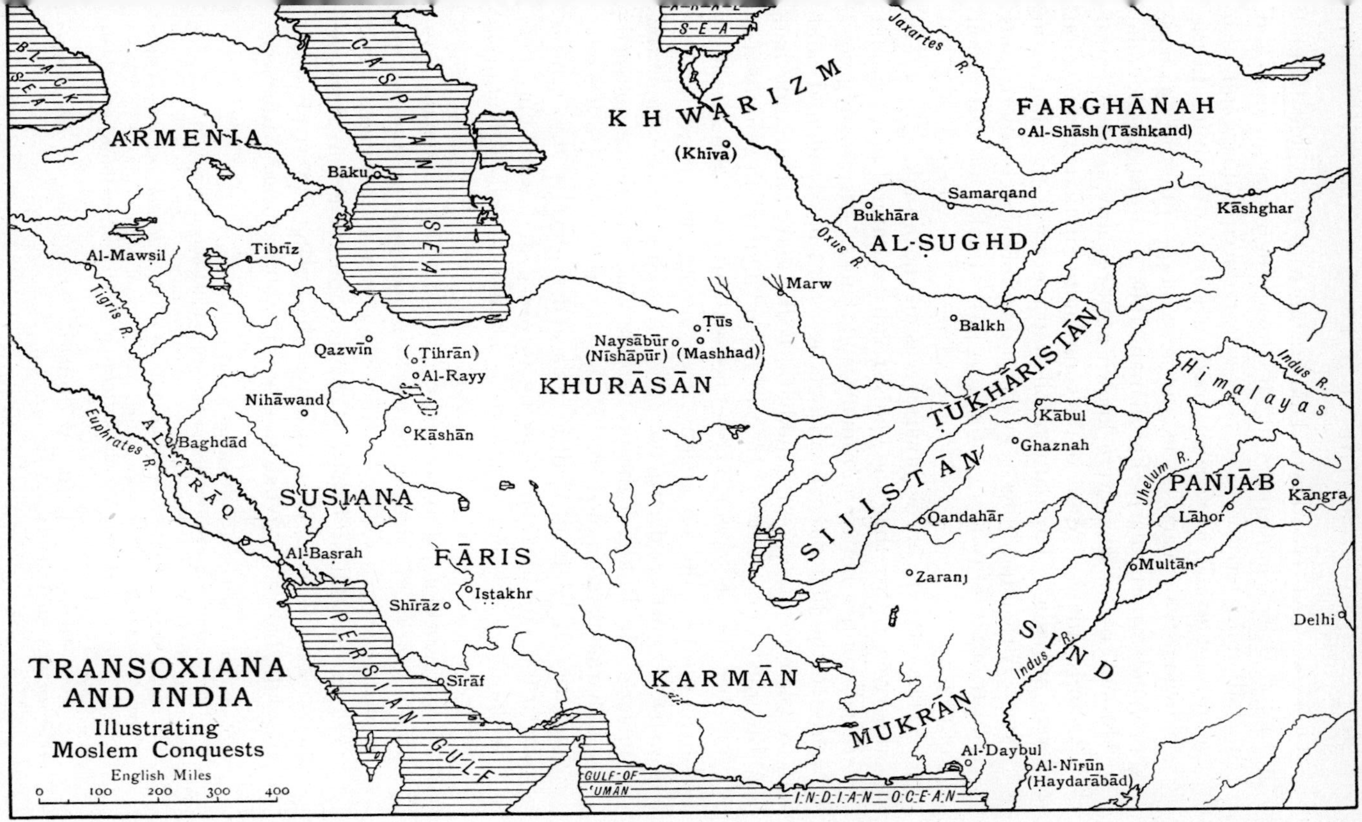

TRANSOXIANA AND INDIA
Illustrating Moslem Conquests

Qutaybah recovered lower Ṭukhāristān with its capital Balkh.[1] In 706–9 he conquered Bukhāra in al-Ṣughd (Sogdiana) and the adjoining territory. In 710–12 he reduced Samarqand (also in al-Ṣughd) and Khwārizm (modern Khīva) west of it. In the following two years he led an expedition into the Jaxartes provinces, particularly Farghānah, thus establishing nominal Moslem rule in what were known until recently as the Central Asian Khānates. Many of the communities in that entire region were nomadic. The pattern followed there was the same as in North Africa and other regions: raids, followed by more raids and tribute, refusal to continue to pay, attacks and conclusion of peace.

The crossing of the Jaxartes was an epoch-making event, as this river, rather than the Oxus, formed a natural political and racial frontier between Iranians and Turks. Its crossing constituted the first direct challenge by Arabs to Mongoloids and by Islam to Buddhism. Bukhāra, Balkh and Samarqand[2] had Buddhist monasteries. In Samarqand Qutaybah fell upon a number of idols to which he set fire with his own hand, resulting in a number of conversions from among devotees who had expected instant destruction to him who dared outrage the images. In Bukhāra the fire temple was likewise demolished. Bukhāra, Samarqand and Khwārizm were soon to become nurseries of Islam in Central Asia and to develop into centres of Arabic culture corresponding to Marw and Naysābūr (Per. Nīshāpūr) in Khurāsān, and to al-Baṣrah and al-Kūfah in al-ʿIrāq.

"Beyond the river" incorporated

The work of Qutaybah was continued by his lieutenant Naṣr ibn-Sayyār[3] and his successors. Appointed by the Caliph Hishām (724–43) as the first governor over Transoxiana, Naṣr used first Balkh and then Marw as capital. From Marw he had to reconquer (738–40) most of the territory overrun earlier by Qutaybah. Qutaybah was presumably satisfied with plant-

[1] Baktra of the Greeks. Balādhuri, p. 419.

[2] The ruler of Sogdiana resided at Samarqand and bore a Persian title *ikhshīd*, also borne by the king of Farghānah. The native rulers of these as well as Khwārizm and al-Shāsh, who too bore Persian titles (*khudāh, shāh, dihqān*), were perhaps related by marriage to the khān or khāqān of the Western Turks. The Arabs applied "Turk" to any non-Persian north-east of the Oxus. See ibn-Khurdādhbih, pp. 39-40; Yaʿqūbi, vol. ii, p. 479.

[3] Ibn-al-Athīr, vol. iv, p. 416; W. Barthold, *Turkestan down to the Mongol Invasion*, 2nd ed. (Oxford, 1928), p. 192.

ing Arab military agents who collected taxes and functioned side by side with native rulers. Kāshghar in Chinese Turkestan, allegedly conquered by Qutaybah (715),[1] was not reached until this time. When al-Walīd II ascended the throne (743), he recalled Naṣr and ordered him to come to Damascus with all kinds of strange hunting birds and musical instruments; but the caliph was assassinated while his governor was still on the way. By 751 Naṣr's successors had occupied al-Shāsh (Tāshkand), north-east of Samarqand, thus definitely establishing the supremacy of Islam in Central Asia, a supremacy that was not to be disputed any further by the Chinese. What lies "beyond the river" was at last fully incorporated into the extensive empire of the caliphs.

Conquest in India

While Qutaybah and Naṣr were conducting their successful campaigns in the eastern theatre of war, another general was moving southward into India. This was Muḥammad ibn-al-Qāsim al-Thaqafi, son-in-law of al-Ḥajjāj. His column comprised 6000 Syrian troops.[2] In 710 Muḥammad subdued Mukrān, pushed on through what is now called Baluchistan and in 711–712 reduced Sind, the lower valley and delta of the Indus. There he captured the seaport al-Daybul, which had a statue of the Buddha (Ar. Budd) "rising to a height of forty cubits",[3] and al-Nīrūn (modern Ḥaydarābād). In the following year the conquest was extended north as far as Multān, in south Panjāb, and the foot of the Himalayas. Multān was the seat of a national Buddhist shrine at which the invaders fell upon a large number of priests and pilgrims whom they took captive. So vast was the wealth plundered from this shrine that it became known by the name "the house of gold".[4] Multān served for years as the capital of Arab India and the outpost of Islam there.

Against the Byzantines

It was also in this period that some of the most determined attacks against the Byzantines were undertaken. In his early reign and while ibn-al-Zubayr was contesting the caliphate, ʿAbd-al-Malik paid tribute (A.H. 70/689–90) to the "tyrant of the Romans", as well as to his Christian allies, the Jurājimah, who had by that time established themselves in Lebanon.[5] But

[1] Ibn-al-Athīr, vol. v, p. 2.
[2] Balādhuri, p. 436.
[3] Yaʿqūbi, vol. ii, p. 346.
[4] Balādhuri, p. 440.
[5] See above, pp. 448-9.

shortly after that ʿAbd-al-Malik was in a position to take the offensive against the eternal enemy. In 692 his troops defeated those of Justinian II at the Cilician Sebastopolis. ʿAbd-al-Malik's successor, al-Walīd, pressed the offensive. About 707 his army occupied Tyana (al-Ṭawānah), the strongest fortress of Cappadocia. After capturing Sardis and Pergamum the way was open to Constantinople, to which Sulaymān's brother and general Maslamah laid his memorable but futile siege, August 716 to September 717.[1] Armenia, which had been overrun (644–5) while Muʿāwiyah was still governor of Syria but had taken advantage of ibn-al-Zubayr's debacle to revolt, was again reduced under ʿAbd-al-Malik.[2]

North Africa

Likewise Ifrīqiyah had to be reconquered at this time. So precarious was the hold of Muʿāwiyah's general ʿUqbah [3] on the land that it had to be evacuated by his successor. In ʿAbd-al-Malik's caliphate Ḥassān ibn-al-Nuʿmān al-Ghassāni (693–*ca.* 700) put an end to Berber resistance and Byzantine authority. With the aid of a Moslem fleet he drove the Byzantines from Carthage (698) and other coast towns. He then pursued and defeated their ally the Berber leader, a prophetess (Ar. *kāhinah*) [4] who held a mysterious control over her followers. The heroine was killed in the Awrās Mountain (Algeria) near a well that still bears her name, Bīr al-Kāhinah.

Ḥassān was followed by the celebrated Mūsa ibn-Nuṣayr. Under him the government of Ifrīqiyah, administered from al-Qayrawān, was divorced from Egypt and held directly from the caliphate in Damascus. Mūsa was born near Beirut. His father was a Syrian Christian captive who fell into the hands of Khālid ibn-al-Walīd with other boys while studying the Gospels at a church in ʿAyn al-Tamr in al-ʿIrāq.[5] It was Mūsa who extended the boundaries of the province westward as far as Tangier (Ṭanjah).

The conquests of Ḥassān and Mūsa brought the Berbers [6] permanently within the fold of Islam. Most of the Berbers who

[1] See above, p. 446. [2] Balādhuri, p. 160. [3] See above, p. 437.

[4] Balādhuri, p. 229; ibn-Khaldūn, vol. vii, pp. 8-9; ibn-ʿIdhāri, *al-Bayān al-Mughrib fi Akhbār al-Maghrib*, ed. R. Dozy (Leyden, 1848), vol. i, pp. 20-24.

[5] Others maintain that Mūsa was a Lakhmid, still others a Yamanite. Cf. Balādhuri, p. 230; ibn-ʿIdhāri, vol. i, p. 24.

[6] Eng. "Berber" and Ar. *Barbar* presumably come from L. *barbari* (originally Gr.), barbarians, a term applied by the Latinized cities of Roman Africa to all natives who did not adopt the Latin tongue.

were then on the fertile strip of land bordering on the sea were Christians. Among them Tertullian, Cyprian, Augustine and other saints and princes of the early Christian Church had flourished. The Byzantine settlers, as well as the Roman before them, were confined to the coastal towns. They represented a culture that remained alien to these nomads and semi-nomads of North Africa. Toward the Moslem Arabs the Berbers felt more affinity. As Hamites they were closer of kin to the Semites. Then they were all on the same cultural level. Moreover, the ancient Phoenician conquest and colonization of that region must have had its facilitating effects. Arabic tradition makes the majority of Berbers of Canaanite origin.[1] Punic, like Arabic a Semitic tongue, was still used in out-of-the-way places until shortly before the Moslem conquest. This explains the seemingly inexplicable miracle of so speedy and complete an Islamization and Arabicization of the Berbers. No sooner were they conquered than they were pressed into service, used as fresh relays in the continued forward march of Islam.

Conquest of Spain

The subjugation of North Africa as far as the Atlantic[2] opened the way for the conquest of south-western Europe. The momentous step was taken in 710, when the thirteen-mile strait was crossed by an Arab army for the first time. Plunder was the immediate objective. The raid developed into a conquest, the conquest of the entire Iberian peninsula.[3] The conquest was followed by occupation and control which lasted in part or in full for almost eight centuries. This successful campaign into the south-western part of Europe was the last and one of the most sensational military operations undertaken by the Arabs. It marked the acme of the Africo-European expansion, just as the conquest of Turkestan marked the height of the Asiatic expansion.

Ṭāriq crosses the strait

In its swiftness of execution and completeness of success this expedition into Spain holds a unique place not only in Arab but in medieval European annals. In July 710 a Berber band of four hundred foot and one hundred horse, under a client of Mūsa named Ṭarīf, landed on the tiny peninsula which

[1] Ṭabari, vol. i, p. 516; Mas'ūdi, vol. iii. pp. 239-40; ibn-al-Faqīh, p. 83. See above, p. 103.

[2] Ibn-'Abd-al-Ḥakam, pp. 203-5.

[3] Ar. al-Andalus, from Vandals, the German tribe that had overrun Spain.

formed almost the southernmost tip of the European continent. Whether Ṭarīf was a Berber or an Arab is still uncertain.[1] The peninsula has since borne the name of the general Jazīrat (isle of) Ṭarīf (Sp. Tarifa).[2] Encouraged by Ṭarīf's success and by the dynastic trouble in the Visigothic kingdom of Spain, Mūsa dispatched in 711 another freedman of his, Ṭāriq ibn-Ziyād. At the head of 7000 men, most of whom were, like him, Berbers, Ṭāriq landed near the mighty rock which has since immortalized his name, Gibraltar.[3] The ships, tradition asserts, were provided by a semi-legendary person, Julian,[4] Byzantine count of Ceuta.[5] The motive for his co-operation is not determined. The story of the violation of his beautiful daughter by the Visigothic usurper Roderick, offered in explanation, is apocryphal. In fact the entire story of the conquest has been richly embellished by both Arab and Spanish reporters.

A decisive victory

Reinforced, Ṭāriq at the head of 12,000 men encountered on July 19, 711, the army of Roderick at the mouth of the Barbate River [6] on the shore of the lagoon of the Janda.[7] Treachery in the Visigothic camp, instigated by relatives of the dethroned king, a son of Witiza,[8] contributed to the routing of the Spaniards, who numbered 25,000. Roderick himself disappeared and was heard of no more.

This turned out to be a decisive victory. The march of Moslem arms throughout the peninsula went on unchecked. Ṭāriq with the bulk of the army headed toward the capital Toledo. On his way he sent detachments against neighbouring

[1] Cf. al-Maqqari, *Nafḥ al-Ṭīb min Ghuṣn al-Andalus al-Raṭīb*, ed. Dozy, Wright *et al.* (Leyden, 1855), vol. i, p. 159; ibn-Khaldūn, vol. iv, p. 117; ibn-ʿIdhāri, vol. ii, p. 6; tr. Fagnan, vol. ii, p. 7; *Akhbār Majmūʿah fi Fatḥ al-Andalus*, ed. Lafuente y Alcántara (Madrid, 1867), p. 6 (text), p. 20 (tr.).

[2] Mentioned by al-Idrīsi, *Dhikr al-Andalus* (extracts from *Nuzhat al-Mushtāq*), ed. and tr. Don Josef A. Conde (Madrid, 1799), pp. 11, 35, 44.

[3] Ar. Jabal (mount of) Ṭāriq. Idrīsi, p. 36.

[4] Ulyān in Balādhuri, p. 230; Yulyān in *Akhbār*, vol. i, p. 4; ibn-ʿIdhāri, vol. ii, p. 6; Maqqari, vol. i, p. 159; ibn-ʿAbd-al-Ḥakam, p. 206; Yūliyān in ibn-al-Athīr, vol. iv, p. 444. Perhaps his real name was Urban or Olban.

[5] Sp. from Ar. Sabtah, ultimately from L. Septem Fratres (seven brothers). Idrīsi, p. 12.

[6] Now called Salado. Ar. Wādi Bakkah (Lakkah) corrupted into Sp. Guadilbeca and confused with Guadelete. Cf. Stanley Lane-Poole and Arthur Gilman, *The Moors in Spain* (New York, 1911), pp. 14, 23.

[7] Ar. al-Buḥayrah (the lake).

[8] Ar. Ghayṭasah, Ghīṭishah, etc. Roderick is Ar. Ludhrīq, Lazrīq, Rudhrīq. Maqqari, vol. i, pp. 160, 161; ibn-ʿAbd-al-Ḥakam, p. 206; ibn-ʿIdhāri, vol. ii, p. 8; ibn-Khaldūn, vol. iv, p. 117; *Akhbār*, p. 8; Masʿūdi, vol. i, p. 359.

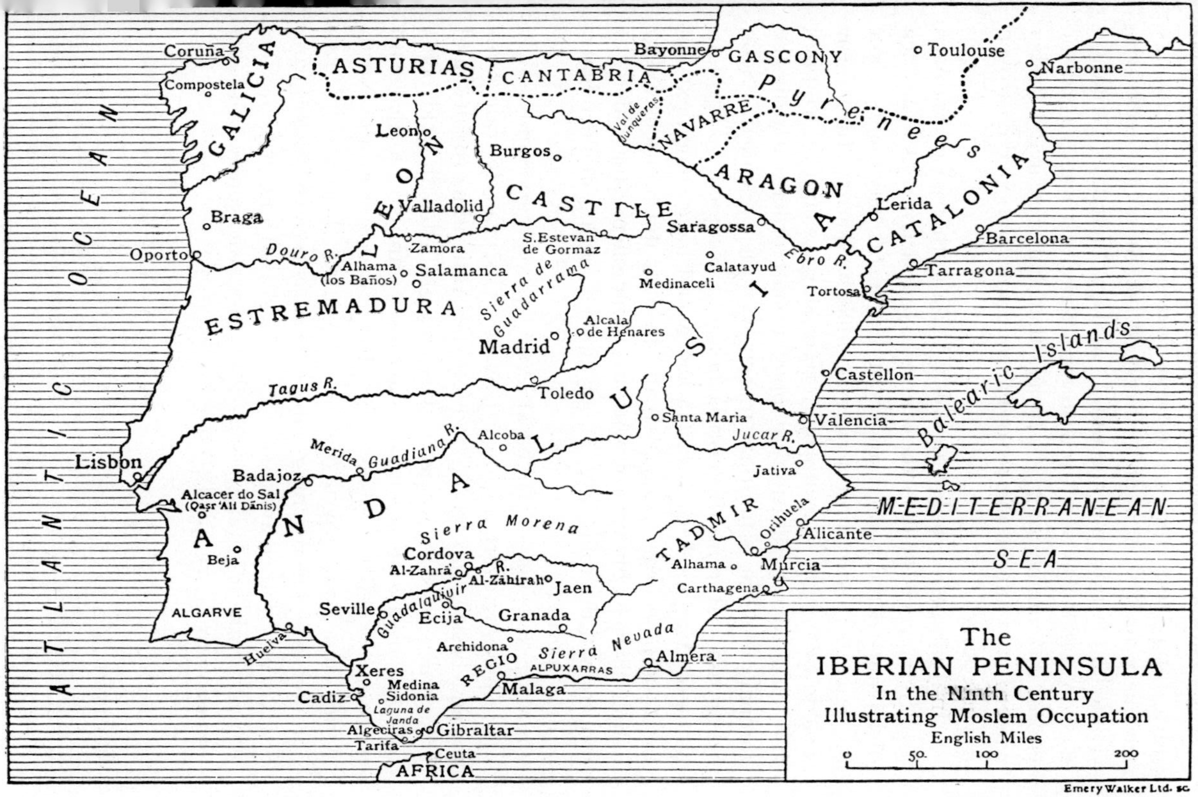

From Hitti, "History of the Arabs"

towns. Seville, a strongly fortified city, was by-passed. Cordova, future resplendent capital of Moslem Spain, fell through treachery on the part of a shepherd, so the story goes, who pointed out a breach in the wall.[1] Malaga offered no resistance. Toledo was betrayed by Jewish citizens. That was toward the end of the summer of 711. In less than half a year the Berber raider found himself master of half of Spain. He had destroyed a whole kingdom.

Mūsa follows

In June of the following year Mūsa with 10,000 Arabians and Syrians [2] rushed to the scene. He did not relish the idea of having all the honour and booty go to his lieutenants. For objective he chose those towns avoided by Ṭāriq. In or near Toledo he caught up with his former slave, whom he whipped and chained for refusing to obey a halt order early in the campaign.[3] The triumphal march was then resumed. Soon Saragossa in the north was reached and occupied. The highlands of Aragon, Leon and Galicia would have come next but for a caliphal order from al-Walīd in distant Damascus. The caliph charged his viceroy with the same offence for which the viceroy had disciplined his subordinate — acting independently of his superior.

A triumphal procession

Mūsa left his son ʿAbd-al-ʿAzīz in command and slowly made his way overland toward Syria. His princely train comprised, besides his staff, 400 of the Visigothic royalty and aristocracy, wearing their crowns and girdled with gold belts, followed by a long retinue of slaves and captives [4] loaded with treasures of booty. The triumphal passage through North Africa and South Syria forms a favourite theme with Arab chroniclers.[5] On reaching Tiberias, Mūsa received orders from Sulaymān, brother and heir of the sick al-Walīd, to delay his arrival at the capital so that it might synchronize with his accession to the caliphal throne.[6]

[1] Ibn-ʿIdhāri, vol. ii, pp. 10-11; *Akhbār*, p. 10. Cf. Maqqari, vol. i, pp. 164-5.

[2] Ṭabari, vol. ii, p. 1253.

[3] Ibn-ʿIdhāri, vol. ii, pp. 17-18; ibn-ʿAbd-al-Ḥakam, p. 210.

[4] 30,000 (!) according to Maqqari, vol. i, p. 144; cf. ibn-al-Athīr, vol. iv, p. 448.

[5] Ibn-ʿAbd-al-Ḥakam, pp. 210-11; ibn-ʿIdhāri, vol. ii, pp. 21-2; ibn-al-Qūṭīyah, *Taʾrīkh Iftitāḥ al-Andalus* (Madrid, 1868), p. 10; pseudo-ibn-Qutaybah, *Qiṣṣat Fatḥ al-Andalus* (taken from *al-Imāmah w-al-Siyāsah* and issued as supplement to ibn-al-Qūṭīyah), pp. 138, 140 *seq.*

[6] Cf. al-Marrākushi, *al-Muʿjib fi Talkhīṣ Akhbār al-Maghrib*, R. Dozy, 2nd ed. (Leyden, 1881), p. 8; tr. E. Fagnan, *Histoire des Almohades* (Algiers, 1893), p. 10.

Evidently Mūsa ignored the orders. In February 715 he made his impressive entry into Damascus and was received by al-Walīd, though some say by the newly installed caliph Sulaymān. The royal reception was held with great dignity and pomp in the courtyard of the newly and magnificently built Umayyad mosque, adjoining the caliphal palace. What a memorable day in the history of triumphant Islam! No such numbers of Western princes and fair-haired European captives were ever seen offering homage to the commander of the believers. If any single episode can exemplify the zenith of Umayyad glory, it is this. Foremost among the trophies Mūsa offered the caliph was the priceless table (*mā'idah*) which Ṭāriq had seized from the Toledo cathedral. Gothic kings had vied with each other in embellishing this table with precious stones. Legend assigns the original workmanship to jinn in the service of King Solomon, from whose temple it was carried away by Romans into their capital and thence by Goths into Spain. Ṭāriq, so the story goes, had secreted one of its legs when Mūsa wrested it from him in Toledo, and now dramatically produced the missing part as proof of his own exploit.[1]

Al-Walīd's successor disciplined Mūsa and humiliated him. After making him stand until exhausted in the sun, he dismissed him from office and confiscated his property. Mūsa met the same fate that many a successful general and administrator in Islam had met. The conqueror of Africa and Spain was last heard of begging for sustenance in a remote village of al-Ḥijāz.[2]

Spain was now incorporated in the Syrian empire. Mūsa's successors carried on the work of rounding out the conquered territory in the east and north. Half a dozen years after the landing of the first Arab troops on Spanish soil, their successors stood facing the towering and mighty Pyrenees.

Such seemingly unprecedented conquest would not have been possible but for internal weakness and dissension. The population of the country was Spanish-Roman; the rulers were

Explanation of the conquest

[1] Maqqari, vol. i, pp. 167, 172; ibn-'Abd-al-Ḥakam, p. 211; ibn-al-Athīr, vol. iv, pp. 448-9; ibn-Khallikān, vol. iii, pp. 26-7; *Nabdhah min Akhbār Fatḥ al-Andalus* (ext. *al-Risālah al-Sharīfīyah ila al-Aqṭār al-Andalusīyah*, supplement to ibn-al-Qūṭīyah, Madrid, 1868), pp. 193, 213. See *Arabian Nights*, No. 272.

[2] Maqqari, vol. i, p. 180; cf. ibn-Khallikān, vol. iii, p. 27.

Teutonic Visigoths (West Goths) who had occupied the land in the early fifth century. They ruled as absolute, often despotic, monarchs. For years they professed Arian Christianity and did not adopt Catholicism, the denomination of their subjects, until the latter part of the following century. The lowest stratum of the society was held in serfdom and slavery and, with the persecuted Jews, contributed to the facility with which the conquest was achieved.

The Pyrenees crossed

In 717 or 718 Mūsa's third successor, al-Ḥurr ibn-ʿAbd-al-Raḥmān al-Thaqafi [1] crossed the mountains that separate Spain from France. These were raids and they were continued by his successor al-Samḥ ibn-Mālik al-Khawlāni. The object was to seize the reputed treasures of convents and churches. In 720, under the Caliph ʿUmar II, al-Samḥ captured Narbonne (Ar. Arbūnah), to be later converted into a huge citadel with an arsenal. In the following year an unsuccessful attempt was made on Toulouse, seat of Duke Eudes of Aquitaine, in which al-Samḥ was killed. Thereby the first victory by a Germanic prince over Arabs was registered.

The battle of Tours

Twelve years later ʿAbd-al-Raḥmān ibn-ʿAbdullāh al-Ghāfiqi, al-Samḥ's successor as amīr over Spain, undertook the last and greatest expedition across the Pyrenees. Having vanquished Duke Eudes on the banks of the Garonne, he stormed Bordeaux and pushed northward to Poitiers, outside of whose walls he set a basilica on fire. Thence he headed toward Tours. Tours held the shrine of St. Martin, apostle to the Gauls. Its votive offerings provided the chief attraction to the invader.

Between Poitiers and Tours ʿAbd-al-Raḥmān's way was intercepted by Charles, mayor of the palace at the Merovingian court. Not a king in name, Charles was a king in fact. His valour had subdued many enemies and forced Eudes to acknowledge the sovereignty of the northern Franks.

After seven days of skirmishing the battle raged. It was an October Saturday in 732. The Frankish warriors, mostly foot, knew how to protect themselves against the cold weather with wolfskins. In the thick of the battle they stood shoulder to shoulder, forming a hollow square, firm as a rock and inflexible as a block of ice — to use the words of a Western historian.[2]

[1] Ibn-ʿIdhāri, vol. ii, pp. 24-5; ibn-al-Athīr, vol. v, p. 373.

[2] André Duchesne, *Historiae Francorum scriptores*, vol. i (Paris, 1936), p. 786.

Without giving way they hewed down the light cavalry of the enemy as it attacked them. ʿAbd-al-Raḥmān fell. Darkness separated the combatants. Under cover of night the invaders stole away and vanished. It was not until the morning that Charles realized what he had done. He had won a victory. His surname then became Martel (hammer).

To the Moslems this battlefield was simply a *balāṭ*[1] *al-shuhadā'*,[2] a pavement of martyrs, a martyr being anyone killed in war against non-Moslems. To the Christians, however, it marked a turning-point in the military career of their eternal foe. European historians would see in Paris and London mosques, where cathedrals now stand, and fezes where hats are worn, had the outcome of the battle been otherwise.[3] In reality nothing was decided on the battlefield of Tours. The Moslem wave, already about a thousand miles from its starting-point in Gibraltar — to say nothing about its base in al-Qayrawān — had already spent itself and reached a natural limit. Moreover, the army's morale had been lowered by internal discord. Jealousy thrived between Arabs and Berbers. The Berbers complained that they were allotted the arid central plateau while the Arabs appropriated for themselves the most smiling provinces of Andalusia, this despite the fact that the Berbers had carried the brunt of the battle. The Arabs themselves were far from being united by common feeling and purpose. The old feud between North Arabians (Muḍarites)[4] and South Arabians (Yamanites) was reasserting itself. And now sectarian differences were adding their contribution. The Muḍarites were Sunnites, but some of the Yamanites were now Shīʿites or Shīʿite sympathizers. The Berbers expressed their difference by espousing another doctrine, the Khārijite.[5]

Though checked at Tours the Arab raids in other directions did not cease. In 734 Avignon was captured; nine years later Lyons was pillaged. The fact, however, remains that Tours does indicate the extreme limit of the victorious march of Islam. Its year 732 marks the centennial of the Prophet's death. A

Damascus the capital

[1] See above, p. 448, n. 2.

[2] *Akhbār*, p. 25; Maqqari, vol. i, p. 146. The battle was fought on a paved Roman road. Cf. John 19: 13.

[3] Gibbon, *Decline and Fall*, vol. vi, pp. 15 *seq*. See also Lane-Poole, pp. 29-30.

[4] The Muḍar and Rabīʿah, both of North Arabian origin, were often included under the collective term Maʿadd. Cf. above, p. 452.

[5] See above, p. 433.

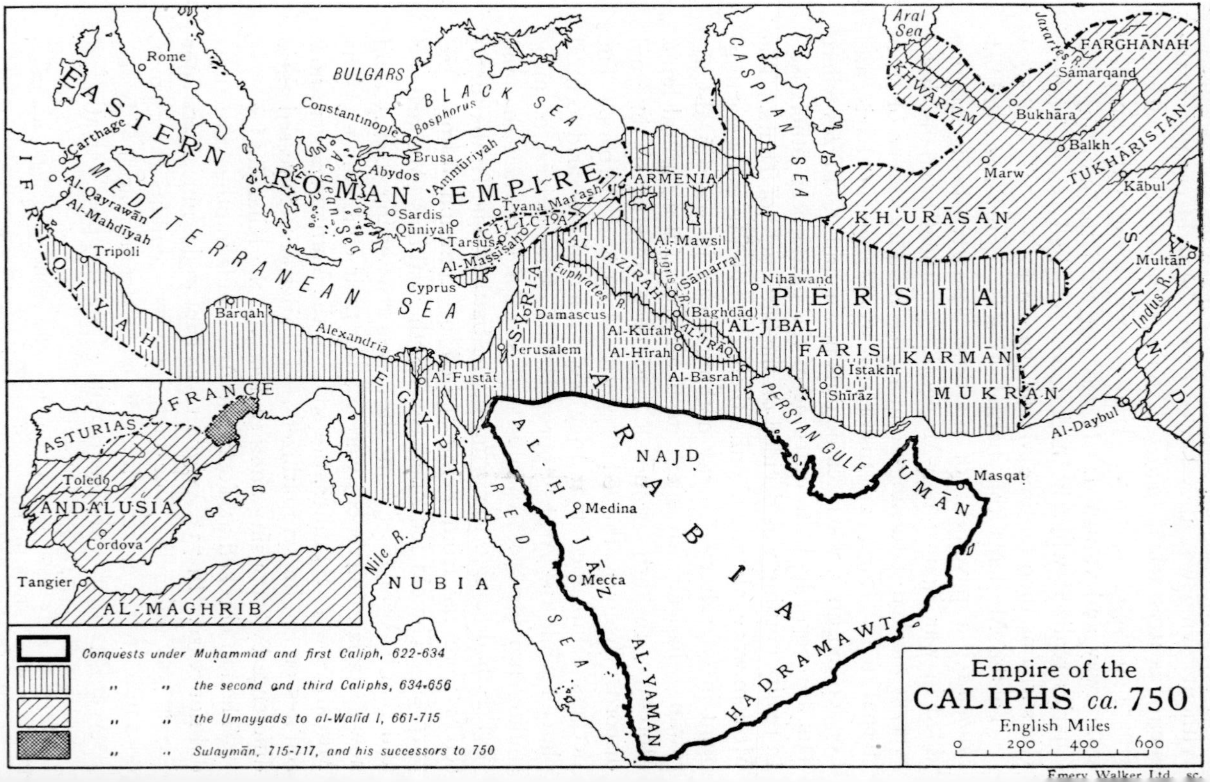
Empire of the
CALIPHS ca. 750
English Miles
0 200 400 600
Conquests under Muḥammad and first Caliph, 622-634
" " the second and third Caliphs, 634-656
" " the Umayyads to al-Walīd I, 661-715
" " Sulaymān, 715-717, and his successors to 750
EASTERN ROMAN EMPIRE
MEDITERRANEAN SEA
BLACK SEA
CASPIAN SEA
Aral Sea
PERSIAN GULF
RED SEA
Aegean Sea
BULGARS
Rome
Carthage
Al-Qayrawān
Al-Mahdīyah
Tripoli
IFRĪQIYAH
Barqah
Alexandria
EGYPT
Al-Fusṭāṭ
Nile R.
NUBIA
Constantinople
Bosphorus
Brusa
Abydos
'Ammūriyah
Sardis
Qūniyah
Tyana
Mar'ash
CILICIA
Tarsus
Al-Maṣṣīṣah
Cyprus
SYRIA
Damascus
Jerusalem
ARMENIA
AL-JAZĪRAH
Euphrates R.
Tigris R.
Al-Mawṣil
Sāmarrā
(Baghdād)
Al-Kūfah
Al-Ḥīrah
AL-'IRĀQ
Al-Baṣrah
Nihāwand
PERSIA
AL-JIBĀL
FĀRIS
Iṣṭakhr
Shīrāz
KARMĀN
MUKRĀN
KHURĀSĀN
KHWĀRIZM
Jaxartes R.
FARGHĀNAH
Samarqand
Bukhāra
Balkh
Marw
TUKHĀRISTĀN
Kābul
Multān
Indus R.
SIND
Al-Daybul
ARABIA
NAJD
AL-ḤIJĀZ
Medina
Mecca
AL-YAMAN
ḤAḌRAMAWT
'UMĀN
Masqaṭ
FRANCE
ASTURIAS
Toledo
ANDALUSIA
Cordova
Tangier
AL-MAGHRIB
Emery Walker Ltd. sc.

pause here and now to survey the entire situation may be worth while. A hundred years after the death of the founder of Islam,

From J. Sauvaget, J. Weulersse and M. M. L. Écochard, " Damas et la Syrie Sud " (Damascus)

DAMASCUS FROM THE MINARET OF THE UMAYYAD MOSQUE

In the foreground is the tomb of Salāḥ-al-Dīn, in the rear the citadel and behind it Mount Qāsiyūn cut by the gorge of Barada

his followers were the masters of an empire greater than that of Rome at its zenith — an empire extending from the Bay of Biscay to the Indus and the confines of China and from the

Aral Sea to the cataracts of the Nile. The capital of this huge domain was Damascus, the oldest living city, the one which reportedly Muḥammad hesitated to enter, because he wished to enter paradise but once.[1] The city was set like a pearl in an emerald girdle of gardens (*ghūṭah*). Through the ages these gardens relied upon snow-fed brooks from Anti-Lebanon for their existence From the north rushes Barada to fling tassels of silver streams across the outstretched plain. From the south comes Pharpar (Abana) laden with tribute from the copious springs of Mount Hermon. Yāqūt,[2] the great geographer of the early thirteenth century, claims that he visited all four spots considered earthly paradises and found Damascus the first among them. "To sum up," he continues, "nothing attributed by way of description to the heavenly paradise is not found in Damascus." [3] The city overlooked a plain stretching southwestward to that venerable patriarch of Lebanon crests, Mount Hermon, called by the Arabs al-Jabal al-Shaykh (the greyhaired peak),[4] because of its turban of perpetual snow. In the centre of the city stood the Umayyad mosque, a gem of architecture that still attracts lovers of beauty. Near by lay the caliphal palace, called al-Khaḍrā', because of its green dome.[5] In his palace the caliph held his formal audiences. Dressed in gorgeous flowing robes, he would sit, cross-legged, on a square throne covered with richly embroidered cushions. Paternal relatives, arranged according to seniority, stood on the right side; maternal relatives on the left; courtiers, poets and petitioners behind.

Nationalizing the state

It was only natural for the state on attaining maturity to Arabicize its administration and nationalize its institutions. Until now Greek had persisted in Syria as the language of the public registers; Pahlawi and certain local dialects had survived in al-'Irāq and the eastern provinces. There was no choice in the matter. The Moslem conquerors, fresh from the desert and ignorant of book-keeping and finance, had to retain in the exchequer Greek-, Pahlawi- and other non-Arabic-writing officials. By this time, however, some of these secretaries had undoubtedly mastered Arabic, and some Arab officials had

[1] For other traditions extolling Damascus see ibn-'Asākir, vol. i, pp. 46 *seq.*

[2] *Buldān*, vol. ii, p. 589. [3] *Buldān*, vol. ii, p. 590. [4] See above, p. 41, n. 6.

[5] Ibn-Jubayr, *Riḥlah*, ed. William Wright (Leyden, 1907), p. 269, l. 3; *Aghāni*, vol. vi, p. 159.

mastered the intricacies of secretarial details. It was time for Arabic to replace all other languages as the official language of the bureaus. The transition was necessarily slow, beginning under ʿAbd-al-Malik and continuing during the reign of his son. That may be inferred from the fact that certain authorities

From "Katalog der orientalischen Münzen, Königliche Museen zu Berlin" (Walter de Gruyter & Co., Berlin)

AN IMITATION IN GOLD OF A BYZANTINE COIN WITH ARABIC INSCRIPTION

Retaining on the obverse the figures of Heraclius, Heraclius Constantine, and Heracleonas, and on the reverse a modified Byzantine cross

ascribe the change to the father, others to the son.[1] Thus in the course of a millennium three written languages succeeded each other in Syria: Aramaic, Greek and Arabic. In al-ʿIrāq and its dependencies the Umayyad viceroy al-Ḥajjāj substituted

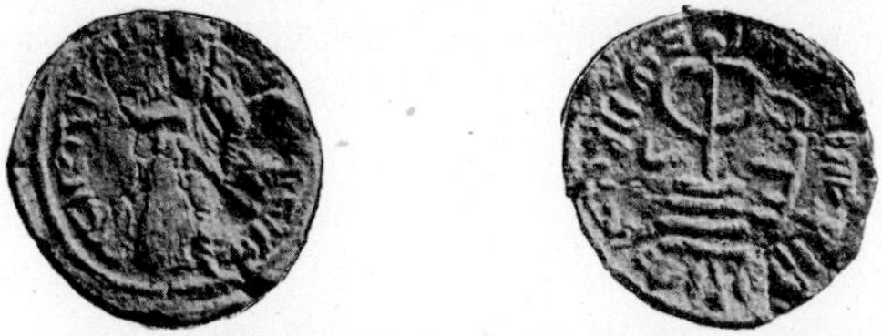

From "Katalog der orientalischen Münzen, Königliche Museen zu Berlin" (Walter de Gruyter & Co., Berlin)

COPPER COIN OF ʿABD-AL-MALIK

Bearing on the obverse his image and his name and on the reverse ȹ on four steps together with the *shahādah* and the mint name, Baʿlabakk. An imitation of the Byzantine dinar

Arabic for the dialects in the chancellery. As to the extent to which the population was Arabicized, that will be treated in the next chapter.[2]

With the change of language went a change in coinage. Hitherto the Byzantine coinage, found current in Syria at the time of conquest, was left undisturbed.[3] In certain cases

[1] *ʿIqd*, vol. ii, p. 322; Māwardi, pp. 349-50; Balādhuri, pp. 193, 300-301. Balādhuri naïvely ascribes the cause to a trivial occurrence, urination of a Greek clerk in an inkwell. [2] Pp. 484-5. [3] Balādhuri, pp. 465-6.

koranic superscriptions were stamped on the coins. A few gold and silver pieces were struck in imitation of Byzantine and Persian types. Muʻāwiyah issued some copper pieces on which the portrait of the king holding a cross was replaced by that of the caliph brandishing a sword. But it was not until the time of ʻAbd-al-Malik (695) that the first purely Arabic dinars and dirhams [1] were struck.[2] In the following year al-Ḥajjāj minted silver in al-Kūfah.[3]

Postal service

Moreover, ʻAbd-al-Malik developed a regular postal service (*barīd*) [4] designed primarily to meet the needs of government officials and their correspondence. In this he built on the foundation laid by his great predecessor Muʻāwiyah.[5] ʻAbd-al-Malik promoted the service through a well-organized system knitting together the various parts of his far-flung empire. To this end relays of horses were used between Damascus and the provincial capitals. Postmasters were installed, charged among other duties with the task of keeping the caliph posted on all important happenings in their respective territories. Al-Walīd made use of the system for his building operations.

Fiscal and other reforms

Other changes in this period involved taxes and fiscal matters. In theory the only tax incumbent on a Moslem, no matter what his nationality might be, was the alms-tax (*zakāh*); but in practice only the Moslem of Arabian origin usually enjoyed this privilege. Taking advantage of the theory, new converts to Islam, particularly from al-ʻIrāq and Khurāsān, began under the Umayyads to desert their farms and villages in favour of the cities with the hope of joining the Arab army as *mawāli* (singular *mawla*, client). This term was used later for freedmen but at this time bore no connotation of inferior status. From the standpoint of the treasury the movement constituted a double loss, for at conversion the taxes were supposedly reduced and upon joining the army a special subsidy was due. As a measure of remedy al-Ḥajjāj ordered such men restored to their farms [6] and reimposed the high tribute origin-

[1] See above, p. 436, n.

[2] Ṭabari, vol. ii, p. 939; Balādhuri, pp. 240, 466-70.

[3] Cf. Yāqūt, *Buldān*, vol. iv, p. 886.

[4] Al-ʻUmari, *al-Taʻrīf bi-al-Muṣṭalaḥ al-Sharīf* (Cairo, 1312), p. 185. Ar. *barīd* is an ancient Semitic word from *brd*, "to send" Cf. Esth. 8:10; Iṣfahāni, *Ta'rīkh*, p. 39.

[5] *Fakhri*, p. 148.

[6] Mubarrad, p. 286.

ally paid, the equivalent of the land-tax (*kharāj*) and poll-tax (*jizyah*).

Al-Ḥajjāj's enactment resulted in so much dissatisfaction among Neo-Moslems, that the pious caliph ʿUmar II (717–20) considered it wise to re-establish the old principle ascribed to his earlier namesake [1] — that a Moslem, whether Arabian or *mawla*, need pay no tribute whatsoever.[2] When an official in Khurāsān objected that the numerous conversions were adversely affecting the treasury and suggested testing the new converts by ascertaining whether they had gone through

By courtesy of E. T. Newell
From "Numismatic Notes and Monographs", No. 87 (*New York*, 1939)

A BYZANTINE WEIGHT VALIDATED BY AL-WALĪD (d. 715)

Bearing on the obverse a cross with the inscription ΓB, i.e. two ounces, and on the reverse a Kufic inscription stating that the caliph has recognized this as equivalent to two *waqīyahs*. Probably the earliest inscribed Moslem weight thus far found

circumcision, ʿUmar replied: "Verily God sent His Prophet as a missionary and not as a circumciser".[3] ʿUmar insisted, however, that the land for which *kharāj* was paid should, on the conversion of its owner, be considered joint property of the Moslem community, with the understanding that the original owner might continue to use it as a leaseholder.[4] Since the poll-tax was a comparatively low item, the treasury thus continued to receive its main income from the land-tax.

ʿUmar's policy was not successful. It diminished the state revenue in proportion as it increased the number of city clients.[5] Berbers, Persians and others flocked to Islam for the pecuniary

[1] See above, pp. 422-3. [2] Balādhuri, p. 426.
[3] Ṭabari, vol. ii, p. 1354; ibn-al-Athīr, vol. v, p. 37.
[4] Ibn-ʿAsākir, vol. iv, p. 80; Yaʿqūbi, vol. ii, p. 362; ibn-al-Jawzi, *Sīrat ʿUmar ibn-ʿAbd-al-ʿAzīz* (Cairo, 1331), pp. 88-9.
[5] Ibn-al-Jawzi, pp. 99-100.

privileges that accrued. Later practice reverted to the system of al-Ḥajjāj with minor modifications.

Other reforms undertaken by al-Ḥajjāj relate to Arabic orthography. To distinguish such similarly written letters as *bā'*, *tā'* and *thā'*, *dāl* and *dhāl* he introduced diacritical marks, and to remove ambiguity in vocalization he adapted from Syriac certain signs (*ḍammah* (*u*), *fatḥah* (*a*) and *kasrah* (*i*)) to be inserted above and below the letters.

The architectural monuments which stand out among the great achievements of this period will be treated in a later chapter (XXXVIII).

CHAPTER XXXVII

POLITICAL AND SOCIAL CONDITIONS UNDER THE UMAYYADS

THE administrative divisions of the Umayyad empire followed in the western provinces the Byzantine pattern and in the eastern provinces the Persian. The main provinces were nine: (1) Syria-Palestine; (2) al-Kūfah, which included al-ʿIrāq; (3) al-Baṣrah with Persia, Sijistān, Khurāsān, al-Baḥrayn, ʿUmān and probably Najd and al-Yamāmah; (4) Armenia; (5) al-Ḥijāz; (6) Karmān and the frontier districts of India; (7) Egypt; (8) Ifrīqiyah; (9) al-Yaman and the rest of South Arabia. Out of these, five vice-royalties developed: that of al-ʿIrāq, which included most of Persia and eastern Arabia with al-Kūfah as capital; that of al-Ḥijāz, which embraced al-Yaman and Central Arabia; the vice-royalty of al-Jazīrah (the northern part of the Tigro-Euphrates region), with which went Armenia, Ādharbayjān and parts of eastern Asia Minor; that of Egypt, which combined both Upper and Lower; and finally Ifrīqiyah, whose capital was al-Qayrawān and which comprised northern Africa west of Egypt, together with Spain and the Mediterranean islands.

Provincial government

The threefold governmental function of political administration, tax collection and religious ministry was directed by three types of officials. The viceroy (*amīr, ṣāḥib*) had under him provincial governors (sing. *ʿāmil*), whom he appointed and for whose conduct he was responsible. As viceroy he had full charge of the political as well as military administration of his domain. In certain cases revenues were collected by a special officer (*ṣāḥib al-kharāj*) responsible directly to the caliph. The chief source of income was tribute from subject peoples. All provincial expenses were met from local income; only the balance went to the caliphal treasury.

The first purely judicial officials in the provinces received their appointments from the governors. Many such judges [1]

[1] Sing. *qāḍi*, Anglicized kazy, kasi, cadi and in six other forms.

were installed in the Umayyad period, recruited as a rule from among scholars learned in the Koran and Islamic tradition. Their jurisdiction was limited to Moslem citizens; non-Moslems were allowed autonomy under their own religious heads, especially in personal matters relating to marriage, divorce and inheritance. Besides judging cases these officials administered pious foundations (sing. *waqf*) and estates of orphans and imbeciles.

Bureau of registry

Created by Muʿāwiyah, the bureau of the seal (*dīwān al-khātim*) was a sort of state chancery charged with the duty of making and preserving one copy of each official document before sealing and dispatching it.[1] The first part of the Arabic name suggests Persian origin.[2] By ʿAbd-al-Malik's time a whole state archive had developed in Damascus.[3]

Military organization

Like the Byzantine army, after which it was modelled, the Umayyad army was divided into five corps: centre, two wings, vanguard and rearguard. The last Umayyad caliph Marwān II (744–50) abandoned this formation in favour of the small compact body termed *kurdūs* (cohort).[4] In outfit and armour the Arab warrior was hard to distinguish from his Greek counterpart. The cavalry used plain, rounded saddles like the ones still in fashion in the Near East. The heavy artillery comprised the ballista (*ʿarrādah*), mangonel (*manjanīq*) and battering-ram (*kabsh*, *dabbābah*). Such heavy engines together with the baggage were transported on camels behind the army.

The core of the army at Damascus consisted of Syrians and Syrianized Arabs. The Sufyānid caliphs maintained a standing army of 60,000, entailing a yearly expenditure of 60,000,000 dirhams.[5] Yazīd III (744) reduced all annuities by ten per cent, which won him the sobriquet of *nāqiṣ* (diminisher, also deficient). Under his successor, the last of the dynasty, the army probably numbered not more than 12,000.[6]

The Arab fleet was likewise an imitation of the Byzantine model and was manned mostly by Syrians.[7] The galley, with

[1] Ṭabari, vol. ii, pp. 205-6; *Fakhri*, p. 149.

[2] Cf. Balādhuri, p. 464.

[3] Masʿūdi, vol. v, p. 239.

[4] Ṭabari, vol. ii, p. 1944; ibn-al-Athīr, vol. v, p. 267, ll. 7-8; ibn-Khaldūn, vol. iii, p. 165, l. 16 (cf. p. 195, ll. 25-7).

[5] Masʿūdi, vol. v, p. 195.

[6] Erroneously given as 120,000 in *Fakhri*, p. 197; abu-al-Fidāʾ, vol. i, p. 222. See below, p. 531.

[7] See above, p. 426.

a minimum of twenty-five seats on each of the two lower decks, was the fighting unit. Each seat held two rowers; the hundred or more rowers in each ship were armed. Those who specialized in fighting took up their positions on the upper deck.

Royal life

Caliphal life in Damascus was fully regal in contrast with that of Medina, which had been on the whole simple and patriarchal.[1] Relations with the Umayyad caliphs began to be regulated by protocol. Ceremonial clothes with the name of the caliph and religious sentences embroidered on their borders came into use possibly in 'Abd-al-Malik's days. The cloth was manufactured by Copts in Egypt, who also prepared the papyrus scrolls [2] for writing purposes. This caliph ordered that Moslem formulas replace the cross and the Trinity at the head of the scrolls. The Persian word *ṭirāz*, applied to embroideries, brocades, robes of honour and other material manufactured for the sole use of the royalty, suggests that in this the caliphs followed Iranian rather than Byzantine models.

The evenings of the caliph were set apart for entertainment and social intercourse. Mu'āwiyah's pastime was listening to tales. He imported a story-teller, 'Abīd ('Ubayd ?) ibn-Sharyah, all the way from al-Yaman to relate to him deeds of the heroes of the past.[3] Rose sherbet, still enjoyed in Damascus and other Eastern towns, was a favourite drink.

Some, however, desired a stronger beverage. Mu'āwiyah's son Yazīd was the first confirmed drunkard among the caliphs. His intemperance won him the sobriquet Yazīd *al-khumūr* (of wines).[4] Among those who participated in his drinking bouts was a pet monkey, abu-Qays, whom he trained to drink with him. Yazīd is said to have drunk daily, whereas al-Walīd I drank every other day; Hishām once every Friday; and 'Abd-al-Malik only once a month, but then so heavily as to necessitate the use of emetics.[5] Most of this information about the lighter side of the caliphs' lives comes from the *'Iqd*, *Aghāni* [6] and similar literary works which should not be taken too literally. Yazīd II's weakness was for singing girls as well as wine. Most

[1] See above, p. 428.
[2] Sing. *qirṭās*, from Gr.; Balādhuri, p. 240.
[3] See below, pp. 492-3.
[4] *Ansāb*, vol. iv B, p. 30; *'Iqd*, vol. iii, p. 403; Nuwayri, *Nihāyah*, vol. iv, p. 91.
[5] Cf. *'Iqd*, vol. iii, p. 404.
[6] Vol. i, p. 3, gives as criterion for the choice of data: " elegance that pleases the onlooker and entertains the hearer "

of his time he spent with his two favourite songstresses, Sallāmah and Ḥabābah. And when Ḥabābah was choked on a grape which he had playfully thrown into her mouth, the passionate young caliph fretted himself to death.[1] But the prize in drinking should be awarded to his son al-Walīd II (743–4), an incorrigible libertine (*khalīʿ*), whose favourite pastime reportedly was to go swimming in a pool of wine of which he would gulp enough to lower the surface.[2] He is said to have once opened the Koran and as his eyes fell upon the passage "And every froward potentate was brought to naught",[3] he was so enraged that he shot the sacred book to pieces with his bow and arrow.[4] The *Aghāni* [5] has preserved an eye-witness's report of one of this caliph's debauched parties, some of which were held in his desert palace by al-Qaryatayn, midway between Damascus and Palmyra. Those among the caliphs who maintained reasonable self-respect would screen themselves behind curtains which separated them from the entertainers; but not this al-Walīd.[6]

Innocent pastimes

Several caliphs and courtiers engaged in more innocent pastimes such as hunting, dicing and horse-racing. Polo (*jūkān*, from Per. *chawgān*) was introduced from Persia probably toward the end of the Umayyad period and soon became a favourite and fashionable sport with the ʿAbbāsids. Cock-fights at that time were not infrequent. The chase was one of the early sports of Arabia, where the saluki (*salūqi*, from Salūq in al-Yaman) dog was at first exclusively used. The cheetah (*fahd*) was used later. The Persians and Indians had trained this animal long before the Arabians. Yazīd I was the first great hunter in Islam; he trained the cheetah to ride on the croup of his horse. His hunting dogs wore gold anklets and each had a special slave assigned to it.[7] Al-Walīd I was one of the first caliphs to institute and patronize public horse-races.[8] His brother Sulaymān had planned a national competition in horse-racing when death overtook him.[9] In a course organized by their brother Hishām, 4000 racers from the royal and other stables took part, "which finds no parallel in pre-Islamic or

[1] *Al-ʿUyūn w-al-Ḥadā'iq* (1865), pp. 40-41; cf. *Aghāni*, vol. xiii, p. 165.
[2] Al-Nawāji, *Ḥalbat al-Kumayt* (Cairo, 1299), p. 98.
[3] Sūr. 14:18.
[4] *Aghāni*, vol. vi, p. 125.
[5] Vol. ii, p. 72.
[6] Al-Jāḥiẓ, *al-Tāj fi Akhlāq al-Mulūk*, ed. Aḥmad Zaki (Cairo, 1914), p. 32.
[7] *Fakhri*, p. 76.
[8] Masʿūdi, vol. vi, pp. 13-17
[9] Ibn-al-Jawzi, *Sīrat*, p. 56.

Islamic annals ".[1] A daughter of this caliph evidently kept a stud.[2]

Royal harem

The harem of the caliphal household apparently enjoyed a relatively large measure of freedom. They undoubtedly appeared veiled in public, veiling (*ḥijāb*) being an ancient Semitic custom sanctioned by the Koran.[3] ʿĀtikah, the beautiful daughter of Muʿāwiyah, was the subject of love poems addressed to her by a Meccan poet who happened to catch a glimpse of her face through the lifted veils and curtains as she was on a pilgrimage. The poet did not hesitate to follow her to her father's capital. Here the caliph found it expedient to "cut off the poet's tongue" by the usual procedure of offering a subsidy. He, moreover, found him a suitable wife.[4] A granddaughter of Muʿāwiyah, also named ʿĀtikah, reportedly locked the door of her room when angry with her husband-caliph, the powerful ʿAbd-al-Malik, and refused to open it until a favourite courtier rushed weeping and falsely announced that one of his two sons had killed the other and that the caliph was on the point of executing the fratricide.[5] Another poet, Waḍḍāḥ al-Yaman, ventured to make love to a wife of al-Walīd I in Damascus, the caliphal threats notwithstanding. For his audacity he finally paid with his life.[6] This poet and other good-looking men veiled themselves on festive occasions as a protection against the evil eye.[7] The harem system, with its concomitant auxiliary of eunuchs, was not fully instituted until the days of al-Walīd II.[8] The eunuch institution was based on the Byzantine model; most of the early eunuchs were Greeks.[9]

The capital

The city of Damascus cannot have changed much in character and tone of life since its Umayyad days. Then, as now, in its narrow covered streets the Damascene with his baggy trousers, heavy turban and red pointed shoes rubbed shoulders with the sun-tanned Bedouin in his flowing gown surmounted

[1] Masʿūdi, vol. v, p. 466. [2] *Al-ʿUyūn w-al-Ḥadāʾiq* (1865), p. 69, l. 12.
[3] See above, pp. 174, 388, fig.; Sūr. 33:53, 55.
[4] *Aghāni*, vol. vi, pp. 158-61.
[5] Masʿūdi, vol. v, pp. 273-5.
[6] *Aghāni*, vol. vi, pp. 36 *seq.*; vol. xi, p. 49.
[7] *Aghāni*, vol. vi, p. 33.
[8] *Aghāni*, vol. iv, pp. 78-9.
[9] J. B. Bury, *The Imperial Administrative System in the Ninth Century* (London, 1911), pp. 120 *seq.*; Charles Diehl, *Byzance: grandeur et décadence* (Paris, 1919), p. 154.

by the *kūfīyah* (head shawl) and *'iqāl* (head band). Occasionally a European-dressed *Ifranji* [1] passed by. A few women, all veiled, crossed the streets; others stole glimpses through the latticed windows of their homes overlooking the bazaars and public squares. There was no right or left rule of way, no part of the passage reserved for riders or pedestrians. Amidst the confused crowd an aristocrat might be seen on horseback cloaked in a silk *'abā'* and armed with a sword. The screaming voices of sherbet sellers and sweetmeat vendors competed with the incessant tramp of passers-by and of donkeys and camels laden with the varied products of the desert and the sown. The entire city atmosphere was charged with all kinds of smell. The demand on eye, ear and nose was overwhelming.

As in Ḥimṣ, Aleppo (Ḥalab) and other towns the Arabians lived in separate quarters of their own according to their tribal affiliation. These quarters (sing. *ḥārah*) are still well marked. The door of the house usually opened from the street into a courtyard. In the centre of the courtyard stood a large basin with a flowing jet emitting intermittently a veil-like spray. An orange or citron tree flourished by the basin. It was the Umayyads who, to their eternal glory, supplied Damascus with a water system unexcelled in its day and still functioning. The name of one of them, Yazīd I, is still borne by a canal from the Barada which he dug or more probably widened.[2] The luxurious gardens outside of Damascus, al-Ghūṭah, owe their very existence to this river, which sends off other canals to spread freshness and fertility throughout the city. About sixty remaining public baths, some with mosaics and decorated tiles, testify to the richness and distribution of its water supply.[3]

Society

The population of the empire was divided into four social classes. At the top stood the ruling Moslems, headed by the caliphal family and the aristocracy of Arabian conquerors. Down to the 'Abbāsid period the Arabs constituted a social hereditary caste. How numerous was this class cannot be exactly ascertained. It should be borne in mind that few of

[1] A Frank, a word used for all Europeans, especially common during the Crusades.

[2] Iṣṭakhri, p. 59; cf. H. Sauvaire, "Description de Damas: 'Oyoûn et-Tawârîkh, par Mohammed ebn Châker", *Journal asiatique*, ser. 9, vol. vii (1896), p. 400.

[3] For more consult M. Écochard, *Les Bains de Damas* (Beirut, 1942).

the Arabs and Bedouins were interested in agriculture and that they mostly congregated in cities. Lebanon was naturally avoided. The mountain does not seem to have received an influx of Arabs till the ninth and succeeding centuries. According to a late tradition the Tanūkh, who figured prominently in the political affairs of Lebanon, did not enter it till the early ninth.[1] The Tanūkh were not very numerous and, like other feudal families, left no descendants.[2] The banu-ʿĀmilah spread to its southern part after the eleventh.[3] In Syria the banu-Ḥamdān, who established a dynasty in Aleppo,[4] did not reach there until the middle of the tenth. The banu-Mirdās,[5] who succeeded them, reached Aleppo in the early eleventh. It is interesting to note that none of these tribes came directly from the desert; they were all previously domesticated in the Ḥīrah or some other region of the Fertile Crescent. As for the Bedouin tribes today in control of the Syrian Desert, their migration there is comparatively recent. The ʿAnazah did not figure prominently till the second half of the seventeenth century, succeeding the Shammar, who had come from Najd. The Ruwalah are a branch of the ʿAnazah. These were the last great Bedouin migrations to Syria.[6]

Some Arabians, even Bedouins, no doubt drifted into country places and established villages. The village development followed a clear line of transition from a temporary settlement to a semi-permanent pastoral-agricultural unit to the permanent village establishment. Most villages had as nucleus a spring of water with due consideration to ease of defence and fertility of soil. Traits of tribal life and organization, such as family solidarity, exaltation of individual prowess, hospitality, predominance of personal touch in all human relations, are still manifest and highly prized in the Syrian and Lebanese society.

[1] Al-Shidyāq, *Ta'rīkh al-Aʿyān fi Jabal Lubnān* (Beirut, 1859), p. 224; cf. Ṣāliḥ ibn-Yaḥya, *Ta'rīkh Bayrūt*, ed. L. Cheikho (Beirut, 1902), p. 65, where Tanūkh from whom the Buḥtur were descended is not made a member of the Tanūkh tribe but a descendant of the Lakhmid al-Mundhir ibn-Mā'-al-Samā'.

[2] Cf. Fu'ād Ḥamzah, *Qalb Jazīrat al-ʿArab* (Cairo, 1933), p. 233.

[3] See above, p. 411, n. 3.

[4] See below, pp. 564 *seq*.

[5] See below, pp. 580-81.

[6] Consult Waṣfi Zakarīya, *ʿAshā'ir al-Sha'm*, vol. i (Damascus, 1945), pp. 117-118.

The Arabian army which conquered Syria numbered some 25,000.[1] Under Marwān I the number of Arabian Moslems in the military registers of Ḥimṣ and its district (*jund*) was 20,000. Under al-Walīd I, Damascus and its district, which included the Phoenician coast, had 45,000 registered. On this basis the number of Moslems in Syria toward the end of the first century after the conquest could not have exceeded 200,000 out of an estimated population of 3,500,000.[2] As for the population of Lebanon the bulk remained Aramaicized Phoenicians. A small minority in all conquered lands, the Arabians were the same minority everywhere; and that is why they were able to play the important rôle they did in the unifying of the vast majority.

The Arab concentration in cities was such that Arabic by that time had become the urban language. As the country folk came to these cities to sell their products or practise their crafts, they acquired the new tongue without necessarily forsaking the old one. The indigenous intellectuals also found it convenient to acquire Arabic in order to qualify for government posts.

The number of country people who readily accepted the new faith must have been fewer than those who accepted the new language, mainly because the Umayyad caliphs, with the exception of the pious 'Umar II,[3] did not favour conversion especially from among owners of arable land. Umayyad liberalism was not only political but religious and intellectual also. The capital and the large cities may by the end of the Umayyad era have presented the aspect of Moslem towns, but the other places, more particularly the mountain regions, preserved their native features and ancient culture pattern. Umayyad Syria reared one of the greatest theologians and hymnologists of the Eastern Church, St. John of Damascus, and her sons gave Christendom five popes; two of whom were canonized.[4] Lebanon remained Christian in faith and Syriac in speech for centuries after the conquest. Indeed, what came to an end with the conquest was the physical conflict; the

[1] See above, pp. 415-16.

[2] Lammens, *La Syrie*, vol. i, pp. 119-20; cf. above, pp. 279, 292.

[3] See above, pp. 475-6.

[4] John V (685–6), St. Sergius (687–701), Sisinnius (708), Constantine (708–15), St. Gregory III (731–41); see below, p. 499.

religious, ethnic, social and above all linguistic conflicts had just begun.

Next below the Arabian Moslems stood the Neo-Moslems. Those were natives who because of force, pressure or persuasion professed Islam and were thereby in theory, though not in practice, admitted to the full rights of Islamic citizenship. Such converts usually attached themselves as clients (*mawāli*) to some Arabian tribe and became members thereof. Clients

As clients the neophytes formed the low stratum of Moslem society, a status which they bitterly resented. Their espousal of the Shīʿite cause in al-ʿIrāq and the Khārijite in Persia was one way in which they expressed their dissatisfaction. Some of them, however, embraced the new faith with such zeal that they became its fanatic exponents ready to persecute their former co-religionists. Clients were naturally the first within the Moslem society to devote themselves to learned studies and the fine arts. They mediated their old traditions and culture to their new co-religionists. As they demonstrated their superiority in the intellectual field, they began to contest with them political leadership. And as they intermarried with them they diluted the Arabian stock and ultimately made the term *ʿArab* applicable to all Arabic-speaking Moslems regardless of the original ethnic relationship.

The third class consisted of members of tolerated sects, professors of revealed religions, i.e. Christians, Jews and Ṣābians (*Ṣābi'ah*), with whom the Moslems had entered into a covenant relationship. The tolerated status was granted to Christians and Jews as *ahl al-kitāb* (people of the book, Scripturaries) by Muḥammad himself [1] and was partly due to the esteem in which the Prophet held the Bible and partly to the fact that a number of Arabian tribes on the Syro-ʿIrāqi border, like the Ghassān, Bakr, Taghlib, Tanūkh, were already Christianized. The Ṣābians were granted this privilege [2] on the assumption that they were monotheists. These people were identical with the Mandeans, the so-called Christians of St. John, and still survive in the marshes at the mouth of the Euphrates. In Arabia proper, however, consequent to an alleged statement by Muḥammad, no non-Moslems were tolerated, the only exception being a small Jewish community Dhimmis

[1] Koran 9:29; 2:99, 103; 3:62-5, etc. [2] Koran 2:59; 5:73; 22:17.

in al-Yaman. This recognition of tolerated sects was predicated on disarming their devotees and exacting tribute from them in return for Moslem protection (*dhimmah*). This was Islam's solution of the minority problem.

In this status dhimmis enjoyed, against the payment of land and capitation tax, a measure of toleration. Not being members of the dominant religious community they held an inferior position socially and politically. In matters of civil and criminal judicial procedure they were left under their own spiritual heads (unless a Moslem was involved).[1] Moslem law was considered too sacred to be applicable to non-Moslems. Essential parts of this system survived through the Ottoman era and the mandatory régimes. The theory of inseparability between religion and nationality was an ancient Semitic one and not a Moslem invention.

The tolerated status was, after Muḥammad, extended to the fire-worshipping Zoroastrians (Magians, *Majūs*), the star worshippers of Ḥarrān (pseudo-Ṣābians), the heathen Berbers and others. Though not devotees of a revealed religion and technically outside the pale of Islam, these were offered by the Moslem invaders the three choices: Islam, the sword or tribute, rather than the first two only. Abu-Yūsuf,[2] the distinguished judge under Hārūn al-Rashīd, expressly states that — in addition to Scripturaries — polytheists, fire-worshippers and idolaters may be accepted as protected citizens of a Moslem state.

In Syria the dhimmis were well treated until the days of ʿUmar II. One conspicuous exception was the case of the chief of the Christian tribe of Taghlib who was put to death by al-Walīd I for refusing to profess Islam.[3] Evidently the Moslems were less tolerant of Christians who were descended from Arabian stock, as illustrated by this case and the case of the Tanūkh. The Tanūkh of the neighbourhood of Qinnasrīn were summoned to Islam at the time of the conquest of Syria and some of them responded;[4] others, of the neighbourhood of Aleppo, were forced to adopt Islam by the ʿAbbāsid al-Mahdi (775–85), who demolished their churches. In Egypt the Copts, after expressing their individuality by several risings against their Moslem overlords, finally succumbed in the days of the

[1] Consult Koran 5:47-52.
[2] *Kharāj*, p. 79, ll. 15-17.
[3] *Aghāni*, vol. x, p. 99.
[4] Balādhuri, pp. 144-5.

ʿAbbāsid al-Ma'mūn (813–33).[1] Christians and Jews pursued their usual means of livelihood though some, such as the manufacture and sale of wine and the conduct of gambling games, were taboo to Moslems. Drinking and gambling houses, where dicing was a favourite pastime, continued to flourish and were patronized even by Moslems. Monks were experts in wine-making and in honey, fruit and flower raising. In connection with the monasteries, some of them must have maintained special guest rooms for entertainment and pleasure. Al-ʿUmari, himself a Damascene (d. 1349), cites many cases in which caliphs and other Moslems patronized monasteries and convents for drinking and pleasure, not all of the innocent variety. This was especially true of al-Walīd ibn-Yazīd.[2] In one instance this caliph so much appreciated the wine of a monastery that he filled the stone basin, which he with the collaboration of his brother had emptied, with silver pieces. From Lebanon wine was exported as far as Medina. A Ḥijāzi poet who attended so many all-night parties that his wife's suspicion was aroused, explained to her, " Deprive me not of an honourable companion who ne'er speaks ill of others. . . . It is wine from the villages of Beirut,[3] pure, faultless, or from the land of Baysān. Forsooth we drank it until it caused us to stagger." [4]

Dis-abilities imposed by ʿUmar

ʿUmar's fame does not rest primarily on his piety or his remission of taxes on neophyte Moslems. He was the first caliph in Islam to impose humiliating restrictions on his Christian subjects — measures wrongly ascribed to his earlier namesake.[5] He issued regulations excluding Christians from public offices, forbidding their wearing turbans and requiring them to cut their forelocks, don distinctive clothes with girdles of leather, ride without saddles, erect no places of worship and pray in subdued voices. The penalty for a Moslem's killing of a Christian, he further decreed, was only a fine, and a Christian's testimony against a Moslem was not acceptable in court. It may be assumed that such legislation was enacted in response to popular demand. In administration, business and industry the Arabian

[1] Al-Kindi, *Ta'rīkh Miṣr wa-Wulātuha*, ed. Rhuvon Guest (Leyden, 1912), pp. 73, 81, 96, 116, 117; al-Maqrīzi, *al-Mawāʿiẓ w-al-Iʿtibār bi-Dhikr al-Khiṭaṭ w-al-Āthār* (Būlāq, 1270), vol. ii, p. 497.

[2] Ibn-Faḍl-Allāh al-ʿUmari, *Masālik al-Abṣār fi Mamālik al-Amṣār*, ed. Aḥmad Zakī, vol. i (Cairo, 1924), pp. 321-22, 349, 351-2, 355-6.

[3] Cf. above, pp. 97, 297-8.

[4] *Aghāni*, vol. ii, pp. 86, 88.

[5] See above, p. 422. Ibn-ʿAbd-al-Ḥakam, pp. 151-2.

Moslems, still predominantly illiterate, could offer no competition to the indigenous Christians. The Jews, who were fewer than Christians and often held meaner jobs, were evidently included under some of these restrictions and excluded from government posts. It should be noted that wearing distinctive dress to designate differing peoples was somewhat practised before Islam in the Near East and that some of these enactments were not enforced after 'Umar's day.

Slaves

At the bottom of the social ladder stood the slaves. Slavery was an ancient Semitic institution the legality of which the Old Testament admitted. Islam accepted the institution and legislated to ameliorate the condition of the slave [1] (*'abd*). Canon law forbade the Moslem to enslave his co-religionist, but did not guarantee liberty to an alien slave on adopting Islam.

In early Islam, slaves were recruited by purchase, kidnapping, raiding and from unransomed prisoners of war, including women and children. Soon the slave trade became brisk and lucrative in all Moslem lands. East and Central Africa supplied black slaves; Farghānah and Chinese Turkestan yellow ones, the Near East and south-eastern Europe white ones. The institution was a self-perpetuating one. Islamic law considers the offspring of a female slave by another slave, by any man other than her master, or by her master in case he does not admit the fatherhood of the child, likewise a slave. But the offspring of a male slave by a free woman is considered free.

Between master and female slave concubinage was made permissible by koranic legislation. The children of such a union belong to the master and are therefore free. The status of the concubine is then raised to that of "child's mother" (*umm walad*). In this state the husband-master can neither sell her nor give her away; at his death she is declared free. The liberation of a slave has always been looked upon as a good work (*qurbah*) bringing the master nearer to God. A liberated slave enjoyed the status of a client (*mawla*) to his former master and was entitled to inherit his patron's estate in case of death without heirs.

In the melting-pot process which resulted in the amalgamation of Arabians and non-Arabians, slaves, no doubt, played a

[1] Koran 4:40, 29-30; 24:33.

significant rôle. This was true of the royalty as well as the commonalty. In Yazīd III the proud tradition of pure-blooded Arab caliphs was broken. Yazīd's mother was a royal Persian princess captured in Khurāsān and sent by al-Ḥajjāj as a present to al-Walīd; whereas Yazīd's brother-successor, Ibrāhīm, was the son of an obscure concubine, perhaps a Greek.[1] The mother of Ibrāhīm's successor, Marwān II, was a Kurdish slave.[2] According to one report, she was already pregnant with Marwān when his father acquired her,[3] which would make the last Umayyad not an Umayyad at all. This encroachment by slave females on the position of the free-born Arab woman continued and increased steadily in the ʿAbbāsid period.[4]

General state of economy

Syria's severance from the Byzantine empire considerably reduced her maritime trade, but that was somewhat compensated for by new markets opened by the acquisition of Persia and Central Asia. The ships plying the Mediterranean had their decks fastened with iron nails and covered with tar to prevent leakage, but those in the Persian Gulf and eastern waters had decks bound with cords prior to the time of al-Ḥajjāj, who ordered the Mediterranean model followed.[5] Al-Ḥajjāj's ships reached distant Ceylon and were at times attacked by Indian pirates.[6] In addition to the shipbuilding factory of Muʿāwiyah at Acre,[7] ʿAbd-al-Malik founded one in Tunis.[8] His son Hishām transferred the factory from Acre to Tyre, where it remained till the days of the ʿAbbāsid al-Mutawakkil.[9] Under one of the last Umayyad governors of al-Baṣrah the canals in that city and its precincts numbered "120,000", on which small boats plied, a number which was doubted by the tenth century geographer al-Iṣṭakhri,[10] who visited the place in person.

These canals, like those of Damascus, were mainly for irrigation. Agriculture on the whole did not suffer in Syria in spite of the greed of the exchequer. Islamic prohibition against wine was not, except to a limited extent, detrimental to viticulture, a flourishing activity since remote antiquity.

[1] *ʿIqd*, vol. ii, pp. 333, 352; Yaʿqūbi, vol. ii, pp. 401, 403; Ṭabari, vol. ii, p. 1874; Masʿūdi, vol. vi, pp. 31-2.

[2] Yaʿqūbi, vol. ii, p. 404; Ṭabari, vol. iii, p. 51.

[3] *Ansāb*, vol. v, p. 186.

[4] See below, p. 535.

[5] Ibn-Rustah, *al-Aʿlāq al-Nafīsah*, ed. M. J. de Goeje (Leyden, 1891), pp. 195-196.

[6] Balādhuri, p. 435.

[7] See above, p. 426.

[8] Ibn-Khaldūn, *Muqaddamah*, p. 211.

[9] Balādhuri, p. 118.

[10] P. 80.

CHAPTER XXXVIII

HIGHER ASPECTS OF LIFE UNDER THE UMAYYADS

As Syrians, ʿIrāqis, Persians, Copts and Berbers joined the bandwagon of Islam and intermarried with Arabians, the gap between Arabians and non-Arabians was bridged. The follower of Muḥammad, no matter what his original nationality might have been, would now adopt the Arabic tongue and pass for an Arab. The Arabians themselves brought no science, no art, no tradition of learning, no heritage of culture from the desert. The religious and linguistic elements were the only two novel cultural elements they introduced. In everything else they found themselves dependent upon their subjects. In Syria and the other conquered lands they sat as pupils at the feet of the conquered. Theirs was another case of the victors led captive by the vanquished. What Greece was to the Romans Syria was to the Arabians. When, therefore, we speak of Arabian medicine or philosophy or mathematics what we mean is not something that was necessarily the product of the Arabian mind or cultivated by the inhabitants of the Arabian peninsula but the learning that was enshrined in Arabic books written by men who were themselves Syrians, Persians, ʿIrāqis, Egyptians or Arabians — Christians, Jews or Moslems — who drew their material from Greek, Aramaean, Indo-Persian and other sources.

Intellectual life in the Umayyad period was not on a high level. In fact the whole period was one of incubation. Its closeness to the dark pre-Islamic age (*jāhilīyah*), the frequence of its civil and foreign wars and the instability of its economic and social conditions militated against the possibility of high intellectual attainment. But in it the seeds were sown to come into full bloom in the ʿAbbāsid caliphate.

Grammar and lexicography

The study of Arabic grammar was one of the first disciplines cultivated in this period. It was necessitated by the linguistic needs of Neo-Moslems eager to learn the Koran, hold government positions and push ahead with the conquering class. It is significant that the first scientific study of the Arabic language was begun in al-Baṣrah, near the Persian border, and was conducted mainly for foreign converts and partly by them. It was in this city that the legendary founder of Arabic grammar, abu-al-Aswad al-Du'ali (d. 688) flourished. The noted biographer ibn-Khallikān [1] naïvely explains the origin of this science in these words: "'Ali laid down for al-Du'ali the basic principle that the parts of speech are three: noun, verb and particle, and then asked him to found a complete treatise thereon". In fact Arabic grammar went through a process of slow, long development and bears striking marks of the influence of Greek logic and Sanskrit linguistics.

Another Baṣrite scholar, al-Khalīl ibn-Aḥmad (d. *ca.* 786), compiled the first Arabic dictionary, *Kitāb al-'Ayn*. In it he seems to have followed the Sanskrit system, which begins with the guttural *'ayn*. Biographers ascribe to al-Khalīl the discovery of Arabic prosody and the formulation of its rules,[2] still followed today.

Religious tradition and canon law

The twin sciences of lexicography and philology arose as a result of the study of the Koran and the necessity of expounding it. The same is true of the most characteristically Moslem literary activity, the science of tradition, *ḥadīth* (narrative), technically a saying or act attributed to the Prophet or to one of his Companions. The Koran and tradition lay at the foundation of theology and *fiqh* (law), the obverse and reverse of sacred law. Of this period, from which hardly any literature has come down to us, we know only a few traditionists and jurists. Most renowned among them were al-Ḥasan al-Baṣri (d. 728) and ibn-Shihāb al-Zuhri (d. 742). Al-Baṣri was believed to have personally known more than seventy Companions. Orthodox Sunnis never tire of quoting his devout sayings, and Sufis never shook off the influence of his ascetic piety.[3] Al-Zuhri was so deeply absorbed in his study of tradition that his wife once remarked, "By Allah, these books of yours are worse to me than three rival wives could be".[4] Al-Kūfah, which rivalled al-Baṣrah as an intellectual centre, produced 'Āmir ibn-Sharāḥīl al-Sha'bi

[1] Vol. i, pp. 429-30.
[2] Ibn-Khallikān, vol. i, p. 307.
[3] For more on him consult ibn-Khallikān, vol. i, pp. 227-9.
[4] Ibn-Khallikān, vol. ii, p. 223; abu-al-Fidā', vol. i, pp. 215-16.

(d. *ca.* 728), who is said to have heard traditions from some hundred and fifty Companions [1] which he related from memory without putting down a single line in black and white. Al-Sha'bi was sent by 'Abd-al-Malik on an important mission to the emperor in Constantinople.

Roman law, directly or through the Talmud and other media, did undoubtedly affect certain phases of Islamic law, especially in Umayyad Syria and Egypt. Those phases were contractual transactions (*mu'āmalāt*) [2] and state monopolies such as coinage, official seals, papyrus for documents and other public utilities. The Arabs followed the Byzantine precedent in regarding these commodities and utilities as state monopolies, in considering it the state duty to protect its citizens against forgery, counterfeit, contraband and other abuses connected with them, and in administering heavy punishments.[3] The channels of transmission were the administrative departments inherited by the Arab state and Moslem converts from former Byzantine subjects. In Arabic legal vocabulary no loan words from Greek or Latin are met, though certain terms in Arabic have the same meaning as corresponding Latin ones.[4] Nor do we know of any book on Roman law translated into Arabic. All the major schools of Moslem jurisprudence, it should be remembered, flourished in non-Byzantine territory, al-'Irāq and al-Ḥijāz.[5] One minor school founded by a Syrian, al-Awzā'i (d. 774), did not survive.[6]

Historio-graphy

History writing started in the form of tradition (*ḥadīth*) and was one of the earliest disciplines cultivated by Arab Moslems. The stimuli for historical research were provided by the interest of the believers in collecting old stories about the Prophet and his Companions, the necessity of ascertaining the genealogical relationship of each Moslem Arab in order to determine the amount of state stipend to be received and the desire of the early caliphs to scan the proceedings of kings and rulers before them. 'Abīd ('Ubayd),[7] who was summoned to Damascus to inform Mu'āwiyah about " the early kings of the Arabians and

[1] Al-Sam'āni, *al-Ansāb*, ed. Margoliouth (Leyden, 1912), fol. 334 recto; cf. ibn-Khallikān, vol. i, p. 436.

[2] M. Ḥamīdullāh, " Influence of Roman on Moslem Law ", *Hyderabad Academy Studies*, No. 6 (1943), pp. 43 *seq.*

[3] Balādhuri, pp. 262-70.

[4] See below, p. 556.

[5] See below, p. 556.

[6] See below, p. 555.

[7] See above, p. 479.

their races ",[1] composed for his royal patron *Kitāb al-Mulūk wa-Akhbār al-Māḍīn* (the book of kings and the history of the ancients), which was still in wide circulation at the time of the historian al-Mas'ūdi [2] (d. 956). Another one of those versed in the " science of origins " (*'ilm al-awā'il*) was Wahb ibn-Munabbih (d. *ca.* 728), a Yamanite Jew who probably professed Islam. One of his works (*al-Tījān*), dealing with the kings of Ḥimyar, has recently been published.

Public speaking in its varied forms attained in the Umayyad epoch heights unsurpassed in later times. It was employed by the *khaṭīb* as an instrument of religion in the Friday noon sermons, resorted to by the general as a means for arousing military enthusiasm and depended upon by the governor for instilling patriotic feeling in his subjects. The sermonettes of al-Ḥasan al-Baṣri, delivered in the presence of 'Umar II and partly preserved in the latter's biography,[3] the patriotic speeches of Ziyād ibn-Abīh [4] and the fiery orations of al-Ḥajjāj [5] are among the most prized literary treasures handed down to us from that early age.[6] Oratory

Early official correspondence must have been brief, concise and to the point. It was not till the days of the last Umayyads that the flowery, long-drawn-out style was introduced. Ibn-Khallikān [7] ascribes its introduction to the court secretary 'Abd-al-Ḥamīd al-Kātib (i.e. the scribe, d. 750). Its conventional, polite phraseology betrays Persian patterns. Persian literary influence may also be detected in the many early wise sayings and proverbs. Correspondence

The strenuous period of conquest and expansion produced no poet in a nation that had a long tradition of poetry. Nor was Islam favourable to the chief of the Muses.[8] But with the accession of the worldly Umayyads, the old contacts with the goddesses of wine, song and poetry were re-established. The greatest measure of literary progress was then achieved in the field of poetical composition. Poetry

[1] *Fihrist*, p. 89, l. 26; Wahb ibn-Munabbih, *al-Tījān fi Mulūk Ḥimyar* (Ḥaydarābād, 1347), pp. 312-13; ibn-Khallikān, vol. ii, p. 365.

[2] Vol. iv, p. 89.

[3] Ibn-al-Jawzi, *Sīrah*, pp. 121-6.

[4] See above, p. 436.

[5] See above, p. 454.

[6] For other specimens consult ibn-Qutaybah, *'Uyūn al-Akhbār*, vol. ii (Cairo, 1928), pp. 231-52; al-Jāḥiẓ, *al-Bayān w-al-Tabyīn*, vol. i (Cairo, 1926), pp. 177 *seq.*, vol. ii (1927), pp. 47 *seq.*; *'Iqd*, vol. ii, pp. 172 *seq.*

[7] Vol. i, p. 350; cf. Mas'ūdi, vol. vi, p. 81.

[8] Koran 26 : 24-7; 36 : 69; 69 : 41.

One of the earliest of Umayyad poets was Ka'b ibn-Ju'ayl (d. *ca.* 705) of the Taghlib tribe, which was then partially Islamized. Though a Moslem, Ka'b takes oaths by the Lord of the Christians and Moslems and holds the readers of the Evangels and the Koran in the same high esteem.[1] In his poetry Christian influence is more apparent than in that of his fellow Taghlibite the Christian al-Akhṭal.

Al-Akhṭal [2] (*ca.* 640–*ca.* 710) was the poetical champion of the Umayyad cause against the theocratic party. He had no hesitancy in satirizing the Companions when requested by Yazīd, whereas Ka'b had.[3] As poet of the court he would enter Mu'āwiyah's palace with a cross dangling from his neck. But Christianity must have sat lightly on the heart of this wine-bibbing, licentious poet who addressed these words to his pregnant wife as she rushed to touch the garment of a passing bishop and succeeded only in reaching the tail of the donkey he was riding: "He and the tail of his ass — there is no difference!" [4]

Al-Akhṭal was one of a trio which dominated the poetical scene of the age. The other two were the vitriolic Jarīr (d. *ca.* 729), court poet of al-Ḥajjāj,[5] and the dissolute al-Farazdaq (640–732), the poet laureate of 'Abd-al-Malik and his sons al-Walīd, Sulaymān [6] and Yazīd. All three poets were satirists as well as panegyrists. In their panegyrics, on which they lived, they performed the same function as that of the party press today. Their satires were often directed against each other. As poets they stand among those with whom Arabic criticism has found none to compare since their time.

Under the Umayyads the poet of love makes his first full appearance. The peninsular school had for its chief exponent 'Umar ibn-abi-Rabī'ah (d. *ca.* 719), prince of Arabic erotic poetry. A Qurayshite,[7] 'Umar specialized in making love to

[1] Khalīl Mardam, "Ka'b ibn-Ju'ayl al-Taghlibi", *Majallat al-Majma' al-'Ilmi al-'Arabi*, vol. xix (1944), pp. 15-24, 104-12.

[2] Two collections of his poems have been published as *Shi'r al-Akhṭal*, ed. A. Ṣāliḥāni (Beirut, 1891, 1905).

[3] Ibn-Qutaybah, *Kitāb al-Shi'r w-al-Shu'arā'*, ed. M. J. de Goeje (Leyden, 1902–4), pp. 301-4.

[4] *Aghāni*, vol. vii, p. 183.

[5] Ibn-Qutaybah, *Shi'r*, p. 287. For other samples of his poetry see his *Dīwān* (Cairo, 1313), vol. i.

[6] Ibn-Qutaybah, *Shi'r*, pp. 297-8. For Farazdaq's eulogies of his patrons see his *Dīwān*, ed. R. Boucher (Paris, 1875), *passim*. Consult also *Aghāni*, vol. viii, pp. 186-97; vol. xix, pp. 2-52; ibn-Khallikān, vol. iii, pp. 136-46.

[7] *Aghāni*, vol. i, p. 32. On his life and works see Jibrā'īl Jabbūr, *'Umar ibn-abi-Rabī'ah*, 2 vols. (Beirut, 1935–9).

beautiful damsels pilgrimaging in the Holy Cities. In language of intense passion and exquisite felicity he immortalized his feeling toward the fair sex.

If ʿUmar represented free love in poetry, his contemporary Jamīl al-ʿUdhri (d. 701) stood for innocent love of the platonic type. His people, the banu-ʿUdhrah, were a Christian tribe settled in al-Ḥijāz. His verses addressed to Buthaynah, of the same tribe,[1] breathe a spirit of tenderness unmatched in that age. As a representative of the lyric type of poetical composition Jamīl had a rival in the semi-legendary Majnūn Layla [2] (he who is crazy because of Layla, d. *ca.* 699 [3]). Qays ibn-al-Mulawwaḥ, for that is supposedly his name, was infatuated with a woman of the same tribe who reciprocated his love but was forced by her father to marry another. Crazed with despair, Qays passed the rest of his life wandering half naked among the hills and vales of his native Najd singing the beauty of his beloved and yearning for a glimpse of her. Only when her name was mentioned would he return to his senses. Majnūn Layla became the hero of numberless romances, Arabic, Turkish and Persian, extolling the power of undying love.

Besides love poetry political poetry makes its debut at this time. The occasion was the historic nomination of Yazīd to the caliphate,[4] when Miskīn al-Dārimi was requested to compose and publicly recite appropriate verses.[5] This type of poetry culminated in the odes of ibn-Qays al-Ruqayyāt [6] (d. 704) addressed to ʿAbd-al-Malik. In this period also the first attempt to compile ancient pre-Islamic poetry was made and that by Ḥammād al-Rāwiyah (i.e. the transmitter, *ca.* 713–72). Of Persian origin, Ḥammād spoke Arabic with an accent. He was one of those famed in Arabic annals for their phenomenal memories. Once, so the story goes, he offered to recite to al-Walīd II — himself a poet [7] — of the pre-Islamic poems alone, rhyming in each of the letters of the alphabet, one hundred different odes for each letter. After listening in person and by

[1] Ibn-Qutaybah, *Shiʿr*, pp. 260-68; *Aghāni*, vol. vii, pp. 77-100.
[2] *Aghāni*, vol. i, p. 169, quoted by ibn-Khallikān, vol. i, p. 148.
[3] Al-Kutubi, *Fawāt al-Wafayāt* (Būlāq, 1283), vol. ii, p. 172.
[4] See above, p. 440.
[5] *Aghāni*, vol. xviii, pp. 71-2; cf. ibn-Qutaybah, *Shiʿr*, p. 347.
[6] See his *Dīwān*, ed. N. Rhodokanakakis (Vienna, 1902), pp. 67 *seq.*
[7] Consult his *Dīwān*, ed. F. Gabrieli (Damascus, 1937), in which *khamrīyāt* (wine odes) are prominent.

proxy to 2900 odes, the caliph felt satisfied and ordered 100,000 dirhams to the reciter.[1]

The closeness of Umayyad poetry to Islam and to Jāhilīyah poetry endowed it with purity of style, strength of expression and natural dignity that raised it to the position of a model for all generations to come. Its techniques and motifs set the pattern and provided the mould into which the Arabic poet's individual feeling and composition has since been cast. His inability since then to dissociate himself from his literary heritage and produce a composition which belongs to timeless humanity has been well marked. Grammar text-books have always drawn their illustrations mostly from pre-Islamic and Umayyad poetry.

Education

Education of the formal type was not common in those days. The Umayyads sent their young sons to the *bādiyah*,[2] the eastern desert, where they could acquire the pure Bedouin Arabic, practise riding and learn the chase. The precedent was set by Muʿāwiyah, who sent there his son and future successor. The public considered him educated who could read and write, use the bow and arrow and swim. Indeed he was more than educated who mastered these skills; he was *kāmil*, a perfect man.[3] Swimming as an educational ideal must have evolved through life on the Mediterranean coast. The ethical ideals of education, as gleaned from literature, tried to preserve values highly prized in Bedouin life: courage, endurance in face of trouble (*ṣabr*), regard to the rights and obligations of neighbourliness (*jiwār*), manliness (*murū'ah*), generosity, hospitality and fulfilment of solemn promises.

Beginning with the caliphate of ʿAbd-al-Malik the private tutor (*mu'addib*) becomes a standing figure in the court. One of the instructions the tutor of this caliph's sons received from the father was: "Teach them to swim and accustom them to little sleep".[4] ʿUmar II was inclined to resort to corporal punishment in case his children violated the rules of Arabic grammar.[5] The piety of this caliph is reflected in the official instructions he handed to their tutor: "Let the first moral

1 Ibn-Khallikān, vol. i, p. 292; *Aghāni*, vol. v, pp. 164-5. See *ʿIqd*, vol. iii, pp. 137-8.

2 See above, p. 440.

3 Ibn-Saʿd, vol. iii, pt. 2, p. 91, ll. 10-11, cf. vol. v, p. 309, ll. 7 *seq.*; *Aghāni*, vol. vi, p. 165, l. 9.

4 Mubarrad, p. 77, ll. 6-7.

5 Yāqūt, *Muʿjam al-Udabā'*, ed. Margoliouth, vol. i (Leyden, 1907), pp. 25-6.

lesson impressed upon them be hatred of means of amusement, whose initiative is from the devil and whose consequence is God's wrath ".[1]

From the rise of Islam the only schools that the masses desirous of education could attend were the mosque schools. These had their curricula centred on the Koran and ḥadīth. Their teachers were Koran readers (*qurrā'*). The Koran readers were thus the earliest teachers in Islam: they are still the only teachers in country and out-of-the way places. 'Umar I as early as 638 sent such teachers in all directions and ordered the people to meet with them in mosques on Fridays. The first man to distinguish himself as teacher in Egypt was a judge sent there in 746 by 'Umar II.[2] In al-Kūfah, al-Ḍaḥḥāk ibn-Muzāḥim (d. 723), mentioned among the tutors of 'Abd-al-Malik's sons,[3] conducted an elementary school (*kuttāb*) where no tuition fees were charged.[4]

Science: medicine

Arab science was based on the Greek and had its start with medicine. Moslem regard for medical science is echoed in a tradition ascribed to the Prophet: " Science is twofold: That which relates to religion and that which relates to the body ".

At the Arab conquest of Western Asia, Greek science was no longer a living force. It was rather a tradition in the hands of Greek- or Syriac-writing commentators and practitioners. To this category belonged the physicians of the Umayyads. Outstanding among them were ibn-Uthāl, the Christian doctor of Mu'āwiyah,[5] and Tayādhūq, the Greek doctor of al-Ḥajjāj.[6] A Jewish physician of Persian origin, Māsarjawayh of al-Baṣrah translated in 683, in the days of Marwān ibn-al-Ḥakam, a Syriac medical treatise originally composed in Greek by a Christian priest in Alexandria named Ahrūn.[7] This was the first scientific book in the language of Islam. Marwān's grandson al-Walīd is credited with segregating persons afflicted with leprosy, blindness and other chronic diseases and making special provision for their treat-

[1] Ibn-al-Jawzi, *Sīrah*, pp. 257-8. Consult Jāḥiẓ, *Bayān*, vol. ii, pp. 138-143.

[2] Kindi, *Wulāh*, p. 89; al-Suyūṭi, *Ḥusn al-Muḥāḍarah fi Akhbār Miṣr w-al-Qāhairh* (Cairo, 1321), vol. i, p. 154.

[3] Jāḥiẓ, *Bayān*, vol. i, p. 175.

[4] Ibn-Sa'd, vol. vi, p. 210.

[5] Ibn-abi-Uṣaybi'ah, *'Uyūn al-Anbā' fi Ṭabaqāt al-Aṭibbā'* (Cairo, 1882), vol. i, p. 116.

[6] Ibn-abi-Uṣaybi'ah, vol. i, p. 121.

[7] Ibn-al-'Ibri, p. 192.

ment.[1] This was the first institution for the sick in Islam. ʿUmar II is said to have transferred the schools of medicine from Alexandria, where the Greek tradition flourished, to Antioch and Ḥarrān.[2]

Alchemy

Closely related to medicine was alchemy, one of the earliest disciplines cultivated by Arabs. In it as in medicine the later Arabs made a distinct contribution. Khālid (d. 704 or 708), son of Yazīd I, is credited by legend with being the first scientist and philosopher (*ḥakīm*) of Islam. He, according to the *Fihrist*,[3] was the first to undertake translating Greek and Coptic works on alchemy, medicine and astrology. The element of truth in this allegation is that the Arabs received their earliest impulses and their scientific knowledge from Greek sources. Legend goes on to associate the name of this Umayyad prince with that of Jābir ibn-Ḥayyān (Latinized Geber). Jābir flourished long after this time (*ca.* 776) and will be treated later. Likewise the alchemical and astrological treatises ascribed to Jaʿfar al-Ṣādiq (700–65),[4] one of the twelve Shīʿite imāms, have been proved spurious by modern scholarship.[5]

Schools of thought

The Umayyad period also saw the beginnings of several religio-philosophical movements often referred to as sects. Contact with Christianity in Syria provoked theological speculation that led to the rise of some of these schools. One of them was the Muʿtazilah, a school of rationalism founded in al-Baṣrah by Wāṣil ibn-ʿAṭā' (d. 748). The major doctrine of the Muʿtazilites (seceders) was that he of the Moslems who commits a mortal sin (*kabīrah*) secedes from the ranks of believers but does not thereby become an unbeliever; he then occupies a medial position between the two.[6] A pupil of al-Ḥasan al-Baṣri, who for a time leaned toward this doctrine, Wāṣil made it a cardinal point in Muʿtazilite belief. Another cardinal

[1] Ibn-al-ʿIbri, p. 195; Ṭabari, vol. ii, p. 1196; Maqrīzi, *Khiṭaṭ*, vol. ii, p. 405.

[2] Ibn-abi-Uṣaybiʿah, vol. i, p. 116, ll. 25-6.

[3] Pp. 242, 354. Cf. Julius Ruska, *Arabische Alchemisten*, I. *Chālid Ibn Jazīd Ibn Muʿāwija* (Heidelberg, 1924), pp. 8 *seq.*

[4] *Fihrist*, p. 317, l. 25; ibn-Khallikān, vol. i, p. 300; Ḥājji Khalfah, *Kashf al-Ẓunūn ʿan Asāmi al-Kutub w-al-Funūn*, ed. Fluegel, vol. ii (Leipzig, 1837), pp. 581, 604; vol. iii (London, 1842), pp. 53, 128.

[5] J. Ruska, *Arabische Alchemisten*, II. *Ǧaʿfar Alṣādiq, der sechste Imām* (Heidelberg, 1924), pp. 49-59.

[6] Masʿūdi, vol. vi, p. 22; vii, p. 234; cf. Shahrastāni, p. 33; al-Baghdādi, *Uṣūl al-Dīn* (Istanbul, 1928), vol. i, p. 335; do., *Mukhtaṣar*, p. 98; al-Nawbakhti, *Firaq al-Shīʿah*, ed. H. Ritter (Istanbul, 1931), p. 5.

doctrine was a denial of the co-existence with God of the divine attributes, such as power, wisdom, life, on the ground that such conceptions tend to destroy the unity of God, Islam's basic and most important dogma. Moreover, they weakened the conception of God's omnipotence in favour of the demands of justice. Hence the Muʿtazilites' favourite description of themselves: "the partisans of justice and unity". Their movement attained its height under the ʿAbbāsid al-Ma'mūn [1] in Baghdād, which began intellectually where al-Baṣrah and al-Kūfah ended.

The doctrine of free will was at this time held by another group called Qadarites (from *qadar*, power), as opposed to the Jabrites (from *jabr*, compulsion).[2] The Qadarīyah arose as a reaction against the harsh predestination of Islam, a corollary of God's almightiness as stressed in the Koran,[3] and betrays Christian influence. To them man was the author of his own acts. This was the earliest philosophical school in Islam and claimed an extensive membership including two caliphs, Muʿāwiyah II and Yazīd III.[4]

St. John of Damascus

Chief among the agents through whom Christian lore and Greek thought found their way into Islam was St. John of Damascus (*ca.* 676–*ca.* 748). Joannes Damascenus, surnamed Chrysorrhas (golden stream) on account of his oratorical gifts, wrote in Greek but was a Syrian who no doubt spoke Aramaic at home and knew, in addition, Arabic. His debates with Moslems on free will and predestination inaugurated the short-lived movement toward rationalism in Islam.[5] He taught that God created the world and then let it go on with its momentum.[6] John began his career as a boon companion to Muʿāwiyah's son Yazīd and then succeeded to the high position in the government held by his father as councillor. Early in Hishām's caliphate (*ca.* 724) he retired to a life of asceticism and devotion in the monastery of St. Sāba, south-east of Jerusalem.

St. John produced several monumental works [7] chief among which was the *Fountain of Wisdom*, in which he collated and

[1] See below, p. 541.
[2] Cf. al-Īji, *Kitāb al-Mawāqif*, ed. Th. Soerensen (Leipzig, 1848), pp. 334, 362.
[3] Sūrs. 3:25-26; 15:21; 42:26; 43:10.
[4] Cf. ibn-Ḥazm, *al-Fiṣal fi al-Milal w-al-Ahwā' w-al-Niḥal*, vol. iii (Cairo, 1347), p. 31.
[5] See below, p. 541.
[6] See his "Exposition of the Orthodox Faith", in *Nicene and Post-Nicene Fathers*, ser. 2, vol. ix, p. 39.
[7] Migne, *Patrologia Graeca*, vols. xciv-xcvi.

epitomized the ideas of the leading ecclesiastical writers who preceded him. The first *summa theologica* that has come down to us, this work was used by Peter Lombard and Thomas Aquinas and became the standard for the great Scholastics that followed. Many of John's works were translated into Latin; he was regarded as a saint by both the Greek and the Latin Churches. Of special interest to us are the two dialogues between a Christian and a Saracen which he wrote and which emphasize the divinity of Christ and the freedom of human will.[1] The work was intended as an apology for Christianity, a manual for the guidance of Christians in their arguments with Moslems. It was probably based on debates in the caliph's presence in which John himself took part and shows that he was at home in both the Koran and the ḥadīth.[2] As for the story of the ascetic Barlaam and the Hindu prince Josaphat,[3] perhaps the most famous religious romance of the Middle Ages, its ascription to St. John is erroneous. The real author was an obscure monk by the name of John who had lived in St. Sāba a couple of centuries earlier. The story is a Christian version of the life of the Buddha, who under the name of Josaphat (or Iosaph), was, strangely enough, made a saint and canonized by both the Latin and the Greek Churches.

From S. Joannes Damascenus, "Opera", ed. J. Billium (Paris, 1619)

ST. JOHN OF DAMASCUS

[1] Migne, vol. xciv, cols. 1585-98; vol. xcvi, cols. 1335-48.
[2] Cf. above, p. 439.
[3] Migne, vol. xcvi, cols. 857-1250.

One conspicuous activity in St. John's life was his defence of images as an instrument of worship, emphasizing that what is worshipped is not the material of the image but that which is imaged.[1] This was the time when Emperor Leo the Isaurian, perhaps with an eye to currying favour with the Moslems, was making strenuous efforts to suppress icons. John thereby incurred imperial wrath. Shortly before his death he toured Syria fighting the iconoclasts and even visited Constantinople at the risk of his life. Ritual in its varied aspects was of vital significance in his estimation. He himself composed hymns (some of which are still used in Protestant hymnals) which mark the highest attainment of beauty in Church poetry. He was the last of the Greek Fathers. As theologian, orator, apologist, polemicist, codifier of Byzantine art and hymnologist, St. John stands out as an ornament to the body of the Church under the caliphate.

The Qadarite-Muʿtazilite movement was the first step on the way to weakening universal Moslem orthodoxy. The Murji'ite was the second. The fundamental article of faith in this sect consisted in the suspension (*irjā'*) of judgment against believers who commit sins and in not declaring them infidels.[2] To the Murji'ites works were irrelevant to faith. This doctrine arose in justification of the position of the Umayyad caliphs, who were accused of suppressing the religious law. To the followers of this doctrine the fact that the Umayyads were nominally Moslems sufficed; as the *de facto* political leaders of Islam homage was due them from all. ʿAli as well as Muʿāwiyah were both servants of God and by God alone must they be judged. In the tolerant atmosphere of this school was reared the great divine abu-Ḥanīfah (d. 767), founder of the first of the four orthodox schools of jurisprudence in Islam.[3] Murji'ites

Like the Murji'ite the Khārijite was a religio-political school of thought. It dates from earlier times when certain followers of ʿAli became indignant on his submittal of his claim to the caliphate to arbitration.[4] Once supporters of ʿAli, the Khārijites became his deadly enemies. They aimed at maintaining the Khārijites

[1] *Nicene and Post-Nicene Fathers*, ser. 2, vol. ix, p. 88.
[2] Cf. Baghdādi, *Mukhtaṣar*, pp. 122-3; ibn-Ḥazm, vol. ii, p. 89.
[3] See below, p. 555. [4] See above, p. 433.

primitive democratic principles of puritanical Islam and in pursuit of their aim caused rivers of blood to flow in the first three centuries of Islam. They opposed the prerogative conferred on the Quraysh that the caliph should be one of their number,[1] forbade the cult of saints with its attendant local pilgrimages and prohibited Sufi fraternities. Today they survive as Ibāḍites (commonly Abāḍites), after ibn-Ibāḍ [2] of the second half of the first Moslem century, and are scattered in Algeria, Tripolitania, ʿUmān and Zanzibar.

The Shīʿah

More important than all these was the Shīʿah, one of the two hostile camps into which early Islam was split on the all-important issue of the caliphate. The other camp was the Sunnite.[3] It was in the Umayyad period that the Shīʿah took its definite form. The differentiating element between Shīʿites (partisans of ʿAli) and Sunnites (orthodox) was the imāmship, successorship to Muḥammad and leadership of Islam. The Shīʿites cling to the belief in ʿAli and ʿAli's sons as the only true imāms with the same persistence with which Catholics cling to the belief in the successorship of Peter. The Prophet made a revelation, the Koran, the intermediary between God and man; the Shīʿites made a person, the imām,[4] the intermediary. To the Sunnite " I believe in Allah the one God " and " I believe in the revelation of the Koran, which is uncreated from eternity ", the Shīʿites added another article of faith: " I believe that the imām especially chosen by Allah as the bearer of a part of the divine being is the leader to salvation "

The Sunnite view makes the caliph secular head of the Moslem community, leader of the believers and protector of the faith, but bestows no spiritual authority on him.[5] In opposition to that the Shīʿite view confines the imāmate to the

[1] Ibn-al-Jawzi, *Naqd al-ʿIlm w-al-ʿUlamāʾ* (Cairo, 1340), p. 102.

[2] Baghdādi, *Mukhtaṣar*, pp. 87-8; Īji, p. 356; Shahrastāni, p. 100.

[3] From *sunnah*, custom, use; technically the theory and practice of the catholic Moslem community.

[4] Koran 2:118; 15:79; 25:74; 36:11, where the word occurs in its basic, non-technical meaning, he who precedes or leads. It is ordinarily applied to the person who in the canonical services indicates the ritual movements. Originally the Prophet, and after him the caliphs or their delegates, fulfilled this function. Ibn-Khaldūn, *Muqaddamah*, pp. 159-60.

[5] Īji, pp. 296 *seq.*; Māwardi, pp. 23-4; al-Nasafi, *ʿUmdat ʿAqīdat Ahl al-Sunnah*, ed. W. Cureton (London, 1843), pp. 28-9.

family of 'Ali and makes the imām not only the sole legitimate head of the Moslem society but also the spiritual and religious leader whose authority is derived from a divine ordinance (*naṣṣ*). As such the lineal descendant of Muḥammad through 'Ali and Fāṭimah becomes endowed with a mysterious power transmitted to him by heredity.[1] He then stands above any human being and enjoys impeccability (*'iṣmah*). Later Sunnite tradition ascribed in varying degrees immunity from sin and error to the prophets only, especially to Muḥammad.[2] Extremists among Shī'ites went so far as to consider the imām the incarnation of the Deity. The Mahdi hypothesis developed later and held out the expectation of a saviour-leader who would usher in a new era of liberty and prosperity, undoubtedly a reflex of Messianic and allied ideas.

Of all Moslem lands al-'Irāq proved to be the most fertile soil for the germination of 'Alid doctrines. After the beginning of the sixteenth century Persia became the bulwark of Shī'ism. In all there are today some 35,000,000 Shī'ites, about 12 per cent of the Moslem body.[3] In Lebanon and Syria, where they go by the name Matāwilah (i.e. partisans of 'Ali), they number roughly 130,000. Within the Shī'ah itself an almost unlimited number of minor sects arose, including heterodoxies and extremists who are no longer acknowledged as Shī'ites. Like a magnet Shī'ism attracted to itself all sorts of non-conformists and malcontents — economic, social, political and religious. Some of the heterodoxies which arose in early Islam were in reality veiled protests against the victorious religion of the Arabians and gradually gravitated to the bosom of the Shī'ah as the strongest representative of opposition to the established order. The Ismā'īlites, the Qarmaṭians, the Druzes, the Nuṣayris and the like, with whom we shall deal later, were all historical offshoots of the Shī'ah.

Muḥammad may have looked with disfavour upon music, as he did upon poetry,[4] only because of the association with pagan religious rites. A ḥadīth makes him declare all musical Music

[1] Shahrastāni, pp. 108-9; Mas'ūdi, vol. i, p. 70.

[2] Ibn-Ḥazm, vol. iv, pp. 2-25; Īji, pp. 218 *seq.*; I. Goldziher in *Der Islam*, vol. iii (1912), pp. 238-45.

[3] If Shī'ite heterodoxies, such as Yazīdis, Assassins and 'Ali-Ilāhis, are added the total would reach approximately 45,000,000, 15 per cent of the Moslem body.

[4] Sūr. 26:224-6.

instruments the devil's muezzin, serving to call men to his worship.[1] Most Moslem legists and theologians frowned on music and musicians, but the masses expressed their view in the adage: " Wine is as the body, music as the soul, and joy is their offspring ".[2]

No sooner had the awe inspired by Islam worn off than male and female professional singers and musicians began to make their appearance. In the Umayyad era Mecca, and more particularly Medina, became a nursery of song and a conservatory of music.[3] They attracted gifted artists from outside and supplied the Damascus court with an ever-increasing stream of talent. The second Umayyad caliph, Yazīd I, himself a composer, introduced singing and musical instruments into the court.[4] It was he who initiated the practice of holding grand festivities in the royal palace which featured wine and song. ʿAbd-al-Malik patronized Saʿīd ibn-Misjaḥ (Musajjaḥ ?, *ca.* 714) of the Ḥijāz school, perhaps the greatest musician of the entire Umayyad age. Saʿīd was a Meccan negro client. He reportedly toured Syria and Persia and put Byzantine and Persian songs into Arabic.[5] In addition, he is credited with the systematization of Arabian musical theory and practice of classical times. Al-Walīd I, the patron of art and architecture, summoned ibn-Surayj (d. *ca.* 726), regarded as one of the four great singers of Islam,[6] and Maʿbad (d. 743), a Medinese mulatto, to the capital, where the caliph received them with great honour. Maʿbad continued to be a court favourite under Yazīd II and al-Walīd II.[7] This Yazīd reinstated poetry and music as an adjunct to royal life after a lapse during the caliphate of the austere and puritanical ʿUmar II. His episodes with the songstresses Ḥabābah and Sallāmah are well known.[8] The licentious al-Walīd II, himself a lute player and song composer, welcomed to his court a host of musician singers.

[1] Consult Nuwayri, *Nihāyah*, vol. iv, pp. 132-5; al-Ghazzāli, *Iḥyā' ʿUlūm al-Dīn* (Cairo, 1334), vol. ii, pp. 238 *seq.*; A. J. Wensinck, *A Handbook of Early Muhammadan Tradition* (Leyden, 1927), p. 173; Henry G. Farmer, *A History of Arabian Music to the Thirteenth Century* (London, 1929), pp. 24-5.

[2] Nawāji, p. 178. Consult Nuwayri, vol. iv, pp. 136 *seq.*

[3] *ʿIqd*, vol. iii, p. 237.

[4] *Aghāni*, vol. xvi, p. 70; cf. Masʿūdi, vol. v, pp. 156-7.

[5] *Aghāni*, vol. iii, p. 84.

[6] *Aghāni*, vol. i, p. 98.

[7] *Aghāni*, vol. ii, pp. 19 *seq.*; Masʿūdi, vol. vi, p. 4

[8] See above, pp. 479-80.

Notes were then known but transmitted by word of mouth from one generation to another. The *Aghāni* is replete with verses set to music in Umayyad days, but not a solitary note has been preserved in it. Hishām bestowed his patronage on an artist from al-Ḥīrah, Ḥunayn by name. So widely spread was the cultivation of musical art under the Umayyads that it provided their rivals, the ʿAbbāsid party, with an effective argument in their propaganda aimed at undermining the house of the " ungodly usurpers ".

Painting

Moslem hostility toward representational art does not manifest itself until early ʿAbbāsid times. It evidently reflects views of converted Jews and a residue of the primitive notion that he who holds the likeness of another is in a position to exercise magical influence on that person.

Most theologians have since ʿAbbāsid days maintained that the representation of animate objects is the prerogative of the deity. Words were put into the mouth of the Prophet to the effect that those to be most severely punished on the judgment day are the *muṣawwirūn*, portrayers (painters and sculptors).[1] Since then no representation of human beings has occurred anywhere on mosques, though it did in a few cases on palaces and in manuscripts. Practically all decorative motifs have been derived from geometry and from the vegetable kingdom.

The frescoes of Quṣayr ʿAmrah, the Transjordanian hunting lodge of al-Walīd I, are the earliest illustrations of Moslem pictorial art. They betray workmanship of Christian painters. The walls depict six royal personages including the caliph himself and his Visigothic adversary Roderick.[2] Other figures are symbolic, representing Victory, Philosophy, History and Poetry. A hunting scene depicts a lion attacking a wild ass. Other pictures portray nude dancers, musicians and merrymakers. Nowhere else have ancient Moslem murals been preserved in such perfect condition.

The recent excavations at Khirbat al-Mafjar,[3] three miles north of Jericho, revealed an elaborate Umayyad winter palace with walls decorated with human and animal motifs. Work-

[1] Al-Bukhāri, *al-Jāmiʿ al-Ṣaḥīḥ* (Būlāq, 1296), vol. vii, p. 61.

[2] See above, p. 464.

[3] Work begun in 1935 by the Palestine Department of Antiquities. Consult " Excavations at Khirbet el Mefjer ", *Quarterly of the Department of Antiquities in Palestine*, vol. v (1936), pp. 132-8; vol. vi (1937), pp. 157-68.

men's graffiti mention the name of Hishām (724–43), leaving no doubt as to the identity of its builder. A statue in the round represents a girl carrying a bouquet of flowers. A panel displays a group of plump dancing girls with lipstick and with finger and

Department of Antiquities, Amman

A MOSAIC FLOOR AT KHIRBAT AL-MAFJAR

A stylized pomegranate tree has two gazelles grazing under it, while a third is attacked by a lion. Brilliantly hued, the mosaic is surrounded by a border which gives it a tapestry-like effect

toe nails painted scarlet. A whole menagerie of birds, rabbits and other animals is exhibited. The art displays an unmistakable ultimate relation to that of the Hellenized Nabataeans The palace was evidently destroyed by earthquake in 746, before its completion.

Palaces in the desert

The Umayyad caliphs, as we learned before,[1] had country places to which they resorted to escape contagious diseases,[2]

[1] P. 440. [2] Ṭabari, vol. ii, p. 1784.

lead rural life and satisfy their nostalgia for the desert. The fringes of the Syrian Desert (al-Bādiyah), especially in its southern part, are strewn with remains of palaces and hunting lodges, either erected by Umayyad architects on Byzantine and Persian patterns or restored by them. Some no doubt were originally Roman fortresses.[1]

ʿAmrah and al-Mafjar are but two samples of such palaces. Both names, as well as the names of most of the others, are modern, not occurring in classical literature. On account of its extraordinary mural paintings Quṣayr [2] is the best known among them. Built by al-Walīd I between 712 and 715 it was discovered for the learned world in 1898.[3]

Another well-known palace in this region is al-Mushatta (Bedouin pronunciation Mshatta, winter resort),[4] built by al-Walīd II, who was addicted to the chase and less innocent pastimes. The magnificently carved façade of this beautiful chateau is now in a Berlin museum.[5] The newly discovered Khirbat al-Munyah (garden), to the north-west of Lake Tiberias, was also built by this caliph. Two excavated dinars agree in their dating with an inscription which declares him the one who ordered the building.[6] This caliph also occupied al-Qasṭal,[7] about twenty miles south of ʿAmmān. Al-Qasṭal is said by an early historian [8] to have been built by the Ghassānid al-Ḥārith ibn-Jabalah.[9] If correct, the palace would be pre-Islamic. Al-Walīd made use of another villa in that neighbourhood, al-Azraq [10] (the blue one). His father Yazīd II either built or restored Muwaqqar,[11] of which few remains are left. Nothing

[1] See above, p. 289.

[2] Diminutive of *qaṣr*, castle; from L. *castrum* through Syriac.

[3] Alois Musil, *Ḳuṣejr ʿAmra und andere Schlösser östlich von Moab*, pt. I (Vienna, 1902), pp. 5 *seq.*; do., *Ḳuṣejr ʿAmra*, I. *Textband* (Vienna, 1907). Musil thought al-Walīd II built it.

[4] Cf. Musil, *Arabia Deserta*, p. 408; do., *Palmyrena*, p. 279, where he makes this and other palaces summer, rather than winter, resorts.

[5] Consult Brünnow and Domaszewski, *Provincia Arabia*, vol. ii, pp. 105-70; B. Schulz and J. Strzygowski, "Mschatta", *Jahrbuch der Königlich-preuszischen Kunstsammlungen*, vol. xxv (1904), pp. 205-373.

[6] "Khirbat Minya", *Quarterly of the Department of Antiquities in Palestine*, vol. vi (1937), pp. 215-16; vol. vii (1938), pp. 49-51.

[7] From Latin *castellum*, castle, through Syriac. *Yāqūt*, vol. iv, p. 95; Ṭabari, vol. ii, p. 1784.

[8] Ḥamzah al-Iṣfahāni, p. 117.

[9] Cited above. p. 402.

[10] Ṭabari, vol. ii, p. 1743.

[11] Yāqūt, vol. iv, p. 687. Al-Balqā', where Muwaqqar, al-Qasṭal and other structures stood, was the eastern Jordan district comprising Moab.

From B. Moritz, " Bilder aus Palästina, Nord-Arabien und dem Sinai " (Dietrich Reimer Verlag, Berlin)

FAÇADE OF AL-MUSHATTA

is known about Qaṣr al-Ṭūba (Tawbah?), south-east of Muwaqqar.

Farther north on the Bādiyah border lie in ruins other castles, some of which have not yet been studied. Most important among these is Usays [1] (modern Says), lying eighty-

Department of Antiquities, Amman

QUṢAYR 'AMRAH, AN UMMAYYAD HUNTING LODGE IN THE SYRIAN DESERT

three miles east of Damascus. This is a fortified site with an irrigation system dependent on winter rain. It is perhaps the work of al-Walīd I and one of the earliest surviving structures of its kind.

Two other palaces in that region go by the name Ḥayr (Ḥair [2]). Many caliphal residences evidently had walled gardens in which wild game was kept for hunting. Forty miles north-east of Tadmur lies the first of these Ḥayrs dis- Qaṣr al-Ḥayr

[1] Yāqūt, vol. i, p. 271; Musil, *Palmyrena*, p. 282; J. Sauvaget, "Les Ruines omeyyades du Djebel Seis", *Syria*, vol. xx (1939), pp. 239-56.

[2] "Ḥā'ir" in Miskawayh, *Tajārib al-Umam*, ed. D. S. Margoliouth, vol. i (Cairo, 1914), p. 159, l. 15. The word comes from Syriac and means enclosed area. It is related to *ḥīrah*, camp; see above, p. 404.

covered, Qaṣr al-Ḥayr al-Sharqi (the eastern) to distinguish it from al-Gharbi (the western), lying between Tadmur and al-Qaryatayn. Its enclosure is about five miles long and almost a mile wide. Built by Hishām in 729, it has recently been supposed by one scholar to be the Ruṣāfah [1] ascribed to this caliph.[2] Hishām was attached to al-Ruṣāfah, where he died and was buried.[3] The machicolation (*saqqāṭah*), known in Syria in pre-Islam and in Europe at the end of the twelfth century, was employed at this Qaṣr.

About forty miles south-west of Tadmur lies Qaṣr al-Ḥayr al-Gharbi, built in 727 by the same caliph, as an extant inscription declares. It was evidently the residence of Hishām before he moved to al-Ruṣāfah. This al-Ḥayr may have been al-Zaytūnah of Arab historians,[4] originally a Byzantine or Roman castle. Its remarkable decorations include statues of two women at the entrance which reflect Palmyrene art. Among the pictures are two songstresses, one of whom is using a five-stringed lute.[5]

The decorations of this Qaṣr, now in the Syrian National Museum at Damascus, fill a gap between the Byzantine and the Islamic art. They combine and harmonize Sāsānid, Byzantine and Syrian elements. The motifs begun here were carried into al-Maghrib and developed to their highest possibilities in Cordova and Granada. The ʿAbbāsids followed the Umayyads in building Ḥayr gardens. Their temporary capital Sāmarra had one described by the geographer al-Yaʿqūbi,[6] who says that it held " wild animals : gazelles, wild asses, deer, hares and ostriches kept in by an enclosing wall in a fine open tract ". The Romans showed no interest in zoological gardens till the imperial period, which suggests Eastern influence.[7]

[1] See above, p. 391.

[2] J. Sauvaget in *Bulletin d'études orientales*, vol. v (1935), pp. 136-7; do., " Remarques sur les monuments omeyyades ", *Journal asiatique*, vol. ccxxxi (1939), pp. 1-13. For more on this structure consult Henri Seyrig, *Antiquités syriennes*, ser. 1 (1934), pp. 1-3; ser. 2 (1938), pp. 1-9; K. A. C. Creswell, *Early Muslim Architecture*, pt. 1 (Oxford, 1932), p. 330.

[3] Ṭabari, vol. ii, p. 1729.

[4] Ṭabari, vol. ii, p. 1467.

[5] This would discredit the ascription of the fifth string to the celebrated Ziryāb, who died *ca.* 852; see Hitti, *History of the Arabs*, p. 598.

[6] *Buldān*, p. 263.

[7] For more on this palace consult D. Schlumberger, " Les Fouilles de Qasr el-Heir el-Gharbi ", *Syria*, vol. xx (1939), pp. 195-238, 324-73; Jaʿfar al-Ḥasani, " Qaṣr al-Ḥayr ", *Majallat al-Majmaʿ al-ʿIlmi al-ʿArabi*, vol. viii (1941), pp. 337-45.

The Caliph Sulaymān (715–17) took up his residence in a city which he built, al-Ramlah in Palestine. This is the only town established by the Arabs in Syria.[1] Traces of the caliphal palace could be seen there until the early twentieth century and the minaret of his White Mosque, as rebuilt by the Mamlūks, is still standing. This mosque, after the Umayyad Mosque of Damascus and the Dome of the Rock in Jerusalem, became the third leading sanctuary of Syria.

Mosques: the Dome of the Rock

For fully half a century after the conquest of Syria Moslems worshipped in converted churches and erected no special mosques. In Damascus they divided not the church itself, as tradition states, but the sacred enclosure. Damascene worshippers entered through the same gate; the Christians turned left and the Moslems right.[2] At the occupation of Ḥamāh its church, styled "the greater" by a local historian,[3] was converted into the Great Mosque (*al-Jāmiʿ al-Kabīr*). The east and west façades of the church are still intact.[4] Likewise the Great Mosque of Ḥimṣ [5] and that of Aleppo [6] were originally Christian places of worship. Christian relics and Roman columns are still visible in the Ḥimṣ sanctuary.

First among the mosques built in Syria was the Dome of the Rock [7] (Qubbat al-Ṣakhrah) in Jerusalem. The Dome was erected by ʿAbd-al-Malik in 691 on a site which once held the Temple of Solomon and represents the earliest Moslem monument surviving. To the right of the Rock Muḥammad halted on his nocturnal journey and thence he was translated heavenward on his miraculous mount.[8] As the Prophet's halting station and the first *qiblah* in Islam (the point toward which the first believers turned in prayer), Jerusalem acquired early sanctity in Moslem eyes. Then there were weighty political considerations. The Umayyads aimed at a sumptuous place of worship to divert the current of Syrian pilgrimage from Mecca, then in an anti-caliph's hands,[9] and to outshine the Church of

[1] *Al-ʿUyūn w-al-Ḥadā'iq fi Akhbār al-Ḥaqā'iq*, ed. T. G. J. Juynboll (Leyden, 1853), p. 40.

[2] Creswell, pt. 1, p. 134.

[3] Abu-al-Fidā', vol. i, p. 168.

[4] Creswell, p. 14.

[5] Balādhuri, p. 131; Maqdisi, p. 156.

[6] Balādhuri, pp. 146-7.

[7] Wrongly called by Europeans the Mosque of ʿUmar, who in 638 on visiting Jerusalem (see above, p. 418) may have erected a simple place of worship of timber or brick.

[8] Hitti, *History of the Arabs*, p. 114.

[9] Yaʿqūbi, vol. ii, p. 311; see above, pp. 452-3.

the Holy Sepulchre and Christian cathedrals of Syria.[1] To this end ʿAbd-al-Malik employed native architects and artisans trained in the Byzantine school. The edifice was modelled after that of the cathedral of Buṣra.[2] Its bronze doors, decorated with incrustation in silver, a distinguished achievement of Byzantine artists, are among the oldest dated ones of their

From C. A. Raven, "Palestine in Pictures" (Cambridge)

THE DOME OF THE ROCK AND THE DOME OF THE CHAIN

kind. Qāshāni and mosaic decoration was lavishly used in the original structure and later in its renovation. Qāshāni involves the use of square or hexagonal glazed tiles, sometimes figured with floral or geometrical designs, and goes back to Persian origin as the name indicates.[3] The mosaic technique can be traced to Babylonian days. ʿAbd-al-Malik left a Kufic inscription around the inside of the dome which represents one of the oldest Islamic writings extant. About a century and a quarter later the structure underwent restoration by the ʿAbbāsid al-

[1] Maqdisi, p. 159.
[2] Dussaud, *Syrie antique*, p. 10; cf. M. S. Briggs, *Muhammadan Architecture in Egypt and Palestine* (Oxford, 1924), p. 37.
[3] Kāshān, a city in Media; Yāqūt, *Buldān*, vol. iv, p. 15.

Ma'mūn, who unscrupulously substituted his own name for that of 'Abd-al-Malik's but fortunately failed to change the date.[1]

East of this edifice stands an elegant little cupola called Qubbat al-Silsilah (dome of the chain), which served as a treasure house (*bayt al-māl*) of the Rock. Its structure and decoration belong to the same period. To make the place inviolable Moslem tradition manufactured a chain which Solomon stretched across and which a truthful witness could grasp without producing any effect on the chain, but not a perjurer.

Close to the Dome 'Abd-al-Malik erected another mosque, the Aqṣa,[2] of which the Dome is in reality the shrine. In local usage al-Masjid[3] al-Aqṣa includes the entire sacred area of some thirty-four acres with its dervish monasteries (sing. *takīyah*, *zāwiyah*) and public fountains (sing. *sabīl*), some of which were built later by Mamlūk and Ottoman sultans. Al-Ḥaram al-Sharīf (the noble sanctuary) is another designation for this area, where once stood a Jewish temple, a Christian church and a heathen (Roman) sanctuary, making it one of the most hallowed places on the surface of the earth. On the site of al-Aqṣa there was a church dedicated to St. Mary by Justinian; its ruins were utilized in the construction of the mosque. Rebuilt by the 'Abbāsid al-Manṣūr, following an earthquake, the Aqṣa was modified by the Crusaders and restored to Islam in 1187 by Ṣalāḥ-al-Dīn (Saladin).

The Aqṣa Mosque

Next in chronology and importance was the Umayyad Mosque of Damascus. It was not until 705 that 'Abd-al-Malik's son al-Walīd seized from his Christian subjects the Cathedral of St. John the Baptist and converted it into this mosque,[4] one of the sublimest places of worship in the world. After the three Ḥarams of Mecca, Medina and Jerusalem, the

The Umayyad Mosque

[1] Following is a literal translation: HATH BUILT THIS DOME THE SERVANT OF GOD 'ABD[ULLĀH AL-IMĀM AL-MA'MŪN CO]MMANDER OF THE BELIEVERS IN THE YEAR TWO AND SEVENTY.—MAY GOD ACCEPT OF HIM AND FAVOUR HIM! AMEN.

[2] "The farther mosque", from a supposed reference in the Koran (17:1) to the site. It was this passage that gave rise to the story of Muḥammad's nocturnal journey. According to *Fakhri*, p. 173, al-Walīd was the builder. For the earliest description consult ibn-al-Faqīh, pp. 100-101, written *ca.* 903, and Maqdisi, pp. 169-171, *ca.* 985.

[3] "Place of bowing down", whence "mosque" through Italian and French.

[4] Ibn-'Asākir, vol. i, p. 200; abu-al-Fidā', vol. i, pp. 209-10.

Umayyad Mosque is still considered the fourth holiest place in Islam. The cathedral stood on the site of a temple consecrated

From J. Sauvaget, J. Weulersse and M. M. L. Écochard "Damas et la Syrie Sud" (*Damascus*)

THE UMAYYAD MOSQUE OF DAMASCUS

to Jupiter Damascenus, originally the Syrian Hadad,[1] and modelled after the temple of the Sun at Palmyra. To justify

[1] See above, p. 172.

the seizure by the Moslems, who until then had shared with its Christian owners a part of the temenos, tradition claimed that at the time of conquest the two contingents led respectively by Khālid and abu-ʿUbaydah [1] entered the city simultaneously, one coming from the east by force and the other from the west by capitulation, and met unknowingly in the middle of the cathedral. The resting-place of the head of St. John is still shown under a richly gilded dome in the mosque. Another Christian relic is a Greek inscription over the lintel of the southern portal of the enclosure: "Thy kingdom, O Christ, is an everlasting kingdom, and Thy dominion endureth throughout all generations".[2]

For seven years, we are told, al-Walīd pursued the project, expending on it the entire land revenue from Syria.[3] Not satisfied with local talent he drafted Persian and Indian craftsmen and requested a hundred Greek artisans from the Byzantine emperor.[4] Multicoloured mosaics and rare marbles adorned its upper walls and ceiling. Murals of gold and precious stones representing trees and cities, and witnessed by the Syrian geographer al-Maqdisi,[5] were plastered later by some pious ruler, to be rediscovered in 1928.[6] A comparative study of the decorations reveals native Syrian, rather than Greek Byzantine, workmanship.

On the north side of the mosque al-Walīd constructed a minaret [7] which was used as a beacon tower and became a model for similar structures in Syria, North Africa and Spain, to which it was introduced by ʿAbd-al-Raḥmān I. This is the oldest purely Moslem minaret still standing. The two minarets on the south side stand on earlier church towers.[8] Al-Ghazzāli (d. 1111) tells us that he isolated himself in the north minaret

[1] See above, p. 414.
[2] Cf. Ps. 145:13; Heb. 1:8.
[3] Maqdisi, p. 158; cf. *al-ʿUyūn w-al-Ḥadāʾiq*, p. 7.
[4] Ibn-ʿAsākir, vol. i, p. 202; *al-ʿUyūn* raises the figure to 100,000, of whom some were used in Mecca and Medina. Cf. Ṭabari, vol. ii, p. 1194; abu-al-Fidā', vol. i, p. 210; ibn-Jubayr, p. 261.
[5] P. 157; cf. Iṣṭakhri, p. 57; ibn-Rustah, p. 326; *al-ʿUyūn*, pp. 8-9.
[6] E. de Lorey and M. van Berchem, *Les Mosaïques de la mosquée des Omayyades à Damas* (Paris, 1930); Creswell, pp. 119-20.
[7] From Arabic *manārah*, lighthouse; also called *ṣawmaʿah* (ibn-ʿAsākir, vol. i, p. 200), monk's cell; *miʾdhanah*, place from which the muezzin calls to prayer, came later into general use.
[8] Cf. Yāqūt, vol. ii, p. 593.

for daily contemplation and devotion.[1] The Syrian type of minaret, a plain square structure, is clearly descended from the watch or church tower. The slender, tapering, round style, reminiscent of classical Roman columns, was a later adoption by the Turks, who introduced it into Syria as exemplified in the Mosque of Khālid at Ḥimṣ.

The Damascus mosque enjoys the further distinction of being the first one in which the semicircular niche for prayer (*miḥrāb*) appears. In it the horseshoe arch is also evident. Burned in 1069 and again in 1400 (by Tamerlane) and for the last time in 1893, the edifice still holds its place in Moslem eyes as the fourth wonder of the world.[2]

Al-Walīd, greatest among Umayyad builders, was also responsible for rebuilding the Mosque of Medina, enlarging and beautifying that of Mecca, erecting in Syria a number of schools, hospitals [3] and places of worship and for removing a dome of gilded brass from a church in Ba'labakk to the mosque built by his father in Jerusalem. In his reign, peaceful and opulent, whenever people in Damascus got together fine buildings formed the chief topic of conversation.[4]

In the palaces and mosques left by the Umayyads the harmonization of Arabian, Persian, Syrian and Greek elements is accomplished and the resultant synthesis called Moslem art makes its start. The Arabian element is endless repetition of small units to which one could add or from which he could subtract without materially affecting the whole. The columns of the Cordova Mosque illustrate the point. The motif suggests the monotony of the desert, the seemingly endless rows of trunks of date palms in an oasis or the legs of a caravan of camels. The Persians contributed delicacy, elegance, multicolour. In Umayyad Syria the ancient Semitic and the intruding Greek elements and motifs were reconciled and pressed into the permanent service of Islam.

[1] Al-Ghazzāli, *al-Munqidh min al-Ḍalāl* (Cairo, 1936), p. 27; cf. ibn-Khallikān, vol. ii, p. 246.

[2] Ibn-al-Faqīh, p. 106; ibn-'Asākir, vol. i, p. 198; Yāqūt, vol. ii, p. 591.

[3] See above, pp. 497-8.

[4] Ṭabari, vol. ii, pp. 1272-3.

CHAPTER XXXIX

THE SYRIAN CHRISTIAN CHURCH

The East Syrian Church

BEFORE the rise of Islam the Syrian (*Suryānī*) Christian Church had split into several communities. There was first the East Syrian Church or the Church of the East. This communion, established in the late second century, claims uninterrupted descent in its teachings, liturgy, consecration and tradition from the time the Edessene King Abgar allegedly wrote to Christ asking him to relieve him of an incurable disease and Christ promised to send him one of his disciples after his ascension.[1] This is the church erroneously called Nestorian, after the Cilician Nestorius,[2] whom it antedates by about two and a half centuries. The term Nestorian was applied to it at a late date by Roman Catholics to convey the stigma of heresy in contradistinction to those of its members who joined the Catholic Church as Uniats and received the name Chaldaeans. The first patriarch of the Chaldaean rite was the metropolitan of Diyār Bakr consecrated in 1681.

With its God-and-man doctrine of Christology,[3] its protest against the deification of the Virgin Mary and its unusual vitality and missionary zeal, this Church at the rise of Islam was the most potent factor in Syrian culture which had impressed itself upon the Near East from Egypt to Persia. Members of this community from the fourth century onward had studied and translated Greek philosophical works and spread them throughout Syria and Mesopotamia. From Edessa the Church extended eastward into Persia. Toward the end of the fifth century the bishop of the Sāsānid capital Seleucia-Ctesiphon declared himself patriarch of the Eastern Church. In 762,

[1] For copies of the correspondence consult Sa'īd ibn-Baṭrīq (Eutychius), *al-Ta'rīkh al-Majmū' 'ala al-Taḥqīq w-al-Taṣdīq* (Beirut, 1909), pp. 263-4.

[2] For more on him consult Assemani (al-Sam'āni), *Bibliotheca Orientalis*, vol. iii, pt. 1 (Rome, 1725), pp. 35-7 ; see above, p. 371.

[3] In contrast to the orthodox doctrine which held that while in Christ two natures existed, these were moulded into one person ; cf. above, pp. 371-2.

when Baghdād was founded, the patriarchate moved to the ʿAbbāsid capital, where it enjoyed caliphal favour. Even under Islam this Church had an unparalleled record of missionary activity. Sepulchral and other evidences attest the existence of Syrian churches in Marw, Harāt (Herat), Samarqand and other places of Central Asia going back to the mid-sixth century.

About the same time missionaries of this " Protestantism of the East " had penetrated south to India, where Christianity had struck root a couple of centuries earlier. Syrian churches arose on the west coast of India, especially Malabar, and in Ceylon. Members of the Syrian rite in India acquired the name " Christians of St. Thomas ", after the apostle whom unreliable tradition makes the first teacher of Christianity in India. Christian immigrants from Baghdād and other Moslem cities reinforced in the eighth and ninth centuries this community, whose fame spread to the West, resulting in an embassy which King Alfred of England sent to that distant land.

But the crowning missionary achievement was in the Far East. In the seventh to the ninth centuries, and again in the twelfth and fourteenth, Syrian monks penetrated to China. The first missionaries arrived at Sian Fu in 635, when the Moslem army was conquering Persia. A stele commemorating in Chinese and Syriac the names and labours of sixty-seven missionaries was erected " on the seventh of the first month of 781 of the Christian era " and now stands in that city.[1] Not far from this place a Nestorian monastery, now a Taoist temple, can still be seen. After an existence of over seven hundred years (635–1367) this Syrian Church in China, cut off from a mother which because of Islam was becoming too weak to reinforce it, was swallowed up by local cults, Taoist sects and Moslem communities. It lives in the Chinese records as the " luminous religion ".[2] Its cultural traces are still visible in the Syriac characters in which Mongol and Manchu were written [3] and in the technique and decoration of bookbinding in Turkestan, which are related to the style used by the Copts in Egypt and were presumably transmitted by these Syrian Christians.[4]

[1] P. Y. Saeki, *The Nestorian Documents and Relics in China* (Tokyo, 1937), pp. 35, 68.

[2] Saeki, pp. 65, l. 15, 457, l. 7; cf. 449, l. 10. [3] See above, p. 371.

[4] Mehmet Aga-Oglu, *Persian Bookbindings of the Fifteenth Century* (Ann Arbor, 1935), p. 1. For more on the Nestorians consult Assemani, vol. iii, pt. 2.

The East Syrian Church was represented at the beginning of the first world war by 190,000 members domiciled around Urmiyah, al-Mawṣil (Mosul) and Central Kurdistan.[1] Those who survived have since drifted into al-ʿIrāq and Syria. As an ethnic group they would rather be called Assyrians, an appellation that does not seem inappropriate when the physical features of many of them are compared with the Assyrian type as portrayed on the monuments.

From P. Y. Saeki, "The Nestorian Documents and Relics in China" (Tokyo)

THE SYRIAN MONUMENTAL COLUMN IN SIAN FU, DATED A.D. 781

THE SYRIAC AND CHINESE INSCRIPTIONS ON THE LOWER PART OF THE MONUMENT

The West Syrian Church

The western branch of the Syrian Church, with its God-man Christology [2] and its exaltation of the Virgin to celestial rank, was comparatively lacking in missionary endeavour. Its theology was Monophysite, giving prominence to the unity of Christ at the expense of the human element. In Syria the Monophysite communion was called by hostile Greeks Jacobite after Jacob

[1] A. Yuhanan, *The Death of a Nation* (New York, 1916), pp. 8-9.

[2] Cf. above, p. 371.

Baradaeus, bishop of Edessa in the mid-sixth century.[1] The Ghassān and other Syrian Arabs adopted this creed before the advent of Islam.[2] The so-called Jacobite Church was preponderant in Syria as the miscalled Nestorian was preponderant in Persia. Syriac [3] was and has remained the language of both Churches; but Greek was also taught in the cloisters, and the Jacobites seconded the efforts made by the Nestorians in transmitting Greek thought to Syria and then to Islam. Qinnasrīn was a great centre in North Syria for disseminating Monophysite doctrine and Greek knowledge. Jacobite scholars were depositories of whatever sciences were cultivated or transmitted in those days.

Some two hundred thousand communicants of this venerable Church survived until the early twentieth century in the neighbourhood of Mārdīn, Diyār Bakr and Armenia.[4] Since then they have been decimated, the remnant taking refuge in Syria and Lebanon. The patriarchate has its present seat at Ḥimṣ. They object to the term Jacobite, to which they prefer the designation Orthodox or Old Syrians (*Suryān*). Those of them who in recent times adopted the Roman Catholic rite form the Syrian Catholic Church with its patriarchal seat in Lebanon. This is a Uniat offshoot corresponding to the Chaldaean.

Besides the Jacobite Church of Syria, the Armenian Church and the Coptic-Ethiopic Church are independent descendants of the Monophysite rite. The triumph of the Church of the Syrians over those of Armenia, Egypt and Ethiopia was another conspicuous achievement of Syrian society and culture. With all their interest in Greek learning the two sister Syrian Churches of the East and of the West, be it remembered, arose and developed as a reaction of the Syrian society against the Hellenizing influences of Byzantium and Rome. Treated as "heresies" by these two Christian capitals, both Jacobitism and Nestorianism were basically protests against foreign intrusion and against the process of syncretism that was turning Christianity, a Syrian religion, into a Greco-Roman institution.

[1] See above, pp. 371-2. Assemani devotes most of his *Bibliotheca Orientalis*, vol. ii, to a study of the Monophysites and Jacobites.

[2] See above, p. 403.

[3] This term after the Aramaeans were Christianized was considered by them preferable to the term Aramaic. See above, pp. 170-71.

[4] Yuhanan, p. 9.

Both Churches " survive today as fossils of an extinct Syriac society ".[1]

Another offshoot of the ancient Church of Syria was the Maronite, which owes its origin to its patron saint Mārūn (Maron, Maro [2]). An ascetic monk about whose life not much is known, Mārūn lived between Antioch and Qūrus (Qūrush, Cyrrhus), where he died about 410. He is presumably the " Maron, the monk priest " to whom John Chrysostom on his way to exile addressed an epistle soliciting his prayers and news.[3] After his death, so tradition asserts, Mārūn's disciples carried his remains to a place near Apamea (Afāmiyah) on the Orontes, where a monastery was erected in his memory. Conflict with Jacobites led to a massacre in this monastery of three hundred and fifty monks, whose memory is still celebrated in the Maronite calendar. Lebanon offered a better refuge and the new sect struck root in its northern soil. There the amalgamation took place with the Mardaites, who had also filtered from the north.[4] The Maronites

If Mārūn was the saint of the new sect, Yūḥanna Mārūn (Joannes Maro, d. *ca.* 707) was the hero and founder of the new nation. He is probably the Mārūn from whom the congregation received its name. Born at Sarūm, near Antioch, Yūḥanna studied Syriac and Greek in Antioch before joining the monastery on the Orontes. He pursued his studies in Constantinople and was consecrated bishop of al-Batrūn in Lebanon. His headquarters were first in Samār Jubayl and later in Kafarḥayy, where he established a monastery and was buried. Under him the Maronite community developed into an autonomous nation which with one arm kept the Moslem caliph [5] at a distance and with the other the Byzantine emperor. When in 694 Justinian II desired to subdue the Maronites, his troops, after destroying the monastery on the Orontes, were routed by Yūḥanna at Amyūn.[6] Since then the Maronites have isolated themselves and developed the kind of individualism that characterizes mountaineers. For a time Qannūbīn,[7] carved in

[1] Toynbee, vol. v, p. 127. [2] From Syriac meaning " the small lord ".

[3] For Arabic translation consult al-Duwayhi, *Ta'rīkh al-Ṭā'ifah al-Mārūnīyah*, (Beirut, 1890), pp. 19-20. [4] See above, p. 448. [5] See above, p. 449.

[6] For more on him see Assemani, vol. i, pp. 496-520.

[7] Syr. from Gr. for monastery; one of the few Greek place names surviving in Lebanon.

the solid rock of rugged Lebanon, provided a seat for the Maronite patriarchate, which has since moved into Bakirki in the neighbourhood of Beirut.

The Maronite leaders of the mid-seventh century were friendly with the Emperor Heraclius, and the entire sect has been charged with espousing his Monothelite cause.[1] Saʿīd ibn-Baṭrīq (fl. *ca.* 931) was one of the first to make this assertion.[2] His Moslem contemporary al-Masʿūdi [3] held the same views. Saʿīd was followed by William of Tyre,[4] historian of the Crusades, who states that " the heresy of Maro and his followers is and was that in our Lord Jesus Christ there exists, and did exist from the beginning, one will and one energy only ". William estimates their number at forty thousand and goes on to say that in 1180 they repudiated their heresies and returned to the Catholic Church; but Maronite apologists, beginning with al-Duwayhi [5] (d. 1704) and ibn-Namrūn [6] (d. 1711), have claimed continued orthodoxy for their Church throughout the ages.[7] A modern Maronite author [8] claims that there was another Maron, a Monothelite of Edessa, who died about 580 and whose followers these authors confused with the Lebanese Maronites. There is no doubt that in this period of the Crusades the Maronites attracted the attention of Rome but union was not effected till the eighteenth century. Their Church, which may be considered the national Church of Lebanon, has retained till the present day its Syriac liturgy and non-celibate priesthood and Rome has failed to include in its list of saints either of its reputed eponymous founders. The 1942 census gives the number of Maronites in Lebanon as 318,211, more than any other religious body in that republic. Recent Maronite emigrants have carried their rite into Italy, France, North and South America, Australia and other parts of the civilized world.

The Melkites

The East and the West Syrian Churches with their ramifica-

[1] See above, p. 417. [2] Ibn-Baṭrīq, p. 12. [3] *Tanbīh*, p. 154.

[4] *History*, tr. Emily A. Babcock and A. C. Krey, vol. ii, p. 459.

[5] Pp. 292 *seq.*

[6] Fausto (Murhij) Naironi, *Dissertatio de origine, nomine, ac religione Maronitharum* (Rome, 1679).

[7] Among the recent apologists Afrām al-Dayrāni, *al-Muḥāmāh ʿan al-Mawārinah wa-Qiddīsīhim* (Beirut, 1899); Yūsuf al-Dibs, *Taʾrīkh Sūrīyah*, vol. v (Beirut, 1900), pp. 156 *seq.*

[8] Bernard G. al-Ghazīri, *Rome et l'Église syrienne-maronite* (Paris, 1906), pp. 31-3, 44-5.

tions did not comprise all Syrian Christians. There remained a small body which succumbed under the impact of Greek theology from Antioch and Constantinople and accepted the decrees of the Council of Chalcedon (451). Thereby this community secured orthodoxy and not only escaped excommunication but obtained protection, even patronage, from the state church and the imperial city. By way of reproach their opponents centuries later nicknamed them Melkites,[1] royalists. Melkite ranks must have been recruited mainly from city-dwellers and descendants of Greek colonists. Gradually Greek replaced Syriac as the language of ritual and the Syriac liturgy gave place to the Byzantine. Hundreds of manuscripts in European and Oriental libraries indicate that the victory of Greek was not complete till the early seventeenth century.[2] Though supported by the ruling state the Melkite community remained comparatively weak and was confined to North Syria, Palestine and Egypt. Their Syrian descendants maintain one patriarchate in Damascus and another in Jerusalem and are now known as Greek Orthodox.[3]

In recent years, strangely enough, " Melkite " has been exclusively employed to designate Christians drawn from the Orthodox Church and attached to Rome. They, however, claim old and uninterrupted communion with the Roman Catholic Church. At present they number about one-half of the Orthodox community estimated at about 230,000. Their patriarch maintains a residence in Egypt and another in Lebanon. The majority of the Greek Catholics and of the Greek Orthodox live in Syria, rather than in Lebanon.

Interaction with Islam

To the Syrian Christian, infant Islam could not have appeared as entirely alien or exotic; in fact it must have appeared more like a new Judaeo-Christian sect than a new religion. In general, Islam's hostility to Christianity was one of rivalry rather than of conflicting ideology. Writing immediately after the conquest, a patriarch of the Eastern Church [4] describes the new masters in the following glowing terms: " The Arabs, to whom God at this time has granted dominion

[1] Less corectly Melchites, from Syr. *malka*, king.

[2] Isḥāq Armalah, *al-Malakīyūn: Baṭriyarkīyatuhum al-Anṭākīyah* (Beirut, 1936), pp. 102, 104-15; Ḥabīb al-Zayyāt in *al-Mashriq*, vol. xxxvii (1939), p. 174.

[3] For a list of the patriarchs consult Armalah, pp. 26 *seq.*

[4] Išoʿyahb III, " Liber epistularum ", in *Scriptores Syri*, ser. II, vol. lxiv, ed. Rubens Duval (Paris, 1904–5), text p. 251, ll. 13-19, cf. p. 252, ll. 8-12, tr. p. 182.

over the world, are, as you know, among us. But they are not enemies of Christianity. On the contrary they praise our faith and honour the priests and saints of the Lord and confer benefits upon the churches and monasteries." Certain Orientalists [1] go as far as making Islam in many respects an heir of Syrian Christianity. John of Damascus regarded Muḥammad as a heretic rather than the founder of a new faith and confounded Islam with Arianism, which discounted the divinity of Christ.[2] John tells his Moslem opponents, " When you call us associators (*mushrikūn*), we call you mutilators ", and asks why should Christians be blamed for bowing before the cross when the Moslems do the same before the Black Stone. So supercilious an attitude was no doubt encouraged by his being a cleric writing in a foreign tongue. ʿUmar II evidently considered it easy to convert Leo the Isaurian by addressing a theological epistle to him, which the emperor attempted to refute by correspondence.[3]

The oneness of God and the last judgment were favourite themes equally in koranic literature and in the Apocryphal gospels and ascetic writings.[4] St. Ephraim (d. *ca.* 373), revered by both branches of the Syrian Church as the greatest preacher they produced, depicts the abode of bliss in these materialistic colours :

I witnessed the dwelling places of the just and the just themselves, dripping with ointments, giving forth pleasant odours, wreathed in flowers and adorned with fruits. . . . When the just lie at the table, the trees offer them shade in the clear air. Flowers grow beneath them and fruits above. . . . Swift winds stand before the blessed, ready to do their will. One of the winds wafts appeasement, another causes drink to flow. One wind is filled with oil, another with ointment. . . . Whoever has abstained from wine on earth, for him do the vines of Paradise yearn. Each one of the trees holds out to him a bunch of grapes. And if a man has lived in chastity, females receive him in a pure bosom.[5]

[1] E.g. Carl H. Becker, *Islamstudien*, vol. i (Leipzig, 1924), pp. 16-18, 386 *seq.*

[2] Migne, *Patrologia Graeca*, vol. xciv, cols. 763-74. See above, p. 371.

[3] Theophanes, *Chronographia*, p. 399; Maḥbūb (Agapius of Manbij), " Kitāb al-ʿUnwān ", in *Patrologia Orientalis*, vol. viii (Paris, 1912), p. 503.

[4] Consult William Wright, *Apocryphal Acts of the Apostles*, 2 vols. (London, 1871).

[5] Sancti Ephraem Syri, *Opera omnia* (Rome, 1743), p. 563; cf. Tor Andrae, tr. Theophil Menzil, *Mohammed: the Man and his Faith* (New York, 1936); Koran 88:4-16; 55:46-78.

The distinction between obligatory and supererogatory works was common to both religions. In the practice of ritual and adoration there were many resemblances. The Syrian Church had recognized three canonical prayers in the daytime and two at night long before the five Moslem prayers were instituted. Night vigils described in the Koran (73 : 1-8, 20) recall monastic practice and ascetic piety. Monks observed fixed bodily postures in time of prayer, involving genuflections and touching the ground with the forehead. The hair of the head of a monk fell off in front from the number of times he hit it on the ground in supplication.[1] A pre-Islamic poem describes a monk with a callous on the forehead comparable to that on a goat's knee.[2]

As Christians turned Moslem, they naturally carried over with them old ideas and practices, some of which were perpetuated in the sects and heterodoxies. The gap was further bridged as early narrators of ḥadīth borrowed events from the life of the founders of Christianity and ascribed them to the founder of Islam. Muḥammad is reported to have commended " him who gives alms only in secret, so that his left hand knows not what his right hand does " [3] and proclaimed that God said: " I have prepared for my righteous servants what eye hath not seen, nor ear heard, nor hath it entered into the heart of man ".[4] Even a version of the Lord's Prayer is put in Muḥammad's mouth.[5] Through the Sufi institution of later days Christian ascetic piety opened another channel into the heart of Islam.

Loan words

The Syriac-speaking Christian readily recognized many key words in Islamic vocabulary. Arabic *furqān* (salvation,[6] Koran 8 : 29, 42), *āyah* (sign, 2 : 37; 3 : 9), *kāhin* (soothsayer, priest, 52 : 29; 69 : 42), *sujūd* (prostration, 2 : 19; 68 : 42, 43), *sifr* (book, 62 : 5), *qissīs* [7] (monk, 5 : 85), *ṣalāh* (ritual prayer, 2 : 2, 40; 24 : 57), *zakāh* (alms, 2 : 40, 77, 104) and many others were loan words from Syriac or Aramaic.[8] Many other church and ecclesiastical terms from Syriac were Arabicized, as illustrated

[1] John of Ephesus in *Patrologia Orientalis*, vol. xvii, p. 40.
[2] L. Cheikho, *al-Naṣrānīyah wa-Ādābuha* (Beirut, 1919), p. 178.
[3] Cf. Matt. 6 : 3-4.
[4] Cf. 1 Cor. 2 : 9.
[5] Hitti, *History of the Arabs*, p. 396.
[6] In sūr. 25 used as a synonym of Koran.
[7] This word and the preceding occur in the Koran only in plural.
[8] For other words consult Arthur Jeffery, *The Foreign Vocabulary of the Qur'ān* (Baroda, 1938).

by *ishbīn* (godfather), *burshān* (wafer), *tilmīdh* (disciple), *shammās* (deacon), *'imād* (baptism), *kanīsah* (church), *kārūz* (preacher), *nāqūs* (gong). The Greek loan words were not quite so numerous and included: *ṭaqs* (rite), *qandalaft* (sexton), *injīl* (Evangel), *usquf* (bishop), *shidyāq* (subdeacon), *abrashīyah* (parish), *zunnār* (girdle).[1] Several Greek words found their way into Arabic through Syriac: *khūri* (priest), *baṭriyark* (patriarch), *iskīm* (monk's hood), *harṭūqi* (heretic).

Ortho-graphy

In one other respect did Syriac make a significant contribution to Arabic, orthography. The Arabic characters themselves, as we learned before,[2] were derived from Nabataean, a sister of Syriac.

In its earliest form Arabic writing entirely lacked the diacritical points which now serve to distinguish letters formerly written alike. It was also destitute of vocalization, all its characters being consonantal. In the course of the first Moslem century diacritical points, of possible Nabataean origin, as well as vowel signs were introduced and put into limited use. A single dot over the letter was employed to indicate the *a* sound; a dot below the letter to indicate the *i* sound.[3] But that was precisely what the East Syrians had been doing for a long time. Toward the end of that century, and following again the Syriac practice, the dots were elongated into the supralinear and infralinear dashes still in use. These are the reforms ascribed by tradition to al-Ḥajjāj.[4] The same Syriac system of vowel pointing lies at the basis of the Hebrew system, which the Masorites borrowed after A.D. 750.[5]

[1] For more consult Georg Graf in *Zeitschrift für Semitistik und verwandte Gebiete*, vol. vii (1929), pp. 225 *seq.*; vol. ix (1939), pp. 234 *seq.*; see below, p. 547.

[2] Pp. 169, 384.

[3] The sign for the *u* sound was evidently borrowed from the letter *w*.

[4] See above, p. 476.

[5] Frank R. Blake in *Journal, American Oriental Society*, vol. lx (1940), pp. 391-413.

CHAPTER XL

FALL OF THE UMAYYAD DYNASTY

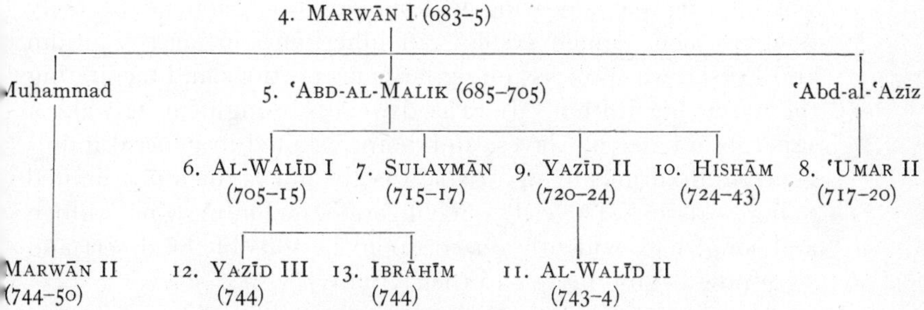

Tree showing the genealogical relationship of the Marwānid caliphs of the Umayyad dynasty

The Umayyad power passed its zenith with the reign of al-Walīd (705–15). Only two distinguished rulers may be noted after him, ʿUmar II and Hishām.

A devout caliph

ʿUmar (717–20) stood out as the only pious caliph in a reputedly worldly régime. His ideal was to follow in the footsteps of his maternal grandfather, the second orthodox caliph, whose namesake he was. His devotion, frugality and simplicity are emphasized by his biographer, who asserts that the caliph wore clothes with so many patches and mingled with his subjects so freely that when one came to petition him he found it difficult to recognize him.[1] During his reign the theologians had their day. Hence the saintly reputation he acquired in Moslem history. ʿUmar abolished the practice introduced by Muʿāwiyah of cursing ʿAli from the pulpit at the Friday prayers.[2] He introduced fiscal reforms which failed of survival but nevertheless substantially contributed toward the equal treatment of Arab and non-Arab Moslems and the ultimate fusion of the sons of conquerors and conquered.[3]

The last able Umayyad

Hishām (724–43) was rightly considered by Arab historians

[1] Ibn-al-Jawzi, pp. 173-4, 145 *seq.* [2] *Fakhri*, p. 176. [3] See above, p. 475.

as the last statesman of the house of Umayyah.[1] His four successors were incompetent if not dissolute and degenerate. When his son, Muʿāwiyah, ancestor of the Spanish Umayyads, met his death while hunting, the father remarked, "I brought him up for the caliphate and he pursues a fox!"[2] His governor over al-ʿIrāq, who appropriated for himself 13,000,000 dirhams after squandering of the state revenue nearly thrice that sum, was apprehended and forced to make repayments.[3] His case was one of many, proving widespread corruption in the body politic. The eunuch system, an inheritance from Byzantium and Persia, was now assuming large proportions and facilitating the harem institution. Increased wealth brought in its wake a superabundance of slaves, and both resulted in general indulgence in luxurious living. Nor was the moral turpitude limited to high classes. The vices of civilization, including wine, women and song, had evidently seized upon the sons of the desert and were now beginning to sap their vitality.

Four incompetent caliphs

Hishām's successor al-Walīd II, a physically strong and handsome man, was more of a virtuoso in music and poetry than an adept in state affairs.[4] He took time from his life of pleasure in the desert to be enthroned in the capital and then resumed his usual career. The ruins of his palaces still adorn the desert.[5] More serious, however, were the mistakes he made in designating his two minor sons, whose mother was a freedwoman, as heirs to the caliphate and then in alienating the Yamanites (South Arabians), who formed the bulk of the Arab population of Syria. The principle of heredity in the caliphate, introduced by Muʿāwiyah,[6] conflicted with the time-honoured tribal principle of seniority in succession. The problem was further complicated when the founder of the Marwānid branch designated two of his sons, ʿAbd-al-Malik and ʿAbd-al-ʿAzīz, as his consecutive successors.[7] The lack of an accepted clear-cut principle of caliphal succession was, of course, not conducive to stability and continuity. As for the Yamanites they were the party on whose shoulders the Syrian throne was raised. Their feud with the Qaysites (North Arabians) was deep-rooted and

[1] Masʿūdi, vol. v, p. 479; cf. Yaʿqūbi, vol. ii, p. 393; ibn-Qutaybah, *Maʿārif*, p. 185.
[2] Ṭabari, vol. ii, pp. 1738-9.
[3] Ṭabari, vol. ii, p. 1642; Yaʿqūbi, vol. ii, p. 387.
[4] *Aghāni*, vol. vi, pp. 101 *seq.*
[5] See above, p. 507.
[6] See above, p. 440.
[7] Yaʿqūbi, vol. ii, p. 306.

destined to last till recent times.[1] A conspiracy headed by Yazīd, cousin of al-Walīd, used Yamanite insurgents to track the caliph and murder him south of Palmyra.[2]

The reign of Yazīd III (744), first caliph born of a slave mother,[3] was marked by disturbances in the provinces. His brother and successor Ibrāhīm, after a reign of only two months, was obliged to abdicate in favour of a distant cousin, Marwān II (744–50), who, like his two predecessors, was the son of a slave concubine.[4]

When Marwān was installed, anarchy was already on the march throughout the whole domain. An Umayyad claimant arose in Syria, a Khārijite one rebelled in al-ʿIrāq and leaders in Khurāsān refused to acknowledge the caliph's authority. Marwān moved his seat of government to Ḥarrān, where he could rely upon Qaysite support and deal more effectively with his two worst enemies — the ʿAlids and the ʿAbbāsids.

ʿAlids and ʿAbbāsids

To the Shīʿites the Umayyads were but ungodly usurpers who had perpetrated an unforgivable, unforgettable wrong against ʿAli and his descendants. The unswerving devotion of the Shīʿites to the house of the Prophet made them the focus of popular interest and sympathy. Their camp gradually became the rallying point of the dissatisfied, politically, socially and economically. Since ʿAli had chosen al-Kūfah for capital, al-ʿIrāq had been their stronghold. The ʿIrāqis, moreover, nurtured a grudge against the Syrians for depriving them of the seat of the caliphate. Sunnite pietists joined the band of critics who charged the house of Umayyah with worldliness, secularism and neglect of koranic law.

Like the Shīʿites the ʿAbbāsids took advantage of the general chaotic condition to press their own claim to the throne. Their claim was based on the proposition that as descendants of an uncle of the Prophet[5] they had a prior claim on the

[1] See above, p. 452. [2] Yaʿqūbi, vol. ii, p. 400; *Fakhri*, p. 182.
[3] Ṭabari, vol. ii, p. 1874; Masʿūdi, vol. vi, pp. 31-2.
[4] Yaʿqūbi, vol. ii, pp. 403, 404; Masʿūdi, vol. vi, p. 47.
[5] Hāshim
  |
ʿAbd-al-Muṭṭalib
  |
ʿAbdullāh — Abu-Ṭālib — AL-ʿABBĀS
  | |
MUḤAMMAD — ʿALI + Fāṭimah

caliphate as compared with the banu-Umayyah.

The Khurāsānians

Another factor that entered into the situation was the discontent felt by non-Arabian Moslems in general and Persian Moslems in particular because of the treatment accorded them by Arabian Moslems. Far from being granted the equality promised by Islam, these neophytes were actually reduced to the status of clients (*mawāli*).[1] In certain cases they were not even granted exemption from the capitation tax paid by them when still dhimmis. The resentment reached its height in Persia, whose more ancient and venerable culture was acknowledged even by the Arabians. The soil of Khurāsān in the north-east proved especially fertile for the germination of Shīʿite-ʿAbbāsid seed. The Shīʿah doctrine struck a responsive chord in Khurāsānian hearts. Under the guise of Shīʿah Islam, old Iranianism was reasserting itself.

Only one element was still missing — leadership, leadership under which Shīʿite, ʿAbbāsid, Persian and other anti-Umayyad forces could coalesce and march against the common foe. That leadership was at last supplied by abu-al-ʿAbbās ʿAbdullāh, a great-great-grandson of al-ʿAbbās. His success in securing control of the entire anti-Umayyad machine was largely due to the clever use of propaganda. For headquarters the ʿAbbāsids had chosen a seemingly innocent and aloof village south of the Dead Sea,[2] al-Ḥumaymah, but in reality a strategic place for reaching caravans, travellers and pilgrims from all over the world of Islam. In it would-be missionaries were indoctrinated and from it sent on their secret mission. At al-Ḥumaymah the earliest and one of the most subtle and successful propaganda acts of political Islam was played. Nothing was comparable to it until the rise of the Fāṭimids.[3]

Revolt breaks out

Action began in Khurāsān. It was June 747. The seditious movement was headed by the ʿAbbāsid agent abu-Muslim al-Khurāsāni, himself a freedman of obscure origin.[4] The banner he unfurled was black, a colour he had adopted for his garments in mourning over the murder of a descendant of ʿAli in Khurāsān. That became the distinctive colour of the rising dynasty. At the head of an army composed of Yamanite Arabs (of the Azd tribe)

[1] See above, pp. 474, 485.

[2] Yaʿqūbi, vol. ii, pp. 356-7; *Fakhri*, pp. 192-3; Ṭabari, vol. iii, p. 34; Yāqūt, vol. ii, p. 342; Musil, *Northern Heǧâz*, pp. 56-61 and map in pocket.

[3] See below, p. 577.

[4] *Fakhri*, p. 186.

and Iranian peasants, abu-Muslim made a successful entry into the capital Marw. The Umayyad governor of Khurāsān, Naṣr ibn-Sayyār, appealed in vain to Marwān, pointing out the threatening danger.[1] He even had recourse to poetry:

I see the coal's red glow beneath the embers
And 'tis about to blaze!
The rubbing of two sticks enkindles fire,
And out of words come frays.
"Oh! is Umayya's House awake or sleeping?"
I cry in sore amaze.[2]

But the caliph had enough trouble to keep him busy at home. Here the rebellion fomented by Yamanites had spread from Palestine to Ḥimṣ. In al-ʿIrāq the Khārijites were again on the march.[3] Personally Marwān was no mean soldier. For his perseverance in warfare he had won the title of al-Ḥimār (ass), a label that then bore no stigma. He was credited with the change from fighting in lines (*ṣufūf*), a practice hallowed by association with the Prophet's method of battling, to that of cohorts (*karadīs*),[4] small units more compact and consequently more mobile. But now he stood helpless in a situation that was hopeless. Clearly the Umayyad sun was fast approaching its setting.

Final blow

The fall of Marw was followed by that of Nihāwand and other Persian cities, which opened the way to al-ʿIrāq. Here al-Kūfah, its chief city and the hiding-place of abu-al-ʿAbbās, fell without determined opposition. On October 30, 749, in its principal mosque homage was paid to him as caliph.[5] Throughout the eastern provinces the white flag was in retreat before the black. Marwān resolved on a last, desperate stand. With 12,000 troops [6] he moved from Ḥarrān and was met (January 750) on the left bank of the Greater (Upper) Zāb, an affluent of the Tigris, by the opposition under the leadership of ʿAbdullāh ibn-ʿAli, an uncle of the new caliph. The battle raged for nine days. The will to win was no more on the Syrian side. Gone were its days of high morale and inspiring leadership. Its defeat was now decisive.

1 Ṭabari, vol. ii, pp. 1953 *seq.*; Dīnawari, pp. 359 *seq.*
2 Nicholson, *Literary History*, p. 251; *Fakhri*, p. 194.
3 Ṭabari, vol. ii, pp. 1943-9.
4 See above, p. 478.
5 Yaʿqūbi, vol. ii, pp. 417-18; Ṭabari, vol. iii, pp. 27-33; Masʿūdi, vol. vi, pp. 87, 98.
6 Ṭabari, vol. iii, p. 47 (cf. p. 45); see above, p. 478, n. 6.

One after the other of the Syrian towns opened their gates to ʿAbdullāh with his Khurāsāni-ʿIrāqi troops. Only Damascus put up the semblance of a fight. A few days of siege were enough to reduce the proud capital (April 26, 750). ʿAbbāsid cavalry were stabled in its great mosque for seventy days. The victorious army pushed south to Palestine. Thence a detachment was rushed after the fleeing caliph. Outside a church at Būṣīr,[1] Upper Egypt, Marwān was overtaken and killed (August 5, 750). His head and caliphal insignia were sent to abu-al-ʿAbbās.[2]

What to do with the rest of the Umayyads was the next chief concern of ʿAbbāsid policy. Extermination was the fate agreed upon and the execution was entrusted to ʿAbdullāh. The implacable commander-in-chief shrank from no measure calculated to wipe out of existence the kindred enemy. Even tombs in Damascus, Qinnasrīn and other burial-places were violated, their corpses crucified and other remains thrown out. The body of Hishām was disentombed from al-Ruṣāfah, lashed eighty times and then burned to ashes.[3] Only the tombs of Muʿāwiyah and the pious ʿUmar were spared. On June 25, 750, ʿAbdullāh invited eighty Umayyad princes to a banquet at abu-Fuṭrus, ancient Antipatris, on the ʿAwjā' River near Jaffa; and as they started the feast, his executioners started to mow them down, one by one. Over the still warm bodies of the dead and the dying leathern covers were spread, and the general with his lieutenants continued in the enjoyment of the repast to the accompaniment of human groans.[4] Agents and spies scoured Moslem lands hunting down fugitive scions of the fallen family. Several "sought refuge in the bowels of the earth",[5] as its surface became unsafe for them.

A dramatic escape

One person escaped the general massacre, ʿAbd-al-Raḥmān ibn-Muʿāwiyah, grandson of the Caliph Hishām. This nine-

[1] Also Abūṣīr, probably Būṣīr al-Malaq in the Fayyūm. Consult Sāwīrus ibn-al-Muqaffaʿ, *Siyar al-Baṭārikah al-Iskandarānīyīn*, ed. C. F. Seybold (Hamburg, 1912), pp. 181 *seq.*; Ṭabari, vol. iii, pp. 49-50.

[2] Masʿūdi, vol. vi, p. 77.

[3] Masʿūdi, vol. v, p. 471; cf. Yaʿqūbi, vol. ii, pp. 427-8. See *Fakhri*, p. 204.

[4] Yaʿqūbi, vol. ii, pp. 425-6; Masʿūdi, vol. vi, p. 76; ibn-al-Athīr, vol. v, pp. 329-30; Mubarrad, p. 707; *Aghāni*, vol. iv, p. 161, cf. pp. 92-6; *Fakhri*, pp. 203-4; Theophanes, p. 427. Compare the story of Jehu's extermination of Ahab's house (2 K. 9: 14-34) and the destruction of the Mamlūks of Egypt by Muḥammad ʿAli (below, p. 692); Jurji Zaydān, *Taʾrīkh Miṣr al-Ḥadīth*, 3rd ed., Cairo, 1925, vol. ii, pp. 160-62.

[5] Ibn-Khaldūn, vol. iv, p. 120.

teen-year-old youth first hid himself in a Bedouin camp on the left bank of the Euphrates in North Syria. The camp was one day startled by the sight of approaching black standards. ʿAbd-al-Raḥmān dashed into the river. His brother, six years his junior, followed. The ʿAbbāsid pursuers were on their heels. Taking their promise of amnesty seriously, the younger yielded and returned from midstream, only to be slain. The elder kept on and gained the opposite bank.[1]

Disguised, ʿAbd-al-Raḥmān trudged on his way southward. In Palestine he was joined by his faithful and able freedman Badr. A price was set on the head of the fugitive prince and he barely escaped assassination at the hands of the governor of North Africa. Friendless and penniless he threaded his way through the length of North Africa. After five years of wandering he landed in Spain (755), conquered and held by his ancestors. There he established himself in the following year as the undisputed master of the peninsula. For capital he chose Cordova, reputedly a Carthaginian foundation, which blossomed into the seat of a new kingdom and a brilliant culture. ʿAbd-al-Raḥmān endeavoured to fashion his state after that of Damascus. He inaugurated an enlightened, beneficent régime, which on the whole conducted itself in the best tradition of its Damascene predecessors. Fourteen years before his arrival the Syrian army of twenty-seven thousand sent by Hishām under Balj ibn-Bishr al-Qushayri against the Berbers in Spain had established itself in military fiefs throughout the principal districts of the Mediterranean Spanish border.[2] The contingents from Damascus, Ḥimṣ, Qinnasrīn, Jordan and Palestine were installed in Elvira, Seville, Jaen, Malaga and Medina Sidonia respectively. The colonists gave their new places of settlement Syrian geographic names. Climatic and other physical similarities helped to make the newcomers feel at home. As the Syrians conquered the land, Syrian songs, poetry and art conquered the people of the land. From Spain and Portugal several of these cultural elements were later introduced into the New World. Arab geographers began to refer to Spain as a Syrian province, but the battle of the Zāb reduced Syria itself to an ʿAbbāsid province.

[1] *Akhbār*, pp. 52-4; ibn-al-Athīr, vol. v, p. 377.
[2] *Akhbār*, p. 31; cf. ibn-al-Qūṭīyah, pp. 14-15; Marrākushi, p. 9.

CHAPTER XLI

SYRIA AN ʿABBĀSID PROVINCE

WITH the Umayyad fall the hegemony of Syria in the world of Islam ended and the glory of the country passed away. The ʿAbbāsids chose al-ʿIrāq for headquarters. Al-Kūfah, close to the Persian border, was the new capital. The Syrians awoke after the humiliating defeat at al-Zāb to the realization that the centre of Islamic gravity had left their land and shifted eastward. As a last resort they set their hopes on an expected descendant of Muʿāwiyah, a Sufyāni,[1] to appear Messiah-like and deliver them from their victorious ʿIrāqi rivals. To the present day this expectancy is vaguely alive in the hearts of Syrian Moslems.

A new era

Meantime abu-al-ʿAbbās was busy consolidating his newly acquired domain. In the inaugural address previously delivered at al-Kūfah he had assumed the title of al-Saffāḥ (bloodshedder),[2] which gave a hint of the new policy. The incoming dynasty was to depend more than the outgoing on the use of force in the execution of its plans. For the first time the leathern bag ready to receive the head of the executioner's victim found a place near the imperial throne. The new caliph surrounded himself with theologians and legists, giving the infant state an atmosphere of theocracy as opposed to the secular character (*mulk*) of its defunct predecessor. On ceremonial occasions he hastened to don the mantle (*burdah*) of his distant cousin, the Prophet.[3] The well-geared propaganda machine which had worked to undermine public confidence in the old régime was now busy

[1] Ṭabari, vol. iii, p. 1320; ibn-Miskawayh, *Tajārib al-Umam wa-Taʿāqub al-Himam*, ed. de Goeje and de Jong, vol. ii (Leyden, 1871), p. 526; Yāqūt, vol. iv, p. 1000; *Aghāni*, vol. xvi, p. 88; H. Lammens, *Études sur le siècle des Omayyades* (Beirut, 1930), pp. 391-408.

[2] Ṭabari, vol. iii, p. 30, l. 20; ibn-al-Athīr, vol. v, p. 316.

[3] Genealogical tree showing the kinship between the ʿAbbāsids and Muḥammad (see facing page):

entrenching the new régime in public esteem. Authority, the zealous propagandists proclaimed, should forever remain in the 'Abbāsid house, to be finally yielded to Jesus (*'Īsa*), the Messiah.[1] To this was later added the warning that should the 'Abbāsid caliphate be destroyed, the entire universe would be disorganized.[2] Anti-Umayyad, pro-'Abbāsid ḥadīths were fabricated wholesale. Even Umayyad names were effaced from inscriptions on buildings[3] and the style of Umayyad pulpits in mosques was modified.

The real difference between this and the preceding caliphate, however, lay in the fact that the 'Abbāsid was oriented Persiaward. Persian protocol pervaded the court, Persian ideas dominated the political scene and Persian women prevailed in the royal harem. It was an empire of Neo-Moslems in which the Arabs formed but one of the component parts. If the Umayyad was in a sense a successor state of the East Roman Empire, the 'Abbāsid was in a wider sense a successor state of the Chosroes. The 'Abbāsid régime called itself *dawlah*, new era, and a new era it was. The 'Irāqis felt relieved from Syrian tutelage. The Shī'ites felt avenged. Persians found high posts in the government open to them; they introduced and occupied a new office, the vizirate, highest after the caliphate. Khurāsānians flocked to man the caliphal bodyguard. The Arabian aristocracy was eclipsed. Arabian-

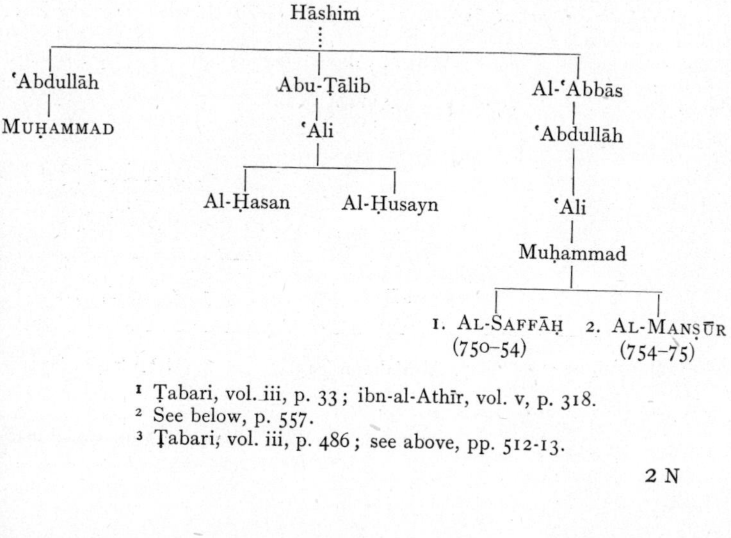

[1] Ṭabari, vol. iii, p. 33; ibn-al-Athīr, vol. v, p. 318.
[2] See below, p. 557.
[3] Ṭabari, vol. iii, p. 486; see above, pp. 512-13.

ism fell but Islam under a new guise, that of Persianism, marched triumphantly on.

Third in chronological order, after the Orthodox (*Rāshidūn*) and the Umayyad, the caliphate founded by al-Saffāḥ (750–54) and his brother abu-Ja'far al-Manṣūr (754–75) was the longest-lived and the most celebrated of all the caliphates. All the thirty-five caliphs who succeeded the second caliph were his lineal descendants. Al-Manṣūr chose for capital the site of a Christian Persian-named village Baghdād (given by God)[1] on the lower west bank of the Tigris. The Dār al-Salām (abode of peace), as the city was officially named, was built with a double surrounding wall of brick, a deep moat and a third inner wall rising to a height of ninety feet. Lying in that same valley which had furnished sites for some of the mightiest cities of antiquity, the city of al-Manṣūr soon fell heir to the power and prestige of Ctesiphon, Babylon, Nineveh and other capitals of the ancient Orient. Scene of the legendary adventures brilliantly commemorated by Shahrazād in *The Thousand and One Nights* and seat of the two luminous reigns of Hārūn al-Rashīd (786–809) and al-Ma'mūn (813–33), Baghdād has lived in legend and in history as the peerless symbol of the glory of Islam. The reigns of these two caliphs endow the whole dynasty with a halo that has not yet faded away. The dynasty enjoyed its prime between the reigns of the third caliph, al-Mahdi (775–85), and that of the ninth, al-Wāthiq (842–7).[2]

[1] Al-Ya'qūbi, *Kitāb al-Buldān*, ed. M. J. de Goeje (Leyden, 1892), p. 235; Balādhuri, p. 294.

[2] Genealogical tree of the 'Abbāsid caliphs under whom the empire reached its prime:

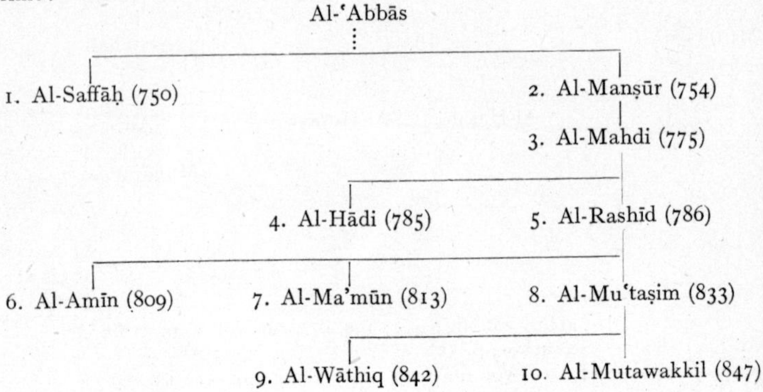

After al-Wāthiq the state starts on its downward course until al-Musta'ṣim (1242–58), thirty-seventh of the line, when it is utterly destroyed by the Mongols. For over five centuries the successors of al-Saffāḥ and al-Manṣūr reigned, though they did not always rule.

Traitors and suspects disposed of

The first governor of 'Abbāsid Syria was none other than 'Abdullāh, hero of al-Zāb. At the death of al-Saffāḥ he disputed with his other nephew al-Manṣūr the caliphate, relying on a huge disciplined army presumably massed for use against the Byzantines. After butchering 17,000 Khurāsānian troops, whom he did not trust, he moved with the rest of his men, mostly Syrians, eastward.[1] He was met by abu-Muslim at Naṣībīn (November 754) and defeated. After seven years' imprisonment he was ceremoniously conducted into a house the foundations of which had been reportedly laid on salt surrounded by water. He was soon buried under its ruins.[2] Abu-Muslim was then virtually independent governor of Khurāsān, the idol of his people and the ruthless suppressor of all personal and official enemies. So successful was he that 'Abbāsid suspicions were aroused. On his way back he was induced to stop and see the caliph at al-Madā'in (Ctesiphon). In the course of an audience with al-Manṣūr, the Persian, to whose sword after that of 'Abdullāh the 'Abbāsids owed their throne, was treacherously put to death.[3]

The turn of the 'Alids came next. These had assumed that the 'Abbāsids were fighting their battles but were now disillusioned. To abu-al-'Abbās and his cohorts, "the people of the house" (*ahl al-bayt*) meant their own family and not that of 'Ali and Fāṭimah. The 'Alids persisted in claiming for their imāms the sole right to preside over the destinies of Islam, thus reducing the 'Abbāsid caliphs to the position of usurpers. Their movement again went underground but never missed an opportunity to rise in open revolt. The renowned Mālik ibn-Anas, founder of the one of the four orthodox systems of jurisprudence that is still dominant throughout North Africa, absolved the Shī'ah from their oath of allegiance to the 'Abbāsids. An early revolt headed by two great-grandsons of

[1] Ṭabari, vol. iii, pp. 101-2.
[2] Ṭabari, vol. iii, p. 330; Ya'qūbi, vol. ii, p. 443.
[3] Ṭabari, vol. iii, pp. 105-17; Dīnawari, pp. 376-8.

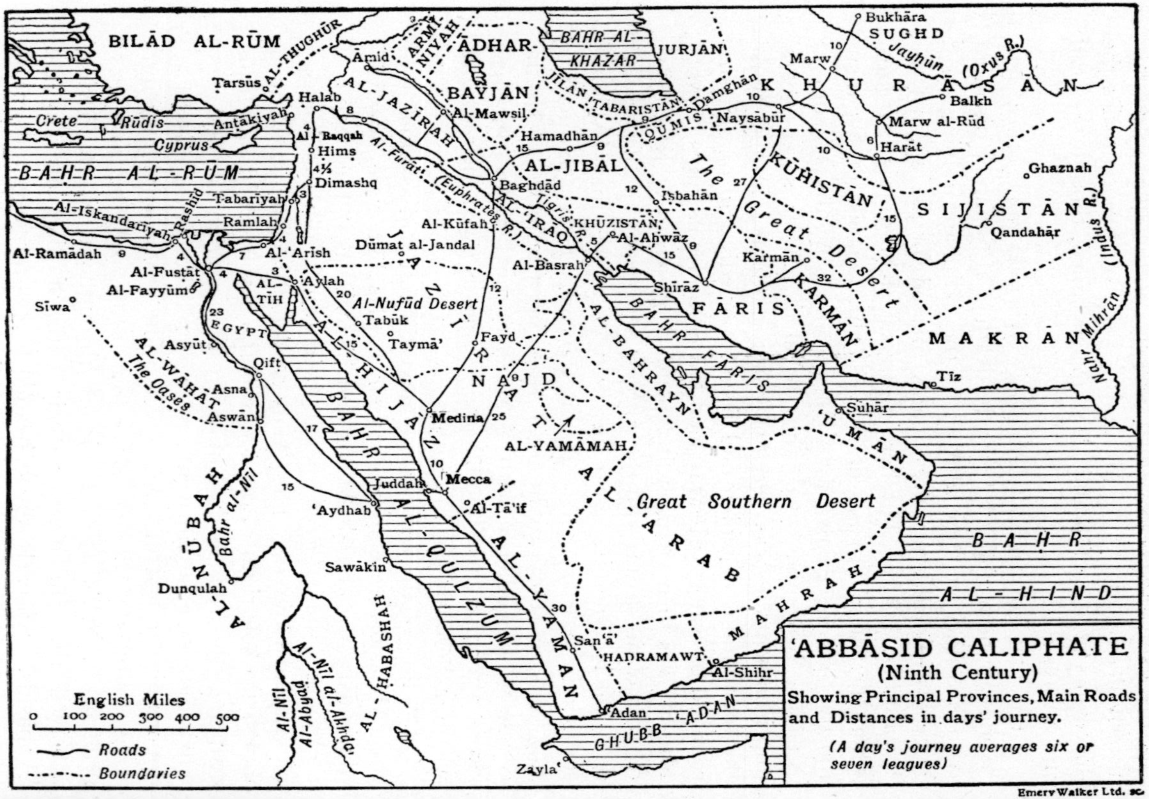

'ABBĀSID CALIPHATE
(Ninth Century)
Showing Principal Provinces, Main Roads and Distances in days' journey.
(A day's journey averages six or seven leagues)

Emery Walker Ltd. sc.

al-Ḥasan, Muḥammad and Ibrāhīm, was ruthlessly crushed.[1] Muḥammad, surnamed al-Nafs al-Zakīyah (the pure soul), was gibbeted in Medina (December 762). His brother Ibrāhīm was decapitated (February 763) near al-Kūfah and his head was dispatched to the caliph.[2]

One more group of Shīʿite collaborators had to be liquidated, the Barmakids. This was the Persian vizirial family exalted by al-Manṣūr. Descended from a Buddhist high priest (*barmak*), the members of this family achieved such distinction and displayed such generosity in the use of their wealth that the word *barmaki* has come down to the present day as meaning generous. Their prestige was too much for the strong-willed Hārūn, who in and after 803 annihilated them and confiscated their estate, said to have amounted to 30,676,000 dinars in cash exclusive of furniture and real estate.[3]

With the removal of the capital to distant Baghdād the hereditary Byzantine enemy ceased to be of major concern. The disturbances accompanying the removal gave the emperors a chance to push the imperial border farther east along the empire boundary of Asia Minor and Armenia. Al-Manṣūr and

[1] Genealogical tree of the descendants of ʿAli :

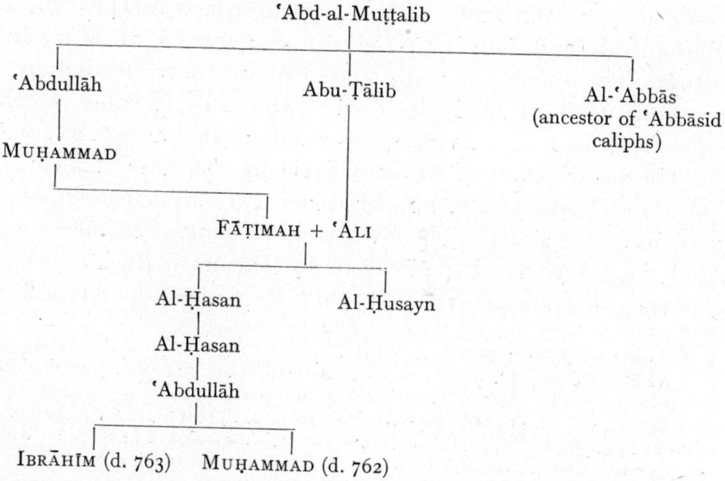

[2] Ṭabari, vol. iii, pp. 245-65, 315-16; Masʿūdi, vol. vi, pp. 189-203; Dīnawari, p. 381.

[3] *ʿIqd*, vol. iii, p. 28; Ṭabari, vol. iii, p. 680; Ṭabari, vol. iii, pp. 676-7; Masʿūdi, vol. vi, pp. 387-94; *Fakhri*, p. 288. Cf. ibn-Khaldūn, vol. iii, pp. 223-4; *Kitāb al-ʿUyūn*, pt. 3, pp. 306-8.

his successors took pains to fortify the *thughūr* of Syria and the seaports of Lebanon.[1] In 782 [2] when still a prince, Hārūn led his forces as far as Byzantium and exacted from the regent Irene a heavy tribute. As caliph he conducted from his favourite residence al-Raqqah in North Syria a series of raids into the "land of the Romans".[3] In 838 his son al-Muʿtaṣim made one last incursion into that land. Therewith the more than a century and a half long struggle between the caliphal and the Byzantine states came to an end.

Unrest in Syria, Lebanon and Palestine

The Syrians lost no time, after the loss by their country of its privileged position, in expressing their opposition by word and deed. Their attitude became worse as the days went by and left them excluded from government offices. A rejoinder by one of them to al-Manṣūr's remark that the people were lucky to escape the plague in his days, typifies the then prevailing sentiment: "God is too good to subject us to the pest and your rule at the same time".[4] In the case of the Christians the situation was aggravated by unfair extortion and increased taxation. Two full centuries had to elapse before the subjects of banu-Umayyah were reconciled to being subjects of banu-al-ʿAbbās.

Their first governor, ʿAbdullāh, found himself on assuming office in 750 confronted with several uprisings in Ḥawrān, al-Bathanīyah and Qinnasrīn led by ex-generals in Marwān's army. The rebels of Ḥimṣ and Tadmur were headed by a descendant of Muʿāwiyah, Ziyād, who was accepted as the expected Sufyāni. His camp near Salamyah counted 40,000.[5]

The polarization of Moslem Syria by the Arab dualism of Qays and Yaman, who appear under a multiplicity of names, was now intensified. The ʿAbbāsids in general favoured and used the Qaysites. Especially under Hārūn al-Rashīd, whose governor in Damascus was Ibrāhīm, a nephew of ʿAbdullāh,[6]

1 Balādhuri, p. 163; see above, p. 442.

2 *Kitāb al-ʿUyūn*, pt. 3, p. 278, dates the expedition 163 (A.D. 780), Yaʿqūbi (vol. ii, pp. 478, 486) 164 and Ṭabari (vol. iii, pp. 503-4) 165.

3 Ṭabari, vol. iii, pp. 696, 709-10; Yaʿqūbi, vol. ii, p. 519, l. 14, p. 523, l. 2; Dīnawari, pp. 386-7; Masʿūdi, vol. ii, pp. 337-52. The ruins of al-Raqqah, which owes its foundation to Seleucid II, show the grand scale on which it was rebuilt by al-Rashīd and fortified by al-Maʾmūn.

4 Ibn-ʿAsākir, vol. iii, p. 392.

5 Ibn-al-Athīr, vol. v, pp. 331 *seq.*

6 The precarious position in Syria necessitated the appointment of members of the ʿAbbāsid family. Ibrāhīm's father was Ṣāliḥ, brother of ʿAbdullāh. At times over different parts of Syria different governors were appointed; Yaʿqūbi, vol. ii, p. 461.

was strife bitter. In Damascus, Ḥawrān, al-Balqā', the Jordan and Ḥimṣ blood was shed.[1] For two years the district of Damascus was the scene of relentless warfare supposedly because a water-melon was filched from a Yamanite garden by a member of the opposing party.[2] The caliph, after considering leading a punitive expedition in person, entrusted it in 795 to a Barmakid general who completely disarmed the warring factions, " leaving not a lance or horse ".[3] The convulsions accompanying the struggle for the throne between al-Amīn and al-Ma'mūn, sons of Hārūn, had repercussions in Syria. Syrian troops finding themselves (811/12) encamped with Khurāsānians at al-Raqqah deserted wholesale as a ringleader harangued, " Down with the black banner! . . . To your homes! To your homes! Death in Palestine is preferable to life in Mesopotamia." [4] In the turbulent days of al-Amīn another Sufyāni, 'Ali by name, unfurled the white banner. A ninety-year-old learned man, the pretender won a host of followers, including the governor of Sidon, seized Ḥimṣ and besieged Damascus, which he captured after expelling the 'Abbāsid agent.[5]

In 829 al-Ma'mūn visited Syria and made a fresh survey of its lands with a view to increasing the revenue from it.[6] Four years later he visited Damascus to test the judges there and enforce his decree that no judge who did not subscribe to the Mu'tazilite view of the creation of the Koran could hold office.[7] Several of his predecessors had visited Syria on their way to the pilgrimage or to battle against the Byzantines. They were all kept informed by their governors and a special agent of information (*ṣāḥib al-barīd*, postmaster), who was in reality chief of secret police.[8] The Mu'tazilite doctrine, which the caliph espoused, was in direct opposition to the later orthodox view. The rationalistic movement had its inception under the Umayyads.[9]

Palestine was the scene of the next major outbreak. Here A veiled rebel

[1] Dīnawari, p. 383; ibn-al-Athīr, vol. vi, pp. 86 *seq.*, 129, 519.
[2] Abu-al-Fidā', vol. ii, p. 14; ibn-al-Athīr, vol. vi, p. 87.
[3] Ṭabari, vol. iii, p. 639.
[4] Ṭabari, vol. iii, pp. 844-5.
[5] Ya'qūbi, vol. ii, p. 532; ibn-al-Athīr, vol. vi, p. 172; Ṭabari, vol. iii, p. 830.
[6] Ibn-'Asākir, vol. iv, pp. 107-8. For his visit to Jerusalem see above, pp. 512-13.
[7] Ya'qūbi, vol. ii, p. 571.
[8] Hitti, *History of the Arabs*, p. 325.
[9] See Hitti, *History of the Arabs*, p. 429.

a Yamanite Arab of obscure origin unfurled the white banner (840/41). Curiously enough he always appeared in public veiled, hence his nickname al-Mubarqaʻ. His followers, said to have numbered a hundred thousand, were recruited mainly from the rural district and peasant class, indicating economic as well as political motivation. To them he was a Sufyāni. Taking advantage of the ploughing season, the ʻAbbāsid general at the head of a thousand troops sent by the Caliph al-Muʻtaṣim attacked their headquarters and carried the veiled rebel to Sāmarra, temporary ʻAbbāsid capital.[1]

Damascus a temporary capital

In the reign of al-Mutawakkil, al-Muʻtaṣim's son, the fire of revolt blazed again in Damascus (854/5). The people slaughtered their ʻAbbāsid governor and were subsequently put to the sword for three consecutive days by a Turkish general sent by the caliph at the head of a band of seven thousand horse and three thousand foot, who also plundered the whole city.[2] That Damascus should shortly after that be chosen as the residence of the caliph seems incredible. In 858 al-Mutawakkil transferred his seat to it possibly to escape the arrogant domination of his praetorian guard, consisting mostly of turbulent, undisciplined Turks who were originally mercenaries and slaves taken into the service by his predecessor. The humid climate of the city, its violent wind and abundant fleas drove the capricious caliph out in thirty-eight days.[3]

Anti-Christian legislation

The pattern of behaviour set by Syrian rebels in the early ʻAbbāsid period was followed for years to come. At this time, however, a new element was introduced, intensification of discontent on the part of Christians due to harsh conditions imposed on them. Before al-Mutawakkil we hear of only one serious uprising by the Christians of Lebanon. It occurred in 759–60 when Ṣāliḥ ibn-ʻAli, brother of ʻAbdullāh, was governor. Driven to arms by fresh exactions and encouraged by the presence of a Byzantine fleet in the waters of Tripoli, a band burst from its headquarters in al-Munayṭirah,[4] high in the Lebanon, and plundered several villages in al-Biqāʻ. Their leader was a youthful mountaineer of huge physique who

[1] Ṭabari, vol. iii, pp. 1319-22; ibn-ʻAsākir, vol. v, pp. 311-12.

[2] Ibn-ʻAsākir, vol. vi, pp. 47-8.

[3] Ṭabari, vol. iii, pp. 1435-6; Yaʻqūbi, vol. ii, p. 601; ibn-ʻAsākir, vol. iv, pp. 288-9.

[4] See below, p. 622.

audaciously styled himself king. Drawn into an ambuscade near Baʿlabakk the Lebanese band was cut down by ʿAbbāsid cavalry. In retaliation Ṣāliḥ uprooted the mountain villagers, many of whom took no part in the revolt, and had them dispersed all over Syria.[1] The protest addressed to the governor by a celebrated legist, al-Awzāʿi of Baʿlabakk and Beirut,[2] is worthy of recording:

The expulsion from Mt. Lebanon of dhimmis who were not a party to the rebellion whose perpetrators you have either killed or sent back home has no doubt been a subject of your knowledge. How then could the many be punished for the crime of the few and how could they be expelled from their homes and lands so long as God Himself hath decreed, "Nor doth any sinning one bear another's burden"?[3] Surely no decree has a greater claim on our final acceptance and permanent obedience. And no command is more worthy of observance and consideration than that of the Messenger of Allah, who proclaimed: "He who oppresses one bound to us by covenant and charges him with more than he can do, verily I am the one to overcome him by argument".[4]

Before al-Mutawakkil his grandfather Hārūn had re-enacted some of the anti-Christian and anti-Jewish measures introduced by ʿUmar II.[5] In 807 he ordered all churches erected since the Moslem conquest demolished. He also decreed that members of tolerated sects should wear the prescribed garb.[6] But evidently much of this legislation was not enforced.[7] In 850 and 854 al-Mutawakkil revived the discriminatory legislation and supplemented it by new features which were the most stringent ever issued against the minorities. Christians and Jews were enjoined to affix wooden images of devils to their houses, level their graves even with the ground, wear outer garments of honey colour (yellow), add two honey-coloured patches on the sleeves, one sewn on the back and the other on the front, and ride only on mules and asses with wooden saddles marked by two pomegranate-like balls on the cantle.[8] On account of this distinctive dress the dhimmis came to be mock-

[1] Ibn-ʿAsākir, vol. v, p. 341.
[2] See below, p. 555.
[3] Koran 6:164.
[4] Balādhuri, p. 162; cf. tr., p. 251.
[5] See above, pp. 487-8.
[6] Ṭabari, vol. iii, pp. 712-13; ibn-al-Athīr, vol. vi, p. 141.
[7] Cf. Laurence E. Browne, *The Eclipse of Christianity in Asia* (Cambridge, 1933), pp. 46 *seq.*
[8] Ṭabari, vol. iii, pp. 1389-93, 1419.

ingly called "spotted" (*arqaṭ*).[1] Basing their contention on a koranic charge that the Jews and the Christians had corrupted the text of their scriptures,[2] the contemporary jurists further emphasized that no testimony of a Jew or Christian was admissible against a Moslem. No other major persecution occurred until the days of the Fāṭimid Caliph al-Ḥākim (996–1021).

Subsequent to the promulgation of these laws by al-Mutawakkil a violent outbreak took place in Ḥimṣ in which Christians and Moslems participated. It was repressed after a vigorous resistance (855). The leaders were decapitated or flogged to death and then crucified at the city gate, all churches, with the exception of one which was added to the Great Mosque, were demolished and all Christians banished from the tumultuous city, which was evidently still predominantly Christian.[3]

Normally the major disability under which dhimmis laboured was the capitation tax (*jizyah*). This was in theory the price paid for freedom of residence and worship and for the right of receiving protection of life and property. The contract was, therefore, cancelled in case of refusal to pay the tax, rising in revolt, espionage in behalf of a foreign state or offering asylum to an enemy of the state. Other grounds were gradually added to include fornication with a free Moslem woman, leading a Moslem to apostasy and violating the sanctity of God, His Messenger or His Book. A Moslem could not embrace Christianity or Judaism without risking his life. A dhimmi, if considered undesirable, could be expelled from Moslem territory. Most Moslem schools of jurisprudence would not administer capital punishment for the homicide of a dhimmi by a Moslem. A non-Moslem was not denied the right of presenting himself before a Moslem court, if he chose so to do. If one party in a case was a Moslem, it had, of course, to go to a Moslem judge. When a case involved members of two differing dhimmi communities, one Christian and the other Jewish, Moslem law took no cognizance of it unless the parties failed to agree on the choice of the tribunal. If a husband embraced Islam and the wife was Scripturary, the marriage remained

[1] Jāḥiẓ, *Bayān*, vol. i, p. 79, l. 28.

[2] Sūrs. 2:70; 5:16-18.

[3] Ṭabari, vol. iii, pp. 1422-4; ibn-al-Athīr, vol. vii, pp. 59-60; Yaʿqūbi, vol. ii, p. 599. See above, p. 511.

valid; but if the wife embraced Islam, the husband had to follow suit within three months, in which all conjugal relations were interrupted, or be divorced. A dhimmi could not inherit from a Moslem.

Islamization

Thus far Syria seems to have maintained its general Christian character, but now the situation began perceptibly to change. Of the Christian banu-Tanūkh in the vicinity of Aleppo five thousand had already obeyed the behest of the 'Abbāsid Caliph al-Mahdi and embraced Islam.[1] The Tanūkhs who entered Lebanon east of Beirut in the early ninth century were one of the first Moslem Arab families to establish themselves in the mountain. In that thinly populated district still known as al-Gharb these Tanūkhs carved for themselves a principality over which they ruled for centuries. The 'Abbāsids used them as a check against the Maronites of northern Lebanon and against the Byzantines coming by sea. The Crusaders found them in Beirut and its vicinity. Before the Tanūkhs the eponymous founder of the Arislān family, which traces its descent to the Lakhmids, had established himself in al-Gharb.[2] A disciple of al-Awzā'i, his descendants still form the high aristocracy of the Druzes. It may be assumed that after al-Mutawakkil many Christian families in Syria, exclusive of Lebanon, flocked to the fold of Islam. They were actuated mainly by the desire to escape the humiliating disabilities and tribute and to acquire social prestige or political influence. The Christian ranks had earlier been thinned by migration into Asia Minor and Cyprus. The second phase of Moslem conquest, the conquest of Islam as a religion, was thus insured. The first was the conquest of Moslem arms accomplished in less than a decade in Syria.

The conquest of Arabic

The third phase was the linguistic.[3] The linguistic victory was the slowest and the last. In this field of struggle the subject peoples of Syria and other lands offered the greatest measure of resistance. They showed themselves more ready to give up political and even religious loyalties than linguistic ones. The literary Arabic won its victory before the spoken did. Syrian

[1] Ibn-al-'Ibri, *Chronicon Syriacon*, ed. and tr. P. J. Bruns and G. G. Kirsch (Leipzig, 1789), vol. ii (text), p. 133; vol. i, pp. 134-5 (tr.); see above, p. 486.

[2] *Maḥāsin al-Masā'i fi Manāqib al-Imām abi-'Amr al-Awzā'i*, ed. Shakīb Arislān (Cairo), pp. 19-20; Shidyāq, pp. 646-7.

[3] See above, pp. 484-5.

scholars under caliphal patronage began to compose in Arabic long before Syrian peasants adopted the new tongue.[1] The oldest dated Christian manuscript in Arabic that has come down to us was composed by abu-Qurrah (d. 820) and copied in 877 at St. Sāba, near Jerusalem.[2] It is preserved in the British Museum. The author, a disciple of St. John of Damascus, was Melkite bishop of Ḥarrān. Islamization no doubt facilitated and accelerated Arabicization, and transition from one Semitic tongue to another did not present too many linguistic difficulties.

By the early thirteenth century, toward the end of the ʿAbbāsid era, the victory of Arabic as the medium of everyday communication was virtually complete. Linguistic islands remained, occupied by non-Moslems: Jacobites, Nestorians and Maronites. Throughout the Crusading period many such islands existed. When around 1170 Benjamin of Tudela[3] visited Mount Sinai he found on its summit a Syrian place of worship and at its base a village whose inhabitants spoke the "Chaldean language". In Maronite Lebanon the native Syriac put up a desperate and prolonged fight. It lingered there until the late seventeenth century.[4] Indeed Syriac is still spoken in three villages in Anti-Lebanon: Maʿlūla, Bakhʿah and Jubbʿadīn[5]. It is still used in the Maronite and other liturgies of the Syrian Churches. In their ritual the Maronites also use *garshūni*,[6] Arabic written in Syriac script. No such attachment was shown by Greek-speaking Syrians to their mother tongue, while only one Arabic inscription in Greek characters has been found. It is a biblical inscription (Ps. 78: 20-31, 56-61) evidently from the end of the eighth century and was discovered in the Umayyad Mosque.[7]

As non-Arabians were Islamized and Arabicized they

[1] See below, p. 550.

[2] Theodorus abu Ḳurra, *De cultu imaginum*, ed. and tr. I. Arendzen (Bonn, 1897); Qusṭanṭīn al-Bāsha, *Mayāmir Thāwadūrus abi-Qurrah* (Beirut, 1924?).

[3] *Itinerary*, vol. i (London, 1840), p. 159.

[4] Consult Hitti, *al-Lughāt al-Sāmīyah al-Maḥkīyah fi Sūrīya wa-Lubnān* (Beirut, 1922), pp. 30-34.

[5] Consult G. Bergsträsser, *Neuaramäische Märchen und andere Texte von Maʿlūla* (Leipzig, 1915); Anton Spitaler, *Grammatik des neuaramäischen Dialekts von Maʿlūla* (Hamburg, 1938).

[6] Less correctly *karshūni*; from Syr. *garshūn*, foreign.

[7] Paul Kahle, *Die arabischen Bibelübersetzungen* (Leipzig, 1904), pp. xiv, 32-3.

attached themselves to Arabian tribes as clients [1] and were gradually assimilated. The old caste line between Arabians and non-Arabians, old Moslems and Neo-Moslems, was obliterated. All became Arabs. Later, in the Mamlūk period, the sedentary population was styled *awlād* (descendants of) *al-'Arab*, a term still in use, to distinguish it from *A'rāb*, Bedouins.[2] A large part of the Aramaic-speaking people of Syria and al-'Irāq hitherto referred to derogatorily as *Anbāṭ* (Nabataeans)[3] or *'ulūj* (foreigners, speaking an unintelligible language) was no more in existence. Aram, as the native name of Syria, gave way to a new one al-Sha'm, " the left ", because it lay to the left of the Ka'bah, in contrast to al-Yaman, which lay to its right.[4] Thus was the entire Semitic world Arabicized under the 'Abbāsids. For the first time the consciousness of unity engendered by the use of a common tongue and the profession of a common faith prevailed.

Syriac did not disappear without leaving its indelible imprint over the Syro-Lebanese Arabic. It is primarily this imprint that distinguishes this dialect from those in neighbouring lands. The traces are clear in the morphology, phonetics and vocabulary. The domestic and agricultural vocabulary is especially rich in Syriac borrowings.[5] The month names come directly from Syriac, which received most of them from Akkadian.[6]

[1] See above, p. 485.
[2] See below, p. 641, n. 1.
[3] Mas'ūdi, *Tanbīh*, pp. 78-9.
[4] Mas'ūdi, vol. iii, pp. 139-40.
[5] For illustrations consult Michel T. Féghali, *Étude sur les emprunts syriaques dans les parlers du Liban* (Paris, 1918); do., *Le Parler de Kfar'abīda* (Paris, 1919); Yūsuf Ḥubayqah in *al-Mashriq*, vol. xxxvii (1939), pp. 290-412; Ighnāṭiyūs Afrām in *Majallat al-Majma' al-'Ilmi al-'Arabi*, vol. xxiii (1948), pp. 161-82, 321-46, 481-506; vol. xxiv (1949), pp. 3-21, 161-81, 321-42, 481-99; vol. xxv (1950), pp. 3-22, etc.; Anīs Furayḥah, *Mu'jam al-Alfāẓ al-'Āmmīyah fi al-Lahjah al-Lubnānīyah* (Jūniyah, 1947). For ecclesiastical loan words see above, pp. 525-6.
[6] Beginning with December and January: *kānūn* I and II, firepot; *shubāṭ*, striker, fatal; *ādhār*, cloudiness; *nīsān*, banner, warfare; *ayyār*, seed produce; *ḥazīrān*, harvest; *tammūz*, son of fresh water (see above, p. 117, n. 1); *āb*, bulrushes; *aylūl*, jubilation; *tishrīn* I and II (Oct. and Nov.), dedication (to the sun-god).

CHAPTER XLII

SYRIAN CONTRIBUTION TO ARAB RENAISSANCE

Translations from Greek

MORE than any other one people the Syriac-speaking Christians contributed to that general awakening and intellectual renaissance centred in ʿAbbāsid Baghdād which became and remained the chief glory of classical Islam. Between 750 and 850 the Arab world was the scene of one of the most spectacular and momentous movements in the history of thought. The movement was marked by translations into Arabic from Persian, Greek and Syriac. The Arabian Moslem brought with him no art, science or philosophy and hardly any literature; but he did bring along from the desert a keen intellectual curiosity, a voracious appetite for learning and a number of latent talents. In the Fertile Crescent he fell heir to Hellenistic science and lore, which was unquestionably the most precious intellectual treasure at hand. In a few decades after the foundation of Baghdād (762) the Arabic-reading public found at its disposal the major philosophical works of Aristotle and the Neo-Platonic commentators, the chief medical writings of Hippocrates and Galen, the main mathematical compositions of Euclid and the geographical masterpiece of Ptolemy. In all this the Syrians were the mediators. The Arabians knew no Greek, but the Syrians had been in touch with Greek for over a millennium. For two centuries before the appearance of Islam Syrian scholars had been translating Greek works into Syriac. Long before ʿUmar II transferred the philosophical school of Alexandria to Antioch an intense wave of translation had swept the monasteries of the Syrian Church. The people who had opened the treasures of Greek science and philosophy to the Persians were now doing the same to the Arabs. The same people who before Islam were instrumental in cultivating the main elements of Greek culture, spreading them eastward and propagating them in the schools of Edessa (al-Ruhā'), Nisibis (Naṣībīn), Ḥarrān and Jundi-Shāpūr were now busily engaged in passing those elements on to the Arabic-reading world. As in Roman days they had functioned as agents of material civilization transmitting the products of the East to the West,[1] so were they now the agents of Western culture in Eastern society.

Especially did the clergy among them realize the importance of Aristotelian logic and Neo-Platonic philosophy for theological controversies, then the breath of intellectual life. Even the Gospels whose original Aramaic was lost [2] had to be done from Greek. The Septuagint itself was translated into Syriac. Edessa, whose school opened in 373, was the chief centre of intellectual Syriac activity. One of its professors made the first translation of Porphyry's *Isagoge*, the recognized manual on logic commonly prefixed to Aristotle's *Organon*. This work of Aristotle was done later by another Syrian, George, who in 686 was installed bishop of the Arab tribes.[3] His parish comprised the Tanūkh, the Taghlib and other tribes of the Syro-Mesopotamian desert. Another Syrian, who flourished on the eve of the Moslem conquest, wrote a commentary on Aristotle's *Hermeneutica*. Syriac commentaries served as models for Arabic ones. When in 439 the Emperor Zeno closed the Edessene institution, its ejected teachers migrated across the eastern border to Ḥarrān, then under Persian rule, and opened or reopened a Christian academy there. Other victims of Byzantine policy which sought rigid religious uniformity throughout the empire found asylum in Persian territory.

Besides philosophy and theology medicine and astronomy attracted Syrian attention. Astronomy, viewed from the astrological standpoint, was allied to medicine. In 555 Kisra Anūsharwān established at Jundi-Shāpūr an academy of medicine and philosophy, many of whose distinguished professors were Christians using Syriac as a medium of instruction. One of these was Jūrjīs (George) ibn-Bakhtīshūʿ ("Jesus hath delivered"), dean of the academy, whom al-Manṣūr in 765 summoned for medical advice. Invited by the caliph to adopt Islam, Jūrjīs replied that he preferred the company of his fathers, be they in heaven or in hell.[4] Jūrjīs became the founder

[1] See above, pp. 297-8, 353-5. [2] See above, p. 168.

[3] Assemani, vol. i, pp. 494-5; Rubens Duval, *La Littérature syriaque* (Paris, 1907), pp. 353, 377; Barhebraeus, *Chronicon ecclesiasticum*, ed. and tr. J. B. Abbeloos and T. J. Lamy (Louvain, 1872), vol. i, cols. 303-6.

[4] Al-Qifṭi, *Ta'rīkh al-Ḥukamā'*, ed. J. Lippert (Leipzig, 1903), pp. 158-60; *Fihrist*, p. 296; ibn-al-ʿIbri, pp. 213-15; ibn-abi-Uṣaybiʿah, vol. i, p. 125.

of a family of physicians which for six or seven generations almost monopolized the entire court medical practice. His son Bakhtīshū' (d. 801) was the chief physician of the Baghdād hospital under al-Rashīd.

Ḥunayn ibn-Isḥāq

Yūḥanna (Yaḥya) ibn-Māsawayh (Latin Mesuë), a Christian pupil of another Bakhtīshū', supposedly translated for al-Rashīd several manuscripts, mainly medical, which the caliph had brought back from raids into Asia Minor.[1] Yūḥanna's pupil Ḥunayn ibn-Isḥāq (Johannitius, 809–73) stands out as one of the greatest translators and noblest characters of that age. A member of the Eastern Syrian Church, Ḥunayn was born in al-Ḥīrah and appointed by al-Ma'mūn chief of Bayt al-Ḥikmah (house of wisdom), that combination of academy, library, museum and bureau of translation which the caliph had established. In his work Ḥunayn was assisted by his son Isḥāq [2] and his nephew Ḥubaysh ibn-al-Ḥasan.[3] The father was more proficient in Greek and evidently did the initial draft of the translation into Syriac, which his collaborators rendered into Arabic. Most of Aristotle's and Galen's works [4] were thus made available to the Arabic student. Ḥunayn is said to have also translated Hippocrates' medical treatises and Plato's *Republic*. A comparison of these translations shows that in all cases the Syriac was closer to the Greek and that the Arabic was a paraphrase of the Syriac. Ḥunayn was more than a translator. Al-Mutawakkil appointed him his private physician and once committed him to jail for refusing to concoct a poison for an enemy.

A pupil of Ḥunayn, Yaḥya ibn-'Adi (d. 974), revised a number of the existing versions and prepared fresh translations of Aristotle's *Poetics* and of Plato's *Laws* and *Timaeus*. Yaḥya belonged to the Western Syrian community, which produced other scholars who followed their co-religionists of the Eastern community and improved on their works. Another contemporary of Ḥunayn was Qusṭa ibn-Lūqa of Ba'labakk (d. *ca.*

[1] Ibn-al-'Ibri, p. 227; ibn-abi-Uṣaybi'ah, vol. i, p. 175; Qifṭi, p. 380.

[2] Ibn-Khallikān, vol. i, p. 116.

[3] *Fihrist*, p. 297; ibn-al-'Ibri, p. 252; ibn-abi-Uṣaybi'ah, vol. i, pp. 187, 203.

[4] Ḥunayn used the Syriac translations of some Galenic works already done by Job of Edessa (Ayyūb al-Ruhāwi, *ca.* 760–835). See Job of Edessa, *Book of Treasures*, ed. A. Mingana (Cambridge, 1935), pp. xix-xx; Barhebraeus, vol. iii, cols. 181-2.

912), who distinguished himself as translator of mathematical and philosophical works. Qusṭa knew Greek, Syriac and Arabic. He journeyed to Byzantine lands in quest of manuscripts on which he worked at Baghdād. He died in Armenia, where

بسم الله الرحمن الرحيم رب يسر واعن
جوامع المقالة الاولى من كتاب جالينوس في تدبير الاصحا
نقل ابي زيد حنين بن اسحق

Princeton University Library, Garrett Collection

GALEN IN ARABIC, MANUSCRIPT

First lines of a chapter in Ḥunayn ibn-Isḥāq's translation of Galen, *Kitāb al-Ṣināʿah al-Ṣaghīrah*, copied A.H. 572 (A.D. 1176/7). The MS. antedates any Greek or Latin MSS. extant and contains sections not yet edited or translated into any modern European language

he was honoured by a monumental tomb, leaving sixty-nine original works and seventeen translations.[1]

The Syrians were indifferent to Greek poetry and drama and so were the Arabs. A Maronite astrologer in the service of al-Mahdi, Thāwafīl (Theophile) of Edessa by name, made translations of Homer's *Iliad* and *Odyssey*, which did not survive.[2]

[1] *Fihrist*, p. 295; Qifṭi, pp. 262-3; G. Gabrieli in *Rendiconti della Reale Accademia dei Lincei*, ser. 5, vol. xxi (Rome, 1912), pp. 361-82.

[2] Assemani, vol. i, pp. 521-2; ibn-al-ʿIbri, p. 220, where he is made a member of the Lebanese Church; cf. Ghazīri, p. 44; above, p. 522; Dibs, *Taʾrīkh Sūrīyah*, vol. iii, p. 297.

Ṣābians

Not only Christian but pagan Syrians made a major contribution to Arab intellectual life. These were the Ṣābians, more correctly pseudo-Ṣābians,[1] whose seat was Ḥarrān. Being star-worshippers and heirs of the Babylonian tradition, the Ṣābians had interested themselves in astronomy and allied sciences from time immemorial. As lovers of Hellenistic science they stood on a par with their Christian compatriots. Outstanding among their scholars was Thābit ibn-Qurrah (*ca.* 836–901). He and his disciples are credited with translating the bulk of Greek astronomical and mathematical works, including those of Ptolemy and Archimedes.[2] Moreover, they revised earlier translations. Ḥunayn's translation of Euclid, for instance, was revised by Thābit.[3] Thābit was succeeded by a son, two grandsons and one great-grandson — all of whom made names for themselves. His son Sinān was forced by a caliph to accept Islam.[4] Ḥunayn's son Isḥāq was also converted to Islam.[5]

It may be assumed that other mathematical and astronomical elements were transmitted by Aramaeans and Syrians living on Babylonian territory. Algebra (*al-jabr*), for example, appears as a full-fledged science from the pen of the renowned al-Khwārizmi (d. 850). The Babylonians had a term for this science and it is the same word, *gabru*. The assumed Syriac links here are missing.[6]

Original contribution

Clearly the bulk of Syriac literature consisted of translations and commentaries and was lacking in originality and creativeness. Only a few representative pieces have survived. In one field, however, the ascetic mystical, Syrian divines were more than copyists and imitators. It is in this same field that the parallelism to Sufi material is striking. Isaac of Nineveh, who

[1] Hitti, *History of the Arabs*, p. 358.

[2] *Fihrist*, pp. 267, 268; ibn-abi-Uṣaybi'ah, vol. i, pp. 218-20.

[3] Ibn-Khallikān, vol. i, pp. 177, 298.

[4] *Fihrist*, p. 302; ibn-abi-Uṣaybi'ah, vol. i, pp. 220-21.

[5] Al-Bayhaqi, *Ta'rīkh Ḥukamā' al-Islām*, ed. Muḥammad Kurd-'Ali (Damascus, 1946), p. 19.

[6] The scientific terms borrowed from Greek and Latin directly or through Syriac and still current in Arabic may be illustrated by *falsafah* (philosophy), *jighrafīyah* (geography), *mūsīqa* (music). Other Latin and Greek words were Arabicized at various times: *kūrah* (district), *iskilah* (port), *nūti* (sailor, cf. Eng. nautical), *sayf* (Gr. *ksiphos*, sword). Persian loan words in Arabic may be illustrated by *bustān* (garden), *daydab* (sentry), *sarāwīl* (trousers), *ṣawlajān* (pall-mall, sceptre).

flourished in the late sixth century, emphasizes in his epistles and discourses the contemplative life, which he considers the second soul and the spirit of revelation, and asserts that it cannot be born in the womb of reason. He therefore admonishes his followers to seek solitude and while therein to think there is no other in the created world except the person himself alone and God on whom he thinks.[1] Another Syrian Christian mystic, Simon of Ṭaibūtheh (d. *ca.* 680), taught that at least a part of knowledge is apprehended not by words but through the inward silence of the mind and that that type of knowledge is the highest of all for it reaches the hidden Godhead.[2]

Moslem contribution: abu-Tammām

The finest talent of Moslem Syria of this period expressed itself through the medium of poetical composition. Two of its sons, abu-Tammām and al-Buḥturi, achieved the distinction of becoming court poets to ʿAbbāsid caliphs.

Ḥabīb ibn-Aws [3] abu-Tammām (*ca.* 804–*ca.* 850) was born in a place called Jāsim, Ḥawrān, of a Christian father who was a druggist. On his embracing Islam the young man attached himself to the Ṭayyi' tribe. Like other literati of his land he roamed through the world of Islam, visiting Egypt, where he worked as a water carrier, al-Ḥijāz, Armenia, Persia and al-ʿIrāq, before he settled in Baghdād. He joined the Caliph al-Muʿtaṣim in his new capital Sāmarra and accompanied him on his victorious expedition against ʿAmmūrīyah (Amorium, 838), which he celebrated in an ode [4] that is still committed to memory by Arab youth. True to type, he enjoyed the cup, the lute and the damsel and paid little heed to the dictates of religion.[5] His claim to glory rests not only on his original compositions but also on his compilation of *al-Ḥamāsah*,[6] which contains masterpieces of Arabic poetry from pre-Islamic days to his time. We owe this treasure of Arabic literature to the

[1] For more on Isaac consult Assemani, vol. i, pp. 444-63.

[2] Margaret Smith, *An Early Mystic of Baghdad* (London, 1935), p. 101, n. 2.

[3] A corruption of Tadūs (Theodosius?); ibn-Khallikān, vol. i, p. 214; al-Suyūṭi, *Ḥusn al-Muḥāḍarah*, vol. i, p. 267.

[4] *Dīwān abi-Tammām*, ed. Shāhīn ʿAṭīyah (Beirut, 1889), pp. 15-18; cf. al-Ṣūli, *Akhbār abi-Tammām*, ed. Khalīl M. ʿAsākir *et al.* (Cairo, 1937), pp. 109-13.

[5] Masʿūdi, vol. vii, p. 151.

[6] Al-Tibrīzi, *Sharḥ Dīwān al-Ḥamāsah*, 3 vols. (Būlāq, 1296); G. G. Freytag, *Hamasae carmina*, 2 vols. (Bonn, 1847–51); Friedrich Rückert, *Hamâsa*, 2 vols. (Stuttgart, 1846).

simple fact that the author on one of his journeys was marooned, because of excessive snow which blocked the roads, in the home of a cultured gentleman in Hamadhān (Ecbatana) whose library possessed collections of anthologies by Arabs of the desert and of other lands. Abu-Tammām used his leisure hours in perusing the collections.[1] His last days he spent in al-Mawṣil, where he was buried.

Al-Buḥturi

His younger contemporary abu-ʿUbaydah al-Walīd al-Buḥturi (*ca.* 820–97) was born in Manbij (Hierapolis) and belonged to the Buḥtur clan of the Ṭayyi' tribe.[2] He was reportedly discovered by abu-Tammām, who heard him in Ḥimṣ recite an original poem and recommended him to the people of Maʿarrat al-Nuʿmān, who engaged him at a salary of 4000 dirhams. Al-Buḥturi admired abu-Tammām and followed in his steps. In Baghdād he became the laureate of al-Mutawakkil and his successors, by one of whom, al-Muʿtazz, he was especially favoured. So avaricious was al-Buḥturi that he would wear dirty garments and almost starve his slave and brother to death.[3] Typical of his class, this poet employed his talent to extort remuneration from influential and wealthy personages under threat of changing his encomiums to lampoons. His *Dīwān* [4] offers illustrations of persons whom he both eulogized and satirized. It also reveals his interest in wine [5] and his ability to describe palaces, pools and wild animals [6] — a rather rare feature in Arabic poetry. Besides his *Dīwān* al-Buḥturi compiled a book of *Ḥamāsah*,[7] which was never regarded with the same esteem by Arab philologists as that of his predecessor. Arab critics have through the ages held al-Buḥturi as one of the trio which tops the list of ʿAbbāsid poets, the other two being abu-Tammām and al-Mutanabbi'.[8] "Probably most European critics would find Buḥturi less brilliant than Mutanabbī, yet far more poetical than Abū Tammām." [9]

Dik al-Jinn

Of a much lower calibre was ʿAbd-al-Salām ibn-Raghbān (777–849), nicknamed Dīk al-Jinn (the cock of the jinn) on

1 Ibn-Khallikān, vol. i, p. 468.
2 Yāqūt, *Udabā'*, vol. vii, p. 226.
3 *Aghāni*, vol. xviii, p. 170.
4 Vol. i (Constantinople, 1300), pp. 75, 87, 117-19.
5 Vol. ii, pp. 176, 189.
6 Vol. i, pp. 108, 16, 51, 111.
7 Ed. R. Geyer and D. S. Margoliouth (Leyden, 1909).
8 See below, p. 567.
9 D. S. Margoliouth, art. "al-Buḥturi", *Encyclopaedia of Islām*.

account of his ugly features and green eyes. A native of Ḥimṣ, Dīk never left his homeland. He was probably descended from a Christian converted to Islam at the battle of Mu'tah.[1] Dīk is of special interest because in his verses, only a few of which have survived, he championed the cause of the vanquished peoples against the Arabian pretensions and asserted the superiority of the Syrians, by which he meant Arabicized Syrians, over the Arabians. He may therefore be considered a harbinger of that interesting intellectual movement termed Shuʿūbīyah,[2] which assumed political aspects in Persia and other lands. Dīk was a moderate Shīʿite and a poor one at that. He squandered his patrimony in pleasure and dissipation. In a fit of jealousy he fatally stabbed his wife, originally a Christian slave of his, and was thereafter convinced of her innocence and visited and tortured by her phantom, as pathetically described in his own verses.[3]

Al-Awzāʿi

In the non-poetical realm one man stands out, the theologian and jurist ʿAbd-al-Raḥmān ibn-ʿAmr al-Awzāʿi.[4] Born in Baʿlabakk in 707, he flourished in Beirut, where he died in a public bath in 774. His shrine (*maqām* [5]) is still standing in the sands south of the city. He had a reputation for learning, asceticism and moral courage [6] and was described by a biographer as the " imām of Syria, than whom no one more erudite existed in that land ".[7] Al-Awzāʿi taught that if a dhimmi fought in a Moslem army he was entitled to the same share of booty as a Moslem.[8] When al-Manṣūr visited Syria he heard al-Awzāʿi preach and greatly admired him. The legal system worked out by this jurist had a vogue in Syria for about two centuries before it was supplanted by the Ḥanafite and Shāfiʿite systems, and in al-Andalus and al-Maghrib for about forty years before it was replaced by the Mālikite.[9]

[1] *Aghāni*, vol. xii, p. 142; ibn-Khallikān, vol. i, p. 525. See above, p. 409.

[2] " Pertaining to the peoples ", i.e. non-Arabians, from a koranic verse 49 : 13.

[3] Ibn-Khallikān, vol. i, pp. 526-7; *Aghāni*, vol. xii, pp. 143-6.

[4] So called after either a Yamanite tribe or a suburb of Damascus; Yāqūt, vol. i, pp. 403-4; ibn-al-Athīr, *al-Lubāb fi Tahdhīb al-Ansāb* (Cairo, 1357), pp. 74-5; Ṭabari, vol. iii, p. 2514; abu-al-Fidā', vol. ii, p. 7.

[5] See above, p. 433, n. 4.

[6] See above, p. 543.

[7] Ibn-Khallikān, vol. i, p. 493. For more on him consult *Maḥāsin al-Masāʿi*, ed. Arislān.

[8] Al-Ṭabari, *Ikhtilāf al-Fuqahā'*, ed. Joseph Schacht (Leyden, 1933), pp. 121, 141.

[9] Ṣāliḥ, p. 23.

Not much is known about the Awzāʿi system, but probably it bore no traces of the Roman law which had prevailed in Syria, where he laboured, and which was taught on a grand scale in Beirut,[1] where he lived. Criminal law in Islam and civil law as it related to marriage, inheritance, usury and other matters are divinely revealed. Only in contractual transactions (*muʿāmalāt*) are there similarities between the two systems. In Arabic and Latin legal terminology certain terms signify the same thing: *fiqh* and jurisprudence, *fatwa* and opinion, *ijmāʿ* and consensus, *ʿādah* and custom, *maṣlaḥah ʿāmmah* and public interest; but that does not necessarily imply dependence. Loan words or Arabicized Greek and Latin words are not found. Nor do we know of any Roman or Byzantine law book translated into Arabic.

[1] See above, pp. 325 *seq.*

CHAPTER XLIII

SYRIA AN ADJUNCT OF MINOR STATES

The Ṭūlūnids

THE first sign of internal decay in the ʿAbbāsid régime was the rise of the Turkish bodyguard under the immediate successors of al-Ma'mūn (d. 833). Like the Janissaries in Ottoman history this corps became too powerful for the caliph and at times held him in abject submission to its will.[1] Except for short intervals thereafter the ʿAbbāsid power was steadily on the decline. The caliphate was committing gradual suicide preliminary to its receiving the *coup de grâce* at the hands of Hūlāgu and his Mongol hordes (1258). As it was disintegrating petty dynasties, mostly of Arab origin, were parcelling out its domains in the west; while other dynasties, mostly Turkish and Persian, were performing the same operation in the east.

First among those with which Syria was concerned was the Ṭūlūnid dynasty (868–905). This short-lived dynasty was founded by Aḥmad ibn-Ṭūlūn (868–84), whose father was a

The American Numismatic Society

A COIN OF IBN-ṬŪLŪN

Obverse and reverse of a gold dinar of Aḥmad ibn-Ṭūlūn struck at Miṣr (Cairo) A.H. 270 = A.D. 883/4

Turk sent from Bukhāra as a present to al-Ma'mūn.[2] Aḥmad began his unusual career when his stepfather, newly appointed fief holder and governor over Egypt, sent him ahead of him as his deputy. No sooner had the ambitious young man arrived than he planned to take advantage of the distance that separated

[1] See above, p. 542.

[2] Ibn-Khaldūn, vol. iii, p. 295; vol. iv. p. 297.

him from the central government and practise independence.[1] On authorization from the caliph he increased his troops, reportedly to a hundred thousand, and marched against a rebel in Syria — the land of rebels, against ʿAbbāsid rule. This gave ibn-Ṭūlūn an entrée into that neighbouring country. On the death of its governor in 877 the time was deemed ripe for full occupation. The Egyptian army marched through al-Ramlah in the south to Damascus, Ḥimṣ, Ḥamāh and Aleppo in the north without opposition. Only Antioch closed its gates and was reduced after a short siege.[2] In A.H. 266 (879/80) Aḥmad proclaimed himself ruler of both lands. The practical test of independence had come in 875 when the Caliph al-Muʿtamid, hard pressed for cash, demanded but did not receive it from his Egyptian viceroy.

This was a turning-point in the history of Egypt. It then and there embarked upon its career as an independent state, a position which it maintained with one important interruption for centuries to come. Syria throughout this long period went with Egypt, as it did in Pharaonic days. The old connection, severed about a thousand years before, was thus re-established. The land of the Nile profited by the change, at least to the extent of having its entire revenue spent within its territory, but the position of its Syrian adjunct was not improved.

A typical military dictator, Aḥmad ruled with an iron hand. He built a powerful military machine on which he depended for the maintenance of his throne. Its core was a bodyguard of 24,000 Turkish and 40,000 Negro slaves from each one of whom he exacted an oath of allegiance. As if to justify his usurpation of power in the eyes of his subjects, he launched a programme of public works that had no parallel since Pharaonic days. He adorned his capital al-Fusṭāṭ and its new quarter al-Qaṭāʾiʿ [3] with magnificent buildings, one of which was a hospital and the other a mosque. The hospital [4] cost 60,000 dinars and was the first of its kind in Egypt. The income of special property in Syria was set aside for its maintenance. The mosque, which

[1] Yaʿqūbi, vol. ii, pp. 615 *seq.*; Ṭabari, vol. iii, p. 1697.

[2] Ibn-Khaldūn, vol. iv, pp. 300-301; Kindi, ed. Guest, pp. 219 *seq.*

[3] "The Wards"; Maqrīzi, vol. i, pp. 313 *seq.*

[4] Ar. *bīmāristān*, see below, p. 642, n. 1. Ibn-Taghri-Birdi, *al-Nujūm al-Zāhirah fi Mulūk Miṣr w-al-Qāhirah*, ed. T. G. J. Juynboll, vol. ii (Leyden, 1855), p. 11; Kindi, p. 216.

still bears his name, is considered one of the grandest monuments of Moslem Egypt. Its structure cost twice that of the hospital [1] and follows in certain particulars the style of the school of Sāmarra, where Aḥmad had spent his youth. Its minaret is the oldest surviving in Egypt. This introduction of an ʿIrāqi pattern, however, did not oust the older Syro-Hellenic one and did not far extend its sway. The Mosque of ibn-Ṭūlūn remains as the only great example of that style.

On the Syrian shore ʿAkka was fortified by ibn-Ṭūlūn and a naval base was established in it. So strong was the tower that topped its double wall that three centuries later it thwarted for almost two years the combined efforts of two Crusading monarchs and in 1799 proved impregnable against the assaults of Napoleon's field artillery.[2] The Syrian geographer al-Maqdisi [3] reports that his own grandfather was summoned from Jerusalem to perform the unusual task of constructing a harbour in the water, which he did by fastening strong beams side by side and placing rocks on them. A gate was built in the middle and long chains were laid which ships entering the harbour at night could pull and thus signal their arrival.

Khumārawayh

Aḥmad was succeeded by his extravagant and dissolute twenty-year-old son Khumārawayh (884–95), one of thirty-three children of whom seventeen were boys.[4] Khumārawayh erected a palace with a "golden hall", whose walls were covered with gold and decorated with bas-reliefs of himself, his wives and songstresses.[5] The garden was rich in exotic trees planted around gilded water tanks, and in flowers growing in beds shaped to spell Arabic words. The palace had also an aviary, a zoological enclosure and a pool of quicksilver. The dynast could lie on leather cushions, moored on the surface of this pool by silken cords fastened to silver columns, and rock himself cosily to sleep.[6]

Under Khumārawayh the Ṭūlūnid domain extended from Barqah to the Euphrates and even beyond to the Tigris. On his accession in 892, al-Muʿtaḍid, the ablest and most energetic

[1] Ibn-Taghri-Birdi, vol. ii, p. 8; ibn-Khallikān, vol. i, p. 97.
[2] See below, p. 690.
[3] Pp. 162-3; quoted by Yāqūt, vol. iii, pp. 707-8.
[4] Ibn-Taghri-Birdi, vol. ii, p. 21; Suyūṭi, vol. ii, p. 11.
[5] Ibn-Taghri-Birdi, vol. ii, pp. 57-8; Maqrīzi, vol. i, pp. 316-17.
[6] Ibn-Taghri-Birdi, vol. ii, pp. 58-9; Maqrīzi, vol. i, p. 317.

ʿAbbāsid caliph of the period of decay, recognized the *status quo* and confirmed the Egyptian sovereign and his heirs in the possession of this vast territory for thirty years in return for an annual tribute of 300,000 dinars. The caliph even sought and secured the hand of Khumārawayh's beautiful daughter Qaṭr-al-Nada (dewdrop). The father settled on her a dowry of a million dirhams — so the story goes — and presented her with a thousand mortars of gold and other objects " the like of which had never been given before ".[1]

Khumārawayh's extravagance left the treasury empty. His addiction to pederasty, according to one report,[2] so enraged his slaves that they fell upon him one night in his villa outside Damascus and slaughtered him. His body was carried to Egypt for burial, and as it was being lowered into its grave, seven Koran readers chanting on the adjacent tomb of his father happened to be repeating: " Seize ye him and drag him into the mid-fire of hell ".[3] His young son and successor Jaysh (895–6) was murdered six months later by his own troops, who were alienated for lack of funds.[4]

The Qarmaṭians

The turbulent reign of Jaysh's brother Hārūn (896–904) was rendered more turbulent by the advent of the Qarmaṭians (Carmathians). This extreme Shīʿite sect, related to the Ismāʿīlite and Fāṭimid, received its name from an ʿIrāqi peasant Ḥamdān Qarmaṭ.[5] Fundamentally its organization was that of a secret, communistic society, with initiation as a requisite for admission. About 890 Ḥamdān occupied his new headquarters near al-Kūfah. Nine years later his followers were masters of an independent state on the western coast of the

[1] Ibn-Khallikān, vol. i, p. 310. Cf. ibn-Khaldūn, vol. iv, pp. 307-8; Ṭabari, vol. iii, pp. 2145-6; ibn-Taghri-Birdi, vol. ii, p. 55.

[2] Ibn-ʿAsākir, vol. v, p. 178.

[3] Sūr. 44:47.

[4] Subjoined is a tree of the Ṭūlūnid dynasty:

1. AḤMAD IBN-ṬŪLŪN (868–84)
- 2. KHUMĀRAWAYH (884–95)
  - 3. JAYSH (895–6)
  - 4. HĀRŪN (896–904)
  - Qaṭr-al-Nada
- 5. SHAYBĀN (904–5)

[5] Consult Bernard Lewis, *The Origins of Ismāʿīlism* (Cambridge, 1940), pp. 19-22. *Qarmaṭ* is probably Aramaic for " secret teacher ".

Persian Gulf. From these two centres they spread devastation in all directions. Throughout the Umayyad period Moslem Syria followed the orthodox Sunnite line; but the imposition of the hated ʿAbbāsid régime opened the way for the introduction of ʿAlid doctrines which now prepared the people for the reception of Qarmaṭian views. Just as in Byzantine Syria the people endeavoured to assert their nationality by espousing Christian doctrines considered heretical by Byzantium, so were they now ready to adopt ultra-Shīʿite, anti-ʿAbbāsid beliefs. The Qarmaṭian move against Syria was led by ibn-Zikrawayh.[1] After defeating the Ṭūlūnid garrison he laid siege to Damascus, reduced Ḥimṣ, destroyed a large number of the people of Ḥamāh and Maʿarrat al-Nuʿmān and almost annihilated the population of Baʿlabakk. Salamyah, later an Ismāʿīlite-Assassin centre, surrendered. From many Syrian pulpits his name was cited in the Friday prayers as that of the expected Mahdi

In 902 the caliph sent against the Qarmaṭians an able general who, after defeating them and securing the allegiance of the Syrian vassals, set out for the conquest of Egypt. Meantime Hārūn was assassinated and succeeded by his uncle Shaybān (904–5).[2] In 904 the ʿAbbāsid general reached the Ṭūlūnid capital al-Qaṭāʾiʿ, razed it to the ground, cut off twenty Ṭūlūnid heads and carried the remaining male members of this house in chains to the imperial capital. In the following year the last Sufyāni on record unfurled the white flag in Syria and he too was captured and sent to Baghdād.[3] The people who had once been described as acknowledging no other authority than that of the banu-Umayyah[4] had evidently at long last become demoralized and reconciled to alien rule.

The Ikhshīdids

The general who in the name of the Ṭūlūnids defended Damascus against the Qarmaṭians was a Turk from Farghānah, Ṭughj by name,[5] whose son Muḥammad managed to inherit the Ṭūlūnid legacy. After a brief interval of precarious ʿAbbāsid sway in Egypt and Syria, Muḥammad established himself at al-Fusṭāṭ in 935 as the ruler of Egypt.[6] Four years later the Caliph al-Rāḍi, in response to Muḥammad's request, bestowed

[1] Ṭabari, vol. ii, pp. 2221-2.
[2] Kindi, pp. 247-8.
[3] Ṭabari, vol. iii, p. 2277.
[4] Maqdisi, pp. 293-4.
[5] Ibn-Saʿīd, *al-Mughrib fi Ḥula al-Maghrib*, ed. K. L. Tallqvist (Leyden, 1899), p. 5.
[6] Miskawayh, vol. i, pp. 332, 366, n.; ibn-Taghri-Birdi, vol. ii, p. 270.

upon him the old Iranian princely title al-Ikhshīd, thereby raising him above his peers. In the nineteenth century an Ottoman sultan conferred on his Egyptian viceroy a similar Persian title, Khedive. Following the Ṭūlūnid precedent, al-Ikhshīd began to cast covetous eyes on Egypt's northern neighbour, most of which was held and successfully defended by an adventurer ibn-Rā'iq.[1] Upon ibn-Rā'iq's death in 941 the vice-royalty of al-Ikhshīd over Syria and Egypt, together with Mecca and Medina, was recognized by the caliph and the Buwayhid overlords of Baghdād. For centuries hence the fortunes of al-Ḥijāz were linked with those of Egypt. In 944 the Ikhshīd obtained from the imperial government hereditary rights for his family in the lands he acquired.

A Negro ruler

Before he had time enough to warm his throne, al-Ikhshīd had his authority challenged in North Syria by the rising power of the Ḥamdānids, represented by their illustrious son Sayf-al-Dawlah, who installed himself in Aleppo. The armed conflicts took place mostly during the reigns of al-Ikhshīd's two sons. Unūjūr,[2] who was born in Damascus, where his father had died, succeeded Sayf in 946 under the tutelage of a Negro eunuch named abu-al-Misk Kāfūr (musky camphor).[3] Sayf-al-Dawlah's attempts to overrun all Syria were frustrated by this able regent, who defeated the Ḥamdānid troops in two engagements and compelled Sayf to recognize Egypt's overlordship. Kāfūr continued to hold the reins of government during the reign of Unūjūr's brother abu-al-Ḥasan 'Ali (960–66).[4] 'Ali was buried

[1] For the battles with him consult the contemporary historian Kindi, pp. 288-291; Miskawayh, vol. i, p. 414; ibn-Sa'īd, pp. 37 *seq.*; ibn-al-Athīr, vol. viii, p. 272.

[2] Unjūr, Anjūr; cf. ibn-Sa'īd, p. 45; ibn-Taghri-Birdi, vol. ii, p. 315; Kindi, p. 294; ibn-Khaldūn, vol. iv, p. 314; ibn-al-Athīr, vol. viii, p. 343; Miskawayh, vol. ii, p. 104. See also F. Wüstenfeld, *Die Statthalter von Ägypten zur Zeit der Chalifen*, pt. iv (Göttingen, 1876), p. 37.

[3] Ibn-Khallikān, vol. ii, p. 186.

[4] Ṭughj
|
1. MUḤAMMAD AL-IKHSHĪD (935–46)
|
2. ABU-AL-QĀSIM UNŪJŪR (946–60) | 3. 'ALI (960–66) | * * 4. ABU-AL-MISK KĀFŪR (966–8)

3. 'ALI (960–66)
|
5. AḤMAD (968–9)

The stars indicate a master-slave relationship.

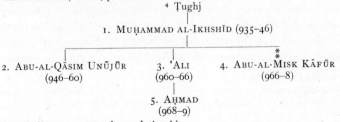

in Jerusalem, where his brother and father were interred. For two years after that the Negro ruled as a sovereign over a state which included besides Egypt and Syria a part of Cilicia with its chief city Tarsus.[1] Originally a harelipped Abyssinian slave whom al-Ikhshīd had bought from an oil dealer for eighteen dinars, Kāfūr was the first illustration in Islamic history of sovereigns who rose to high eminence from the lowliest origins. His enfranchisement, according to a story, was due to the fact that he kept his eyes fastened on his master while the eyes of all other slaves and servants had turned toward an elephant and a giraffe which the master had just received as a present. This slave could not miss for an instant the opportunity of serving his master if need be, and his extraordinary vigilance was amply rewarded.[2]

Kāfūr's name, like that of his adversary Sayf, has been immortalized by the greatest poet of the age, al-Mutanabbi', in verses which almost every school child in the Arab world today commits to memory. The verses were first composed in praise of the Egyptian potentate and later — after his failure to reward the poet with the high office to which he aspired — in ridicule of him.[3]

Fall of the Ikhshīdids

Kāfūr was succeeded by Aḥmad abu-al-Fawāris (968–9), an eleven-year-old lad unable to cope with the problems of the day. The Ḥamdānids were threatening from the north, the resurgent Qarmaṭians from the east and, more dangerously, the Fāṭimids [4] from the west. The Fāṭimid caliphate, which arose in Tunis in 909, had for years carried on secret correspondence with 'Alids and other sympathizers in Egypt. It was now time to act. In 969 its dashing general Jawhar had no difficulty in routing the Ikhshīdid army and entering al-Fusṭāṭ (July 6). The name of the Caliph al-Mu'izz was forthwith introduced into the public prayers and struck on the new coins. The Ikhshīdid vassal in Damascus, a cousin of abu-al-Fawāris, made a faint attempt to save Syria. Jawhar sent against him a general who defeated his troops at al-Ramlah and took him prisoner. Thereupon were Palestine and Central Syria incorporated into the emerging Fāṭimid empire.[5]

[1] Ibn-Khallikān, vol. ii, pp. 185-9; ibn-Khaldūn, vol. iv, pp. 314-15; ibn-Taghri-Birdi, vol. ii, p. 373.

[2] Ibn-Sa'īd, pp. 46-7.

[3] See below, pp. 567-8.

[4] See below, pp. 577 *seq.*

[5] Kindi, pp. 297-8.

The Ikhshīdid dynasty (935–69), like its predecessor the Ṭūlūnid (868–905), had an ephemeral existence. They followed the same pattern of behaviour, the pattern that typifies the case of many other states which, in this period of disintegration, broke off from the imperial government. Both made lavish use of state moneys to curry favour with their subjects and thereby ruined the treasuries. Neither of them had any national basis in the land over which it tried to rule; neither could rely upon a strong coherent body of supporters of its own race among its subjects. Being intruders the rulers had to recruit their body-guards, which were also their armies, from alien sources. Such a rule could be maintained only so long as the arm which wielded the sword remained strong.

The Ḥamdānids: Sayf-al-Dawlah

The banu-Ḥamdān, successors of the Ikhshīdids in northern Syria, took their name from Ḥamdān ibn-Ḥamdūn of the Taghlib tribe, which was once Christian and produced the famous Umayyad poet al-Akhṭal.[1] Ḥamdān made his military and political debut in the late ninth century when he took possession of the fortress of Mārdīn.[2] His successors, after several conflicts and reconciliations with the caliphs, extended their sway into al-Mawṣil, a large part of Mesopotamia and northern Syria. The most distinguished among them was abu-al-ʿAli Ḥasan, who in 944 wrested from the Ikhshīdid vassal Aleppo, Antioch and Ḥimṣ [3] and subsequently received from the caliph the honorific title of Sayf-al-Dawlah (the sword of the state, i.e. the ʿAbbāsid, 944–67). By the bestowal of such high-sounding titles the caliphs meant to leave the impression that the recipient — in reality independent — was under their control. Sayf and his successors were tolerant Shīʿites and preserved the caliph's name in the Friday prayer. Sayf chose Aleppo [4] for capital perhaps because of its ancient citadel and its proximity to the frontier fortresses which he intended to defend against the new wave of Byzantine inroads. For the first time since Amorite days [5] the northern metropolis became the seat of an important government. In it the new ruler erected a magnificent palace with three baths and running water. A stream

[1] See above, pp. 439, 494.
[2] Ṭabari, vol. iii, p. 2141.
[3] Ibn-Saʿīd, p. 41.
[4] Ḥalab, called al-Shahbā' (grey) possibly because of its whitish stones.
[5] See above, p. 68

surrounded the palace and a garden and racecourse adjoined it.[1]

Sayf's domain covered North Syria, a section of Cilicia and a large part of northern Mesopotamia. He even established a foothold in Armenia with the aid of Kurdish supporters;[2] his mother was a Kurd. By marrying a daughter of al-Ikhshīd he hoped to be left in peaceful possession of his territory. Damascus he failed to reduce.[3] A frontier province, his principality consumed much of its time and energy struggling with the Byzantines. Sayf was the first after a long interval to take up the cudgels seriously against the Christian enemies of Islam. This Ḥamdānid-Byzantine conflict may be considered a significant chapter in the prehistory of the Crusades. As a warrior the Ḥamdānid prince had a worthy peer in the Byzantine emperor Nicephorus,[4] with whom the historians record about ten engagements. Success was not always on Sayf's side. In 962 he even temporarily lost his own capital after a brief siege in which his palace, symbol of his glory, was destroyed.[5] The repercussion was felt in Baghdād, where a demonstration staged by the people, who demanded that the caliph in person lead an expeditionary force, resulted in nothing more than tears from the caliph's eyes.[6] The death of Sayf in 967[7] and the ensuing internal discord enabled Nicephorus and his successors to push their advance, occupy a large part of North Syria and impose an ephemeral Byzantine suzerainty over the Ḥamdānid realm. In 968 Nicephorus again captured Aleppo and added Antioch, Ḥimṣ and the towns between. His successor John Zimisces[8] reduced six years later not only the coastal towns of Beirut, Jubayl, ʿArqah, Ṭarṭūs, Jabalah and al-Lādhiqīyah but such inland places as Ṣihyawn and Baʿlabakk. Antioch remained in Byzantine hands for over a century (968–1084).

Aleppo was not recaptured by the Ḥamdānids until 975. Its citadel held out for two more years. Sayf's son Saʿd-al-Dawlah had his hands full fighting a cousin claimant in Ḥimṣ before he

[1] Ibn-al-Shiḥnah, *al-Durr al-Muntakhab fi Ta'rīkh Ḥalab* (Beirut, 1909), pp. 60-61, 133.

[2] Miskawayh, vol. ii, p. 161.

[3] Ibn-Saʿīd, p. 42.

[4] Nicephorus II Phocas (963–9), Niqfūr of Arabic chronicles.

[5] Ibn-al-Athīr, vol. viii, pp. 401-2; Miskawayh, vol. ii, pp. 192-4.

[6] Miskawayh, vol. ii, p. 201, n.

[7] For a collection of Arabic texts relative to Sayf consult Marius Canard, *Sayf al Daula* (Algiers, 1934).

[8] Ar. ibn-al-Shumushqīq; ibn-al-Qalānisi, pp. 12-14.

felt secure in his succession. Meantime a disloyal vassal in Aleppo had signed a treaty with the Byzantines agreeing to the payment of tribute, which Sa'd refused to acknowledge. In 985 Sa'd besieged Qal'at Sam'ān,[1] then in Byzantine hands, sacked it and killed its monks or sold them into slavery. In the reign of Sa'd's successor Sa'īd-al-Dawlah (991–1001)[2] a new foe was looming on the southern horizon, the Fāṭimids. Hard pressed, the Ḥamdānid prince appealed to the Emperor Basil for aid. The Byzantine ruler rushed with 17,000 men to Aleppo and the enemy dispersed for the time being. But Sa'īd had afterwards to acknowledge Fāṭimid suzerainty. Being young he had a regent over him whose daughter he married. The regent now coveted the throne for himself and poisoned both his son-in-law and daughter. For two years after that he held the regency in the name of the Fāṭimid caliphs over Sa'īd's two sons 'Ali and Sharīf (1001–3). In 1003 he sent the two young princes to Cairo with the Ḥamdānid harem and appointed his own son co-regent. This was the last episode in the life of the Ḥamdānid dynasty, which was the second and last Arab dynasty to rise on Syrian soil.

The glamorous circle of Sayf-al-Dawlah

The life-cycle of the Ḥamdānid dynasty did not suffer in essence from that of its two predecessors, the Ikhshīdid and the Ṭūlūnid. A dominant leader carves a principality for himself, is followed by incompetent successors; the state moneys are squandered; discord within and foes without bring the story to an end. In this case the munificence of Sayf in his patronage of science and art was the first great drain on the treasury.

Sayf surrounded himself in his gorgeous palace with a circle of literary and artistic talent that could hardly be matched except by that of the Baghdād caliphs in their heyday. It comprised the renowned philosopher and musician al-Fārābi, the distinguished historian of Arabic literature al-Iṣbahāni, the eloquent

[1] See above, pp. 364-5.

[2] 1. Sayf-al-Dawlah abu-al-Ḥasan 'Ali (944–67)
|
2. Sa'd-al-Dawlah abu-al-Ma'āli Sharīf (967–91)
|
3. Sa'īd-al-Dawlah abu-al-Faḍā'il Sa'īd (991–1001)
|
4a. Abu-al-Ḥasan 'Ali (1001–3) | 4b. Abu-al-Ma'āli Sharīf (1001–3)

preacher ibn-Nubātah (d. 984),[1] the philologist ibn-Khālawayh, the grammarian ibn-Jinni (d. 1002),[2] the warrior-poet abu-Firās and, above all, the illustrious bard al-Mutanabbi'.

Sayf-al-Dawlah — may God favour him, gratify his wishes and make Paradise his abode! — was the luminous spot of his age and the pillar of Islam. By him the frontiers were guarded and the state affairs well managed. . . . It is said that after the caliphs no monarch gathered around him so many shaykhs of poetry and stars of learning. After all, a monarch is like a market, people bring to him what is in demand by him. Sayf himself was a literateur, a poet and a lover of poetry.[3]

Abu-al-Ṭayyib Aḥmad ibn-al-Ḥusayn received his surname al-Mutanabbi' (prophecy claimant, 915–65 [4]) because in his youth he claimed the gift of prophecy, attempted an imitation of the Koran and was followed by a number of admirers, especially in al-Lādhiqīyah and the Syrian Desert. The Ikhshīdid governor of Ḥimṣ cast him into prison, where he remained for almost two years and from which he went out cured from his prophetic illusion but not from his vanity, self-assertiveness and self-admiration, which accompanied him throughout his life. Here is his own estimate of his work: Al-Mutanabbi'

My deep poetic art the blind have eyes to see,
  My verses ring in ears as deaf as deaf can be.
They wander far abroad while I am unaware,
  But men collect them watchfully with toil and care.

. . . .

The desert knows me well, the night, the mounted men,
  The battle and the sword, the paper and the pen! [5]

The man who sang his own praise in such glowing terms had a humble origin. He was born in al-Kūfah of a father who worked as water carrier. When still a lad he moved with the

[1] His *Khuṭab* (sermons) have appeared in several Cairo and Beirut editions.
[2] Son of a Turkish slave, noted for his commentary on al-Mutanabbi'.
[3] Al-Tha'ālibi (d. 1037), *Yatīmat al-Dahr fi Shu'arā' Ahl al-'Aṣr* (Damascus, 1303), vol. i, pp. 8-9.
[4] The thousandth anniversary of his death was celebrated in Syria in 1935 (A.H. 1354); see *Al Mutanabbi: Recueil publié à l'occasion de son millénaire* (Beirut, 1936); cf. R. Blachère, *Un Poète arabe: Abou-ṭ-Ṭayyib al-Motanabbî* (Paris, 1935), pp. 66 *seq.*
[5] Al-Wāḥidi, *Sharḥ Dīwān al-Mutanabbi*, ed. Fr. Dieterici (Berlin, 1861), pp. 483-4; Nicholson, p. 307.

family to Syria. After roaming about in quest of a patron he settled in Aleppo as the laureate of Sayf-al-Dawlah; the two names have ever since remained inseparably linked. The proud poet insisted on reciting his compositions in the princely presence while sitting and without bowing down to kiss the ground. Throughout his audiences with Kāfūr he would keep his shoes on and his sword in his belt.[1] On the way back and forth he would ride with two of his slaves fully armed. The reason given for deserting the Syrian court in favour of the Egyptian is that the poet had an argument with Sayf's teacher ibn-Khālawayh, who struck him with a key on the face. Disappointed in his Egyptian patron al-Mutanabbi' stole away to Baghdād and Persia. On his way back he was killed with his son by a marauding band of Bedouins who made away with the autograph copy of his *Dīwān*.[2]

Outstanding among the odes in his *Dīwān* are those depicting the glories of Sayf's campaigns against the Byzantines. It is a question whether or not those panegyrics did not contribute more than the exploits themselves to making Sayf the myth he is in Arabic annals. In them the poet appears as the consummate phrasemaker in the Arabic language. Nuggets of wise sayings add to the value of the composition; the poet personally lived a moral life in contrast to members of his class in his day. In places the style appears bombastic and ornate, the rhetoric florid and the metaphor overdone — but not to the Easterner. Such is the hold that this poet has had upon the imagination of Arabic speakers that he is still generally considered the greatest in Islam. In him and his two predecessors, abu-Tammām and al-Buḥturi, Arabic poetry reached its full maturity, if not its zenith. With few exceptions the decline after this was steady.

Abu-Firās

Al-Mutanabbi' had a close competitor in abu-Firās al-Ḥārith ibn-abi-al-ʿAlā' al-Ḥamdāni (932–68), a cousin of Sayf-al-Dawlah and his comrade at arms. For one verse his patron is said to have bestowed on abu-Firās a fief near Manbij, the annual income of which amounted to a thousand dinars. In 962 the gallant poet was taken as a prisoner to Constantinople

[1] Ibn-Khallikān, vol. i, p. 64.

[2] Besides Dieterici's edition there is one by Naṣīf al-Yāziji, *al-ʿUrf al-Ṭayyib fi Sharḥ Dīwān abi-al-Ṭayyib* (Beirut, 1882).

and was ransomed after four years.[1] Some of his most touching poems were composed in captivity.[2] An ode of his extolling the ʿAlids and berating the ʿAbbāsids is still a favourite in Shīʿite circles.[3] It was he who, after the death of Sayf, claimed independent control over Ḥimṣ and fell fighting against troops sent by Sayf's son.[4]

Lesser lights in the poetical firmament of this age included the versatile Kushājim and the euphuistic al-Wa'wā'. Of Hindu origin,[5] Kushājim (d. *ca.* 971) owes his curious name to a combination of the first letters of the Arabic words for writer, poet, literateur, polemicist and astrologer—all of which he supposedly was. A native of al-Ramlah, he embarked on his career as a cook for Sayf-al-Dawlah. Some of the poetry he composed describes different dishes and drinks.[6] To his many accomplishments he added that of medicine and wrote a book on zoology. Al-Wa'wā' (d. 999), a Damascene of Ghassānid origin, is remembered by an ode in which he describes a damsel crying and biting her lip in the following terms: "She caused pearls to rain from narcissus, watered with them the roses and bit the jujubes with her hailstones".[7]

Other than poets

The court of Sayf-al-Dawlah was graced by other than poets. A historian of literature and music, al-Iṣbahāni, and a philosopher-musician, al-Fārābi, are worthy of note. Abu-al-Faraj al-Iṣbahāni (Iṣfahāni, 897–967), a lineal descendant of the last Umayyad caliph but of Shīʿite leanings, was born in Iṣbahān. From his royal relatives in Spain he received gifts in recognition of books dedicated to them. Sayf bestowed on him a thousand gold pieces for an autograph copy of his monumental *Kitāb al-Aghāni*[8] (book of songs), which is much more than what it professes to be. It is related that a contemporary learned

[1] Ibn-Khallikān, vol. i, pp. 225-6.

[2] Consult his *Dīwān*, ed. Nakhlah Qalfāṭ (Beirut, 1900); tr. in part, Rudolph Dvořák as *Abû Firâs: ein arabischer Dichter und Held* (Leyden, 1895). See also Thaʿālibi, vol. i, pp. 22-62.

[3] For text consult his *Dīwān*, ed. Sāmi al-Dahhān (Beirut, 1944), vol. iii, pp. 348-56; Canard, pp. 325-33.

[4] See above, pp. 565-6.

[5] Masʿūdi, vol. viii, p. 318.

[6] Masʿūdi, vol. viii, pp. 394-5, 399-400. See also his *Dīwān* (Beirut, 1313), pp. 44-5, 50, 51, 83, 84, 85, 179-80.

[7] Al-Wa'wā', *Dīwān*, ed. J. Krachkovsky (Leyden, 1914), pp. 47, 137; Kutubi, vol. ii, p. 182.

[8] 20 vols. (Būlāq, 1285); R. E. Brünnow edited vol. xxi (Leyden, 1888) and I. Guidi issued the index (Leyden, 1900).

vizir who ordinarily carried along with him on his travels thirty camel loads of reading matter happened on a copy of *al-Aghāni* and was ever thereafter content with it alone as a companion.[1]

Al-Fārābi

Muḥammad abu-Naṣr al-Fārābi (Alpharabius) was a Turk from Fārāb, Turkestan.[2] He lived in Syria as a Sufi, satisfied with an honorarium of four dirhams per day from Sayf. In 950, aged eighty, he died at Damascus, to which he had accompanied his patron. Al-Fārābi was one of the earliest Moslem thinkers to attempt a harmonization of Greek philosophy and Islam. His system was a syncretism of Aristotelianism, Platonism and Sufism. His people conferred on him the unique title of "the second teacher" after Aristotle, who was the first. He became the intellectual ancestor of ibn-Sīna and all other subsequent Moslem philosophers. His major works are *Risālat Fuṣūṣ al-Ḥikam* (epistles containing bezels of wisdom),[3] *Risālah fi Ārā' Ahl al-Madīnah al-Fāḍilah*[4] (treatise on the opinions of the inhabitants of the superior city) and *al-Siyāsah* (*Siyāsāt*) *al-Madanīyah* (political economy).[5] In the last two the author presents his conception of an ideal city, which he conceives as a hierarchical organism analogous to the human body. His city is clearly modelled after Plato's *Republic*.

More than a philosopher, al-Fārābi was a fair physician and mathematician, an occult scientist and an excellent musician. His three works on music, headed by *Kitāb al-Mūsīqi al-Kabīr* (the great book of music),[6] mark him as one of the greatest, if not the greatest, of all Arabic music theorists. Indeed he was a practitioner, too. He was able — so goes the story — to play a lute of his own manufacture in the Ḥamdānid salon and make his listeners laugh, cry or go to sleep — as he wished.[7]

Al-Maqdisi, geographer

While the Ḥamdānids ruled in North and the Fāṭimids in

[1] Ibn-Khallikān, vol. ii, p. 11.

[2] Ibn-abi-Uṣaybi'ah, vol. ii, p. 134; Qifṭi, p. 277; ibn-Ḥawqal, p. 390.

[3] Published by Friedrich Dieterici in his *Die Philosophie der Araber im IX. und X. Jahrhundert n. Chr.*, vol. xiv (Leyden, 1890), pp. 66-83.

[4] Published at Cairo, 1323, and also by Dieterici, *Philosophie der Araber*, vol. xvi (Leyden, 1895), who also translated it as *Der Musterstaat von Alfārābi* (Leyden, 1900).

[5] (Ḥaydarābād, 1346.)

[6] Extracts by J. P. N. Land appeared in *Actes du sixième congrès international des orientalistes*, pt. 2, sec. 1 (Leyden, 1885), pp. 100-168. Fr. tr. by Rodolphe d'Erlanger, *La Musique arabe*, vols. i, ii, al-Fārābī (Paris, 1930-35).

[7] Ibn-Khallikān, vol. ii, p. 501.

South Syria there flourished in Palestine one of the most original and meritorious geographers, al-Maqdisi (Muqaddasi, 946–*ca.* 1000). Born in Jerusalem (*Bayt al-Maqdis*) under the Ikhshīdids, he started at the age of twenty travels that took him through all Moslem lands excluding Spain, India and Sijistān. In 985 he embodied the information he thus gathered in a book entitled *Aḥsan al-Taqāsīm fi Ma'rifat al-Aqālīm* (the best of classification for the knowledge of climates).[1] In its composition, as he says in the introduction, he was guided primarily by personal observation and experience rather than by books. His predilection seems to have been in favour of the Shī'ah and the Fāṭimids. At his time the Shī'ah did represent the intellectual and progressive wing of Islam.

Thanks to the works of al-Maqdisi and other geographers who began to flourish in this age, our knowledge of the economic and social conditions of tenth century Syria reaches a height unattained before. No Latin, Greek or Semitic geographer ever left us material comparable to this Arabic material in quality and quantity. Al-Maqdisi surveys trade, agriculture, industry and general education. He refers, among many other things, to iron ores in the "mountains of Beirut",[2] the abundant trees and hermits in Lebanon,[3] the sugar and glassware products of Tyre, the cheese and cotton goods of Jerusalem and the cereals and honey of 'Ammān.[4] He characterizes Syria as a "blessed region, the home of cheap prices, fruits and righteous people".[5] Al-Maqdisi's Persian contemporary ibn-al-Faqīh[6] emphasizes the ascetics and woods in Lebanon and makes special mention of its apples. Another Persian, ibn-Khurdādhbih (d. *ca.* 912), enumerates the districts of Syria, indicating the roads and the distances between cities.[7] 'Arqah, Tripoli, Beirut and other coastal and inland towns were still strongly fortified. On the whole the general impression one receives from a perusal of these and other contemporaneous sources is favourable so far as the standard of living is concerned. People generally lived a happy, useful life — judged by the authors' standards. Christians and Jews do not seem to have been worse off under

[1] Ed. M. J. de Goeje (Leyden, 1877).

[2] P. 184; al-Idrīsi, *Nuzhat al-Mushtāq, Dhikr al-Sha'm*, ed. J. Gildemeister (Bonn, 1885), p. 16. See above, pp. 35, 277; below, p. 656.

[3] P. 188. [4] P. 180. [5] P. 179. [6] Pp. 112, 117.

[7] Pp. 74 *seq.*, 95 *seq.*

the petty dynasts of Egypt and Syria than under the ʿAbbāsids. Most of the scribes in Syria, if not all of them, and most of the physicians were still Christians.[1] In 992 Syria was visited by an earthquake which, however, did not do as much damage as that of 859/60, in which al-Lādhiqīyah and Jabalah were almost wiped out of existence and Antioch lost fifteen hundred buildings.[2] In the preceding century Syria had suffered from at least two earthquakes, in 738 and 746.

Dark ages begin

Black clouds, however, were thickening in the horizon; times of trouble lay ahead. After the mid-tenth century Fāṭimid armies of Berbers and Egyptians resumed their incursions from the south; fanatic Qarmaṭian hordes of ʿIrāqis and Persians were again overrunning the land from the north-east. Saljūq and other unruly Turkish tribes were soon to follow, pouring in from the north. Clearly the dark ages in the history of Syria had begun. A state bordering on anarchy prevailed. Pillage, fire and slaughter marched in the wake of the invaders. Leading cities — Aleppo, Damascus, Jerusalem — were tossed like a ball from one alien hand to another. Toward the end of the eleventh century Frankish and other Crusading bands were winding their way from the north-west into the torn, tortured land. Before the Crusades were over, waves of Mongol tribes were rolling over Syria from north to south. The slave dynasty of nondescript Mamlūks was superseded in its rule, or rather misrule, by the Ottoman Turks. The blackout continued throughout until the middle of the nineteenth century.

[1] Maqdisi, p. 183, ll. 4, 7-8.

[2] Ṭabari, vol. iii, pp. 1439-40.

CHAPTER XLIV

BETWEEN SALJŪQS AND FĀṬIMIDS

THE major powers that arose with the dismemberment of the ʿAbbāsid state were not those treated in the preceding chapters but the ones to be treated now, the Saljūqs and the Fāṭimids. These two powers parcelled out Syria between them; the Saljūqs held its northern part and the Fāṭimids the southern. The former were Turks, the latter allegedly Arabs.

Ṭughril in Baghdād

The eponymous founder of the Saljūq house was a Turkoman chief of the Ghuzz tribe in Turkestan who, with his rough nomadic clan, moved to the region of Bukhāra,[1] where they evidently embraced Islam. His grandson Ṭughril pushed his conquests westward through Persia and in 1055 stood at the head of his band at the very gate of Baghdād. There was but one course for the powerless Caliph al-Qā'im to follow, to exchange one master for another — the Shīʿite Persian Buwayhids for the Sunnite Turkish Saljūqs.[2] The new Saljūq ruler assumed the title of *sulṭān* (he with authority). He is the first Moslem ruler whose coins bear this title. With his successors the designation became regular. In the wake of Ṭughril's victory hordes of Turks, Saljūq and others, were funnelled into Western Asia and spread all over that region. Gradually they were Islamized and Arabicized.

Under Ṭughril's nephew and successor Alp Arslān (hero-lion, 1063–72) and the latter's son Malikshāh (1072–9), the Saljūq domain attained its greatest dimensions, from the borders of Afghanistan to the frontiers of the Byzantine empire in western Asia Minor. In 1070 Alp advanced against the Mirdāsids in North Syria and occupied Aleppo, leaving the Mirdāsid governor as his vassal.[3] Alp's general Atsiz, a Turkoman from Khwārizm, pushed into Palestine and captured al-

[1] Ibn-al-Athīr, vol. ix, pp. 321-2.

[2] Ibn-Khallikān, vol. i, pp. 107-8; ibn-Taghri-Birdi, ed. Popper, vol. ii, pt. 2, p. 225.

[3] Ibn-al-Athīr, vol. x, pp. 43-4; see below, pp. 580-81.

Ramlah, Jerusalem and other towns as far south as 'Asqalān, whose Fāṭimid garrison held out.[1] In 1076 he occupied Damascus and exasperated its people with his exactions. Alp's son Tutush recaptured Damascus two years later and killed Atsiz.[2] In 1071 Alp won a decisive victory over the Byzantines at Manzikert, north of Lake Van, and took the emperor himself prisoner. All Asia Minor then lay open to the Turks. Hordes of them rushed into Anatolia and northern Syria. Turkish generals penetrated as far as the Hellespont. With one stroke the traditional frontier separating Islam from Christendom was pushed four hundred miles west. For the first time Turks gained a foothold in that land — a foothold that was never lost.

The fragmentation of the vast sultanate soon followed. Different Saljūq amīrs received different subdivisions. That of Asia Minor (Rūm) was held by a cousin of Alp, Sulaymān, who in 1077 established himself in Nicaea (Nīqiyah, Iznīq), not far from Constantinople. In 1084 the capital shifted south-east to Iconium (Qūniyah, Koniah). In the same year Antioch was recovered for Islam from the Byzantines by the Saljūqs.[3] No hold on Asia Minor could be secure as long as Byzantines remained entrenched in the rear. It was a son of Sulaymān, Qilij Arslān, whom the first bands of Crusaders encountered (1096) as they crossed Asia Minor *en route* to Syria.[4] One of the various Turkish states which followed the Saljūqs of Rūm about 1300 was that of the Ottomans, traditionally another branch of the Ghuzz.[5]

The Saljūqs of Syria

The Saljūq dynasty of Syria was founded by Alp's son Tutush, who in 1094 gained possession of Aleppo.[6] The city was still the leading one of North Syria and a worthy seat of a principality. Tutush fell in battle the following year and his son Riḍwān (1095–1113) became after him lord of Aleppo while another son, Duqāq, established himself over Damascus.[7] The two amīrs were soon involved in a family war [8] and a couple of years later Duqāq was forced to recognize the overlordship of

[1] Ibn-'Asākir, vol. ii, p. 331; ibn-Khaldūn, vol. v, pp. 145-6.
[2] Ibn-Khallikān, vol. i, p. 168. [3] See above, p. 565. [4] See below, p. 591.
[5] See below, p. 661. [6] Ibn-al-Athīr, vol. x, pp. 157-8.
[7] Ibn-Khallikān, vol. i, p. 168.
[8] Ibn-al-Qalānisi, pp. 130-32; ibn-al-Athīr, vol. x, p. 168; ibn-Khaldūn, vol. v, p. 148.

his brother. In 1096 a brother-in-law of Tutush who held Jerusalem as fief surrendered it to the Fāṭimids. It was Fāṭimid rule which the Crusaders found on their arrival in the Holy Land. Riḍwān was a partisan of the Ismāʿīli Assassins and the Aleppines were then evidently mostly Shīʿites and Ismāʿīlites.[1] But the Sunnites hated him. For a month he ordered the name of the Fāṭimid caliph, also of the Ismāʿīli denomination, recited in the Friday prayer, but then reverted to the ʿAbbāsid name. Riḍwān was one of those with whom the Crusaders were repeatedly involved in battle in North Syria. He maintained his hold on Aleppo against the Frankish attacks but his attempt at relieving Antioch, besieged in 1098, failed.[2]

Riḍwān was succeeded in 1113 by his sixteen-year-old son Alp Arslān, a feeble-minded debauchee, who was assassinated by his regent in Aleppo shortly after his installation.[3] A brother, Sulṭān Shāh, ruled under a regent for three years. In 1117 a Turkoman officer in the Saljūq army, Īl-Ghāzi ibn-Urtuq got possession of Aleppo.[4] The seat of the branch of the Urtuqid dynasty which he established lay at Mārdīn. He was a redoubtable warrior against the Crusaders.

In 1128 Aleppo was annexed by another warring Turk, ʿImād-al-Dīn (pillar of the faith) Zangi,[5] of al-Mawṣil, whose father was once a slave in the service of Malikshāh and later a

The Atābegs

[1] Ibn-al-Athīr, vol. x, p. 349; ibn-al-Qalānisi, p. 142; ibn-Khaldūn, vol. v, pp. 153-4.

[2] See below, p. 592.

[3] Ibn-al-Qalānisi, pp. 189, 198; Kamāl-al-Dīn, "Muntakhabāt min Ta'rīkh Ḥalab", in *Recueil des historiens des croisades: historiens orientaux*, vol. iii (Paris, 1884), pp. 602-3, 605-6.

A genealogical table of the Saljūqs of Syria (1094–1117):

1. Tutush ibn-Alp Arslān (1094–5)

2. Riḍwān (at Aleppo, 1095–1113) — 2. Duqāq (at Damascus, 1095–1104)

(sons of Riḍwān:) 3. Alp Arslān (1113–14) — 4. Sulṭān Shāh (1114–17)

[4] Ibn-al-Qalānisi, p. 199.

[5] Founder of the Atābeg dynasty of al-Mawṣil and Syria. The *atābegs* (Tur. *ata*, "father" + *beg*, "prince", cf. Atatürk) were originally guardians or tutors of the young Saljūq princes and finally replaced them in supreme power. Abu-Shāmah, *al-Rawḍatayn fi Akhbār al-Dawlatayn*, vol. i (Cairo, 1287), p. 24.

lieutenant in Tutush's army.[1] In the following years Ḥamāh, Ḥimṣ, Ba'labakk and Damascus were added to the Zangid realm. Zangi was the anti-Crusading hero who in 1144 wrested Edessa from Frankish hands [2] and inaugurated the series of victories which were continued by his son Nūr-al-Dīn and his son's successor Ṣalāḥ-al-Dīn (Saladin).[3] He was the builder of medieval al-Mawṣil. Another Turkish Atābeg was Ṭughtagīn,[4] a freedman of Tutush, who had entrusted him with the education of his son Duqāq. Following the norm of other regents, Ṭughtagīn usurped the sovereign power and was recognized as the ruler of Damascus shortly after the death in 1104 of his protégé, whose mother he had married.[5] In 1116 the Great Saljūq sultan in Baghdād appointed Ṭughtagīn governor of Syria with the right to regulate taxes and levy armies. Ṭughtagīn allied himself with Īl-Ghāzi and they jointly warred against the Franks.[6] Both were heavy drinkers; Īl-Ghāzi would at times remain under the influence of alcohol for "twenty days" at a stretch. Once Īl-Ghāzi sent him a Frankish prisoner, lord of Ṣihyawn, with the hope that he would scare the prisoner and exact a higher ransom. But Ṭughtagīn, who was then drinking heavily in his tent, simply drew his sword and decapitated the unfortunate lord, explaining later that he had no better way of scaring him.[7] In 1112 Tyre, then under the Fāṭimids, appealed to Ṭughtagīn for aid against the Crusaders. The relief he brought was temporary. The seaport was entered in 1124 by the Crusaders.[8]

The line started by Ṭughtagīn bore the name of his son and

[1] Kamāl-al-Dīn in *Recueil*, vol. iii, pp. 703 *seq.*; ibn-al-Athīr, "Ta'rīkh al-Dawlah al-Atābakīyah", in *Recueil*, vol. ii, pt. 2, pp. 10 *seq.*

[2] Kamāl-al-Dīn in *Recueil*, vol. iii, pp. 685-6; ibn-al-Athīr in *Recueil*, vol. ii, pt. 2, pp. 118-19; ibn-Khallikān, vol. i, p. 344; Dhahabi, vol. ii, pp. 38, 40; abu-Shāmah, vol. i, pp. 33-4, 36-7.

[3] See below, pp. 600 *seq.*

[4] Turkish for "warrior falcon", the Daldequin of Western historians. His Arabic honorific title was Ẓahīr-al-Dīn, "the supporter of religion". Most of these Turkish generals assumed pompous Arabic titles: Īl-Ghāzi (champion of his people) took "Najm-al-Dīn" (the star of religion), Tutush took "Tāj-al-Dawlah" (the crown of the state) and Riḍwān, "Fakhr-al-Mulūk" (the pride of kings).

[5] Ibn-al-Qalānisi, p. 190; ibn-Khallikān, vol. i, p. 169; ibn-Khaldūn, vol. v, p. 155; ibn-Taghri-Birdi, vol. ii, pt. 2, p. 388.

[6] Kamāl-al-Dīn in *Recueil*, vol. iii, pp. 620 *seq.*

[7] Usāmah, pp. 119-20; tr., pp. 149-50.

[8] Ibn-Taghri-Birdi, vol. ii, pt. 2, pp. 336-7.

successor Būri.[1] It was superseded in 1154 by the Zangid atābegs, whose achievements will be recorded later.[2]

The Fāṭimids established

The rise of the Fāṭimid caliphate, like that of the 'Abbāsid,[3] was closely related to Syria. An insignificant out-of-the-way town, Salamyah,[4] south-east of Ḥamāh, became in the late ninth century the residence and seat of activity of the head of the Ismā'īli Assassins. His name was Muḥammad al-Ḥabīb (the beloved) and he was supposed by his followers to be the great-grandson of the Imām Ismā'īl ibn-Ja'far al-Ṣādiq, himself a descendant of 'Ali and Fāṭimah through al-Ḥusayn.[5] True to Ismā'īlite principles al-Ḥabīb had his secret agents throughout the Moslem world working for the undermining of Sunnite power and the re-establishing of the true Islam of Shī'ism. After the 'Abbāsid [6] this was the most effective and formidable propagandist machine in the political history of Islam.

An able agent (*dā'i*) of his, named abu-'Abdullāh al-Ḥusayn al-Shī'i, a native of al-Yaman, met in Mecca and converted several Berber pilgrims of the Quṭāmah (Qiṭāmah) tribe in North Africa. In 893 he accompanied them to Tunis, shrewdly worked himself into a position of leadership and persistently fought to displace the century-old Aghlabid régime. When sure of success he invited the head of the sect from Salamyah, now 'Ubaydullāh son of Muḥammad al-Ḥabīb. At Sijilmāsah the disguised 'Ubaydullāh was detected and imprisoned by the Aghlabid governor (905). In 909 al-Shī'i succeeded in dethroning the Aghlabid ruler, freeing 'Ubāydullāh and establishing him in Raqqādah as the new master of the realm.[7]

[1] Table of the Būrids, atābegs of Damascus (1103–54):

1. Ṭughtagīn (1103–28)
   - 2. Būri (1128–32)
   - 3. Ismā'īl (1132–4)
   - 4. Maḥmūd (1134–8)
   - 5. Muḥammad (1138–9)
     - 6. Abaq (1139–54)

[2] Pp. 599-600. [3] See above, p. 530.

[4] This form is older and more correct than Salamīyah; a corruption of Greek Salamias; cf. Canard, p. 235; Dussaud, *Topographie*, pp. 201, 244, 252.

[5] See above, p. 539, n. 1. [6] See above, p. 530.

[7] Maqrīzi, vol. ii, pp. 10-11; ibn-Khaldūn, vol. iv, pp. 31 *seq.*

ʿUbaydullāh proclaimed himself the expected Mahdi. A new caliphal dynasty was born, the Fāṭimid, also called the ʿAlid and the ʿUbaydite (ʿUbaydīyah). This was no mean dynasty. Its rise constituted a deliberate challenge to the current leadership of Islam by the ʿAbbāsids. At its height it controlled all North Africa, western Arabia and Syria. It was the only major Shīʿite caliphate and the last of the medieval caliphates of Islam.

History has shrouded the pedigree of ʿUbaydullāh with a veil of mystery. He was presumably born in Salamyah — not far from Ḥimṣ, which had supplied the Roman throne with some of its occupants [1] — and so was his son and successor.[2] Critics point out that his line of noble ancestry is variously given and therefore not genuine. Some go as far as saying that the real Mahdi was killed in the Sijilmāsah jail and that the ʿUbaydullāh who emerged thence was but a Jew who impersonated him and played the Mahdi rôle. Others assert that ʿUbaydullāh, far from being an ʿAlid or even an Arab, was in fact a descendant of the Persian ʿAbdullāh ibn-Maymūn al-Qaddāḥ, the second founder after Ismāʿīl of the Ismāʿīlite sect,[3] which had by now become a curious mixture of extreme Shīʿite heretical views, Persian mystic concepts, Syrian gnostic elements and rationalistic views. Pro-ʿAbbāsid historians generally denounce the legitimacy of the Fāṭimid claim. Among modern European scholars several accept the genuineness of the ancestry.[4]

Their vast domain

ʿUbaydullāh (909–34) founded a new capital south-east of al-Qayrawān and named it after himself al-Mahdīyah. His third successor al-Muʿizz (952–75) moved in 973 to Egypt, where his victorious general Jawhar had laid (969) the foundation of a new capital Cairo (al-Qāhirah, the triumphant), destined to become the most populous city of the African continent. In it he built the great university-mosque al-Azhar (the bright one), the oldest extant institution of higher learning

[1] See above, p. 340.

[2] Ibn-Ḥammād, *Akhbār Mulūk bani-ʿUbayd*, ed. M. Vonderheyden (Algiers, 1927), pp. 6, 18; ibn-Khallikān, vol. i, p. 488.

[3] Ibn-Khallikān, vol. i, p. 487; ibn-Taghri-Birdi, vol. ii, pt. 2, p. 112.

[4] P. H. Mamour, *Polemics on the Origin of the Fatimi Caliphs* (London, 1934), pp. 16 *seq.*, 43 *seq.*, 124 *seq.*; W. Ivanow, *Ismaili Tradition concerning the Rise of Fatimids* (Oxford, 1942), pp. xvii-xix, pp. 27 *seq.*, 127 *seq.* (Eng.); cf. Lewis, p. 22.

and still one of the largest educational institutions in the world. Originally a Christian slave probably from Sicily, Jawhar was bought in al-Qayrawān by a Moslem master and rose to the dizzy height of an empire builder.[1] He it was who in 969 drove the Ikhshīdids from Egypt and Syria.[2]

But in Syria Jawhar had many other opponents to contend with. There were the Qarmaṭians, under al-Ḥasan ibn-Aḥmad al-Aʿṣam, receiving aid and encouragement from the ʿAbbāsids. For a time it looked as if al-Aʿṣam would have the upper hand. He occupied Damascus, forced the Fāṭimids to retreat from all the land and ventured to pursue them to their own capital Cairo.[3] Then there were the Byzantines, eager to take advantage of any fresh opportunity and renew their assault on the land they once ruled. Nor were the Turks quiescent. A general of theirs, Aftakīn (Alaftakīn), gained possession of Damascus and started a series of raids on the whole country. It was natural for the Turks and Qarmaṭians to join hands against a common foe. In 977 the second Egyptian Fāṭimid caliph al-ʿAzīz took the field in person and inflicted a crushing defeat on the allied forces outside al-Ramlah.[4] Al-ʿAzīz extended his domain in Syria, especially along the coast, but failed to reduce Aleppo, mainly because of Byzantine intervention.[5] Under him the Fāṭimid empire reached its farthest limits. His sovereignty was recognized from the Atlantic to the Red Sea and in al-Ḥijāz, al-Yaman, Syria and even al-Mawṣil.[6] For fast communication with Syria he used carrier pigeons, a hundred and twenty of which were once used for carrying plums from Damascus to his palace in three or four days. His favourite concubine was a Christian, one of whose brothers the caliph appointed bishop over Cairo and the other over Jerusalem. His vizir was a Christian, ʿĪsa ibn-Nasṭūrūs, whose deputy in Syria was a Jew, Manashsha (Manasseh) ibn-Ibrāhīm. Both were charged with favouritism toward their co-religionists. As the caliph was one day galloping on a fast mule, a woman cast in his way a placard which read: "By Him who glorified the Christians through ʿĪsa and the Jews through Manashsha and

[1] Ibn Khallikān, vol. i, pp. 209-13; Maqrīzi, vol. i, pp. 352, 377 *seq.*

[2] See above, p. 563.

[3] Ibn-Khaldūn, vol. iv, pp. 50-51.

[4] Ibn-al-Qalānisi, pp. 18-19; ibn-Khaldūn, vol. iv, p. 52.

[5] Ibn-al-Qalānisi, p. 29.

[6] Ibn-Taghri-Birdi, vol. ii, pt. 2, p. 10; ibn-Khallikān, vol. iii, p. 54.

mortified the Moslems through you, how about having pity on the Moslems and removing the disabilities under which I have been labouring ?"[1]

Precarious hold

The Fāṭimid hold on Syria was rather precarious and unstable. Not only was it contested by Qarmaṭians, Saljūqs, other Turks and Byzantines but occasionally by natives too, and Bedouins from the desert. In the second year of al-Ḥākim's reign (996–1021)[2] a sailor from Tyre, ʿAllāqah, had the nerve to strike money in his name and declare his city independent. For a time he defied the Egyptian army and with the aid of a Byzantine flotilla stood against the Egyptian fleet. But at last he had to surrender his besieged city and suffer flaying and crucifixion.[3] His skin was filled with hay and exhibited in Cairo.

The Mirdāsids

During al-Ḥākim's reign the Bedouins from the Syrian Desert were encouraged by the prevailing disorders to begin serious raids against Syria. In 1023 Ṣāliḥ ibn-Mirdās, chief of

[1] Cf. Ibn-al-Qalānisi, p. 33; ibn-Taghri-Birdi, vol. ii, pt. 2, p. 4; Suyūṭi, vol. ii, p. 14; abu-al-Fidā', vol. ii, p. 138.

[2] Table of Fāṭimid caliphs:

1. Al-Mahdi (909–34)
2. Al-Qā'im (934–46)
3. Al-Manṣūr (946–52)
4. Al-Mu'izz (952–75)
5. Al-ʿAzīz (975–96)
6. Al-Ḥākim (996–1021)
7. Al-Ẓāhir (1021–35)
8. Al-Mustanṣir (1035–94)

9. Al-Mustaʿli (1094–1101) — (Muḥammad)
10. Al-Āmir (1101–30) — 11. Al-Ḥāfiẓ (1130–49)

(Yūsuf) — 12. Al-Ẓāfir (1149–54)
14. Al-ʿĀḍid (1160–71) — 13. Al-Fā'iz (1154–60)

[3] Ibn-al-Qalānisi, pp. 50-51; ibn-Khaldūn, vol. iv, pp. 56-7.

the Kilāb tribe, wrested the capital of North Syria from Fāṭimid control. The Mirdāsid line held Aleppo, with varying fortunes, for over half a century (1023–79). They allied themselves with the Kalb and the Ṭayyi' tribes. The Kalb blockaded Damascus (1025) and the Ṭayyi' set al-Ramlah on fire (1024). Brigandage, highway robbery and lawlessness which started with the Saljūqs were still thriving throughout the land. But Aleppo itself seems to have maintained its prosperous look. The Persian Ismā'īli traveller Nāṣir-i-Khusraw,[1] who visited it in 1047, refers to merchants there from al-'Irāq, Egypt and Asia Minor and to the customs levied by the Mirdāsids on the merchandise. A letter written to a friend by a Christian Baghdādi physician, ibn-Buṭlān, who visited the city about the same time, gives a bird's-eye view of Mirdāsid Aleppo. The city was enclosed within a wall of white stone with six gates. The ancient castle stood by its wall, and the summit of its hill was crowned by two churches and a mosque. There were six other churches and a congregational mosque in the city (indicating a surprisingly large Christian population). There was also a small hospital. People drank rain water from reservoirs. One market hall had twenty cloth merchants who, for the last twenty years, had been transacting business at the rate of twenty thousand dinars a day.[2]

A blind poet-philosopher: al-Ma'arri

The spirit of the age, with its political anarchy, social decay, intellectual pessimism and religious scepticism, was reflected in the poetry of a North Syrian, abu-al-'Alā' al-Ma'arri (973–1057), whose surname reveals his birthplace, Ma'arrat al-Nu'mān. Abu-al-'Alā' was descended from the Yamanite tribe of Tanūkh. At the age of four he lost one eye as a result of a smallpox attack and later the other. This physical mishap soured him further. The blind young man acquired whatever education he could at Aleppo. Later he visited Baghdād twice.[3] While there the second time he held intercourse with rationalists, Mu'tazilites and philosophers of the Greek schools and joined the circle of a freethinker, but had to hasten back home in 1010, after nineteen months, because of the illness of his mother, who died before his arrival. In Baghdād he probably came in

[1] *Sefer Nāmeh*, ed. Charles Schefer (Paris, 1881), p. 10; tr., p. 32.
[2] Yāqūt, *Buldān*, vol. ii, pp. 306-8.
[3] Ibn-Khallikān, vol. i, p. 59; Yāqūt, *Udabā'*, vol. i, p. 162.

contact with Hindus, who converted him to vegetarianism. "For forty-five years after that he would not eat meat." [1] The remaining years of his life he lived as a bachelor in his native town and is said to have willed that the following verse of his composition be inscribed on his tombstone:

This wrong was by my father done
To me, but ne'er by me to one.[2]

The little income he lived on was earned from his lectures. When the Fāṭimid caliph al-Mustanṣir, al-Ḥākim's grandson, occupied Maʿarrah, he offered its poet all that was in its treasury, but it was refused.[3] Al-Maʿarri lived most of the time in seclusion, referring to himself as *rahīn al-maḥbasayn*, the double-prison (home and blindness) inmate. On one occasion he went out to a suburb of Maʿarrah to plead before Ṣāliḥ ibn-Mirdās the case of sixty insurgent notables of his town whom Ṣāliḥ had taken into custody; they were forthwith released.

Unlike the poets of his day al-Maʿarri did not devote his talent to eulogizing princes and potentates with a view to receiving remuneration; the ode he composed in his early career extolling Sayf-al-Dawlah was evidently never presented to the prince.[4] His later works embody his pessimistic, sceptic philosophy of life and his rational approach to its problems. He included among his correspondents the chief Ismāʿīli propagandist. In his *Risālat al-Ghufrān* (epistle of forgiveness)[5] al-Maʿarri peopled the limbo with reputed heretics and free-thinkers enjoying themselves and discussing textual criticism. It was this treatise that supposedly had a stimulative effect on Dante's *Divine Comedy*.[6] His *Luzūmīyāt*[7] contains some of his most popular poems, in certain of which he anticipates ʿUmar

[1] Yāqūt, vol. i, p. 170.
[2] Ibn-Khallikān, vol. i, p. 59; Nicholson, p. 317.
[3] Yāqūt, vol. i, p. 178.
[4] Al-Maʿarri, *Dīwān: Saqṭ al-Zand*, ed. Shākir Shuqayr (Beirut, 1884), pp. 4 *seq.*
[5] Ed. Kāmil Kīlāni, 2 pts. (Cairo, 1923); partially translated by R. A. Nicholson in *Journal, Royal Asiatic Society* (1900), pp. 637-720; (1902), pp. 75-101, 337-62, 813-47.
[6] Miguel Asín, *Islam and the Divine Comedy*; tr. H. Sunderland (London, 1926).
[7] *Aw Luzūm Ma la Yalzam*, ed. ʿAzīz Zand, 2 vols. (Cairo, 1891–5); parts of it and of *Saqṭ* translated by Ameen F. Rihani as *The Quatrains of abu'l-Ala* (London, 1904).

al-Khayyām. In his *al-Fuṣūl w-al-Ghāyāt* [1] al-Maʿarri tried to imitate the Koran, a sacrilege in Moslem eyes. The philosophy advocated in this work is basically Epicurean. The following verses illustrate his unorthodoxy:

We laugh, but inept is our laughter;
  We should weep and weep sore,
Who are shattered like glass and thereafter
  Re-moulded no more! [2]

Take Reason for thy guide and do what she
  Approves, the best of counsellors in sooth.
Accept no law the Pentateuch lays down:
  Not there is what thou seekest — the plain truth. [3]

Ḥanīfs [Moslems] are stumbling, Christians all astray,
Jews wildered, Magians far on error's way.
We mortals are composed of two great schools —
Enlightened knaves or religious fools. [4]

Al-Maʿarri was one of the few Arabic poets who rose above limitations of time and place to the realm of universal humanity. The thousandth anniversary of his birthday was celebrated in 1944, under the auspices of the Arab Academy of Damascus, in Damascus, Aleppo, al-Lādhiqīyah and Maʿarrat al-Nuʿmān. Delegates from Syria, Lebanon, Transjordan, al-ʿIrāq and Egypt participated and Orientalists from Europe and America contributed essays. The celebration in Damascus was described as the greatest in the cultural history of that city. [5] In connection with these festivities his tomb at his birthplace was renovated and made a public shrine.

The Druzes

The Caliph al-Ḥākim (996–1021) was responsible for the birth of a new sect in Islam, Druzism. The sect derives its name from a Persian Bāṭinite [6] missionary Muḥammad ibn-

[1] Ed. Maḥmūd H. Zanāti, vol. i (Cairo, 1938).
[2] Abu-al-ʿAlā', *Rasā'il*, ed. D. S. Margoliouth (Oxford, 1898), p. 131; Nicholson, p. 316.
[3] *Luzūmīyāt*, vol. i, p. 394; Nicholson, p. 323.
[4] *Luzūmīyāt*, vol. ii, p. 191; Nicholson, p. 318.
[5] *Al-Mahrajān al-Alfi li-abi-al-ʿAlā' al-Maʿarri* (Damascus, 1945), p. 9.
[6] Ar. *bāṭin*, inner, esoteric. This term was applied by orthodox Moslems to those who maintained that the Koran should be interpreted allegorically and that religious truth could be ascertained by the discovery of an inner meaning of which the outer (*ẓāhir*) was but a veil intended to keep the truth from the eyes of the uninitiate. The Ismāʿīlites and Qarmaṭians were Bāṭinites.

Ismāʿīl al-Darazi (Per. for tailor), who was the first to offer public divine veneration to this Fāṭimid caliph.[1] This doctrine of the incarnation of the deity (*Mawlāna*, our lord) in human form, the last and most important manifestation being al-Ḥākim, is basic in the Druze system. The prophets are of comparatively little consequence.

Finding no response for his new creed among the Egyptians, al-Darazi migrated to Wādi al-Taym,[2] at the foot of Mount Hermon in Lebanon, where the hardy freedom-loving mountaineers, evidently already impregnated with ultra-Shīʿite ideas, were ready to give him a hearing.[3] Here he fell in battle in 1019 and was succeeded by his rival Ḥamzah ibn-ʿAli, surnamed al-Hādi (the guide), also a Persian.[4] When al-Ḥākim was assassinated, probably as a result of a conspiracy by his own household, al-Hādi denied his death and proclaimed that he had gone into a state of temporary occultation (*ghaybah*), whence his triumphal return (*rajʿah*) should be expected.[5] Al-Muqtana Bahā'-al-Dīn (d. 1031), Ḥamzah's right hand in the propagation of the new cult, addressed epistles as far as India and Constantinople,[6] but later enunciated a new policy, that pending the "absence" of al-Ḥākim no part of the religion should be divulged or promulgated — a policy doubtless dictated by the desire for safety on the part of a small heterodox minority struggling for existence. Since then "the door has been closed"; no one could be allowed entrance or exit. The hidden imām idea had been elaborately worked out, prior to the rise of Druzism, by a number of ultra-Shīʿite groups (*ghulāh*), chief among which was the Ismāʿīlite.

In his *al-Risālah al-Masīḥīyah* (the Christian epistle)[7] Bahā'-al-Dīn identifies Ḥamzah with the Messiah. In other epistles directed to the Christians he calls them "saints" and

[1] Ibn-Taghri-Birdi, vol. ii, pt. 2, p. 69.

[2] So called after Taym-Allāh (formerly Taym-Allāt), an Arabian tribe which, after having settled in the Euphrates region and become Christianized, moved into southern Lebanon; Ṭabari, vol. i, pp. 2489-90, 2031.

[3] Ibn-Taghri-Birdi, vol. ii, pt. 2, p. 70.

[4] Ibn-Ḥajar al-ʿAsqalāni, "Rafʿ al-Iṣr ʿan Quḍāt Miṣr", in Kindi, ed. Guest, p. 612, calls him al-Zūzani (from Zūzan, in eastern Persia).

[5] For a translation of an excerpt of this proclamation consult Hitti, *The Origins of the Druze People and Religion* (New York, 1928), pp. 61-4.

[6] For a translation of an excerpt of his epistle to Constantine VIII consult Hitti, pp. 64-7.

[7] For a translation of an excerpt consult Hitti, pp. 68-70.

"assemblies of saints", hoping thereby to win them over to his faith. He uses parables that recall those of the New Testament. This would seem to indicate that he was a Christian apostate.[1]

Ḥamzah in behalf of al-Ḥākim absolved his followers of the cardinal obligations of Islam, including fasting and pilgrimage, and substituted precepts enjoining veracity of speech, mutual aid among the brethren in faith, renunciation of all forms of false belief and absolute submission to the divine will. The last precept, involving the concept of predestination, has continued to be a potent factor in Druzism, as in orthodox Islam. Another feature of this cult is the belief in the transmigration of souls. The idea came originally to Islam from India and received an increment of Platonic elements. The Muʿtazilites and Bāṭinites had long before the time of al-Ḥākim accepted some form of the doctrine of metempsychosis, which is still held by modern mystics of Persia and by Bahāʾis. The operation of the second precept of Ḥamzah, enjoining mutual aid, has made of the Druzes an unusually compact self-conscious community presenting more the aspects of a religious fraternal order than those of a sect, and that despite the fact that the community itself is divided into two distinctly marked classes: the initiate (*ʿuqqāl*, wise) and the uninitiate (*juhhāl*, ignorant). The sacred writings, all handwritten, are accessible to the initiated few only and the meeting-places are secluded rooms on hills outside the villages, where Thursday evening sessions are held.

As they tried to gain a permanent footing in southern Lebanon, the Druzes found themselves in conflict with an already established Islamic heterodoxy, the Nuṣayrīyah, whose followers were subsequently driven out into northern Syria, their present habitat. The Druzes had to struggle against other neighbours — Shīʿites and Sunnites. From their original home in southern Lebanon they later spread into the Shūf district, east of Beirut, where the Crusaders found them and where they still flourish. In no city were they able to thrive. The first mention of the Druze people in European literature occurs in the travels of Benjamin of Tudela[2] (*ca.* 1169), when

[1] Silvestre de Sacy, *Exposé de la religion des Druzes* (Paris, 1838), vol. i, p. 83, n. 1.

[2] Vol. i, p. 61.

they were confined to Wādi al-Taym. From al-Shūf some of them, as a result of Qaysite-Yamanite blood feuds, migrated in the early eighteenth century into Ḥawrān in Syria.[1] The influx was augmented by malcontents from Lebanon in the nineteenth century. In Ḥawrān they now number about eighty-six thousand as against seventy-nine thousand in Lebanon. Throughout their entire history they have shown remarkable vigour and exercised in Lebanese and Syrian national affairs influence quite disproportionate to their number.

The Nuṣayrīyah

Another surviving offshoot of the Ismā'īlite body is the Nuṣayrīyah. Its name is derived probably from that of Muḥammad ibn-Nuṣayr of al-Kūfah (fl. late ninth century), a partisan of the eleventh 'Alid imām al-Ḥasan al-'Askari (d. 874).[2] The earliest important references to ibn-Nuṣayr and his followers occur in the writings of Ḥamzah and other early Druze polemicists. The last founder of the sect according to their manuscripts was Ḥusayn ibn-Ḥamdān al-Khaṣībi (d. *ca.* 957), an Ismā'īlite protégé of the Ḥamdānids of Aleppo.[3]

Not much is known about this religion, which is secretive in character, hierarchical in organization and esoteric in doctrine. Its sacred writings have not been exposed to the same extent as those of the Druzes, many of which came to light as a result of communal wars in the nineteenth century. Finding itself a small heterodoxy amidst a hostile majority, the cult chose to go underground. There it has remained, a partially unsolved religious riddle of the Near East.

This much, however, is known. In company with other ultra-Shī'ites (*ghulāh*), the Nuṣayris deify 'Ali. To them he is the final and most important incarnation of the deity.[4] Their late counterparts are the Takhtajis (woodcutters) of western Anatolia, the Qizil-Bāsh (red-heads) of eastern Anatolia and the 'Ali-Ilāhis ('Ali-deifiers) of Persia and Turkestan. The Nuṣayris are, therefore, sometimes referred to as 'Alawites, a name which became current after the French organized the region centring on al-Lādhiqīyah into a separate state under

[1] See above, pp. 42-3.

[2] See above, pp. 450, 502. Cf. abu-al-Fidā', *Taqwīm*, p. 232, n. 3, where the founder is made Nuṣayr, a freedman of 'Ali.

[3] L. Massignon in *Actes du XVIII congrès international des orientalistes* (Leyden, 1931), p. 212.

[4] Shahrastāni, pp. 143-5.

the name Alaouite. In the Crusading chronicles they are termed Nazarei. The cult represents an imposition of extreme Shīʿite ideas directly on a pagan body. In other words it is a survival of pagan Syrian cults under the guise of a Shīʿite heterodoxy. Its adepts must have passed directly from paganism to Ismāʿīlism.[1] Later they appropriated certain superficial Christian features. For instance, they celebrate a mass-like rite, observe Christmas [2] and Easter and bear such names as Matta (Matthew), Jibrāʾīl (Gabriel), Yūḥanna (John), Hīlānah (Helen). Their initiated shaykhs, who correspond to the Druze *ʿuqqāl*, are organized in a three-class hierarchy. The rest of the community constitute the uninitiated masses. Unlike the Druzes, they admit no women into the initiated class. Their meetings are held at night in secluded places. Charges of nocturnal orgies and phallic worship have been brought against them as against other groups who practise their religion in secret.[3]

Today some three hundred thousand Nuṣayris, mostly peasants, occupy the mountainous region of northern and central Syria and are scattered as far as Turkish Cilicia.

Persecution of Christians

On the whole the Christians and Jews fared well under the Fāṭimid régime. It was only during al-Ḥākim's reign that they were re-subjected to the old humiliating disabilities initiated by ʿUmar II and al-Mutawakkil [4] and put under new ones imposed by this caliph, whose mother and vizir were Christians. To the earlier regulations governing clothing to distinguish dhimmis externally from Moslems, which he reactivated, al-Ḥākim in 1009 added that when Christians were in public baths they should display a five-pound cross dangling from their necks, and Jews an equally weighty frame of wood with jingling bells.[5] In the same year he demolished several Christian churches, chief among which were Our Lady in Damascus and the Holy Sepulchre in Jerusalem. By way of implementing the koranic prohibition against wine,[6] he ordered all grapevines uprooted; any such plantation in Egypt must have been under Christian

[1] *Kitāb al-Iʿtibār*, ed. Hitti, pp. 159-60; *Arab-Syrian Gentleman*, p. 190.
[2] R. Strothman in *Der Islam*, vol. xxvii, No. 3 (1946), pp. 175-9.
[3] Conder, *Syrian Stone-Lore*, p. 423, n.
[4] See above, pp. 487-8, 542-4.
[5] Ibn-Khallikān, vol. iii, p. 5; Saʿīd ibn-Baṭrīq, p. 195; Maqrīzi, vol. ii, p. 288; ibn-Ḥammād, p. 54.
[6] For a translation of his edict consult Hitti, *Origins*, pp. 59-60.

cultivation. The caliph invited those of the dhimmis who were unwilling to abide by his regulations to profess Islam or else migrate to the land of the Romans. It seems that in his time, almost four centuries after Muḥammad, the Christians in Egypt and Syria equalled, if not outnumbered, their Moslem compatriots. Twenty years later al-Ḥākim's son and successor al-Ẓāhir, following a treaty with the Byzantine emperor, restored

The American Numismatic Society

A COIN OF AL-ẒĀHIR

Obverse and reverse of a gold dinar of the Fāṭimid caliph al-Ẓāhir struck at Ṣūr (Tyre) A.H. 424 = A.D. 1032/3

the destroyed churches, including the Holy Sepulchre. But the fact remains that the destruction of this shrine of Christendom was a contributory cause of the Crusades.

The behaviour of the blue-eyed Ḥākim, who was enthroned when eleven years old and died at the age of thirty-six, shows strange contradictions. He built an academy in Cairo only to destroy it with its professors three years later. He legislated against sexual immorality and went so far as prohibiting the appearance of women in the Cairo streets. He issued edicts against banquets and music and included certain dishes and chess playing. So freakish was his behaviour that anti-Fāṭimid writers charged him with abnormal psychology.[1] Freakish behaviour of Christian saints, Moslem dervishes and Hindu fakirs is familiar in Oriental annals.

More interested in luxurious living than state administration, al-Ḥākim's successors were unable to maintain order at home or sovereignty abroad. In 1023 Aleppo, capital of North Syria, was wrested away by the Bedouin Mirdāsids; in 1071

[1] Ibn-Khallikān, vol. iii, pp. 4-7; ibn-Khaldūn, vol. iv, pp. 59-61; ibn-Taghri-Birdi, vol. ii, pt. 2, pp. 62 *seq.*; Suyūṭi, *Ḥusn*, vol. ii, pp. 14-15; ibn-al-Qalānisi, pp. 66-7, 79-80; Maqrīzi, vol. ii, pp. 285-9; ibn-Ḥammād, pp. 54-5.

Jerusalem, metropolis of southern Syria, fell into Saljūq hands and five years later Damascus followed suit.[1] In 1098 Jerusalem was recaptured from the Urtuqid vassals of the Saljūqs, only to fall the following year into the hands of a strange and unexpected enemy — the Crusaders.

[1] See above, pp. 573-4, 580-81.

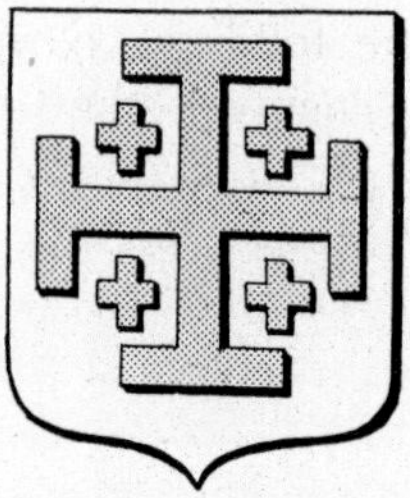

COAT OF ARMS OF THE KINGDOM OF JERUSALEM
On a field of silver a cross potent between four crosslets, gold

CHAPTER XLV

MEETING OF EAST AND WEST: THE CRUSADES

ON November 26, 1095, Pope Urban II, a Frenchman by birth, delivered a fiery speech at Clermont in south-eastern France urging the believers to " enter upon the road to the Holy Sepulchre, wrest it from the wicked race and subject it " to themselves. Judged by its results this was perhaps the most effective speech in history. " *Deus lo volt* " (God wills it) became the rallying cry and was reiterated throughout Europe, seizing high and low as if by a strange psychological contagion.

Complexity of motivation

The response, however, was not all motivated by ideology supplied by the Church. Besides the devout there were the military leaders intent upon new conquests for themselves; the merchants, especially of Genoa, Venice and Pisa, whose interest was more commercial than spiritual; the romantic, the restless, the adventurers ever ready to join a spectacular movement; the criminals and sinful who sought penance through pilgrimage to the land " where His feet once stood "; and the economically and socially depressed individuals to whom " taking the cross " was more of a relief than a sacrifice.[1]

[1] For more on conditions in Europe consult August C. Krey, *The First Crusade* (Princeton, 1921), pp. 24-43.

Other factors, of international character, were involved. The pope's choice of southern France as stage for his initial appeal was not without design. That part of Europe had been overrun by Moslem hordes from Spain.[1] In fact for the past four and a half centuries Islam had been on the offensive against Christendom, first through the Byzantine Empire and then through Spain, Sicily and Italy.[2] It was time for a Christian reaction. Moreover, the year before Urban made his public appeal, the Byzantine emperor Alexius Comnenus, whose Asiatic possessions had been overrun by Saljūqs almost as far as Constantinople,[3] had solicited papal aid against the Moslem invasion. The pope viewed the solicitation as providing an opportunity for healing the schism between the Greek Church and Rome, effected forty years earlier, and establishing himself as head of Christendom.

The first Crusade

By the spring of 1097 some hundred and fifty thousand men, mostly Franks and Normans, had responded. Constantinople was the rendezvous. They bore the cross as a badge; hence the designation Crusaders. The first of the campaigns was thus launched. Its route lay across Asia Minor, then the domain of Qilij Arslān. In June of that year Nicaea, Saljūq headquarters, was captured. In the next month Dorylaeum (modern Eski-Shehr) fell.[4] This victorious march restored to the Byzantine emperor, who had exacted from almost all the Crusading leaders an oath of feudal allegiance, the larger portion of Asia Minor.

The first Latin principality

After crossing the Taurus, the leaders began squabbling among themselves and planning local conquests each for himself. Baldwin, one of the leaders of the Lotharingians from the Rhineland, swung eastward into a territory occupied by Christians. Here al-Ruhā' (Edessa), then under Armenian rule, was occupied early in 1098.[5] The first Latin state was

[1] See above, pp. 463 *seq.*

[2] For the Aghlabid conquest of Sicily from Tunis consult Hitti, *History of the Arabs*, pp. 602, 605, 617, 622.

[3] See above, pp. 573-4.

[4] *Gesta Francorum et aliorum Hierosolymitanorum*, ed. Heinrich Hagemeyer (Heidelberg, 1890), pp. 197, 208; Fulcher, *Historia Hierosolymitana*, ed. Hagemeyer (Heidelberg, 1913), p. 192; ibn-al-Qalānisi, p. 134; tr. H. A. R. Gibb, *The Damascus Chronicle of the Crusades* (London, 1932), p. 42. For a general bibliography on the Crusades consult Claude Cahen, *La Syrie du Nord à l'époque des croisades* (Paris, 1940), pp. 3-104.

[5] Matthew of Edessa, *Chronique*, ed. E. Dulaurier (Paris, 1858), p. 218.

thus founded as the county of Edessa, with Baldwin as its prince. This future king of Jerusalem married an Armenian princess and settled temporarily in the north. Another Crusading chief, Tancred, one of the leaders of the Normans of southern Italy and Sicily, had turned westward into Cilicia, whose population was likewise Armenian with an admixture of Greek. He occupied Tarsus and its territory.

Meantime the bulk of the Crusading army was pouring into Syria, its main objective. North Syria, as noted above, was under virtually independent Saljūq amīrs; South Syria was under the Fāṭimid caliphs.[1] The whole land had for years been a bone of contention between Sunnite Turks and Shīʿite Egyptians. Other parts were held by local Arab chieftains. Tripoli and its territory, for instance, had been since 1089 under the Shīʿite banu-ʿAmmār;[2] Shayzar on the Orontes had been since 1081 under the banu-Munqidh.[3] Local feuds, fraternal jealousies, problems of dynastic succession had engendered a chronic state of political instability. The population itself was far from being able to present a common front. Schismatic communities honeycombed the land: Druzes in southern Lebanon, Nuṣayris in the northern mountains of Syria, Ismāʿīlites and later Assassins inland from the Nuṣayris.[4] Among the Christians the Maronites of northern Lebanon were still speaking Syriac.[5]

Antioch, the second principality

Antioch was the first Syrian city in the way of the Crusading army. It was held by a Saljūq amīr, Yāghi-Siyān,[6] who had received his appointment from the third Great Saljūq (after Ṭughril and Alp Arslān), Malikshāh of Baghdād. As the cradle of the first organized Christian church,[7] this city was of special significance to the Crusaders. The siege was long and arduous (October 2, 1097 to June 3, 1098). Attempts at relief by Riḍwān of Aleppo and Duqāq of Damascus were repelled.[8] The operations were directed by Bohemond, kinsman of Tancred and leader of the Normans, and supported by the Italian fleet,

[1] See above, pp. 579-80.
[2] Consult G. Wiet in *Mémorial Henri Basset* (Paris, 1928), vol. ii, pp. 279-84; ibn-Taghri-Birdi, vol. ii, pt. 2, p. 267.
[3] See below, p. 621.
[4] See above, pp. 583, 586.
[5] See above, p. 521.
[6] Name erroneously transcribed in ibn-al-Athīr, vol. x, p. 187; abu-al-Fidā', vol. ii, p. 220; ibn-Khaldūn, vol. v, p. 20.
[7] Acts 11:26.
[8] See above, pp. 574-6.

which, on this and later occasions, supplied food and siege engines against fortified towns on or near the coast. But it was treachery on the part of a disgruntled Armenian commander of one of the towers that sealed the fate of the city.[1]

No sooner, however, had the besiegers made their entry than they found themselves besieged. Karbūqa, a Saljūq adventurer who had wrested al-Mawṣil from the Arab banu-ʿUqayl,[2] had just arrived from his capital with reinforcements. The suffering from plague and starvation in the course of the twenty-five days that ensued was perhaps the worst ever experienced by Franks[3] in Syria.[4] Only a miraculous event could raise their morale and save the day. The event took the shape of the discovery of the "holy lance", which had pierced the Saviour's side as He hung upon the cross and which had lain buried in an Antiochian church. In a bold sortie the Crusaders repelled the besiegers. Bohemond, the shrewdest and ablest of all the Christian leaders, remained in charge of the newly acquired principality, Antioch and its territory. The Byzantine emperor expected the re-annexation of Antioch to his empire but was disappointed. Even more disappointed was Raymond of Toulouse, wealthy leader of the Provençals, whose men had made the sensational discovery and who sought the lordship of Antioch. Another legend connected with the struggle for Antioch relates to Saint George, regarded by local tradition as a native of al-Ludd (Lydda),[5] who had been put to death under Diocletian (303) and now came to the aid of the harassed Crusaders.[6]

Along the coast

Count Raymond pushed southward. Maʿarrat al-Nuʿmān, native town of al-Maʿarri, was committed to the flames and

[1] Kamāl-al-Dīn in *Recueil*, vol. iii, pp. 580 *seq.*; ibn-al-Qalānisi, p. 135.

[2] At first tributary to the Ḥamdānids (see above, p. 564), the ʿUqaylids succeeded them in al-Mawṣil.

[3] Ar. *Ifranj*, a word which since the Crusades has become synonymous with Europeans.

[4] They even dug up and devoured dead bodies of beasts; William of Tyre, vol. i, p. 271; ibn-al-Qalānisi, p. 136.

[5] William of Tyre, vol. i, p. 332; Ṣāliḥ, p. 16.

[6] Introduced into Europe by the Normans, Saint George was adopted in the fourteenth century as patron saint of England. In the Syrian churches, where his name was connected with the conquest of a dragon and the delivery of a royal princess, he vied for first place in popularity with Saint Sergius (see above, p. 391). The bay of Beirut, on the shore of which he supposedly slew the monster, still bears his name (Khalīj Mār Jurjis). Ludolph von Suchem, *Description of the Holy Land*, tr. Aubrey Stewart (London, 1895), p. 135.

its population was destroyed.[1] Following the Orontes valley, he reached and occupied Ḥiṣn al-Akrād,[2] commanding the strategic pass between the coastal plains and those of the Orontes. Strongly fortified ʿArqah, birthplace of a member of the Syrian dynasty of Roman emperors [3] and now in the amīrate of Tripoli, resisted the siege from February to mid-May. In March, Baldwin's brother, Godfrey of Bouillon (capital of Lower Lorraine), who had marched south by the coast and laid siege to Jabalah, joined Raymond. Under pressure from his own men, who were impatient to reach Jerusalem, and through inducement by presents from ibn-ʿAmmār, amīr of Tripoli, Raymond lifted the siege. Anṭarṭūs,[4] where he hit the shore, offered no resistance. Communication with the Italian fleet was hereafter possible. The coastal route was followed, the same route trodden by Alexander [5] and other conquerors. Al-Lādhiqīyah was avoided presumably because it was being occupied by naval forces of the Byzantines, who had become alienated from the Latins.[6] In al-Batrūn the Crusaders established contacts with the Maronites, " a stalwart race, valiant fighters ", who provided greatly needed guides.[7] Following Tripoli's precedent, the amīr of Beirut offered money and a bountiful supply of provisions.[8] The gardens of Sidon, where the Crusaders pitched their tents by the running water, provided a welcome resting-place for a few days. ʿAkka was reached as early as May 24. Evidently garrisons existed only in a few of the major cities, and the foreign warriors neither molested the natives nor were molested by them. The march must have looked more like a promenade. Passing through Caesarea and Arsūf, they swerved inland through al-Ramlah and on June 7 stood facing the main goal of the entire expedition, the holy city.

[1] Ibn-al-Athīr, vol. x, p. 190, copied by abu-al-Fidā', vol. ii, p. 221. Cf. *Gesta Francorum*, p. 387; Kamāl-al-Dīn in *Recueil*, vol. iii, pp. 586-7.

[2] Literally " castle of the Kurds ", today Qalʿat al-Ḥiṣn; Crac des Chevaliers of the Franks. This " Crac " was originally " Crat ", a corruption of " Akrād ", and is not the same word that appears in Crac de Montréal or Crac des Moabites (below, p. 596, n. 4). Crac des Chevaliers rose on the site of an early fortress built by an amīr of Ḥimṣ in 1031 who planted in it a military colony of Kurds.

[3] See above, p. 344.

[4] Tortosa of the Latin chronicles; see below, p. 609.

[5] See above, p. 232.

[6] Cahen, p. 222.

[7] William of Tyre, vol. ii, p. 459; vol. i, p. 330; Ludolph von Suchem, p. 135.

[8] William of Tyre, vol. i, p. 331.

Jerusalem seized

The Crusaders then numbered some forty thousand, of whom about a half were effective troops.[1] The Egyptian garrison may be estimated at a thousand. At the end of a month's siege conducted by Godfrey, Raymond and Tancred, the city was stormed (July 15) and its population, regardless of age and sex, was subjected to an indiscriminate slaughter. An Arab source [2] puts the number of victims above 70,000, an Armenian [3] at 65,000 and a Latin refers to "heaps of heads and hands and feet to be seen throughout the streets and squares".[4] A third Latin state, by far the most important, came into existence in Syria. At its head stood Godfrey, a devout leader and hard fighter. Allegedly reluctant to wear a crown of gold where the Saviour had worn a crown of thorns, Godfrey chose the title "defender of the Holy Sepulchre".[5]

Godfrey's reign was short, lasting but one year. In it he had a successful encounter with the Egyptians near 'Asqalān which contributed to rendering the Latin position in Jerusalem more secure. This seaport, however, remained the seat of a Fāṭimid garrison and the base of its fleet.[6] Jaffa (Yāfa), which lay in ruins when the Crusaders passed by, was now occupied and special privileges were given therein to the Pisans. Haifa (Ḥayfa) was occupied with the aid of a Venetian fleet.[7] Meantime Tancred was penetrating inland to the Jordan region. Without a hold on the hinterland, as well as the coast, the position of Latin Jerusalem would remain precarious. Baysān, on the route between the Mediterranean and Damascus, was one of his early acquisitions. Nābulus voluntarily submitted. Tancred took up his residence in Tiberias as Godfrey's vassal. In March 1101 he relinquished his fief to succeed his uncle Bohemond of Antioch, who had been taken captive by a Turk while on a campaign in the north.

Baldwin, first king

Godfrey's brother Baldwin, count of Edessa, was called and installed king on Christmas day 1100. He was the real founder

[1] Cf. "Annales de Terre sainte", *Archives de l'orient latin*, vol. ii (Paris, 1884), pt. 2, p. 429; Raimundus de Agiles, "Historia Francorum qui ceperunt Jerusalem", in Migne, *Patrologia Latina*, vol. clv, p. 657; William of Tyre, vol. i, p. 349.

[2] Ibn-al-Athīr, vol. x, p. 194.

[3] Matthew of Edessa, p. 226.

[4] Agiles, p. 659; cf. William of Tyre, vol. i, pp. 370-72.

[5] Agiles, p. 654.

[6] Ibn-Muyassar, *Akhbār Miṣr*, ed. Henri Massé (Cairo, 1919), pp. 39 *seq.*

[7] Ibn-al-Qalānisi, p. 139; ibn-Khallikān, vol. i, p. 101.

of the Latin kingdom. His immediate task was to reduce the coast towns and thus insure sea communication with the homeland and forestall hostile action by the Egyptian fleet. In the seamen of the Italian republics he found eager and greedy allies. These men insisted on a share of the booty, special quarters in the captured towns under the jurisdiction of their own republics and the right of importing and selling merchandise without the payment of taxes[1] — thus enjoying privileges associated with the capitulations. Accordingly Arsūf and Caesarea (Qaysārīyah) were seized in 1101 with the aid of the Genoese and agreed to pay tribute pending a period of truce.[2] Strongly walled ʿAkka capitulated three years later as a result of attacks by Pisan and Genoese ships. In 1110 Beirut was besieged by land and sea for eleven weeks ending May 13, on which it was stormed and many of its inhabitants were slaughtered. The adjacent pine grove, still standing, provided wood for constructing towers, hurling missiles and scaling the city walls.[3] In the same year Sidon was occupied with the aid of a Norwegian fleet of fifty-five ships.[4]

Baldwin extended his kingdom southward, too, with a view to capturing at least part of the Red Sea and Indian Ocean trade. South of the Dead Sea he built (1115) a formidable fortress, al-Shawbak,[5] to guard the caravan route from Damascus to Egypt and al-Ḥijāz. His successors followed the same policy of tightening their grip on the land by constructing castles. Al-Shawbak and al-Karak were the two most strategically located among the seven fortresses in that region.[6] On Baldwin's death in 1118, the kingdom had attained its highest limits, from al-ʿAqabah to Beirut. Secure on its peninsula, Tyre remained in Moslem hands till 1124,[7]

1 William of Tyre, vol. i, pp. 434, 455.

2 Albert of Aix, "Historia Hierosolymitanae expeditionis", Migne, vol. clxvi, p. 575.

3 W. B. Stevenson, *The Crusaders in the East* (Cambridge, 1907), pp. 58-9; William of Tyre, vol. i, pp. 484-5; ibn-al-Qalānisi, pp. 167-8; Ṣāliḥ, pp. 28-9.

4 Ibn-al-Athīr, vol. x, pp. 336-7; ibn-al-Qalānisi, p. 171.

5 Called by the Latins Mons Regalis (Mont Royal, Montréal). According to early chronicles Crac de Montréal refers to its sister to the north-east, Crac des Moabites (biblical Kir of Moab), Ar. al-Karak, planted *ca.* 1140. This "Crac" is a corruption of Ar. *karak*, from Aram. *karkha*, town.

6 For more on these castles consult Camille Enlart, *Les Monuments des croisades*, 2 vols. (Paris, 1925–8).

7 See above, p. 576.

and ʿAsqalān as late as 1153. In breadth the kingdom did not reach far beyond the Jordan.

Expansion in the north

The Latin countries to the north were likewise expanding. Raymond,[1] who had had his eye on Tripoli (Ṭarābulus) ever since he passed there, returned after the capture of Jerusalem and laid siege to the town. In order to isolate it he built in 1103 a castle, Château Pèlerin,[2] on an adjacent hill named Mons Pelegrinus (pilgrims' hill). The site soon became the centre of a Latin quarter. The siege dragged slowly on despite reinforcements from the neighbouring mountain.[3] Tripoli had a population of 20,000 and its main industries were glass and paper. At intervals adjacent towns were reduced, mostly with the aid of a Genoese fleet. Al-Marqab marked the northern limit of the county of Tripoli, Jubayl the southern limit. Tripoli itself did not fall until 1109, four years after Raymond's death. Evidently the city had become a centre of Shīʿite learning under the banu-ʿAmmār with schools and libraries, all of which were now obliterated.[4] Al-Maʿarri was among the notables who had used the Tripoli library.

Farther north al-Lādhiqīyah was seized by Tancred in 1103 and Apamea three years later. Both were added to the principality of Antioch, which at times included parts of Cilicia.

At the death of Baldwin II (1118–31) the Latin kingdom with its fiefs stood complete. All three Latin states in the north — Tripoli, Antioch and Edessa — owed nominal allegiance to the king of Jerusalem. The success was remarkable and must have inspired the Franks with confidence and an optimistic outlook. But in reality the prospects were not so bright. Except in the very north and south, the area was limited to the littoral — a narrow Christian territory set against a dark background of Islam. Not a town was more than a day's march from the enemy. Inland cities, such as Aleppo,[5] Ḥamāh, Ḥimṣ, Baʿlabakk,[6] Damascus, were never conquered, though

[1] Because he was called Raymond of Saint-Gilles, the Arabs referred to him as Ṣanjīl or ibn-Ṣanjīl.

[2] Repaired by the Turks, this Qalʿat Ṭarābulus was used by them as a prison, and in the second world war as an anti-aircraft station by the British.

[3] Ibn-Khaldūn, vol. v, p. 186.

[4] Ibn-al-Qalānisi, p. 163; ibn-al-Athīr, vol. x, pp. 333-4; Sibṭ ibn-al-Jawzi, *Mirʾāt al-Zamān*, ed. James R. Jewett (Chicago, 1907), p. 17; William of Tyre, vol. i, pp. 477-8.

[5] William of Tyre, vol. ii, p. 22.

[6] William of Tyre, vol. ii, p. 413.

occasionally attacked. At times they paid tribute; Damascus paid it to Baldwin II in 1126.[1] The fertile Biqāʻ lay within the territory of this city. In their own states the Franks were but

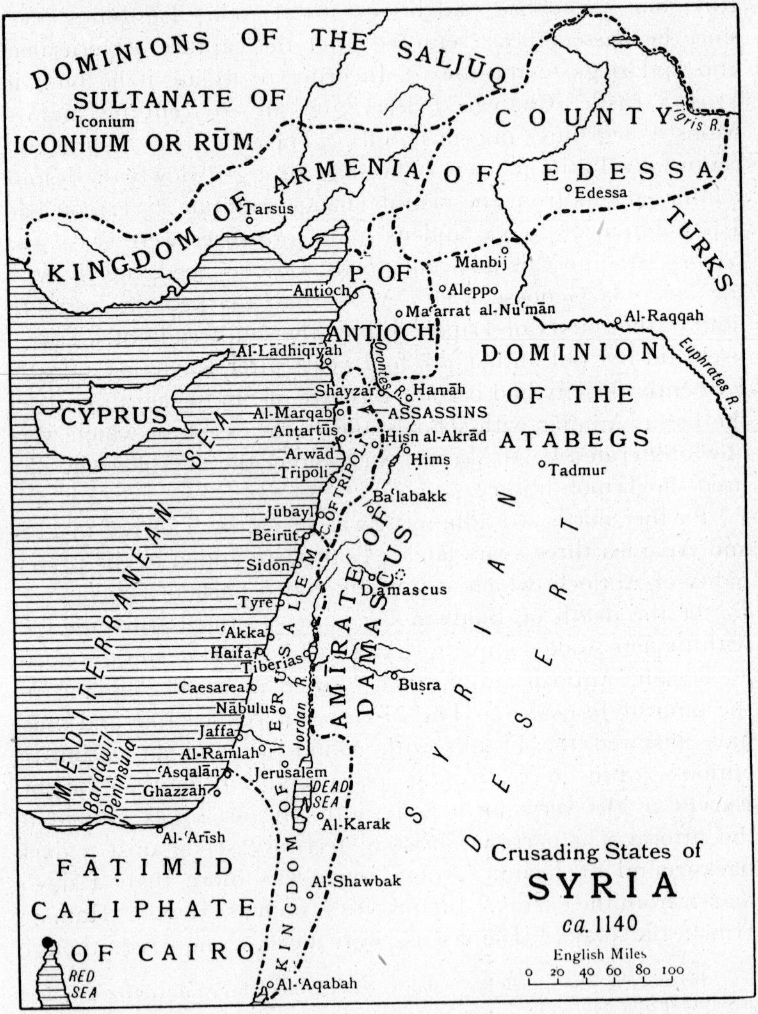

thinly dispersed. Even in Jerusalem and other occupied cities they never formed more than a minority. After the capture of Jerusalem a number of them, considering their vows fulfilled,

[1] In the year beginning Sept. 1156 its ruler Nūr-al-Dīn paid 8000 dinars; ibn-al-Qalānisi, p. 336.

sailed back home. Clearly such exotic states could hold their own only as long as they received a constant supply of fresh recruits from home and the forces of opposition were not unified under strong leadership.

Moslem reaction: Zangi

With the rise of the blue-eyed Turkish Atābeg Zangi (1127–1146), lord of al-Mawṣil and Aleppo,[1] the elements of unification and leadership began to make their appearance. With Zangi a series of anti-Crusading heroes commenced. His were the first hammer-strokes under which the Latin states were to crumble away. The first blow fell on al-Ruhā', northern bulwark of these states. A four-week siege in 1144 ended in its capture from Joscelin II.[2] First among the states to rise, al-Ruhā' was the first to fall. Its fall marks the beginning of the turn of the tide in favour of Islam. On the European side it provoked the so-called second Crusade (1147–9).

The usual classification of the Crusades, however, into a fixed number of campaigns is artificial, as the stream was somewhat continuous and the line of demarcation not sharply drawn. A more satisfactory division would be into first a period of Latin conquest extending to 1144; second a period of Moslem reaction inaugurated by Zangi and culminating in the brilliant victories of Ṣalāḥ-al-Dīn; and third a period of petty wars, coinciding roughly with the thirteenth century, in which the Ayyūbids and the Mamlūks figured and which ended in driving all Crusaders out of the land.

Nūr-al-Dīn

The championship of the Islamic cause passed from Zangi to his son Nūr-al-Dīn (the light of the faith) Maḥmūd. More capable than his father, Nūr in 1154 wrested Damascus from a successor of Ṭughtagīn,[3] thereby removing the last barrier between Zangid territory and Jerusalem. For many years past Damascus had been a virtual ally of Jerusalem.[4] Ṣarkhad (Ṣalkhad), Buṣra, Bāniyās under the Ismā'īlites and other towns in the Damascene territory at times sought Latin aid in their wars against other Moslems.[5] The banu-Faḍl of the

[1] See above, p. 576.
[2] Abu-Shāmah, vol. i, pp. 36-7; ibn-al-Athīr in *Recueil*, vol. ii, pt. 2, pp. 118 *seq.*
[3] See above, p. 576; ibn-al-Athīr, vol. xi, pp. 130-31.
[4] Ibn-al-Qalānisi (who at this time held a high position in the Damascus government), pp. 308-9; William of Tyre, vol. ii, pp. 76-7, 105-6, 147-8, 224; abu-Shāmah, vol. i, p. 77.
[5] Ibn-al-Qalānisi, pp. 289-90, 314, 316; abu-al-Fidā', vol. iii, pp. 2-3.

Ṭayyi', perhaps the most influential of the tribes in the Syrian Desert, allied themselves at times with the Franks and at other times with the Fāṭimids.[1] Latin Jerusalem had in its service a body of light cavalry, called Turcopuli (sons of Turks),[2] recruited from Moslems, besides an infantry corps of Armenians and a contingent of Maronite archers.[3] With the seizure of Damascus the Nūrid realm extended from al-Mawṣil to Ḥawrān. The crescent was extending its horn southward.

Realizing the decrepit condition of the Fāṭimids and the advantage of placing Jerusalem where it could be crushed between an upper and a lower millstone, Nūr dispatched an able lieutenant of his, Shīrkūh, to Egypt. Here he succeeded in 1169, through diplomatic and military victories, in receiving the vizirate under the Caliph al-'Āḍid (1160–71). Two months after his investiture Shīrkūh died and his mantle fell on his brother's son Ṣalāḥ-al-Dīn (the rectitude of the faith, Saladin) ibn-Ayyūb.[4]

Enter Ṣalāḥ-al-Dīn

Al-Malik al-Nāṣir (the defender-king) al-Sulṭān Ṣalāḥ-al-Dīn Yūsuf was born in Takrīt on the Tigris in 1138 of Kurdish parents. When a year old he moved with the family to Ba'labakk, over which his father Ayyūb (Job) was appointed commander by Zangi. The interests of the young man were evidently theological, rather than military. Only reluctantly did he accompany his uncle in 1164 on his first Egyptian campaign.[5] The trip, however, marked the beginning of a new career, a career devoted to the pursuit of three objectives: replacing Shī'ite with Sunnite Islam in Egypt, uniting Egypt and Syria under one sceptre and pressing the holy war against the Franks. The first proved to be the easiest to realize. As al-'Āḍid lay on his deathbed in 1171, Ṣalāḥ as vizir simply substituted in the Friday prayer the name of the contemporary 'Abbāsid caliph al-Mustaḍī'. Thus came to its end the Fāṭimid caliphate. Incredible as it may seem, the momentous change

1 Ibn-Khaldūn, vol. vi, pp. 6 *seq.*; A. S. Tritton in *Bulletin, School of Oriental and African Studies*, vol. xii (1948), p. 567.

2 'Imād-al-Dīn, p. 425; Usāmah, p. 51; tr. p. 79.

3 Cf. Jacques de Vitry, *The History of Jerusalem*, tr. Aubrey Stewart (London, 1896), p. 79.

4 Abu-Shāmah, vol. i, pp. 160-61; Sibṭ ibn-al-Jawzi, p. 175.

5 Ibn-al-Athīr, vol. xi, p. 223; abu-Shāmah, vol. i, p. 155; abu-al-Fidā', vol. iii, p. 47.

was effected without even "the butting of two goats".[1] Thereby Ṣalāḥ became the sole ruler of Egypt. The second ambition of his life was realized when his Syrian suzerain Nūr-al-Dīn passed away. A few minor engagements snatched Syria from the hands of the eleven-year-old son of Nūr, Ismā'īl.[2] With the first two goals attained, the third entered the range of vision.

As adjuncts of Egypt, Cyrenaica and al-Ḥijāz immediately became parts of the newly rising Syro-Egyptian domain. Ṣalāḥ's elder brother Tūrān-Shāh added Nubia and al-Yaman. The 'Abbāsid caliph granted Ṣalāḥ in 1175 at his own request a diploma of investiture over all these lands, thereby giving away what in reality was not his to give but what it was flattering to him not to refuse. The incorporation of al-Mawṣil and its Mesopotamian dependencies rounded out the sultanate.[3] Nūr-al-Dīn's dream of enveloping the Franks and crushing them to death was becoming a reality through the achievements of his more illustrious successor.

The decisive encounter: Ḥiṭṭīn

At last Ṣalāḥ was free to concentrate on "the infidels". The hour of peril for the Latin kingdom struck when, after a six-day siege, Tiberias fell and the Moslem army moved to the adjacent Ḥiṭṭīn (Ḥaṭṭīn).[4] There the battle was joined July 3 to 4, 1187. The heat was intense. Exhausted from the long march and crazed with thirst, the heavy-armoured Franks were surrounded by light-armoured Moslems and subjected to an incessant shower of arrows the like of which they never experienced before. Of the 20,000 knights[5] and footmen only a few remained alive through apostasy or escape; the rest were slaughtered or captured. The prisoners' procession was headed by none other than the king of Jerusalem, Guy de Lusignan. He was received in a way worthy of his high office by a magna-

[1] Ibn-al-Athīr, vol. xi, p. 242; abu-al-Fidā', vol. iii, p. 53; cf. abu-Shāmah, vol. i, pp. 200-201.

[2] Ibn-al-Athīr, vol. xi, pp. 274-5.

[3] Ibn-al-Athīr, vol. xi, pp. 319-21.

[4] The "horns" (*qurūn*) of Ḥiṭṭīn tower 1700 feet above the Sea of Galilee and represent the crater of an extinct volcano. Tradition assigns the Sermon on the Mount to this site.

[5] Templars and Hospitallers. The Templars, so called because their first residence was near the site of Solomon's Temple, were organized about 1119 to protect pilgrims on their way to the Holy Land. The Hospitallers, or Knights of St. John of Jerusalem, sprang from an earlier organization established to maintain hostels (not hospitals) for pilgrims and later devoted to military pursuits. Both orders took monastic vows.

nimous and chivalrous sultan. But his companion Reginald of Châtillon, lord of al-Karak,[1] merited and received a different treatment. In violation of treaty relations, he had more than once attacked pilgrim and commercial caravans as they passed by his castle on the main route south of Jerusalem. The sultan's sister was once in such a caravan. As adventurous as he was unscrupulous, Reginald had with his Red Sea fleet harassed both the Nubian and the Arabian coasts; he even landed on the holy soil of al-Ḥijāz and moved toward Medina. When within a short day's march from the holy city itself, he was driven back by Egyptians transported on a hurriedly constructed fleet. It was rumoured that he aimed at removing the Prophet's body to al-Karak and charging a heavy fee for Moslem pilgrims to view it.[2] Ṣalāḥ had sworn to slay him with his own hand and the time had come for the fulfilment of his oath. The drink of cold water taken by the chained captive in his captor's tent did not guarantee impunity according to Arab hospitality rites, as it was not offered but requested. Guy shook in his boots as Ṣalāḥ slew his captive but was reassured by him: "A king does not kill a king".[3]

The destruction on the day of Ḥiṭṭīn of the Frankish army, which comprised besides the capital's garrison contingents from the other states, sealed the fate of the Latin kingdom. After a week's siege Jerusalem capitulated on October 2. Ṣalāḥ's treatment of the Frankish populace stood in sharp contrast with the treatment accorded the Moslems eighty-eight years earlier. Those who could ransom themselves individually did so; the poor were allowed forty days to collect a lump sum for ransom and the rest were sold as slaves. The lands of the evacuated Franks were purchased by troops and native Christians.[4] From Jerusalem the tide of conquest continued, engulfing such fortifications as al-Shawbak and al-Karak in the south, Kaw-

[1] See above, p. 596, n. 4.

[2] Ibn-Jubayr (pp. 58-60) witnessed in Alexandria the remnant of his army, chained on to camels and facing the tails, as they were led to execution to the sound of drums. Abu-al-Fidā', vol. iii, pp. 68-9.

[3] Abu-Shāmah, vol. ii, pp. 75 *seq.*, who gives an eye-witness' report; ibn-al-Athīr, vol. xi, pp. 352-5; Bahā'-al-Dīn ibn-Shaddād, *Sīrat Ṣalāḥ-al-Dīn* (Cairo, 1317), pp. 27, 60-65; tr. *'Saladin': or, What Befell Sultan Yūsuf* (London, 1897), pp. 42-3, 110-17; 'Imād-al-Dīn al-Iṣfahāni, *al-Fatḥ al-Qussi fi al-Fatḥ al-Qudsi*, ed. C. de Landberg (Leyden, 1888), pp. 22-8; Ernoul and Bernard le Trésorier, *Chronique*, ed. M. L. de Mas Latrie (Paris, 1871), pp. 172-4.

[4] Ibn-Khaldūn, vol. v, p. 311.

kab,[1] al-Shaqīf [2] and Ṣihyawn (Saone) to the north. ʿAsqalān, ʿAkka, Ṣafad, Ṭarṭūs, Jabalah, al-Lādhiqīyah, all fell before the end of 1189.[3] Only Tyre, Tripoli and Antioch, other than smaller towns and castles, remained in Frankish hands.[4]

ʿAkka, centre of activity

The loss of the holy city aroused Europe and inspired the "Third Crusade". In it participated the three mightiest sovereigns of Western Europe, Frederick Barbarossa of Germany, Philip Augustus of France and Richard I Cœur de Lion of England. Legend and history have collaborated to make this campaign, with Richard and Ṣalāḥ as its chief heroes, one of the truly spectacular and romantic periods in Occidental and Oriental annals.

The king of Germany took the land route and was drowned crossing a river in Cilicia. Discouraged, many of his followers returned home. ʿAkka was decided on by the Syrian Latins as providing the key for the restoration of the lost domain. Against it marched all available warriors augmented by the new arrivals from Europe. King Guy led the attack despite the fact that he had pledged his honour to Ṣalāḥ after Ḥiṭṭīn never again to bear arms against him. The city was besieged. Ṣalāḥ rushed to its rescue and pitched his camp facing the enemy.

> About the trench was fought the battle
> 'Twixt God's men and the pagan cattle.[5]

The Franks had the decided advantage of a fleet and up-to-date siege artillery. For two years (August 27, 1189 to July 12, 1191) the operations, considered among the major ones in the military annals of the Middle Ages, dragged on. The Moslem governor of Beirut used native Christian mariners dressed like Franks and accompanied by pigs to carry food by sea to the besieged city.[6] Spectacular feats of valour are recorded on

[1] A newly built Crusading castle north of Baysān by the Jordan. Its full name was Kawkab al-Hawā' (the star of the sky), Belvoir in Latin sources.

[2] The Belfort of Latin chronicles. Hanging like an eagle's nest on a precipitous rock 1500 feet above al-Līṭāni River (Leontes), this fortress commands the mountain pass from Damascus to Sidon. Its full name, Shaqīf (Syr. for huge rock) Arnūn (Syr. for rushing stream, cf. Arnon, above, p. 167), suggests its ancient origin. Arnūn is considered by some a corruption of Arnold.

[3] Al-Maqrīzi, *Kitāb al-Sulūk li-Maʿrifat al-Mulūk*, ed. M. Muṣṭafa Ziyādah, vol. i, pt. 1 (Cairo, 1934), pp. 99-101.

[4] Ibn-Shaddād, pp. 65 *seq.*; ʿImād-al-Dīn, pp. 136 *seq.*; Ernoul and Bernard, pp. 179 *seq.*, 251.

[5] Ambroise, *The Crusade of Richard Lion-Heart*, tr. Merton J. Hubert, John L. La Monte (New York, 1941), p. 145.

[6] Abu-Shāmah, vol. ii, p. 161.

both sides. A Damascene coppersmith forewent the sultan's in favour of Allah's reward for having burned three of the besiegers' towers with explosives he compounded.[1] One flint stone taken from Sicily by Richard for his mangonels reportedly destroyed thirteen 'Akkans and was exhibited to Ṣalāḥ as a curiosity. Swimmers and carrier pigeons were employed between Ṣalāḥ and the beleaguered town. The dead body of such a swimmer was washed out and the 'Akkans received the money and letters he carried, prompting Ṣalāḥ's biographer [2] to remark: "Never before has it been known that someone received a trust in his lifetime and delivered it after his death" Finally, after Ṣalāḥ had sought but did not receive aid from the caliph, the garrison surrendered.

Included in the conditions of surrender were the restoration of the "true cross", captured at Ḥiṭṭīn, and the release of the garrison on the payment of 200,000 gold pieces.[3] But the money was not paid in a month and the Lion-Hearted ordered the twenty-seven hundred captives slaughtered.[4]

Rich in romantic ideas, Richard proposed a marriage between his sister and Ṣalāḥ's younger brother al-Malik al-'Ādil with the understanding that the couple would receive as a wedding present both 'Akka and Jerusalem and therewith the Christian-Moslem conflict would end [5] Al-'Ādil's son, al-Malik al-Kāmil, was in May 1192 ceremoniously knighted by Richard. His uncle Ṣalāḥ had been years before similarly admitted to the honours of Christian knighthood. Richard and Ṣalāḥ exchanged gifts but never met. On November 2, 1192, peace was concluded on the general basis that the coast belonged to the Latins and the interior to the Moslems and that the Christian pilgrims should not be molested. Palestine was partitioned. Richard bade Syria farewell and returned home:

> Ah, Syria, I now commend
> You to the Lord God! May He lend
> Me time enough, if He so will
> That I may yet relieve your ill!
> For still I think to succour you.[6]

[1] Ibn-Khaldūn, vol. v, p. 321.
[2] Ibn-Shaddād, p. 120.
[3] Abu-Shāmah, vol. ii, p. 188; 'Imād-al-Dīn, p. 357; ibn-al-'Ibri, pp. 386-7; abu-al-Fidā', vol. iii, pp. 83-4.
[4] Benedict of Peterborough, ed. W. Stubbs (London, 1867), vol. ii, p. 189; ibn-Shaddād, pp. 164-5.
[5] Cf. abu-al-Fidā', vol. iii, p. 84.
[6] Ambroise, p. 447.

Early in March of the following year Ṣalāḥ died of fever, aged fifty-five. His tomb, still standing by the Umayyad Mosque, is one of the most revered shrines in the Syrian capital.

More than a warrior and champion of orthodox Islam, Ṣalāḥ was a builder and a patron of learning. He founded schools, seminaries and mosques in both Egypt and Syria and included

The American Numismatic Society

A COIN OF ṢALĀḤ-AL-DĪN

Obverse and reverse of a silver dirham of Ṣalāḥ-al-Dīn struck at Dimashq (Damascus), A.H. 573 = A.D. 1177/8

in his cabinet two learned vizirs, al-Qāḍi al-Fāḍil [1] and ʿImād-al-Dīn al-Iṣfahāni.[2] His private secretary and biographer was Bahā'-al-Dīn ibn-Shaddād.[3] The vast collection of treasures of the Fāṭimid court [4] which fell into his hands on the overthrow of the caliphate, he distributed among his men, leaving nothing for himself. One of those treasures was a seventeen-dirham sapphire as weighed by the historian ibn-al-Athīr [5] in person. Styled *al-jabal* (the mountain), this stone, " which shone at night like a lamp ", supposedly once belonged to the Saljūqs, the ʿAbbāsids — of whom al-Rashīd one day dropped it into the Tigris — and the Chosroes.[6] Nūr-al-Dīn's estate Ṣalāḥ passed on to the deceased ruler's son. The estate he himself left amounted to forty-seven dirhams and one gold piece,[7] but the memory he left is still a priceless treasure in the heritage of

[1] Ibn-Khallikān, vol. i, pp. 509 *seq.*; al-Subki, *Ṭabaqāt al-Shāfiʿīyah al-Kubra* (Cairo, 1324), vol. iv, pp. 253-4.

[2] Ibn-Khallikān, vol. ii, pp. 495 *seq.*; Suyūṭi, *Ḥusn*, vol. i, p. 270. His *al-Fatḥ* was drawn upon in the composition of this chapter.

[3] Ibn-Khallikān, vol. iii, pp. 428 *seq.* His *Sīrah* has been extensively used in this chapter.

[4] Maqrīzi, vol. i, pp. 414-16; ibn-Taghri-Birdi, ed. Popper, vol. iii, pt. 1, pp. 85-6.

[5] Vol. xi, p. 242.

[6] Ibn-al-Athīr, vol. vi, p. 74; vol. x, p. 266; Masʿūdi, vol. vii, p. 376; Ṭabari, vol. iii, pp. 602, 1647.

[7] Abu-al-Fidā', vol. iii, p. 9.

the Arab East. The memory of his chivalry is almost equally cherished in Europe, where it has touched the fancy of English minstrels as well as modern novelists.[1]

After Ṣalāḥ-al-Dīn's death

With the death of the great hero of Islam the third period in Crusading history begins, that of dissension and petty wars covering a century. Throughout the thirteenth century European public sentiment remained indifferent to these campaigns. Only those of St. Louis, king of France, in the middle of that century, could be compared with the first Crusade as being motivated by religious considerations. Several of the Crusades of this period were directed against Egypt with the expectation of reaching the Red Sea and participating in the opulent commerce of the Indian Ocean and on the pretext that the occupation of Dimyāṭ (Damietta) or Alexandria, for instance, might result in an exchange for Jerusalem. The Moslems also had lost the spirit of the *jihād*. What was equally serious they had lost the unified leadership and a united domain. Syria was partitioned among Ṣalāḥ's three sons, but shortly thereafter Ṣalāḥ's younger brother al-ʿĀdil acquired sovereignty over Egypt and most of Syria.[2] Throughout his rule al-ʿĀdil (*ca.* 1199–1218, the Saphadin [3] of Latin chronicles) tried to maintain cordial relations with the Franks. This policy aimed at peace and the furtherance of trade with the Italians.

From al-ʿĀdil sprang a variety of Ayyūbid branches which reigned in Egypt, Damascus and Mesopotamia. Other branches arose in Ḥimṣ, Ḥamāh and al-Yaman.[4] In the course of the ensuing dynastic turmoils one after another of Ṣalāḥ's conquests — Beirut, Ṣafad, Tiberias, even Jerusalem (1229) — reverted to Frankish hands. Jerusalem was turned over by al-Kāmil (1218–38), son of al-ʿĀdil, to Frederick II, king of Sicily, in accordance with a ten-year treaty in which al-Kāmil was guaranteed Frederick's aid against his enemies, most of whom were Ayyūbids.[5] Al-Kāmil's nephew, however, al-Malik al-Ṣāliḥ Najm-al-Dīn, utilized in 1244 a contingent of Khwārizm

[1] A Damascene poet who knew Ṣalāḥ personally attacked the character of the lame Ṣalāḥ; ibn-ʿUnayn, *Dīwān*, ed. Khalīl Mardam (Damascus, 1946), pp. 6, 210-11; another contemporary poet ibn-al-Sāʿāti, *Dīwān*, ed. Anīs K. al-Maqdisi, vol. i (Beirut, 1938), pp. 19-21, devotes several odes to the glorification of the hero.

[2] See below, p. 627.

[3] From his honorific title Sayf-al-Dīn (the sword of religion). Ibn-Khallikān, vol. ii, p. 446.

[4] See below, pp. 627-9.

[5] Abu-al-Fidā', vol. iii, p. 148; ibn-al-Athīr, vol. xii, p. 315.

Turks, dislodged from their Central Asian abode by Chingīz Khān, to restore the city to Islam. But the Franks were in no position to capitalize on Moslem dissension. They themselves were in as bad a situation, with rivalries between Genoese and Venetians, jealousies between Templars and Hospitallers and quarrels among the leaders. In these quarrels it was no more unusual for one side to secure Moslem aid against the other than it was for the Moslems to secure Christian aid against other Moslems.[1]

St. Louis

The mid-thirteenth century was marked by the advent of Louis, king of France and leader of the " sixth Crusade " (first directed against Egypt). Louis spent four years in Syria (1250–1254), where he fortified Jaffa, Caesarea, ʿAkka and Sidon.[2]

The American Numismatic Society

A CRUSADING COIN

Obverse and reverse of a silver bezant with Arabic inscription struck by the Crusaders at ʿAkka about A.D. 1250. The obverse bears the mint, the date and the legend: " One God, one faith, one Baptism "; the reverse: " The Father, the Son, the Holy Ghost, one God ".

Ruins of the castle in Sidon, garrisoned by Templars, where he stayed, are still standing. Of all the Crusading leaders his, by far, was the purest, the noblest character — that of a real saint.

Baybars, leader of the counter-Crusade

A new and unexpected danger, however, was now threatening from the East: the Tartars. Mongol hordes were flooding northern Syria and advancing southward. Concurrently Ayyūbids were giving way to Mamlūks.[3] Fourth among these was al-Malik al-Ẓāhir Baybars (1260–77), who inaugurated the series of sultans who dealt the final blows to Latin Syria. Baybars checked in Palestine the Mongols' first advance,[4] recovered their Syrian conquests, reunited Egypt and Syria and was then able to pursue the holy war. From 1263 to 1271

[1] See above, p. 599. [2] Joinville, pp. 223-331. [3] See below, p. 629.
[4] See below, p. 631.

he conducted almost annual raids against the Frankish establishments. One after the other they yielded. Even the Templars and the Hospitallers, who, entrenched in strong castles, formed the bulwark of the Latin states, were unable to withstand his reiterated blows. In 1263 Baybars occupied al-Karak and demolished the venerated church of Nazareth (al-Nāṣirah). Two years later he captured Caesarea by surprise, and after a forty-day siege received the surrender of Arsūf from the Hospitallers.[1] In 1266 Ṣafad capitulated and its garrison of two thousand Templars were executed, despite amnesty granted by him.[2] The walls of the city still bear the inscription of "the Alexander of his age and the pillar of his faith"; the bridge he built across the Jordan shows a lion on each side of his inscription. In 1268 Jaffa was seized, Shaqīf Arnūn capitulated, and what is more significant, Antioch surrendered. Of Antioch's garrison and people 16,000 were put to the sword and reportedly 100,000 were led to captivity. A young boy fetched twelve dirhams and a young girl five. The city itself, with its ancient citadel and world-renowned churches, was given to the flames, a blow from which it has never recovered.[3]

The fall of Antioch, second of the Latin states to be founded, had its demoralizing effect. A number of minor Latin strongholds were thereupon abandoned. In 1271 the tenacious Ḥiṣn al-Akrād, principal retreat of the Hospitallers and the most admirable of all medieval castles in preservation, surrendered after a short siege (March 24 to April 8). For many years this castle, which belonged to the count of Tripoli and could house as many as two thousand at a time, watched the passage connecting the northern Lebanon littoral with Syria, just as al-Shaqīf watched the southern passage. It headed the list of the mountain-type castles set to dominate the passes that led from the Moslem hinterland to the Frankish seaboard. Other forts of the same type were Miṣyāf,[4] al-Qadmūs, al-Kahf and

[1] Ibn-al-Furāt, *Ta'rīkh*, ed. Costi K. Zurayq, vol. vii (Beirut, 1942), p. 82.

[2] Al-Maqrīzi, *Kitāb al-Sulūk fi Ma'rifat Duwal al-Mulūk*, tr. M. Quatremère, *Histoire des sultans mamlouks* (Paris, 1854), vol. i (pt. 2), pp. 29-30; abu-al-Fidā', vol. iv, p. 3.

[3] Ibn-al-'Ibri, p. 500; Maqrīzi, tr. Quatremère, vol. i (pt. 2), pp. 52-4; abu-al-Fidā', vol. iv, pp. 4-5.

[4] Also Maṣyāf, Maṣyād, Maṣyāt, Maṣyāth; see art. Maṣyād, *Encyclopaedia of Islām*; Usāmah, p. 148; tr., p. 177; Dussaud *et al.*, *Syrie antique*, pl. 128. Ismā'īlites still live there.

al-Khawābi, all of which belonged to the Assassins, allies of the Hospitallers. These fortifications, of which Miṣyāf was the strongest, lay in the Nuṣayrīyah region and were now reduced. Both Anṭarṭūs [1] (Tortosa), principal fortress of the Templars,[2] and al-Marqab,[3] garrisoned by Hospitallers, hastened to make peace. These two castles represented the coastal type planted

Photo taken 1923

ḤIṢN AL-AKRĀD, CRAC DES CHEVALIERS, ONE OF THE STRONGEST AND LARGEST OF THE CRUSADER CASTLES

This castle stood sentinel over the Ḥimṣ-Tripoli road

to control the maritime road and ports and to defend them against the fleet centred in Egypt. Of the Ṭarṭūs castle not much is left, but al-Marqab is still perched like a dreadnought on a hill. The famous geographer al-Idrīsi,[4] who visited Syria shortly before this time, cites no less than sixteen forts between Beirut and al-Lādhiqīyah. Modern research indicates that the Byzantine art of fortification lies at the base of the development

[1] Antaradus (opposite the isle of Aradus), modern Ṭarṭūs; Ṭaraṭūs in Yaqūt, vol. iii, p. 529.

[2] Their chief inland stronghold was Chastel Blanc, now Burj Ṣāfīta, a Greek Orthodox church.

[3] "Watchtower", Castrum Mergathum, Margat.

[4] Ed. Gildemeister, pp. 16-23.

of the military Crusading architecture in both its Christian and Moslem aspects.[1]

The Assassins

The Assassins were a Neo-Ismā'īlite order inaugurated by al-Ḥasan ibn-al-Ṣabbāḥ, who in 1090 set up his headquarters in a fortress, Alamūt,[2] in the Alburz Mountain. They acquired their name from Arabic *ḥashīsh*,[3] the intoxicating hemp (marijuana), to which they supposedly resorted when they operated. The order was a secret organization headed by a grand master below whom stood priors followed by propagandists. Near the bottom were the *fidā'is*[4] ready to execute at all cost the grand master's orders. The *fidā'is* made free and treacherous use of the dagger against Christians and Moslems alike; they made assassination an art.

About the same time that the Crusaders were entering Syria from the north-west the Assassins were entering it from the north-east. Their first important convert was the Saljūq amīr Riḍwān[5] (d. 1113); their first stronghold was Bāniyās.[6] By 1140 they had acquired several strongholds in mountainous North Syria, a procedure in which they followed their Persian kinsmen. Qadmūs was the first to be acquired (1133). William of Tyre[7] estimates their number at 60,000. To the Europeans the Syrian grand master was the *vieux de la montagne*. His seat was at Miṣyāf.[8] For thirty years, beginning about 1162, Rāshid[9]-al-Dīn Sinān held this high office. It was his men who made two unsuccessful attempts on the life of Ṣalāḥ-al-Dīn;[10] Rāshid was bribed by a Damascene vizir loyal to the memory of Nūr-al-Dīn. Ṣalāḥ attacked Miṣyāf but did not reduce it. He in turn was suspected of having used Assassins

1 Paul Deschamps, *Le Crac des Chevaliers* (Paris, 1934), vol. i, pp. 43 *seq.*; cf. T. E. Lawrence, *Crusader Castles* (London, 1936), vol. i, pp. 13-15.

2 The fortress hangs like an eagle's nest, which is probably the meaning of the word, on the rough road between the Caspian shores and the Persian highlands.

3 Indian *bhang* (Ar. *banj*). References to a drug that acted as an antidote for sorrow and "robber of the mind" occur in Babylonian literature.

4 Variant *fidāwi*, one ready to offer his life for a cause. Cf. ibn-Baṭṭūṭah, vol. i, pp. 166-7.

5 See above, p. 575.

6 See above, p. 599.

7 Vol. ii, p. 691; cf. Burchard of Mount Zion, tr. Aubrey Stewart (London, 1896), p. 105, where their number is made 40,000.

8 Benjamin of Tudela (*ca.* 1169), vol. i, p. 59, makes Qadmūs the seat.

9 (Not Rashīd); abu-al-Fidā', vol. iii, p. 89; ibn-Khallikān, vol. ii, p. 521.

10 Abu-al-Fidā', vol. iii, pp. 60, 61.

against Conrad of Montferrat, titular king of Jerusalem, who was killed in 1192 by a band disguised as Christians.[1] Another prominent Frank for whose death the Assassins were responsible was Count Raymond II of Tripoli (*ca.* 1152). Sinān's successor was visited by a Frankish count in his mountain castle with its high turrets guarded by white-clad Assassins. On a signal from the master two of the sentinels threw themselves from their turrets to be torn to pieces on the rocks below.[2] The story shows that religious zeal rather than intoxicating drugs motivated the blind obedience and unquestioning loyalty of the Assassins.

In 1172 the Old Man of the Mountain sent envoys to the king of Jerusalem to discuss the possibility of conversion on the part of his men to Christianity. This was in line with the practice of dissimulation (*taqīyah*) authorized by ultra-Shīʿite tenets. Fearing the loss of tribute which the Assassins were then paying the Templars, these knights murdered the envoys.[3] When in ʿAkka St. Louis received an Assassin delegation with presents, including ornaments and beasts of crystal, amber, a ring and a shirt. The shirt meant that Louis was as close to Rāshid as his own body. Louis reciprocated.[4] Two knights who spoke Arabic served as interpreters. Before Louis' departure from France the Assassins had made an attempt on his life, indicating that their field of operation extended as far as Western Europe. Eastward they operated as far as Mongolia, where they tried to assassinate one of the Great Khāns. With Baybars' destruction of their Syrian nest, which for years had hatched intrigue and murder, the Syrian Assassin power was forever crushed.

The last of the Crusading colonies

The work begun by Baybars against the Franks was continued by his equally energetic and zealous successor Qalāwūn (1279–90). His title al-Malik al-Manṣūr (the victorious king) was well deserved. On April 15, 1282, Qalāwūn renewed the truce negotiated by Baybars with the Templars of Anṭarṭūs for another period of ten years and ten months. A treaty with similar terms was signed three years later with the princess of

[1] Ibn-al-Athīr, vol. xii, p. 51; Jacques de Vitry, pp. 116-17; Ambroise, pp. 334-5.
[2] Marinus Sanuto, "Liber secretorum", in Bongars, *Gesta Dei per Francos* (Hanau, 1611), vol. ii, p. 201.
[3] William of Tyre, vol. ii, pp. 392-4; Burchard, pp. 105-6.
[4] Joinville, pp. 250 *seq.*

Tyre, who then held Beirut.[1] After a siege of thirty-eight days ending May 25, 1285, al-Marqab yielded. Its outer walls still show numberless arrowheads imbedded between the stones. The Ayyūbid historian-amīr abu-al-Fidā',[2] then a lad of twelve years, had his first military experience on this occasion. Its Hospitallers were escorted to Tripoli.[3] Four years later this town, the largest still in Frankish hands, was captured and levelled to the ground. So oppressive was the odour from the corpses lying thick on the islet outside the port that abu-al-Fidā'[4] could not stand it. Tripoli was rebuilt several years later not on its former site but several miles from the sea, where it now stands.

Amidst preparations against 'Akka, the only place of military importance left, Qalāwūn died and was succeeded by his son al-Ashraf (1290–93). Al-Ashraf invested 'Akka for

From Henri Lavoix, "Monnaies à légendes arabes frappées en Syrie par les Croisés"

A FRANKISH DINAR STRUCK AT 'AKKA IN 1251

Bearing Arabic inscription

over a month, using ninety-two catapults, before he stormed it on May 18, 1291. He slaughtered its Templar defenders in violation of a safe-conduct he had granted them. Abu-al-Fidā'[5] took part in the siege. The city was practically wiped out of existence.[6]

[1] Maqrīzi has preserved the texts of both treaties, ed. Quatremère, vol. ii (pt. 3), pp. 172-6, 177-8, tr. pp. 22-31, 212-21; cf. treaties preserved in ibn-al-Furāt, vol. vii, pp. 204-6, 262-72.

[2] Vol. iv, p. 22.

[3] Ibn-al-Furāt, vol. viii, pp. 17-18.

[4] Vol. iv, p. 24; cf. ibn-al-Furāt, vol. viii, pp. 80-81. Idrīsi, p. 18, reports four islands in the port of Tripoli. Those visible today can hardly be so called.

[5] Vol. iv, pp. 25-6; Maqrīzi, tr. Quatremère, vol. ii (pt. 3), pp. 125-9.

[6] Rebuilt in the eighteenth century, its citadel was later used by the British as a prison and blasted by Zionist terrorists in May 1947.

'Akka's capture sealed the fate of the few remaining coastal towns. Tyre was abandoned on the same day and Sidon on July 14. Beirut capitulated on July 21 and Anṭarṭūs on August 3. 'Athlīth (Castrum Peregrinorum, Château Pèlerin), deserted by its Templars, was demolished about mid-August.[1]

Service des Antiquities de Syrie

THE ISLET OF ARWĀD

The Templars of Arwād held out for eleven years more. Over the gateway of the ruins of this islet's castle the Lusignan coat of arms — a lion and a palm — is still visible. With the fall of Arwād the curtain fell on the last scene of the most spectacular drama in the history of the conflict between East and West.

[1] Ṣāliḥ, p. 42; abu-al-Fidā', vol. iv, p. 26; Sanuto in Bongars, vol. ii, pp. 231 *seq*.

CHAPTER XLVI

CULTURAL INTERACTION

RICH in picturesque and romantic incidents, the Crusades were rather disappointing in intellectual and cultural achievement. On the whole they meant much more to the West in terms of civilizing influences than they did to the East. They opened new horizons — industrial, commercial and colonial — before the eyes of Europeans. The states they built in Syria correspond to modern colonial empires, and the merchant or pilgrim rather than the returned soldier was the principal culture carrier. In the East they left a legacy of ill will between Moslems and Christians the effects of which are still noticeable.

The impact on the West: science and literature

Islamic culture in the Crusading epoch was already decadent in the East. For some time it had ceased to be a creative force.[1] In science, literature, philosophy all its great lights had been dimmed. Moreover, the Franks themselves were on a lower cultural level. Nationalistic animosities and religious prejudices thwarted the free play of interactive forces between them and the Moslems and left them in no responsive mood. No wonder, then, that we know of only one major scientific work done from Arabic into Latin throughout the whole period, al-Majūsi's [2] *Kāmil al-Ṣināʿah al-Ṭibbīyah*, or *al-Kitāb al-Maliki* (the perfect in the medical art, or the royal book). This was done at Antioch in 1127 by a Pisan named Stephen. A minor work translated also in Antioch (1247) was *Sirr al-Asrār* (*Secretum secretorum*), a pseudo-Aristotelian treatise on occult science which had a wide vogue in the late Middle Ages. Systematic hospitalization in the Occident probably received a fresh stimulus from the Orient. A number of hospices and hospitals, chiefly lazar-houses,[3] begin to spring up in twelfth century Europe. Syrian leper houses may thus be considered ancestors of European hospitals.

[1] See above, p. 572.
[2] His first name ʿAli ʿAbbās, Latinized Haly Abbas; he died in 994.
[3] Cf. above, pp. 497-8.

In literature the influence was even slighter and more difficult to detect. Stories, some of which were of Persian and Indic origin, were transmitted and appear strangely altered in the *Gesta Romanorum* and other collections. Chaucer's *Squieres*

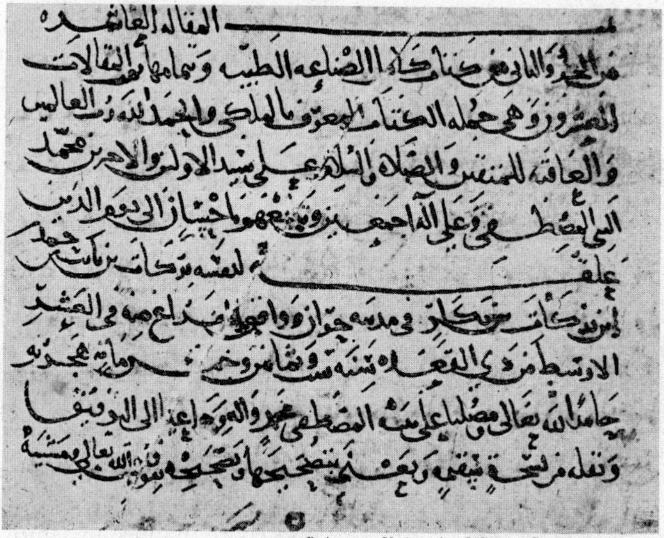

Princeton University Library, Garrett Collection

COLOPHON OF AL-MAJŪSI'S GREAT WORK ON MEDICINE, MANUSCRIPT

This *al-Kitāb al-Maliki* by 'Ali ibn-al-'Abbās al-Majūsi, copied A.H. 586 (A.D. 1190), is one of only two known complete copies. It was the only major scientific work done into Latin by the Crusaders and taken back to Europe

Tale has an *Arabian Nights* antecedent; Boccaccio's *Decameron* contains a number of tales derived orally from Oriental sources. The Holy Grail legend preserves elements of undoubted Syrian origin.

Military art

In Syria the Franks learned the use of the crossbow,[1] the wearing of heavier mail by knight and horse, the employment of the tabor and naker[2] in military bands, the conveying of military intelligence by carrier pigeons and the use of fire for signalling at night.[3] They also acquired the practice of

[1] See Ludolph von Suchem, p. 135.

[2] Ar. *ṭunbūr* and *naqqārah*.

[3] Consult Ṣāliḥ, pp. 60-61; al-Ẓāhiri, *Zubdat Kashf al-Mamālik*, ed. P. Ravaisse (Paris, 1894), pp. 116-17; Qalqashandi, vol. viii, pp. 392-4; 'Umari, pp. 196-7. Cf. Suyūṭi, *Ḥusn*, vol. ii, p. 186.

celebrating victory by illumination and were introduced to the knightly sport of tournament. In fact the whole institution of chivalry was promoted on Syrian soil. Contact with Moslem knights encouraged the use of armorial bearings and heraldic devices. The double-headed eagle, of Sumerian antiquity, was used by Zangi on his coins and by the Urtuqids as a badge. It passed on to the knights of the Round Table and to Byzantium and was adopted in 1345 by German emperors. The heraldic idea finally reached the United States, which uses an eagle as its emblem. The fleur-de-lis, known to the Elamites and Assyrians, appears for the first time in Moslem heraldry as the blazon of Nūr-al-Dīn, Zangi's son. It frequently occurs on Ayyūbid and Mamlūk coins. Adopted by the Franks, it passed on to France and later to Canada. The rosette was popular with the Ayyūbids and the Mamlūks. Many Mamlūks bore names of animals, the corresponding images of which they blazoned on their shields. Baybars' crest was a lion.[1] "Azure" (Ar. *lāzaward*) and other heraldic terms testify to the enduring effect of Moslem knighthood.

ARMS OF FRANCE

Early coats of arms of France showed many fleurs-de-lis on a blue field

The order of Templars, which, like that of the Hospitallers, was the nearest approach to harmonizing war and religion — an old achievement in Islam — followed in its organization a pattern similar to that of the Assassins. At the bottom of the Christian order stood the lay brothers, esquires and knights, corresponding to the *lāṣiqs* (associates), *fidā'is* and *rafīqs* (comrades). The knight wore a white mantle with a red cross mark, the *rafīq* a white mantle with a red cap. In the higher brackets the counterparts of the prior, grand prior and grand master were the *dā'i*, *dā'i kabīr* (superior propagandist) and

[1] L. A. Mayer, *Saracenic Heraldry* (Oxford, 1933), pp. 7, 26, 107.

shaykh al-jabal (old man of the mountain).[1] Then there was another secret order, *futūwah*, in which Arab chivalry sought to express itself. The order was reformed and patronized by the ʿAbbāsid al-Nāṣir (1180–1225), who might have been impressed by the Crusading orders. The initiate was also called *rafīq* and wore distinctive trousers (*sarāwīl*). Ṣalāḥ-al-Dīn's brother al-ʿĀdil and al-ʿĀdil's sons wore such trousers. Syria had an active branch that went by the name Nubuwīyah.[2]

Most conspicuous among all Crusading remains in Syria are the many castles still crowning its hills. Then come the churches. In the churches the Franks employed the familiar Romanesque and Gothic styles but the Byzantine and Syrian motifs of decoration. The Church of the Holy Sepulchre and the Dome of the Rock were imitated in several ecclesiastical buildings of the "round temple" type in England, France, Spain and Germany. Many of the Crusader churches have since been converted into mosques. Among these are the great cathedral of Notre-Dame in Tyre, where the historian William of Tyre[3] was archbishop (1175–85); the church of Sidon erected by the Hospitallers, now al-Jāmiʿ al-Kabīr (the great mosque); the cathedral of St. John of Beirut, now the ʿUmari Mosque, constructed in 1110 by King Baldwin;[4] and the cathedral of Our Lady in Anṭarṭūs, the most beautiful and best preserved of all, which was an object of pilgrimage. The structure was begun in 1130 and housed a picture supposedly painted by Luke and an altar over which Peter allegedly celebrated the first mass.[5] A recent minaret was added to this edifice, which no doubt stood on the site of an early Christian church. Al-Balamand (Belmont), near Tripoli, now a Greek Orthodox monastery, was built by Frankish monks in 1157.[6]

Architecture

For long generations before the Crusades pilgrims frequented the Holy Land and traders visited the eastern shores of the Mediterranean. The Crusading movement accelerated forces already in operation and popularized in Europe Oriental pro-

Agriculture and industry

[1] See above, p. 610.
[2] Ibn-al-Athīr, vol. xii, p. 268; *Fakhri*, p. 434; ibn-Jubayr, p. 280.
[3] Vol. ii, p. 411; Enlart, vol. ii, pp. 353 *seq.*
[4] Ṣāliḥ, p. 58; Enlart, vol. ii, pp. 69 *seq.*
[5] Joinville, p. 328; Jacques de Vitry, pp. 20-21; Dussaud *et al.*, *Syrie antique*, pls. 117, 118; Enlart, vol. ii, pp. 403 *seq.*
[6] Enlart, vol. ii, pp. 45 *seq.*

ducts, some of which must have been previously known. The problem of tracing origins is further complicated by the fact that while the Syrian bridge was open for traffic two other bridges, the Sicilian and the Spanish, were in operation too, thus making it difficult to determine the exact route taken by any particular commodity.

While in Syria the Franks were introduced to or acquired a taste for certain native and tropical products with which the

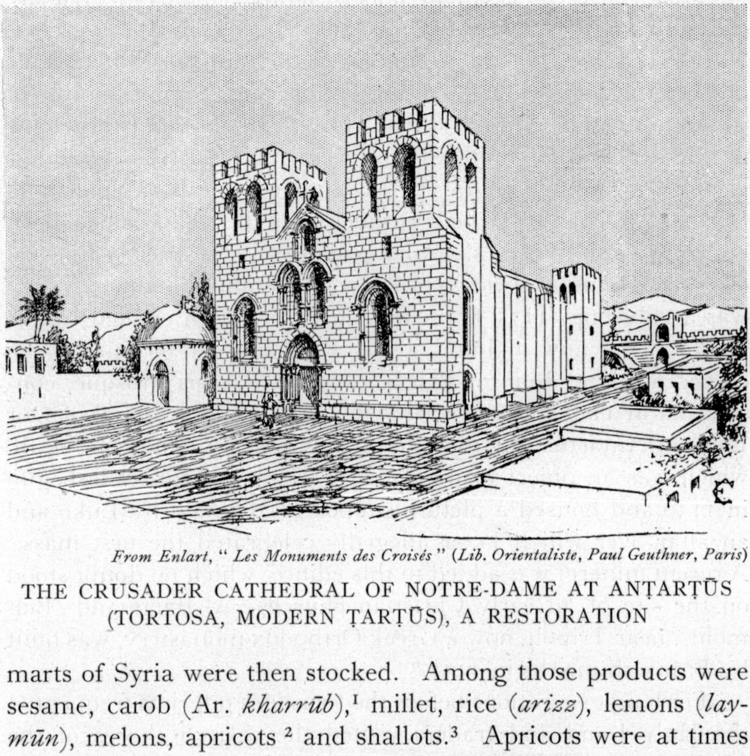

From Enlart, " Les Monuments des Croisés " (Lib. Orientaliste, Paul Geuthner, Paris)

THE CRUSADER CATHEDRAL OF NOTRE-DAME AT ANṬARṬŪS (TORTOSA, MODERN ṬARṬŪS), A RESTORATION

marts of Syria were then stocked. Among those products were sesame, carob (Ar. *kharrūb*),[1] millet, rice (*arizz*), lemons (*laymūn*), melons, apricots [2] and shallots.[3] Apricots were at times called the plums of Damascus. The Syrian capital specialized in sweet scents and damask rose (*Rosa damascena*). Attars (Ar. *'iṭr*) and fragrant volatile oils, of Persian origin, incense and other aromatic gums of Arabia, together with other spices, perfumes and sweetmeats became favourites. Cloves and

[1] Originally Assyrian; see above, p. 138, n. 5.
[2] From Ar. *baraqrūq*, originally L. *praecoquum*, early ripe.
[3] Shallots and scallions received their name from Ascalon ('Asqalān).

similar *aromatics*, pepper and other condiments, alum, aloes and several drugs found their way into the European kitchen and store, first in the East and subsequently in the West. Fantastic ideas were readily accepted about the precious spices originating in Paradise and floated down the Nile to be fished out at its mouth.[1] In Egypt ginger (*zanjabīl*) was added to the Crusader menu. More important than all these articles was sugar (*sukkar*), with the cane of which the Franks familiarized themselves on the Lebanese maritime plain. Arab traders had introduced sugar-cane from India or south-eastern Asia, where it must have originally grown wild. Hitherto honey was the ingredient used by Europeans for sweetening foods and medicines. Tyre and its environs, home of William [2] (d. *ca.* 1190), greatest among the historians of the Crusades, was especially rich in sugar-cane plantations. With sugar went a variety of soft drinks, sweetmeats and candy (*qandah*). In Europe windmills make their appearance in 1180 in Normandy, where they were called *turquois* (Turkish). Water wheels (sing. *nāʿūrah*, noria) antedate windmills in Europe, but those near Bayreuth, Germany, follow the Syrian type. This contrivance had existed in Syria since Roman days.

In matters of fashion, clothing and home furnishing new desires were likewise sharpened if not created. The Franks became convinced that not only native foods but native clothes were preferable. Men began to grow beards, wear flowing robes and cover the head with a scarf (*kūfīyah*). Women wore Oriental gauze ornamented with sequins (*sikkah*) and sat on divans (*dīwān*), listening to the lute (*al-ʿūd*) and rebab (*rabābah*); they even veiled in public.[3] Warriors, pilgrims, sailors and merchants returned with rugs, carpets and tapestries, which had been fixtures in Near Eastern homes from time immemorial. Fabrics such as damask, muslin, baldachin,[4] sarcenet (Saracen stuff), atlas (*aṭlas*), taffeta,[5] velvet, silk, satin [6] came to be appreciated as never before. Camlets (*khamlah*) and furs

[1] Joinville, p. 104. Old French *épices* (spices) came to mean bribe for the judge.

[2] Vol. ii, p. 6; Joinville, p. 310.

[3] Ibn-Jubayr, p. 333.

[4] These three words perpetuate the names of three cities: Damascus, al-Mawṣil (Mosul) and Baghdād.

[5] Ar. *tafta*, from Per. *tāftah*.

[6] From Ar. *zaytūni*, a corruption of Chinese Tsʿien-tʿang, a city in China from which this silk originally came.

acquired wider vogue. Damascene and Cairene jewels were in great demand. Ṣalāḥ-al-Dīn's brother al-ʿĀdil reportedly used jewelry to bribe Frankish wives to hold back their husbands from warfare. Oriental luxuries became Occidental necessities. Mirrors of glass replaced those of steel. The rosary, of Hindu origin, was used by Syrian Christians and then Sufi Moslems before it got into the hands of Roman Catholics. Pilgrims sent back home reliquaries of native workmanship which served as models for European craftsmen. Arras and other European centres began to imitate wares, rugs and fabrics of Oriental manufacture. With cloth and metallic wares went dyestuffs and new colours such as lilac (*laylak*), carmine and crimson (*qirmizi*). Oriental work in pottery, gold, silver, enamel and stained glass was also imitated.[1]

International exchange

In the twelfth and thirteenth centuries maritime activity and international trade were stimulated to a degree unattained since Roman days. The introduction of the compass, of which presumably the Moslems made the first practical use, was a great aid in navigation. Before the Moslems the Chinese had discovered the directive property of the magnetic needle. Among the Europeans Italian sailors were the earliest users of the compass.[2] The enhanced flow of trade necessitated new demands, one of which was for ready cash on the part of pilgrim and Crusader. This demand helped establish a money economy and increase the supply and circulation of currency. Banking firms were organized in the Italian city republics with branch offices in the Levant. The need was also felt for letters of credit.[3] The *Byzantinius Saracenatus*, bearing Arabic inscription, was perhaps the earliest gold coin struck by the Latins. The first consuls reported in history were Genoese accredited to ʿAkka in 1180. They presided over local Genoese courts, witnessed seal contracts, wills and deeds, identified new arrivals of their nationals, settled disputes and on the whole performed duties analogous to those of modern Western consuls in the Near East.

Social contacts

During the Crusades the periods of peace, it should be

[1] See below, p. 639.

[2] Consult George Sarton, *Introduction to the History of Science*, vol. iii (Baltimore, 1947), pp. 714-15.

[3] Eng. "cheque" goes back to Ar. *ṣakk*.

remembered, were of longer duration than the periods of war. Thus ample opportunity was provided for forging amicable and neighbourly bonds between Easterners and Westerners. Once the language barrier was removed the Frank must have discovered that after all the Moslem was not the idolater he was thought to be and that he shared in the Judaeo-Christian and Greco-Roman heritage of the European. We hear of many Crusaders, Reginald of Châtillon and William of Tyre for example, who mastered Arabic,[1] but of no Arabs who spoke French or Latin. The tolerance, breadth of view and trend toward secularization which usually result from mingling of men of different faiths and cultures seem in this case to have accrued to the Western rather than the Eastern society. Certain shrines in the Holy Land were venerated by Christians, Moslems and Jews alike. On the social and economic level Christians and Moslems mixed freely,[2] traded horses, dogs and falcons, exchanged safe-conducts and even intermarried. A new progeny from native mothers arose and was designated Pullani.[3] Among modern Lebanese and Palestinians, especially in Ihdin (Lebanon) and Bethlehem, are quite a few with blue eyes and fair hair. Certain Christian families, such as the Faranjīyah (Frankish), the Ṣalībi (Crusading), the Duwayhi (from de Douai ?), the Bardawīl (Baldwin)[4] and the Ṣawāya (Savoie ?) have preserved traditions or names suggesting European origins. The villages of Sinjīl (Saint-Gilles) and al-Raynah (Reynaud) in Palestine perpetuate two Frankish names.

Usāmah's testimony

In his memoirs Usāmah ibn-Munqidh (1095–1188) gives the clearest first-hand picture of interracial association. A friend of Ṣalāḥ-al-Dīn, Usāmah defended his picturesque ancestral castle on the Orontes, Shayzar, against Assassins and Franks. Never did this castle fall into Crusading hands. He himself fraternized with Franks in time of peace. To him the comparatively free sex relations among the Franks, " who are void of all zeal and jealousy ",[5] was simply shocking. Their methods of ordeal by

[1] See above, p. 611.

[2] Ibn-Jubayr, pp. 287-8, 298, 302; Usāmah, *I'tibār*, pp. 131, 134; *Arab-Syrian Gentleman*, pp. 161, 163-4.

[3] Poulains, " kids ", " young ones ".

[4] Marino Sanuto, *Secrets for True Crusaders to Help Them to Recover the Holy Land*, tr. Aubrey Stewart (London, 1896), " Sabaquet Baridoil, where King Baldwin died ". This is Sabkhat Bardawīl on the Mediterranean coast of Sinai.

[5] *I'tibār*, p. 135; *Arab-Syrian Gentleman*, p. 164.

water and duel [1] were far inferior to the Moslem judicial procedure of the day. Especially crude by contrast was their system of medication. Two members of a Frankish family at al-Munayṭirah were properly treated by a native Christian physician until a European was summoned. The latter laid the ailing leg of one of the patients on a block of wood and bade a knight chop it off with one stroke of the axe. He then shaved the head of the other patient, a woman, made a deep cruciform incision on it and rubbed the wound with salt — to drive off the devil. Both patients expired on the spot. The native physician, himself the narrator of the story, concludes with these words: "Thereupon I asked them whether my services were needed any longer, and when they replied in the negative I returned home, having learned of their medicine what I knew not before".[2]

Effects on Syria

In general the effects of the Crusades on Syria were disastrous. Fearing the return of the Franks, some of whom had simply moved across the water to Cyprus, the Mamlūks undertook the dismantling of ʿAkka, Arsūf, Caesarea, Tyre, Tripoli and other ports.[3] The Ayyūbids had destroyed ʿAsqalan.[4] After ʿAkka Tyre had become the most flourishing city of Frankish Syria. Ibn-Jubayr [5] found it unsurpassed as a fortified town; abu-al-Fidā',[6] a century later, found it in ruins and desolation. Dissident Moslem elements, comprising Shīʿites, Ismāʿīlites and Nuṣayrīyah, who then, according to ibn-Jubayr,[7] outnumbered the Sunnites and had on varied occasions compromised their loyalty by aiding Franks, were now decimated; their remnant sought refuge in Central Lebanon and al-Biqāʿ. Earlier al-Ashraf had exacted from the Druzes outward conformity to Sunnite Islam, but the conformity did not last long. Baybars had forced the Nuṣayris to build mosques in their villages, but he could not force them to pray in them. Instead, they used the buildings as stables for their cattle and beasts of burden.[8] In pursuit of the "scorched earth" policy Mamlūk

[1] *Iʿtibār*, pp. 138-9; *Arab-Syrian Gentleman*, pp. 167-8.

[2] *Iʿtibār*, pp. 132-3; *Arab-Syrian Gentleman*, p. 162.

[3] Consult abu-al-Fidā', *Taqwīm*, p. 239; ibn-Baṭṭūṭah, *Tuḥfat al-Nuẓẓār fi Gharā'ib al-Amṣār*, vol. i, pp. 129-30; cf. Idrīsi, p. 11.

[4] Consult ibn-Baṭṭūṭah, vol. i, p. 126.

[5] P. 304. [6] *Taqwīm*, p. 243. [7] P. 280.

[8] Ibn-Baṭṭūṭah, vol. i, p. 177.

sultans methodically ravaged Lebanon. Especially disastrous was al-Nāṣir's campaign of 1306, which resulted in the virtual annihilation of the people of Kisrawān.[1] The Shī'ites of that region were replaced by Kurds and Turkomans; Maronites from the north pushed on later to fill the vacancy. The defence of Beirut against recurring sea incursions was entrusted in 1294 by the sultans to the Buḥtur family, who were installed amīrs of al-Gharb. To this family the chronicler Ṣāliḥ ibn-Yaḥya [2] belonged. Lebanon then became less oriented westward; it assumed the general aspect that it has maintained till modern times. In fact all Syria had in it by then almost every element of civilization it possessed until the early nineteenth century, when a fresh wave of Western ideas and cultural elements began to break on its shore.

Native Christians suffered no less than schismatic Moslems. A measure of hostility was engendered between the Syrian Christians and their Moslem neighbours that was hardly attained before and that is not yet entirely abated. Alarmed by the actively helpful attitude of the Christians of Edessa and Antioch, the Moslem rulers of Jerusalem extorted "all the money and goods in the possession of the Christian inhabitants" [3] of the city and drove them out with the exception of the aged, the sick, the women and the children. When the Crusaders entered the city, they found few survivors. In Lebanon the Maronites were accorded by the Latins all the ecclesiastical and civil rights that pertained to members of the Roman Catholic Church.[4] After the capture of Beirut in 1191 by Ṣalāḥ-al-Dīn thousands of Maronites migrated to Cyprus, where four thousand of their descendants still live. The Armenian and Jacobite communities entered into closer friendly relations than ever before with the Latins, but the *rapprochement* led to no union.

The *jihād* spirit which animated the Mamlūks in their counter-Crusades seems now to have been canalized against Copts and Syrian Christians. Toward the end of his reign Qalāwūn (1279–90) issued edicts excluding his Christian subjects from governmental offices. In 1301 Sultan al-Nāṣir [5]

[1] Ṣāliḥ, p. 136. Native tradition derives the name of this district from a Mardaite leader; Shidyāq, p. 201.

[2] P. 63.

[3] William of Tyre, vol. i, p. 334.

[4] See above, p. 522. Consult Pierre Dib, *L'Église maronite* (Paris, 1930), pp. 186-90.

[5] On him see below, p. 634.

reactivated the old anti-dhimmi laws enjoining Christians and Jews to wear distinctive dress and refrain from horse and mule riding;[1] Sultan al-Ṣāliḥ did likewise in 1354.[2] Al-Nāṣir went beyond that: he ordered the abolition of a national Coptic feast[3] and padlocked many Christian churches in Egypt. This wave of anti-Christian feeling is further reflected in the contemporaneous literature. Speeches, *fatwas* (legal opinions) and *khuṭbahs* (sermons) inflamed the populace. The writings of the Syrian theologian ibn-Taymīyah (1263–1328) embody the reactionary spirit of the age.[4] Born in Ḥarrān, ibn-Taymīyah, an ardent follower of ibn-Ḥanbal, flourished in Damascus, where he lifted his voice high in condemnation of saint worship, vows and pilgrimage to shrines. His principles were later adopted by the Wahhābis who today dominate the religious and political life of Najd and al-Ḥijāz. His tomb and that of ibn-ʿAsākir can be seen on the campus of the Syrian University.

Another type of literature flourished now which may be termed counter-propaganda. It extolled the virtues of Jerusalem, recommended pilgrimage to it and insisted that the Prophet had proclaimed prayer in its mosque a thousand times more meritorious than in any other, excepting the two of Mecca and Medina. Even a preacher of the Umayyad Mosque in Damascus, ibn-al-Firkāḥ[5] (d. 1329), subscribed to these views. Alongside this genre arose the *sīrah*, a form of historical romance extolling the exploits, real or imaginary, of some Arab hero. Ṣalāḥ-al-Dīn, Baybars and ʿAntarah became the heroes of such romances. ʿAntarah was a pre-Islamic poet-warrior, but his romance (*Sīrat ʿAntar*), judged by its latest historical allusions, was conceived in Syria in the early twelfth century. Story-tellers in the cafés of Cairo, Beirut, Damascus and

[1] See above, p. 542.

[2] Qalqashandi, vol. xiii, pp. 377-81; ibn-Taghri-Birdi, ed. Popper, vol. v, p. 133.

[3] Maqrīzi, vol. i, p. 69.

[4] On them consult Kutubi, vol. i, pp. 48-9; Henri Laoust, *Essai sur les doctrines sociales et politiques de Taki-d-Dīn Aḥmad b. Taimīya* (Cairo, 1939), pp. 634-9.

[5] "Bāʿith al-Nufūs li-Ziyārat al-Quds al-Maḥrūs", tr. Charles D. Matthews, *Palestine — Mohammedan Holy Land* (New Haven, 1949), pp. 1 *seq.* Ibn-al-Jawzi (d. 1200) of Baghdād wrote a treatise *Faḍā'il al-Quds* (the excellences of Jerusalem), described in Philip K. Hitti, Nabih A. Faris and Buṭrus ʿAbd-al-Malik, *Descriptive Catalogue of the Garrett Collection of Arabic Manuscripts in the Princeton University Library* (Princeton, 1938), No. 586.

Baghdād drawing their tales from it and *Sīrat al-Ẓāhir* (Baybars) attract larger audiences than when reciting tales from the *Arabian Nights*.

Feudalism

The Frankish states of Syria were established on feudal principles that prevailed in Europe, but some of the fief holders were natives. As a Moslem land Syria had a feudal system of its own since the days of conquest. Conquerors — whether caliphs, sultans or amīrs — granted fiefs (sing. *iqṭā'*) to their generals and high officials, who in turn parcelled out the land locally among subordinates and tenants. At the lowest level serfs and slaves tilled the soil. The collection of land-tax (*kharāj*) [1] from non-Moslems was leased out to influential persons. The 'Abbāsid caliphs replaced farming to the highest bidder by hereditary farming, the farmer paying a fixed and constant rent. The Fāṭimids and Mamlūks continued the Islamic usage.[2] In medieval Europe, however, an aristocracy of landowners had risen which occupied fortified homes in country places, established reciprocal relationship with the royalty and exercised direct control over those below them. No such aristocracy arose in Arab Islam. The fief holders as a rule lived in cities and were content with deriving the necessary income from their country possessions. The feudal organization introduced by the Franks left no traces on the local tenure of the land aside from making the military fief for a time, under the Ayyūbids, the principal form of agrarian relationship. Nor did Frankish monarchy leave permanent effect on the political institutions of Syria; but the Church which stood beside the monarchy is still represented by the Latin patriarchate of Jerusalem.

Missionary activity

An interesting by-product of the Crusades was the initiation of Christian missionary work among Moslems. Convinced, by the failure of these wars, of the futility of the military method in dealing with Moslems, men like Raymond Lull (d. 1314) began to advocate concentration on peaceful methods. A Catalan, Raymond was the earliest European to emphasize Oriental studies as an instrument of pacific campaign in which persuasion should replace violence. He himself studied Arabic

[1] See above, p. 423.

[2] Qalqashandi, vol. xiii, pp. 123 *seq.*, 139 *seq.* Consult A. N. Poliak, *Feudalism in Egypt, Syria, Palestine, and the Lebanon* (London, 1939), pp. 18 *seq.*

from a slave. With Raymond the Crusading spirit turned into a new channel: converting the Moslem rather than exterminating him.

The Carmelite order, still active in Syria, was founded in 1157 by a Crusader in that country and named after one of its mountains. Early in the thirteenth century two other monastic orders, the Franciscan and the Dominican, were founded and their representatives were stationed in many Syrian towns. In the last years of that century Beirut had a large Franciscan church.[1] In 1219 the founder of the Franciscan order, St. Francis of Assisi, visited the Ayyūbid court in Egypt and held a fruitless religious discussion with al-Kāmil. A Dominican bishop, William of Tripoli, wrote one of the most learned treatises in medieval times on the Moslems (*Tractus de statu Saracenorum*), bringing out points in which Islam and Christianity agree and advocating missionaries rather than soldiers for the recovery of the Holy Land. Like William of Tyre he was native born but of European parentage.

[1] Ṣāliḥ, p. 149; Enlart, vol. ii, p. 79.

CHAPTER XLVII

AYYŪBIDS AND MAMLŪKS

THE sultanate built by Ṣalāḥ-al-Dīn, extending from the Nile to the Tigris, was partitioned among his heirs, none of whom inherited his genius. His son al-Malik al-Afḍal (the superior king) succeeded to his father's throne in Damascus, but in 1196 he was succeeded by his uncle al-ʿĀdil of Egypt. In 1250 the Damascus branch was incorporated with that of Aleppo, which was swept away after a decade by the Mongol avalanche of Hūlāgu.[1] Ṣalāḥ-al-Dīn's second son, al-ʿAzīz (the mighty, 1193–8), followed his father on the Egyptian throne but al-ʿAzīz' son was supplanted in 1198 by the same al-ʿĀdil, who in both cases took advantage of the dissension among his nephews. It was these dynastic feuds which afforded the Franks an opportunity to regain some of their lost territory.

[1] Genealogical tree of the Ayyūbids of Damascus:

Ayyūb
- Ṣalāḥ-al-Dīn
  - 1. Al-Afḍal (1186–96)
- 2. Al-ʿĀdil Sayf-al-Dīn (1196–1218)
  - 3. Al-Muʿaẓẓam Sharaf-al-Dīn (1218–27)
    - 4. Al-Nāṣir Ṣalāḥ-al-Dīn (1227–8)
  - 5. Al-Ashraf Mūsa (1228–1237)
  - 6. Al-Ṣāliḥ Ismāʿīl (1237, again 1240–1245)
  - 7. Al-Kāmil Muḥammad of Egypt (1237–8)
    - 8. Al-ʿĀdil of Egypt (1238–40)
    - 9. Al-Ṣāliḥ Najm-al-Dīn of Egypt (1240, again 1245–9)
      - 10. Al-Muʿaẓẓam Tūrān-Shāh of Egypt (1249–50)

11. Al-Nāṣir Ṣalāḥ-al-Dīn of Aleppo (grand-nephew of al-Afḍal) (1250–60) —— 10. Al-Muʿaẓẓam Tūrān-Shāh of Egypt (1249–50)

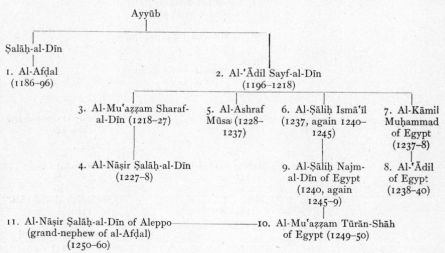

In 1200 al-'Ādil appointed one of his sons over Mesopotamia. The third son of Ṣalāḥ, al-Ẓāhir, succeeded his father at Aleppo.[1] The Ḥamāh petty branch, founded by a nephew of Ṣalāḥ-al-Dīn, survived the Mongol invasion of 1260, which two years earlier had annihilated the 'Abbāsid caliphate in Baghdād, and continued under the Mamlūks until 1341, thus outlasting all other branches of the house.[2] It numbered in its line the historian-king abu-al-Fidā' (d. 1332).[3] A minor branch, that of Ḥimṣ, was descended from an uncle of Ṣalāḥ- al-Dīn. It was destroyed by the Mamlūk Baybars in

[1] Tree of the Ayyūbids of Aleppo:

Ṣalāḥ-al-Dīn
|
1. Al-Ẓāhir Ghiyāth-al-Dīn (1186–1216)
|
2. Al-'Azīz Ghiyāth-al-Dīn (1216–36)
|
3. Al-Nāṣir Ṣalāḥ-al-Dīn (1236–60)

[2] There was a brief interval (1298–1310) in which other governors ruled under the Mamlūks.

[3] Tree of the Ayyūbids of Ḥamāh:

Nūr-al-Dīn Shāhanshāh (brother of Ṣalāḥ-al-Dīn)
|
1. Al-Muẓaffar I Taqi-al-Dīn (1178–91)
|
2. Al-Manṣūr Nāṣir-al-Dīn (1191–1220)
|
- 3. Al-Nāṣir Ṣalāḥ-al-Dīn (1220–29)
- 4. Al-Muẓaffar II Taqi-al-Dīn (1229–44)
  - 5. Al-Manṣūr Sayf-al-Dīn (1244–84)
    - 6. Al-Muẓaffar III Taqi-al-Dīn (1284–98)
  - (al-Muẓaffar 'Ali)
    - 7. Al-Mu'ayyad abu-al-Fidā' (1310–32)
      - 8. Al-Afḍal Muḥammad (1332–41)

1262.[1] Another minor branch, that of Ba'labakk, traced its descent from Tūrān-Shāh, brother of Ṣalāḥ-al-Dīn.[2]

Ayyūbids supplanted by Mamlūks

Of the many Ayyūbid branches the Egyptian was the chief. Several in this line held both Cairo and Damascus. One of them was al-Ṣāliḥ Najm-al-Dīn Ayyūb,[3] who died in November 1249 leaving a widow Shajar-al-Durr (the tree of pearls). Formerly a Turkish or Armenian slave in the harem of the Baghdād caliph al-Musta'ṣim, Shajar was freed by al-Ṣāliḥ after having borne him a son. For three months she kept the news of her husband's death a secret, pending the return of his son Tūrān-Shāh from a trip to Mesopotamia. Tūrān proved to be *persona non grata* to the slaves (*mamlūks*) and was murdered with the connivance of his stepmother. The daring and energetic woman thereupon proclaimed herself queen of the Moslems;[4] a six-year-old scion of the Damascus Ayyūbids, al-Ashraf Mūsa, was accorded the honour of joint sovereignty with her. For eighty days Shajar, the only Moslem woman to rule a country in North Africa and Western Asia, continued to exercise sole sovereignty over the lands which had produced Zenobia and Cleopatra. She had coins struck in her name[5] and had herself mentioned in the Friday prayer. When her former caliph-master addressed a scathing note to the amīrs of Egypt: "If ye have no man to rule you, let us know and we will send you one",[6] they chose her commander-in-chief 'Izz-

[1] Tree of the Ayyūbids of Ḥimṣ:

Shīrkūh (Ṣalāḥ-al-Dīn's uncle)
|
1. Al-Qāhir Nāṣir-al-Dīn (1178–85)
|
2. Al-Mujāhid Ṣalāḥ-al-Dīn (1185–1239)
|
3. Al-Manṣūr Nāṣir-al-Dīn (1239–45)
|
4. Al-Ashraf Muẓaffar-al-Dīn (1245–62)

[2] For the names of this and the Karak branch consult E. de Zambaur, *Manuel de généalogie et de chronologie* (Paris, 1927), p. 98.

[3] Consult genealogical tree, above, p. 627.

[4] Abu-al-Fidā', vol. iii, p. 190; Maqrīzi, *Khiṭaṭ*, vol. ii, p. 237.

[5] With the exception of certain coins struck in India and Fārs, hers are the only ones bearing a Moslem woman's name.

[6] Suyūṭi, *Ḥusn*, vol. ii, p. 39.

al-Dīn Aybak [1] for sultan and she did the next best thing — married him. Aybak spent the first years of his reign crushing the legitimist Ayyūbid party of Syria who considered themselves successors to their Egyptian kinsmen, deposing the child joint-king al-Ashraf and disposing of his own general who had distinguished himself against Louis IX. On hearing that he was contemplating another marriage, the queen had him murdered at his bath after a ball game. Her turn then came. Battered to death with wooden shoes by the slave women of her husband's first wife, her body was cast from a tower in the citadel of Cairo.[2]

Baḥri Mamlūks

Aybak (1250–57) was the first of the Mamlūk sultans. The series is unique in dynastic annals, for, as the name [3] indicates, this dynasty — if it could be so called — was a dynasty of slaves, slaves of varied races and nationalities constituting a military oligarchy in an alien land. When one of them died, quite often it was not his son but a slave or a mercenary of his who had won distinction and eminence who succeeded him. Thus the bondman of yesterday would become the army commander of today and the sultan of tomorrow. For almost two and three-quarter centuries the slave sultans dominated by the sword one of the most turbulent areas of the world. Generally uncultured and bloodthirsty yet they endowed Cairo with some architectural monuments of which it still rightly boasts. Two other services to the cause of Islam were rendered by them: they cleared Syria and Egypt of the remnant of the Crusaders and they definitely checked the redoubtable advance of the Tartar Mongol hordes of Hūlāgu and of Tīmūr (Tamerlane).[4] But for that, the entire course of culture and history in Western Asia and Egypt might have been different.

Originally purchased in the slave markets of Moslem Russia and the Caucasus to form the personal bodyguard of the Ayyūbid al-Ṣāliḥ,[5] the first Mamlūks started a series which is somewhat arbitrarily divided into two dynasties, Baḥri (1250–

[1] He was a Turk, as the name, *ay* moon + *beg* prince, indicates. Maqrīzi, tr. Quatremère, vol. i (pt. 1), p. 1.

[2] Qal'at al-Jabal. Ibn-Khallikān, vol. iv, p. 64; ibn-al-Athīr, vol. x, pp. 60, 160.

[3] *Mamlūk*, "possessed", "slave", especially applied to one who is not black.

[4] See below, p. 655. Arab historians use *Tatar* and *Mughūl* indiscriminately.

[5] Abu-al-Fidā', vol. iii, p. 188; ibn-Khaldūn, vol. v, p. 373.

1390) and Burji (1382–1517). The Baḥris received their name from the Nile,[1] on an islet in which their barracks stood. They were mostly Turks and Mongols; the Burjis were largely Circassians.[2] Their rise was followed a decade later by the advent of the Mongols. Once more Syria became a battlefield of two contending powers.

Mongol invasions

Fresh from the destruction of the caliphate of Baghdād and the Assassin nest of Alamūt, the Mongol horde under Hūlāgu, grandson of Chingīz Khān, made its ominous appearance in North Syria. Aleppo was the first victim. Fifty thousand of its people were put to the sword — giving a taste of what was to come. Ḥārim and Ḥamāh came next. A general was dispatched to besiege Damascus, while Hūlāgu returned to Persia because of the death of his brother, the Great Khān. Latin Antioch turned into a Mongol satellite. Louis IX and the pope thought an alliance with the invaders would help in the struggle against the Moslems. Shamanism was the official religion of the newcomers — as it was of their cousins the Turks — but among them were some Christian descendants of converts by early Syrian missionaries.[3] It was a Christian general, Kitbugha, who overran and devastated most of Syria. The reigning Mamlūk was Quṭuz (1259–60), who had executed Hūlāgu's envoys.[4] The issue was settled at 'Ayn Jālūt (Goliath's spring), near Nazareth. In this battle Baybars led the vanguard under Quṭuz and administered a crushing defeat to the intruders. Kitbugha's body was left on the field.[5] The remnant of his army was pursued and chased out of Syria. In recognition of his military service Baybars expected to receive Aleppo as a fief but the sultan disappointed him. On the way homeward from Syria a fellow-conspirator addressed the sultan and kissed his hand while Baybars stabbed him in the neck. The murderer succeeded the murdered.

Fourth in the series, Baybars [6] was the first great sultan, the

[1] Colloquially referred to as *baḥr*, sea.

[2] Ibn-Khaldūn, vol. v, p. 369, and Suyūṭi, *Ḥusn*, vol. ii, p. 80, designate them as the "Turkish dynasty".

[3] See above, pp. 518-19.

[4] The letter they carried is preserved in Maqrīzi, tr. Quatremère, vol. i (pt. 1), pp. 101-2.

[5] Abu-al-Fidā', vol. iii, pp. 209-14; Maqrīzi, ed. Quatremère, vol. i (pt. 1), pp. 98, 104 *seq.*; ibn-Khaldūn, vol. v, p. 544.

[6] For table of Baḥri Mamlūks, see below, p. 633.

real founder of Mamlūk power. His first laurels he won on the battlefield against the Mongols but his crown of glory was won against the Crusaders.[1] More than a military figure he was a great administrator. He dug canals, improved harbours and connected his two capitals in Egypt and Syria by a swift postal service modelled on the Persian-'Abbāsid system. He could play polo in both cities during the same week.[2] He launched public projects, renovated mosques — including the Dome of the Rock — restored citadels — among which was that of Aleppo — and established religious and charitable endowments.[3] His mausoleum in Damascus is now used as a library bearing his epithet, al-Ẓāhirīyah. This library houses one of the oldest manuscripts on paper, *Masā'il* (questions of) *al-Imām Aḥmad ibn-Ḥanbal*, bearing the date A.H. 266 (879/80).[4]

The Mongol peril was only temporarily averted. Pushed by forces not fully determined from their abode in Central Asia, where they had roamed as far as the borders of the Chinese empire, the Mongols came in waves reminiscent in certain features of the Semitic and the Teutonic waves of earlier days. Hūlāgu's son and successor Abāqa, who chose Tibrīz for capital, renewed the attack on Syria. The Mongols were then flirting with Christianity, and Abāqa entered negotiations with the pope, Edward I of England and other European rulers urging a fresh Crusade to drive the Mamlūks out of Syria. Though superior in number and reinforced by Armenians, Georgians and Persians the Mongol army was badly beaten in 1280 at Ḥimṣ.[5] After straddling the fence for a time the Mongols jumped to the Islamic side and there remained. This invasion took place in the reign of Qalāwūn (1279–90), the outstanding Mamlūk figure after Baybars. Like his predecessor, Qalāwūn was a Turkish slave whose title al-Alfi (thousander) indicates the high price, a thousand dinars, paid for him.[6]

The adoption of Islam as the state religion by the seventh Īl-Khān Ghāzān Maḥmūd, who was brought up as a Buddhist, did not spare Syria further invasions, two of which followed.

[1] See above, pp. 607-8.
[2] Ibn-al-Furāt, vol. vii, p. 82.
[3] An imposing list of his public works appears in Kutubi, vol. i, pp. 113-15.
[4] Cf. Hitti, *History of the Arabs*, p. 347.
[5] Abu-al-Fidā', vol. iv, pp. 15-16; Maqrīzi, tr. Quatremère, vol. ii (pt. 3), pp. 36-40; ibn-Khaldūn, vol. v, pp. 545-6.
[6] Suyūṭi, *Ḥusn*, vol. ii, p. 80; Maqrīzi, tr. Quatremère, vol. ii (pt. 3), p. 1.

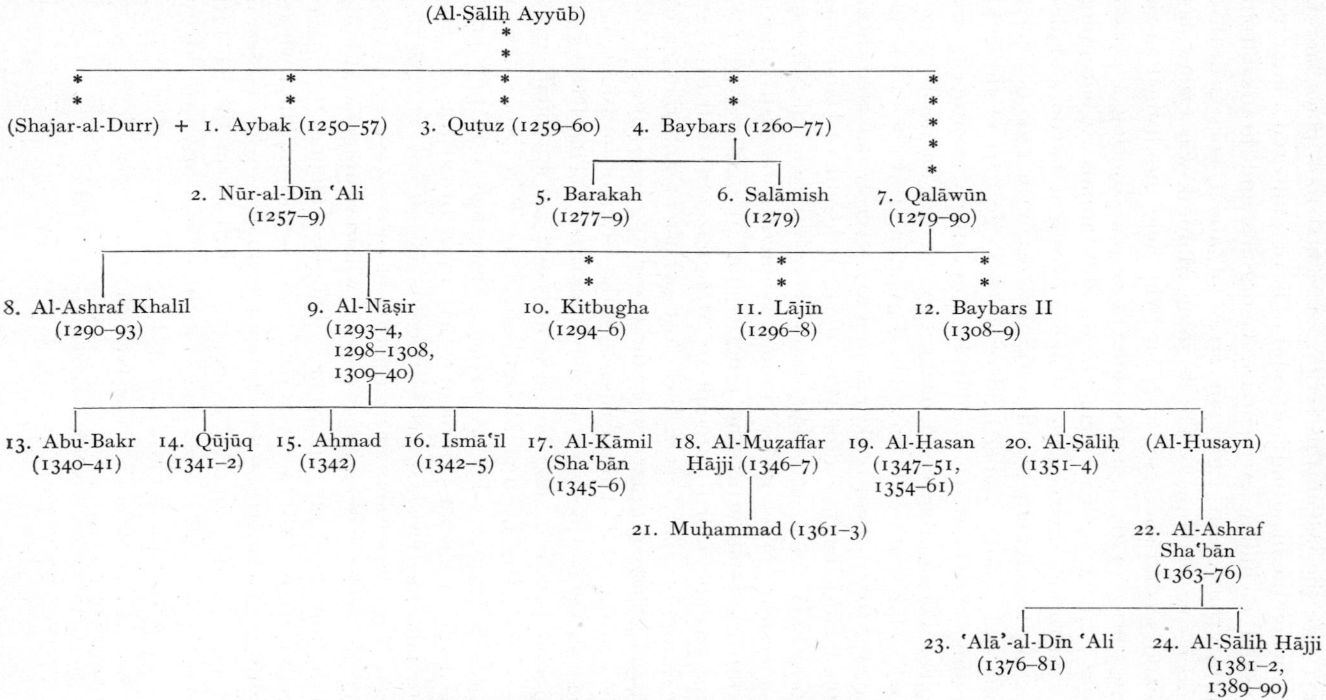

Note.—Starred lines indicate a master and slave relationship.

They were the last in this series. The first took place late in 1299, when the invading host, said to have numbered a hundred thousand including Armenians, Georgians and Franks from Cyprus, routed an Egyptian army of about one-third that number east of Ḥimṣ.[1] The reigning Mamlūk was Qalāwūn's son and second successor al-Nāṣir, who held the distinction of ruling thrice (1293–4, 1298–1308, 1309–40), covering a period longer than any other ruler's in Mamlūk annals. Continuing their victorious march, the Mongols wrought havoc and destruction throughout North Syria, and early in 1300 occupied Damascus, whose citadel held out. A large part of the city, including its suburb al-Ṣāliḥīyah, was utterly destroyed. A revolt in Persia prompted Ghāzān's return, but his troops penetrated as far south as Gaza. The Egyptian army then took the offensive, rolled them back and in 1303 severely defeated them on the historic battlefield of Marj al-Ṣuffar,[2] south of Damascus. Abu-al-Fidā',[3] who was later restored by his friend al-Nāṣir to his ancestral princedom in Ḥamāh, scouted in his native town for the Egyptian army and reported the Mongol movements. Thus was the fourth attempt to Mongolize Syria frustrated. The Mamlūks had beaten the most persistent and dangerous enemy Egypt had to face since the beginning of Islam.

As in the case of the Crusades,[4] the Mongol invasions had disastrous consequences for the minorities. The Druzes of Lebanon, whose 12,000 bowmen harassed the Egyptian army on its retreat before the Mongols in 1300, were brought to a severe reckoning. The Armenians saw their unhappy land repeatedly devastated in and after 1302 by al-Nāṣir. His Christian and Jewish subjects suffered.

Burji Mamlūks

Al-Nāṣir was followed in a period of forty-two years (1340–1382) by twelve descendants, none of whom distinguished himself in any field of endeavour. The last among them was al-Ṣāliḥ Ḥājji (1381–2, 1389–90), an incompetent child whose reign was first interrupted and then terminated by a Circassian, Barqūq. Barqūq founded a new line called Burji (1382–1517), after the towers (Ar. *burj*, sing.) of the citadel in Cairo, where they were first quartered as slaves.[5] With the exception of two

[1] Ṣāliḥ, p. 174; Maqrīzi, tr. Quatremère, vol. ii (pt. 4), p. 146.
[2] See above, p. 414.
[3] Vol. iv, p. 50. Ibn-Khaldūn, vol. v, pp. 548-9.
[4] See above, pp. 622 *seq.*
[5] Maqrīzi, *Khiṭaṭ*, vol. ii, p. 241.

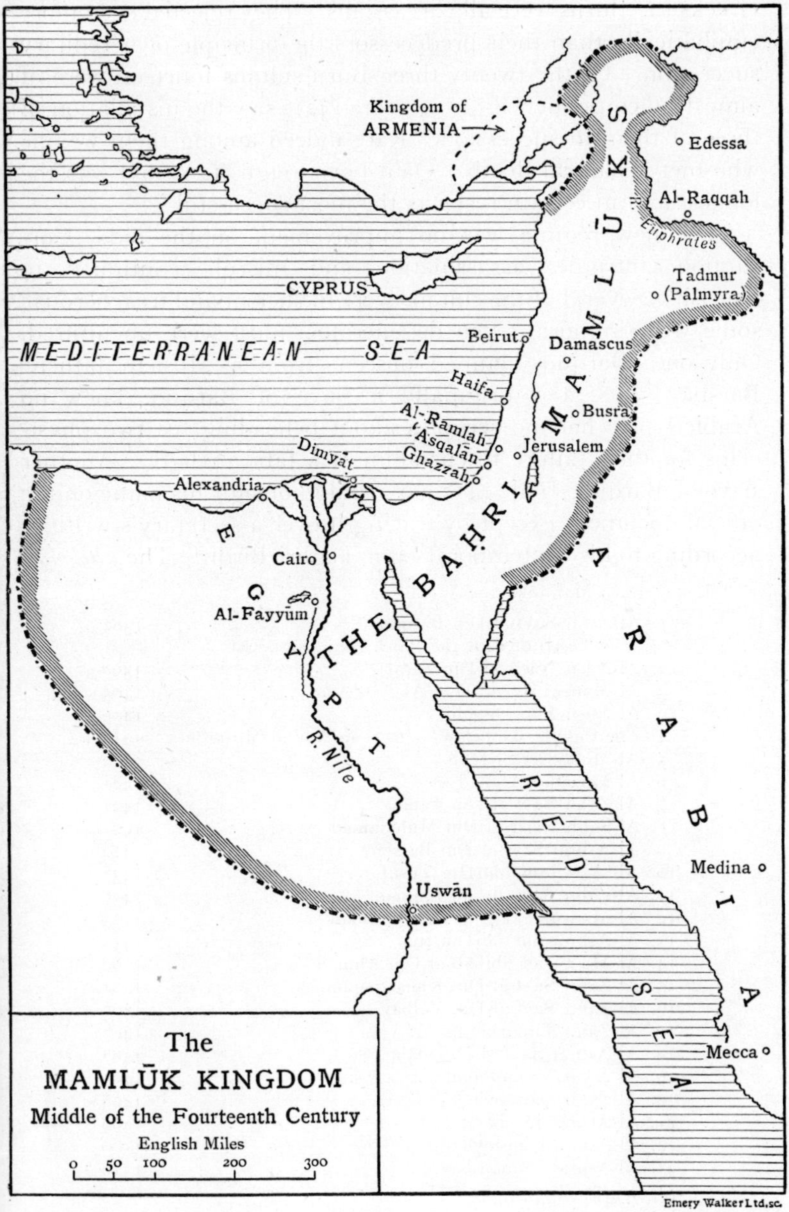

Emery Walker Ltd. sc.

From Hitti, "History of the Arabs"

Greeks the Burjis were all Circassians. They rejected even more emphatically than their predecessors the principle of hereditary succession. Of the twenty-three Burji sultans fourteen were of almost no consequence. One year, 1421, saw the installation of three of them in succession. Rare indeed among them was he who met a natural death. Qā'it-bay's reign (1468–95) was the longest and in certain respects the most successful.[1]

The new régime was no improvement on the old. Corruption, intrigue, assassination and misrule continued to flourish. Several of the sultans were inefficient and treacherous; some were immoral, even degenerate; most were uncultured. Only one, Barqūq, claimed descent from a Moslem father.[2] Barsbāy (1422–38), originally a slave of Barqūq, knew no Arabic.[3] He had no scruples about beheading his two physicians for their failure to cure him of a fatal malady. Another slave of Barqūq, Īnāl (1453–60), could not sign his name on the official document except by tracing it over a secretary's writing, according to his contemporary ibn-Taghri-Birdi.[4] The *ghilmān*

[1] List of Burji Mamlūks:

1.	Al-Ẓāhir Sayf-al-Dīn Barqūq (interrupted by the Baḥri Ḥājji, 1389–90)	1382
2.	Al-Nāṣir Nāṣir-al-Dīn Faraj	1398
3.	Al-Manṣūr 'Izz-al-Dīn 'Abd-al-'Azīz	1405
	Al-Nāṣir Faraj (again)	1406
4.	The Caliph (see below, p. 657) al-'Ādil al-Musta'īn	1412
5.	Al-Mu'ayyad Shaykh	1412
6.	Al-Muẓaffar Aḥmad	1421
7.	Al-Ẓāhir Sayf-al-Dīn Ṭaṭar	1421
8.	Al-Ṣāliḥ Nāṣir-al-Dīn Muḥammad	1421
9.	Al-Ashraf Sayf-al-Dīn Barsbāy	1422
10.	Al-'Azīz Jamāl-al-Dīn Yūsuf	1438
11.	Al-Ẓāhir Sayf-al-Dīn Jaqmaq	1438
12.	Al-Manṣūr Fakhr-al-Dīn 'Uthmān	1453
13.	Al-Ashraf Sayf-al-Dīn Īnāl	1453
14.	Al-Mu'ayyad Shihāb-al-Dīn Aḥmad	1460
15.	Al-Ẓāhir Sayf-al-Dīn Khushqadam	1461
16.	Al-Ẓāhir Sayf-al-Dīn Yalbāy	1467
17.	Al-Ẓāhir Timurbugha	1467
18.	Al-Ashraf Sayf-al-Dīn Qā'it-bāy	1468
19.	Al-Nāṣir Muḥammad	1495
20.	Al-Ẓāhir Qānṣawh	1498
21.	Al-Ashraf Jān-balāṭ	1499
22.	Al-Ashraf Qānṣawh al-Ghawri	1500
23.	Al-Ashraf Ṭūmān-bāy	1516–17

[2] Suyūṭi, *Ḥusn*, vol. ii, p. 88.

[3] His was not a unique case; consult al-Isḥāqi, *Akhbār al-Uwal fi Man Taṣarraf fi Miṣr min al-Duwal* (Cairo, 1296), p. 210.

[4] Vol. vii, p. 559.

(boy slaves) institution, for the practice of unnatural sex relations, was again in full bloom as in ʿAbbāsid days. Several Mamlūks, beginning with Baybars, were charged with pederasty. Not only the sultans but the amīrs and the entire oligarchy were more or less corrupt. The tenure of even the ablest official seldom lasted more than three years; one judge was appointed and dismissed ten times.

Though the Mamlūk régime was unique, the Mamlūk administration was but a continuation of the Fāṭimid-ʿAbbāsid system. Syria was divided into half a dozen provinces (sing. *niyābah*) following the general division under the Ayyūbids. These were Aleppo, Ḥamāh, Damascus, Tripoli, Ṣafad and al-Karak. Originally slaves of some sultan, the governors of the provinces were generally recruited from the military class (*arbāb al-suyūf*, lords of the sword)[1] as opposed to the learned class (*arbāb al-aqlām*, lords of the pen). In general they were independent of one another, each with a court reproducing on a small scale that of Cairo. The animosities and disturbances in the federal capital were often reflected in the provincial ones. The change of a Mamlūk sultan usually provoked a rebellion on the part of a governor in Damascus or some other Syrian province.[2] The Gharb of Lebanon was enfeoffed to its native chiefs, the Buḥturids of the Tanūkh.[3] Administration of Syria

Because of its historic background Damascus, where Baybars — organizer of the Mamlūk sultanate — often held his court, had an advantage over its sister provinces. One of its governors, Tangiz (1312–39), was acknowledged as regent over Syria during al-Nāṣir's third reign. His province (*mamlakat Dimashq*,[4] kingdom of Damascus) included the whole of Palestine, with the exception of the petty provinces of Ṣafad and al-Karak, and extended north to Beirut, Ḥimṣ and Tadmur. Tangiz brought water to Jerusalem and restored the tower (*burj*) of Beirut, where he also built hostels (sing. *khān*) and public baths.[5] After an unusually long and beneficent reign

[1] Qalqashandi, vol. ix, p. 253.

[2] For more on government of Syria consult Gaudefroy-Demombynes, pp. xix *seq.*, 29 *seq.*; Walther Björkman, *Beiträge zur Geschichte der Staatskanzlei im islamischen Ägypten* (Hamburg, 1928), pp. 101 *seq.*, 157 *seq.*; ʿAli Ibrāhīm Ḥasan, *Dirāsāt fi Taʾrīkh al-Mamālīk al-Baḥrīyah* (Cairo, 1944), pp. 248-53.

[3] Ṣāliḥ, pp. 81 *seq.*

[4] ʿUmari, p. 176; cf. Ẓāhiri, p. 131.

[5] Ibn-Baṭṭūṭah, vol. i, p. 121; Ṣāliḥ, pp. 155-6.

he fell into disgrace and was put to death in a prison in Alexandria.[1]

Famine and plague

Almost the entire Mamlūk era was punctuated with periods of drought, famine and pestilence. Earthquakes added their quota to the general devastation. The pages of the chronicles of the era are covered with reports of woe and disaster.[2] The leading historian of the age, al-Maqrīzi,[3] devotes an entire work to the famines of Egypt to the year 1405, in which he wrote. Ibn-Taghri-Birdi[4] reports at least four plagues of great severity in the fourteenth century (1348–9, 1359–61, 1362–3, 1389). In the fifteenth century no less than fourteen serious outbreaks are recorded in different chronicles, averaging one every seven years. The "black death" (*al-fanā' al-kabīr*), which in 1348 to 1349 wrought havoc in Europe, lingered in Egypt for seven years. Its victims in the capital, according to the estimates of ibn-Iyās,[5] reached the incredible figure of 900,000. Gaza reportedly lost in one month 22,000 and Aleppo an average of five hundred per day. A large number of the victims were foreigners and children who had not acquired a sufficient degree of immunity. Owing to these calamities and Mamlūk misgovernment, the entire population of Egypt and Syria, it is estimated, was reduced to about one-third of its former size.

Trade and industry

The economic situation was aggravated by taxation and policies which were unsound if not predatory. The wars against Franks and Mongols led to the imposition of burdensome taxes in both Egypt and Syria, including thirty-three and one-third per cent on rents, which caused endless complaints. Not only horses and boats but necessities of life, such as salt and sugar, were heavily taxed. Some sultans monopolized certain commodities and manipulated prices to their advantage. Others

[1] Ibn-Iyās, *Badā'i' al-Ẓuhūr fi Ta'rīkh al-Duhūr*, vol. i (Cairo, 1893), p. 172; Maqrīzi, *Khiṭaṭ*, vol. ii, pp. 54-5.

[2] E. G. Ṣāliḥ, pp. 144, 242; ibn-al-Furāt, vol. viii, p. 209, 212; ibn-Taghri-Birdi, vol. vii, pp. 528-42; do., *Ḥawādith al-Duhūr fi Mada al-Ayyām w-al-Shuhūr*, ed. William Popper (Berkley, 1942), pp. 11, 37, 312, 319. For the Ayyūbid period consult Maqrīzi, *Sulūk*, ed. Ziyādah, vol. i, pt. 1, pp. 130-33, 156-8, 248.

[3] *Ighāthat al-Ummah bi-Kashf al-Ghummah*, eds. Muḥammad M. Ziyādah and Jamāl-al-Dīn M. al-Shayyāl (Cairo, 1940).

[4] Vol. v, pp. 70-76, 154, 185, 408, 507.

[5] Vol. i, p. 191; cf. ibn-Taghri-Birdi, vol. v, p. 71.

debased the currency and contributed to the inflationary spiral.[1] As the people became impoverished, the rulers waxed rich. Without an abundance of wealth the sultans could not have erected those architectural monuments of which Egypt still rightfully boasts.[2]

Happily some of the economic loss was offset by increased trade subsequent to the Crusading enterprise. The concessions offered by al-ʿĀdil [3] and Baybars to the Venetians and other European merchants stimulated exchange of commodities and made Cairo a great *entrepôt* of trade between East and West. Syrian silk shared with perfumes and spices first place in the export trade. Glass and manufactured articles stood next on the list.[4] Damascus, Tripoli, Antioch and Tyre were among the leading centres of industry. Some of the silk in the Syrian market was imported from China; spices came from Arabia and other tropical lands; pearls were brought from the Persian Gulf to the ports of Jaffa and Tripoli.[5] When a governor of Damascus sent his agent to the Shūf district of Lebanon to explore the possibility of the use of mulberry branches for arrows, the Lebanese were greatly disturbed.[6] In the bazaars of Aleppo, Damascus, Beirut one could buy ivory- and metal-work, dyed cloth, carpets and enamelled pottery. The neighbourhood of Beirut produced olive oil and soap [7] as it does today. Pans of saltworks are still visible in ʿAthlīth and other places along the coast.[8]

Syrians did not depend entirely on foreigners for their export trade. As early as Ṣalāḥ-al-Dīn's day their merchants took up residence in Constantinople, where the emperor in compliance with Ṣalāḥ's request built a mosque for them and their Egyptian colleagues in reciprocation for privileges enjoyed by Byzantine merchants in Syria and Egypt. No other foreign merchants were permitted permanent residence in the Byzantine capital. A German clergyman, Ludolph von Suchem, who visited the Holy Land in 1336 to 1341, was most favourably

[1] Maqrīzi, *Ighāthah*, pp. 70-72; ibn-Taghri-Birdi, *Ḥawādith*, pp. 310-12.

[2] See below, p. 648.

[3] See above, p. 606.

[4] See E. Rey, *Les Colonies franques de Syrie* (Paris, 1883), pp. 204, 214-34.

[5] Hilmar C. Krueger, "The Wares of Exchange in the Genoese-African Traffic of the Twelfth Century", *Speculum*, vol. xii (1937), pp. 64, 71.

[6] Ṣāliḥ, p. 225.

[7] Ṣāliḥ, p. 229.

[8] Conder, p. 451.

impressed by the signs of prosperity in Damascus,[1] "the glorious city of Acre" and other Syrian towns.

The streets within the city [Acre] were exceeding neat, all the walls of the houses being of the same height and all alike built of hewn stone, wondrously adorned with glass windows and paintings, while all the palaces and houses in the city were not built merely to meet the needs of those who dwelt therein, but to minister to human luxury and pleasure. . . . The streets of the city were covered with silken cloths, or other fair awnings, to keep off the sun's rays. At every street corner there stood an exceeding strong tower, fenced with an iron door and iron chains. All the nobles dwelt in very strong castles and palaces along the outer edge of the city. In the midst of the city dwelt the mechanic citizens and merchants, each in his own special street according to his trade.[2]

Ibn-Jubayr,[3] who visited Damascus under Ṣalāḥ-al-Dīn, styles it "the bride of the cities" in which he sojourned and describes in detail the timepiece in its mosque which in the day showed progress of time by the operation of two brass falcons and at night by a scheme of special lights. The same timepiece was noted by Benjamin of Tudela.[4]

In Lebanon

With remarkable dexterity the feudal chiefs of Lebanon practised the Machiavellian art of political manœuvring long before the Florentine statesman lived. Through the turmoils that saw the installation over them of Fāṭimids, Ayyūbids, Franks, Mamlūks and Tartars they played the game. When the Crusaders occupied Beirut and Sidon the banu-Buḥtur amīrs of al-Gharb held some of the adjacent territory as fiefs and offered military service to the Franks.[5] Those amīrs did not hesitate to enter into the same relationship with the Mamlūks.[6] The Buḥturid fiefs comprised such small villages as Shimlān, ʻAynāb and Bayṣūr never mentioned before in history and still in existence.[7] In the struggle between Tartars and Mamlūks those amīrs had at times representatives in both camps — a feat that insured their being on the winning side no matter which it was.[8] The policy of watchful waiting and double crossing was practised on those shores in the fourteenth century before Christ;[9] it continued to be practised until the days of Fakhr-al-Dīn and al-Amīr Bashīr.[10]

[1] Pp. 129-32. [2] Ludolph von Suchem, p. 51. [3] Pp. 260, 270-71.
[4] Vol. i, pp. 84-5. [5] Ṣāliḥ, pp. 74-5, 83-4, 111-12; cf. above, p. 599.
[6] Ṣāliḥ, p. 81. [7] Ṣāliḥ, pp. 81, 128, 197, 198-9, 234-5; see above, p. 637
[8] Ṣāliḥ, pp. 93-4, 242-8. [9] See above, p. 71. [10] See below, pp. 665-6.

Although a number of Arab tribes had penetrated into the mountain, mainly from the south,[1] parts of it remained wooded. Bears and boars, even lions and onagers were, as late as the fourteenth century, encountered.[2] Syria also had such animals as attested by Usāmah,[3] who cites wild asses, gazelles, lions, boars, hyenas and leopards. Wild fruits and edible plants together with an abundance of fresh water made the mountain a favourite haunt for ascetics and hermits of both religions. A late twelfth century author [4] devotes chapters to such men and women in the mountains of Lebanon and Syria. Ibn-Jubayr [5] notes with pleasant surprise the kind treatment accorded by neighbouring Christians to these solitaries. Sufi literature has preserved many legendary tales about such men. A Moslem Lebanese ascetic, who one day missed his one-loaf ration coming from an undetermined source, sought alms from the nearest farmhouse. The Christian farmer gave him two barley loaves but the dog pursued the ascetic and did not cease barking until he had deprived him of both loaves and his garment. When the ascetic remarked how greedy the dog was, God put in the canine mouth words to this effect: I guard my master's home and flocks and often go without food when there is none for him or me. But you, deprived but one day of your ration, insisted on coming to us and seeking aid. Who of the two then is more greedy, you or I? [6]

Despite its political turmoils and economic periods of depression Syria enjoyed under the Nūrids and Ayyūbids, in particular under Nūr-al-Dīn and Ṣalāḥ-al-Dīn, the most

Cultural activity: hospitalization

[1] See above, p. 483; Lammens, *Syrie*, vol. ii, pp. 8-14. In the literature of the period the Arabians domiciled in Syria and Egypt became known as *awlād* (descendants of) *al-'Arab* (ibn-Taghri-Birdi, vol. v, p. 367, l. 10; see above, p. 547); *'Arab* was used especially for Bedouins (ibn-Taghri-Birdi, *Ḥawādith*, p. 13, l. 3, p. 47, l. 15, p. 193, l. 21), though the koranic word for them, *'Urbān*, was not entirely abandoned (ibn-Taghri-Birdi, *Ḥawādith*, p. 12, l. 20, p. 190, l. 3, p. 692, ll. 15, 17; do., vol. vi, p. 749, ll. 1, 3; al-Jabarti, *'Ajā'ib al-Āthār fi al-Tarājim w-al-Akhbār* (Cairo, 1297), vol. i, p. 379, l. 9; p. 417, l. 30; ibn-al-Furāt, vol. vii, p. 178, l. 11; Qalqashandi, vol. xiii, p. 5, vol. ix, p. 254; Ẓāhiri, p. 136.

[2] Ṣāliḥ, pp. 113, 193; ibn-Baṭṭūṭah, vol. i, p. 185.

[3] *I'tibār*, pp. 220, 218, 193, 223-4, 144-5, 126, 103-12; *Arab-Syrian Gentleman*, pp. 248-9, 246-7, 223, 251-2, 231, 173-4, 133-42.

[4] Ibn-al-Jawzi, *Ṣifwat al-Ṣafwah*, vol. iv (Ḥaydarābād, 1356), pp. 314-21, 323-7. See above, p. 571.

[5] P. 287.

[6] Al-Makki, *Nuzhat al-Jalīs wa-Munyat al-Adīb al-Anīs* (Cairo, 1293), pp. 58-9.

flourishing era in its artistic and educational activity. Its capital Damascus still bears evidences of the architectural works of these two rulers. Nūr renovated the walls of the city with its towers and gates and erected public buildings, some of which remained in use until recent times. Especially significant was the hospital bearing his name,[1] now used as a commerce school building.[2] The funds for this structure came from the ransom of a Frankish prisoner.[3] Ibn-Jubayr,[4] who visited the hospital in 1184, found it with an endowment yielding fifteen dinars daily and staffed with wardens keeping a record of the cases and expenses and with physicians attending the patients and prescribing foods and free medicines. The historian ibn-al-Athīr received treatment in this institution and when he protested that he could well afford to pay for the drugs he was told that no one ever spurned Nūr's bounty. According to this historian,[5] Nūr built other hospitals and hostels throughout the domain The site of the hospital in Aleppo [6] was determined by slaughtering a sheep and hanging four parts of it in four quarters of the city. The quarter where the meat in the morning "smelled better" than the others was chosen. The same experiment was ascribed to al-Rāzi, who chose the site for Baghdād hospital about two and a half centuries earlier.[7] The Egyptian official and author al-Ẓāhiri [8] visited the Damascus hospital around 1428 accompanied by an amiable Persian pilgrim who, attracted by the comforts accorded the patients, feigned illness and was admitted. On feeling his pulse and examining him thoroughly, the head physician realized there was nothing wrong with the gentleman but nevertheless prescribed fattened chickens, fragrant sherbets, fruits, savoury cakes and other delicacies.

[1] Al-Māristān al-Nūri; ibn-Jubayr, p. 283. Ar. *māristān*, of which the older form is *bīmāristān* (ibn-Khallikān, vol. ii, p. 521), comes from a Persian word meaning home for the sick. Ibn-Jubayr refers to an older hospital which was evidently built by the Saljūq Duqāq ibn-Tutush (above, p. 574) rather than al-Walīd (above, pp. 497-8).

[2] Ṣalāḥ-al-Dīn al-Munajjid in *al-Mashriq*, vol. xlii (1948), p. 251. For a description of the building consult Ernst Herzfeld, "Damascus: Studies in Architecture", *Ars Islamica*, vol. ix (1942), pp. 2-18; J. Sauvaget, *Les Monuments historiques de Damas* (Beirut, 1932), pp. 49-53.

[3] Maqrīzi, vol. ii, p. 408. [4] P. 283. [5] Vol. xi, p. 267.

[6] Ibn-al-Shiḥnah, pp. 230-31; for more on this hospital consult Ahmed Issa, *Histoire des bimaristans à l'époque islamique* (Cairo, 1928), pp. 203-5.

[7] Ibn-abi-Uṣaybi'ah, vol. i, pp. 309-10.

[8] Pp. 44-5.

When the time came, however, he wrote a new prescription: "Three days are the limit of the hospitality period".

Medicine

This hospital was equipped with a library and served as a medical school. Ibn-abi-Uṣaybiʿah [1] has preserved the name of its first physician-professor, abu-al-Majd ibn-abi-al-Ḥakam, and a long sketch of the life of its distinguished dean under the Ayyūbid al-ʿĀdil, Muhadhdhab-al-Dīn ibn-al-Dakhwār (1169/1170–1230). There is evidence to show that physicians, pharmacists and oculists were examined and given certificates (sing. *ijāzah*) before being allowed to practise their professions. In the manuals for the guidance of *al-muḥtasib*, the official responsible for law enforcement, his duties with respect to phlebotomists, cuppers, physicians, surgeons, bone-setters and druggists are clearly set, indicating a certain measure of state control.[2] One of ibn-al-Dakhwār's brilliant students was ibn-al-Nafīs,[3] who, after serving as the dean of the Qalāwūn [4] hospital in Cairo, returned to Damascus, where he died in 1288/9. He was a physician "who would not prescribe medicine when diet sufficed". In his *Sharḥ Tashrīḥ al-Qānūn*, a commentary on ibn-Sīna's major work, ibn-al-Nafīs contributed a clear conception of the pulmonary circulation of the blood three centuries before the Portuguese Servetus, to whom the discovery is usually credited. Syrian oculists (sing. *kaḥḥāl*) produced the only two major Arabic works of the thirteenth century: *al-Kāfi fi al-Kuḥl* (the sufficient work on collyrium) by Khalīfah ibn-abi-al-Maḥāsin, who flourished in Aleppo about 1256, and *Nūr al-ʿUyūn wa-Jāmiʿ al-Funūn* (the light of the eyes and compendium of arts) by Ṣalāḥ-al-Dīn ibn-Yūsuf, who practised in Ḥamāh about 1296. So confident was Khalīfah of his surgical skill that he did not hesitate to remove a cataract from a one-eyed man.[5] All these men, however, lived in the late twilight of Islamic science.

To this period belongs the most distinguished historian of medicine the Arab world produced, Muwaffaq-al-Dīn Aḥmad ibn-abi-Uṣaybiʿah (1203–70). Himself a physician and son of a Damascene oculist, ibn-abi-Uṣaybiʿah studied under ibn-al-

[1] Vol. ii, pp. 155, 239-43.
[2] Ibn-al-Ukhūwah, *Maʿālim al-Qurba fi Aḥkām al-Ḥiṣbah*, ed. Reuben Levy (Cambridge, 1938), pp. 159-70 (text), 54-9 (tr.).
[3] Subki, vol. v, p. 129.
[4] See above, p. 632.
[5] Consult Sarton, vol. ii, pp. 1101-2.

Dakhwār and in Cairo and botanized with the celebrated Spanish Moslem ibn-al-Bayṭār. His masterpiece, *'Uyūn al-Anbā' fi Ṭabaqāt al-Aṭibbā'* [1] (sources of information on the classes of physicians), almost unique in Arabic literature, is an elaborate collection of some four hundred biographies of Arab and Greek physicians, many of whom were also philosophers, astronomers, physicists and mathematicians. The nearest approach to this work was that of a contemporary Egyptian, al-Qifṭi [2] (1172–1248), who spent the latter part of his life at Aleppo, where he acted as vizir to its Ayyūbid rulers. One of the sources of ibn-abi-Uṣaybi'ah [3] on Greek philosophy was an Egyptian of Damascene origin, abu-al-Wafā' Mubashshir ibn-Fātik,[4] who in 1053 compiled a book entitled *Mukhtār al-Ḥikam wa-Maḥā-sin al-Kalim* that was translated into Spanish in the first half of the thirteenth century and then into Latin, French and English. The English edition, *Dictes and Sayings of the Philosophers*, issued in 1477 by William Caxton, was the first book printed in that language with a date and place of printing. For over four centuries the literary descendants of this Arabic work continued to influence the thoughts and writings of Western Europeans.

Madrasahs

Together with the hospitals went schools and mosques. The Nūrids introduced into Syria the type of schools styled *madrasahs* (collegiate mosques). The madrasah was not an intellectual descendant of al-Ma'mūn's Bayt al-Ḥikmah (house of wisdom) established in 830 in Baghdād — which was a general academy of sciences and arts — but rather of the Niẓāmīyah founded in Baghdād in 1067 and named after the Persian vizir of the early Saljūq sultans. The madrasahs were mosque schools, theological seminaries and law academies founded by the state to inculcate and propagate orthodoxy. In them the doctrines approved by Sunnite religion and Moslem scholasticism were studied and taught. Teachers and students received their pay from endowments (sing. *waqf* [5]) connected with the institutions and as a rule lodged in them. The teachers

[1] First edited by "Imru'-al-Qays ibn-al-Ṭaḥḥān" [August Müller], 2 vols. (Cairo, 1882), then republished with additional pages, corrections and index by August Müller, 2 vols. (Königsberg, 1884).

[2] *Ikhbār al-'Ulamā' bi-Akhbār al-Ḥukamā'* (*Ta'rīkh al-Ḥukamā'*), ed. Julius Lippert (Leipzig, 1903).

[3] Vol. i, pp. 9, 16, 21, 28, 30, 38, 41, 43, 47, 50.

[4] Yāqūt, *Irshād*, vol. vi, p. 241; Qifṭi, p. 269.

[5] See above, p. 478.

were jurisconsults (*faqīhs*), theologians (*ʿulamāʾ*) and traditionists. No civil career was normally open to an aspirant who did not receive his training in a madrasah. Realizing the value of such institutions for the state, the Nūrids and after them the Ayyūbids made full use of them. Nūr-al-Dīn built such schools not only in Damascus but in Aleppo, Ḥimṣ, Ḥamāh and other Syrian towns.[1] Three of his schools in Damascus are the oldest monuments of their kind that have come down to us. They follow the cruciform style of Persian origin. In one of them, al-Madrasah al-Nūrīyah, described by ibn-Jubayr [2] as "one of the finest school buildings in the world", Nūr was buried. The simple inscription on the stone is still legible: "This is the tomb of the martyr Nūr-al-Dīn ibn-Zangi, may God have mercy on him". The mausoleum is still held in reverence by the Damascenes. Its dome is of the type termed *muqarnaṣ*,[3] often described as stalactite but in reality corbelled. Through this building the connection between the school, mausoleum (*turbah*) and mosque was established in Syria.

Nūr was equally munificent in mosque building. That of Ḥamāh still bears his name, al-Nūri. It was provided with running water, as all his large mosques, hospitals and madrasahs were. Besides, he reconstructed mosques in several cities including Aleppo, whose citadel he renovated. His inscription on a western tower of the citadel is still visible. Nūr's inscriptions are a landmark in Arabic palaeography signalizing the age in which the old angular Kufi gave place to the common rounded *naskhi*.

The Ayyūbids followed in the Nūrids' footsteps. Ṣalāḥ-al-Dīn's brother al-ʿĀdil resumed the building of a school begun by Nūr and was buried in it. This is the ʿĀdilīyah, now housing the Arab Academy of Damascus.[4]

Ṣalāḥ-al-Dīn vied with Nūr-al-Dīn in architectural and educational patronage. His contemporary ibn-Jubayr [5] found in Damascus twenty schools, a hundred public baths, forty lavatories

[1] Ibn-Khallikān, vol. ii, p. 521; ibn-al-Athīr, vol. xi, p. 267. For more on the schools in Aleppo consult J. Sauvaget, *Alep* (Paris, 1941), pp. 122-4, 148.

[2] P. 284. Consult al-Nuʿaymi, *al-Dāris fi Taʾrīkh al-Madāris*, ed. Jaʿfar al-Ḥasani (Damascus, 1948), pp. 606-7.

[3] Defined in Arabic dictionaries as "scale-shaped". The word is an adaptation of the same Greek word whence "cornice" comes; Herzfeld in *Ars Islamica*, vol. ix (1942), p. 11.

[4] Nuʿaymi, p. 359.

[5] Pp. 283, 288.

THE ANCIENT CITADEL OF ALEPPO (QAL'AT ḤALAB), RESTORED BY NŪR-AL-DĪN (d. 1174)

To the left of the entrance is a Byzantine tower repaired and now used as a Moslem minaret (sing. *dār li-al-waḍū'*, place for ablution) and a large number of dervish "monasteries",[1] most of them with running water. It

From Dussaud, Deschamps and Seyrig, "La Syrie" (Paul Geuthner, Paris)

KHĀN AL-ṢĀBŪN (THE SOAP CARAVANSARY), ALEPPO
An elegant structure of the Mamlūk period

was Ṣalāḥ who introduced the dervish sanctuary and the madrasah into Egypt, the madrasah to combat the widely spread

[1] Sing. *khānaqāh*, from Per.

Shīʿite doctrine.[1] In Jerusalem he built a hospital, a school and a monastery all bearing his name, al-Ṣalāḥi.[2] These were the three types of institutions favoured by the Nūrids.

Mamlūk architecture and decoration

The Ayyūbid school of Syrian architecture was continued in Mamlūk Egypt, where it is still represented by some of the most exquisite monuments Arab art ever produced. Strength, solidity and excessive decoration characterize this school. Its decorative motifs assume infinite grace on its durable material of fine stone. In the thirteenth century Egypt received fresh Syro-Mesopotamian influences through refugee artists and artisans from Damascus, Baghdād and al-Mawṣil who had fled Mongol invasions. The influence is apparent in schools, mosques, hospitals, dervish monasteries and palaces. The far-famed al-Qaṣr al-Ablaq (the multicoloured palace), built by the Mamlūk al-Nāṣir in 1314, was modelled after a palace in Damascus. The ornamentation of Ayyūbid and Mamlūk monuments enhanced their architectural beauty. Among the Ayyūbid innovations was a tendency toward elaboration in detail, greater elegance of proportion and increase in the number of stalactites. There was also a breakaway from the tradition of the plain square towers. In the Baḥri Mamlūk period the elaborate type of minaret evolved from the Ayyūbid. The finest minarets, however, belong to the Burji period, in which Arab architecture — as represented in the mosques — achieved its greatest triumphs.[3]

Exquisite specimens of iron-work, copper-work, glassware and wood-carving have come down to us from the Ayyūbid-Mamlūk age. Especially noteworthy among copper utensils are vases, ewers, trays, chandeliers, perfume burners and Koran cases, all with rich decoration.

In spite of the dazzling profusion of its motives, this decoration, with its powerful Kufic script, its running patterns of conventionalized foliage, its interlacing patterns, rosettes, arabesques and occasional heraldic motives, retains a vigour and sureness of touch that make it

[1] Ibn-Khallikān, vol. iii, p. 521; Suyūṭi, vol. ii, pp. 156, 158; cf. Maqrīzi, vol. ii, p. 363.

[2] Ibn-Khallikān, vol. iii, p. 516; Maqrīzi, vol. ii, p. 415.

[3] René Grousset, *The Civilizations of the East*, vol. i, *The Near and Middle East*, tr. Catherine A. Phillips (New York, 1931), p. 235; M. van Berchem, *Matériaux pour un corpus inscriptionum Arabicarum*, pt. 2, vol. i (Cairo, 1922), pp. 87 *seq.*

not only a delight to the eye, but also — and this is, in our opinion, the secret of Arab decoration — a delight to the intelligence.[1]

Damascus was especially noted for its "gold-like" basins and ewers inlaid with figures, foliage and other delicate designs

Courtesy of the Walters Art Gallery, Baltimore

A BRASS INCENSE BURNER MADE IN MAMLŪK SYRIA, SECOND HALF OF THE THIRTEENTH CENTURY

Inlaid with silver its lower part is decorated with units of scrolling stems symmetrically composed and coalescing with water-fowls

in silver. An Italian traveller[2] who visited the city in 1384/5 noted that "if the father should be a goldsmith, the sons can never thereafter be engaged in any other craft than this . . . so that by force of circumstances they are obliged to be perfect

[1] Grousset, p. 234.

[2] Simone Sigoli in Cesare Angelini, *Viaggi in Terrasanta* (Florence, 1944), p. 227.

masters of their craft". Bronze ornaments from doors of mosques bear witness to the good taste of the age. The wood carvings with their floral and geometrical designs indicate freedom from the formulas of Fāṭimid art. A bottle in the Arab

From René Grousset, "The Civilizations of the East", vol. i, "The Near and Middle East" (Alfred A. Knopf, New York)

COPPER TRAY WITH METAL INLAY REPRESENTING MAMLŪK ART OF THE FOURTEENTH CENTURY IN DAMASCUS

Museum at Cairo bearing the name of al-Nāṣir Ṣalāḥ-al-Dīn, sultan of Damascus and Aleppo (1250–60), is one of the oldest specimens of enamelled glass. Mosque lamps preserved in this and other museums prove that Syria was still ahead of any European land in the technique of glass manufacture.[1]

[1] Sarton, vol. iii, p. 173.

Intellectual endeavour

Viewed intellectually the entire Ayyūbid-Mamlūk period was one of compilation and imitation rather than of origination. Nevertheless Damascus and Cairo, especially after the destruction of Baghdād and the disintegration of Moslem Spain, remained the educational and intellectual centres of the Arab world. The schools, founded and richly endowed in these two cities, served to conserve and transmit Arab science and learning.

Illuministic Sufism

In Sufism certain significant developments took place. Aleppo under al-Malik al-Ẓāhir, son of Ṣalāḥ-al-Dīn, was the scene of the activity of an extraordinary Sufi, Shihāb-al-Dīn al-Suhrawardi (1155–91), founder of the doctrine of illumination (*ishrāq*) [1] and of a dervish order. According to this doctrine light is the very essence of God, the fundamental reality of all things and the representative of true knowledge, perfect purity, love and goodness. Clearly such theories combine Zoroastrian — more especially Manichaean — Neo-Platonic and Islamic ideas. Plotinus and Manes were the ancestors of al-Ishrāq.[2] Al-Suhrawardi was himself born in Persia. The Neo-Platonic ideas filtered at least in part through Christian, mainly Syrian, sources. The conception of God in terms of light is found in the Koran (24 : 35). Long before al-Suhrawardi, al-Ghazzāli devoted a whole treatise, *Mishkāt al-Anwār* (the niche for lights),[3] to this idea. To al-Ghazzāli, too, God is the one real light, from which all other lights are but rays or reflections. Before him Christian mystics had hinted at a spiritual light permeating the universe and itself a radiation of divinity and the essence of all things. During al-Ghazzāli's sojourn in Syria he must have come in contact with mystical teachings of Christians belonging to the Greek Church. His main endeavour was to reconcile orthodox Islam with Sufi mysticism. Al-Suhrawardi contributed several works [4] of which *Ḥikmat al-Ishrāq* [5] (the wisdom of illumination) is the most important. Intoxicated with his mystical fervour this young Sufi so incensed the conservative theologians that on their insistence he

[1] Consult Ḥājji Khalfah, vol. iii, pp. 87 *seq.*

[2] Consult Arthur J. Arberry, *An Introduction to the History of Ṣūfism* (London, 1942), p. 32.

[3] (Cairo, 1322); tr. W. H. Gairdner (London, 1924).

[4] For a list consult ibn-Khallikān, vol. iii, pp. 257-8; ibn-abi-Uṣaybiʿah, vol. ii, pp. 170-71. One of his odes quoted in ibn-Khallikān is still chanted, especially in Sufi circles.

[5] (Teheran, 1316).

was starved or strangled to death on orders from the defender of the faith Ṣalāḥ-al-Dīn.[1] Hence his epithet *shaykh maqtūl* (the murdered master). His tomb lies near the post-office building of Aleppo.

Ibn-ʿArabi

Another Ishrāqi Sufi of foreign birth who spent his last days in Syria was Muḥyi-al-Dīn ibn-ʿArabi (1165–1240).[2] Ibn-ʿArabi was more of a pantheistic philosopher; in fact he is considered the greatest speculative genius of Islamic mysticism. Probably to escape restrictions then imposed on liberal thought in his native Spain, where al-Ghazzāli's works had been burned, ibn-ʿArabi, following a pilgrimage to Mecca in 1202, made Damascus his home. There his tomb, enshrined in a mosque built by the Ottoman sultan Salīm I, is still visited. The true mystic in ibn-ʿArabi's judgment has but one guide, the inner light, and will find God in all religions.[3] Raymond Lull [4] and other Christian mystics bear traces of ibn-ʿArabi's influence. In his *al-Futūḥat al-Makkīyah* [5] (Meccan revelations) and *al-Isrā' ila Maqām al-Asra* [6] (the nocturnal journey toward the station of the Most Magnanimous), ibn-ʿArabi develops the favourite theme involving Muḥammad's ascension to the seventh heaven.[7] A considerable number of details relating to scenes, episodes, topography and architecture in Dante's *Divine Comedy* have their precedents in these two works of ibn-ʿArabi and other Islamic writings.[8]

Biography

One of the earliest professors in Dār al-Ḥadīth (school of tradition) al-Nūrīyah of Damascus was ibn-ʿAsākir [9] (1105–1176), author of *al-Ta'rīkh al-Kabīr* (the great history), in which he sketched the lives of almost all personages who had ever been connected with that city. Of the eighty volumes of this work few have survived.[10] As a biographer, ibn-ʿAsākir was eclipsed by another product of the Damascene schools,[11] Shams-al-Dīn

[1] Ibn-Shaddād, pp. 302-3; Suhrawardi, *Thalāth Rasā'il*, ed. and tr. Otto Spies and S. K. Khatak (Stuttgart, 1935), p. 98; ibn-Khallikān, vol. iii, p. 260.

[2] A. E. Affifi, *The Mystical Philosophy of Muḥyid Dín-Ibnul ʿArabi* (Cambridge, 1939), pp. 3, 5, 47, 108, 183-4.

[3] Ibn-ʿArabi, *Tarjumān al-Ashwāq*, ed. and tr. Nicholson (London, 1911), pp. 19, 67.

[4] See above, p. 625. [5] 2nd ed., 4 vols. (Cairo, 1293). [6] (Cairo, 1252).

[7] Koran 17:1. [8] See above, p. 582.

[9] Kutubi, vol. i, p. 333; Yāqūt, *Irshād*, vol. v, pp. 139-46; Subki, vol. iv, pp. 273-7. Nuʿaymi, pp. 100, 104, 105.

[10] Ed. ʿAbd-al-Qādir ibn-Badrān, 7 vols. (Damascus, 1329–51).

[11] See above, p. 644.

(sun of the faith) Aḥmad ibn-Khallikān, foremost among all Moslem biographers. Born in Irbil (Arbela), ibn-Khallikān was appointed in 1261 chief judge of Syria.[1] This high position he held in Damascus, with a seven years' interval, until shortly before his death in 1282. Ibn-Khallikān produced the earliest dictionary of national biography in Arabic, *Wafayāt al-Aʿyān wa-Anbā' Abnā' al-Zamān* [2] (obituaries of eminent men and sketches of leading contemporaries), a collection of biographies. The author took pains to establish the correct orthography of names, fix dates, trace pedigrees, ascertain the significant events and on the whole produce as accurate and interesting portrayals as possible. A continuation of this work was penned by al-Kutubi (the bookseller, *d.* 1363) of Aleppo under the title *Fawāt al-Wafayāt*.[3]

A more prolific but less thorough biographer than ibn-Khallikān was Ṣalāḥ-al-Dīn Khalīl ibn-Aybak, known as al-Ṣafadi after his birthplace (1296–1363).[4] Son of a Turkish slave, al-Ṣafadi studied in Damascus under the grammarian abu-Ḥayyān al-Tawḥīdi and later associated with the traditionist-historian al-Ḥāfiẓ al-Dhahabi (1274–1348) [5] and the canon lawyer Tāj-al-Dīn al-Subki (*ca.* 1327–70).[6] So voluminous was al-Dhahabi's history of Islam that it deterred copyists, baffled book collectors and consequently failed of survival. Al-Ṣafadi held the post of treasurer of Damascus. The work for which he is best known is *al-Wāfi bi-al-Wafayāt* [7] (adequate treatment of obituaries) in thirty volumes, in the extant part of which the lives of some fourteen thousand rulers, judges and literati are portrayed. This is the largest biographical dictionary in Islam. Ibn-Khallikān's *Wafayāt* has 865 biographies, al-Kutubi's *Fawāt* 506 and ibn-abi-Uṣaybiʿah's *ʿUyūn* about 400. In the introduction to his dictionary al-Ṣafadi worked out a manual of

[1] Subki, vol. v, pp. 14-15; Suyūṭi, vol. i, pp. 265-6.

[2] Several editions. The one used here is in 3 vols. (Cairo, 1299); tr. de Slane, 4 vols. (Paris, 1843–71).

[3] 2 vols. (Cairo, 1283). For a criticism of ibn-Khallikān's approach as compared with Plutarch's consult Gustave E. von Grunebaum, *Medieval Islam* (Chicago, 1946), pp. 279-80.

[4] Subki, vol. vi, pp. 94-103.

[5] Of his many works only *Duwal al-Islām*, 2 vols. (Ḥaydarābād, 1337), was used above.

[6] His *Ṭabaqāt al-Shāfiʿīyah al-Kubra*, 6 vols. (Cairo, 1324), was drawn upon in the writing of this section.

[7] Ed. H. Ritter, vol. i (Istanbul, 1931).

historical method, "the first of its kind produced anywhere in the world".[1] Al-Ṣafadi supplements the works of his predecessors, particularly ibn-Khallikān and Yāqūt. Originally a Greek slave, Yāqūt wrote an important dictionary of learned men, *Muʿjam al-Udabāʾ* (*Irshād*), but he is better known for his geographical dictionary, *Muʿjam al-Buldān*.[2] This masterpiece of literature was completed in 1228 at Aleppo and dedicated to its vizir al-Qifṭi.[3] Yāqūt died in that city.

History and geography

Closely related to biography and geography is history. Among the Syrian historians cited in the foregoing pages are abu-Shāmah (1203–68),[4] whose chief work, *Kitāb al-Rawḍatayn fi Akhbār al-Dawlatayn*,[5] was mainly the history of Nūr-al-Dīn and Ṣalāḥ-al-Dīn, and abu-al-Fidāʾ (1273–1332), one of the last Ayyūbid rulers of Ḥamāh,[6] whose *Taʾrīkh*[7] condenses and continues the more voluminous history of ibn-al-Athīr (d. 1234). Abu-al-Fidāʾ was born in Damascus, whither his parents had fled from the Mongols. So popular was his history that it was continued, summarized and abridged by later writers. Equally worthy was his contribution to geography. In the introduction to his *Taqwīm al-Buldān*[8] (tables of the lands) he argues for the sphericity of the earth and cites the loss or gain of one day as one travels around it. This Syrian author may perhaps be considered "the greatest historiogeographer of the period irrespective of nationality or religion".[9] A contemporary and fellow-countryman of abu-al-Fidāʾ, Shams-al-Dīn al-Dimashqi (Damascene, d. 1326/7), produced a cosmographical treatise, *Nukhbat al-Dahr fi ʿAjāʾib al-Barr w-al-Baḥr* (choice piece of the age relative of the marvels of land and sea),[10] which is poorer than the *Taqwīm* in its mathematical aspects but richer in its physical, mineral and ethnic information. Another, ibn-Faḍl-Allāh al-ʿUmari, who, after serving as chancellor in the Mamlūk court, at Cairo returned to his birthplace in Damascus, where he

[1] Sarton, vol. iii, p. 309.
[2] Ed. F. Wüstenfeld, 6 vols. (Leipzig, 1866–73).
[3] See above, p. 644.
[4] Kutubi, vol. i, pp. 322-5.
[5] 2 vols. (Cairo, 1287–8).
[6] See above, p. 628.
[7] 4 vols. (Constantinople, 1286).
[8] Ed. M. Reinaud and MacGuckin de Slane (Paris, 1840); tr. M. Reinaud, vols. (Paris, 1848).
[9] Sarton, vol. iii, p. 308.
[10] Ed. A. F. Mehren (St. Petersburg, 1865); Fr. tr. by Mehren (Copenhagen, 1874).

died of the plague (1349), produced two important works: *Masālik al-Abṣār fi Mamālik al-Amṣār* (paths of the eyes through the kingdoms of the main towns) [1] and *al-Taʿrīf bi-al-Muṣṭalaḥ al-Sharīf* (acquainting [the reader] with the noble epistolary style),[2] a manual for administrators and diplomats.

The names of the two leading historians in the Mamlūk period, the Egyptian al-Maqrīzi and the Tunisian ibn-Khaldūn, are connected with Syria. Al-Maqrīzi (1364–1442), whose valuable *al-Khiṭaṭ* [3] was repeatedly cited in the above pages, was of Baʿlabakkan ancestry and held a professorship in Damascus. As chief judge of Egypt, his younger contemporary ibn-Khaldūn (1332–1406) in 1401 accompanied the Mamlūk sultan al-Nāṣir Faraj to Damascus on his campaign against Tīmūr and was received as an honoured guest by the dreadful Mongol. Ibn-Khaldūn's *Muqaddamah* (prolegomena),[4] which is the first volume in his comprehensive history,[5] entitles him to the distinction of being the greatest philosopher of history Islam produced. In his attempt to interpret historical happenings and national traits on economic, geographic, physical and other secular bases, ibn-Khaldūn had no predecessor in Islam and remains without a worthy successor.

This array of biographers, geographers, historians and encyclopaedic scholars, beginning with ibn-ʿAsākir and ending with ibn-Khaldūn, makes Syria and Egypt of the Ayyūbid and Mamlūk period without peer among the lands of Islam.

The onslaught on Syria by Tīmūr Lang (Tamerlane) was Tīmūr
the last in the Mongol series. Tīmūr claimed descent from Chingīz Khān.[6] Like a cyclone he and his hordes swept from Central into Western Asia leaving havoc and ruin in their wake. For the fourth or fifth time Syria lay prostrate at Mongol feet.[7] For three days in October 1400 Aleppo was given over to plunder. Its citadel was perhaps for the first time taken by

[1] Ed. Aḥmad Zaki, vol. i (Cairo, 1924). For a critical appreciation consult ʿAbd-al-Laṭīf Ḥamzah, *al-Ḥarakah al-Fikrīyah fi Miṣr fi al-ʿAṣrayn al-Ayyūbi w-al-Mamlūki al-Awwal* (Cairo, 1947), pp. 324-7.

[2] (Cairo, 1314).

[3] 2 vols. (Cairo, 1270).

[4] Earlier than the Cairo (1284) edition is that of M. Quatremère, 3 vols. (Paris, 1858); tr. de Slane, 3 vols. (Paris, 1862–8, ed. Boutboul, Paris, 1934–8).

[5] Vol. vi (Cairo, 1284), pp. 379 *seq.*, contains his autobiography, the best source of his life.

[6] Cf. ibn-ʿArab-Shāh, *ʿAjāʾib al-Maqdūr fi Akhbār Tīmūr* (Cairo, 1285), p. 6.

[7] See above, pp. 631-2.

storm, the invader having sacrificed of his men enough to fill the moat with their corpses. Some twenty thousand of the city's inhabitants were slaughtered; severed heads were built into a platform ten cubits high by ten in circumference.[1] The city's priceless schools and mosques built by Nūrids and Ayyūbids were forever destroyed. The routing of the Egyptian army of Sultan Faraj opened the way to Damascus. Its citadel held out for a month. In violation of the capitulation terms the city was plundered and committed to the flames. Thirty thousand of its men, women and children were shut up in its great mosque, which was then set on fire. Of the building itself only the walls were left standing. The cream of Damascene scholars, craftsmen, artisans, armourers, steel workers[2] and glass manufacturers were carried away to Tīmūr's capital, Samarqand, there to implant these and other minor arts. Damascus lost its leadership in damascening. From the pen of ibn-Taghri-Birdi,[3] whose father was chief armour-bearer of Faraj, we have a graphic description of the entire Syrian campaign. This was perhaps the heaviest blow that the city, if not the whole country, ever suffered.

By 1402 the wild conqueror had crushed the Ottoman army at Ankara, captured Brusa and Smyrna and taken Bāyazīd I prisoner.[4] Fortunately for the mamlūks Tīmūr died in 1404. His successors exhausted themselves in internal struggles which made possible the reconstitution of the Ottoman power in Asia Minor and later the rise of the Ṣafawid dynasty in Persia.

Ottomans against Mamlūks and Ṣafawids

Rivalry between the Mamlūk and the Ottoman sultanates for supremacy in Western Asia asserted itself in the second half of the fifteenth century. The Ṣafawid state became involved in the early sixteenth. Ottoman-Mamlūk relations were strained in the days of Khushqadam (1461–7), who unlike his Turkish and Circassian Mamlūk predecessors was a Greek,[5] and Muḥammad II, conqueror of Constantinople. But hostilities did not break out till 1486, when Qā'it-bāy contested with the Otto-

[1] Ibn-Taghri-Birdi, vol. vi, pt. 2, 52; cf. ibn-Iyās, vol. i, p. 327.

[2] Iron ore came presumably from neighbouring Lebanon; see above, pp. 35, 277, 571.

[3] Vol. vi, pt. 2, p. 5, l. 14, pp. 50 *seq.* Cf. Mīrkhwānd, *Ta'rīkh Rawḍat al-Ṣafā'* (Teheran, 1270), Bk. VI; Maqrīzi, vol. ii, p. 241.

[4] Ibn-'Arab-Shāh, p. 6; ibn-Iyās, vol. i, p. 334; vol. iii, p. 48.

[5] Ibn-Taghri-Birdi, vol. vii, p. 685.

man Bāyazīd II the possession of Adana, Tarsus and other border towns. Towards the end of his reign this Mamlūk sultan sent a message to the pope threatening reprisals on the Christians of Syria as Ferdinand was destroying the last Islamic power in Spain. Shortly after that hostilities began between Ottomans and Persians resulting in the swift destruction of the Ṣafawid army and the occupation of Mesopotamia by Salīm I (1512–20). The Ṣafawids were ardent Shī'ites and established their rite as the state religion. Salīm charged that the Mamlūk Qānṣawh al-Ghawri (1500–16) had entered into treaty relations with the Ṣafawid Shah against him and had harboured various political refugees.

Marj Dābiq: a decisive victory

Meantime Qānṣawh had moved northward under the pretext of acting as an intermediary between the two contestants.[1] In his train were the chief judges of his realm and the puppet caliph al-Mutawakkil. This caliph was a descendant and successor of al-Mustanṣir (uncle of the last 'Abbāsid caliph in Baghdād), whom Baybars had in 1261 installed in Cairo merely to confer legitimacy upon his crown and give his court an air of primacy in Moslem eyes.[2] Qānṣawh sent a special envoy to Salīm, who thought of no better way of insulting him than to shave his beard and send him back, on a lame donkey, with a declaration of war. The two armies were locked in battle on August 24, 1516, on the blood-stained field of Marj Dābiq, north of Aleppo. The seventy-five-year-old Qānṣawh, who had begun his career as a slave of Qā'it-bāy, fought valiantly but hopelessly. He could not depend upon the loyalty of his Syrian governors nor could he match his troops with the redoubtable Janissaries[3] with their superior equipment. Khā'ir Bey, the treacherous governor of Aleppo, who was entrusted with the command of the left wing, deserted with his men at the first charge.[4] The Turkish army employed artillery, muskets and other long-range weapons which the Egyptian army, comprising Bedouin and Syrian contingents, was unfamiliar with or dis-

[1] Al-Qaramāni, *Akhbār al-Duwal wa-Āthār al-Uwal* (Baghdād, 1282), pp. 219-20.

[2] Maqrīzi, tr. Quatremère, vol. i (pt. 1), pp. 146-68; ibn-Khaldūn, vol. v, pp. 382-3; abu-al-Fidā', vol. iii, p. 222; Suyūṭi, *Ḥusn*, vol. ii, pp. 49-52; ibn-Iyās, vol. i, pp. 100-101.

[3] Tur. *yeni-cheri*, new troops, name given to the regular infantry recruited mainly from young captured Christians and largely responsible for the Ottoman conquests.

[4] Ibn-Iyās, vol. iii, pp. 46, 51.

dained to use, clinging to the antiquated theory that personal valour is the decisive factor in combat. Gunpowder [1] and "heavy guns mounted on wagons drawn by horses" [2] were also used by the Turks. In the heat of the battle Qānṣawh was stricken with apoplexy and fell from his horse. Salīm's victory was complete. He seized the caliph and later took him to Constantinople, but the claim that the caliph transmitted to the Ottoman sultan the dignity of his office is a nineteenth century fiction. In the citadel of Aleppo Salīm found Mamlūk treasures estimated in millions of dinars. In mid-October he moved on to Damascus. Syria passed quietly into Ottoman hands, where it was to remain for four full centuries. Its people, as on many a previous occasion, welcomed the new masters as deliverers from the old.

Mamlūk rule abolished

From Syria the Ottoman army streamed south into Egypt, where Ṭūmān-bāy, a slave of Qānṣawh, had been proclaimed sultan. The two armies met on January 22, 1517, outside Cairo. "Plastered with shots and bullets" [3] the Egyptian army was soon routed. Ṭūmān-bāy fled to a Bedouin camp where he was betrayed and later (April 17) hanged at one of Cairo's main gates.[4] Egypt was no more a sovereign state. Al-Ḥijāz, with its two holy cities, automatically became a part of the rising Ottoman empire. In the first Friday congregational services Egyptian preachers invoked Allah's blessing on the conqueror in these words:

> O Lord! uphold the sultan, son of the sultan, ruler over both lands and the two seas, conqueror of both hosts, monarch of the two ʿIrāqs, minister of the two Holy Cities, the victorious king Salīm Shāh. Grant him, O Lord, Thy precious aid; enable him to win glorious victories, O Ruler of this world and the next, Lord of the universe.[5]

A new era dawned upon the Arab world: that of domination by the Ottoman Turks.

[1] Evidently a Chinese invention, gunpowder was introduced by the Mongols about 1240 into Europe, where its use for projective purposes through firearms was later developed; cf. Sarton, vol. iii, pp. 722-3. The first mention of artillery (*madāfiʿ*) in Syrian history is perhaps in Yaḥya, p. 229, where Genoese seamen bombard Beirut in 1382.

[2] Qaramāni, p. 220.

[3] Ibn-Iyās, vol. iii, p. 97.

[4] Ibn-Iyās, vol. iii, p. 115; Suyūṭi, vol. ii, p. 90; Qaramāni, p. 220; cf. Saʿd-al-Dīn, *Tāj al-Tawārīkh*, vol. ii (Constantinople, 1280), p. 361.

[5] Ibn-Iyās, vol. iii, p. 98.

PART V

UNDER THE OTTOMAN TURKS

CHAPTER XLVIII

SYRIA A TURKISH PROVINCE

FROM modest beginnings in the early fourteenth century the petty Turkish state in western Asia Minor rose in the course of the following two centuries to a dominant position in Western Asia, south-eastern Europe and north-eastern Africa. Its rise was one of the major facts in modern history. The term Turk appears for the first time about A.D. 500 as name of a nomadic people in Central Asia.[1] In the sixth century Turkish peoples succeeded in establishing nomadic states extending from Mongolia and the northern frontier of China to the Black Sea. If the Arabians were parasites of the camel, the Turks were parasites of the horse. They drank its milk, ate its flesh and rode on it to victory. They used stirrups and bows and arrows. Mobility was the chief advantage they possessed over their foes. In Turkestan they came in contact with Indo-European peoples, and it was in this region that the Arab conquerors of the late seventh and early eighth centuries first encountered Turkish-speaking people.[2] When at last those of them to be designated Ottoman reached Asia Minor, they found the country already partly Turkicized by their Saljūq cousins.[3] Both Saljūqs and Ottomans traditionally belonged to the Ghuzz tribe or federation of tribes.

The Ottoman state

The eponymous founder of the Ottoman state and dynasty was a semi-historical leader ʿUthmān[4] (1299–1326), whose name, assuming its genuineness, indicates that by that time his clan was beginning to be or was Islamized.[5] With the adoption of Islam thousands of religious, scientific and literary terms from Arabic, and some from Persian, found their way into the

[1] See above, p. 437. [2] See above, pp. 458 *seq.*

[3] See above, pp. 573 *seq.*

[4] On him consult Mehmed Fuad Köprülü, *Les Origines de l'empire ottomane* (Paris, 1935), pp. 87 *seq.*; Paul Wittek, *The Rise of the Ottoman Empire* (London, 1938), pp. 7-9; Joseph von Hammer, *Geschichte des osmanischen Reiches*, vol. i (Pest, 1827), pp. 40 *seq.*

[5] On the early religion of the Turks, see above, p. 631.

Turkish language. With little written literature [1] of its own this language in the meantime adopted the Arabic characters, which remained in use until the reforms of Muṣṭafa Kemāl in 1928. For about sixty-six years after its foundation in about 1300 the Ottoman state was a frontier amīrate with Brusa (Bursa) as capital after 1326.[2] From 1366 to 1543 it was a kingdom with Adrianople (Edirne) as capital.[3] The conquest of Constantinople in 1453 by Muḥammad II the Conqueror (al-Fātiḥ, 1451–1481) marks the emergence of the empire. Thus did this Moslem Turkish state fall heir to the Byzantine empire, to which it later successively added several states of the Arab caliphate. The Ottoman empire attained its height under Sulaymān I the Magnificent (al-Qānūni, the lawgiver, 1520–66), son of the conqueror of Syria and Egypt, Salīm I. Under Sulaymān the greater part of Hungary was reduced, Vienna was besieged, Rhodes was occupied and North Africa, exclusive of Morocco, acknowledged the political authority of the Sublime Porte (*al-Bāb al-ʿĀli*) in Constantinople.[4] The failure of the second

[1] Syriac script was used by Turks in Central Asia; see above, pp. 169, 518.

[2] Genealogical table of the first Ottoman rulers:

1. ʿUthmān I (1299)
|
2. Ūrkhān (1326)
|
3. Murād I (1359)

[3] 3. Murād I (1359)
|
4. Bāyazīd I (1389–1401)
|
Sulaymān (claimant, 1403–10) — 5. Muḥammad I (1403) (sole ruler 1413) — Mūsa (claimant, 1410–13)
|
6. Murād II (1421)
|
7. Muḥammad II (1451)

[4] 7. Muḥammad II (1451)
|
8. Bāyazīd II (1481)
|
9. Salīm I (1512)
|
10. Sulaymān I (1520)
|
11. Salīm II (1566)
|
12. Murād III (1574)

attempt to capture Vienna in 1683 marked the beginning of the end. The empire under Sulaymān extended from Budapest on the Danube to Baghdād on the Tigris and from the Crimea to the first cataract of the Nile. No such state was built by Moslems in modern times. It was also one of the most enduring Moslem states. From 1300 to 1922, when the empire came to an end, thirty-six sultans, all in the direct male line of ʿUthmān, ruled.[1]

Administrative divisions of Syria

It was Sultan Salīm I (1512–20) who incorporated the Arab world in the Ottoman empire.[2] After his decisive victory at Marj Dābiq he triumphantly entered Ḥamāh and Ḥimṣ, both of which capitulated. Salīm then received the submission of Tripoli, Ṣafad, Nābulus, Jerusalem and Gaza, " none of which

[1]
- 12. Murād III (1574)
  - 13. Muḥammad III (1595)
    - 14. Aḥmad I (1603)
      - 16. ʿUthmān II (1618)
      - 17. Murād IV (1623)
      - 18. Ibrāhīm (1640)
        - 19. Muḥammad IV (1648)
          - 22. Muṣṭafa II (1695)
            - 24. Maḥmūd I (1730)
            - 25. ʿUthmān III (1754)
          - 23. Aḥmad III (1703)
            - 26. Muṣṭafa III (1757)
              - 28. Salīm III (1789)
            - 27. ʿAbd-al-Ḥamīd I (1774)
              - 29. Muṣṭafa IV (1807)
              - 30. Maḥmūd II (1808)
                - 31. ʿAbd-al-Majīd (1839)
                  - 33. Murād V (1876)
                  - 34. ʿAbd-al-Ḥamīd II (1876)
                  - 35. Muḥammad V Rashād (1909)
                  - 36. Muḥammad VI Waḥīd-al-Dīn (1918–22)
                - 32. ʿAbd-al-ʿAzīz (1861)
        - 20. Sulaymān II (1687)
        - 21. Aḥmad II (1691)
    - 15. Muṣṭafa I (1617, 1622)

[2] See above, pp. 657-8.

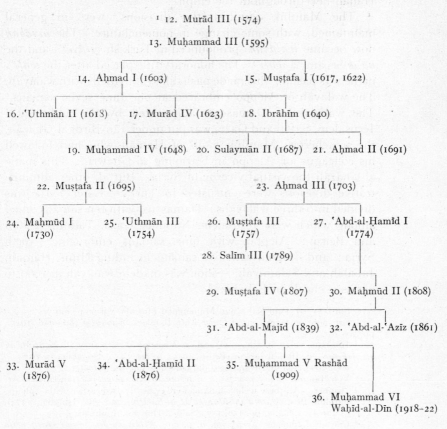

put up any resistance whatsoever ".[1] On his way back from Egypt he lingered long enough in Syria to consolidate his position and organize the new domain. For purposes of taxation he empowered a commission to draw up a cadastre of the whole land, reserving a large portion of the fertile plain of al-Biqāʿ and the rich valley of the Orontes to the crown.[2] The Mamlūk procedure of farming out (*talzīm*) tax collection to the highest bidder was, of course, retained. The Ḥanafite rite of jurisprudence, preferred by the Ottomans, was given official status in Syria.[3] An Aleppine jurist, Ibrāhīm al-Ḥalabi (d. 1594), wrote *Multaqa al-Abḥur* (confluence of the seas), which was first published in Constantinople and became a handbook of Ḥanafi law throughout the empire.

The Mamlūk administrative divisions[4] were in general maintained, with some change in nomenclature. The *niyābah* now became *walāyah* (pronounced in Turkish *vilāyet*), and the *nā'ib* became a *wāli*.[5] The honorary title placed after the *wāli's* name was pasha ; this made pashalik synonymous with walāyah. The walayāh of Aleppo embraced at one time seven sanjāqs.[6] The walāyah of Damascus, augmented by the addition of Jerusalem, Ṣafad and Gaza, was put under Jān-Birdi al-Ghazāli, the treacherous Mamlūk nā'ib of Ḥamāh who had followed his colleague of Aleppo in betraying al-Ghawri.[7] This made al-Ghazāli the virtual viceroy of Syria. But all other administrative divisions were entrusted to Turks. Later Syria was divided into three walāyahs : Damascus, with ten sanjāqs, chief among which were Jerusalem, Nābulus, Gaza, Tadmur, Sidon and Beirut ; Aleppo, with nine sanjāqs embracing North Syria ; and Tripoli, with five sanjāqs including Ḥimṣ, Ḥamāh, Jabalah and Salamiyah. Sidon was made a walāyah in 1660 to act as a check on Lebanon.[8]

[1] Ibn-Iyās, ed. Paul Kahle and Muḥammad Muṣṭafa, vol. v, p. 149.

[2] For more on taxes consult Ömer Lûtfi Barakan, *Kanunlar* (Istanbul, 1945), pp. 206 *seq.*

[3] Ibn-Iyās, vol. v, p. 238 ; al-Ghazzi, *al-Kawākib al-Sā'irah bi-Aʿyān al-Mi'ah al-ʿĀshirah*, ed. Jibrā'īl Jabbūr (Beirut, 1945), p. 210. [4] See above, p. 637.

[5] *mutaṣarrifīyah* and *mutaṣarrif* did not come into use till later.

[6] Von Hammer, vol. ii, p. 477, n.d. Tur. *sanjāq* (Ar. *sanjaq*) is a translation of Ar. *liwā'*, banner. All these technical terms were evidently used earlier by the Saljūqs.

[7] Farīdūn Bey, *Majmūʿah Munsha'āt al-Salāṭīn*, 2nd ed. (Istanbul, 1274), p. 455 ; Ibn-Iyās, vol. v, pp. 156, 157 ; Saʿd-al-Dīn, vol. ii, pp. 364-5.

[8] Consult Lammens, *Syrie*, vol. ii, p. 60 ; *Relazioni dei consoli veneti nella Siria*, ed. G. Berchet (Turin, 1866), pp. 89, 126.

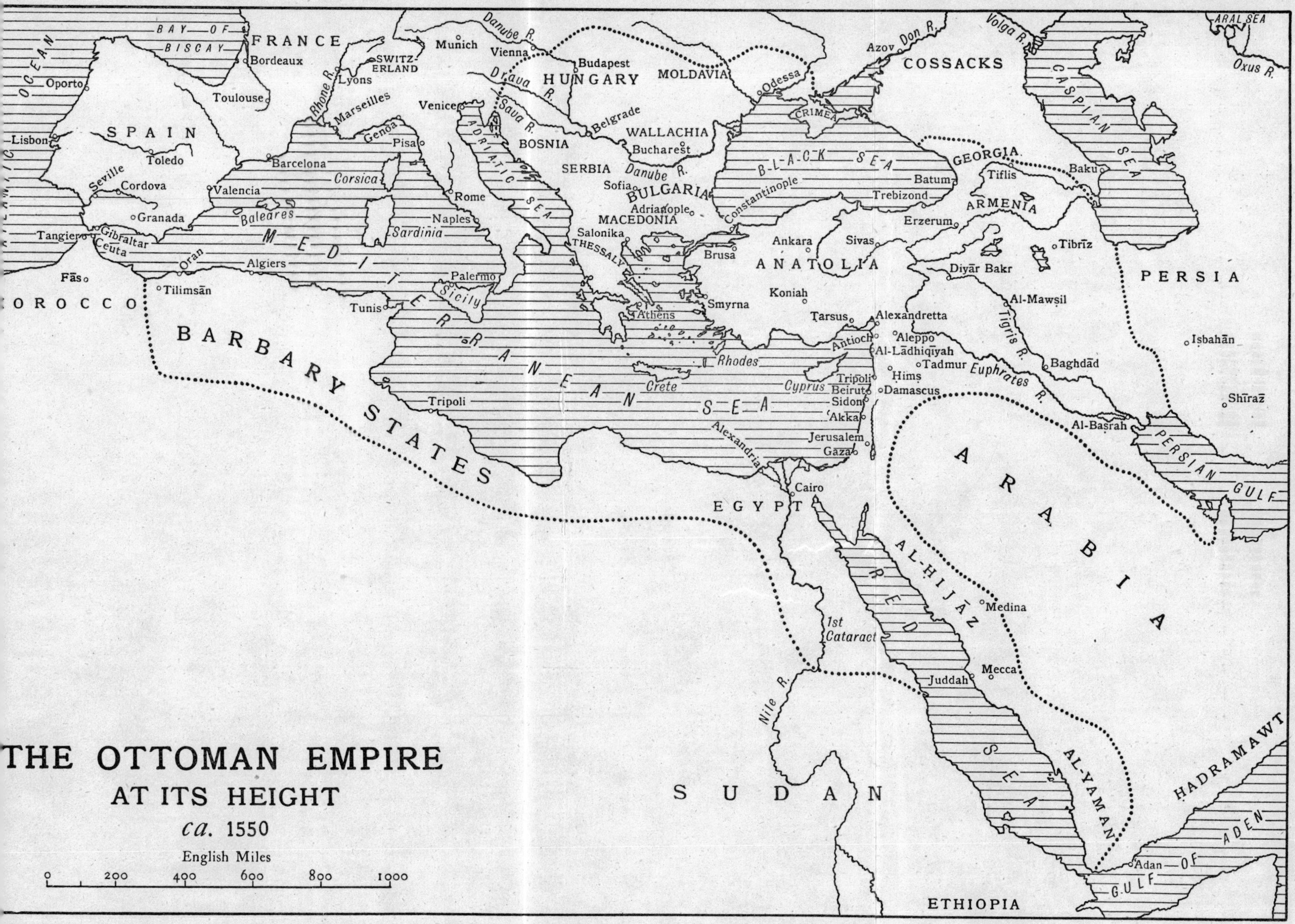

THE OTTOMAN EMPIRE AT ITS HEIGHT

ca. 1550

In 1724 Ismā'īl Pasha al-'Aẓm, founder of a prominent Damascene family, was entrusted with the walāyah of Damascus. His son As'ad, who began his career as governor of Sidon and then of Ḥamāh, was one of the best known wālis of Damascus under the Ottomans. He was also in charge of the holy pilgrimage and must have amassed a large fortune. His palace in Ḥamāh, now housing a native school, is one of the show places of the city on the Orontes. More sumptuous is that of Damascus built about 1749 and considered the most beautiful Arab monument of the century. Its style, woodwork and mosaic exemplify the finest in Islamic art at its decline. Its marble was imported from Italy. Partly destroyed in the uprising against the French mandate in 1925, it was renovated and occupied by the Institut Français de Damas. Other members of this Syrian family were appointed over Damascus, Sidon or Tripoli, but unlike the Lebanese governors they remained loyal to the Ottoman sultan despite the fact that several of them were degraded and had their property confiscated. Ismā'īl spent some of his last days in jail and As'ad was treacherously killed in the bath by orders from Constantinople.[1]

Special position of Lebanon

Lebanon, however, with its hardy Druze and Maronite mountaineers, deserved a different treatment. Expediency dictated that its native feudal lords be recognized,[2] especially since the real danger came from Egypt and Persia. While in Damascus Salīm received a delegation of Lebanese amīrs headed by Fakhr-al-Dīn I al-Ma'ni[3] of al-Shūf, Jamāl-al-Dīn (Arislān ?[4]) of al-Gharb and 'Assāf al-Turkumāni of Kisrawān.[5] Fakhr-al-Dīn who, according to a Lebanese chronicler,[6] had advised his men at Marj Dābiq, " Let's wait and see on what the victory will be and then join it ", now appeared before the Ottoman sultan, kissed the ground and delivered a most eloquent prayer :

O Lord, perpetuate the life of him whom Thou hast chosen to administer Thy domain, made the successor (*khalīfah*) of Thy covenant,

[1] Muḥammad Kurd-'Ali, *Khiṭaṭ al-Sha'm*, vol. ii (Damascus, 1925), pp. 289, 290-91 ; Ḥaydar al-Shihābi, *Ta'rīkh*, ed. Na''ūm Mughabghab (Cairo, 1900), p. 769. *Les Guides bleus : Syrie — Palestine — Iraq — Transjordanie* (Paris, 1932), pp. 124, 303-4.

[2] See above, pp. 637, 640.

[3] On the origin of this family see Shidyāq, pp. 247-8.

[4] Ḥaydar, p. 561. For the Arislān family see above, p. 545. Jamāl belonged to the Yamanite faction, the Tanūkhs to the Qaysite.

[5] See above, p. 623.

[6] Ḥaydar, p. 560.

empowered over Thy worshippers and Thy land and entrusted with Thy precept and ordinance; he who is the supporter of Thy luminous law, the leader of the pure and victorious nation, our lord and master of our favours, the commander of the believers.[1] . . .

Impressed by his eloquence and seeming sincerity, Salīm confirmed Fakhr-al-Dīn and the other Lebanese amīrs in their fiefs, allowed them the same autonomous privileges enjoyed under the Mamlūks and imposed on them a comparatively light tribute [2] Fakhr-al-Dīn was recognized as the leading chieftain of the mountain (*sulṭān al-barr*). Thereafter the Ottoman sultans dealt with their Lebanese vassals either directly or through a neighbouring Syrian wāli. As a rule these vassals acted independently, transmitted their fiefs to their descendants, offered no military service to the sultan, exercised the right of life and death over their subjects, exacted taxes and duties and at times even concluded treaties with foreign powers.

Al-Ghazāli

Al-Ghazāli signalized his loyalty to the new régime by apprehending the Buḥturid Tanūkh [3] leaders of al-Gharb, who remained loyal to the Mamlūks, and jailing them in the citadel of Damascus. He decapitated both ibn-al-Ḥanash, the Arab chieftain of Sidon and al-Biqā' who refused to submit,[4] and ibn-al-Ḥarfūsh, head of a Shī'ite family in al-Biqā', and forwarded their heads, together with other Bedouin heads from the mountain of Nābulus, to Constantinople. But he who betrayed his first masters could not long remain loyal to the new ones. Taking advantage of the death of Salīm in 1520, al-Ghazāli proclaimed himself in the Umayyad Mosque an independent sovereign under the title al-Malik al-Ashraf (the most noble king), struck coins in his own name and tried to induce his former colleague Khā'ir Bey, whom Salīm had rewarded with the vice-royalty of Egypt, to follow his example. But Aleppo did not openly support al-Ghazāli and Sulaymān sent against him an army which, on January 27, 1521, destroyed the Syrian rebels and killed al-Ghazāli at al-Qābūn, near Damascus. The punishment the Syrian capital and its environs received was

[1] Ḥaydar, p. 561; cf. Duwayhi, p. 152; Shidyāq, p. 251.

[2] Kisrawān's share was only 4200 gold piastres; Duwayhi, p. 152; 'Īsa I. al-Ma'lūf, *Ta'rīkh al-Amīr Fakhr-al-Dīn al-Thāni* (Jūniyah, 1934), p. 9, n. 1.

[3] See above, pp. 545, 637, 640. One of these princes had visited Salīm in Damascus and offered him Arab steeds; ibn-Sabāṭ, supplement to Ḥaydar, p. 596, and to Ṣāliḥ, p. 269. Cf. Shidyāq, p. 246.

[4] Ḥaydar, p. 596.

even more severe than that meted out earlier by Tīmūr.[1] About a third of the city and its villages was utterly destroyed.[2] Ever since then the name of the Janissaries has become associated in the Syrian mind with destruction and terror.

The system of administration

Ottoman political theory, at least as understood by the average wāli, held that the conquered peoples, especially if non-Moslems, were flocks (raia, raya [3]) to be shepherded for the benefit of the conqueror. The terminology, borrowed from the vocabulary of Bedouin life in Arabia, expressed traditional concepts in the minds of the descendants of Central Asiatic nomads. As human cattle the conquered were to be milked, fleeced and allowed to live their own lives so long as they gave no trouble. Mostly peasants, artisans and merchants, they could not aspire to military or civil careers. But the herd needs watchdogs. These were recruited mainly from war prisoners, purchased slaves and Christian children levied as a tribute and then trained and brought up as Moslems. All recruits were put through a rigorous system of training in the capital covering many years. They were subjected to keen competition and careful screening; the mentally bright among them were further prepared for governmental positions and the physically strong for military service. The toughest were drafted into the infantry corps termed Janissary. The governing and the military class in the empire came at first almost exclusively from this source.[4] Grand vizirs, vizirs, admirals, generals, provincial governors were once slaves and so they remained. Their lives and property were always at the disposal of their sultan master, who never hesitated to exercise his right of ownership. History does not record the creation of a parallel machine. It left the house of ʿUthmān as the only aristocracy in the empire, wielding absolute power in the administration of the state and for its defence.

Another basis of classification was religious affiliation. From time immemorial Near Eastern society was stratified in terms of belief rather than of race and within the religious

[1] See above, p. 656.

[2] Ibn-Iyās, vol. v, pp. 363, 371, 376-8, 418-19; Qaramāni, pp. 316-17.

[3] From Ar. *rayāʿa*, pl. of *raʿīyah*, herd. In 1856 the term was replaced by the less obnoxious one *tabaʿah*, followers, subjects.

[4] Albert H. Lybyer, *The Government of the Ottoman Empire* (Cambridge, 1913), pp. 45 *seq.*; Barnette Miller, *The Palace School of Muhammad the Conqueror* (Cambridge, 1941), pp. 6 *seq.*, 81, 95.

community the family rather than the territory was the nucleus of organization. Hence in the minds of the people religion and nationality were inextricably interwoven. Each of the religious groups of the Ottoman empire was termed a millet.[1] The two largest millets were those of Islam and the Rum (Greek Orthodox).[2] Armenians and Jews were also classified as millets. According to this system all non-Moslem groups were organized into communities under religious heads of their own who also exercised certain civil functions of importance. This amounted to a provision for the government of subject minorities. Europeans — Venetians, Dutch, French and English — domiciled in the land were likewise treated as millets. In 1521 Sulaymān signed with the Venetians a treaty, set out in thirty chapters,[3] which confirmed privileges previously enjoyed under the Byzantines. The French obtained their first capitulations fourteen years later[4]; the English followed in 1580. Originally intended as concessions from a strong sovereign, rather than exactions from a weak one, the capitulations gave extraterritorial privileges to foreigners and lingered as a humiliating institution until the dissolution of the empire.

Abuses and attempts at reform

The Ottoman wāli was no improvement on his predecessor the Mamlūk nā'ib, who likewise was recruited from the slave class. Besides, he was farther removed from the central government and therefore freer from its control. But that did not make much difference, as corruption in the capital was as rife as in the provinces. Wālis often bought their appointments there and entered upon their duties with the main desire of promoting their own interests. Not a few returned to Constantinople to face execution and confiscation of property. Exploitation went hand in hand with instability. In the first hundred and eighty-four years of its career as an Ottoman city Damascus witnessed no fewer than a hundred and thirty-three

[1] From Ar. *millah*, religion, nationality.

[2] The Turks took Arabic *rūm*, a contraction of the word for Romans, and applied it to all Ottoman subjects of the Greek Orthodox faith irrespective of nationality or language. The term is retained to the present day despite the fact that the Greek Orthodox owe no allegiance to Rome. The Saljūqs designated their sultanate in Anatolia "Rūm" (see above, p. 574) because it was conquered from the Eastern Roman Empire.

[3] Late Lat. *capitula*, chapters, whence "capitulations".

[4] For the terms consult I. de Testa, *Recueil des traités de la porte ottomane*, vol. i (Paris, 1864), pp. 15 *seq*.

wālis, of whom only thirty-three held their office as long as two years each.[1] Aleppo evidently did not fare much better. A Venetian consul there reports nine pashas in three years.[2] At times pashas engaged in bloody conflicts against one another with utter disregard of the central government. Occasional visits by Janissaries added to the misery of the people, most of whom, however, were manifestly reconciled to their fate. The general attitude seems to have been one of passivity, frustration, distrust of leadership and pessimism as to the result of effort. The old spirit of rebellion which had often flared under 'Abbāsid and Fāṭimid misrule was by this time apparently dead. Clearly the dark ages which began under the Saljūq Turks [3] were getting darker under the Ottoman Turks. While Europe was entering upon her age of enlightenment, Syria was groping in Ottoman darkness.

The need for introducing drastic reforms and curbing abuses of officials was early felt by Muṣṭafa Köprülü, grand vizir from 1689 to 1691, whose promulgation of new regulations for the better treatment of non-Moslems foreshadowed the attempted reforms of the three bold sultans, Salīm III (1789–1807), Maḥmūd II (1808–39) and 'Abd-al-Majīd I (1839–61). All these reform regulations, however, remained ink on paper. Those of Salīm, entitled *Niẓām-i Jadīd* (new regulations), were opposed by the Janissaries and corrupt officials. Those of 'Abd-al-Majīd, entitled *Khaṭṭ-i Sharīf* (the noble rescript) of Gül-Khāné (1839), and *Khaṭṭ-i Humāyūn* (imperial rescript, 1856), aimed at removing the disabilities under which the raya laboured, guaranteeing the lives, property and honour of all subjects irrespective of creed and race, abolishing the farming out of taxes and considering all people of whatever tongue or millet equal before the law. But no effective implementation was provided for these *tanẓīmāt* (reform regulations), which were, moreover, premature.[4] Powerful conservative theologians opposed them, foreigners who enjoyed extra-territoriality did not like them and even Jewish and Christian money-changers (sing. *ṣarrāf*) objected to the features involving non-farming out of

[1] Lammens, *Syrie*, vol. ii, p. 62.
[2] *Relazioni*, p. 121.
[3] See above, p. 572.
[4] For Turkish text consult Luṭfi, *Ta'rīkh* (Constantinople, 1303), vol. vi, pp. 61-64; Enver Z. Karal, *Osmanli Tarihi*, V, *Nizam-i Cedit ve Tanzimat Devirleri* (Ankara, 1947), pp. 266-72; for French see de Testa, vol. v, pp. 140-43, 132-7.

taxes. The reforming attempts of Salīm, who had not been immured as had his predecessors,[1] cost him his throne. His second successor Maḥmūd, greatest among modern sultans, rendered a national service when, on a memorable day of June 1826, he ordered the guns trained on the barracks where the Janissaries were mustered and wholly destroyed them. It was this Maḥmūd who adopted the fez (*ṭarbūsh*) as a headgear and, interestingly enough, was called the *giaur*[2] sultan by his subjects.

Abortive constitutional measures

The next champion of the cause of liberalism and reform was a grand vizir, Midḥat Pasha. Midḥat began his career at the age of twenty-two as a government official in Damascus. For years thereafter he worked ardently but secretly with a few kindred souls to provide his country with a constitutional régime. The first results became apparent when Murād V issued on July 15, 1876, a proclamation in which the word for constitution[3] was used for the first time in an official document. After a three-month reign Murād became insane and was succeeded by his brother ʿAbd-al-Ḥamīd II, who on December 23 solemnly proclaimed the promulgation of a constitution and the institution of a representative parliament. The draft was proposed by Midḥat as grand vizir and modelled on the French and Belgian constitutions. The new document proclaimed that all subjects were to be known as Ottomans and be personally free and that Islam was the religion of the state. It provided for the protection of all recognized religions, guaranteed the freedom of the press within the limits of the law and established the principle of popular representation through a parliament of two chambers, one of deputies and one of senators, the deputies to be elected for four years and to represent each a constituency of 50,000. ʿAbd-al-Ḥamīd, as later events showed, aimed by the introduction of this liberal measure at warding off threatening encroachment on his sovereignty and at winning Western European sympathy, rather than at the amelioration of the

[1] His predecessor ʿAbd-al-Ḥamīd I (1774–89) refused to observe the usual practice of confining the heir apparent in a carefully guarded kiosk in the seraglio. "Seraglio" comes from It. *serraglio*, an enclosure of palisades, and was confused with Tur. *sarāy*, palace, from Per. *serāy*, building, inn.

[2] From Per. *gaur*, infidel; applied derogatorily by Turks to non-Moslems, especially Christians.

[3] Ar. *qanūn asāsi*, used again by his successor ʿAbd-al-Ḥamīd; *ʿIlmīyah Sālnāmehsi* (Constantinople, 1334), pp. 20-50.

condition of his people. In the following February he banished Midḥat and the following year he dissolved the parliament. Under pressure from England, however, Midḥat was recalled and appointed governor of Syria, soon thereafter to be banished to al-Ṭā'if in al-Ḥijāz, where he was presumably assassinated by agents of the Porte in 1883.[1]

Social and economic aspects

Neither the political nor the ethnic structure of Syria was seriously affected by the Ottoman conquest. The only radical change in the Ottoman period was incidental and involved the desert population.[2] Turks came and went as officials but there was no Turkish colonization of the land. At heart they and their Syrian subjects always remained strangers to one another A few thousand Moslem Circassians drifted into North Syria and Transjordan after the Russo-Turkish war of 1877, and several thousand Armenian refugees found haven in Lebanon after the first world war. Arabic remained the language of the people. It borrowed only a few Turkish words, mostly relating to politics, army and food.[3]

Syrian economic life underwent a steady decline for which Ottoman maladministration, however, was not entirely to blame. The Ottoman conquest of the Arab East coincided with changes in the international trade routes that left that region economically insignificant. The foundation of the prosperity of those lands, as repeatedly noted above,[4] rested on trade, especially India-to-Europe trade. The discovery in 1497 of the sea route from Europe to India around the Cape of Good Hope by the Portuguese navigator Vasco da Gama, the rounding of the southern tip of South America in 1520 by another Portuguese Ferdinand Magellan with the ensuing discovery of the Philippine Islands, the memorable westward voyage in 1492 of the Genoese Christopher Columbus which discovered America, these and related events changed the course of the great trade routes. The centre of world activity and civilization consequently shifted westward. In the inauguration of the age of exploration and discovery that therewith dawned the Arab

[1] His life was published by his son Ali Haydar Midhat Bey, London, 1903.

[2] See above, p. 483.

[3] E.g. *bāsha* (Tur. *pāsha*); *bayraq* (Tur. *bayrāq*), flag; *balṭah*, axe; *jāwīsh* (Tur. *chāwush*), sergeant; *burghul* (Tur. *bulghur*), crushed wheat; *qāwarmah* (Tur. *qāwurmah*), minced and spiced cooked meat. Certain Turkish words borrowed by Arabic were of Persian or Greek origin.

[4] Pp. 296, 353 *seq.*, 620, 639.

peoples had no share. Their ships were swept from the eastern seas by the Portuguese commander Affonso de Albuquerque, who between 1503 and 1515 gave his countrymen control over the Persian Gulf and the Indonesian trade. The Portuguese were thus able to circumvent the Mediterranean corsairs and to by-pass Arab lands, whose population belonged to a different faith and whose merchants levied high tariffs on transit merchandise. The Mediterranean, hitherto a middle sea, was no longer filling that position; it had to wait three and a half centuries, till the opening of the Suez Canal, before it could resume its place as a highway and a battlefield.

Syrian merchants had hereafter to depend more upon the overland trade. As the terminus of the route leading to Baghdād and al-Baṣrah, Aleppo began to flourish as a centre of internal trade for the empire and of international trade between Europe and Asia. It eclipsed for the time being Damascus, as the ports of Alexandretta and Tripoli eclipsed Beirut.[1] In fact it remained until the mid-seventeenth century the principal market of the entire Near East.[2] A sizable Venetian colony grew in Aleppo. Their consular reports refer to arrivals at both Aleppo and Damascus of caravans with spices from India. Spices were in special demand for preserving meat in those pre-refrigeration days.

Venetian traders in the Syrian cities and ports soon had a competitor in the French, whose earliest consulate was established in Aleppo. A French consul there in 1683 thought that the city was "the largest, most beautiful and richest in the entire Ottoman empire after Constantinople and Cairo".[3] The capitulations granted Francis I by Sulaymān in 1535[4] laid the basis of French trade and led to French supremacy in the Levant. In 1740 Maḥmud I signed a treaty with Louis XV putting not only French pilgrims to the Holy Land but all other Christians visiting the Ottoman empire under the protection of the French flag. These concessions served as the basis of the French claim to protect all Catholic Christians of Syria.[5]

[1] On these seaports consult F. Charles-Roux, *Les Échelles de Syrie et de Palestine au XVIIe siècle* (Paris, 1928), pp. 5 *seq.*

[2] Sauvaget, *Alep*, p. 201.

[3] D'Arvieux, *Mémoires* (Paris, 1735), vol. vi, p. 411.

[4] See above, p. 668.

[5] De Testa, vol. i, pp. 186 *seq.*; F. Charles-Roux, *France et chrétiens d'orient* (Paris, [1939]), pp. 68-77.

Besides Aleppo the French had settlements (factories) in Alexandretta, al-Lādhiqīyah, Tripoli, Sidon, Acre and al-Ramlah. English merchants followed the French and both gradually replaced the Venetians and Genoese in the Syrian cities and ports. The foundation of the Levant Company in 1581 under Queen Elizabeth started the migration of English businessmen to Syria. Again Aleppo was the centre.[1] Consular reports reveal some fifty British merchants there in 1662. Shakespeare [2] cites the case of a sailor's wife whose "husband's to Aleppo gone". The entire European colony numbered about two hundred.[3] These traders tried to satisfy the Western taste for Eastern luxuries promoted during the Crusades. Through their activity the old land routes were reactivated. The list of native products was headed by silk from Lebanon, cotton from Palestine, wool and oil. Competition with the sea traders was keen but the Portuguese insistence on high, almost monopolistic, prices gave the traders in Syria their chance.

The merchants of each nation had a khān (hostel) of their own allocated by the government. A typical khān was a two-story quadrangular structure enclosing a courtyard. The ground floor was used for the merchandise, the upper as lodging quarters for the merchants. They were mostly bachelors and wore native clothes. As a measure of safety they were not permitted out in Aleppo after sunset. Thanks to the capitulations they enjoyed the privilege of exemption from the jurisdiction of local courts. Several of these khāns are still standing. That built under Fakhr-al-Dīn II (d. 1635) in Sidon for the French is today occupied by the Sisters of St. Joseph.

No enduring benefits evidently accrued to Syria from this new development in its trade, which was largely in European hands. The population of the land continued on its downward course in wealth and in numbers. Volney,[4] who visited Aleppo in 1784 or 1785, estimates that of the three thousand two hundred taxable villages in the walāyah of Aleppo at the beginning of the Ottoman period there were only about four hundred left, which seems incredible. He did not think the city had more

[1] Alfred C. Wood, *A History of the Levant Company* (Oxford, 1935), pp. 11 *seq.*, 75 *seq.*

[2] *Macbeth*, act I, sc. 3.

[3] Grant, *Syrian Desert*, p. 93.

[4] *Voyage en Syrie et en Égypte*, 2nd ed. (Paris, 1787), vol. ii, p. 135.

than a hundred thousand inhabitants,[1] though consular reports of the late sixteenth century make its population two to four times as many.[2] A leading Turkish historian [3] states that as late as about 1740 the tax-gatherer's office in Aleppo was still greatly coveted because its holder could amass enough to buy a vizirate on his return to the capital.

On the heels of European businessmen came missionaries, teachers, travellers and explorers. The door was thus opened to modern influences, one of the most pregnant facts in the history of Ottoman Syria. The missionaries were Jesuits, Capuchins, Lazarites and members of other Catholic orders. Their activity was centred in the native Christian communities and resulted in the founding of the Uniat Churches — Syrian and Greek — in the seventeenth and eighteenth centuries.[4] Lebanon under Fakhr-al-Dīn II and his successors especially welcomed Western cultural influences.[5] In one of its villages, ʿAyn Ṭūrah, the Jesuits, who had been operating in the land since 1625,[6] established in 1734, in collaboration with the Maronites, what may be called the first important modern school. When forty years later their order was temporarily suppressed, the Lazarites occupied their posts.

Cultural aspects

Intellectually the period was one of sterility. Oppressive rule, high taxation, economic and social decline are not conducive to creative or original work in art, science or literature. The era of compilation, annotation, abridgment and imitation which had its beginnings centuries before continued with fewer and poorer productions. Throughout the Ottoman age no Syrian poet, philosopher, artist, scientist or essayist of first order made his appearance. Illiteracy was widespread, almost universal. Judges were appointed whose mastery over the written word was deficient. A few intellectuals, like the historian Naʿīma of Aleppo (*ca.* 1665–1716), were attracted to the imperial capital and fully Ottomanized.

Among the Arabic chroniclers and biographers utilized in the composition of this chapter were Aḥmad ibn-Sinān al-

[1] Volney, vol. ii, p. 139. [2] *Relazioni*, pp. 59, 102.

[3] Jawdat, *Taʾrīkh*, vol. iii (Constantinople, 1309), p. 269.

[4] See above, pp. 520, 523. Consult *Lubnān* (Beirut, 1334), pp. 300 *seq.*

[5] See below, p. 683.

[6] For some of their early reports consult Antoine Rabbath, *Documents inédits pour servir à l'histoire du christianisme en orient*, vol. i (Paris, 1905), pp. 30 *seq.*

Qaramāni (1532–1610),[1] who was in the government service at Damascus; Najm-al-Dīn al-Ghazzi (1570–1651),[2] traditionist and professor in Damascus; and Muḥammad al-Muḥibbi (1651–1699), who also held a professorial chair in Damascus. All three were of Damascene nativity. Damascus was evidently an intellectual centre until the beginning of the eighteenth century and Aleppo a financial centre. Al-Muḥibbi was educated in Constantinople and acted for some time as assistant judge in Mecca. His principal work is a collection of twelve hundred and ninety biographies of celebrities who died in the eleventh Moslem century (1591–1688). Damascus provided the locale in which al-Maqqari of Tilimsān (d. 1632) compiled between 1628 and 1630, from material brought with him from Morocco, the voluminous work considered the chief source of information for the literary history of Spain.[3] Another Damascene of note was ʿAbd-al-Ghani al-Nābulusi (1641–1731), a Sufi and traveller, most of whose works are still unpublished.[4]

Three chroniclers cited in this chapter were Maronite Lebanese. Patriarch Isṭifān al-Duwayhi (1625–1704), when sixteen years old, went to the Maronite seminary in Rome, which was founded in 1584 by Pope Gregory XIII for training Maronite students for clerical life. Al-Amīr Ḥaydar al-Shihābi (*ca.* 1761–1835)[5] had his villa at tiny Shimlān, overlooking Beirut. Ṭannūs al-Shidyāq (d. 1859), a native of al-Ḥadath, near Beirut, and a judge under the Shihāb amīrs, compiled the annals of the feudal families of Lebanon.

The Maronite seminary in Rome afforded these Christians of Lebanon a unique educational facility. Some of the brightest among their youth were picked for training in it and either returned to their homeland to occupy high ecclesiastical positions or remained in Rome to teach and write. One of the earliest distinguished graduates was Jibrāʾīl al-Ṣahyūni (Latinized Sionita, 1577–1648), who, after teaching Syriac and Arabic in Rome, transferred to the chair of Semitic languages at the

[1] For his biography consult al-Muḥibbi, *Khulāṣat al-Athar fi Aʿyān al-Qarn al-Ḥādi-ʿAshar* (Cairo, 1284), vol. i, pp. 209-10. [2] Muḥibbi, vol. iv, pp. 189-200.

[3] *Nafḥ al-Ṭīb min Ghuṣn al-Andalus al-Raṭīb*, ed. R. Dozy *et al.*, 3 vols. (Leyden, 1855–60).

[4] *Dhakhāʾir al-Mawārīth fi al-Dalālah ʿala Mawāḍiʿ al-Ḥadīth*, 4 vols. (Cairo, 1934).

[5] On his life consult Ḥaydar, *Lubnān fi ʿAhd al-Umarāʾ al-Shihābīyīn*, ed. Asad Rustum and Fuʾād A. al-Bustāni (Beirut, 1933), vol. i, pp. v-viii.

Sorbonne in Paris. There he collaborated in the compilation of the polyglot Bible. He was succeeded in his work on the polyglot by his fellow-Lebanese, Ibrāhīm al-Ḥāqilāni (Ecchelensis, 1600–64), who had also studied at Rome and was professor of Arabic and Syriac in the college of the Propaganda there. In 1646 al-Ḥāqilāni was appointed to a chair at the Collège de France. The Paris polyglot was the first to include Syriac and Arabic versions. Another product of the Maronite seminary, and perhaps the most distinguished of them all, was Yūsuf Sam'ān al-Sam'āni (Assemani, 1687–1768), to whose efforts the Vatican library owes many of the finest manuscripts in its Oriental collection. The researches of al-Sam'āni on these manuscripts in Syriac, Arabic, Hebrew, Persian, Turkish, Ethiopic and Armenian, for the sake of which he undertook two trips to the East, were embodied in his voluminous *Bibliotheca Orientalis* (4 volumes, Rome, 1719–28), still a major source of information on the Churches of the East. In 1736 al-Sam'āni was delegated by the pope to the Maronite synod held at al-Luwayzah in Lebanon, through which the Maronites were brought into closer contact with the papal see.[1] It was the work of these Rome-educated Maronite scholars that made modern Europe for the first time fully conscious of the importance of Near Eastern languages and literatures, especially in their Christian aspects.

The printing press

The monastery of Qazḥayya in Lebanon had the privilege of being the seat of the first press in the Arab East. The press, whose origin is unknown but which was perhaps introduced from Rome by one of those Lebanese scholars, produced in 1610 the Psalms in the Syriac language and in Arabic written in Syriac characters.[2] Syriac was then still in use among Maronites as attested by travellers and resident Europeans. D'Arvieux,[3] who visited North Lebanon in 1660, reports that the bishop of Ihdin spoke perfect Arabic and Syriac. By the end of the century Syriac as a spoken language was probably dead. Volney's [4] inquiries revealed its use in only two villages in Anti-Lebanon, in one of which it is still spoken.[5]

[1] On al-Sam'āni's contribution to effect *rapprochement* between the Maronites and Rome consult Dibs, vol. ix, pp. 483-7; Rabbath, vol. i, pp. 181-2.

[2] Garshūni, see above, p. 546. Consult Louis Cheikho, "Ta'rīkh Fann al-Ṭibā'ah fi al-Mashriq", *al-Mashriq*, vol. iii (1900), pp. 251-7, 355-62.

[3] Vol. ii, p. 407. [4] Vol. i, pp. 331-2. [5] See above, p. 546.

The first Arabic press with Arabic characters in the East made its appearance in 1702 at Aleppo. Its origin too is shrouded in mystery. It followed by one hundred and eighty-eight years the Arabic press at Fano, Italy, the first of its kind in the world.[1] This Italian press owed its invention probably to papal interest and may have been the ancestor of the Aleppine press. Other establishments followed in Lebanon. Their output was mostly religious and linguistic, supplementing the work of the schools. Slowly but surely the implementation for embarking on a new cultural life was being forged.

[1] Consult Hitti, " The First Book Printing in Arabic ", *The Princeton University Library Chronicle*, vol. iv (1942), pp. 5-9.

CHAPTER XLIX

THE MAʿNS AND THE SHIHĀBS: LORDS OF LEBANON

THE preliminary exposure of the entire Syrian country to Western cultural influences, treated in the preceding chapter, and the emergence of Lebanon as a separate political entity, to be treated in this one, are two of the most significant developments in the Ottoman period. Around these two developments and the general misrule of the Ottoman government most of the events in the history of this entire period may be grouped.

With the Ottoman conquest the Maʿns began to replace the Tanūkhs [1] as masters of central and southern Lebanon. To the north of them were the ʿAssāfs, whose chief was confirmed by Salīm over Kisrawān with the addition of Jubayl.[2] The height of the ʿAssāf power was reached under the long amīrate of Manṣūr (1522–80), whose authority extended from near Beirut to ʿArqah north of Tripoli. The ʿAssāfs had their seat at Ghazīr, where some of their buildings' remains can still be seen. In 1590 the political heritage of this family passed to its rivals the banu-Sayfa (Sīfa ?) of Tripoli, who were responsible for the murder of the last ʿAssāfid ruler.[3] The Sayfas were of Kurdish origin. In the case of all these feudal families the head amīr would usually parcel out the fief among subordinate amīrs, *muqaddams* (front men) or shaykhs. The Shihābs, for instance, successors of the Maʿns, had under them in the early eighteenth century the Janbalāṭs [4] over al-Shūf, the abu-al-Lamʿs over al-Matn, the Talḥūqs over the Upper Gharb, the Arislāns over the Lower

[1] Some of their buildings are still standing in ʿAbayh, where the shrine of al-Sayyid ʿAbdullāh al-Tanūkhi (d. 1480) is frequented by Druze pilgrims.

[2] See above, p. 665.

[3] Duwayhi, p. 181; Ḥaydar, *Taʾrīkh*, p. 60; Shidyāq, p. 181.

[4] A Kurdish family from the Aleppo region whose original name was Jānbūlād; Shidyāq, p. 130. The Janbalāṭs are now Druzes and bear the honorific hereditary title of shaykh. The Shihābs bear the title of amīr; some of them are still Moslems but the majority are Maronites.

Gharb and the Khāzins over Kisrawān.[1] As for the Maronites, they had their own muqaddams, one of whose functions was to raise and transmit the tribute due the Ottoman government. Prominent among the muqaddams were those of Basharri, al-Batrūn and Jubayl.[2] As Druzes and Maronites the Lebanese were mostly subject to their own laws administered by the religious heads of their respective communities under the millet system.

That Lebanon under its local feudal lords fared better than Syria under its Turkish governors is indicated by the increase in its population through natural causes and immigration. The comparative safety and stability it enjoyed attracted Sunnites from al-Biqā' to Sāḥil 'Alma and neighbouring villages and Shī'ites from Ba'labakk to Jubayl and other places in Kisrawān. Maronites from the Tripoli district expanded southward to the foothills north of Jūniyah, and Druzes expanded northward to Brummāna and other villages in al-Matn.[3]

The struggle for power on the local and national levels, by peaceful and forceful methods, occupied no small part of the time and energy of the amīrs, muqaddams and shaykhs. At times these feudal chiefs found themselves in armed conflict with their suzerain in Constantinople. In 1584, while a convoy of Janissaries was passing through Lebanon, they were attacked and robbed of large sums of money which represented taxes from Palestine and Egypt on their way to the treasury in the capital. Enraged, the sultan sent a punitive expedition against Yūsuf Sayfa — in whose district the robbery took place — and destroyed many of his villages by fire. Then another expedition was directed against the Druzes to the south on the charge that they were the ones who perpetrated the crime. The Turkish commander — Ibrāhīm Pasha, wāli of Egypt — slaughtered five to six hundred of the Druze delegation which went to meet him at 'Ayn Ṣawfar [4] and reportedly 60,000 of the people, whom he first disarmed. The amīr of Jabal al-Durūz (mountain of the

1 The abu-al-Lam's were raised from muqaddams to amīrs by a Shihāb governor in 1711 (Shidyāq, p. 67); originally Druzes they are now entirely Maronites. The Talḥūqs came to Lebanon from North Africa in the retinue of the Fāṭimids (cf. Shidyāq, p. 155) and are now Druze shaykhs. The Khāzins are Maronite shaykhs; Shidyāq, pp. 71 *seq.*

2 For more on the muqaddams consult Shidyāq, pp. 217-23.

3 Duwayhi, p. 153; Shidyāq, p. 215.

4 Duwayhi, p. 178; Ḥaydar, *Ta'rīkh*, pp. 618-19.

Druzes, as that part of Lebanon was then called) was then Qurqumāz (Qurqumās), who in 1544 had succeeded his father Fakhr-al-Dīn I. Qurqumāz took refuge in Qal'at Nīḥa (Shaqīf Tīrūn), near Jazzīn. While there he died, perhaps poisoned by an agent of the Porte. His father before him was treacherously killed by the wāli of Damascus. Qurqumāz left a twelve-year-old son, named Fakhr-al-Dīn after his grandfather, and a widow who hid him with the Khāzins in Kisrawān.[1]

Fakhr-al-Dīn II

Young Fakhr-al-Dīn succeeded his father in 1590. Under him the Ma'nid power reached its zenith. He was undoubtedly the ablest and most fascinating figure in the history of Ottoman Lebanon if not of all Syria. He embarked on his career with three ambitions burning in his heart: building up a greater Lebanon, severing the last links between it and the Porte and setting it on the road of progress. All three no doubt represented tendencies among his people. By intermarriage, bribery, intrigue, treaties and battles — the recognized media of the day — he sought to achieve his political purposes.

After receiving from the sultan the sanjāqs of Beirut and Sidon, Fakhr moved against his neighbour Yūsuf Sayfa, whose daughter he had married, and wrested control of northern Lebanon from his hands after several engagements. The Shī'ite banu-Ḥarfūsh of Ba'labakk and the Bedouin chiefs of the Biqā' and of the region south as far as Galilee submitted to the rising lord of Lebanon. Sultan Aḥmad I was too busy fighting Hungarians and Persians to bother with a Lebanese vassal. Besides, he had in 1606 a rebel on his hands, 'Ali Jānbūlād,[2] Kurdish chief who usurped the walāyah of Aleppo. Fakhr lost no time in entering into an alliance with the Aleppo dictator. According to George Sandys,[3] English traveller who visited Lebanon in 1610, the sea-coast from the Dog River to Mount Carmel and the cities of Ṣafad, Bāniyās, Tiberias and Nazareth were included in Fakhr's territory. The southward expansion brought under his command castles which since Crusading days dominated strategic roads and sites. The addition of the rich al-Biqā' increased his income enough to enable him to organize a trained, disciplined army, with a core of professional soldiers,

[1] Shidyāq, p. 81; Ma'lūf, p. 48.
[2] An ancestor of the Lebanese Janbalāṭs; see above, p. 678, n. 4.
[3] *A Relation of a Journey*, 2nd ed. (London, 1621), pp. 211-12.

to replace the old irregulars whose chances of standing against Janissaries were nil.[1] The income left was enough to employ spies in his rivals' and enemies' courts and to bribe Ottoman officials.[2]

Another source of revenue was the trade he encouraged especially with the Florentines, whose ships provided Lebanese silk, soap, olive oil, wheat and other cereals with a lucrative foreign market. In 1608 the lord of Lebanon signed with Ferdinand I, the Medici grand duke of Tuscany, whose capital Florence was, a treaty containing a secret military article clearly directed against the Porte.[3] Thereupon the sultan, prompted by his Damascus wāli Ḥāfiẓ Pasha, resolved to take action against his audacious vassal and put an end to his separatist and expansionist policy. An army was sent against him in 1613 from Damascus but could not accomplish much in the mountains. But when a fleet of sixty galleys appeared to blockade the coast, prudence dictated retirement on Fakhr's part. Three ships which happened to be at the port of Sidon carried him with one of his wives and a retinue to his friends and allies in Italy.[4] His son 'Ali, assisted by his brother Yūnus, was entrusted with the amīrate.

Fakhr remained in Europe five years (1613–18) during which he visited Leghorn, Florence, Naples, Palermo, Messina, Malta and other places of interest and became imbued with ideas which strengthened rather than weakened the earlier ones he entertained. Only one disappointment he had: his attempt to return with an expeditionary force from the European powers and the pope proved futile. While he was there the legend that the Druzes were descended from a Crusading count de Dreux was manufactured.[5]

On his return he lost no time in taking measures to regain whatever territories were lost in his absence especially to the banu-Sayfa. The death of their chief Yūsuf removed from the

[1] Muḥibbi, vol. iii, p. 267; cf. d'Arvieux, vol. i, p. 438.

[2] Cf. d'Arvieux, vol. i, p. 457.

[3] For this and other treaties with the grand dukes consult P. Paolo Carali. [Qara'li], *Fakhr ad-Dīn II e la corte di Toscana* (Rome, 1936–8), vol. i, pp. 146 *seq.*, vol. ii, p. 52; G. Mariti, *Istoria di Faccardino grand-emir dei Drusi* (Livorno, 1787), pp. 74 *seq.*

[4] Aḥmad al-Khālidi al-Ṣafadi, *Ta'rīkh al-Amīr Fakhr-al-Dīn*, ed. Asad Rustum and Fu'ād A. al-Bustāni (Beirut, 1936), pp. 17-19.

[5] Volney, vol. ii, pp. 40-41.

way his father-in-law and greatest foe. The way was open both north and south. Once again the old Lebanese state was re-established and stretched. In 1622 the Porte bestowed on him the sanjāqs of ʿAjlūn and Nābulus. Two years later it considered it expedient to recognize the *fait accompli* and acknowledge

From Giovanni Mariti, " Istoria di Faccardino grand-emir dei Drusi " (Livorno, 1787)

FAKHR-AL-DĪN AL-MAʿNI II, AMĪR OF LEBANON, 1590–1635

Fakhr lord of ʿ*Arabistān*, from Aleppo to the borders of Egypt. This diminutive man, whose enemies described him as so short that if an egg dropped from his pocket to the ground it wouldn't break,[1] was the only one able to maintain order, administer justice and insure regular taxes [2] for himself and the sultan.

The year after his elevation to the governorship of Syria his men engaged Muṣṭafa Pasha, wāli of Damascus, in a battle at ʿAnjar in al-Biqāʿ and captured him. But Fakhr immediately

[1] Maʿlūf, p. 211. Sandys, p. 210: " His name is Faccardine; small of stature, but great in courage and achievements: about the age of forty; subtill as a foxe, and not a little inclining to the Tyrant. He never commenced battell, nor executeth any notable designe, without the consent of his mother."

[2] Ar. colloquial *mīri*, from *al-māl al-amīri*, money due the government.

released the prisoner.[1] During the next eleven years the amīr was free to pursue the third ambition of his life — modernizing Lebanon. In his public and private projects he employed architects, irrigation engineers and agricultural experts he brought from Italy. Documents show that he invited missions from Tuscany to introduce the Lebanese farmer to improved methods of tilling the soil and made requests for cattle to improve the local breed.[2] He embellished and fortified Beirut, where he built an elaborate residence with a magnificent garden. Maundrell [3] in 1697 visited this garden in which stood several pedestals for statues "from whence it may be inferr'd, that this emir was no real mahometan". His unfinished palace in Sidon stood opposite the khān built there for the French.[4] In this period the Capuchin mission entered Sidon and established centres in Beirut, Tripoli, Aleppo, Damascus and in certain villages of the Lebanon.[5] The Jesuits and Carmelites entered the country about the same time.[6] In the interest of agriculture he encouraged migration of Christians from North to South Lebanon. According to Volney,[7] Christian families migrated to Lebanon "daily" from Syria to escape Turkish rule. He also welcomed to Lebanon his friends the Janbalāṭs of Aleppo. He admitted into his intimacy European missionaries, merchants and consuls, all of whom enjoyed the capitulations initiated by Sulaymān. Consular reports show he protected European merchants in Sidon against pirates.[8] Throughout his career he had for counsellors Maronites, first among whom was abu-Nādir al-Khāzin, who also commanded his troops. He raised the status of this family, which had protected and reared him as an orphan, from that of commoners to that of shaykhs by once addressing its head in a letter "dear brother" (*al-akh al-ʿazīz*) — such was the protocol of the day.[9] Under the hereditary governorship of Kisrawān by this family, Kisrawān became a

[1] Maʿlūf, p. 232; cf. Duwayhi, pp. 198-9.

[2] Carali, vol. ii, p. 52.

[3] P. 54. The ascription by Volney, vol. ii, p. 172 of the planting of the pine grove outside of Beirut to Fakhr is erroneous, as the grove has stood there since the Crusades. He very likely reforested the place.

[4] See above, p. 673. The ancestral seat of the Maʿns was in Baʿaqlīn; their remains survive there and in neighbouring Dayr al-Qamar.

[5] Consult Rabbath, vol. ii, pp. 464-72.

[6] See above, p. 674; Duwayhi, p. 203.

[7] Vol. ii, p. 68.

[8] *Relazioni*, p. 163.

[9] Maʿlūf, p. 71.

flourishing Christian district.[1] For a time he had the distinguished scholar al-Ḥāqilāni [2] as agent in Italy. Through him he deposited money in a Florentine bank which his descendants a century later tried, through the aid of the other scholar al-Samʿāni, to recover, but in vain.[3]

Fakhr's sympathetic attitude toward the Christians made some ascribe Christianity to him. According to Sandys,[4] "he was never knowne to pray, nor ever seen in a Mosque". D'Arvieux [5] thought that the amīr had the religion of his people, "who had no religion". It is likely that he and the other Maʿns professed Islam before the Ottoman authorities and the outside world and practised Druzism with their people. A document claims that in 1633 he was baptized by a Capuchin father who was his physician.[6]

The amīr's social and economic programme did not make him neglect the military needs of his realm. The revenue from the increased trade, especially from the seaports of Tripoli and Sidon, sufficed for both demands. The cultivation of mulberry trees was then flourishing. The annual income of his amīrate was estimated at nine hundred thousand gold pounds, of which forty-three thousand went to the imperial treasury. With up-to-date material from Tuscany he equipped an army of forty to a hundred thousand, mostly Maronites and Druzes, and renovated some of the old castles. A castle crowning a hill in Tadmur still bears his name. This increased scale of armament, his negotiations with Europeans and his sympathy with Christianity attracted once more the suspicious eye of the sultan to him. In 1633 Murād IV ordered his wāli in Damascus, Kūchūk Aḥmad Pasha, to march against Fakhr-al-Dīn at the head of a vast army mustered from Anatolia and Egypt. Meantime a fleet under Jaʿfar Pasha began to operate against the coastal castles and ports. Fakhr-al-Dīn's subordinates, the Sayfas, Ḥarfūshes and Yamanites, began to desert him. His gallant son ʿAli, who held Ṣafad, fell in battle at Wādi al-Taym at the

[1] Shidyāq, p. 85.
[2] See above, p. 676; Carali, vol. i, pp. 402-3.
[3] Carali, vol. ii, pp. 315-18, 378-88.
[4] P. 210.
[5] Vol. i, p. 367.
[6] Carali, vol. ii, pp. 640 *seq.* A cross is said to have been found in his clothes at his death; Maʿlūf, p. 275; cf. F. Wüstenfeld, *Fachr ed-Dīn der Drusenfürst und seine Zeitgenossen* (Göttingen, 1886), pp. 167-8.

foot of Mount Hermon.[1] The amīr's requests for aid from his Italian allies went unheeded. For months he hid in Qal'at Nīḥa and then in an almost inaccessible cave in the mountain outside of Jazzīn, where he was at last discovered and led in chains with three of his sons to Constantinople (about February 10, 1635).[2] Eloquence, which once saved his grandfather's amīrate,[3] saved his neck — but only for a short time. Pleaded he before the sultan:

> Verily I am a misunderstood man. No troops did I ever muster except by order of your vizirs and representatives; no castles did I build except for the defence of the realm; and no men did I kill except those who rebelled against the Ottoman state. I captured the rebels' fortresses only to deliver them to the Ottoman government. Moreover I insured the safety of the pilgrims' road [to Mecca] against Bedouin aggression; I delivered the taxes to the imperial treasury at the times they were due; and I enforced the noble Islamic law [*sharī'ah*] with strict adherence to its ordinances and regulations.[4]

The banished amīr lived on borrowed time until news was received by the Porte that his relatives and followers were not obeying the new authority established. On April 13, 1635, he was beheaded with three of his sons who accompanied him and his body was exhibited for three days in a mosque.[5] The independent greater Lebanon of which he dreamed and which he successfully initiated was again attempted by a successor of his, al-Amīr Bashīr al-Shihābi,[6] but was not fully realized until 1943.

Period of anarchy

Lebanon entered upon a period of anarchy following the removal of Fakhr-al-Dīn from the political scene. 'Ali 'Alam-al-Dīn,[7] whom Kūchūk Aḥmad in the name of the sultan appointed over southern Lebanon, followed a partisan policy, confiscated the Ma'ns' property and persecuted them. In the course of a dinner to which he was invited at 'Abayh, he had his men fall upon his hosts, the Tanūkhs, and slaughter them. Those who were not there were pursued until the entire family was exterminated.[8] The opposition was headed by

[1] Muḥibbi, vol. i, p. 386.
[2] Duwayhi, pp. 204-5; Shidyāq, pp. 330-35; Ma'lūf, pp. 272-82; Carali, vol. ii, pp. 340-56.
[3] See above, pp. 665-6.
[4] Ma'lūf, p. 273; cf. Shidyāq, p. 336.
[5] Carali, vol. ii, pp. 355-6.
[6] See below, pp. 691 *seq.*
[7] Originally Tanūkhs, the 'Alam-al-Dīns headed the Yamanite faction and were therefore opposed to their Qaysite kinsmen; Shidyāq, p. 114.
[8] Ḥaydar, *Ta'rīkh*, p. 719; Shidyāq, pp. 114-15.

Mulḥim son of Yūnus and nephew of Fakhr-al-Dīn,[1] who for years contested the control of the region and succeeded in regaining a precarious hold under suspicious Ottoman supervision. The régime was continued under Mulḥim's son Aḥmad, who in 1697 died childless. The Maʿn family thereby became extinct.

The Shihābs succeed the Maʿns

At a national conference held at al-Sumqānīyah, near Baʿaqlīn, the Lebanese notables elected al-Amīr Bashīr al-Shihābi of Rāshayya as their governor (*ḥākim*), and communicated their decision to the wāli of Sidon with the assurance that they would pay through him the taxes, some of which were evidently still due Aḥmad.[2] Evidently the Lebanese spirit of home rule was not entirely dead. Turkey, herself in danger of being destroyed by European powers, was content so long as the taxes were guaranteed.

The Shihābs now entered upon the political heritage of the Maʿns. They held the reins of government until 1841, using the old techniques: bribing Ottoman officials, rising against weak sultans, playing one chief or one party against another and thus maintaining their hold on the mountain. They never adopted the Druze creed of their people, although their Druze people may have so considered some of them. Centuries of tight-rope walking made Lebanese politicians adept in the practice of dissimulation.

On representations from Ḥusayn, a young son of Fakhr-al-Dīn who had been taken to Constantinople, Ottomanized and sent as ambassador to India, Bashīr [3] was made regent pending the attainment of majority by al-Amīr Ḥaydar al-Shihābi of Ḥāṣbayya, son of Aḥmad Maʿn's daughter. Ḥaydar's amīrate (1707–

[1] Genealogical tree of the Maʿn family:

- 1. Fakhr-al-Dīn I (d. 1544)
  - 2. Qurqumāz (Qurqumās, 1544–85)
    - 3. Fakhr-al-Dīn II (1590–1635)
    - Yūnus
      - 4. Mulḥim (1635–57)
        - 5. Aḥmad (d. 1697)

[2] Ḥaydar, *Lubnān*, pp. 3-4; Shidyāq, pp. 358-9; Maʿlūf, p. 401.

[3] Usually referred to as Bashīr I to distinguish him from his illustrious successor Bashīr II; see below, p. 691.

1732) was signalized by the utter destruction of the Yamanite party at the battle of 'Ayn Dārah in 1711.[1] Some members of the defeated faction migrated to Ḥawrān, where they laid the basis of a new Druze community.[2] The unpopular 'Alam-al-Dīns were tracked down and exterminated. For the valour they displayed in this battle the abu-al-Lam's were made amīrs.[3] With the Yamanite power crushed, Ḥaydar was free to reorganize the feudal system with his partisans — Janbalāṭs, abu-al-Lam's and al-Khāzins — at the helm. The Yamanite Arislāns he made share their district with the Talḥūqs.[4] His son and successor Mulḥim (1732–54) added al-Biqā' and Beirut[5] to his domain but kept his residence at Dayr al-Qamar. This made him clash with the 'Aẓm wālis of Sidon and Damascus.[6]

After the crushing of the Yamanites a new alignment in Lebanese party politics resulted in two factions: Janbalāṭi and Yazbaki. The Janbalāṭs had then become one of the most powerful and wealthy Druze families. The Yazbakis received their name from a leader of the 'Imād family, which was also Druze and came originally from the Mawṣil district.[7] The alignment went beyond the aristocracy and involved the Maronites. The feud which began in the last decades of the eighteenth century lingered until the first decades of the twentieth. Mulḥim abdicated in 1754 and his two brothers contested the amīrate after him. One, Manṣūr, leaned toward the Janbalāṭs; the other, Aḥmad, favoured the Yazbakis. Aḥmad was the father of the historian Ḥaydar, repeatedly cited in this chapter. The period of civil disturbance lasted until Yūsuf, son of Mulḥim, attained majority and succeeded to the amīrate.[8] At a national assembly held at al-Bārūk in 1770 Manṣūr announced that he was tired of the affairs of the state and ready to abdicate in favour of his nephew Yūsuf, who was thereupon proclaimed governor of the mountain.[9] The wāli of Damascus was notified accordingly. The district over which Yūsuf ruled extended from Tripoli to Sidon.

[1] Shidyāq, pp. 364-5. [2] See above, p. 43. [3] See above, p. 679, n. 1.
[4] See above, p. 679, n. 1. [5] Ḥaydar, *Lubnān*, pp. 37, 40.
[6] See above, p. 665. [7] Shidyāq, p. 162.
[8] Sa'd al-Khūri, a Maronite from Rashmayya and member of a family that has given the Republic of Lebanon two of its presidents, was his guardian; Ḥaydar, p. 783; Shidyāq, p. 377. Yūsuf raised the family rank to that of shaykh; Ḥaydar, *Ta'rīkh*, p. 849.
[9] Ḥaydar, *Ta'rīkh*, p. 807; Shidyāq, pp. 386-7.

Al-Shaykh Ẓāhir al-ʻUmar

By this time two other persons were on the scene to share the limelight with the Shihābi amīr: Ẓāhir al-ʻUmar and Aḥmad al-Jazzār. With their rise Palestine begins to compete with Lebanon for a front place in the historical parade. Aleppo and Damascus keep in the background. The urban and country population in and around these two cities must have been low in number and in morale.

A Bedouin whose father was made by Bashīr I shaykh under the governor of the Ṣafad district, young Ẓāhir al [Āl]-ʻUmar, entered the political arena about 1737 by adding Tiberias to his Ṣafad domain.[1] With the aid of the Shīʻites of Upper Galilee, who were especially oppressed by Turkish officials and ready to follow any leader who promised relief, Ẓāhir resolved to rid the region of its rulers. Nābulus and Nazareth submitted. Acre was the next large prize that fell into his hands (1750).[2] The city had been partly in ruins since Crusading days and the usurper fortified it, made it his residence and used it for exporting silk, cotton, wheat and other Palestinian products to foreign markets. A benevolent dictator, Ẓāhir stamped out lawlessness, encouraged agriculture and assumed a tolerant attitude toward his Christian subjects. His biographer [3] reports on the testimony of an eye-witness that as Ẓāhir was once passing on horseback by the Virgin Mary's church in Nazareth, he alighted, knelt and vowed to keep an oil lamp burning in the church in case of victory. "Even a woman could travel around carrying gold in her hand without fear of being molested by anyone." [4] His financial obligations to the Ottoman government he regularly met, for he realized that to the government it made no great difference who the agent was, Turk or Arab, so long as the cash was forthcoming.

At this time Turkey was embroiled in a bitter struggle with Russia under Catherine and its prestige throughout the East was at a low ebb. In Egypt ʻAli Bey dared defy the sultan and send his agent abu-al-Dhahab [5] to seize Damascus and other

[1] Volney, vol. ii, p. 85; Shidyāq, p. 360; Ḥaydar, *Ta'rīkh*, p. 801; Mikhā'īl N. al-Ṣabbāgh (al-ʻAkkāwi), *Ta'rīkh al-Shaykh Ẓāhir al-ʻUmar al-Zaydāni*, ed. Qusṭanṭīn al-Bāsha (Ḥarīṣa), pp. 31-3 (where the dates are not accurate).

[2] Volney, vol. ii, p. 89; Ṣabbāgh, pp. 41-4.

[3] Ṣabbāgh, p. 48.

[4] Ṣabbāgh, p. 50.

[5] A slave of ʻAli, abu-al-Dhahab (the father of gold) was so generous with the distribution of gifts that he acquired this epithet; Jabarti, vol. i, p. 417.

Syrian towns which he did in 1771. Ẓāhir had entered into alliance with 'Ali, whose aim was to resuscitate the old Mamlūk rule. With the co-operation of a Russian fleet which bombarded Sidon, Ẓāhir occupied this city in 1772.[1] The Russians also bombarded Beirut and plundered it. Yūsuf Shihāb allied himself with the wāli of Damascus against the new upstart. A squadron was sent from Constantinople to lend its aid. With the co-operation of the land forces it seized Sidon in 1775 and blockaded Ẓāhir in his strongly fortified capital. Turkish bullets proved ineffective against Acre's walls but Turkish gold had its effect upon its garrison, bringing about Ẓāhir's death. In the Syrian army which tried to defend Sidon against Ẓāhir was one Aḥmad al-Jazzār, before whose adventures those of Ẓāhir pale.

Aḥmad Pasha al-Jazzār

A Christian Bosnian by birth, Aḥmad committed a sex crime when a boy, fled to Constantinople, sold himself to a Jewish slave dealer and landed in the possession of 'Ali Bey in Cairo. His master used him as an executioner. The technique he developed and the delight he took in his work earned him the surname of *al-jazzār* (the butcher), a surname in which he ever thereafter took pride and which he successfully endeavoured to live up to. From Egypt he fled to Syria, where for the military service he rendered against Ẓāhir he was rewarded with the governorship of Sidon.[2] For a short time he held Beirut but refused to acknowledge the authority of Yūsuf. Beirut's population then, according to Volney,[3] who passed through it, was only about six thousand.

Al-Jazzār extended his authority southward and succeeded Ẓāhir in Acre. He further fortified the city by forced labour from neighbouring villages, built a small fleet, organized a cavalry corps of eight hundred Bosnians and Albanians and an infantry corps of some one thousand Maghribis. The partial monopoly he exercised over the trade of his district enabled him to defray all necessary expenses and live in luxury. The large mosque he built in Acre is still standing. His ambition carried him beyond the confines of Palestine and the littoral of Lebanon. In 1780 he received a firman making him wāli over Damascus. For almost a quarter of a century after that he ruled as virtual

[1] Ṣabbāgh, p. 115; Shidyāq, p. 389; Ḥaydar, *Lubnān*, p. 93.
[2] Ḥaydar, *Ta'rīkh*, pp. 811, 827.
[3] Vol. ii, p. 170.

viceroy of Syria and arbiter of Lebanese affairs. No major setback marred his career, ended in 1804 by natural death, a rather unique record in the Syrian annals of the period. The Turks had their hands full with a new and powerful internal enemy, the Wahhābis of Arabia, and that was part of the explanation.

The high-water mark in al-Jazzār's career was attained in 1799, when he checked the advance of Napoleon. The French

From F. B. Spilsbury, "Picturesque Scenery in the Holy Land and Syria" (London, 1803)

AḤMAD PASHA AL-JAZZĀR OF ACRE CONDEMNING A CRIMINAL

invader had conquered Egypt and marched triumphantly along the Palestinian coast until he reached the gates of al-Jazzār's capital. With the aid of the English fleet under Sir Sidney Smith, al-Jazzār successfully defended Acre from March 21 to May 20, when Napoleon was forced to retreat with an army decimated by plague. French inscriptions can still be read on tombstones marking soldiers' burials on Mount Carmel.

A usurper dictator, the lord of Acre ruthlessly cut down his enemies and rivals, crushed the Shīʿite and Bedouin partisans of his predecessor and on the whole terrorized Syria and Lebanon. His name still lives there as a synonym of cruelty. A native chronicler, Mushāqah,[1] reports that his grandfather, an official in the government, witnessed one day more than forty outside the city wall arrayed for execution by impalement. The last four were spared on the intercession of this official. The same author reports that once when al-Jazzār's suspicions were aroused against his harem, he had all thirty-seven of them dragged, one after the other, to a burning pyre by his eunuchs.[2] In Lebanon he pitted one party against another, patronized the Janbalāṭs and, following a battle in Qabb Ilyās in 1788 in which Yūsuf was routed, requested the people to elect Bashīr al-Shihābi.[3] Yūsuf was hanged in the prison of Acre.[4]

Bashīr II

Bashīr's position as governor-general of Lebanon was at first precarious. The sons of his predecessor, Yūsuf, were actively conspiring against him and his patron al-Jazzār was turning against him for failing to support him in the struggle against Napoleon. Forced to retire, he fled in 1799 to Egypt on one of Sidney Smith's ships.[5] The British then became his friends.

[1] Mīkhā'īl Mushāqah, *Mashhad al-'Ayān bi-Ḥawādith Sūrīya wa-Lubnān*, ed. Mulḥim K. 'Abduh and Andarāwus H. Shakhāshīri (Cairo, 1908). A valuable but poorly edited source.

[2] Mushāqah, p. 54.

[3] Genealogical tree of the Shihābs:

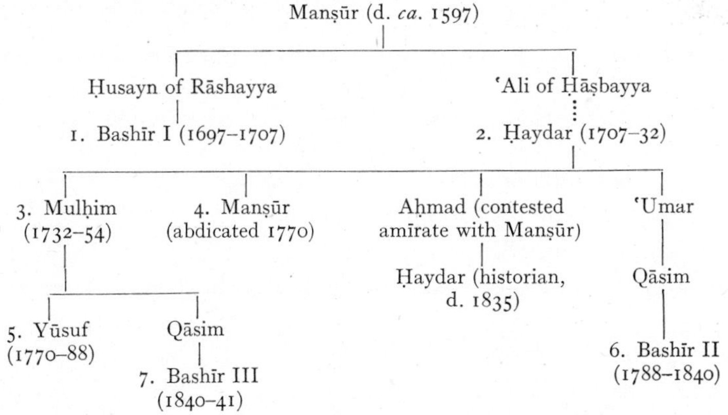

[4] Consult Ḥaydar, *Ta'rīkh*, p. 856; Mushāqah, p. 46; Shidyāq, pp. 419-20, 427.

[5] Ḥaydar, *Lubnān*, pp. 201 *seq.*

After a few months' absence he returned to crush his domestic foes and consolidate his domain. Yūsuf's sons were blinded before they were punished by death. Al-Biqā' was re-attached to Lebanon, the desires of the Damascus wāli notwithstanding. His policy toward the Turks was now one of firmness and friendliness. Early in 1810, when the Wahhābis of Najd, emerging from the desert, burst through the Syrian frontier and were threatening 'Ajlūn and southern Ḥawrān, Bashīr was there with 15,000 Lebanese to help drive them back.[1] At the head of his victorious men he paid Damascus a visit. He was no longer a local chieftain but was playing a part in Syrian affairs and in disputes between rival wālis of Damascus and Tripoli. This, however, forced another period of exile on him (1821–2), which he spent again in Egypt.[2] There he struck up a significant friendship with Muḥammad 'Ali, viceroy of the country and founder of its royal family.

When a few years later Muḥammad 'Ali launched his campaign against Turkey through Syria, Bashīr cast his lot with him. The Egyptian viceroy had expected—by way of compensation for the services he had rendered his Turkish suzerain on the battlefield of Greece in the war of its people for independence, and the battlefield of Arabia where the Wahhābis were crushed—at least the addition of Syria to his vice-royalty. But his expectation was not fulfilled. Lebanese troops stood side by side with the Egyptians in the siege of Acre in 1831.[3] Thanks to Bashīr's co-operation the task of Ibrāhīm Pasha, son of Muḥammad 'Ali and commander of the Egyptian expedition, was rendered comparatively easy. Ibrāhīm captured Damascus, routed the Turkish army at Ḥimṣ, crossed the Taurus and struck into the heart of the land of the Turks. He came close to administering the final blow to the "sick man of Europe". He was then forced to withdraw by England, Austria and Russia. In Syria his régime was ended in 1840. Muḥammad 'Ali's ambition to establish an Arab empire with himself at its head turned out to be a daydream. As yet there was no foundation in the consciousness of the people for such a state.[4] It was eighty-five

[1] Ḥaydar, *Lubnān*, pp. 556-7. [2] Ḥaydar, *Lubnān*, pp. 724-8.

[3] Mushāqah, p. 101; Shidyāq, pp. 567-8; Ḥaydar, *Lubnān*, pp. 832 *seq*.

[4] Cf. Asad J. Rustum, *The Royal Archives of Egypt and the Origins of the Egyptian Expedition to Syria* (Beirut, 1936), pp. 47 *seq*., 83 *seq*.

years before another potentate entertained such ambitious schemes. This was al-Sharīf Ḥusayn of Mecca, whose attempt was equally premature.

On the expulsion of Ibrāhīm the Turks called Bashīr to account. A British ship took him early in the autumn of 1840 to Malta.[1]

The exile in Malta was allowed to transfer to Constantinople, where he died in 1850. His remains were translated in

From Dussaud, Deschamps and Seyrig, " La Syrie " (Paul Geuthner, Paris)

THE PALACE OF AL-AMĪR BASHĪR II, BAYT AL-DĪN

Built in 1811, in the Arab style of the preceding centuries, this palace is now a museum

October 1947 to the grounds of the princely palace he erected in his days of glory at Bayt al-Dīn. No other such picturesque and sumptuous villa exists in the mountain. Water Bashīr brought to it in a nine-mile aqueduct from ʿAyn Zaḥaltah, whose spring is fed by snow and rain falling on a cedar-covered hill. The Lebanon of Bashīr prospered no less than that of Fakhr-al-Dīn. Bashīr built roads, renovated bridges and set

[1] Mushāqah, pp. 132-4; Shidyāq, pp. 620-21.

Beirut on its way to becoming what it is today, the gateway of Lebanon and Syria. The city was avoided by the Maʿns and Shihābs partly because of its exposure to piratical and other hostile attacks. Fakhr and Bashīr fought not only for an independent but also for a greater Lebanon, one that would embrace with the mountain the coastal towns and the eastern plain. Both encouraged foreign trade relations. Both welcomed political refugees and religious minorities. Bashīr offered refuge to a number of Druze families from Aleppo and to Greek Catholics. In contrast to his unprepossessing Maʿnid predecessor, the Shihābi had pronounced physical features. His eagle eyes, tiger face and wavy beard inspired awe and reverence. He was doubtless a Christian but did not consider it *politique* to profess his faith. His father was the first Shihābi to forsake Islam in favour of Maronitism. If Fakhr-al-Dīn was the first modern Lebanese, Bashīr was the second. In the Maʿnid tradition the Shihābi opened the door still wider to Western cultural, particularly educational, influences. To his people he is known as Bashīr al-Kabīr (the great), a name that has become legendary in their mountain saga. Anecdotes extolling his equity, sternness, wisdom and ability are still told and retold around fireplaces.

In 1840 another Bashīr,[1] who had taken part in the rising of the Lebanese against Ibrāhīm Pasha when he tried to disarm and overtax them,[2] and who had co-operated with the Ottomans and the British in expelling him, was appointed governor of Lebanon. The Ottomans, who were carrying out a policy of centralization initiated by Maḥmūd the reformer, were now convinced more than ever that the only way of keeping the mountain under control was to sow the seeds of discord and stir up strife between its Christian and Druze population. Hitherto, as noted above,[3] the alignment in the mountain ran across the denominations and arrayed Qaysites against Yamanites, or Yazbaki against Janbalāṭi. The civil strife between Christians and Druzes thus engendered began in 1841 and culminated in the massacre of 1860, which brought about European inter-

[1] See above, p. 691, n. 3.

[2] For the rebels' manifesto consult Fīlīb and Farīd al-Khāzin, *Majmūʿat al-Muḥarrarāt al-Siyāsīyah*, vol. i (Jūniyah, 1910), pp. 3-5.

[3] P. 687.

vention.[1] A French army occupied Lebanon for about a year. The estimated number of Christians massacred in 1860 is 11,000, and of those who perished by destitution 4000.[2]

An internationally recognized autonomous Lebanon

By the organic statute of 1861, revised in 1864, an autonomous system of government was allowed the mountain under a Christian governor-general (*mutaṣarrif*) of the Catholic faith designated by the Porte and approved by the signatory powers.[3] This chief executive was appointed for a renewable term of five years and assisted by an elective administration council of twelve representatives from the different religious communities. Sub-governors (sing. *qā'im-maqām*) administered the seven districts into which the new province, Mutaṣarrifīyat Jabal Lubnān, was divided after being stripped of Beirut, Sidon, Wādi al-Taym and eastern al-Biqā'. The government maintained its own judiciary and preserved order by a local militia. No Turkish troops were quartered in it, no tribute was sent to Constantinople and no military service was required of its citizens.

This autonomous Mount Lebanon, though stripped of certain strategic areas that lay within its natural boundary, entered upon an era of relative tranquillity and prosperity that was hardly matched in any other province of the empire. New roads were opened, high villages were converted into summer resorts and a narrow-gauge railway was constructed connecting Beirut with Damascus. The handicap under which its people had through the ages laboured, difficulty of internal communication, which was partly responsible for their political failure to form a united state, was being slowly overcome. Summer resorts capitalized on the beauty nature generously lavished on the mountain. The scantiness of its natural resources found part compensation in the facilities it enjoyed for overseas trade, and the poverty of its soil served to stimulate its sons, as it did their ancestors, to become the principal traders and colonists of the Levant. The saying became current: Happy is he who possesses even a goat's enclosure in the Lebanon. The increasing

1 William Miller, *The Ottoman Empire and its Successors, 1801–1927* (Cambridge, 1936), pp. 300-303; J. F. Scheltema, *The Lebanon in Turmoil* (New Haven, 1920), is a rather inaccurate translation of a good Arabic source.

2 Colonel Churchill, *The Druzes and the Maronites under the Turkish Rule from 1840 to 1860* (London, 1862), p. 219; cf. Khāzin, vol. ii, p. 99.

3 To the representatives of France, England, Russia, Prussia and Austria, who signed the 1861 statute, the representative of Italy was added in 1864.

prosperity was reflected in overpopulation, especially among the Christian elements, which sought relief through emigration. The fertility of the women of the mountain was in striking contrast with the barrenness of its soil.[1] Beginning with the eighties of the last century, Lebanese emigrants have sought new abodes for themselves and their families in Egypt, America, Australia and other parts of the civilized world. In the United States alone it is estimated that no less than a quarter of a million are of Lebanese descent.[2]

The series of mutaṣarrifs opened with an especially able man, Dā'ūd Pasha, who restored to the Lebanon a part of its lost territory, established for the Druzes a school in 'Abayh that still bears his name and struggled against the feudal lords in the south and the clerical party in the north. The latter was led by Yūsuf Karam, who after a number of military engagements was banished to Italy, where he died. The second successor of Dā'ūd, Rustem Pasha, subsequently ambassador in London, was an equally firm and economical administrator.[3] The privileged position enjoyed by Lebanon was abolished by the Turks in the first world war. Its charter served as a model for Crete and on the whole it was " the most successful example of autonomy applied to a Turkish province ".[4]

[1] Miller, p. 300.

[2] Cf. *Arabic-Speaking Americans* (Institute of Arab American Affairs) (New York, 1946), p. 4; Philip K. Hitti, *The Syrians in America* (New York, 1924), pp. 62-5. In America the Lebanese are still generally known as Syrians.

[3] List of mutaṣarrifs: Dā'ūd (1861–8), Franco, Naṣri (1868–73), Rustem (1873–83), Wāṣa (1883–92), Na''ūm (1892–1902), Muẓaffar (1902–7), Franco, Joseph (1907–12), Koyoumjian, Ohannes (1912–15). Of these Dā'ūd and Koyoumjian were of Armenian, Franco and Rustem of Italian, Wāṣa of Albanian and Muẓaffar of Polish origins.

[4] Miller, p. 306.

CHAPTER L

THE CONTEMPORARY SCENE

THE contemporary period in the life of the Arab East as exemplified by Syria and Lebanon is distinguished by the emergence and operation of potent forces that involve and relate to Western penetration and imperialism, the rise of local nationalism, the struggle for independence and the inception and spread of the Pan-Arab movement. These forces are dynamic and interactive. They are responsible for the most significant happenings of the last century and a half.

Political penetration

The nineteenth century opened with three major European powers competing for preponderant influence in a shrinking Ottoman empire that had been on the defensive for about a century. These were France, Russia and Great Britain. Austria had somewhat retreated; Prussia was still a second-rate power; Italy was non-existent. France's interest rested on economic considerations, a policy of prestige, the time-honoured capitulations and the traditional friendly relations with the Catholic and Maronite minorities. Especially significant were the capitulations of 1740 which placed all pilgrims to the Holy Land under French protection.[1]

The humiliating defeat administered by Russia to Turkey and signalized by the treaty of Kuchuk Kainarji (1774) practically substituted Russian influence for French. Russian interest dates from the days of Peter the Great and Catherine [2] and stems from the country's landlocked position and consequent desire to seek warm water seaports and from her professed sympathy with the Greek Orthodox community. The treaty of Kuchuk Kainarji recognized the czars as the protectors of that community. Conflicting claims on the part of France and Russia for the protection of the holy places was one of the causes of the Crimean War (1854–6). England, not a territorial neighbour of Turkey, had since the sixteenth century developed special

[1] See above, pp. 667-8.

[2] See above, pp. 688-9.

interest because of her overland trade relations with India and the Far East, as well as the Near East.[1] With the beginning of the disintegration of the Ottoman empire England's interest transcended commercialism into imperialism; she neither wanted to see Turkey dismembered nor wished Russia installed on the Bosphorus. It was this rivalry between the great powers that gave Turkey a new lease of life and insured her prolonged existence. The so-called Near Eastern question was in the last analysis the problem of expanding at the expense of the Ottoman empire and filling up the vacuum created by the gradual disappearance of this once mighty power.[2]

Before the close of the nineteenth century a new Western power had begun to loom on the Ottoman horizon: Germany. Her *Drang nach Osten* policy, initiated by Kaiser Wilhelm, soon gave her the ascendancy in Turkish Affairs. This was the time of ʿAbd-al-Ḥamīd II (1876–1909), one of the most reactionary rulers to ascend the throne of ʿUthmān. In the Kaiser the sultan found a new and welcome friend. The German emperor and empress visited Constantinople in 1898 and proceeded to Jerusalem and Damascus, where he laid a wreath at the tomb of Ṣalāḥ-al-Dīn. In a fiery speech he assured the sultan and with him "the three hundred million Moslems who revere him as the caliph" that the German emperor was, and would remain at all times, their friend.[3] Subsequently the concession for the Baghdād railway, bisecting North Syria, was given to a German company.[4] Thus was Berlin to be connected with Baghdād. This railway was one of the factors leading to the first world war. Meantime German officers were sent to reorganize the Ottoman army.

The Ḥamīdian régime

The point of departure in ʿAbd-al-Ḥamīd's policy was that the state should be more Asiatic than European. By way of implementation he resorted to an antiquated institution, the caliphate, which he tried to revivify. In the hope of retaining the loyalty of the non-Turkish Moslem elements in the empire and winning over all Moslems outside its boundaries, he tried

[1] See above, p. 673; M. V. Seton-Williams, *Britain and the Arab States* (London, 1948), pp. 1-5, 101 *seq.*

[2] Miller, p. 1.

[3] George Antonius, *The Arab Awakening* (Philadelphia, 1939), p. 77.

[4] Edward Mead Earle, *Turkey, the Great Powers and the Bagdad Railway* (New York, 1923), pp. 67-71.

to assert the earlier political power of the caliphate with its ideal of Pan-Islam. Gradually he succeeded in reducing his ministers to the position of secretaries and in concentrating the administration of the realm in his own hands. He put the press under strict censorship, abolished whatever measure there was of freedom of speech and spread an elaborate system of delation and espionage over the whole empire. In constant fear for his throne and life, he withdrew more and more into a life of seclusion behind the walls of his Yildiz palace. Wholesale arrests and executions coupled with the massacre of the Armenians won him the title of the " red sultan ".

In pursuance of his Pan-Islamic policy the sultan-caliph completed in 1908 the Ḥijāz railway, which connected Constantinople with Medina, passing through Syria from north to south, at a cost of £3,000,000, a third of which was raised by voluntary contributions from Moslems all over the world. It was this al-Ḥijāz railway whose bridges Lawrence helped to blow up in the first world war.[1] The engineers were Germans and the official in charge was a Syrian, Aḥmad ʿIzzat Pasha, the sultan's private secretary. Another Syrian, abu-al-Huda al-Ṣayyādi, exercised a strange influence over the caliph as his imām.

After thirty years of dictatorial reign ʿAbd-al-Ḥamīd awoke one July day in 1908 to find himself helpless in the face of a revolution led by officers in his own army. This was the work of the Committee of Union and Progress, the striking arm of a secretly organized society known as the Young Turks. The Young Turks were successors of the Young Ottomans, to whom Midḥat [2] belonged. The society had its inception at Geneva in 1891 through the activity of youthful reformers and students and was later moved to Paris. Its aim was to achieve a constitution of the Western type with an elective parliament and to break down the barriers of the millet system, thereby bringing about a homogeneous democratic state. On July 24, 1908, ʿAbd-al-Ḥamīd reluctantly announced the restoration of the constitution of 1876 [3] and the following day ordered the abolition of espionage and censorship and the release of all political

[1] T. E. Lawrence, *Seven Pillars of Wisdom* (New York, 1938), pp. 198-203, 207-11.

[2] See above, pp. 670-71.

[3] See above, p. 671.

prisoners. On December 10 he opened the parliament with a flourish and declared in a speech from the throne that the earlier parliament was only temporarily suspended pending the adequate preparation, through education, of the citizenry. Meantime a wave of optimism and enthusiasm had engulfed the entire nation. In Beirut, Damascus, Aleppo, Jerusalem and other towns of the empire the proclamation of the constitution was hailed with bonfires, orations and fireworks. The nightmare, it was believed, was gone. A new day had dawned. "Turkey, it appeared, had been converted overnight into a Utopia." [1] But ʿAbd-al-Ḥamīd had no more intention of preserving the constitution of 1908 than that of 1876. Caught intriguing with the reactionaries and staging a counter-revolution in April 1909, he was replaced by his doddering brother, Muḥammad Rashād. Authority remained in the hands of the committee.

Union and Progress

The new régime had more patriotic zeal than experience or political sagacity. Its policy of Ottomanization — reducing all racial and religious elements in the state into a common Ottoman denominator — was bound to fail. The Arabs interpreted the new *ḥurrīyah* (liberty) to mean freedom to realize their own national aspirations and to promote their own cultural individuality including language. Soon separatist movements began to assert their claims. With the failure of Ottomanization the Young Turks turned to the discredited Ḥamīdian policy of Pan-Islam. Domestic troubles were aggravated by international complications culminating in the war with Italy (1911–12), which caused Turkey the loss of Tripoli and Cyrenaica, her last foothold in Africa, and in the Balkan wars (1912–13), which stripped Turkey of almost the last vestiges of her suzerainty in that area. With all that the triumvirate of Enver, Ṭalʿat and Jemāl was unable to cope. In the world war that ensued Turkey cast her lot with the Central Powers and her performance in the struggle demonstrated the utter failure of Ottomanism and the bankruptcy of Pan-Islam. It led to the emergence of a new Turkey, a national Turkey less hampered by religious and ethnic complications. The architect of this state was a member of the Young Turks party, an officer who had participated in

[1] Harry Luke, *The Making of Modern Turkey* (London, 1936), p. 144.

their revolution. His name was Muṣṭafa Kemāl. His were the only thoroughgoing reforms that reached the masses.

Cultural penetration

Of all the eastern provinces of the empire Lebanon was the one least affected by the disabilities imposed by the Ḥamīdian régime. The measure of self-government it enjoyed after 1861 safeguarded the continued flow of ideas and other cultural elements from Western sources, a flow that had its beginnings in the earliest days and that was reinforced by Fakhr-al-Dīn and Bashīr.[1] The military occupation of Syria by Ibrāhīm Pasha (1831–40),[2] whose father was the first to establish vital contacts between Egypt and the West, opened the Syrian door wider for Western cultural influences. Ibrāhīm removed certain disabilities relating to dress and mounts under which the Christians in Syria had been labouring for ages.[3] It was then that the Jesuit order returned to Lebanon after a period of suspension[4] and American missionary enterprise found a firm lodging. In 1948 the Protestant Church of Syria celebrated its hundredth anniversary. In 1834 the American Press was established in Beirut. The Imprimerie Catholique of the Jesuits followed nineteen years later. Both presses are still going concerns. Translations of the Bible into modern Arabic were issued by both establishments. Jesuit educational activity, which was inaugurated in the early seventeenth century,[5] culminated in the founding in 1874 of the Université Saint-Joseph in Beirut, where the American mission had established in 1866 a college now known as the American University of Beirut. These two universities remain the leading institutions of learning in that part of the world. Native schools, presses, newspapers, magazines and literary societies began to flourish. Translations from French and English became numerous and popular.[6] Of all the new ideas thus imported nationalism and political democracy were unquestionably the most potent, the most dynamic.

Nationalism and the struggle for independence

The Arab nationalist awakening had its inception as a purely intellectual movement centring on the study of the Arabic language, history and literature. Its pioneers were mostly Syrian intellectuals, more specifically Christian Lebanese

[1] See above, pp. 683, 693-4.
[2] See above, p. 692.
[3] See above, pp. 542-5, 587-8.
[4] See above, p. 674.
[5] See above, p. 674.
[6] A. H. Hourani, *Syria and Lebanon* (Oxford, 1946), pp. 35-7.

educated at the American University of Beirut.[1] In their hands classical Arabic began to be moulded into a new instrument capable of expressing modern thought. The concept of nationalism, with its stress on secularism and material values, ran counter to the most cherished ideals and traditions of Islam, which at least in theory recognizes no bond other than that of religion. The adoption of nationalism of the latter-day type by the Arabic-speaking peoples and the insurrection of the Sharīf of Mecca, Ḥusayn, in 1916 against the Ottoman Turks shattered any remaining hopes of Pan-Islamic unity and substituted for it Pan-Arab unity, one based on language and secular culture rather than on religion. Lebanon's response to Western Christian stimuli was accelerated by the migration of thousands of its sons to the New World,[2] whence by their writings and return visits they kept the flame of liberty, independence and democracy burning. The Arab congress held in Paris in 1913 was called by Shukri Ghānim, brother of the Syrian deputy to the 1876 Constantinople parliament, and had a preponderantly Syrian membership. Its demands were moderate, including decentralization with administrative and cultural autonomy.

The Syrian intellectuals and champions of Arab nationalism found in neighbouring Egypt a more congenial atmosphere for their activity. Receiving its stimuli mainly from American ideology, the movement drew its inspiration from the past glory and cultural achievements of the Arabic-speaking peoples and looked forward to a consolidated Arab world. It started from a wide base, general Arabism of the non-provincial type. Soon, however, it suffered fragmentation. As the political aspects developed, they became diversified and localized. Egyptian nationalist aspirations parted company with Pan-Arabism in the early 'eighties, when opposition to British occupation became their chief immediate concern. Arab nationalism in Egypt thus asssumed regional colouring to be able more effectively to arouse local public opinion in its drive against the British. In Syria Arab nationalism concentrated its force against Ottoman domination and Turkification and, after the institution of the French mandate in 1919, on opposition to French rule. It

[1] Antonius, pp. 43, 51-5; Hans Kohn, *A History of Nationalism in the East* (London, 1929), pp. 268 *seq.*; Martin Hartmann, *The Arabic Press of Egypt* (London, 1899), pp. 3-13.

[2] See above, p. 696.

acquired fresh strength from the blood of patriots executed by Jemāl Pasha in the course of the first world war.[1] In Palestine, the southern part of Syria amputated and mandated to Great Britain, Arab nationalism was nourished throughout by hostility to the British and to Zionism — which in 1948 eventualized in the birth of Israel — as an intruding nationalist movement of Central and Western European Jews.

In 1921 Transjordan, with a biblical name but no real historical existence, was in turn amputated from Palestine and placed under the Amīr ʿAbdullāh, since 1946 king, who was then threatening to avenge the loss of the Syrian throne temporarily occupied by his brother Fayṣal, later king of al-ʿIrāq.[2] The new amīrate served a good purpose as a buffer state between the British mandated territory and the restless Bedouins of the desert. In 1949 it became the Hāshimite Kingdom of the Jordan.

The fragmentation of nascent Arab nationalism ran parallel to the fragmentation of the Arab territory which, until the first world war, was united under Ottoman rule. Between the first and second world wars the many Arabic-speaking lands of the Ottoman empire fell apart and developed into different states and quasi-nations. Community of language, religion and economic interest, however, operated to bring them together again. After 1940 the movement toward Pan-Arabism was again reactivated and intensified, eventuating in the creation of the Arab League. Reaction against political Zionism as a disruptive, expansive force contributed to this result. Both Syria and Lebanon have been members of the League since its organization in 1945.

Democracy

With the urge for nationalist assertion and the spread of education went an increased desire for more democratic practices in social and political life. Discontent among the farming class provided fertile soil for the reception and germination of new democratic ideas. In the mid-nineteenth century the feudal organization of the two leading Lebanese communities was beginning to show signs of breaking down. But the structure of the Druze feudalism proved to be more substantial than that

[1] For their number and reasons for condemnation consult *La Vérité sur la question syrienne* (Commandement de la IVème armée) (Constantinople, 1916), pp. 158-68.

[2] Hans Kohn, *Nationalism and Imperialism in the Hither East* (London, (1932), pp. 162-4, 177-8; Antonius, pp. 304-5.

of the Maronite; it has survived in a weakened form till the present day. In Syria, too, the feudal organization has not entirely disappeared. In northern Lebanon an agrarian insurrection against the Khāzins[1] and other feudal lords was in full swing when the civil war with the Druzes broke out.[2] Its leader was a farrier from Rayfūn named Ṭāniyūs Shāhīn, who in 1859 succeeded in forming a peasant commonwealth with himself at its head.[3] The Maronite clergy, recruited mostly from the common people, espoused the popular cause. When Dā'ūd Pasha assumed the governorship of the mountain the democratic section of the Maronite community withheld the payment of taxes to a foreigner who was favoured by the local aristocracy. The Maronites had demanded a native governor-general. Yūsuf Karam was the hero of the insurrection.[4] With the winning of the fight against the French for independence the Syrians and Lebanese adopted on a larger scale than ever before Western democratic concepts and institutions and adapted them to their particular needs. Lebanon was first among the Arabic-speaking states to institute a republican form of government. Syria followed. The Republic of Lebanon was fully achieved and generally recognized in 1943; that of Syria two years later.

The exposure of Syria, Lebanon and Palestine in the course of the nineteenth century to fresh economic, scientific and political ideas was more intensive and continuous than that of the seventeenth.[5] It partook more of the character of the exposure of the entire Arab world many centuries earlier to European cultural influences of the Greek variety.[6] In the contemporary period, too, the process of cross-fertilization was general; it embraced the entire Near East, in fact practically all Asia and Africa. Once more the people of the eastern Mediterranean became oriented westward as in Phoenician, Roman and Byzantine days. The resultant conflict between the traditional, static, religious point of view and the modern, scientific, secular point of view was felt most in Moslem communities. Nor was the conflict limited to the higher levels. The entire area, like most other parts of the nineteenth century

[1] See above, pp. 683-4.
[2] See above, pp. 694-5.
[3] Anṭūn D. al-'Aqīqi, *Thawrah wa-Fitnah fi Lubnān* (Beirut, 1938), pp. 83-90.
[4] See above, p. 696.
[5] See above, p. 683.
[6] Discussed above, pp. 548 *seq.*

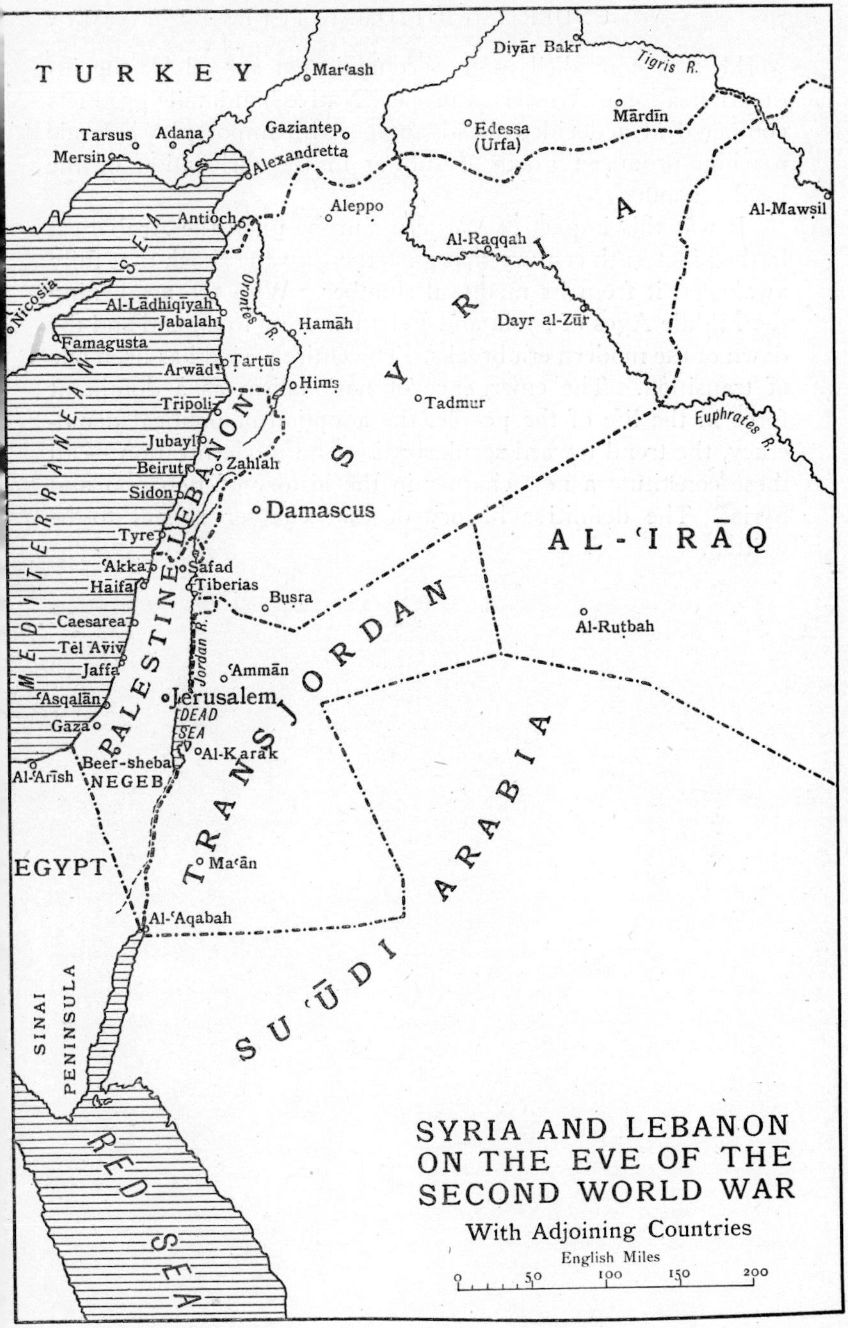

SYRIA AND LEBANON ON THE EVE OF THE SECOND WORLD WAR

With Adjoining Countries

world, was enmeshed in the economic net spread by the industrialization of Western Europe. Native handmade products competed at a decided disadvantage with imported wholesale machine-produced goods, resulting in the dislocation of the local economy.

It was this impact of Western Europe upon the Arab East in the nineteenth century that gave the East the shock that fully awakened it from its medieval slumber. With the awakening the Middle Ages of Syria and Lebanon draw to an end and the dawn of the modern era breaks. The entire period has been one of transition. The emergence of nationalism as a dominant force in the life of the people, the adoption of political democracy, the trend toward secularization and modernization — all these constitute a new chapter in the history of Lebanon and Syria. The definitive history of that chapter is still to be written.

INDEX

Titles of books, as well as Arabic and other Semitic words and technical terms occurring in the text, in italics. Main references indicated in heavy type.

When in the text reference is made to a book for the first time, the title in full — including author, edition (if any), place and date of publication — is given in the footnotes and then indexed. Thereafter, the title is given in an abridged form unless the author's life is sketched and the book is cited again, in which case the title is given in full and indexed for the second time. Books printed in Moslem presses often bear the *hijrah* date, which began A.D. 622.

In pronouncing Arabic words the accent generally falls on the long vowel bearing the macron (–); the ' stands for a glottal stop; the ' for a deep guttural that has no correspondent in English; such dotted letters as *ṣ* and *ṭ* are emphatically sounded; *aw* and *ay* are diphthongs.

The author's thanks are due to Mrs. R. Bayly Winder and Mr. Richard W. Downar, who assisted in the compilation of this index.

Abāḍites, 402. *See also* Ibāḍites
Abana, 41, 472. *See also* Barada
Abāqa, 632
'Abar Nahara, 220
'Abayh, 696
'Abbās, al-Saffāḥ, abu-al-, 530, 531, 532, **534** *seq.*
'Abbāsid: caliphate, 4; cavalry, 532, 543; régime, 535; era, 546; misrule, 669
'Abbāsids, **529** *seq.*
'abd, 488
Abd-Ashirta, 71, 72, 155
'Abd-al-Ḥakam, ibn-, *Futūḥ Miṣr*, 427 n. 2
'Abd-al-Ḥamīd II, **670-71**, 698-700
'Abd-al-Ḥamīd al-Kātib, 493
Abd-Khiba, 161
'Abd-al-Laṭīf Ḥamzah, *al-Ḥarakah al-Fikrīyah*, 655 n. 1
'Abd-al-Majīd I, 669
'Abd-al-Malik, Umayyad: 449, 462, 473; dinars of, 474; tutor under, 496
Abd-Melkarth, 142
'Abd-Rabbihi, ibn-, *al-'Iqd*, 404 n. 4
'Abd-al-Raḥmān I, 515, 532-3
'Abd-al-Raḥmān ibn-'Abdullāh al-Ghāfiqi, 468-9
'Abd-al-Raḥmān ibn-al-Ash'ath, 458
'Abdullāh, son of Ḥusayn, 703
'Abdullāh ibn-'Ali, **531-2**, 540
'Abdullāh al-Ḥusayn al-Shī'i, abu-, 577. *See also* Shī'i, abu-'Abdullāh al-Ḥusayn, al-
'Abdullāh ibn-Maymūn al-Qaddāḥ, 578. *See also* Qaddāḥ, 'Abdullāh ibn-Maymūn, al-
'Abdullāh ibn-al-Zubayr, **451-3**
Abel, F.-M., *Géographie de la Palestine*, 38 n. 4
Abgar, 247, 282, 517
Abgars, the, 308
Abi-Milki, 74
'Abīd ('Ubayd?) ibn-Sharyah, 479, **492-3**
Abraham, 60, 68
Absha, 76
Abulustayn, 443
Abūṣīr, 127
Abydos, in Asia Minor, 446, 447
Abydos, in Egypt, 28, 137
Abyssinian: language, 62
Acheulean: culture, 7 n. 1
Acre: 31, 253; reached by Tigranes, 249; shipyards in, 426, 489; walls of, 689. *See also* 'Akka
Actium, 283
Adad, 77, 172. *See also* Hadad
Adad-nirari I, 152, 162
Adana, 657
Addu, 172. *See also* Hadad
Adhanah, 442
Ādharbayjān, 429, 477
'Adhrā', 414
Adhruḥ, 410, 432
'Āḍid, al-, Fāṭimid, 600
'Ādil, al-: 620, 628; concessions by, 639. *See also* Malik al-'Ādil, al-
'Ādilīyah, 645
'Adlūn: caves of, 9
Adonis, 117, 256
Adonis-Ishtar, 19
Adrianople, 662
Adrianus, rhetorician, 321
Aegean: 247; area, 180
Aelia Capitolina, 340. *See also* Jerusalem

Mosul, 519. *See also* Mawṣil, al-
Mot, 115
Mother Earth, 118
Mother Goddess, 89
Mt. ʿAjlūn, 43
Mt. al-Aqraʿ, 32. *See also* Casius
Mt. Athos, 224
Mt. Baʿli-ra'si, 140
Mt. Carmel: 82; caves of, 9, 10, 38. *See also* Carmel
Mt. Casius, 256, 305
Mt. Gerizim, 197, 198, 274
Mt. Gilead, 43
Mt. Hermon: 35, 40, 41, **42**, 472, 685; timber from, 98
Mt. Hirmil, 248
Mt. Lebanon: 449, 695; copper in, 296; dhimmis of, 543
Mt. Seir, 41, 177
Mt. Silpius, 357
Mt. Sinai, 546
Mt. Tabor, 38
Mousterian: 10; lower, 11; culture, 18
Mouterde, René, *Le Nahr el-Kelb*, 142 n. 4
Mshtta, 507. *See also* Mushatta, al-
mu'addib, 496
muʿāmalāt, 492, 556
Muʿāwiyah I: 411, **425** *seq.*, **431** *seq.*, 449; fleet of, 445; issues coins, 474
Muʿāwiyah II, 445
Mubarqaʿ, al-, 542
Muḍarites, 469
Mughīrah ibn-Shuʿbah, al-, 436
Muhallab, al-, 455
Muḥammad: **410**; in Buṣra, 403
Muḥammad II the Conqueror, 662
Muḥammad ʿAli, **692**
Muḥammad al-Ḥabīb, *see* Ḥabīb, Muḥammad, al-
Muḥammad ibn-al-Ḥanafīyah, 453
Muḥammad ibn-Nuṣayr, 586. *See also* Nuṣayr, Muḥammad, ibn-
Muḥammad ibn-al-Qāsim al-Thaqafi, 461
Muḥammad Rashād, 700
Muḥammad ibn-Ṭughj, 561
Muḥibbi, al-, 675
Muḥibbi, al-, *Khulāṣat al-Athar*, 575 n. 1
muḥtasib, al-, 643
Muʿizz, al-, ʿAbbāsid, 563
Muʿizz, al-, Fāṭimid, 578
Mūjib, al-, 167. *See also* Arnon
Mukhtār al-Ḥikam, 644
Mukrān, 461
Mulḥim, Maʿni, 687
mulk, 441, 534
Müller, W. Max, *Asien und Europa*, 163 n. 4
Multān, 461
Multaqa al-Abḥur, 664
Munayṭirah, al-, 542, 622
Mundhir, al-, Ghassānid, **403-4**
Mundhir, al-, III, 402
Munqidh, banu-, 592
muqaddams, 678
muqarnaṣ, 645
muqātilah, 424
Muqtana Bahā'-al-Dīn, al-, 584. *See also* Bahā'-al-Dīn, al-Muqtana
Murād IV, 684
Murād V, 670
Murji'ites, **501**
Murshilish I, 155, 161
murū'ah, 496
Mūsa ibn-Nuṣayr, **464** *seq.*
Muṣʿab ibn-al-Zubayr, 452
muṣawwirūn, 505
Mushāqah, Mīkhā'īl, *Mashhad al-ʿAyān*, 691 n. 1
Mushatta, al-, 507, 508, 509
Mushrifah, al-, 68. *See also* Qaṭna
mushrikūn, 524
Musil, Alois, *Arabia Deserta*, 391 n. 3; *Palmyrena*, 391 n. 3; *Arabia Petraea*, 409 n. 2; *Northern Ḥeğâz*, 410 n. 2; *Ḳuṣejr ʿAmra*, 507 n. 3
Muslim al-Khurāsāni, abu-, 531
Muslim ibn-ʿUqbah, 451
Muṣṭafa Kemāl, 662, 701
Mustanṣir, al-, Fāṭimid, 582
Mu'tah, 409-10
Muʿtamid, al-, 558
Mutanabbi', al-, 563, **567-8**
mutaṣarrif, 695
mutaṣarrifīyah, 664 n. 5
Muʿtaṣim, al-, 540
Mutawakkil, al-: 542; laureate of, 554
Mutawakkil, al-, puppet caliph, 657
Muʿtazilite: view, 541
Muʿtazilites, **498-9**, 581, 585
Muʿtazz, al-, 554
Muwaqqar, palace, 507, 509
Muwatallish, 156
Muyassar, ibn-, *Akhbār Miṣr*, 595 n. 6
Muzāḥim, 497
Mycenaean: ceramics, 87; weapons, 88; ivory, 89; pottery, 116

Naaman the Syrian, 172
Nabataea: 377, 381, 382, 399; produce of, 383

'Umar, son of Sa'd ibn-abi-Waqqāṣ, 450
'Umar II ibn-'Abd-al-'Azīz: 447, 468, 475, 484, 493, 524, **527**; disabilities imposed by, 487-8, 543; transfers schools, 498, 548
'Umar al-Khayyām, 582-3
'Umar ibn-abi-Rabī'ah, 494-5
'Umari, al-, 487, 654
'Umari, al-, *al-Ta'rīf bi-al-Muṣṭalaḥ*, 474 n. 4, 655 n. 2; *Masālik al-Abṣār*, 487 n. 2; 655 n. 1
Umayyad: empire, 4; caliphs, 391; glory, 467; mosque, 472; poetry, 496; fall, 527 *seq.*
Umayyad Mosque of Damascus, 511, **513-16**
Umayyad Syria, 484
Umayyads: poets of, 494
Umayyah, banu-, 561. *See also* Umayyads
Umm al-Biyārah, 376
Umm al-Jimāl, 367
Umm Qaṭafah: caves of, 9
umm walad, 488
'Unayn, ibn-, *Dīwān*, 606 n. 1
Uni, 127
Uniat, churches, 674
Union and Progress, *see* Committee of Union and Progress
Unis, 127
United States, 197
Université Joseph, 701
Unūjūr, 562
'Uqayl, banu-, 593
'Uqbah ibn-Nāfi', **437-8**
'uqqāl, 585, 587
Ur: 177; tombs of, 138
Urban II, 590
Urdunn, al-, 424
Urfa, 253 n. 3. *See also* Ruhā', al-
Urmiyah, 150, 519
Urtuqid: dynasty, 575
Urtuqids, 616
Urusalim, 161. *See also* Jerusalem
Usāmah ibn-Munqidh, **621-2**
Usāmah ibn-Munqidh, *Kitāb al-I'tibār*, 53 n. 6
Uṣaybi'ah, ibn-abi-, **643-4**
Uṣaybi'ah, ibn-abi-, *'Uyūn al-Anbā'*, 497 n. 5; 644 n. 1
Usays, 509
Uswān, 170, 396. *See also* Aswān
Uthāl, ibn-, 439, 497
'Uthmān, founder of Ottoman state: 661; house of, 667
'Uthmān, Orthodox caliph, 426, 428, **429-30**
Utica, 95
'Uyūn w-al-Ḥadā'iq, al-, 511 n. 1
'Uzza, al-, 385, 402
Uzziah, 198

Valerian, 332, 392
Van Dyck, Cornelius, *al-Mir'āt*, 59 n. 3
Varuna, 150
Vasco da Gama, 671
Venetian: merchants, 95; fleet, 595; colony, 672
Venetians: 607; millet, 668
Venice: 354; merchants of, 590
Venus: temple of, 316
Vergil, 319
Verus, emperor, 302
Vespasian, 316, 339
Via Maris, 289
Vienna, 662, 663
Virgin, the, 37
Virolleaud, Charles, *La Légende phénicienne*, 116 n. 1
Visigothic: kingdom, 464
Visigoths, 468
Vitellius, 287, 294
Vitry, Jacques de, *History of Jerusalem*, 600 n. 3
Vogüé, de, *Inscriptions sémitiques*, 392 n. 1
Volney, 676, 683
Volney, *Voyage en Syrie*, 673 n. 4
Vulgate, 61, 170, 359

Waḍḍāḥ al-Yaman, 481
Waddington, W. H., *Inscriptions grecques*, 385 n. 1
Wādi al-'Arabah, 380, 411. *See also* 'Arabah, al-
Wādi Barissa, 201
Wādi Mūsa, 376
Wādi al-Naṭūf, 14
Wādi al-Sirḥān, 380, 412. *See also* Baṭn al-Sirr
Wādi al-Taym, 584, 586, 695
Wafā' Mubashshir ibn-Fātik, abu-al-, 644
Wahab-Allāth: 393; coins of, 394
Wahb ibn-Munabbih, 493
Wahb ibn-Munabbih, *al-Tījān*, 493 n. 1
Wahhābis, 624, 690, 692
Wāḥidi, al-, *Sharḥ Dīwān al-Mutanabbi'*, 567 n. 5

PRINTED BY R. & R. CLARK, LTD., EDINBURGH